WILEY INTERNATIONAL ENCYCLOPEDIA OF MARKETING

VOLUME 3

CONSUMER BEHAVIOR

WILEY INTERNATIONAL ENCYCLOPEDIA OF MARKETING

Encyclopedia Editors-in-Chief: Jagdish N. Sheth and Naresh K. Malhotra

WILEY INTERNATIONAL ENCYCLOPEDIA OF MARKETING

VOLUME 3
CONSUMER BEHAVIOR

Edited by
Richard P. Bagozzi and
Ayalla A. Ruvio
University of Michigan and
Temple University

⊛WILEY

A John Wiley and Sons, Ltd., Publication

This edition first published in 2011
Copyright © 2011 John Wiley & Sons Ltd

Registered office

John Wiley & Sons Ltd, The Atrium, Southern Gate, Chichester, West Sussex, PO19 8SQ, United Kingdom

For details of our global editorial offices, for customer services and for information about how to apply for permission to reuse the copyright material in this book please see our website at www.wiley.com

ISBN for the 7-volume set (including Cumulative Index) 978-1-405-16178-7

A catalogue record for this book is available from the British Library.

Typeset in 9.5/11 pt EhrhardtMT by Laserwords Private Limited, Chennai, India.
Printed in Singapore by Markono Print Media Pte Ltd.

Contents

Foreword

The scale and scope of marketing knowledge has dramatically changed in the last 20 years owing to four major external forces. The first and foremost is the diffusion and rapid adoption of the Internet and web-based communication. Its impact on marketing is more dramatic than the invention of television, telephone, and even electricity. The Internet is a very rich medium and allows convergence of pictures, print, and voice. It also has global reach. It is emerging as a great social medium as we are experiencing more peer-to-peer (word-of-mouth) communication through Facebook, YouTube, Twitter, and other forms of social media. It enables marketers to not only communicate but also to do transactions with documented and measurable impact of marketing activities such as price, promotion, and placement. With the popularity of smart phones such as the iPhone, it is possible to offer unlimited applications. Finally, the worldwide growth of HDTV and 3D animation is changing the paradigm of customer experience in mass communication.

A second major external force is globalization and the growth of emerging markets such as China and India. Most consumers in emerging markets even today purchase and consume unbranded products and services. However, they are becoming first time buyers of branded products such as cell phones, prepared foods, branded garments, and branded utility (telephone, electricity) and professional services (dentists, doctors). The sheer size of the rising middle class in China and India is shifting the market size and growth toward them. Both are likely to become the largest consumer markets for virtually all products and services. And, as a consequence, there will also be an impact on the purchase and sourcing of industrial products and services.

The third external force is the emergence of global competition, especially from multinationals of emerging economies. Who would have thought that a Brazilian Company (InBev) would acquire the largest beer company (Anheuser-Busch) in the world and South African Beer (SAB) would buy Miller Beer, the number two beer company in America? Similarly, Haier has become the number one appliance maker in the world surpassing Electrolux, Whirlpool, and General Electric. Lenovo has bought out IBM's PC business. The story is the same in industrial markets. For example, the largest tractor company is Mahindra and the largest motorcycle company is Hero Honda, both from India. The scale advantage gained from the size of their domestic market mandates companies from advanced economies to participate in these large emerging markets.

Finally, all advanced countries are aging and aging very rapidly. This has dramatically changed the target market from a fully nested family between the ages of 18 and 35 to empty nested households and aging baby boomers 35 to 50 years old. Their primary concerns are health and wealth preservation, and not appliances, baby clothes, and schools. Consequently, the largest expenditure today is in the health care sector. It was 9% of GDP in 1980 and today it exceeds 15% with an estimated expenditure of $1.5 trillion in the United States.

The objective of this *Wiley International Encyclopedia of Marketing* is to create, compile, and codify this rapidly expanding marketing knowledge into six volumes: *Marketing Strategy*, *Marketing Research*, *Consumer Behavior*, *Advertising and Integrated Communication*, *Product Innovation and Management*, and *International Marketing*.

As Editors in Chief, we believe in two things: First, to motivate the best and the busiest scholars to become Volume Editors and second, to get out of the way by empowering them to select the best authors to write each essay. As a result, there are more than 500 leading experts who have contributed to this six-volume encyclopedia. Each volume is comprehensive and covers a full range of topics from early developments to latest advances. The credit, therefore, goes to our Volume Editors: Roger Kerin and Robert Peterson for *Marketing Strategy*; Wagner Kamakura for *Marketing Research*; Richard Bagozzi and Ayalla Ruvio for *Consumer Behavior*; George Belch and Michael (Mickey) Belch for *Advertising and Integrated Communication*; Barry Bayus for *Product Innovation and Management*; and Daniel Bello and David Griffith for *International Marketing*. We are truly grateful to them for their commitment and hard work in making this a reality.

    We also want to thank the team at John Wiley & Sons who worked on this project for more than two years and through significant internal reorganizations. We are especially grateful to Rosemary Nixon for her patience, calm confidence, and continued support through emotional ups and downs. On reflection, we feel like academic wedding planners, enjoying with a smile and satisfaction now that the task is successfully completed. We also believe this will be a very valuable contribution to the discipline and practice of marketing in serving as a repository of knowledge in these main areas of marketing. We look forward to the impact of these volumes.

Jagdish N. Sheth, Emory University
Naresh K. Malhotra, Nanyang Technical University
Editors-in-Chief

Preface

Consumer behavior continues to be a vibrant and growing field, expanding theoretically, methodologically, and substantively on its own and in conjunction with other fields. All this made the choice of topics for articles in this volume quite difficult.

We identified many areas of basic knowledge in consumer behavior and asked leading scholars to summarize the state of art and science in each area. To arrive at the list of key topics we examined leading textbooks from the past and present, as well as recent encyclopedias with purposes similar to ours. In addition, we surveyed a number of marketing researchers from both academia and consultancy for their recommendations. After synthesizing the information from these diverse sources, and debating the timeliness and relevance of each topic, we pared the list, revised and combined a few suggestions, and added some topics of our own. The result is the 51 short and long entries presented in the table of contents.

Some of the entries focus on theoretical knowledge of consumer behavior that is quite broad in the sense of explaining or describing how and why consumers do what they do across a wide variety of consumption contexts. For example, the entries on "consumer information processing" and "consumer behavior analysis" have relevance for nearly any conceivable consumption behavior despite coming from radically different philosophical orientations. The entries on "consumer decision making," "choice models," and "consumer neuroscience" are also relatively broad in scope.

Many other entries might be best characterized as "focused theories" in the sense of addressing specific consumption phenomena. Instances here include "consumer brand loyalty," "consumer categorization," "cross-cultural psychology of consumer behavior," "how consumers respond to price information," "persuasion," "self-regulation," "social influence," "social networks," and "subcultures." Compared to the early writings on consumer behavior in marketing, which tended to espouse grand theories so to speak or frameworks cataloging the many determinants of consumption, the focused theories discussed in this encyclopedia characterize one important stream of research that, nevertheless, tends to make consumer research fragmented. As the field becomes more scientific, theories become more specific, and methods more controlled, fragmentation in theoretical perspectives become, perhaps, inevitable. Another type of fragmentation can be seen in the many theoretical approaches followed under "consumer information processing" and "consumer decision making," where such theories as prevention–promotion focus and fit, or one or more particular theories from social cognition, social psychology, or cognitive psychology are drawn upon in dozens of applications in consumer research. The combination of the complexity of consumer behavior with a fertile supply of basic research ideas from psychology and elsewhere is sure to contribute to the sense of fragmentation in the field in the years ahead. It is perhaps time for scholars to step back and provide some integration in the field, much as in the spirit that James Bettman (1979) did early on with his "information processing theory of consumer choice" and John Howard (1989) attempted in his "consumer behavior in marketing strategy." Until this happens, consumer researchers today can draw upon the scholarly writings in this encyclopedia to guide their work.

Beyond the broad and focused theory entries in this volume, we note that some entries discuss variables or processes that fit in different ways and to different degrees within the theories. Thus we see that key variables/processes such as "attitudes," "consumer acculturation," "consumer desire," "consumer expertise," "consumer intentions," "consumer involvement," "consumer memory processes," "emotion," "habit in consumer behavior," "implicit consumer cognition," "impulsive and compulsive buying," "knowledge accessibility," "motivation and goals," "optimum stimulation level," and "the role of schemas in consumer behavior research" receive specific treatment.

Finally, for lack of a better classification, we term the remaining entries as instances of specific research contexts or relatively general phenomena. Here we see "brand community," "childhood socialization and intergenerational influences," "consumer aspects of international marketing," "consumer behavior across literacy and resource barriers," "consumer behavior and services marketing," "consumer creativity," "consumer innovativeness," "consumer materialism," "consumer well-being," "consumers' need for uniqueness," "environmental consumer behavior," "family buying," "family life cycle," "hedonism," "on-line consumption," "opinion leadership and market mavens," "possessions and self," "social class," and "variety seeking." Each of these areas might be informed by one or more of the broad and focused theories and include one or more variables/processes noted above, but, for the most part, each of these areas arose early on with its own unique history or more recently emerged in response to new technological innovations or descriptive requisites.

The topics selected for inclusion in this volume certainly do not exhaust the content of consumer behavior. But they provide a sturdy sense of where the field is now and where it is going. We speculate that the field will continue its rich trajectory with more theories added and more variables/processes and contexts/phenomena proposed in the years ahead. One observation that arose with hindsight is the following. Whereas the field has focused heavily on consumer *behavior* it has done little so far to define and study consumer *action*. Action entails what one does in a purposive or expressive manner, and typically is performed with or takes into account other people. There is a need to refine the concept of consumer action and develop theories and hypotheses explaining it. Many of the entries in this volume can be used to inform such theories and hypotheses, but progress here awaits deeper theoretical and philosophical thinking to reconcile, among other difficult issues, those such as determinism and indeterminism or agency, different methodological approaches and their relationship to knowledge generation and validity, consciousness with nonconscious processes, cross-level explanations of phenomena, and individual versus social action.

Richard P. Bagozzi and Ayalla A. Ruvio

About the Editors

Editors-in-Chief

Dr. Jagdish N. Sheth is a renowned scholar and world authority in the field of marketing. Dr Sheth is the Charles H. Kellstadt Chair of Marketing in the Goizueta Business School at Emory University. Prior to this, he was a distinguished faculty member at the University of Southern California, the University of Illinois, Columbia University, and the Massachusetts Institute of Technology. Dr Sheth is the founder of the Center for Relationship Management at Emory University and Center for Telecommunications Management at the University of Southern California. He was a prominent member of the core team during the initial years of the Indian Institute of Management Calcutta, the first Indian Institute of Management. In 2003, he founded the India, China & America Institute, a nonprofit institute providing a sustainable, nongovernmental platform to identify and drive synergies among India, China, and America in the areas of emerging markets, commercial growth, and alignment of policies for the benefit of a vast number of people.

Dr. Naresh K. Malhotra is Nanyang Professor, Nanyang Business School, Nanyang Technological University, Singapore. and Regents' Professor Emeritus, College of Management, Georgia Institute of Technology, USA. He is listed in Marquis *Who's Who in America* continuously since its 51st Edition 1997, and in *Who's Who in the World* since 2000. He received the prestigious Academy of Marketing Science CUTCO/Vector Distinguished Marketing Educator Award in 2005. Recently, he was selected as a Marketing Legend and his refereed journal articles will be published in nine volumes by Sage.

He holds several top research rankings based on publications in top journals. In a landmark study by West et al. (2008) examining publications in the top four marketing journals (JMR, JM, JAMS, and JCR) over a 25-year period from 1977 to 2002, Professor Malhotra has three top-three rankings: ranked number three based on publications in all the four journals combined, ranked number three based on publications in JMR, and ranked number one based on publications in JAMS. He has published 10 papers in JMR. His books on marketing research are global leaders in the field and have been translated into many languages. Dr. Malhotra is an ordained minister of the Gospel, a member and Deacon, First Baptist Church, Atlanta.

Volume Editors

Richard P. Bagozzi is the Dwight F. Benton Professor of Behavioral Science in Management and Professor of Social and Administrative Sciences, College of Pharmacy, at the University of Michigan. A graduate of the PhD program at Northwestern University, he recently received honorary doctorates from the University of Lausanne, Switzerland, and Antwerp University, Belgium. Professor Bagozzi grounds his research in the theories of action and mind, social psychology, philosophy, and statistics. He applies ideas and methods in these fields to the study of consumer behavior, health behavior, organizations behavior, salesperson behavior, ethics, construct validity, and structural equation modeling. Professor Bagozzi also uses the comparative method to investigate cross-cultural behavior and neuroscience procedures to examine personality and decision making.

Ayalla A. Ruvio is Assistant Professor of Marketing in the Fox School of Business at Temple University; she received her PhD from the University of Haifa in Israel, and was a visiting scholar at the University of Michigan. She is a consumer behavior researcher who focuses on issues such as consumers' self-identity, possessions as an extension of the self, consumers' need for uniqueness, and cross-cultural consumer behavior. Dr. Ruvio has published more than 20 papers in refereed journals including *Journal of Academy of Marketing Science, Journal of Business Research, Journal of International Marketing, and Leadership Quarterly*. She has received grants from a number of international foundations including the German-Israel Foundation, and the American Association of University Women.

Contributors

Aaron Ahuvia
University of Michigan-Dearborn, Dearborn, MI, USA

René Algesheimer
University of Zurich, Zurich, Switzerland

Alan R. Andreasen
Georgetown University, Washington, DC, USA

Barry J. Babin
Louisiana Tech University, Ruston, LA, USA

Richard P. Bagozzi
University of Michigan, Ann Arbor, MI, USA

Hans Baumgartner
The Pennsylvania State University, Pennsylvania, PA, USA

Russell Belk
York University, Toronto, Ontario, Canada

James Burroughs
University of Virginia, Charlottesville, VA, USA

Ziv Carmon
INSEAD, Singapore

Robert B. Cialdini
Arizona State University, Arizona, AZ, USA

Catherine A. Cole
University of Iowa, Iowa City, IA, USA

David K. Crockett
University of South Carolina, Columbia, SC, USA

Hélène Deval
Dalhousie University, Halifax, NS, Canada

Utpal M. Dholakia
Rice University, Houston, TX, USA

Claudiu V. Dimofte
Georgetown University, Washington, DC, USA

Aimee Drolet
UCLA Anderson School, Los Angeles, CA, USA

Ronald Earl Goldsmith
Florida State University, Tallahassee, FL, USA

Eric M. Eisenstein
Temple University, Philadelphia, PA, USA

Ronald J. Faber
University of Minnesota, Minneapolis, MN, USA

Fred M. Feinberg
University of Michigan, Ann Arbor, MI, USA

Ayelet Fishbach
University of Chicago, Chicago, IL, USA

Karen E. Flaherty
Oklahoma State University, Stillwater, OK, USA

Mark R. Forehand
University of Washington, Seattle, WA, USA

Gordon R. Foxall
Cardiff University, Cardiff, UK

James W. Gentry
University of Nebraska-Lincoln, Lincoln, NE, USA

Jacob Goldenberg
The Hebrew University of Jerusalem, Jerusalem, Israel and Columbia University, New York, NY, USA

Mitch Griffin
Bradley University, Peoria, IL, USA

Vladas Griskevicius
University of Minnesota, Minnesota, MN, USA

Daniel He
The University of Chicago, Chicago, IL, USA

Paul M. Herr
Virginia Polytechnic and State University, Blacksburg, VA, USA

Michal Herzenstein
University of Delaware, Newark, DE, USA

Elizabeth C. Hirschman
Rutgers University, New Brunswick, NJ, USA

Dawn Iacobucci
Vanderbilt University, Nashville, USA

Elif Izberk Bilgin
University of Michigan-Dearborn, Dearborn, MI, USA

Frank R. Kardes
University of Cincinnati, Cincinnati, OH, USA

Minkyung Koo
University of Illinois, Urbana-Champaign, IL, USA

Robert V. Kozinets
York University, Toronto, Ontario, Canada

Barbara Loken
University of Minnesota, Minneapolis, MN, USA

Tina M. Lowrey
University of Texas at San Antonio, San Antonio, TX, USA

David Mazursky
The Hebrew University, Jerusalem, Israel and Bocconi University, Milan, Italy

John A. McCarty
The College of New Jersey, Ewing, NJ, USA

Kathryn R. Mercurio
University of Washington, Seattle, WA, USA

Kent B. Monroe
University of Illinois, Urbana-Champaign, IL, USA and University of Richmond, Richmond, VA, USA

Elizabeth S. Moore
University of Notre Dame, Notre Dame, IN, USA

John C. Mowen
Oklahoma State University, Stillwater, OK, USA

Dhananjay Nayakankuppam
University of Iowa, Iowa City, IA, USA

Sangdo Oh
University of Illinois at Urbana-Champaign, Champaign, IL, USA

Richard L. Oliver
Vanderbilt University, Nashville, TN, USA

Lisa Peñaloza
Ecole des Hautes Etudes Commerciales du Nord, Lille, France

Rik Pieters
Tilburg University, Tilburg, The Netherlands

Hilke Plassmann
INSEAD, Fontainebleau, France

Marsha L. Richins
University of Missouri, Columbia, MO, USA

Julie A. Ruth
Rutgers University, Camden, NJ, USA

Ayalla A. Ruvio
Temple University, Philadelphia, PA, USA

Crystal Scott
University of Michigan–Dearborn, Dearborn, MI, USA

Seethu Seetharaman
Rice University, Houston, TX, USA

Sharon Shavitt
University of Illinois, Urbana-Champaign, IL, USA

Baba Shiv
Stanford University, Stanford, CA,
USA

L. J. Shrum
University of Texas at San Antonio, San
Antonio, TX, USA

Jayati Sinha
University of Iowa, Iowa City, IA,
USA

Jan-Benedict E. M. Steenkamp
University of North Carolina at Chapel Hill,
Chapel Hill, NC, USA

Leona Tam
Old Dominion University, Norfolk, VA,
USA

Gerard J. Tellis
University of Southern California, Los
Angeles, CA, USA

Patrick T. Vargas
University of Illinois at Urbana-Champaign,
Champaign, IL, USA

Gideon Vinitzky
Ariel University Center, Ariel, Israel

Madhu Viswanathan
University of Illinois at Urbana-Champaign,
Urbana, IL, USA

Kathleen D. Vohs
University of Minnesota, Minneapolis, MN,
USA

Robert S. Wyer, Jr.
University of Illinois at Urbana-Champaign,
Champaign, IL, USA

Haiyang Yang
INSEAD, Singapore

Eden Yin
Cambridge University, Cambridge, UK

Carolyn Yoon
University of Michigan, Ann Arbor, MI,
USA

Judith Lynne Zaichkowsky
Copenhagen Business School, Frederiksberg,
Denmark

attitudes

Paul M. Herr

Any comprehensive treatment of the attitude construct in general and its applications in marketing in particular could easily fill this volume, let alone a single article. Hence, the focus here is to simply identify the construct, describe some of the major stages in its development, and briefly trace its recent history in consumer behavior. Consequently, this article will be far more selective than comprehensive in nature.

EARLY DEVELOPMENT

Throughout this discussion, one is struck by the singular contributions of attitude theorists in social psychology to applications in consumer research. Attitude has long been viewed as a central construct in social psychology, and its role in consumption has been viewed as no less important. Clearly, the ability to elicit from consumers a simple, summary evaluation of goods and services with predictive utility has had strong allure. This appeal, however, is tempered by a history rich with disappointment and debate. Even something as (deceptively) simple as defining the attitude construct (which could also easily fill this volume), not to mention settling debate over the construct's very existence, has filled academic journal pages for many decades. Thurstone's (1928) triumphant claim that attitudes can be measured presupposed both their stable existence and their directive influence on an individual's behavior. Allport's (1935) early definition of attitude continues to guide current thinking about attitude's functional role, as well as spur debate. According to Allport, "An attitude is a mental and neural state of readiness, organized through experience, exerting a directive or dynamic influence upon the individual's response to all objects and situations with which it is related" (1935, p. 810). Central to this definition is attitude's enduring nature, that it is learned through experience, and its directive influence on behavior.

Attitudes' functional role was considered by Katz (1960). His analysis provides compelling reasons why consumers may hold attitudes as well. Katz suggested that individuals might be well-served by holding stable attitudes about persons and objects in their environment, as useful functions might be served by attitudes. Specifically, Katz identified four functions that attitudes might provide. It is a simple extension to note what each provides the consumers. First, consumer attitudes may serve a *utilitarian* function. That is order and structure are provided by knowing which brands fill needs well and which do not. Likewise, a *value expressive* function is served to the extent a consumer is able to identify which brands and products allow them to best express their central values and who they believe themselves to be. Attitudes of both valences about luxury goods may serve this function. An *ego-defense* function is served by attitudes that protect against damage to the self-concept. Finally, a *knowledge* function allows the holder of attitudes to make sense of an otherwise chaotic and disorganized world; knowing which brands are loved and which are hated.

THE THEORY OF REASONED ACTION

The existence of functionally sound reasons to hold attitudes notwithstanding, prominent failures of attitudes to in fact predict behaviors led Wicker (1969) to suggest that attitudes are epiphenomenal; after-the-fact explanations of behavior, rather than guiding influences, and as such should be abandoned as a scientific construct. Two responses to this attack on attitudes are particularly noteworthy, with respect to both their impact within traditional attitude theory and their influence on marketing. First, with their Theory of Reasoned Action Fishbein and Ajzen (1975) attempted to salvage the attitude construct by (i) redefining attitude as an expected value of the sum of an individual's beliefs about an attitude-object, weighted by individual's evaluations of each of those beliefs, (ii) considering the impact of subjective norms for engaging in attitude-relevant behavior, and (iii) weighting the attitude and subjective norms in predicting the individual's intention to engage in a particular behavior. This development's impact on marketing has been profound. The bulk of academic marketing work, as well as marketing practitioners' work in attitudes, employs this framework or variants (and more recently, the Theory of Planned Behavior, Ajzen, 1985).

Academic research explicitly studying consumers generally has taken one of two paths: either directly applying the model to consumption settings (and more recently, applying the models to social marketing settings) or engaging in theoretical discussions of the model itself. Representative of the former research is work by Shimp and Kavas (1984) investigating consumer coupon usage and Hansen, Jensen, and Solgaard (2004) examining online grocery purchase intentions.

A great deal of work has investigated modified versions of the Theory of Reasoned Action, as well as questioned the assumptions of and made extensions to the original model. Representative work includes Bagozzi (1981, 1982), Sheppard, Hartwick, and Warshaw (1988), Miniard and Cohen (1983), and Mitchell and Olsen (1981). Central to this work are concerns for the ability of attitudes (affective judgments) to be fully mediated by expectancy-value judgments, the process by which expectancy-value judgments are expected to influence behavior, and how the entire Theory of Reasoned Action model's components is expected to influence behavior.

THE PROCESS MODEL OF ATTITUDE-BEHAVIOR CONSISTENCY

The second significant response to Wicker's (1969) assault on attitudes was a focus on *how* attitudes may influence behavior (Fazio and Zanna, 1981; Fazio *et al.*, 1986). This latter development shifted focus away from "Do attitudes predict behavior?" to a process question "How do attitudes guide behavior?" Moreover, the definition of attitude proposed in this work is conceptually closer to Allport's definition of four decades earlier, but without the necessity that attitudes be linked to behavior. Rather, that link's existence was left as an empirical question. An attitude is considered to be a learned association between a concept and an evaluation (e.g., an affective categorization of a person or an object). Structurally, this may be represented in memory as a link between a node representing the object or person, and its evaluation (e.g., good, bad, and likable.). Operationally, attitudes may vary in strength, reflecting the strength of the associative link between the object and its evaluation. Relatively weak links reflect relatively weak (or nonexistent) attitudes. Encountering the attitude-object (or its representation) is insufficient to activate the associated evaluation from memory, so the attitude fails to influence behavior directed toward the person or object. Relatively strong links, however, reflect strong attitudes. Simply encountering the attitude-object (or its representation) may automatically activate the individual's evaluation of the person or object from memory. Once activated, the attitude serves as a filter, through which the object and situation are perceived, filtering out attitude-inconsistent information and coloring ambiguous information attitudinally consistent. The individual's behavior is determined by their immediate perceptions of the situation (biased by the attitudinal filter). Attitude-behavior consistency occurs not because of a striving for consistency, or as an end result of a conscious, rational process but rather as a natural end state of the attitude's activation (of which the attitude holder may be wholly unaware). Moreover, for strong attitudes, the activation itself may be automatic and wholly outside the control of the individual (Fazio *et al.*, 1986).

Applications of Fazio's model in marketing have been relatively few, but its applicability is well demonstrated by Fazio, Powell, and Williams (1989). The authors demonstrated that, even after controlling for attitude extremity, product choice was influenced by attitude accessibility. Branded products for which participants held relatively accessible attitudes were more likely to be chosen than products for whom participants held less accessible attitudes. Moreover, prominently positioned products (those placed in the front row of a display) were more likely to be chosen by participants holding less accessible attitudes. That is, their choice was determined by a situational factor (salience of position) rather than an attitudinal factor (strength).

To a considerable extent, attitude's definition has determined the types of models employed in predicting attitude's influence on behavior. While debate over attitude's definition appeared to be subsiding in the last decade of the twentieth century, the distinction between implicit and explicit attitudes has revived interest in definitional matters, and the debate has been rejoined. This distinction will be visited below.

ATTITUDES AND PERSUASION

A central task facing consumer researchers is to understand the conditions under which product and service communications will produce a sufficiently strong attitude to result in consumer choice favoring a given product or service. During the 1980s considerable research addressed exactly this issue, growing out of Chaiken's (1980) Heuristic-Systematic Persuasion model and Petty and Cacioppo's (1986) Elaboration Likelihood models. The models make largely similar predictions. The ELM (Elaboration Likelihood Model) identifies two "routes" to persuasion; central and peripheral. The central route involves cognitively effortful consideration of the arguments (content) of the communication message. Central processing occurs only when the individual is both motivated and able to think about the message and product. If either is lacking (e.g., the individual does not care about the message or product due to irrelevance, or is distracted, or otherwise lacks the cognitive

resources to process the message) the central processing route will be aborted in favor of the peripheral route.

Message-consistent attitudes growing out of the peripheral route to persuasion are based not on the strength of the message arguments, but rather on peripheral cues to message strength, that may be wholly invalid with respect to indicating actual strength of the message. For instance, cues such as number of arguments, length of the argument, communicator attractiveness and confidence all signal that the message may be credible. Without analyzing the actual content of the message, though, a judgment of message credibility is premature. Followers of the peripheral route are insufficiently motivated, or lacking in ability (or both) to effortfully process the content of the message and instead simply rely on the peripheral cues when forming their communication-based attitude.

Central to the ELM is the notion that attitudes changed or formed via the central route will have different effects than will attitudes changed through the peripheral route. Specifically, central route-based attitudes show greater temporal persistence, greater resistance to change, and are better predictors of behavior than attitudes that result mostly from peripheral cues.

The ELM and heuristic-systematic model (HSM) have garnered considerable empirical support, within both the field of consumer behavior and a far-ranging variety of other areas. In a consumer setting, Petty, Cacioppo, and Schumann (1983) exposed participants to print advertisements for a new razor blade. Whether the central or peripheral route would be followed was manipulated by the relevance of the ad to readers. High issue relevance (involvement) was induced by indicating that the razor would be available for purchase in their local market area. It was expected (and confirmed) that this would lead to greater reliance on central processing. Low issue relevance was induced by indicating to participants that the advertised razor would not be available in their market area. Under low relevance conditions, individual's attitudes were most affected by the celebrity status of the product endorsers. In contrast, the quality of product arguments was a more important determinant of the attitudes of individuals exposed to the advertisements under high relevance conditions.

While the ELM and HSM deal primarily with persuasion (attitude change) Fazio's (1990) Mode model addresses how attitudes influence behavior, and reconciles the Theory of Reasoned Action with his own process model. A key distinction between the two models involves the amount of cognitive processing involved in deciding how one will behave in the presence of the attitude object. The Theory of Reasoned Action presents behavior as a reasoned, cognitively cumbersome, and highly deliberative process on the part of the individual. Individuals are said to make systematic use of the information at hand. Salient beliefs about the attitude-object are weighted by their evaluations, summed, and compared with norms to form a behavioral intention. The individual is expected to behave consistently with the intention. Fazio's process model presents an alternative in which activation of an attitude is relatively effortless and automatic. The attitude colors immediate perceptions of the object in the current situation, which in turn may prompt attitudinally congruent behavior. The MODE model suggests that both attitude-behavior processes may occur, but the antecedents of each differ. Specifically, the more cognitively effortful process occurs only when the individual is motivated and has the opportunity to engage in the more taxing process. If either antecedent is absent, the default value is the relatively effortless process of the Fazio model. In the realm of consumer behavior, the expected differences in attitude-to-behavior processes are relatively straightforward. When consumers are highly involved and have the ability to process, they will likely engage in reasoned action. Such cases include big-ticket items, or purchases of considerable significance in some other regard. Frequent purchases or purchases with small downside potential seem more likely to be driven by the relatively effortless, top-down guidance provided by a highly accessible attitude.

IMPLICIT ATTITUDES

A relatively recent development of some significance is the notion of implicit attitudes and the development by Greenwald and his colleagues of the Implicit Association Test (IAT). Greenwald and Banaji (1995) define *implicit attitude* as "... introspectively unidentified (or inaccurately identified) traces of past experience that mediate favorable or unfavorable feeling, thought, or action toward social objects." (p. 8). This definition grew out of the work in social psychology examining "automatic" (as used by Bargh and his colleagues, e.g. Bargh, 1994) behavior, as well as Fazio's definition of attitude as an association (of varying strength) between an object and its evaluation. "Automatic" behavior is said to proceed in an implicit or unconscious fashion. It is characterized by its spontaneous, unplanned nature, over which the actor has neither awareness nor control, nor, most importantly, awareness of (or conscious access to) cognitions (including attitudes) causally precipitating the behavior. Behavior of this type is at an extreme end of the planned-spontaneous behavior continuum.

The implicit nature of attitudes (and their measurement) is interesting and important, according to Nosek, Greenwald, and Banaji (2007) because, "... implicit cognition could reveal traces of past experience that people might explicitly reject because it conflicts with values or beliefs, or might avoid revealing because the expression could have negative social consequences. Even more likely, implicit cognition can reveal information that is not available to introspective access even if people were motivated to retrieve and express it (see Wilson, Lindsey, and Schooler, 2000, for a similar theoretical distinction for the attitude construct specifically) . . .. The term *implicit* has come to be applied to measurement methods that avoid requiring introspective access, decrease the mental control available to produce the response, reduce the role of conscious intention, and reduce the role of self-reflective, deliberative processes" (p. 266).

Greenwald and his colleagues have developed a measure of implicit attitudes (the IAT) that is both widely available and easily used. A description of the test from his website follows:

"In the IAT a subject responds to a series of items that are to be classified into four categories – typically, two representing a concept discrimination such as *flowers* versus *insects* and two representing an attribute discrimination such as *pleasant* versus *unpleasant* valence. Subjects are asked to respond rapidly with a right-hand key press to items representing one concept and one attribute (e.g., *insect*s and *pleasant*), and with a left-hand key press to items from the remaining two categories (e.g., *flowers* and *unpleasant*). Subjects then perform a second task in which the key assignments for one of the pairs is switched (such that *flowers* and *pleasant* share a response, likewise *insects* and *unpleasant*). The IAT produces measures derived from latencies of responses to these two tasks. These measures are interpreted in terms of association strengths by assuming that subjects respond more rapidly when the concept and attribute mapped onto the same response are strongly associated (e.g., *flowers* and *pleasant*) than when they are weakly associated (e.g., *insects* and *pleasant*)." (http://faculty.washington.edu/agg/iat_materials.htm)

The IAT measure is not without its critics. Blanton and Jaccard (2008) note that many variables are confounded with associative strength, and influence the IAT, including the similarity between two objects (De Houwer, Geldof, and De Bruycker, 2005), different degrees of familiarity with stimulus items on the IAT (Brendl, Markman, and Messner, 2001), and "salience asymmetry," of items on the IAT (Rothermund and Wentura, 2004). Reliability concerns with the IAT have also been raised. Steffens and Buchner (2003) found test-retest correlations ranging from 0.50 to 0.62. Greenwald, Nosek, and Sriram (2006) reported average test-retest scores of the IAT across a range of studies of 0.56. Cunningham, Preacher, and Banaji (2001) reported average test-retest correlations over a two week measurement period of 0.27.

Moreover, Han *et al.* (2010) found that the IAT's susceptibility to extrapersonal (essentially nonattitudinal) associations increases its sensitivity to transient contextual influences (that render both reliability and validity suspect). Specifically, the authors compared the IAT with Olson and Fazio's Personalized IAT (in which the evaluative labels include "I" (e.g. "I like" or "I dislike") rather than a general "Like" or "Dislike." This forces respondents to interpret the stimuli in terms of their own experience, rather than the ambiguous interpretation (either personal or normative) that is possible when a nonspecific label (such as "good") is used. In the first experiment, the traditional IAT was found susceptible to mindset priming effects. An earlier experience in an unrelated task influenced how respondents disambiguated the IAT labels, and whether they adopted a normative or a personal focus while completing the IAT. Subsequent experiments revealed that scores on the IAT indicated attitude change when it was unlikely to have occurred, and failed to detect attitude change in a situation when all other indications were that attitude change had in fact occurred. In each case, by personalizing the IAT the influence of contextual factors was eliminated.

In spite of predating the formal development of the implicit attitude construct, the MODE model anticipates its relevance and accommodates its existence in consideration of attitude function surprisingly well. This is partly due to the definition of attitude in both cases as dependent on associative strength, but also due to the MODE model's explicit accounting for how attitudes are expected to influence behavior. That is, a person's awareness of the attitude (or its basis) may have little to do with whether the attitude can influence behavior. As discussed previously, of greater import is the strength of the attitude and the motivation and opportunity of the individual to process. When the association between the object and its evaluation is sufficiently strong, evaluations may be activated automatically upon the encounter of an object-relevant stimulus.

The activated attitude's influence on further evaluative judgments of the attitude-object depends on the individual's motivation and opportunity to engage in elaborate processing of evaluative characteristics of the attitude-object.

Fazio (2007) notes that the correspondence between implicit and explicit measures of attitudes also depends on the motivation and opportunity of the individual. Specifically, he suggests that since the verbal expression of any object-judgment occurs following the automatic activation of any relevant attitude, such attitude-relevant verbal responses may be influenced by motivational factors as well. Hence, greater correspondence between implicit and explicit measures is expected when motivation to deliberate is low and (or) the opportunity to do so is low. When both are high, additional information is likely to be at least to some extent inconsistent with the attitude indicated by the implicit measure, rendering correlation low.

CONCLUSION

Albeit well-intentioned and within constrained limits successful, the quest for a simple measure of attitudes' influence on behavior appears all but finished, and for those interested in simple answers, the news is not good. As noted, though, the journey has provided insight into a far more interesting set of questions, and uncovered relations between attitudinal processing and behavior that are both more interesting and important for a far broader range of attitudinal phenomena than the answer to the simpler "Does attitude predict behavior?" question. Specifically, attitude existence, verbal expressions of, formation, strength, change, resistance to attack, persuasion, conditions under which some kinds of attitudes predict some kinds of behavior for some kinds of people, and attitudes' relations to other constructs have all become substantial areas of investigation in their own right. Each also has much to inform the student of consumer behavior.

See also   *attitude–behavior consistency; consumer categorization; consumer decision making; consumer intentions; consumer involvement; consumer memory processes; implicit consumer cognition; knowledge accessibility; persuasion*

Bibliography

Ajzen, I. (1985) From intentions to actions: a theory of planned behavior, in *Action-control: From Cognition to Behavior* (eds J. Kuhl and J. Beckman), Springer, Heidelberg, pp. 11–39.

Allport, G. (1935) Attitudes, in *A Handbook of Social Psychology* (ed. C.M. Murchison), Clark University Press, Worchester, MA, pp. 798–844.

Bagozzi, R.P. (1981) Attitudes, intentions, and behavior: a test of some key hypotheses. *Journal of Personality and Social Psychology*, **41**, 607–627.

Bagozzi, R.P. (1982) A field investigation of causal relations among cognitions, affect, intentions, and behavior. *Journal of Marketing Research*, **19** (4), 562–583.

Bargh, J.A. (1994) The four horsemen of automaticity: awareness, intention, efficiency, and control in social

cognition, in *Handbook of Social Cognition*, Vol. 1, 2nd edn (eds R.S. Wyer Jr., and T.K. Srull), Erlbaum, Hillsdale, NJ, pp. 1–40.

Blanton, H. and Jaccard, J. (2008) Unconscious racism: a concept in pursuit of a measure. *Annual Review of Sociology*, **34**, 277–2097.

Brendl, C.M., Markman, A.B. and Messner, C. (2001) How do indirect measures of evaluation work? Evaluating the inference of prejudice in the implicit association test. *Journal of Personality and Social Psychology*, **81**, 760–773.

Chaiken, S. (1980) Heuristic versus systematic information processing and the use of source versus message cues in persuasion. *Journal of Personality and Social Psychology*, **39**, 752–756.

Chaiken, S. (1987) The heuristic model of persuasion, in *Social Influence: The Ontario Symposium*, Vol. 5 (eds M.P. Zanna, J.M. Olson and C.P. Herman), Erlbaum, Hillsdale, NJ, pp. 3–39.

Cunningham, W.A., Preacher, K.J. and Banaji, M.R. (2001) Implicit attitude measures: consistency, stability, and convergent validity. *Psychological Science*, **12**, 163–170.

De Houwer, J., Geldof, T. and De Bruycker, E. (2005) The implicit association test as a general measure of similarity. *Canadian Journal of Experimental Psychology*, **59**, 228–239.

Fazio, R.H. (1990) Multiple processes by which attitudes guide behavior: the MODE model as an integrative framework, in *Advances in Experimental Social Psychology*, Vol. 23 (ed. M.P. Zanna), Academic Press, San Diego, pp. 75–109.

Fazio, R.H. (2007) Attitudes as object-evaluation associations of varying strength. *Social Cognition*, **25**, 603–637.

Fazio, R.H., Powell, M.C. and Williams, C.J. (1989) The role of attitude accessibility in the attitude-to behavior process. *Journal of Consumer Research*, **16** (3), 280–288.

Fazio, R.H., Sanbonmatsu, D.M., Powell, M.C. and Kardes, F.R. (1986) On the automatic activation of attitudes. *Journal of Personality and Social Psychology*, **50**, 229–238.

Fazio, R.H. and Zanna, M.P. (1981) Direct experience and attitude-behavior consistency, in *Advances in Experimental Social Psychology*, Vol. 14 (ed. L. Berkowitz), Academic Press, New York, pp. 161–202.

Fishbein, M. and Ajzen, I. (1975) *Belief, Attitude, Intention, and Behavior: An Introduction to Theory and Research*, Addison-Wesley, Reading, MA.

Greenwald, A.G. and Banaji, M.R. (1995) Implicit social cognition: attitudes, self-esteem, and stereotypes. *Psychological Review*, **102**, 4–27.

Greenwald, A.G., Nosek, B.A. and Sriram, N. (2006) Consequential validity of the implicit association test: comment on Blanton and Jaccard. *American Psychologist*, **61**, 56–61.

Han, H.A., Czellar, S., Olson, M.A. and Fazio, R.H. (2010) Malleability of attitudes or malleability of the IAT? *Journal of Experimental Social Psychology*, **46** (2), 286–298.

Hansen, T., Jensen, J.M., and Solgaard, H.S. (2004) Predicting online grocery buying intention: a comparison of the theory of reasoned action and the theory of planned behavior. *International Journal of Information Management*, **24**, 539–550.

Katz, D. (1960) The functional approach to the study of attitudes. *Public Opinion Quarterly*, **24**, 163 204.

Miniard, P.W. and Cohen, J.B. (1983) Modeling personal and normative influences on behavior, *The Journal of Consumer Research*, **10**, 169–180.

Mitchell, A.A. and Olson, J.C. (1981) Are product attribute beliefs the only mediator of advertising effects on brand attitudes? *Journal of Marketing Research*, **18** (3), 318–332.

Nosek, B.A., Greenwald, A.G. and Banaji, M.R. (2007) The implicit association test at age 7: a methodological and conceptual review, in *Automatic Processes in Social Thinking and Behavior* (ed. J.A. Bargh), Psychology Press, pp. 265–292.

Olson, M.A. and Fazio, R.H. (2004) Reducing the influence of extrapersonal associations on the implicit association test: personalizing the IAT. *Journal of Personality and Social Psychology*, **86**, 653–667.

Petty, R.E. (2001) Attitude change: psychological, in *International Encyclopedia of the Social & Behavioral Sciences* (eds J.S. Neil and P.B. Baltes), Pergamon, Oxford.

Petty, R. and Cacioppo, J.T. (1986) The elaboration likelihood model of persuasion, in *Advances in Experimental Social Psychology* Vol. 19 (ed. L. Berkowitz), Academic Press, New York, pp. 123–205.

Petty, R.E., Cacioppo, J.T. and Schumann, D. (1983) Central and peripheral routes to advertising effectiveness: the moderating role of involvement. *Journal of Consumer Research*, **10**, 135–146.

Rothermund, K. and Wentura, D. (2004) Underlying processes in the implicit association test: dissociating salience from associations. *Journal of Experimental Psychology*, **133**, 139–165.

Sheppard, B.H., Hartwick, J. and Warshaw, P.R. (1988) The theory of reasoned action: a meta-analysis of past research with recommendations for modifications and future research. *Journal of Consumer Research*, **15**, pp. 325–343.

Shimp, T.A. and Kavas, A. (1984) The theory of reasoned action applied to coupon usage. *Journal of Consumer Research*, **11**, 795–809.

Steffens, M.C. and Buchner, A. (2003) Implicit association test: separating transsituationally stable and variable components of attitudes toward gay men. *Experimental Psychology*, **50**, 33–48.

Thurstone, L.L. (1928) Attitudes can be measured. *American Journal of Sociology*, **33**, 529–554.

Wicker, A.W. (1969) Attitudes versus actions: the relationships of verbal and overt behavioral responses to attitude objects. *Journal of Social Issues*, **25**, 41–78.

Wilkie, W.L. and Pessemier, E.A. (1973) Issues in marketing's use of multi-attribute attitude models. *Journal of Marketing Research*, **10**, 428–441.

Wilson, T.D., Lindsey, S. and Schooler, T. (2000) A model of dual attitudes. *Psychological Review*, **107**, 101–126.

brand community

Utpal M. Dholakia and René Algesheimer

INTRODUCTION

Much of consumer behavior is social, impelled by social motives and joint decision-making processes, shaped by socially constructed and shared information, and governed by social norms, influences, rituals, traditions, and taboos. Over the last decade, consumer researchers have increasingly turned their attention to social processes. Among other things, they have studied family and couples decision making, social influences on consumer decision making and self-regulation, consumer subcultures, and the effects of community on consumer choices, attitudes, and behaviors.

A social concept that has emerged as important in explaining and understanding consumer behavior is that of a consumer collective called a *brand community*. The concept of brand community is powerful because it reflects both social process and cultural meaning, stems from a number of converging environmental trends such as the ascendance of the Internet, the decline of traditional family and community, and the growing power of individual consumers in marketplace transactions, and influences consequential marketing outcomes. In this article, we elaborate on this concept by providing a definition of brand community, introduce and elaborate on different types of brand communities, and examine the consequences of consumer participation in them.

DEFINITION OF A BRAND COMMUNITY

Brand communities serve many different functions for consumers and firms. For consumers, brand communities act as conduits of information, channels for solving product-related problems and learning how to use its features, places for finding new friends for social support and for meeting existing friends, and as a means for self-expression through creation and sharing of symbolic content. For firms, brand communities are low-cost, high-efficacy marketing programs which can achieve a number of different marketing objectives simultaneously: the abilities to conduct quick and low-cost marketing research with the target audience, deliver prompt customer service at low expense, educate and socialize new customers, strengthen attachment to the firm's brand for existing customers, and increase the frequency and loyalty of customer purchase behaviors.

We define a *brand community* as *a collective of consumers organized around one particular brand, which is sustained through repeated online and/or offline social interactions and communication among its members who possess a consciousness of kind, feel moral responsibility toward one another, and embrace and propagate the collective's rituals and traditions*. Several aspects of this definition are important and worth elaborating on.

Role of brand in brand community. First, a brand community is a social collective organized around one particular brand, which means that the collective comprises of consumers who have at least some heightened enduring interest in that brand. Such an interest may stem from an attachment to the brand itself, from a more general interest in the product category to which the brand belongs, or (more likely) both. In the prototypical example of a brand community involving Harley Davidson Motorcycle owners, the so-called HOG (Harley Owners Group), many members have a fanatical devotion to the Harley Davidson brand, and view the biker lifestyle symbolized by the brand in idealistic terms. Generally speaking, brand community members are among the most ardent enthusiasts of the brand. Consumer researchers have found brand communities comprised of enthusiasts to exist across a range of product categories, from highly complex technological products like enterprise software (e.g., Oracle and Hewlett Packard) and construction equipment (e.g., John Deere), to consumer durables like virtually all brands of cars, motorcycles, and video game consoles, to low-cost consumable food brands like the Nutella chocolate hazelnut spread, Coca-Cola, and Starburst candy.

Role of communication in brand community.   The second part of the definition explains the process by which the brand community sustains itself. Regular social interactions and communication between members, accomplished through online channels such as bulletin boards, chat-rooms, and email lists, and via offline means such as face-to-face meetings, events, and gatherings, is essential not only for the community's business to be conducted but also, perhaps more importantly, for the relationships between community members to form and strengthen. It is through timely and convenient communication ability that the brand community is able to solve the problems of individual members, deliver technical service and support to them, generate consumer feedback and new product ideas, and deepen participants' knowledge of one another and the strength of their relationships. For individual participants, communicating with others within the brand community serves specific functional purposes such as solving a particular product-related problem or learning how to use a product feature, or may simply provide the means to have a pleasant and enjoyable communal experience.

The essential markers of brand community.   The remaining part of our brand community definition describes the three markers that sociologists stipulate as essential for any social collective to be truly considered a community: (i) a consciousness of kind, (ii) a sense of moral responsibility,

and (iii) the knowledge and acceptance of the collective's rituals and traditions.

The first core marker of community, the so-called *consciousness of kind*, refers to the intrinsic connection that community members feel toward one another through a sense of belonging to the group, and a sense of difference or separation from those who are nonmembers. Consciousness of kind is the force driving the cognitive categorization of in-groups and out-groups and biased behavior favoring the in-groups by consumers, and a primary reason why brand communities are such effective marketing programs. Compared to advertising or direct marketing, brand communities muster the consumers' intrinsic interests and motivations in support of the brand, and in opposition to competing brands. For example, Harley Davidson riders belonging to a HOG believe that they share similar attributes, values, and views of life, and thus feel intrinsically connected to each other. At the same time, they may view riders of other brands such as those who own Honda or Suzuki motorcycles in a negative light. Such beliefs and feelings strongly influence their behaviors.

As Cova 1997 points out in introducing the notion of "linking value," even if brand community members have never met before in a face-to-face setting (as is often the case with brand community participants), they can still experience the connection and the feeling that they know one another. The common social link shared with other members through their interest in the brand sustains the community, even without actual physical interaction among its members.

The second core community marker is a feeling or sense of moral responsibility or obligation toward the community itself and other brand community members, and may include a concern for their well-being as expressed through acts of help or social support such as by teaching newer members how to use the product, and educating them about the practices and norms of the community. The sense of moral responsibility can extend to the community as a whole, and is evident when members make the effort to enforce communal rules and shared values such as fairness, and go out of their way to recruit new members to the community. Usually, such a sense of responsibility is cultivated over time as a member participates in and comes to identify with the community. It deepens with the consumer's experience and tenure in the brand community.

Muniz and O'Guinn (2001) insightfully observed that brand communities are *communities of limited liability* in the sense that for individual consumers they are intentional, voluntary, and partial in the level of involvement they engender, yet are vital to contemporary life and convey significant meaning to the consumer.

The third core community marker is the knowledge and acceptance of the brand community's shared rituals and traditions by its members. As a social collective matures into a community, it develops various rituals and traditions. In an important way, it is these rituals and traditions, which may include such things as narratives of the brand's origins and history, celebrations, brand stories and myths, and ritualistic utterances and actions, which create the sense of the in-group and affirm the cohesiveness of brand community members. For example, it is customary for members of eBay's brand community to recount personal acts of devotion to the eBay site in its chat forums, and instances where they converted a friend or a loved one from the use of a competing site such as amazon.com.

In addition to these markers, an important characteristic of the brand community is the dynamics of the collectivity. Rather than being a static, stabilized state of social relations previously defined as a community, brand communities are dynamic and active. As a consequence, community members are neither passive, nor reactive individuals that only behave in accordance to internal forces, for example, compliance or self-esteem, or external forces, for example, group norms, or peer pressure, of the community. Members actively choose their community and decide when to leave it. Furthermore, ongoing interactions between and activities of community members shape and change the appearance and structure of the community itself. For example, how rituals and traditions are celebrated in the community influences the emergence of its cultural symbols. On the other hand, the brand communities' structure, its norms and set of rules, its rituals and traditions

influence individual's future activities, social interaction, and consumption patterns. Overall, one can say that brand communities are not only "produced" by their members but also "reproduced" by social interactions between their members that reinforce the community. Thus, brand communities are dynamic social phenomena.

TYPES OF BRAND COMMUNITIES

In further understanding brand communities, it is important to distinguish between (i) brand communities that are comprised of consumer networks and those that consist primarily of small friendship groups and (ii) brand communities that are centrally managed by the firm's managers versus those that are often decentrally organized and managed through grassroots efforts by customer enthusiasts.

Network-based and small-group-based brand communities. In describing communities, sociologists make the distinction between *neighborhood solidarities*, which they define as tightly bound, densely knit groups with strong relationships between members, and *social networks*, which are loosely bound, sparsely knit networks of members sharing weak and narrowly defined relationships with one another. Whereas neighborhood solidarities tend to be geographically conjoint, where each member knows everyone else and relies on them for a wide variety of social support, social networks are usually geographically dispersed groups that interact with one another for a specific reason, without prior planning.

Social psychologists similarly distinguish between *common bond* and *common identity* groups. Whereas the bond between members is the glue holding the group together in common bond groups, the attachment depends on identification to the whole group, in common identity groups. Common bond groups correspond to neighborhood solidarities and common identity groups to social networks. These distinctions, of viewing the community as either more or less the same small group of individuals with each of whom the consumer has relationships, or viewing it as a venue where numerous, dynamically changing people (strangers or acquaintances) with shared interests or goals meet, is useful in classifying brand communities.

In some instances, the consumer thinks of the brand community primarily as a venue, and only superficially associates it with any particular individual(s) within it. For instance, a consumer may log on to the bulletin-board of a software company because he/she has a problem that needs solving. In this case, his/her main interest is in solving the problem; there is no expectation or inclination to meet, chat, or socialize with any particular community member. Likewise, an engaged *yelp.com* or *amazon.com* consumer may read and benefit from reviews offered by others, without personal knowledge of, or relationships with, the reviewers. A brand community defined this way, that is, as "a network of relationships among consumers organized around a shared interest in the brand and promoted mainly via online channels, where intellectual and utilitarian support is primary and emotional support is secondary" is a *"network-based brand community."*

In other cases, the brand community's member may identify primarily with a specific small group (or groups) of consumers, rather than with the venue in which the community meets. For example, a software developer may log on to the community chat-room specifically to chat with his/her geographically distant buddy group of kindred software developers every week to trade ideas, learn new concepts, and to socialize with them. Here, the developer's focus is on communication with his/her peer group that he/she knows personally, rather than on the brand community venue. Such a brand community, "constituted by individuals with a dense web of relationships and a consciously shared social identity interacting together as a group, in order to accomplish a wider range of jointly conceived and held goals, to express mutual sentiments and commitments, and to maintain existing relationships," is a *"small-group-based brand community."*

Differences between network-based and small-group-based brand communities. There are several important differences between network-based and small-group-based brand communities. First, not surprisingly, the specific group with which the consumer interacts holds greater importance for members of small-group-based when compared to network-based brand communities. This is because the individual knows everyone else personally, and in many cases, may have shared histories and close personal relationships with them. As a result, relationships between community members are stronger, more resilient, and more stable than those in network-based brand communities, where members participate primarily to achieve functional goals (e.g., to trouble-shoot a problem) and have tenuous, short-lived, and easily severed ties.

Accentuating the group's importance for small-group-based brand community members is also why the brand community venue is often only one of a number of places where such groups meet. Online social interactions are supplemented by face-to-face and other offline forms of interactions. For instance, a small group of HOG members may not only chat online with one another periodically in the course of a week but also meet on weekdays for coffee and fellowship, and on weekends for group outings. In contrast, network-based community members are more likely to interact with each other exclusively through the brand community venue.

The two brand communities also differ in the range of activities its members engage in. Network-based community members are likely to engage primarily in narrow, instrumental, brand-related activities. In contrast, small-group-based community members engage in broad-based activities. For Harley riders belonging to small group brand communities, for example, social interactions occur through group rides for purely recreational purposes or for more formal goals such as fundraising (e.g., a rally for raising funds for the victims of an earthquake or a hurricane), competitions, political protests (e.g., anti-helmet law rallies), or community service. Even more frequently, small group members come together to meet at a pub or restaurant or to mutually examine the latest bikes and accessories at a nearby dealership.

These differences create what we call the *loyalty-influence paradox* in brand communities. Customers belonging to small-group-based brand communities are less likely to be loyal to a particular venue offered to them by the firm to interact in than members of network-based brand communities; yet, at the same time, small-group-based brand community members are more likely to be influenced by the social interactions with other members in the venue when they do participate than those belonging to network-based brand communities. Thus, loyalty to the brand community is inversely correlated with its influence on its members.

The distinctions between network-based and small-group-based brand communities also have implications for managers of these communities. Whereas the primary managerial objective in a network-based brand community is to match individual motives, for example, to find members willing to help solve product-related problems of those who have the questions, in the case of small-group-based brand communities, the main goal is to satisfy the motivations of group members to socialize with one another by providing them various applications that facilitate social interactions. Thus, tools and applications such as buddy lists, instant messaging, providing status updates, and sharing of personal history are likely to be more valued in small-group-based brand communities. In contrast, applications that allow specific functional goals to be reached such as an archive of product-related problem solutions, an "ask-an-expert" service, and a reputation system which rewards problem-solving of other members, are more useful in network-based brand communities. The differences also mean that the marketers' role is starkly different in the two cases: to be active information providers and problem solvers in the case of network-based brand communities, but to be more passive and indirect – in the background – in the case of small-group-based brand communities.

Firm-managed and customer-managed brand communities.   In discussing the types of brand communities, another important distinction is between firm-managed and customer-managed brand communities. Many popular brands have many established brand communities, some organized and managed by the firm's professional marketing managers, and others that are grassroots organizations founded and

run independently by customer enthusiasts. For example, Microsoft XBOX 360, the leading video gaming console, has an established brand community (www.xbox.com/Community) hosted on Microsoft's website and managed by Microsoft managers. Concurrently, there are dozens of XBOX brand communities, founded and managed by its fans such as the Brotherhood of the Box (www.bob.com.sg/forum) and Planetxbox360 (forums.planetxbox360.com).

There are several similarities between firm-managed and customer-managed brand communities. First, both communities are comprised of customers who are fans of the brand. Some participants may even have overlapping memberships within the two communities. Second, participants of both communities are interested in the same subject matter, namely news and information about the brand and its competitors. Finally, although consumers ultimately decide which community to join, there is at least some degree of targeting by community managers. For instance, it is quite common to offer referral rewards in cash, kind, or recognition, to existing members to recruit friends, and to use direct marketing approaches such as email invitations to encourage selected customer segments to participate.

Differences between firm-managed and customer-managed brand communities. There are also several significant differences between firm-managed and customer-managed brand communities. Perhaps the most important distinction has to do with the community manager's motives. Firms provide brand communities to their customers *to accomplish marketing objectives.* Some firms use brand communities to gather marketing research insights by monitoring discussions and/or interacting with participants. Others do so to increase participants' loyalty to their products and brands, and to increase their purchase behaviors. Consequently, customers are recruited to join the community through targeted approaches, and the facilities and affordances provided to participants are designed to reach these objectives. It is not uncommon for firms to use established segmentation variables, in particular, demographic variables for recruiting community participants.

This professional recruitment of fans into communities often contradicts with the social motives of the brand's enthusiasts. This may be the reason why acquisitions and transformations of a customer-managed community into firm-managed communities often fail.

In contrast, customer-managed brand communities rarely have specific marketing goals. Instead, the community managers seek to express their love and admiration for the brand through organizing and managing the community. Participants, too, self-select and join the customer-managed brand community because of a shared passion for the brand, which often overlaps with common values, hobbies, and lifestyles. These differences indicate that customers in firm-managed brand communities should be more similar to each other in demographic characteristics, and those in customer-managed brand communities should be more likely to share psychographic commonalities.

The second difference between the two brand communities has to do with managers' constraints in the two cases. As noted earlier, professional managers of firm-managed brand communities are dictated by the firm's marketing objectives and therefore strive for consistency with its other marketing programs. Consequently, their emphasis is on a fit between the tone and content of the communications of the brand community members and the other marketing communications being sent by the firm. For example, a discussion in the brand community criticizing a newly introduced product and discussing its weaknesses will be viewed as inconsistent with the firm's ongoing advertising campaign that extols its virtues. Likewise, managers have an ingrained discomfort with giving customers free reign because of the possibility of unbridled and/or prolonged criticism by them regarding the firm. On the other hand, members of a customer-managed community do trust other members and their opinions more, because the firm's influence is not emergent. Practitioners and researchers are only now beginning to recognize and study these and other differences between firm-managed and customer-managed communities. This is one research area of great future potential, promising to increase our understanding of the scope and workings of brand communities.

CONSEQUENCES OF CONSUMER PARTICIPATION IN BRAND COMMUNITIES

Perhaps the most important reason for the success and growing importance of brand communities stems from the significant, multifaceted and long-lasting effects that participation in brand communities has on consumers. Consumer researchers have found that a key psychological process that occurs due to brand community participation is that the consumer psychologically identifies with the community, which in turn, mediates a number of important firm-relevant outcomes. It is useful, therefore, to understand what identification means, and examine its effects on the psychology and behavior of the brand community participants.

Identification with the brand community. Brand community identification captures the strength of the consumer's relationship with the brand community, whereby the person construes himself or herself to be a member – that is, as "belonging" to the brand community. In contrast to other personal identities, which may render a person unique and separate, this is a shared or collective identity. The consumer's self-esteem is also boosted to the extent that his or her ego-ideal overlaps with that of the others, and acting as the other acts or wants one to act reinforces one's self-esteem. Identification resembles aspects of normative and informational influence, as well as referent power, and is characterized by the community member's social identity. Several studies suggest that social identity, defined in terms of a valued group, such as a brand community, involves cognitive, affective, and evaluative components.

Considering the cognitive component first, identification with the brand community involves categorization processes, whereby the consumer formulates and maintains a self-awareness of his or her membership within the community (e.g., "I see myself as part of the community"), emphasizing his or her perceived similarities with other community members and dissimilarities with nonmembers. The self is perceptually and behaviorally depersonalized in terms of the relevant group prototype. The cognitive component of identification captures the consciousness-of-kind aspect of brand communities.

Next, the affective component of identification implies a sense of emotional involvement with the group, which social psychologists have characterized as an affective commitment to the group and which can also be viewed as kinship between members. Organizational researchers have shown that affective identification influences in-group favoritism and citizenship behaviors toward the organization. Identification means that the consumer agrees (or strives to agree) with the community's norms, traditions, rituals, and objectives, and promotes its well-being. Third, the *evaluative component of social identity – group-based self-esteem* – has been defined as the positive or negative value connotation attached to brand community membership, and arises from evaluations of self-worth derived from membership. Group-based self-esteem has been found to promote actions that produce in-group welfare by social psychologists.

Identification with the brand community is a useful psychological concept to understand consumer psychology in this context because it produces behavioral intentions to engage in brand community participation, and to maintain a positive self-defining relationship with other community members. It also produces a number of interesting and important outcomes. Among the consequences of identification with the brand community are brand relationship quality, learning, oppositional loyalty, and trust in the firm.

Brand relationship quality. Consumer research on brand community has shown that the consumers' integration within the brand community is a function of their relationships with the brand, other community members, the product, and the firm as a whole. Brand relationship quality is the customer's psychological attachment to the brand and its assessment as a satisfactory partner in an ongoing relationship, and is consistent with the idea that consumers frequently view brands, especially well-liked or beloved ones, in human terms, assigning animate characteristics to them. Brand relationship quality captures the extent to which the consumer identifies with the brand and views his or her self-image as close

to or overlapping with the brand's image. It involves cognitive aspects such as the degree to which the consumer believes that the brand's image overlaps with his or her self-image, and emotional elements such as the degree of the consumer's emotional attachment to the brand.

Brand relationship quality and brand community identification share a bidirectional relationship with one another. For some consumers, the consumer's relationship with the brand precedes and contributes to his or her relationship with the brand community. Many consumers first discover and value the brand for the functional and symbolic benefits it provides. A harmonious relationship with the brand can lead consumers to seek out and interact with like-minded consumers who share their enthusiasm. Moreover, an existing identification with the brand facilitates integration and identification with the brand community. For example, even when traditions, such as greeting other brand users, appear peculiar to the consumer, a strong relationship with the brand may help the person accept them and intrinsically endorse these practices.

On the other hand, integration with, and participation in the brand community, strengthens the customer's relationship with the brand. Not only does participation in the brand community provide opportunities for learning about the product and the brand associations (as we discuss below) but also close contact with other brand devotees rubs off on the consumer, increasing the strength of his or her emotional attachment to the brand. In today's environment, many marketers consider brand relationship quality to be the ultimate objective and metric of their marketing actions.

Learning. For complex, frequently evolving products, customers must continuously learn to keep abreast of changes and new developments and to take advantage of these advances. Traditionally, companies have been responsible for educating their customers to fully leverage the company's service offerings. They have done so by getting customers to participate in firm-organized training delivered by the firm's full-time or contracted employees. However, increasingly, many firms supplement this employee-based education model with peer-to-peer education delivered through brand communities, wherein customers assist their peers in learning about the products and their use. Customers thus take over service functions that are customarily performed by employees and act as "partial employees" of the firm. In eBay's Help Forums, for example, many novice sellers are interested in learning about the efficacy of different decision variables such as offering "buy-it-now" options, starting the auction with a low price versus a high price, and so on. Experienced sellers who are Forum members provide this service, bypassing the eBay employees.

The knowledge that a firm's customer possesses regarding its products, in particular, how to choose and use them, is a significant, valuable, and archivable resource, especially for complex products. Many brand communities exist to tap into, and they disseminate this knowledge effectively to the participant base. For the individual member, this knowledge exchange translates into *learning*, which is defined as the customer's perceptions of increase in his or her own product expertise. Often, customers come to these communities for the first time because of the need to solve a specific problem. Once they receive the solution from the community, and hence have learned, they are captivated by the experience and become and stay a member themselves.

In brand communities, customers learn in vicarious and interactive ways, from the anecdotes, suggestions, and ideas of other members. The created knowledge is thus dependant on the members involved rather than on the pure truth. As members not only report short questions and/or manual-like answers but also share information on the situation, intentions, and feelings about an issue or action, they are able to convey the context. The context information contributes substantially to the learning experience, as it stimulates effective thinking, and supports information prioritization and interpretation. Additionally, in most brand communities, participants can access knowledge repositories such as records of prior conversations, product manuals, user guides, "hacks" from other members, and archives of (frequently asked questions (FAQs), that most communities store. The community

site constitutes a knowledge base of all past incidents to aid the solutions of similar problems in the future and is therefore the collective memory of the individual interactions.

Oppositional brand loyalty. Prior consumer research has shown that brand communities strengthen a member's devotion and loyalty to the brand. For many loyal customers, the most important facet of this loyalty is derived from developing and expressing negative perceptions of competing brands. In fact, some researchers argue that this phenomenon of opposition to another brand and its community is the very defining feature of the brand community. *Oppositional brand loyalty*, which is defined here as "the participant's perception that competing brands are inferior to the target brand and should be avoided," benefits the firm by reducing the likelihood that members will purchase competing brand products, strengthening the possibility of future purchases of the firm's brand.

For the brand community participant, the tendency to position the brand against the competition arises from the perception of being threatened, along with a desire for the target brand to maintain its superiority over the competition. Such an adversarial position is fostered by the perceived normative pressure to conform to the brand community's views and to signal this inclination to conform explicitly to the world, and to dissociate from the disfavored brands through means visible to the community.

Trust in firm. *Trust in the firm* is defined as "the brand community member's willingness to rely on the firm, stemming from a confidence in its benevolence, reliability, and integrity." Trust in the firm is important from a managerial standpoint not only because it creates a relationship that is highly valued by the customer, extending beyond the interactions with the brand community, but also because it has been linked directly to organizational performance.

Research has shown that trust in the firm is affected positively by community identification because the shared consciousness inherent in greater social identification supports stronger convictions about the firm's intentions and integrity, leading to greater trust in it. This reasoning is consistent with the influential commitment-trust marketing theory, which posits that shared values between partners positively affect their trust perceptions. Trust in the community's manager and governance structure also contributes to the brand community member's trust in the firm. This is because the beliefs in the benevolence, reliability, and integrity of the brand community manager, along with the discussions in the trusted community regarding the firm's products and brands, elevate the participant's beliefs in the good intentions and reliability about the firm, leading to greater trust in it.

CONCLUSION

Brand communities offer the promise of a marketing program that is synergistic with the intrinsic motivations, interests, and empowerment of contemporary consumers. Widely applicable and increasingly used by mainstream consumers across a range of product and service categories, they represent avenues for marketers to generate a range of positive outcomes for the firm in cost-effective ways. For consumer researchers, brand communities are venues to study a host of psychological and social issues. Brand communities are certain to grow in research importance and practical significance in the coming years.

Bibliography

Algesheimer, R. (2004) *Brand Communities*, Gabler, Wiesbaden.

Algesheimer, R. and Dholakia, U.M. (2006) Community marketing pays. *Harvard Business Review*, **November**, 26–28.

Algesheimer, R., Dholakia, U.M., and Herrmann, A. (2005) The social influence of brand community: evidence from European car clubs. *Journal of Marketing*, **69** (3), 19–34.

Algesheimer, R. and Gurau, C. (2008) Introducing structuration theory in communal consumption behavior research. *Qualitative Market Research*, **11** (2), 227–245.

Almeida, S.O., Dholakia, U.M., and Mazzon, J.A. (2009) The mixed effects of participant diversity and expressive freedom in firm-managed and customer-managed brand communities Working paper, Rice University.

Bagozzi, R.P. (2005) Socializing Marketing. *Marketing – Journal of Research and Management*, **1**, 101–111.

Bagozzi, R.P. and Dholakia, U.M. (2002) Intentional social action in virtual communities. *Journal of Interactive Marketing*, **16** (2), 2–21.

Bagozzi, R.P. and Dholakia, U.M. (2006a) Open source software user communities: a study of participation in Linux user groups. *Management Science*, **52** (7), 1099–1115.

Bagozzi, R.P. and Dholakia, U.M. (2006b) Antecedents and purchase consequences of customer participation in small group brand communities. *International Journal of Research in Marketing*, **23** (1), 45–61.

Cova, B. (1997) Community and Consumption: toward a definition of the 'Linking Value' of products or Services. *European Journal of Marketing*, **31** (3/4), 297–316.

Dholakia, U.M., Bagozzi, R.P., and Pearo, L.K. (2004) A social influence model of consumer participation in network- and small-group-based virtual communities. *International Journal of Research in Marketing*, **21** (3), 241–263.

Dholakia, U.M., Blazevic, V., Weirtz, C., and Algesheimer, R. (2009) Communal service delivery: how customers benefit from participation in firm-hosted virtual P3 communities. *Journal of Service Research*, **12** (2), 208–226.

Latour, B. (2005) *Reassembling the Social. An Introduction to Actor-Network-Theory*, Oxford University Press, Oxford.

McAlexander, J.H., Schouten, J.W. and Koenig, H.F. (2002) Building brand community. *Journal of Marketing*, **66** (1), 38–54.

Muniz, A.M. Jr. and O'Guinn, T.C. (2001) Brand community. *Journal of Consumer Research*, **27** (4), 412–432.

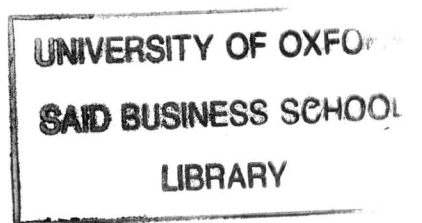

C

childhood socialization and intergenerational influences

Elizabeth S. Moore

"To what extent do family influences experienced during childhood continue to exert influence on our behavior as adults?" This question frames the study of *intergenerational influence*, which is defined as the transmission of information, resources, and beliefs from one family generation to the next. Given the prolonged nature of childhood learning, the fact that some beliefs and attitudes formed within the household persist into adulthood comes as no surprise. It is the *nature* of these influences that is of interest, a topic rooted in socialization theory, and a long-standing area of inquiry in the social sciences (Macoby, 2007).

Socialization is the process through which individuals develop skills, beliefs, and behaviors needed to function successfully in society. It is a primary mechanism by which culture sustains itself. It also helps individuals to develop their personal identities, and assume new roles as they mature. Although socialization is a life-long process, childhood and adolescence are particularly crucial periods of this process.

The family, schools, mass media, religious institutions, and peers contribute in important ways to the socialization process. However, the family is the first and typically most powerful socialization agent, with parents and other family members serving as channels of information, sources of social pressure, and support. Socialization is a bidirectional process with parents and children influencing one another.

Consumer socialization, defined as "processes by which young people acquire the skills, knowledge and attitudes relevant to their

functioning in the marketplace" is one aspect of the broader socialization process (Ward, 1974). Published research provides insight into the development of children's decision-making skills and marketing knowledge, particularly advertising (see John's, 1999 review). It also helps to understand parent–child interaction in household purchase decisions and impacts of parenting style (Carlson and Grossbart, 1988).

Intergenerational consumer research emerged in the 1970s. Since then scholars have shown that these effects are significant, interesting, and potentially important in the marketplace. Early research focused on consumer buying styles. Hill's (1970) longitudinal study showed, for example, that financial planning skills transfer across generations, particularly in families that are poor planners. Parent–child commonalities have also been discovered for choice heuristics, marketplace beliefs, and innovativeness. Interestingly, Cotte and Wood (2004) found that consumer innovativeness is affected by both parents and siblings, but parents are more influential.

Researchers have also examined the transmission of brand and product preferences, outcomes with direct strategic implications. For example, the public versus private nature of consumption for shopping goods may impact family influence levels (Childers and Rao, 1992). Intergenerational impacts are also a source of brand equity for packaged goods, but only for some brands, thus posing strategic challenges for particular marketers (Moore, Wilkie, and Lutz, 2002). These effects are multidimensional (impacting usage, consideration, and preference) and difficult to isolate analytically. Further, many factors are at work in adulthood to sustain or disrupt them.

Current knowledge of intergenerational influences in consumer research is grounded in a relatively small research base. Primary emphasis has been on documenting effects and the forms these take (Moore and Wilkie, 2005). Intriguing challenges lie ahead in the development of new measurement approaches, in understanding the determinants of intergenerational influences, and variation across families.

Bibliography

Carlson, L. and Grossbart, S. (1988) Parental style and consumer socialization of children. *Journal of Consumer Research*, **15**, 77–94.

Childers, T.L. and Rao A.R., (1992) The influence of familial and peer-based reference groups on consumer decisions. *Journal of Consumer Research*, **19**, 198–211.

Cotte, J. and Wood, S.L. (2004) Families and innovative consumer behavior: a triadic analysis of sibling and parental influence. *Journal of Consumer Research*, **31**, 78–86.

Hill, R. (1970) *Family Development in Three Generations*, Schenkman, Cambridge.

John, D.R. (1999) Consumer socialization of children: a retrospective look at twenty-five years of research. *Journal of Consumer Research*, **26**, 183–213.

Macoby, E.E. (2007) Historical overview of socialization research and theory, in *Handbook of Socialization* (eds J.E. Grusec and P.D. Hastings), Guilford Press, New York, pp. 13–41.

Moore, E.S. and Wilkie, W.L. (2005) We are who we were: intergenerational influences in consumer behavior, in *Inside Consumption: Frontiers of Research on Consumer Motives, Goals and Desires* (eds S. Ratneshwar and D.G. Mick), Routledge, London, pp. 208–232.

Moore, E.S., Wilkie, W.L., and Lutz, R.J. (2002) Passing the torch: intergenerational influences as a source of brand equity. *Journal of Marketing*, **66**, 17–37.

Ward, S. (1974) Consumer socialization. *Journal of Consumer Research*, **1**, 1–14.

choice models

Seethu Seetharaman

A brand manager is interested in understanding market demand for his product and how marketing activities influence such demand. Since market demand is simply an aggregation of individual brand choices, numerically quantifying households' brand-choices and their dependence on marketing variables is of central importance to brand managers. Also called *discrete choice models*, brand choice models confront the problem of a household's choice of one brand from a set of mutually exclusive and collectively exhaustive brands within a product category. The model explains households' (observed) brand choices using both *observed* predictor variables (such as brands' prices, advertising activities etc.) and *unobserved* parameters (such as households' brand preferences, price sensitivities etc.), the latter being estimated using consumer choice data.

Consider the example of a household, having decided to buy a bottle of ketchup on a shopping visit, deciding on whether to buy *Heinz* or *Hunts*. The household first evaluates information about the attributes of each brand, for example quality, price, feature advertising (i.e., whether or not a brand is advertised in the newspaper that week) and end-of-aisle display (i.e., whether or not a brand is on display using a shelf talker). If one brand dominates the other along all four attributes, the household chooses the dominant brand. If it dominates the other in some attributes (e.g., price, display), but is dominated by the other brand in other attributes, (e.g., feature advertising, quality) the household's relative preferences for attributes determines which of the two brands the household will buy. A mathematical representation of how a household resolves these trade-offs between attributes in order to choose a brand is called a *brand choice model*. The household is assumed to first express the composite attractiveness of each brand (along the four attributes) using a scalar measure called *utility*. The household is then assumed to choose the brand that offers the higher utility. Since the household's utilities for brands are unknown to the marketing researcher, they must be treated as random variables. For this reason, brand choice models are also called *random utility models*. Next we describe two such random utility models – Logit and Probit.

LOGIT MODEL

We will start with a discussion of the simplest logit model, the binary logit model, and then move on to the multinomial logit model.

Binary logit – a utility theoretic exposition. Let us consider the example of the household choosing between *Heinz* and *Hunts* brands of ketchup at a shopping occasion. Suppose the household's utilities for the two brands at time t are given by U_{1t} and U_{2t} respectively. The household will choose *Heinz* at time t if $U_{1t} > U_{2t}$ and Hunts if $U_{2t} > U_{1t}$. While U_{1t} and U_{2t} are known to the household, they are unknown to the marketing researcher. The marketing researcher specifies these utilities as follows.

$$U_{1t} = V_{1t} + \varepsilon_{1t}$$
$$U_{2t} = V_{2t} + \varepsilon_{2t} \qquad (1)$$

where V_{1t} and V_{2t} are the deterministic components of the utilities at time t, while ε_{1t} and ε_{2t} are the random components of the utilities (that represent the effects of unobserved variables, which are known to the household but unknown to the researcher, that influence households' utilities for brands).[1] The household's probability of choosing each brand is then expressed as follows.

$$\Pr(1) = \Pr(U_{1t} > U_{2t})$$
$$= \Pr(V_{1t} + \varepsilon_{1t} > V_{2t} + \varepsilon_{2t})$$
$$= \Pr(\varepsilon_{2t} - \varepsilon_{1t} < V_{1t} - V_{2t})$$
$$\Pr(2) = \Pr(U_{2t} > U_{1t})$$
$$= \Pr(V_{2t} + \varepsilon_{2t} > V_{1t} + \varepsilon_{1t})$$
$$= \Pr(\varepsilon_{2t} - \varepsilon_{1t} > V_{1t} - V_{2t}) \qquad (2)$$

The deterministic components of the utilities are specified in terms of observed brand attributes as shown below.

$$V_{1t} = V(X_{1t}) = \alpha_1 + X_{1t}\beta$$
$$V_{2t} = V(X_{2t}) = \alpha_2 + X_{2t}\beta \qquad (3)$$

where $X_{1t} = (P_{1t}D_{1t}F_{1t})$ and $X_{2t} = (P_{2t}D_{2t}F_{2t})$ are brand-specific attribute vectors at time t,

where P_{it}, D_{it} and F_{it} stand for price, display and feature of brand i respectively, $\beta = (\beta_1\beta_2\beta_3)'$, is a parameter-vector associated with these attributes,[2] and $\alpha = (\alpha_1\alpha_2)'$ is a vector of brand constants. The random components ε_{1t} and ε_{2t} are assumed to be distributed *iid* Gumbel with location parameter η and scale parameter $\mu > 0$. That is,

$$F(\varepsilon_{1t}) = e^{-e^{-\mu(\varepsilon_{1t}-\eta)}}$$
$$F(\varepsilon_{2t}) = e^{-e^{-\mu(\varepsilon_{2t}-\eta)}} \qquad (4)$$

This implies that $\varepsilon_{2t} - \varepsilon_{1t}$ is distributed logistic with location parameter 0 and scale parameter $\mu > 0$. That is,

$$F(\varepsilon_{2t} - \varepsilon_{1t}) = \frac{1}{1 + e^{-\mu(\varepsilon_{2t}-\varepsilon_{1t})}} \qquad (5)$$

Using 5 in 2 we get

$$\Pr(1) = \frac{1}{1 + e^{-\mu(V_{1t}-V_{2t})}}$$
$$\Pr(2) = \frac{e^{-\mu(V_{1t}-V_{2t})}}{1 + e^{-\mu(V_{1t}-V_{2t})}} \qquad (6)$$

which can be rewritten as

$$\Pr(1) = \frac{e^{\mu V_{1t}}}{e^{\mu V_{1t}} + e^{\mu V_{2t}}}$$
$$\Pr(2) = \frac{e^{\mu V_{2t}}}{e^{\mu V_{1t}} + e^{\mu V_{2t}}} \qquad (7)$$

Substituting 3 in 7 yields

$$\Pr(1) = \frac{e^{\mu(\alpha_1+X_{1t}\beta)}}{e^{\mu(\alpha_1+X_{1t}\beta)} + e^{\mu(\alpha_2+X_{2t}\beta)}}$$
$$\Pr(2) = \frac{e^{\mu(\alpha_2+X_{2t}\beta)}}{e^{\mu(\alpha_1+X_{1t}\beta)} + e^{\mu(\alpha_2+X_{2t}\beta)}} \qquad (8)$$

Equation 8 represents the *binary logit model*. Since the parameter μ is confounded with the scale of the β's, it is usually fixed at 1. This yields the following standard version of the binary logit model.

$$\Pr(1) = \frac{e^{\alpha_1+X_{1t}\beta}}{e^{\alpha_1+X_{1t}\beta} + e^{\alpha_2+X_{2t}\beta}}$$
$$\Pr(2) = \frac{e^{\alpha_2+X_{2t}\beta}}{e^{\alpha_1+X_{1t}\beta} + e^{\alpha_2+X_{2t}\beta}} \qquad (9)$$

The brand choice probabilities in 9 will remain unchanged if a constant is added to all brands' utilities. For this reason, the intercept term associated with one of the brands is fixed (usually at zero). This yields the following *estimable* version of the binary logit model.

$$Pr(1) = \frac{e^{\alpha_1 + X_{1t}\beta}}{e^{\alpha_1 + X_{1t}\beta} + e^{X_{2t}\beta}}$$

$$Pr(2) = \frac{e^{X_{2t}\beta}}{e^{\alpha_1 + X_{1t}\beta} + e^{X_{2t}\beta}} \quad (10)$$

The idea of random utility goes way back to Thurstone (1927). However, a formal exposition of the logit model from random utility primitives, as laid down in this section, first appeared in McFadden (1974).

Binary logit – a regression-based exposition. The binary logit model can also be understood as a regression model, where the dependent variable y_t takes one of two values, that is, 1 or 0. The regression model looks as shown below.

$$Y_t = \pi(X_t) + \varepsilon$$

where

$$\pi(X_t) = \frac{e^{\alpha_1 + X_{1t}\beta}}{e^{\alpha_1 + X_{1t}\beta} + e^{X_{2t}\beta}}$$

and

$$\varepsilon_{1t} = 1 - \pi(X_t) \text{ if } Y_t = 1$$
$$= -\pi(X_t) \text{ if } Y_t = 0 \quad (11)$$

This regression-based representation of a binary logit model is also called a *logistic regression*. There are two key differences between the conventional linear regression model and the logistic regression model: one, unlike the linear regression model where $E(Y_t|X_t) = X_t\beta$ which is *linear* in X_t and *unbounded*, in the logistic regression model $E(Y_t|X_t) = \pi(X_t)$, which is *S-shaped* in X_t and *bounded* between 0 and 1; two, unlike the linear regression model where ε has a *normal* distribution with mean 0 and *constant* variance σ^2, in the logistic regression model ε has a *two-point discrete* distribution with mean 0 and *heteroscedastic* variance $\pi(X_t)[1 - \pi(X_t)]$. Since the observed choice outcome Y_t has a

binomial distribution with parameter $\pi(X_t)$, that is a *logit* function of the marketing variables, this model is also called the *binomial logit* model. Next we will discuss how to estimate the parameters of the binary logit/binomial logit/logistic regression model using consumer choice data.

Maximum likelihood estimation of the binary logit model. Given n independent observations of (X_t, Y_t) the parameters of the logistic regression model are estimated by maximizing the following *likelihood* function.

$$l(\beta) = \prod_{t=1}^{n} \pi(X_t)^{Y_t}[1 - \pi(X_t)]^{1-Y_t} \quad (12)$$

which is equivalent to maximizing the following *log-likelihood* function.

$$L(\beta) = \ln[l(\beta)] = \sum_{t=1}^{n} \{Y_t \ln \pi(X_t)$$
$$+ (1 - Y_t) \ln[1 - \pi(X_t)]\} \quad (13)$$

Maximization involves differentiating $L(\beta)$ with respect to β and setting the resulting expressions to zero. This yields the following $(p + 1)$ *likelihood equations*.

$$\sum_{t=1}^{n} [Y_t - \pi(X_t)] = 0$$

$$\sum_{t=1}^{n} X_{tk}[Y_t - \pi(X_t)] = 0 \, (k = 1, \ldots, p)$$

$$(14)$$

where $p = 3$ stands for the number of predictor variables in the model. Since the likelihood equations are *non-linear* in β, they require special numerical methods for their solution (unlike the linear regression model where the first-order equations are *linear* in β). Optimization modules in programming languages such as SAS, Gauss, Fortran, and so on, automatically employ these numerical methods. One such numerical method is the *Newton-Raphson* method that iterates using the formula

$$\hat{\beta}_{i+1} = \hat{\beta}_i - \left[\frac{\partial^2 L}{\partial \beta \partial \beta'}\right]_{\hat{\beta}_i}^{-1} \left[\frac{\partial L}{\partial \beta}\right]_{\hat{\beta}_i} \quad (15)$$

and converges when $|\hat{\beta}_{i+1} - \hat{\beta}_i|$ is within a predetermined tolerance level ξ. Faster methods, such as the *Davidson Fletcher Powell* (DFP) method, use approximations for the derivatives instead of directly evaluating the derivatives. Solving the likelihood equations using one of these numerical methods yields $\hat{\beta}$ and $\hat{\pi}(X_t)$, the maximum likelihood estimates (MLE) of β and $\pi(X_t)$ respectively. Before MLE became computationally easy to perform, marketing researchers employed an alternative estimation procedure to estimate the parameters of the logit model. This was based on the *logit transformation*

$$\ln\left[\frac{\pi(X_t)}{1 - \pi(X_t)}\right] = \alpha_1 + (X_{1t} - X_{2t})\beta \quad (16)$$

which suggested that one could run a linear regression of $\ln\left[\frac{\pi(X_t)}{1-\pi(X_t)}\right]$ versus $X_{1t} - X_{2t}$ in order to estimate $\hat{\beta}$. In order to do this, researchers would group observations with the same $X_{1t} - X_{2t}$ together, compute the fraction of purchase observations in each group to estimate $\hat{\pi}(X_t)$, and then run a linear regression of $\ln\left[\frac{\hat{\pi}(X_t)}{1-\hat{\pi}(X_t)}\right]$ versus $X_{1t} - X_{2t}$ across groups. For an illustration of this estimation procedure, see Jones and Zufryden (1982). In this approach, heteroscedasticity in the errors must be explicitly adjusted for. This method is now out of vogue since current statistical software packages have MLE routines built into them. Further, MLEs have desirable asymptotic properties, as discussed next.

Asymptotic properties of maximum likelihood estimators. MLEs have desirable asymptotic properties, that is, properties that can be invoked in extremely large samples (such as those available from scanner panel data) and easily derivable compared to small-sample properties. Two of these properties are described below.

1. *Consistency.* This refers to the distribution of the MLE "collapsing" on the true parameter value as the sample gets larger. It implies

the following.

$$\lim_{n\to\infty} \Pr[\beta - \varepsilon < \hat{\beta} < \beta + \varepsilon]$$
$$= 1 \,\forall \varepsilon > 0$$
$$\lim_{n\to\infty} E[(\hat{\beta} - \beta)^2]$$
$$= \lim_{n\to\infty} E[(\hat{\beta} - E\hat{\beta})^2]$$
$$+ [E\hat{\beta} - \beta]^2 = 0 \quad (17)$$

which can be rewritten as

$$p\lim_{n\to\infty} \hat{\beta} = \beta$$
$$\lim_{n\to\infty} \text{MSE}(\hat{\beta}) = \lim_{n\to\infty}[\text{Var}(\hat{\beta})$$
$$+ \text{Bias}(\hat{\beta})^2] = 0 \quad (18)$$

where $\text{MSE}(\hat{\beta})$, $\text{Var}(\hat{\beta})$ and $\text{Bias}(\hat{\beta})$ stand for the mean-squared-error, variance and bias associated with $\hat{\beta}$ respectively. Consistency, therefore, implies that

$$\lim_{n\to\infty} \text{Var}(\hat{\beta}) = 0, \lim_{n\to\infty} \text{Bias}(\hat{\beta})^2 = 0$$
$$(19)$$

If $\hat{\beta}$ is a consistent estimator of β, then $h(\hat{\beta})$ is a consistent estimator of $h(\beta)$ where $h(.)$ is a continuous function. This is called *Slutsky's theorem.*[3] Further, if $\hat{\beta}$ is an MLE of β, then $h(\hat{\beta})$ is an MLE of $h(\beta)$ where $h(.)$ is a continuous function. This greatly simplifies the algebraic derivation of the MLE of a highly non-linear function of model parameters.

2. *Best asymptotic normality (BAN).* The distribution of the MLE can be well approximated by a normal distribution as the sample gets larger as shown below.

$$\lim_{n\to\infty} \sqrt{n}[\hat{\beta} - \beta] \sim N(0, \sigma^2) \quad (20)$$

where σ^2 is called the *asymptotic variance* of the MLE. Further, the MLE is *asymptotically efficient*, that is, σ^2 tends to zero (as $n \to \infty$) faster than the variance of any other consistent estimator.[4] The asymptotic variance of $\hat{\beta}$ is equal to the *Cramer Rao Lower Bound* (i.e., the minimum variance that an unbiased estimator can have), and is estimated as shown below.

$$\text{Var}(\hat{\beta}) = I^{-1}(\hat{\beta})$$

where

$$\mathbf{I}(\hat{\beta}) = - \begin{bmatrix} \frac{\partial^2 L(\beta)}{\partial \beta_1^2} & \frac{\partial^2 L(\beta)}{\partial \beta_1 \partial \beta_2} & \cdots & \frac{\partial^2 L(\beta)}{\partial \beta_1 \partial \beta_p} \\ \cdots & \frac{\partial^2 L(\beta)}{\partial \beta_2^2} & \cdots & \frac{\partial^2 L(\beta)}{\partial \beta_2 \partial \beta_p} \\ \cdots & \cdots & \cdots & \\ \cdots & \cdots & \cdots & \frac{\partial^2 L(\beta)}{\partial \beta_p^2} \end{bmatrix}_{\beta=\hat{\beta}}$$

(21)

where $\mathbf{I}(\hat{\beta})$ is called the *information matrix*. The variance of β_k is simply the kth diagonal element of $\text{Var}(\hat{\beta})$. The information matrix can be written compactly as shown below.

$$\hat{\mathbf{I}}(\hat{\beta}) = X'VX$$

$$V = - \begin{bmatrix} \hat{\pi}_1 & 0 & \cdots & 0 \\ (1-\hat{\pi}_1) & & & \\ \cdots & \hat{\pi}_2 & \cdots & 0 \\ & (1-\hat{\pi}_2) & & \\ \cdots & \cdots & \cdots & \\ \cdots & \cdots & \cdots & \hat{\pi}_n \\ & & & (1-\hat{\pi}_n) \end{bmatrix}$$

(22)

where X is the $n^*(p+1)$ predictor matrix.

If $g(\hat{\beta})$ is a continuous function of $\hat{\beta}$, the asymptotic variance of $g(\hat{\beta})$ can be calculated as the square of the first derivative of $g(\beta)$ with respect to β (evaluated at $\hat{\beta}$) times the asymptotic variance of $\hat{\beta}$. This technique, based on approximating the function $g(\beta)$ as a linear function of β at $\beta = \hat{\beta}$, is called the *delta method*.

Interpreting logit parameters.   In a linear regression, the coefficient β_k stands for the change in y for a unit change in X_k. In a logistic regression, β_k stands for the change in *log-odds* for a unit change in X_k, as shown below.

$$\hat{\beta}_k = \ln \left[\frac{\hat{\pi}(X_k+1)}{1-\hat{\pi}(X_k+1)} \right] - \ln \left[\frac{\hat{\pi}(X_k)}{1-\hat{\pi}(X_k)} \right]$$

(23)

which can also be written as

$$\hat{\beta}_k = \ln \left[\frac{\frac{\hat{\pi}(X_k+1)}{1-\hat{\pi}(X_k+1)}}{\frac{\hat{\pi}(X_k)}{1-\hat{\pi}(X_k)}} \right] = \ln[OR_k] \quad (24)$$

where OR_k stands for the *odds-ratio* based on variable X_k. In other words, the coefficient β_k stands for the *log-odds ratio* based on the variable X_k.

Hypothesis testing.   The *likelihood ratio* (LR) test is used to test hypotheses about parameters of the binary logit model, for example, testing the joint significance of a set of estimates. It is based on the following test statistic.

$$G = -2^* \ln \left[\frac{l^*}{l} \right] = -2^*[L^* - L] \sim \chi_k^2 \quad (25)$$

where L^* is the log-likelihood of the restricted model, L is the log-likelihood of the unrestricted model, k is the number of restrictions. If one used this to test the significance of the estimated price coefficient, L^* will be the log-likelihood of the model estimated after dropping the price variable from the model, and $k = 1$. The LR test is analogous to the F-test in linear regression models.

The *Wald* test is used to test individual significance of estimated parameters. It is based on the following test statistic.

$$W = \frac{\hat{\beta}_k}{\text{S}\hat{\text{E}}(\hat{\beta}_k)} \sim t_1 \quad (26)$$

where $\hat{\beta}_k$ is the MLE of the coefficient of the kth predictor variable and $\text{S}\hat{\text{E}}(\hat{\beta}_k)$ is the estimate of its standard error. One can also construct confidence intervals for parameters using the *Wald* statistic. The *Wald* test is analogous to the *t*-test in linear regression models. The difference between the *Wald* test and the LR test is that the *Wald* test employs the estimates themselves while the LR test uses the log-likelihood values instead. The *Wald* test has lower computational cost since the LR test involves the estimation of two models – restricted and unrestricted. Asymptotically, the two tests are equivalent. In fact, there is another asymptotically equivalent test called the *score test* or *Lagrange multiplier test* that uses derivatives instead.

Assessing model fit. Model fit is typically assessed on the basis of the "distance" between observed Y's and fitted $\hat{Y}$'s. Some of the popular measures of model fit are listed below.

1. *Pearson chi-square statistic.* This is given by

$$\sum_{c=1}^{C} r(Y_c, \hat{\pi}_c)^2 \sim \chi^2_{C-(p+1)} \quad (27)$$

where

$$r(Y_c, \hat{\pi}_c) = \frac{Y_c - m_c \hat{\pi}_c}{\sqrt{m_c \hat{\pi}_c (1 - \hat{\pi}_c)}} \quad (28)$$

where Y_c stands for the number of observed positive responses with *covariate pattern c*. A *covariate pattern* refers to a single set of values for the covariates in a model, for example, price = $1, display = 1, feature = 0. If C refers to the number of distinct values of covariates that are observed in the data $(C \leq n)$, and m_c refers to the number of observations with covariate pattern c, then $\sum_{c=1}^{C} m_c = n$. If the model fits the data well, one would expect this statistic to be less than the critical value from the chi-square table.

2. *Hit rate.* Also called *classification rate*, refers to the percentage of observations that are correctly classified. It is given by

$$\frac{n - \sum_{t=1}^{n} |Y_t - \hat{Y}|}{n} \quad (29)$$

where Y_t is the observed choice outcome at time t and $\hat{Y}_t = 1$ if $\hat{Y}_t > 0.5$. A disadvantage of the *hit rate* measure is that it depends heavily on the distribution of the true probabilities in the sample. If the true probabilities are all close to 0 or 1, most models would do equally well on this criterion. Conversely, if the true probabilities are all close to 0.5, even a good model may not do well on this criterion.

3. *Efron's (1978) R^2.* This is given by

$$1 - \frac{\sum_{t=1}^{n} (Y_t - \hat{\pi}_t)^2}{\sum_{t=1}^{n} (Y_t - \overline{Y})^2} \quad (30)$$

This measure does not suffer from the deficiency of the *hit rate* measure, and is in the same spirit as the R^2 measure in the linear regression model. The numerator of the second term is called *sum of squared residuals*. The use of this measure cannot be defended strongly since the logit model is a heteroscedastic regression model.

4. *McFadden's (1974) Adjusted R^2.* This is given by

$$R^2_{adj} = 1 - \frac{L_p}{L_o} \quad (31)$$

where L_p is the log-likelihood of the full model and L_o is the log-likelihood of a logit model with an intercept only.

5. *Log-likelihood.* The maximized value of the log-likelihood function itself is an intuitive measure of model fit. In order to adjust for the number of parameters in the model, one can use the L-R test to test whether the change in log-likelihood in going from a restricted version of the proposed model to the proposed model is statistically significant. The L-R test requires that the two models being compared are nested models.

6. *Akaike information criterion (AIC).* This is used to compare non-nested models; the measure is given by

$$AIC = -2^* L + 2^* k \quad (32)$$

which adjusts the log-likelihood L based on the number of parameters k.

7. *Schwarz Bayesian criterion (SBC).* This is also used to compare non-nested models, the measure is given by

$$SBC = -2^* L + \ln n^* k \quad (33)$$

which penalizes a highly parameterized model more than the AIC if $n > e^2$.

External validation refers to the evaluation of the above-mentioned goodness-of-fit measures for a model using a *holdout sample* of observations. For example, if one used the first 80% of a household's purchase observations to fit model parameters ("calibration"), one can then evaluate hit rates, adjusted R^2 for the remaining 20% of the household's purchase observations using the estimated model parameters ("holdout validation"). Horowitz and Louviere (1993) propose a holdout validation scheme that takes into account sampling errors in predicted choices. It is based on estimating the linear regression model $Y_t = \alpha \hat{\pi}_t + \varepsilon_{jt}$, and testing the hypothesis $\hat{\alpha} = 1$.

Multinomial logit – a utility theoretic exposition. Let us consider the example of a household choosing between $\mathcal{J}$ brands of laundry detergents – *Tide, Wisk, Surf, Cheer, Bold, Gain, Era, Oxydol, Dreft, Ivory Snow*, and so on, at a shopping occasion. Suppose the household's utilities for the $\mathcal{J}$ brands at time t are given by $U_{1t}, \ldots, U_{\mathcal{J}t}$ respectively. The household will choose *Cheer* (say, brand i) at time t if $U_{it} > U_{jt}$ $\forall j \neq i$. The household's probability of choosing *Cheer* is then expressed as follows.

$$Pr(i) = Pr(U_{it} > U_{jt}, j \neq i) \qquad (34)$$

which can be rewritten as

$$Pr(i) = Pr(U_{it} > \max_{j \neq i} U_{jt}) \qquad (35)$$

which conveniently reduces the problem of making $\mathcal{J}$ pair-wise utility comparisons to making just one pair-wise comparison, that is, between U_i and $\max_{j \neq i} U_{jt}$. If we know the distributions of the two random variables U_i and $\max_{j \neq 1} U_{jt}$, the probability in 35 can be appropriately derived.

We assume the random components in the utilities, ε_{jt}, to be distributed *iid* Gumbel with location parameter η and scale parameter $\mu > 0$. This implies that $U_{jt} = V_{jt} + \varepsilon_{jt}$ is distributed Gumbel with location parameter $\eta + V_{jt}$ and scale parameter $\mu > 0$. The distribution of $\max_{j \neq i} U_{jt}$, is derived as follows:

$$F_{\max_{j \neq i} U_{jt}}(u) = \prod_{j \neq i} F_{U_{jt}}(u)$$

$$= \prod_{j \neq i} e^{-e^{-\mu(u - V_{jt} - \eta)}} = e^{-\sum_{j \neq i} e^{-\mu(u - V_{jt} - \eta)}}$$

$$= e^{-e^{-\mu(u - \frac{1}{\mu} \ln \sum_{j \neq i} e^{\mu(V_{jt} + \eta)})}} \qquad (36)$$

which is distributed Gumbel with location parameter $\frac{1}{\mu} \ln \sum_{j \neq i} e^{\mu(V_{jt} + \eta)}$ and scale parameter μ. Now we can rewrite 35 as follows

$$Pr(i) = Pr(\max_{j \neq i} U_{jt} - U_{it} < 0) \qquad (37)$$

Since the difference between two Gumbel variates (with a common scale parameter μ) is distributed logistic whose location parameter is simply the difference between the location parameters of the two Gumbel variates, 37 can be written as follows

$$Pr(i) = F_{\text{logistic}}(0)$$

$$= \frac{1}{1 + e^{-\mu\left(\eta + V_{it} - \frac{1}{\mu} \ln \sum_{j \neq i} e^{\mu(V_{jt} + \eta)}\right)}} \qquad (38)$$

which can be written in a more convenient form as follows (setting $\eta = 0$)

$$Pr(i) = \frac{e^{\mu V_{it}}}{\sum_{j=1}^{\mathcal{J}} e^{\mu V_{it}}} \qquad (39)$$

which represents the *multinomial logit model* (MNL). Since the parameter μ is confounded with the scale of the β's, it is usually fixed at 1. This yields the following standard version of the MNL model.

$$Pr(i) = \frac{e^{V_{it}}}{\sum_{j=1}^{\mathcal{J}} e^{V_{it}}} = \frac{e^{\alpha_{it} + X_{it}\beta}}{\sum_{j=1}^{\mathcal{J}} e^{\alpha_{jt} + X_{jt}\beta}} \qquad (40)$$

The brand choice probabilities in 40 will remain unchanged if a constant is added to all brands' utilities. For this reason, the intercept term associated with one of the brands is fixed (usually at zero). This yields the following *estimable* version of the MNL model (where the intercept of the $\mathcal{J}$th brand has been fixed at zero).

$$\Pr(i) = \pi_i = \frac{e^{\alpha_{it}+X_{it}\beta}}{\sum\limits_{j=1}^{\mathcal{J}-1} e^{\alpha_{jt}+X_{jt}\beta} + e^{X_{\mathcal{J}t}\beta}} \quad (41)$$

For the first published application of the MNL model to scanner panel data on brand choices, see Guadagni and Little (1983). It is useful to note here that the MNL model is equally derivable using *deterministic utility* (instead of *random utility*) primitives. For example, one could assume that households have deterministic utilities (V_j) for brands, but have probabilistic rules that determine which brands they buy (Luce, 1959). If the probabilistic rule is the *Luce Choice Axiom*, a household's brand choice probabilities are given by

$$\Pr(i) = \pi_i = \frac{V_i}{\sum\limits_{j=1}^{\mathcal{J}} V_j}, \quad (42)$$

which would be identical to the MNL model in 41 if $V_i = e^{\alpha_i + X_i\beta}$.

Maximum likelihood estimation of the MNL model. Given n independent observations of (X_t, Y_t) the parameters of the MNL model are estimated by maximizing the following *likelihood* function.

$$l(\beta) = \prod_{t=1}^{n} \pi_1(X_t)^{Y_{1t}} \pi_2(X_t)^{Y_{2t}} \dots \pi_{\mathcal{J}}(X_t)^{Y_{\mathcal{J}t}} \quad (43)$$

which is equivalent to maximizing the following *log-likelihood* function.

$$L(\beta) = \ln[l(\beta)] = \sum_{t=1}^{n} \{ Y_{1t} \ln \pi_1(X_t)$$
$$+ Y_{2t} \ln \pi_2(X_t) + \dots + Y_{\mathcal{J}t} \ln \pi_{\mathcal{J}}(X_t) \} \quad (44)$$

Maximization involves differentiating $L(\beta)$ with respect to β and setting the resulting expressions to zero. This yields the following $(\mathcal{J}-1)*(p+1)$ *likelihood equations.*

$$\sum_{t=1}^{n} [Y_{jt} - \pi_j(X_t)] = 0, j = 1, \dots, \mathcal{J}-1$$

$$\sum_{t=1}^{n} X_{jkt}[Y_{jt} - \pi_j(X_t)] = 0 \ (k = 1, \dots, p),$$
$$j = 1, \dots, \mathcal{J}-1 \quad (45)$$

Since these equations are *non-linear* in β, they require special methods for their solution. One uses the *Cramer Rao Lower Bound* to estimate the variance-covariance matrix of the estimated parameters as shown below.

$$\text{Var}(\beta) = I^{-1}(\hat{\beta})$$

where

$$\mathbf{I}(\hat{\beta}) = - \begin{bmatrix} \frac{\partial^2 L(\beta)}{\partial\beta_1^2} & \frac{\partial^2 L(\beta)}{\partial\beta_1\partial\beta_2} & \cdots & \frac{\partial^2 L(\beta)}{\partial\beta_1\partial\beta_p} \\ \cdots & \frac{\partial^2 L(\beta)}{\partial\beta_2^2} & \cdots & \frac{\partial^2 L(\beta)}{\partial\beta_2\partial\beta_p} \\ \cdots & \cdots & \cdots & \\ \cdots & \cdots & \cdots & \frac{\partial^2 L(\beta)}{\partial\beta_p^2} \end{bmatrix}$$
$$(46)$$

where $\mathbf{I}(\hat{\beta})$ is called the *information matrix*. The variance of β_k is simply the kth diagonal element of $\text{Var}(\beta)$. The information matrix can be written compactly as shown below.

$$\hat{\mathbf{I}}(\hat{\beta}) = - \begin{bmatrix} \hat{\mathbf{I}}(\hat{\beta})_{11} & \hat{\mathbf{I}}(\hat{\beta})_{12} & \cdots & \hat{\mathbf{I}}(\hat{\beta})_{1\mathcal{J}-1} \\ \cdots & \hat{\mathbf{I}}(\hat{\beta})_{22} & \cdots & \hat{\mathbf{I}}(\hat{\beta})_{2\mathcal{J}-1} \\ \cdots & \cdots & \cdots & \cdots \\ \cdots & \cdots & \cdots & \hat{\mathbf{I}}(\hat{\beta})_{\mathcal{J}-1\mathcal{J}-1} \end{bmatrix}$$

$$\hat{\mathbf{I}}(\hat{\beta})_{jj} = X'V_{jj}X$$
$$\hat{\mathbf{I}}(\hat{\beta})_{jk} = X'V_{jk}X$$

$$V_{jj} = - \begin{bmatrix} \hat{\pi}_{1j} & 0 & \cdots & 0 \\ (1-\hat{\pi}_{1j}) & & & \\ \cdots & \hat{\pi}_{2j} & \cdots & 0 \\ & (1-\hat{\pi}_{2j}) & & \\ \cdots & \cdots & \cdots & \\ \cdots & \cdots & \cdots & \hat{\pi}_{nj-1} \\ & & & (1-\hat{\pi}_{nj-1}) \end{bmatrix}$$

$$V_{ij} = - \begin{bmatrix} \hat{\pi}_{1j}\hat{\pi}_{1k} & 0 & \cdots & 0 \\ \cdots & \hat{\pi}_{2j}\hat{\pi}_{2k} & \cdots & 0 \\ \cdots & \cdots & \cdots & \\ \cdots & \cdots & \cdots & \hat{\pi}_{nj-1}\hat{\pi}_{nk-1} \end{bmatrix}$$

$$(47)$$

where X is the $n^*(p+1)$ predictor matrix.

Role of the scale parameter.   The scale parameter μ of the logit model cannot be identified since it is confounded with the utility parameters β. Hence it is arbitrarily set to 1 when dealing with a given household's brand choices. Suppose we want to compare the estimated price sensitivity of two different households. The estimates are confounded with their respective scale factors. Scale factor differences (i.e., variance differences) between the two households must therefore be isolated before comparing utility parameter estimates across individuals. Otherwise, statistical tests such as the *Chow test* may lead one to falsely conclude that parameter vectors differ between households when indeed they do not. Swait and Louviere (1993) propose a way of testing equality in parameter estimates across datasets that works as follows: first, separate logit models are estimated for the two datasets, yielding maximized log-likelihood of L_1 and L_2 respectively; second, the data from the two datasets are pooled and a logit model is estimated based on the assumption of a common β, but different scale factors for the two datasets. This yields estimates of β and the ratio (μ_2/μ_1) along with the maximized log-likelihood L_μ. An LR test of L_μ versus $L_1 + L_2$ is a test of the hypothesis $H_1 : \beta_1 = \beta_2 = \beta$. Therefore, even though one cannot identify the scale parameter for any given dataset, one can identify the ratio of the scale parameter for two different datasets.

Price elasticities.   One useful managerial measure is the price elasticity of a brand, that is the percentage change in a brand's demand in response to a percentage change in its price. A brand's price elasticities are computed as follows

$$\text{OwnElas}_i = \frac{\partial \pi_{it}}{\partial P_{it}} * \frac{P_{it}}{\pi_{it}}$$

$$\text{CrossElas}_{ij} = \frac{\partial \pi_{it}}{\partial P_{jt}} * \frac{P_{jt}}{\pi_{it}}$$

$$(48)$$

where OwnElas$_i$ and CrossElas$_{ij}$ stand for the own- and cross-price elasticity (with respect to the price of brand j) of brand i, π_{it} and π_{jt} stand for the household's logit probabilities of buying brands i and j respectively at time t, P_{it} and P_{jt} stand for the prices of the ith and jth brands respectively at time t. For a logit model it is easy to show that

$$\text{OwnElas}_i = [1 - \pi_{it}]P_{it}\beta_k$$

$$\text{CrossElas}_{ij} = -\pi_{jt}P_{jt}\beta_k$$

$$(49)$$

which implies that (i) smaller brands have higher own- and cross-price elasticities than larger brands, and (ii) higher priced brands have larger own-price elasticities but smaller cross-price elasticities than lower-priced brands. These restrictions are an artifact of the logit model, and may not necessarily be appropriate for the data in hand.

The IIA property.   In the MNL model, the ratio of a household's choice probabilities for any two brands is unaffected by the presence of other brands in the market. In other words,

$$\frac{P_{it}}{P_{jt}} = \frac{e^{\alpha_{it}+X_{it}\beta}}{e^{\alpha_{jt}+X_{jt}\beta}} = e^{(\alpha_{it}-\alpha_{jt})+(X_{it}-X_{jt})\beta} \quad (50)$$

which is independent of other brands $k \neq i,j$. This property, also called *independence from irrelevant alternatives* (IIA), is unnecessarily restrictive and leads to three types of problems.[5] The first, also called the *similarity problem* (first noted by Debreu, 1960), can be understood as follows. Suppose a household chooses between two brands – *Coke* and *7-Up* – in a two-brand product market. When a new brand – *Pepsi* – is introduced to this market, the logit model would predict that the household's choice probability for the new brand will draw an equal proportion from the household's brand choice probabilities for *Coke* and *7-Up*. However, it is more reasonable to expect that *Pepsi* will draw disproportionately more from *Coke* than from *7-Up*, almost to the extent that the household's choice probability for *7-Up* will remain unchanged. The logit model cannot allow for this. The second problem, called the *dominance problem*, can be understood as follows: suppose a household has equal choice probabilities (i.e.,

0.5) for *Coke* and *7-Up* when only these two brands are available in the product category, and equal choice probabilities (i.e., 0.5) for *Pepsi* and *7-Up* when only these two brands are available. Also suppose that *Pepsi* almost completely dominates *Coke* for the household when both are available, that is, when *Pepsi* and *Coke* are the only available brands, the household's choice probabilities for the two brands are 0.95 and 0.05 respectively. Such a pattern of household choices, while perfectly reasonable, also cannot be represented using a logit model. The third problem, called the *regularity problem*, can be understood as follows: suppose a household has equal choice probabilities (i.e., 0.5) for *Coke* and *7-Up* when only these two brands are available in the product category. However, the household's choice probability for *7-Up* can increase after the introduction of *Pepsi* either because the household ends up switching between cola and non-cola in a desire for variety or because the household ends up valuating *7-Up* higher after the entry of Pepsi on account of *7-Up*'s uniqueness in the product category. The logit model cannot allow for such a probability increase for *7-Up*. To summarize, therefore, the IIA restriction of the logit model leads to at least three types of problems while modeling brand choice data. The IIA restriction is an artifact of the logit model's assumption that the random components of the household's brand utilities (i.e., the ε_j's) are *iid*.

Whether or not the IIA restriction is valid for the data in hand can be assessed on the basis of the "distance" between observed and predicted shares. McFadden, Train and Tye (1977) proposed the following test statistic:

$$\frac{\sum_{m=1}^{M} (S_m - N_m \overline{P}_{jm})^2}{N \overline{P}_j} \sim \chi^2_{M-p-1} \quad (51)$$

where the *n* observations in the data are first ranked from highest to lowest in terms of the predicted choice probabilities for brand *j*, and then sorted into *M* cells such that each cell contains roughly the same number of observations, S_m is the actual number of observed choices for the brand in cell m, N_m is the total number of observations in cell m, $\overline{P}_{jm}$ is the

average predicted choice probability for brand *j* in cell *m*, and $\overline{P}_j$ is the average predicted choice probability for brand *j* in the total sample. If the critical value of the chi-square statistic is not exceeded, the IIA restriction is valid for the data in hand.

PROBIT MODEL

Multinomial probit – a utility theoretic exposition. Let us revisit the example of a household choosing between $\mathcal{J}$ brands of laundry detergents at a shopping occasion (as discussed in the section "Multinomial Logit – A Utility Theoretic Exposition"). Suppose we assume $\varepsilon_t = (\varepsilon_{1t}\varepsilon_{2t} \dots \varepsilon_{\mathcal{J}t})'$ to be distributed $N_{\mathcal{J}}(0, \Sigma)$ we obtain the multinomial probit model (MNP). In other words, the MNP model is based on a normal distribution of errors[6] (instead of a Gumbel distribution of errors as in the MNL model), and does not assume the errors to be *iid* (as does the MNL model). This implies that $U_t = (U_{1t}U_{2t} \dots U_{\mathcal{J}t})' = (V_{1t} + \varepsilon_{1t}V_{2t} + \varepsilon_{2t} \dots V_{\mathcal{J}t} + \varepsilon_{\mathcal{J}t})'$ is distributed $N_{\mathcal{J}}(V_t, \Sigma)$, where $V_t = (V_{1t}V_{2t} \dots V_{\mathcal{J}t})'$. Since the multivariate normal cumulative distribution function (cdf) does not have a closed form, the brand choice probabilities must be written as the following J-dimensional integral.

$$Pr(i) = \pi_{it} = \int_{\varepsilon_{1t}=-\infty}^{V_{it}-V_{1t}+\varepsilon_{it}} \dots \int_{\varepsilon_{it}=-\infty}^{\infty} \dots$$
$$\int_{\varepsilon_{\mathcal{J}t}=-\infty}^{V_{it}-V_{\mathcal{J}t}+\varepsilon_{it}} f(\varepsilon_{1t}, \dots, \varepsilon_{it}, \dots, \varepsilon_{\mathcal{J}t})$$
$$d\varepsilon_{1t} \dots d\varepsilon_{it} \dots d\varepsilon_{\mathcal{J}t} \quad (52)$$

which can be rewritten as the following (J − 1)-dimensional integral

$$Pr(i) = \pi_{it} = \int_{\delta_{1t}=-\infty}^{V_{it}-V_{1t}} \dots \int_{\delta_{i-1t}=-\infty}^{V_{it}-V_{i-1t}}$$
$$\int_{\delta_{i+1t}=-\infty}^{V_{it}-V_{i+1t}} \dots \int_{\delta_{\mathcal{J}t}=-\infty}^{V_{it}-V_{\mathcal{J}t}} f(\delta_{1t}, \dots, \delta_{i-1t}, \delta_{i+1t}$$
$$\dots, \delta_{\mathcal{J}t}) d\delta_{1t} \dots d\delta_{i-1t} d\delta_{i+1t} \dots d\delta_{\mathcal{J}t} \quad (53)$$

where $\delta_{jt} = \varepsilon_{jt} - \varepsilon_{it}$. By explicitly accommodating a general covariance matrix Σ of the error terms, the probit model eliminates the IIA problem associated with the logit model. Specifically, the probit model relaxes two strong assumptions of the logit model: one, that error variances are equal across brands; two, that error covariances are zero. However, relaxing *either* of these two assumptions of the logit model is sufficient to eliminate the restrictive IIA property of the logit model.[7]

Maximum likelihood estimation of the multinomial probit model.   Given *n* independent observations of (X_t, Y_t) the parameters of the MNP model are estimated by maximizing the following *likelihood* function.

$$l(\beta) = \prod_{t=1}^{n} \pi_1(X_t)^{Y_{1t}} \pi_2(X_t)^{Y_{2t}} \ldots \pi_{\mathcal{J}}(X_t)^{Y_{\mathcal{J}t}}$$

(54)

which is equivalent to maximizing the following *log-likelihood* function.

$$L(\beta) = \ln[l(\beta)] = \sum_{t=1}^{n} \{ Y_{1t} \ln \pi_1(X_t)$$
$$+ Y_{2t} \ln \pi_2(X_t) + \ldots + Y_{\mathcal{J}t} \ln \pi_{\mathcal{J}}(X_t) \}$$

(55)

Since the brand choice probabilities, $\pi_i(X_t)$, do not have a closed form (see Equation 52), their evaluation requires Monte Carlo simulation (Lerman and Manski, 1981). This involves generating *g* random draws from the $N_{\mathcal{J}}(V_t, \Sigma)$ distribution characterizing U_t and taking the fraction of draws in which U_{it} is maximal as $\pi_i(X_t)$. As long as *g* is sufficiently large, the simulated value of $\pi_i(X_t)$ will be very close to its exact value (given in Equation 52). Since the maximum likelihood routine maximizes the simulated likelihood function (as opposed to the exact likelihood function), this estimation approach is also called *simulated maximum likelihood* (SML). In order to generate random draws from the $N_{\mathcal{J}}(V_t, \Sigma)$ distribution, one must first simulate a *g*-dimensional vector $v = (v_1 v_2 \ldots v_g)'$ of *iid* draws from the N(0,1) distribution and then use the following equation

$$U_t = Cv + V_t$$

(56)

where

$$\Sigma = CC'$$

(57)

where *C* is a lower-triangular matrix with positive diagonal elements. Equation 57, also called the *Cholesky decomposition*, ensures that Σ is positive definite (which is required by the statistical regularity conditions imposed on the MNP model).

The brand choice probabilities, $\pi_i(X_t)$, can also be evaluated using a numerical approximation approach proposed by Clark (1961). In this approach, the brand choice probability is written as

$$\Pr(i) = \Pr[\max_{j \neq i} (U_{jt} - U_{it}) < 0]$$

(58)

where one approximates the univariate cdf of the random variable $\max_{j \neq i}(U_{jt} - U_{it})$ using recursive formulas for its mean and variance, in order to obtain the desired probability. While this approach is much quicker than Monte Carlo simulation, its bias depends on the (unknown) covariance structure of the brands' random utilities and cannot be controlled by increasing the number of observations.

Smooth recursive conditioning (SRC) simulator.
The Monte Carlo simulation procedure of Lerman and Manski (1981) employs a frequency-based simulator of brand choice probabilities. Such a simulator may be discontinuous in model parameters, which may impede numerical optimization, unless the number of draws is kept very high. Borsch-Supan and Hajivassiliou (1993) employ a Monte Carlo simulation procedure to evaluate $\pi_i(X_t)$ that is computationally superior to the frequency-based simulation procedure of Lerman and Manski (1981). Also called the *smooth recursive conditioning* (SRC) simulator,[8] their Monte Carlo procedure is based on evaluating the (J − 1)-variate integral given in Equation 53.

First Equation 52 is rewritten as shown below.

$$\begin{bmatrix} -\infty \\ \cdot \\ \cdot \\ -\infty \\ -\infty \\ \cdot \\ \cdot \\ -\infty \end{bmatrix} \leq \begin{bmatrix} \delta_{1t} \\ \cdot \\ \delta_{i-1t} \\ \delta_{i+1t} \\ \cdot \\ \delta_{Jt} \end{bmatrix} \leq \begin{bmatrix} V_{it} - V_{1t} \\ \cdot \\ \cdot \\ V_{it} - V_{i-1t} \\ V_{it} - V_{i+1t} \\ \cdot \\ V_{it} - V_{Jt} \end{bmatrix}$$

$$(59)$$

which can be written in vector-form as shown below.

$$a \leq A\varepsilon_t \leq b_t,$$

$$A_{(J-1)*J} = \begin{bmatrix} 1 & & & -1 \\ & 1 & & -1 \\ & & \cdots & -1 \\ & & & \cdots \\ & & -1 & \cdots \\ & & -1 & 1 \\ & & -1 & & 1 \end{bmatrix}$$

$$\varepsilon_t = \begin{bmatrix} \varepsilon_{1t} \\ \cdot \\ \cdot \\ \varepsilon_{it} \\ \cdot \\ \cdot \\ \varepsilon_{Jt} \end{bmatrix} \qquad (60)$$

where

$$a = \begin{bmatrix} -\infty \\ \cdot \\ \cdot \\ -\infty \\ -\infty \\ \cdot \\ \cdot \\ -\infty \end{bmatrix}, b = \begin{bmatrix} V_{it} - V_{1t} \\ \cdot \\ \cdot \\ V_{it} - V_{i-1t} \\ V_{it} - V_{i+1t} \\ \cdot \\ V_{it} - V_{Jt} \end{bmatrix} \quad (61)$$

Therefore, the necessary random draws are from a *truncated multivariate normal* distribution as shown below.

$$A\varepsilon_t \sim N_{J-1}(0, A\Sigma A')$$

such that

$$a \leq A\varepsilon_t \leq b_t \qquad (62)$$

which is equivalent to the following truncated normal distribution (Geweke, 1991).

$$e_t \sim N(0, I)$$

such that

$$a \leq Le_t \leq b_t \qquad (63)$$

where L is the lower-triangular matrix of the Cholesky decomposition

$$LL' = A\Sigma A' \qquad (64)$$

This renders the Monte Carlo simulation to be recursive as shown below[9].

$$e_1 \sim N(0, 1) \; st \; a_1 \leq l_{11}e_1 \leq b_1$$
$$e_2 \sim N(0, 1) \; st \; a_2 \leq l_{21}e_1 + l_{22}e_2 \leq b_2$$
$$e_3 \sim N(0, 1) \; st \; a_3 \leq l_{31}e_1 + l_{32}e_2 + l_{33}e_3 \leq b_3$$

$$(65)$$

and so on.

This means that sequential sampling from univariate truncated normal distributions is sufficient to simulate the desired brand choice probability. Sampling from a univariate truncated normal distribution is achieved using the integral transform theorem as shown below.

$$Z = \Phi^{-1}[\{\Phi(b) - \Phi(a)\}U + \Phi(a)]$$
$$U \sim \text{Unif}(0, 1) \qquad (66)$$

Identifiability of probit model parameters. The identifiability of the parameters of an MNP model cannot be verified directly using the brand choice probabilities (as in the MNL model) since these probabilities do not have closed form expressions. An obvious check for identifiability is to ensure that there is no change of variable that can reduce the number of parameters in V_t and Σ. Identifiability requires one of the brand constants to be restricted to 0 (as in the MNL model), that is, to fix the location. Identifiability also requires that one brand's error variance is restricted to 1, while its error covariances are restricted to 0 (for the same reason that μ is restricted to be 1 in the MNL model), that is, to fix the scale. In more complicated versions of the MNP, one way to check for model identifiability is to check whether the Hessian matrix is negative-definite at convergence.[10] However, this is neither a necessary nor sufficient condition for model identifiability. In fact, even if the MNP model is fully identified, the log-likelihood function is not necessarily globally concave. The only way to check for global maxima is to first identify whether multiple local maxima exist (using different starting values for the parameters) and then pick the largest among the identified local maxima as the global maximum.

For marketing applications of the MNP model to scanner panel data on brand choices, see Papatla and Krishnamurthi (1992) and Chintagunta (1992). An alternative way to relax the IIA restriction is to allow the model coefficients (price, display, feature, and brand constants) in an MNL model to be random. If they follow a joint multivariate distribution, the IIA restriction is removed (even if the brand-specific errors are *iid*). Such an approach has been adopted in an independent probit framework by Hausman and Wise (1978).

OTHER NON-IIA MODELS OF BRAND CHOICE[11]

Because of the computational burden and identification problems associated with the MNP model, marketing researchers have proposed alternative brand choice models that have tractable, closed form expressions, yet avoid the IIA restriction of the MNL model. We discuss some of these models below. All of these models can be estimated using maximum likelihood.

Generalized extreme value (GEV) model. A generalization of the MNL model, first proposed by McFadden (1978), can be written as shown below.

$$\pi_t(i) = \frac{e^{V_{it} + \ln G_i(e^{V_{1t}}, \dots, e^{V_{Jt}})}}{\sum_{j=1}^{J} e^{V_{jt} + \ln G_j(e^{V_{1t}}, \dots, e^{V_{Jt}})}} \quad (67)$$

where $G_i = \frac{\partial G}{\partial y_i}$, and G(.) is a function with the following properties.

1. G is non-negative,
2. G is homogeneous of degree $\mu > 0$, that is, $G(\alpha y_1, \dots, \alpha y_J) = \alpha^\mu G(y_1, \dots, y_J)$,
3. $\lim_{y_i \to \infty} G(y_1, \dots, y_J) = \infty$, for $i = 1, \dots, J$,
4. $\frac{\partial^l G}{\partial y^l} \geq 0$ if l is odd, and $\frac{\partial^l G}{\partial y^l} \leq 0$ if l is even.

The GEV model is consistent with random utility maximization and can be derived by assuming the distribution of the random components of the utilities to be $F(.) = e^{-G(e^{-\varepsilon_1}, \dots, e^{-\varepsilon_J})}$. If $G(e^{V_1}, \dots, e^{V_J}) = \sum_{j=1}^{J} e^{V_j}$, the GEV reduces to the MNL model. If $G(e^{V_1}, \dots, e^{V_J}) = \sum_{a=1}^{A} \left(\sum_{j \in D_a} e^{V_j} \right)^\mu$, where the choice set $(1, \dots, J)$ is partitioned into A non-overlapping subsets, the GEV reduces to the *nested logit* model (described in the next section). In fact, Equation 67 shows that the GEV model extends the MNL model by making the utility of each brand depend not only on its own attributes, but also on other brands' attributes.

Nested logit model. This model allows brands to share unobserved (and observed) attributes, which induces correlations in a household's random utilities across brands. Suppose brand i can be defined as a bundle (a, b) of two attributes.

$$U_{it} = U_{abt} = V_{at} + V_{bt} + V_{abt}$$
$$+ \varepsilon_{at} + \varepsilon_{bt} + \varepsilon_{abt} \quad (68)$$

where V_{at} is the deterministic component of utility common to all brands that share attribute a, V_{bt} is the deterministic component of utility common to all brands that share attribute b, ε_{at} is the random component of utility due to attribute a (i.e., varies only across brands with different a), ε_{bt} is the random component of utility due to attribute b (i.e., varies only across brands with different b), and ε_{abt} is the random component of utility that varies across all brands (i.e., the "usual" random component). Assuming that the three random components – ε_{at}, ε_{bt} and ε_{abt} – are independent of each other, have zero means and variances given by σ_a^2, σ_b^2, and σ^2 respectively, one can show that

$$\text{cov}(U_{ab}, U_{ab'}) = \sigma_a^2$$
$$\text{cov}(U_{ab}, U_{a'b}) = \sigma_b^2 \qquad (69)$$

that is, utilities across brands are correlated.[12]

The estimable version of the nested logit model is obtained by setting one of the two attribute-specific random components to zero, for example, $\varepsilon_{bt} = 0$. Further, one assumes that ε_{abt} is distributed *iid* Gumbel $(0, \mu)$, and ε_{at} is distributed so that Max $_{b \in Da} U_{abt}$ is distributed *iid* Gumbel $(0, \mu')$, where Da refers to the set of all brands that share attribute a. This results in the following marginal probability of a household buying a brand with attribute a.

$$\pi_{at} = \frac{e^{\left(V_{at} + \frac{1}{\mu} \ln \sum_{b \in Da} e^{(V_{bt} + V_{abt})\mu}\right)\mu'}}{\sum_{a'} e^{\left(V_{a't} + \frac{1}{\mu} \ln \sum_{b \in Da} e^{(V_{bt} + V_{a'bt})\mu}\right)\mu'}}$$

$$(70)$$

where $\frac{\mu'}{\mu} = \sqrt{1 - \text{corr}(U_{ab}, U_{ab'})} \leq 1$. The household's *conditional* probability of buying a brand with attribute b, given choice of a brand with attribute a, is given by

$$\pi_{(b|a)t} = \frac{e^{(V_{bt} + V_{abt})\mu}}{\sum_{b' \in Da} e^{(V_{b't} + V_{ab't})\mu}} \qquad (71)$$

Since only the ratio of the two scale parameters is identified, μ is usually restricted to be 1. The estimable version of the nested logit model, therefore, becomes

$$\pi_{it} = \pi_{abt} = \pi_{at}^* \pi_{(b|a)t}$$

$$= \frac{e^{\left(V_a + \ln \sum_{b \in Da} e^{V_b + V_{ab}}\right)\mu'}}{\sum_{a'} e^{\left(V_{a'} + \ln \sum_{b \in Da} e^{V_b + V_{a'b}}\right)\mu'}}$$

$$* \frac{e^{V_{bt} + V_{abt}}}{\sum_{b' \in Da} e^{V_{b't} + V_{ab't}}} \qquad (72)$$

where $\mu' \leq 1$. If $\mu' = 1$ this model reduces to an MNL model. The nested logit model can be understood using a *tree-structure* where the upper level represents the household's choice of attribute a, and the lower level represents the household's choice of attribute b conditional on the choice of attribute a. With three attributes, the estimable nested logit model looks as shown below.

$$\pi_{it} = \pi_{abct} = \pi_{at}^* \pi_{(b|a)t}^* \pi_{(c|ab)t}$$

$$= \frac{e^{(V_{at} + V'_{at})\mu''}}{\sum_{a' \in D} e^{(V_{a't} + V'_{a't})\mu''}}$$

$$* \frac{e^{(V_{bt} + V_{abt} + V'_{abt})\mu'}}{\sum_{b' \in Da} e^{(V_{b't} + V_{ab't} + V'_{ab't})\mu'}}$$

$$* \frac{e^{V_{ct} + V_{bct} + V_{act} + V_{abct}}}{\sum_{c' \in Dab} e^{V_{c't} + V_{bc't} + V_{ac't} + V_{abc't}}} \qquad (73)$$

where

$$V'_{abt} = \ln\left(\sum_{c' \in Dab} e^{V_{c't} + V_{bc't} + V_{ac't} + V_{abc't}}\right)$$

$$V'_{at} = \frac{1}{\mu'} \ln\left(\sum_{b' \in Da} e^{(V_{b't} + V_{ab't} + V'_{ab't})\mu'}\right)$$

$$\mu' \leq 1, \mu'' \leq \mu' \qquad (74)$$

If $\mu'' = \mu'$ this model reduces to the MNL model. While the nested logit model presents a parsimonious way of modeling inter-brand correlations, determining the sequence of attributes in the tree is a subjective decision. Some authors prescribe the estimation of nested logit models with all possible orders of attributes, and pick whichever best describes the observed data. For an application of the nested logit model to scanner panel data on brand choices, see Kannan and Wright (1991).

Batsell and Polking (1985) model. This model allows the ratio of a household's choice probabilities for brands i and j to depend on other brands

34   choice models

in the household's choice set. Specifically,

$$\beta_{ij}^A = \ln\left(\frac{\pi_i^A}{\pi_j^A}\right) = \sum_{I \subset [A-\{i,j\}]} \alpha_{ij}^I \quad (75)$$

where A is the household's choice set, that is, a subset of the full set of brands $\{1,\ldots,J\}$. This implies that the ratio of the brands' choice probabilities is a function of the brands in the choice set A. For example, if $A = \{i,j\}$, $I = (\{\emptyset\})$ and $\beta_{ij}^{ij} = \alpha_{ij}^\emptyset$. If $A = \{i,j,k\}$, $I = (\{\emptyset\},\{k\})$ and $\beta_{ij}^{ijk} = \alpha_{ij}^\emptyset + \alpha_{ij}^k$. If $A = \{i,j,k,l\}$, $I = (\{\emptyset\},\{k\},\{l\},\{k,l\})$ and $\beta_{ij}^{ijkl} = \alpha_{ij}^\emptyset + \alpha_{ij}^k + \alpha_{ij}^l + \alpha_{ij}^{kl}$. The estimable version of this model is given below.

$$P_A(i) = \frac{\prod\limits_{I \subset A} e^{s_i^I}}{\sum\limits_{k \in A} \prod\limits_{I \subset A} e^{s_k^I}} \quad (76)$$

where

$$s_i^I = 0 \text{ for } i \notin I$$
$$\sum_{i \notin I} s_i^I = u_I \quad (77)$$

where u_I is a pre-assigned number. If $s_i^I = 0$ for $I \neq \emptyset$, this model reduces to the MNL model. Once the estimates for $s_i^{I'}s$ are obtained, the $\alpha_{ij}^{I'}s$ are given by

$$\alpha_{ij}^I = s_i^{iI} + s_i^{ijI} - s_j^{jI} - s_j^{ijI} \text{ if } I \cap i,j = \emptyset \quad (78)$$

While this model relaxes the IIA restriction of the MNL model in a more flexible manner than the nested logit model, it involves the estimation of a large number of parameters. Further, unlike the GEV or nested logit models, this model cannot be derived from random utility maximization.

Alternative approaches. The *elimination-by-aspects* (EBA) model of (Tversky, 1972) works on the idea that a household sequentially screens brands based on attributes in order to arrive at an optimal brand choice. This model does not have the IIA property. A *consideration set model* explains a household's brand choice as an outcome of a two-stage process, where the first stage involves the formation of a consideration set, and the second stage involves the optimal choice of brands within the consideration set (see, for example, Roberts and Lattin, 1991). Such a two-stage model also does not have the IIA property. In general, a brand choice model that is consistent with two-stage decision-making on the part of the household eliminates the IIA restriction. Similarly, any brand choice model that allows a brand's utility to depend on the attributes of competing brands (for example, the GEV model) ends up eliminating the IIA restriction. Models that obey this property are called *mother logit* models. While a large number of non-IIA brand choice models have been proposed in the marketing literature, the most popular (in terms of the number of academic papers published on the model) are the multinomial probit and the nested logit models. Among these two, given the sharp rise in computational power in recent years and the natural appeal of the normal distribution to statisticians and econometricians, the multinomial probit model has come to be accepted as the *de facto standard* for brand choice models. Another reason for the increasing popularity of the multinomial probit model is that it provides a more flexible framework to accommodate the effects of unobserved heterogeneity, state dependence, and so on.

ENDNOTES

[1] It is on account of these random components that brand choice models are also called *random utility models.*

[2] It is useful to note that this parameter vector is common across brands.

[3] This is what renders asymptotic properties of estimators to be much more convenient to work with than small-sample properties.

[4] If $\hat\beta$ is a vector, the asymptotic variance of the MLE is a matrix Σ, and asymptotic efficiency implies that $(\Sigma^* - \Sigma)$ is *non-negative-definite,* where Σ^* is the asymptotic variance of any other consistent estimator of β.

[5] The exposition of these problems borrows heavily from Batsell and Polking (1985).

[6] If one viewed the error term to be the sum of a large number of unobserved but independent components, by the *central limit theorem* the error term will tend to be normal.

[7] The probit model solves the *similarity problem* associated with the IIA property (see section on the IIA property), however, the *dominance* and *regularity* problems still remain.

[8] Also called the Geweke-Hajivassiliou-Keane (GHK) simulator, this simulator has been shown to be superior to other simulation algorithms in terms of RMS error by Hajivassiliou, McFadden, and Ruud (1996).

[9] This recursive scheme is also called a *Gibbs cycle* (Geweke 1991).

[10] Since optimizers in software packages such as Gauss, SAS, and others. are *minimizers*, maximum likelihood estimation entails minimization of the negative log-likelihood function. In such a case, the Hessian matrix must be *positive-definite*.

[11] The discussion of the GEV and Nested Logit Models in this section are borrowed from Ben-Akiva and Lerman (1985).

[12] The MNL model, by ignoring attribute-specific random components, that is, ε_{iat} and ε_{ibt}, restricts σ_a^2 and σ_b^2 to be zero.

Bibliography

Batsell, R.R. and Polking, J.C. (1985) A new class of market share models. *Marketing Science*, **4** (3), 177–198.

Ben-Akiva, M. and Lerman, S. (1985) *Discrete Choice Analysis*, MIT Press, Cambridge.

Borsch-Supan, A. and Hajivassiliou, V.A. (1993) Smooth unbiased multivariate probability simulators for maximum likelihood estimation of limited dependent variable models. *Journal of Econometrics*, **58**, 347–368.

Chintagunta, P.K. (1992) Estimating a multinomial probit model using the method of simulated moments: a panel data application. *Marketing Science*, **11** (4), 386–407.

Clark, C. (1961) The greatest of a finite set of random variables. *Operations Research*, **9** (3), 145–162.

Debreu, G. (1960) A review of individual choice behavior: a theoretical analysis. *American Economic Review*, **50** (4), 186–188.

Efron, B. (1978) Regression and ANOVA with zero-one data: measures of residual variation. *Journal of the American Statistical Association*, **73**, 113–121.

Geweke, J. (1991) Efficient Simulation From the Multivariate Normal and Student-t Distributions Subject to Linear Constraints, in *Computing Science and Statistics: Proceedings of the Twenty-Third Symposium on the Interface* (ed. E.M. Keramidas), Fairfax: Interface Foundation of North America, Inc., 571–578

Guadagni, P. and Little, J.D.C. (1983) A logit model of brand choice calibrated on scanner data. *Marketing Science*, **2** (3), 203–238.

Hajivassiliou, V.A., McFadden, D.L. and Ruud, P. (1996) Simulation of multivariate normal rectangle probabilities and their derivatives: theoretical and computational results. *Journal of Econometrics*, **72**, 85–134.

Hausman, J. and Wise, D.A. (1978) A conditional probit model for qualitative choice: discrete decisions recognizing interdependence and heterogeneous preferences. *Econometrica*, **46**, 403–426.

Horowitz, J. and Louviere, J. (1993) Testing predicted choices against observations in probabilistic discrete choice models. *Marketing Science*, **12** (3), 270–279.

Jones, J.M. and Zufryden, F.S. (1982) An approach for assessing demographic and price influences on brand purchase behavior. *Journal of Marketing*, **46** (1), 36–46.

Kannan, P.K. and Wright, G. (1991) Modeling and testing structured markets: a nested logit approach. *Marketing Science*, **10** (1), 58–82.

Lerman, S. and Manski, C. (1981) On the use of simulated frequencies to approximate choice probabilities, in *Structural Analysis of Discrete Data with Econometric Applications* (eds C. Manski and D. McFadden), MIT Press, Cambridge, pp. 305–319.

Luce, R. (1959) *Individual Choice Behavior*, John Wiley & Sons, Inc., New York.

McFadden, D. (1974) Conditional logit analysis of qualitative choice behavior, in *Frontiers in Econometrics* (ed. P. Zarembka), Academic Press, New York.

McFadden, D. (1978) Modeling the choice of residential location, in *Spatial Interaction Theory and Residential Location* (ed. A. Karlquist) North Holland, Amsterdam, pp. 75–96.

McFadden, D., Train, K. and Tye, W.B. (1977) An application of diagnostic tests for the independence of irrelevant alternatives property of the multinomial logit model. *Transportation Research Record*, **637**, 39–45.

Papatla, P. and Krishnamurthi, L. (1992) A probit model of choice dynamics. *Marketing Science*, **11** (3), 189–206.

Roberts, J.H. and Lattin, J.M. (1991) A development and testing of a model of consideration set composition. *Journal of Marketing Research*, **28** (4), 429–440.

Swait, J. and Louviere, J. (1993) The role of the scale parameter in the estimation and comparison of multinomial logit models. *Journal of Marketing Research*, **30** (3), 305–314.

Thurstone, L. (1927) A law of comparative judgment. *Psychological Review*, **34**, 273–286.

Tversky, A. (1972) Elimination by aspects: a theory of choice. *Psychological Review*, **79**, 281–299.

consumer acculturation

Lisa Peñaloza

Consumer acculturation is defined as the general process of adaptation by consumers in the marketplace. While initially theorized for immigrants seeking economic opportunity and quality of life in another nation or fleeing situations of economic conflict or war at home (Peñaloza, 1994), distinct consumption patterns and market relations are forged by minority groups as well, as they adapt to mainstream and other groups in heterogeneous societies (Kjeldgaard and Askegaard, 2006). Such interaction and adaptation is increasingly widespread globally, as families and communities extend beyond national borders. The growing importance of the topic is evident from the 80 odd participants of over 20 nationalities at the May 2009 conference on Immigration, Consumption and Markets organized by Nil Toulouse and Soren Askegaard in Lille, France.

The scope of this body of work is broad, in examining social and market learning and interaction at individual, family, community, societal, and transnational levels (Lindridge, Hogg, and Shah, 2004; Askegaard, Arnould, and Kjeldgaard, 2005; Parreñas, 2005; Nolin, 2006; Peñaloza, 2007). Patterns of adaptation include a varied, dynamic mix of assimilating new consumption tastes and skills, maintaining old ones, resisting new and old forms, swapping or alternating between them (Oswald, 1999; Visconti, 2005), and forming distinctively hybrid consumption patterns based on localized interpretations of global media and market artifacts (Kjeldgaard and Askegaard, 2006) within global labor (Peñaloza, 1995) and financial imperatives (Üçok, 2007).

Consumer research challenges include distinguishing consumption practices across groups and calibrating changes in cultural skills, values, and knowledge, as inflected by social class, race, ethnicity, gender, religion, nationality, and geographic differences, and as played out in increasingly diverse intra- and transnational social and market formations. As cultural artifacts and behaviors are detached from the people creating them and appropriated by other consumers and corporations globally (Grier, Brumbaugh, and Thornton, 2006), concerns of cultural hegemony and homogenization among minority groups coincide with concerns with loss of status and power by the mainstream group, as both seek to maintain cultural identity and integrity. These concerns gain currency with the decreasing size of mainstream cultural groups and as minority consumer subcultures are incorporated by marketers within nations and in market diaspora across the globe.

Work on marketer acculturation examines how marketers learn to serve consumers of various cultures and address them in ways sensitive to relations between groups (Peñaloza and Gilly, 1999). Carried further, acculturation research can provide insight into the identity and vitality of nations by examining the nature of group relations as diverse people coexist and adapt their respective ways of life in consumption, in markets, and in communities. The issue is the role of business in separating, uniting, legitimizing, and excluding groups of people, as tailoring products and services to the mainstream advances, its dominance, even as targeting groups outside a cultural mainstream enables their members to reproduce vital cultural patterns and meanings and thrive. Public policies restricting the language and other cultural expressions of those who are "different" or "other" and excluding them in markets and other social services are the means by which one group dominates the others (Üstüner and Holt, 2007). Such intolerance increases in adverse economic circumstances and may be accompanied by violence, and yet such intolerance can trigger politically oriented consumption and market incorporation that ultimately advances the identity and community of those otherwise excluded (Peñaloza, 2007).

Further research opportunities lie in documenting how market development relies on and fosters forms of difference. Ultimately, the market both integrates and separates (Keating and McLoughlin, 2005). In their integrative function, markets assemble various people under a particular rubric and provide them with the cultural legitimization of a market. Other promising areas of work are investigating the nature of market participation played out within cities and nations, and exploring how immigrants and other minorities attain forms of consumer sovereignty that potentially inform by and impact political participation. It remains to be seen how capitalism and democracy will continue to cross-fertilize each other, with immigrants and minorities serving as test cases.

Bibliography

Askegaard, S., Arnould, E.J., and Kjeldgaard, D. (2005) Postassimilationist ethnic consumer research: qualifications and extensions. *Journal of Consumer Research*, **32**, 160–170.

Grier, S., Brumbaugh, A.M., and Corlis, T. (2006) Crossover dreams: consumer responses to ethnic-oriented products. *Journal of Marketing*, **70**, 35–51.

Keating, A. and McLoughlin, D. (2005) Understanding the emergence of markets: a social constructionist perspective on gay economy. *Consumption, Markets, Culture*, **8**, 131–152.

Kjeldgaard, D. and Askegaard, S. (2006) The glocalization of youth culture: the global youth segment as structures of common difference. *Journal of Consumer Research*, **33**, 231–247.

Lindridge, A., Hogg, M., and Shah, M. (2004) Imagined multiple worlds: how South Asian Women in Britain use family and friends to navigate the border crossings between household and societal contexts. *Consumption, Markets, Culture*, **7**, 211–238.

Nolin, C. (2006) *Transnational Ruptures. Gender and Forced Migration*, Ashgate, London.

Oswald, L. (1999) Culture swapping: consumption and ethnogenesis of middle class hatian immigrans. *Journal of Consumer Research*, **25**, 303–318.

Parreñas, R.S. (2005) *Children of Global Migration: Transnational Families and Gender Woes*, Stanford University Press, Stanford, CA.

Peñaloza, L. (1994) Atravasando fronteras/border crossings. *Journal of Consumer Research*, **21**, 32–54.

Peñaloza, L. (1995) Immigrant consumers: marketing and public policy considerations in the global economy. *Journal of Public Policy and Marketing*, **14**, 83–94.

Peñaloza, L. (2007) Mainstreet U.S.A revisited: market targeting, Latino/a consumer culture, and community. *International Journal of Sociology and Social Policy*, **27**, 234–249.

Peñaloza, L. and Mary G. (1999) arketers' acculturation: the changer and the changed. *Journal of Marketing*, **63**, 84–104.

Üçok, M. (2007) Consumption practices in transnational social spaces: a study of Turkish transmigrants in Denmark. Doctoral dissertation, University of Southern Denmark, Odense.

Üçokner, T. and Holt, D.B. (2007) Dominated consumer acculturation: the social construction of poor migrant women's consumer identity projects in a Turkish squatter. *Journal of Consumer Research*, **34**, 41–56.

Visconti, L. (2005) Attraversate le frontiere/border crossed: processes of cultural alternation in the marketplace. Unpublished Ph.D. dissertation, Management Department, Bocconi University, Milan, Italy.

consumer aspects of international marketing

Claudiu V. Dimofte

THE GLOBAL CONSUMER

The globalization of markets has long defined the research agenda of economists and marketers alike. Yet the perspective that each group tends to employ when approaching the topic varies to a large extent: the former are mostly concerned with the international flows of capital, labor, and goods that imply a large degree of cross-market homogeneity, whereas the latter generally assume cultural heterogeneity and look for locally defined cultural determinants of consumption behavior. On the one hand, marketplace evidence suggests that specific consumption patterns across the globe do show some convergence, such that market segments from culturally and geographically distant nations are developing similar tastes and product preferences. This phenomenon is at the core of what GLOBAL MARKETING STRATEGY has termed the *universal segment* (or *intermarket*) approach to market segmentation: positioning the firm's offerings toward groups of consumers around the world who display similar needs and look for the same product benefits, regardless of location (see Toyota Scion vehicles and MTV programming targeting Generation Y consumers internationally). Furthermore, the ubiquity of the Internet at the center of many nations' social and technological environments allows marketing information to easily diffuse and spill over, to create more uniform consumer knowledge and interests, and to generate relatively consistent brand preferences across borders, as the law of communicating vessels would predict.

On the other hand, the alternative view to this single world economy is the perception of multiple world markets, each described by idiosyncrasies that are deeply rooted in cultural heritage, as determined by local knowledge, beliefs, customs, and so forth. Global marketing textbooks provide a multitude of approaches for segmenting such markets, under the implicit assumption that attempting to standardize one product across national boundaries described by so much cultural variance is practically impossible. For anyone who has ever traveled to a foreign land and has experienced the at once wonder and shock associated with dramatically different people, foods, or customs (ever had a balut egg in the Philippines or exchanged business cards in Japan?), this perspective has immediate resonance. To better understand what global consumers may be about and how marketers can appropriately describe and predict their behavior, it is useful to begin by addressing the topic of consumer culture (*see* SOCIETY, CULTURE, AND GLOBAL CONSUMER CULTURE) in more detail.

Consumer culture. Defining the *culture* construct is no easy theoretical endeavor (*see* SOCIETY, CULTURE, AND GLOBAL CONSUMER CULTURE). In short, culture consists of a society's complex set of beliefs, customs, and other specific forces that shape individuals' perceptions and behaviors and is thought to be a key characteristic of a national environment that produces systematic differences in behavior across borders (Steenkamp, 2001). Whereas some have suggested that clusters of countries may display numerous cultural commonalities and could thus be construed as regional metacultures (Steenkamp, 2001), dealing with the idiosyncrasies of national cultures is a more

intriguing conceptual endeavor. Looking for the dimensions underlying cultural specificity has thus been the main concern of cross-cultural research, in an attempt to bring some uniformity and measurement structure to a highly diverse global environment.

The earliest and arguably the most influential account of cultural variation and its impact on business is that of Hofstede (1980). His framework discusses five dimensions: individualism/collectivism (addressing the individual vs group relationships), power distance (looking at power inequality in terms of hierarchical social layers), masculinity/femininity (dealing with the social implications of gender, such as a focus on success vs quality of life), uncertainty avoidance (handling economic and social uncertainty), and long-term orientation (displaying a cognitive focus on short- vs long-term temporal horizons). The empirical study underlying his research was highly comprehensive and robust, employing over 60 000 respondents across 70 countries. Each of these nations was assigned an index on each dimension, which was then linked with a variety of societal variables (geo-demographics, political, economical, etc.) – an operationalization that no other research has matched.

Relative to other frameworks, Hofstede's (1980) work displays high relevance to a variety of global business contexts (including international marketing), while maintaining a high level of conceptual convergent validity. That said, Schwartz (1994) provides an alternative perspective that – unlike Hofstede's (1980) focus on social dimensions – takes a more individual-level look at specific cultural values. Within a comparably large sample (over 60 000 respondents across 64 nations), Schwartz (1994) uncovers seven universally relevant cultural domains: harmony, egalitarianism, intellectual autonomy, affective autonomy, mastery, hierarchy, and embeddedness. Owing to their complementarity, combining the Hofstede (1980) and Schwartz (1994) frameworks has been suggested as a way to uncover clusters of more manageable regional cultures of interest to marketers (Steenkamp, 2001).

The immediate practical relevance of the cultural specificity that these frameworks address for the marketing efforts of any firm can be observed even within the confines of a particular nation, as in the proverbial cultural melting pot represented by the United States. Simply thinking about the different consumption patterns that the various US ethnic groups display can easily illustrate this point. Reading the grocery shopping lists of families of consumers in the African-American, Hispanic, or Asian ethnic groups will probably reveal very different items, flavors, and quantities. And watching television programming (as well as the associated advertising) on NBC relative to Telefutura or the BET channel will most likely entail highly distinct experiences. The existence of these microcultures (Steenkamp, 2001) contoured along ethnic or other dimensions highlights the importance of studying cultural heterogeneity through a more fine-tuned lens.

Another relevant stream of research addresses what social psychologists have termed individual difference variables describing consumers. In an international marketing context, one must be aware of a variety of social or subjective norms that influence how consumers in a nation perceive or respond to (products from) specific countries (home or foreign). For example, some consumers display a tendency to denigrate foreign products and favor domestic ones, a behavior that renders them ethnocentric with respect to foreign products (*see* BASE OF THE PYRAMID MARKETS: CULTURE INSIGHTS AND MARKETING IMPLICATIONS). A related construct is that of CONSUMER ANIMOSITY, such as that describing reactions of some American consumers to French-made products after this nation's opposition to the 2003 invasion of Iraq (remember those *freedom fries?*). On the opposite end of the spectrum, there are individuals who show a consistent interest in other cultures and global issues or even preference for foreign products. These consumers are generally considered high on worldmindedness (*see* CONSUMER WORLD-MINDEDNESS), affinity (*see* CONSUMER AFFINITY CONSTRUCT), or cosmopolitanism.

If cultural and even individual differences are so prevalent both across nations and within them, what is left of the claim that today's consumer is a global consumer? Keillor, D'Amico and Horton (2001) undertook survey research with consumer samples from the United States, France, and Malaysia to assess the extent to which individuals with such culturally and economically distinct backgrounds would display similar tendencies related to specific aspects of the psychology of consumption. When juxtaposed across four relevant constructs (i.e., national identity, ethnocentrism, social-desirability bias, and response to consumer influence sources), the differences were not remarkable, suggesting that consumers around the globe may indeed become more homogenous in terms of their consumption behaviors. Nevertheless, although a global consumer may be emerging, cultural differences across nations are still highly relevant to international marketing researchers. The next section provides specific considerations in support of this point.

International marketing research. One of the classic debates in the academic field in terms of dealing with the cultural differences that underlie the consumption behavior of individuals across nations is that between the emic and etic perspectives. Paralleling the earlier idiosyncratic-generic dichotomy related to the globalization of consumers and consumption patterns, this debate refers to the choice of theoretical frameworks to be employed in examining cultural differences. The *emic* view argues that such frameworks need to be culture-specific and operationalized via indigenous research techniques and instruments. Alternatively, the *etic* perspective favors the use of already established, universal theoretical frameworks as benchmarks for research pursued in any specific culture (Maheswaran and Shavitt, 2000).[1] A specific charge levied against the latter approach is that too often this established framework is developed by US researchers who simply attempt to apply it in novel cultural contexts, with little adaptation (Sekaran, 1983; Steenkamp, 2001). A potential solution to the emic–etic debate was proposed by Douglas and Craig (2006) in the shape of two iterative research approaches: the *adapted etic* (i.e., explicitly adapting the conceptual model of a base culture to the differences of new research contexts) and the *linked emic* model (i.e., taking the local context as the simultaneous starting point, at multiple research sites).

A related concern for international marketing researchers (academics and practitioners alike) is that of achieving measurement equivalence when it comes to employing specific scales in cross-cultural contexts. Therefore, it is important that not only conceptual equivalence of the target construct(s) be ensured (in particular within an emic theoretical approach) but that instrument equivalence (e.g., in terms of the item and scalar properties of the measure) be achieved as well (Maheswaran and Shavitt, 2000). In terms of construct operationalizations, method and item bias are often a concern in multicountry marketing research, as are the choice and relevance of the particular unit of analysis employed (Douglas and Craig, 2006). Finally, cross-cultural research is also affected by more practical methodological problems, such as the sampling, timing, and specific choice of statistical analyses underlying data collection and study across nations (Sekaran, 1983).

It should be noted that the field of international marketing is a broad one and includes theoretical accounts from multiple disciplines. Whereas the focus of this article is on consumer-level variables that borrow conceptually from social and cognitive psychology, there are complementary perspectives such as the theory of the international firm (e.g., global marketing strategy, *see* GLOBAL MARKETING STRATEGY: PERSPECTIVES AND APPROACHES, and the management of international operations) and the economics of global markets (e.g., international pricing, *see* INTERNATIONAL PRICING OBJECTIVES AND STRATEGIES, and distribution INTERNATIONAL MARKETING CHANNELS) which require similar concern with conceptualization, operationalization, and measurement. The next section bridges the global consumer-global firm dyad by addressing recent literature findings on consumer response to global brands (*see* GLOBAL BRANDING: THREE KEYS FOR GLOBAL BRAND SUCCESS).

CONSUMER RESPONSE TO GLOBAL BRANDS

As is the case with the *culture* construct, there is also considerable ambivalence in the international marketing literature in terms of what a *global brand* actually represents. Much of the

practitioner view on the issue is simply limited to the international, multimarket reach and profit potential that a brand accrues. For example, the Interbrand agency – which compiles its annual top 100 brands list for publication in Business Week – looks in its valuation at a brand's future earnings potential, with the expectation that a certain percentage of its sales come from each market in which it operates. The rival Millward Brown agency and its similar rankings published in the Financial Times require that a brand be present in at least seven countries before it is deemed global; yet by its own admission only 3% of its more than 10 000-brand database achieve this standard.

In terms of the academic research on the topic, the problem of operationalization may be one reason for the lack of a universally accepted definition of the global brand. However, the dimensions that underlie the global brand construct have been researched in a handful of articles, including Dimofte, Johansson and Ronkainen's (2008) work that identified five latent factors: *reach, aspiration, low risk, ethics,* and *standardization.* The authors show that consumers perceive global brands to be widely available, well recognized, standardized, more powerful, more cosmopolitan, and subject to more stringent social responsibility standards than other, more local brands. However, other brand attributes such as higher quality are – perhaps somewhat surprisingly – not necessarily associated a priori with global brands.

Combining the practitioner and academic perspectives may bring into focus a clearer, albeit still imperfect, understanding of what the global brand is about. Thus, as far as consumers, brand managers, and most academics are concerned, a global brand has a strong presence across multiple national markets, which associates it with universal recognition, the promise of long-term financial survival, and the burden of higher social responsibility standards governing its corporate behavior. Yet, the largely positive image inherent to this global brand definition is not universal. Literature suggests that there are important differences in terms of the specific valence that these defining global brand attributes acquire for consumers in the developing versus the developed world. Simply put, whereas the former aspire to the idealistic qualities embodied by a global brand, the latter are significantly less impressed. The next section addresses this dichotomy in more detail.

Global brands in developing versus developed nations.   Alden, Steenkamp and Batra (1999) argue that globally positioned brands might work better in markets that are characterized by lower levels of economic development, since "consumers in these markets may admire the 'economic center' and believe that […] ownership of brands from the West increases the owner's status" (Alden, Steenkamp and Batra, 1999, p. 84). Subsequent work by Batra *et al.* (2000) finds similar evidence that consumers in developing nations perceive nonlocal brands as preferable to local brands.

Holt, Quelch and Taylor (2004) uncover four basic dimensions of global brands *quality signal*, *global myth*, *social responsibility*, and *American values*. Averaging across responses from 12 countries (including the United States), their results also suggest that developing nations consumers aspire to the greater global community and in the process downgrade their own brands relative to global brands.

While the evidence of the attractiveness that global brands entail for consumers in developing nations is consistent in the international marketing literature, things are less clear cut when it comes to consumers in developed nations. On the one hand, Steenkamp, Batra and Alden (2003) investigate US and Korean samples and find that perceived globality positively impacts both perceived brand quality and prestige, including in the United States. On the other hand, Johansson and Ronkainen (2005) analyze the top 150 brands in terms of brand strength from the large cross-country and multiyear database underlying Landor's Brand Asset Valuator (BAV) model. In a survey of these brands across eight developed countries, the authors find that although global brands are held in high esteem, they are not necessarily associated with high levels of quality or other desirable brand attributes. There is also some evidence suggesting that local brands still command deeper customer loyalty than global brands in developed countries. For example, empirical analyses of Young & Rubicam data on brands from the European marketplace show that in such mature markets local brands often do better with consumers than global brands.

To understand this international dichotomy of responses to global brands, Dimofte, Johansson and Bagozzi (2010) evaluate ethnic consumer groups in the United States. Reflecting the aspirational dimension inherent to global brands for consumers in developed nations, the historically more economically disadvantaged African-American and Hispanic market segments are shown to associate global brands with higher product quality, more social status and prestige, as well as superior style. Yet, Caucasian consumers do not find global brands to be any more exciting than other brands, and – although they do perceive them to imply higher social status – they do not think their product quality is necessarily higher, mimicking the findings in developed nations (Dimofte, Johansson and Bagozzi, 2010). However, as a conceptual check, the relationships in a structural equation model show similarity across ethnic groups in the way the global brand associations link up to consumer attitudes and purchase behavior. Those with more positive perceptions of global brands also have more positive attitudes overall and, as one would expect, show higher purchase rates of global brands. Although Caucasians' perceptions and attitudes tend to be less favorable than those of African-American and Hispanic consumers, they nonetheless buy global brands at the same rate as non-Caucasians (Dimofte, Johansson and Bagozzi, 2010).

Other global branding research findings.   The extensive literature on global branding cannot truly be done justice within the limiting confines of a short article, so the final part of this section presents selected findings on the topic from two lines of consumer research – both classic (the country-of-origin effect) and more recent (automatic consumer response to global brands).

A firm's marketing communications, strategic marketplace behavior, and perceived competitive performance create in consumers' minds a particular brand personality and a variety of related brand associations – in short, (*see* PERCEPTION OF BRAND EQUITY). One of these brand associations that is particularly relevant to international marketing researchers involves consumer perceptions of a brand's country of origin (*see* "COUNTRY OF ORIGIN" AS BRAND ELEMENT). The location where a product is made prompts immediate country associations (i.e., a particular country image) that consumers generally incorporate into their brand evaluations and oftentimes produce cognitive biases in terms of attitudes and choice. Consumers tend to evaluate products more favorably when they originate in countries that benefit from a positive image (i.e., stereotypical perceptions describing the likely quality and performance of locally made products).[2] Most of us would likely agree that given a choice and in the absence of price constraints we would prefer a Swiss watch, a French perfume, or a German car. At the same time, similar negative stereotypical perceptions (created or reinforced by significant press coverage) have recently produced an avoidance behavior among many consumers toward products originating in China.

The country-of-origin effect is robust enough to emerge in studies that employ single-cue and multiple-cue product stimuli, within and between-subjects designs, and US and non-US samples. There have been two major cognitive process explanations proposed to underlie this effect. Depending on a consumer's familiarity with a country's products, country image can operate as either an inferential halo or a summary construct. If a consumer is unfamiliar, country image is used as a halo that impacts attribute ratings and, indirectly, brand attitudes (e.g., for Korean automobiles, quality inferences are made based on one's perception of Korean-made things in general). If the consumer is familiar with the country's products, the country image becomes a summarizing construct for the product attributes, directly influencing brand attitudes (e.g., for Japanese electronics, the fact that they are made in Japan is a proxy for high quality).

An interesting cognitive bias related to the country-of-origin effect is presented by Leclerc, Schmitt and Dubé (1994) in their research on consumer response to brand names that merely suggest a specific national origin. The authors show that product evaluations change such that, for example, more hedonic

perceptions follow a French pronunciation relative to an English one for the very same brand name (Leclerc, Schmitt and Dubé, 1994). The fact that merely altering the pronunciation produces biased perceptions of brand attributes (as mediated by country-of-origin inferences) attests to the strength and ubiquity of the effect in daily consumption. This is an important finding, because other research has shown that a product's country of origin heightens or lowers relevant consumer expectations (depending on the direction of the associated country stereotype), with direct implications for subsequent evaluative standards and customer satisfaction (*see* CUSTOMER SATISFACTION/DISSATISFACTION).

Despite the fact that the country-of-origin effect has been widely demonstrated, consumers' reliance on country image when forming attitudes and making choices is generally not acknowledged in self-reports. It has also been shown that country stereotypes can be spontaneously activated by the mere contextual presence of country-of-origin information, with subsequent measurable impact on attribute and product evaluations without consumers' intention or control. A similar finding in terms of American consumers' response to global brands shows that they explicitly deny the importance of brand globality in choice, yet clearly favor them in terms of subsequent behavioral measures (Dimofte, Johansson and Ronkainen, 2008).

The lack of acknowledgement in self-reports could have two possible explanations. On the one hand, it may simply be a matter of conscious self-presentation bias, driven by a strategic desire to appear open-minded and sophisticated when responding to international marketing surveys. On the other hand, it may be that consumers are truly unaware of the biases they hold, and as such unconsciously rely on information such as a brand's country of origin or global nature to inform their subsequent judgments (*see* IMPLICIT CONSUMER COGNITION). To evaluate these alternative explanations in the case of global brands, Dimofte, Johansson and Ronkainen (2008) employed the Implicit Association Test (IAT).[3] The results showed that, compared to local brands, global brands were more closely associated with adjectives such as *ideal* and *desirable*, whereas local brands, by contrast, were seen as more concrete and mundane. The IAT responses did not correlate with self-reported explicit attitudes toward global brands, such that even consumers who were explicitly against globality displayed the same implicit preference for these brands.

CONCLUSIONS

The emergence of global consumption patterns and, at the same time, the complexity involved in understanding the still remaining national differences attest to the importance of research in international marketing. As reviewed in this article, the field is indissolubly linked to the topic of cross-cultural consumer behavior and its applications.

When considering the relevant conceptual and theoretical perspectives employed in research in international marketing, the emic–etic juxtaposition should be carefully assessed in order to ensure the validity of subsequent findings and their relevance to corporate strategy. At the same time, when thinking about the practical aspects of assessing and satisfying consumer needs across the globe, issues such as the appropriate operationalization of constructs and the achievement of measurement equivalence across multinational samples should be at the center of international marketing research. Yet, despite these cross-national cultural differences, a global consumer culture may be emerging, and the field seems well positioned to address it.

Finally, the extensive literature on relevant topics such as the country-of-origin effect and global branding is informative to both academics and practitioners in suggesting that, despite local specifics, the global consumers' behavior is governed by universal social-psychological processes and cognitive biases. Understanding these underlying factors will leave both consumers and firms better off.

ENDNOTES

[1] Others have argued that the international marketing field may benefit from employing established theoretical frameworks that originate in other academic areas.

[2] The level of fit between particular products and countries of origin underlies the product ethnicity construct (*see* PRODUCT ETHNICITY).

[3] The IAT is designed to measure the strength of automatic associations between mental representations of concepts in memory. It requires the rapid categorization of various stimulus objects, such that easier pairings (i.e., faster response latencies) are interpreted as being more strongly associated in memory than more difficult pairings (i.e., slower response latencies).

Bibliography

Alden, D.L., Steenkamp, J.B. and Batra, R. (1999) Brand positioning through advertising in Asia, North America and Europe: the role of global consumer culture. *Journal of Marketing*, **63**, 75–87.

Batra, R., Ramaswamy, V., Alden, D.L. *et al.* (2000) Effects of brand local and nonlocal origin on consumer attitudes in developing countries. *Journal of Consumer Psychology*, **9**, 83–95.

Dimofte, C.V., Johansson, J.K. and Bagozzi, R.P. (2010) Global brands in America: how consumer ethnicity mediates the global brand effect. *Journal of International Marketing*, **18** (3) in press.

Dimofte, C.V., Johansson, J.K. and Ronkainen, I.A. (2008) Cognitive and affective reactions of American consumers to global brands. *Journal of International Marketing*, **16**, 115–137.

Douglas, S.P. and Craig, S.C. (2006) On improving the conceptual foundations of international marketing research. *Journal of International Marketing*, **14**, 1–22.

Hofstede, G. (1980) *Culture's Consequences: International Differences in Work-Related Values*, Sage, Beverly Hills.

Holt, D.B., Quelch, J.A. and Taylor, E.L. (2004) How global brands compete. *Harvard Business Review*, **82**, 68–81.

Johansson, J.K. and Ronkainen, I.A. (2005) The esteem of global brands. *Journal of Brand Management*, **12**, 339–354.

Keillor, B.D., D'Amico, M. and Horton, V. (2001) Global consumer tendencies. *Psychology and Marketing*, **18** (1), 1–19.

LeClerc, F., Schmitt, B.H. and Dubé, L. (1994) Foreign branding and its effect on product perceptions and attitudes. *Journal of Marketing Research*, **31**, 263–270.

Maheswaran, D. and Shavitt, S. (2000) Issues and new directions in global consumer psychology. *Journal of Consumer Psychology*, **9**, 59–66.

Schwartz, S.H. (1994) Beyond individualism/collect-
ivism: new cultural dimensions of value, in *Individualism and Collectivism: Theory, Method, and
Applications* (eds U. Kim, H.C. Triandis, C. Kagit-
cibasi *et al.*) Sage, Thousand Oaks.

Sekaran, U. (1983) Methodological and theoretical issues
and advancements in cross-cultural research. *Journal
of International Business Studies*, 14, 61–73.

Steenkamp, J.B. (2001) The role of national culture
in international marketing research. *International
Marketing Review*, 18, 30–44.

Steenkamp, J.B., Batra, R. and Alden, D.L. (2003)
How perceived brand globalness creates brand value.
Journal of International Business Studies, 34, 53–65.

consumer behavior across literacy and resource barriers

Madhu Viswanathan

With few exceptions (Hill, 1991; Alwitt, 1995; Arnould and Mohr, 2005), much of what is known about consumer behavior has come from studying relatively resource-rich, literate consumers, usually in advanced economies. This article focuses on low-literate, low-income consumers in the United States and subsistence consumers in India, that is, those living in circumstances of widespread poverty. Each of these groups is described and compared and contrasted with what is known about consumer behavior in more conventional settings. Thus, the focus is on consumer behavior across literacy and resource barriers. Implications for marketing in general are also briefly discussed.

LOW-LITERATE LOW-INCOME CONSUMER BEHAVIOR IN THE UNITED STATES

Background.   Literacy relates to reading and writing skills, whereas numeracy relates to counting. Functional literacy relates to posses-sing the reading, writing, and counting skills to function in day-to-day life (Kirsch and Guthrie, 1997). Literacy and functional literacy are used interchangeably in this article. Low literacy, of course, is associated with low income as well, and the discussion emphasizes low-literate,

low-income consumers in the United States, disentangling these two factors where possible. Literacy rates in the United States, until a few decades ago, were reported to be as high as 99%. However, such statistics were based on a question in the Census as to whether an individual was literate. Subsequently, when grade-equivalent tasks were used (e.g., if you are in a certain grade, you should be able to write a check or read a package label), the estimates of low literacy have varied from 20% to considerably higher. Statistics about literacy carry a sense of prestige with them and therefore, often reflect biases at individual and more aggregate state or country levels. The 2002 National Assessment of Adult Literacy (NAAL) showed that at least 22% of US consumers lack skills to perform retail tasks (e.g., calculating unit prices and price discounts, comparing product attributes), and between 34% and 55% lack skills to look up reference materials to identify foods containing a particular vitamin (Kutner, Greenberg, and Baer, 2005).

Method.   In describing literate versus low-literate consumers, it is important to understand that this is a continuum and that there is no demarcation that makes someone nonlit-erate, hence the preference here to use the term, low-literate. Also relevant here is how low-literate consumers can be studied. Exper-iments and surveys are not the most effective approaches, unless very carefully designed (Viswanathan, Gau, and Chaturvedi, 2008a). In this work, observations of classrooms at adult education centers, observations of shopping trips, and interviews of teachers and students were used. Typically, such centers have students divided by grade–equivalent levels, such as 0–4, 5–8, and 9–12, based on reading and math tests administered periodically, that is, ranging from low to moderate levels of literacy. Although a number of insights are offered below, it should be noted that some of them apply more to those at the 0–4 level than say those at the 5–8 level. Both vulnerabilities and strengths of low-literate consumers were observed in this work and that is important to acknowledge as well. Low-literate consumers overcome constraints borne out of their circumstances, sometimes in ingenious ways, and display extraordinary resilience in negotiating a marketplace that assumes a certain level of literacy. Over time, surveys and experiments have been employed as well.

Illustrative findings.   In observations of low-literate consumers while shopping, most striking were the things that literate consumers may take for granted. A typical trip to the grocery store for a literate consumer may involve some trade-offs between price and attributes of products. If the intention is a cash purchase and one is short by a few dollars, it is usually not a big issue to leave behind some items and attribute things to one's forgetfulness. But this typical trip does not begin to describe the kinds of issues that take up much of the effort of low-literate shoppers, particularly those at the low end of the continuum.

Locating a product can take considerable time, when reading signs is difficult or just not possible. Therefore, once a product is located, it may be bought. It is not always easy to be asking store employees for directions, particularly when an individual has spent a lifetime with low literacy and it has been cause for many travails. Identifying the correct volume can be effortful – finding 150 candles involves finding two different packets of a 100 and a 50. With the many different price tags and sales signs, finding the bottom-line price can be very confusing. Also, low-literate individuals may need to rely on written computations to find out the price of multiple units when the price of one is known. "% off" sales signs can be another cause for concern as some may completely avoid them owing to difficulty computing the final price or embarrassment with having to ask a store employee, whereas others may use them some-times, say, when 50% off, as computing half off may be relatively easier. Computing the total on a shopping trip may be difficult, leading to solu-tions such as moving currency bills after each item is added to a cart or visually subtracting from an imagined set of currency bills. Similarly, allowing for taxes can be a significant concern leading to rules of thumb like buying one thing if one has five dollars. Unit prices are essentially abstractions that are difficult to understand and often ignored. Similarly, nutrient values may not be used and "% DVs," serving sizes, and even expiry dates misunderstood or misused.

Adding to cognitive difficulties, issues such as being short of money at the checkout counter are cause for despair, as this is a result of one's low literacy rather than forgetfulness. Similarly, having enough money can be cause for celebra-tion. Underlying their shopping interactions for low-literate consumers is the need to maintain self-esteem and avoid being exposed for their low literacy. Thus, in addition to cognitive issues, emotional issues are also central, with anxiety being a common aspect of seemingly mundane shopping activities.

Cognitive tendencies.   Some of these findings with cognitive tendencies, decision-making aspects, and coping strategies are summarized. A tendency that is most striking is one of concrete thinking, focusing on single pieces of information such as price, without abstracting across, say price and size or price and other attributes (Viswanathan, Rosa, and Harris, 2005; Gau and Viswanathan, 2008). Buying the cheapest product without attention to size is an example of this tendency. It manifests in a number of ways, through seeking familiar stores, learning to use expiry date or other concrete information, such as numerical information, without understanding its meaning. In a study of low-literate peasants in Central Asia in the early 1900s, a Russian psychologist asked participants to view tools (e.g., an axe, a hatchet, a log, and a saw) and asked them to group three of these objects that can be described by a word or belong together (Luria, 1976). Participants responded in terms of how they could chop firewood to stay warm, that is, how they could use what they saw in day-to-day life. Thus, low literacy and difficulty with abstractions tends to lead consumers to think in the immediate, visual, graphic, here-and-now world of how they can use things.

Another cognitive tendency is pictographic thinking (Viswanathan *et al.*, 2005; Gau and Viswanathan, 2008). Although consumers in general depend on pictures, pictographic thinking is qualitatively different. It means viewing text such as brand names not as something to read but as an image, and thus remembering brands to buy through pictorial elements. Pictographic thinking also manifests in visualizing quantities to buy rather than using symbolic information. For instance, when buying an ingredient like sugar to bake a cake, low-literate consumers may visualize baking the cake and pouring sugar into it and buy the package of corresponding size. Pictographic thinking may even involve "counting" by visualizing currency bills. Pattern-matching prescriptions with medicine packages to find the right medicine is another approach. Whereas low-literate consumers may have poorer memory for textual information when compared to consumers with higher literacy, their memory for pictorial information, such as brand signatures, can be as good (Viswanathan *et al.*, 2009). Such improvement in memory appears to arise from familiar pictorial elements.

Decision making, emotional trade-offs, and coping strategies. Decision rules may range from single-attribute decisions (buy the cheapest) to habitual decision making or even random decision making (picking up the first item in a product category that is seen, for a planned or unplanned purchase). As noted earlier, sometimes, locating a product can lead to its purchase. This should be contrasted with conventional decision-making models, which cover a number of steps. Also intertwined with decisions are emotional trade-offs. For instance, low-literate consumers may trade off utility to save embarrassment, as maintaining self-esteem is central when they negotiate the marketplace. Having sufficient money at the counter may be cause for celebration, whereas being "caught" short may be cause for despair. The anxiety associated with negotiating a complex market-place while lacking in literacy and trying to avoid being exposed on this account is the larger emotional context where day-to-day shopping occurs. Along similar lines, Adkins and Ozanne (2005) identify types of low-literate consumers on the basis of dimensions such as acceptance or rejection of stigma arising from low literacy. They find a number of coping strategies including avoidance, dependence on others, self-esteem maintenance, and social deception.

Low-literate consumers cope in a number of ways – depending on others, coming up with rudimentary defensive rules like buying one item from the menu at a time to avoid being short of money, and even giving all the money they have at the checkout counter. Some of the ways in which they cope are ingenious, such as in "counting" by visualizing currency bills. They often depend on others, sometimes even helpful store employees, to help them with shopping and avoid situations and stores that are likely to lead to embarrassment, striving to maintain self-esteem in their interactions.

Low-literate shopping behavior. A model of low-literate shopping behavior is presented in Figure 1 purely for illustrative purposes to contrast low-literate consumer behavior with more conventional consumer behavior. It should be noted that this model captures consumer behavior especially for 0-4 level adult education students, setting up a sharp contrast with consumers with higher levels of literacy. In terms of generic models of decision making, low-literate consumers may bypass or spend minimal effort in steps such as prepur-chase search and evaluation of alternatives. Alternatively, consumers bypass the entire decision process by mimicking others or by delegating responsibility to others. As indicated in the direct link from "need recognition" to "purchase," some consumers may completely delegate decision making to others, highlighting the theme of dependence on others. The first step in the decision-making process is location of a product. Owing to the amount of effort expended in locating a product in the store, location may be followed by purchase. Location of a product may also be followed by obtaining the correct number of units of a product. Alter-natively, the next step may be to expend effort in looking for a price, a distinct step in the process. The process may be "short-circuited" at this point by either reshelving or buying the product caused by lack of success in finding the price. The next step may be reading a price and iter-atively looking for a price owing to confusion in identifying a price tag or interpreting multiple price stickers. Again, the process may be short-circuited through reshelving or purchase. The next step may be to locate the correct volume or number of units needed. In instances where a combination of package sizes are needed, significant effort may be needed in locating the correct packages. Location of needed volume may precede location of a price and reading a

Generic model of
consumer decision making

Generic model of consumer
information processing

Shopping behavior model for
low-literate consumers

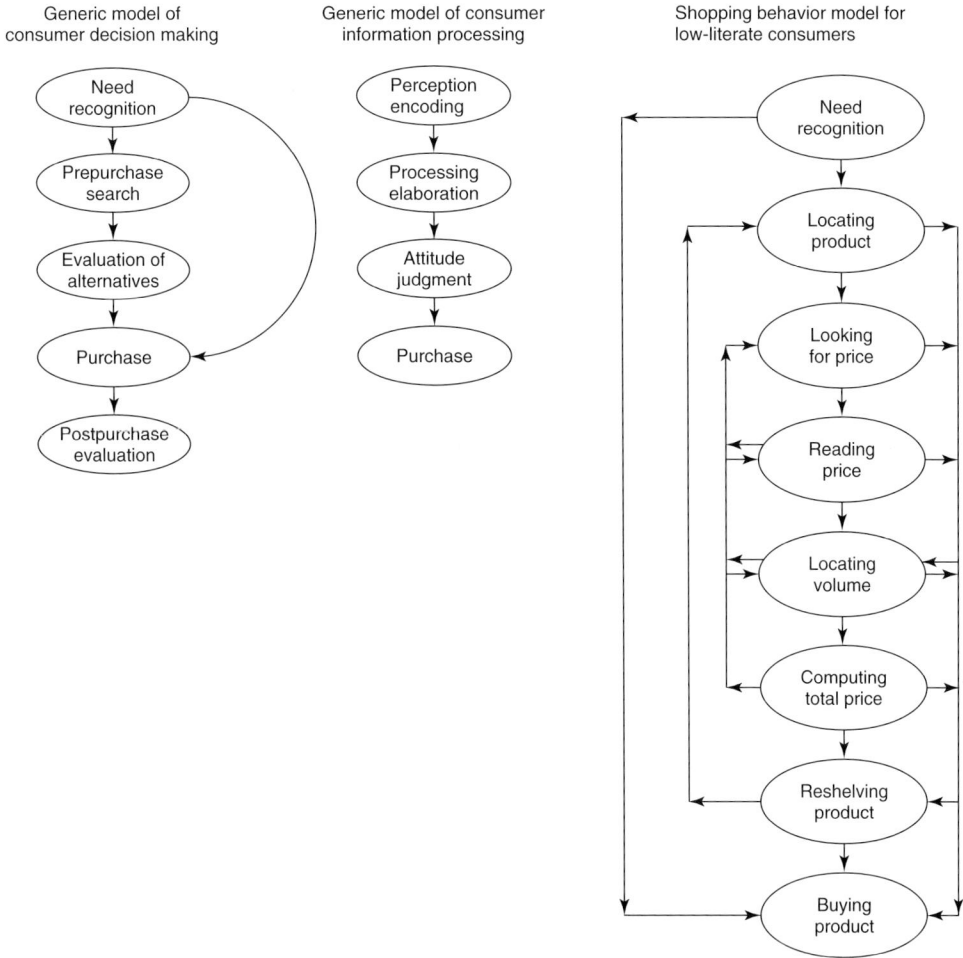

Figure 1 An illustration of shopping behavior for low-literate consumers.

price, and may follow location of a product and may immediately lead to purchase. Location of volume may also be followed by looking for a price and/or reading a price. The next step is to compute a total price with some iteration needed here to perform the computations. Iterations may also be required here in looking for the price again or rereading the price, or identifying the correct volume. Reshelving or purchase culminates the decision-making sequence.

Although not strictly comparable to generic models of decision making and information processing adapted from the literature (Bettman, 1979), the shopping behavior model for functionally low-literate consumers highlights the importance of one or two stages in other models. In contrast to these typical decision-making and information processing models, the emphasis here is on perception of information, leading to surface-level processing of primarily one or very few pieces of product information (e.g., price information), often with error. Whereas typical information processing models include perception, encoding, elaboration, evaluation, and then purchase (Bettman, 1979), the emphasis for low-literate consumers is on perception with regard to location of product and identification of price. Encoding may be of a transient nature, with a view toward completing the immediate purchase task rather than leading to memory and integration with prior knowledge.

Importantly, whereas this model may resemble low-involvement models of decision making and models of repeat purchase in terms of lack of active information seeking and lack of comparison along attributes (cf., Zaichkowsky, 1985), fundamental processing differences are noteworthy. The decision-making process involves bypassing of several steps when compared to traditional decision-making models. Rather than arising from a lack of motivation that characterizes low-involvement decision making and repeat purchases, this process can be quite effortful. Thus, striking differences among consumers who differ in levels of literacy are illustrated by contrasting decision-making processes.

SUBSISTENCE CONSUMER BEHAVIOR

Background.   The discussion now moves further across the resource spectrum to examine subsistence marketplaces and consumer behavior. Research in poverty contexts in India provides the foundation for the discussion. When compared to the United States, such contexts are characterized by more widespread poverty and higher rates of low literacy as well. Much of humanity lives on the equivalent of two to four dollars a day (Prahalad, 2005). However, much of what is known about consumer behavior has been based on studying relatively resource-rich, literate consumers, mostly in advanced economies.

Method.   The work here was in low-income urban neighborhoods and rural areas in South India, using a range of methods including in-depth interviews of buyers and sellers (Viswanathan, 2007; Viswanathan, Gajendiran, and Venkatesan, 2008; Viswanathan, Rosa, and Ruth, 2010). Such subsistence communities are characterized by deprivation on many fronts. Uncertainty pervades every facet of life as basic infrastructure is either unreliable or absent. For example, rural areas are characterized by unreliable transportation or electricity. Central consumption events like cooking a staple, say rice, may be dependent on many factors –

the quality of rice and water, availability of cooking fuel, and so on. There are, of course, many differences between urban and rural areas as well, with the latter having lack of access to markets and shops and more severe infrastructure problems.

Illustrative findings.   In such marketplaces, subsistence consumers often have relationships with a single store, such as a neighborhood retail store that is conveniently located and charges higher prices but allows purchase on credit in times of need, or a larger reseller. Through such relationships, often with the neighborhood retail store owner, subsistence consumers multiply the value of their patronage for a small seller and expect responsive customer service in return. It may be noted here that an understanding of relatively resource-rich settings may lead to misconceptions about subsistence consumer behavior. For instance, it may seem that buying from larger resellers at the beginning of the month and stocking up is the rational course of action. However, this implicitly assumes a stable income and the lack of frequent crises, certainties that are beyond the reach of subsistence consumers. Fear of crises necessitates buying on credit from the neighborhood retailer in exchange for consumer loyalty. Also interesting here is how the longer-term relationship rather than any transaction, and particularly an impersonal one, takes precedence as subsistence consumers and sellers leverage relationships to multiply the economic value and leverage social relations to compensate for the lack of marketplace infrastructure prevalent in resource-rich settings.

Subsistence consumers have to focus on products that serve immediate and basic needs, such as food and clothing, and emergency medical care. Their choices may be between buying a product, making it (e.g., indigenous soap substitute), or, of course, forgoing it. However, they aspire for quality brands that serve their needs and also for products such as cell phones that greatly improve their ability to communicate and can serve vital needs (e.g., for emergencies). They also aspire for a better future, making sacrifices to obtain better education or health care for their children – a driving motivation in many parents' lives. Subsistence consumers are also very adaptive and willing to experiment with new technology, such as cell phones, that serve vital communication needs. Their adaptivity is borne out by the need to survive and the experience of coping with extreme uncertainty in many realms of life that are taken for granted in relatively affluent settings. Thus, to fully understand subsistence consumer behavior, preconceptions that they require only some basic products or that products in demand would have to be of low technology need to be dispelled. Similarly, quality is very central, as scarce resources have to be used for products that will better subsistence consumers' immediate and basic life circumstances. Otherwise, subsistence consumers have the resilience to forgo products or the resourcefulness to make them.

The issues discussed for low literacy in the United States apply in subsistence marketplaces as well, in terms of concrete thinking and pictographic thinking. They engage in concrete thinking, such as in fixating on concrete numbers denoting price, such as maximum retail price, a requirement in the Indian marketplace. However, they may do so without understanding what it means. This is akin to low-literate consumers in the United States who may depend on expiry date without understanding its meaning. Pictographic thinking is also pervasive, such as in pattern-matching prescriptions with medicine labels. Self-esteem issues are also relevant, and although both poverty and low literacy is pervasive, the stigma attached to the latter is perhaps more acute, with lack of education often being attributed with the lack of ability to overcome poverty. Low literacy can lead to fear of conversations in shopping contexts, and feelings of futility about arguing with shopkeepers or questioning quality.

One-to-one interactional marketplaces. In a larger context of widespread and extreme poverty and low literacy, subsistence consumers negotiate the marketplace in ways that require face-to-face interactions and oral communication in the native language. Such communication does not require specific basic literacy skills, but rather knowledge of spoken language that individuals acquire growing up and social skills. Subsistence consumers can learn marketplace skills through conversations and observations on

streets and other public locations. Conversations with sellers can lead to development of skills and self-confidence. Moreover, consumers themselves may often be vendors as a way to subsist and survive, thus learning valuable skills that transfer to their consumer behavior, such as negotiating, counting, and so forth. What is interesting here is the widespread existence of distinct markets in terms of the poor and the higher strata. Clothes can be purchased at department stores or on the sidewalk for diametrically opposite price points.

In this one-on-one interactional marketplace, subsistence consumers may be resource poor but network rich. With an opportunity to participate through oral communications and observations, such a marketplace can be a stepping stone to gaining important skills, awareness of rights, and self-confidence. Word of mouth is powerful, and trust and fairness play important roles. With the life circumstances they face, the human aspects are intertwined with the economic as buyers and sellers negotiate while emphasizing both. Transactions can be fluid, with prices and amounts varied (e.g., weighing can be "adjusted" downward if the price bargained is too low) and buyers constantly demanding customization in offerings. As conversations are not private by and large and word can spread very quickly, sellers have to be careful about waiving payment or treating customers differentially.

This world of social relations also cuts both ways and should not be interpreted to suggest anything but an intensely harsh reality. For instance, noncollateral loan repayments are enforced through public humiliation and buyers and sellers are open to abuse and exploitation. Also relevant here are the many different group influences, whether local community groups or larger family or neighborhood or social strata. Group influences can be accentuated in rural areas where villages are geographically dispersed.

Contrasting low-literate consumer behavior in the United States to subsistence consumers in India. In comparing the two consumer groups discussed here, although speculative and cognizant of the wide range of differences within low-literate consumer behavior in the United States, say between urban and rural areas, and similarly in subsistence consumer behavior, a number of differences are noteworthy. In advanced economies like the United States, the marketplace context assumes a certain level of literacy. Large chain stores use technology to compute and present symbolic package and shelf information that assume a certain level of literacy. Thus, low-literate consumers may be isolated from the marketplace and the development of consumer skills may be impeded when compared to the one-to-one interactional subsistence marketplaces described here. In the latter context, generic products are evaluated in face-to-face interactions with prices determined by enquiry and bargaining, and money and change counted out. Consumers learn skills by being vendors themselves and managing various aspects of a business, rather than through an occupation in a narrowly circumscribed role for a large business as may often be the case in advanced economies. Extreme poverty and the need to get the next meal is in itself a very harsh teacher of consumer lessons. Thus, ironically, the low-literate subsistence consumer may develop some of the functional skills needed to negotiate the one-to-one interactional marketplace, when compared to the low-literate consumer in the United States who has to negotiate a relatively impersonal marketplace that assumes a certain level of literacy.

IMPLICATIONS FOR MARKETING

Each of these streams of research across literacy and resource barriers suggest important implications for marketing. They also represent opportunities for marketers to serve these consumer groups effectively and gain a competitive advantage. Some generic implications that cut across both contexts are noteworthy. First and foremost is the need for literate managers and researchers to understand consumers whom they may not be able to personally relate to in terms of literacy or income. Thus, the most important implication is the need for literate, relatively resource-rich researchers and managers to adopt a mind-set of learning before designing solutions for these contexts. They need to understand consumer behavior in a realm where their own experiences as consumers, although a strength in understanding

conventional consumer behavior, may be quite misleading. Thus, the need to employ innovative research methods to understand these consumer groups is critical. Conducting research in these settings requires setting aside preconceptions and employing an open approach that is conducive to learning from low-literate, low-income, or subsistence consumers. Instead of an approach that assumes literate managers and researchers know better and can design solutions for low-literate, low-income consumers or subsistence consumers, an approach of learning from those with experience and expertise in overcoming constraints and then designing solutions for them is likely to be effective.

Low-literate, low-income consumer behavior.   A number of implications for marketing relate to addressing the cognitive predilections, emotional elements, decision making and coping discussed earlier (Viswanathan, Rosa, and Harris, 2005; Gau and Viswanathan, 2008). Marketers need to develop an understanding of the challenges faced by low-literate consumers and work to create shopping environments that are user friendly. Examples include price display and sale signs, the use of visuals (e.g., semicircles for half off, dollar bills for amount of savings) rather than abstract symbols such as percentages, and the display of final price, perhaps in a color-coded format, rather than having to rely on computations (Viswanathan, Rosa, and Ruth, 2008). The use of common formats to display information such as unit prices may enable low-literate consumers to inform themselves and begin to use such information to make price-size trade-offs. Pictographic representations such as heart signs or weighing machines as well as graphical representations of nutrient levels, instructions, and other pertinent information are other possible ways to design communications to enable usage by low-literate consumers. Store signs can similarly be designed to depict product categories pictorially and help consumers navigate the store. Familiar pictorial elements are a central means by which low-literate consumers may understand and remember information, therefore, the use of pictorial elements at the package, shelf, and store level are very important as well. Technological aids, such as shopping carts with scanning and computing features, would also be helpful to low-literate consumers as they keep track of their total shopping basket.

Perhaps most importantly, marketers should work to address the challenges faced by low-literate consumers that extend beyond the cognitive to the emotional as well. Training store employees to treat low-literate consumers sensitively and respectfully can go a long way toward building trust and, in turn, loyalty as well, and represents the essence of the marketing approach from which a sustainable competitive advantage can accrue. Perhaps most damaging is the perception among low-literate consumers that they are being cheated, emphasizing the need for employees to be trained and sensitized in these issues, while also distinguishing between the consequences of low literacy versus other issues such as those faced by literate, English as second language consumers or by literate but poor consumers. Even if low-literate consumers do not complain, the lingering negative emotions may lead them to avoid future visits to such stores. Employees should be trained to interact with different consumers and to explain store policies clearly and respectfully.

At the level of product design, marketers need to learn to use innovative methods to research the needs of low-literate consumers and incorporate insights into the design of the product, including assembly and interface, as well as its packaging and related communications, such as instructions. This requires adopting a different mind-set than one that literate managers and researchers may typically employ, in order to view the usage of products from the perspective of low-literate consumers. A case in point is in designing the interface for computers and cell phones with visual icons, or the packaging of medical products with respect to dosage information.

A noteworthy issue is that many of these implications will ease shopping for all consumers, irrespective of literacy levels. Pictorial aids are easier to use for all consumers, as illustrated by such examples as displays of foods that specific wines can be served with. Product design that incorporates the perspective of low-literate consumers is similarly likely to enhance ease of use for all consumers. With the plethora of information at the store, simplified display of pricing and other information in consistent formats is likely to enhance the shopping experience for all consumers.

Subsistence consumers. Perhaps the biggest implication to marketers is to understand their own limitations in focusing on subsistence consumers owing to their likely lack of personal connection in terms of poverty, literacy, and culture (Viswanathan, Seth, Gau, and Chaturvedi, 2009). Thus, they need to unlearn preconceptions about these consumers and marketplaces and aim to understand their strengths and vulnerabilities as well as marketplace dynamics, such as between buyers and sellers. With an open mind-set and holistic immersion in the context during data collection or a learning and listening phase, and rigorous consideration of what is different about these settings during analysis, marketers in turn, can bring a fresh perspective and new solutions that stem from deep understanding of a radically different context. Thus, complementary strengths and weaknesses that stem from being unfamiliar with subsistence marketplaces can be used to an advantage. Such immersion should aim to understand broader life circumstances and how products and related support would fit in such contexts and improve individual and community welfare. Critical here is the need to avoid exporting solutions from other markets.

Researching subsistence consumers, in turn, involves a number of cognitive, emotional, and administrative considerations (Viswanathan, Gau, and Chaturvedi, 2008). Marketers should gain insights from "experts" in living in subsistence ranging from consumers to vendors, self-help groups, and community-based organizations. Such bottom-up understanding is essential, given the vast differences across different subsistence contexts as a function of geographic location, local language, and cultural differences.

A fundamental challenge for marketers is to identify central needs that subsistence consumers are willing to spend very scarce resources on. Such needs range from the basic to the aspirational, often accompanied by a motivation to pay a small premium for quality – covering food, clothing, and energy, as well as health care, communication and education. In turn, designing solutions requires understanding broader life circumstances as well as specific product-usage situations, often difficult for affluent marketing managers and researchers. How subsistence consumers use or reuse products and use them for multiple purposes is also important to understand. Given the constant demand for customization in a one-to-one interactional marketplace, providing local entrepreneurs with the ability to configure products and prices to different customers is another important consideration (e.g., products with nutritional additives customized to different segments, such as children and the elderly). In designing solutions, the need to involve subsistence consumers and entrepreneurs is also central, as is the need to address psychological aspects such as engendering trust.

In terms of marketing communications, including informational and educational campaigns, marketers should consider conc-retizing, localizing, and socializing solutions (Viswanathan, Sridharan, Gau, and Ritchie, 2009). Thus, information in concrete form for low-literate audiences who engage in concrete thinking and pictographic thinking, that also reflect local reality and harness the one-to-one interactional marketplace in terms of community interaction are all likely important elements of marketing communications. This is also the case for product interfaces and packages, with a need to visualize benefits and value propositions. In contexts of multifaceted deprivation, marketers should also consider product-relevant support including educational programs. Another impor-tant issue is the need to communicate the value proposition to highlight costs (e.g., including time and effort) and benefits (including hidden benefits such as nutrition to avoid illnesses) (Sridharan and Viswanathan, 2008). Such costs and benefits and the value proposition need to be communicated to low-literate audiences in ways that can be visualized. Communications should also be designed from the bottom up to harness the social networks discussed here, through partnerships with local entrepreneurs and customers. Similarly, distribution should harness social networks, such as through local retailers and community-based organizations and allow for customization at the point of purchase through such means as offering credit.

To implement their plans, marketers need to work with a diverse set of organizations who have been functioning in subsistence marketplaces, in a number of sectors of society, such as local governments and community-based organiza-tions. Lacking the institutions in affluent markets that enable impersonal exchanges, relation-ships with diverse groups and organizations are critical in providing access and effectively implementing plans.

Marketers should also understand how product performance and related company activities work toward improving individual and community welfare (Viswanathan et al., 2009). For instance, subsistence consumers seek products that will better their life circumstances, ranging from nutritious food, to education for their children and communication devices. When products lack these characteristics, subsistence consumers may opt to make or forgo the products rather than spend scarce resources. Therefore, quality and value are extremely important. Moreover, product support through educational programs and other means may be critical in settings where deprivation is multifaceted. In their quest to survive, the human aspects and larger life circumstances are intertwined with economic transactions – in contrast to impersonal transactions in affluent societies with relative certainty regarding infrastructure and institutional support. Thus, issues of trust and fairness are very important and marketers should work to address them. With the one-to-one interactional marketplace described earlier characterized by strong word of mouth, a reputation for trustworthiness and fairness can go a long way in developing a sustainable competitive advantage. Focusing on individual and community welfare may also be helpful in working with diverse organizations to reach and serve markets.

In conclusion, the need to view subsistence consumers as preexisting marketplaces whose dynamics need to be understood by marketers should be emphasized. Rather than view these subsistence marketplaces as parallel markets to sell to, they should be viewed as marketplaces to learn from, to then design solutions for, that may well be transferable to all contexts. As a case in point, creating products for conditions of very scarce recourses and lack of infrastructures, such as, say, distributed energy generators (solar applications), in turn has implications for all contexts in confronting the challenges of the twenty-first century.

In summary, a top-down approach to different elements of marketing assumes certain institutional infrastructure, often lacking in subsistence marketplaces. For instance, marketing research assumes the ability to sample, marketing communications assume mass media, and distribution assumes related infrastructure. With the lack of such infrastructure, subsistence marketplaces rely on social networks to provide some measure of certainty in an extremely uncertain world. Rather than adopt a mind-set of scaling by using top-down approaches, marketers should employ a bottom-up approach to addressing each element of marketing in radically different and diverse subsistence contexts, and aggregate insights from the bottom up.

In conclusion, this article explored consumer behavior across literacy and resource barriers, in sharp contrast to conventional consumer behavior. Both for low-literate, low-income consumers in the United States, and for subsistence consumers in South India, traditional assumptions about consumer behavior do not hold. Rather, unique cognitive, emotional, and social characteristics that characterize such consumer behavior present marketers with challenges as well as opportunities to serve such consumers and develop a sustainable competitive advantage while also improving individual and community welfare.

Bibliography

Adkins, N. and Ozanne, J. (2005) The low literate consumer. *Journal of Consumer Research*, **32** (1), 93–105.

Alwitt, L. (1995) *The Low-Income Consumer: Adjusting the Balance of Exchange*, Sage, Thousand Oaks.

Arnould, E.J. and Mohr, J.J. (2005) Dynamic transformations for base-of-the-pyramid market clusters. *Journal of the Academy of Marketing Science*, **33** (3), 254–274.

Bettman, J.R. (1979) *An Information Processing Theory of Consumer Choice (Duke University)*, Addison-Wesley Publishing Co., Reading.

Gau, R. and Viswanathan, M. (2008) The retail shopping experience for low-literate consumers. *Journal*

of *Research for Consumers*, (15), Consumer Empowerment Special Issue.

Hill, R.P. (1991) Homeless women, special possessions, and the meaning of 'home': an ethnographic case study. *Journal of Consumer Research*, **18** (3), 298–310.

Kirsch, I.S. and Guthrie, J.T. (1997) The concept and measurement of functional literacy. *Reading Research Quarterly*, **13** (4), 485–507.

Kutner, M., Greenberg, E., and Baer, J. (2005) *A First Look at the Literacy of America's Adults in the 21st Century*, National Center for Education Statistics, Department of Education, Washington, DC.

Luria, A.R. (1976) *Cognitive Development: Its Cultural and Social Foundations*, Harvard University Press, Cambridge.

Prahalad, C.K. (2005) *The Fortune at the Bottom of the Pyramid*, Wharton School Publishing, University of Pennsylvania, Philadelphia.

Sridharan, S. and Viswanathan, M. (2008) Marketing in subsistence marketplaces: consumption and entrepreneurship in a South Indian context. *Journal of Consumer Marketing*, Special Issue on Base of the Pyramid Research, **25** (7), 455–462.

Viswanathan, M. (2007) Understanding product and market interactions in subsistence marketplaces: a study in South India, in *Product and Market Development for Subsistence Marketplaces: Consumption and Entrepreneurship Beyond Literacy and Resource Barriers*, Advances in International Management Series (eds J. Rosa, M. Viswanathan, J. Cheng, and M. Hitt), Elsevier, Oxford, pp. 21–57.

Viswanathan, M., Gajendiran, S., and Venkatesan, R. (2008) *Enabling Consumer and Entrepreneurial Literacy in Subsistence Marketplaces*, Springer, Dordrecht.

Viswanathan, M., Gau, R., and Chaturvedi, A. (2008) Research methods for subsistence marketplaces, in *Sustainability Challenges and Solutions at the Base-of-the-Pyramid: Business, Technology and the Poor* (eds P. Khandachar and M. Halme), Greenleaf Publishing, Sheffield.

Viswanathan, M., Rosa, J.A., and Harris, J. (2005) Decision-making and coping by functionally illiterate consumers and some implications for marketing management. *Journal of Marketing*, **69** (1), 15–31.

Viswanathan, M., Rosa, J., and Ruth, J. (2008) *Emerging Lessons – For multinational companies, understanding the needs of poorer consumers can be profitable and socially responsible*, Wall Street Journal/MIT Sloan Online, October.

Viswanathan, M., Rosa, J.A., and Ruth, J., (2010) Exchanges in marketing systems: the case of subsistence consumer merchants in Chennai, India. *Journal of Marketing*, **74**, 1–18.

Viswanathan, M., Seth, A., Gau, R., and Chaturvedi, A. (2009) Internalizing social good into business processes in subsistence marketplaces: the sustainable market orientation. *Journal of Macromarketing*, 29, 406–425.

Viswanathan, M., Sridharan, S., Gau, R., and Ritchie, R. (2009) Designing marketplace literacy education in resource-constrained contexts: implications for public policy and marketing. *Journal of Public Policy & Marketing*, 28 (1), 85–94.

Viswanathan, M., Xia, L., Torelli, C., and Gau, R. (2009) Literacy and consumer memory. *Journal of Consumer Psychology*, 19, 389–402.

Zaichkowsky, J.L. (1985) Measuring the involvement construct. *Journal of Consumer Research*, 12, 341–352.

consumer behavior analysis

Gordon R. Foxall

INTRODUCTION

Although the main theoretical perspective of consumer research has been cognitive, behaviorism receives intermittent mention as a possible contributor, though its potential for understanding consumer choice remains underdeveloped. Some consumer theories incorporate it to deal with routine aspects of consumer behavior, while other treatments approach it as a source of marketer, especially retailer, tactics. The possibility that behaviorism provides insights into the explanation of consumer choice has been neglected. *Consumer behavior analysis* attempts to redress the balance by exploring the nature of behaviorist explanation and its capacity to enlighten consumer research.

Especially in terms of the theoretical and empirical advances made by behavior analysts in the field of verbal behavior and behavioral economics during the last two decades, behaviorism promises to extend the investigation and explanation of consumer behavior beyond the limits of a purely cognitive approach. Behavioral economics, in particular, combines the rigor of operant theory with the methods of experimental economics with the aim of understanding aspects of consumer choice that cognitive consumer psychology has often

neglected, such as gambling, addiction, and health-related behaviors as well as more routine features of consumer behavior such as product and brand choice. Consumer behavior analysis adds to this the contextual framework of consumer decision making in marketing-oriented economies, adding further to the interdisciplinary base of the psychological investigation of economic behavior.

THE BEHAVIORAL PERSPECTIVE MODEL

The original aim of the research program was to ascertain whether a model of consumer choice based on a radical behaviorist framework was feasible, and, if so, what the epistemological nature of such a route to explanation would be (Foxall, 2004a). So the aim has never been to change the paradigm in consumer research in favor of behaviorism, but to test a radical behaviorist depiction of consumer choice to its limit, adding in other approaches to explanation only as and when they became essential. The earliest stages involved critiques of the central explanatory devices assumed in consumer research at the time, notably the ideas that attitudes and intentions inevitably precede, prefigure, and determine consumer behavior, or that novel behavior on the part of consumers was explicable in terms of underlying traits of "innovativeness." The development of the sought-after model of consumer behavior based on radical behaviorism resulted in the behavioral perspective model (BPM), which is an elaboration of the "three-term contingency," the basic explanatory device of operant psychology in which a discriminative stimulus (S^D) marks the occasion on which a particular response (R) is likely to be rewarded or reinforced (S^R), that is, to increase in frequency, or punished (S^P), that is, to decrease. The three-term contingency is usually depicted as

$$S^D : R \longrightarrow S^{R/P}$$

where : indicates that the probability of an operant response is increased in the presence of the S^D, while by definition that response leads to consequences that are reinforcing and/or punishing. The model adapts these key elements to suit the interpretation and prediction of human economic behavior in affluent societies. The BPM is shown in Figure 1.

Consumer choice is the outcome of the consumer's learning history meeting the current consumer behavior setting, the point at which the experience of consumption meets a new opportunity to consume. This intersection is the *consumer situation*, the immediate determinant of approach/avoidance responses involved in purchase and consumption. The *consumer behavior setting* comprises the stimulus antecedents of that behavior, some of which would have been present on earlier consumption occasions. Given the individual's learning history, that is, past choices and the reinforcing/punishing consequences they have had, these initially neutral stimuli are transformed into the discriminative stimuli that set the occasion for current choice; in particular, the individual's consumption history invests them with meaning, in the sense of a capacity to generate specific kinds of approach and/or avoidance behaviors, which produce consequences that regulate the rate of recurrence of the behaviors that produced them. The consumer situation consists also of motivating operations (MOs) such as rules that invest the consequences inherent in the discriminative stimuli with additional motivating or inhibitory power by making the consequences of radical behaviorism appear more or less reinforcing, more or less punishing.

The consumer behavior setting.   Like the three-term contingency, the BPM specifies behaviorally antecedent stimulus conditions (the behavior setting) but combines the concepts of

discriminative stimuli and motivating operations by means of the construct of behavior-setting *scope*, the extent to which these setting elements encourage or inhibit the behavior predicted to occur in such settings. Settings of purchase and consumption are all *relatively* open, but differ from one another along a restricted continuum of closed–open consumer behavior settings. Waiting in line at the bank to pay in a check occurs in a relatively closed consumer behavior setting: there is probably no alternative to being there and waiting until a teller becomes available, standing in an orderly fashion is encouraged both by the physical style of the building and by the social arrangements, deviation from the established behavior program of the setting is likely to be punished by stares or glares. An open consumer behavior setting encourages a wider range of alternative behaviors. In a bar, for instance, all types of beverages and snacks may be available, there may be TV to watch, talking loudly may not be discouraged, and even singing and dancing may be possible. The customer is free to leave at any time, even if only to go to another bar in the vicinity – at least far freer than he or she would be to leave the bank and find another at which to present the check.

Patterns of reinforcement.   The consequences of economic behavior fall into three types: utilitarian reinforcement, which consists in the functional outcomes of behavior, informational reinforcement, which stems from the symbolic outcomes, principally performance feedback, aversive/punishing consequences, and the costs of purchase and consumption. Such aversive outcomes can themselves be subdivided into

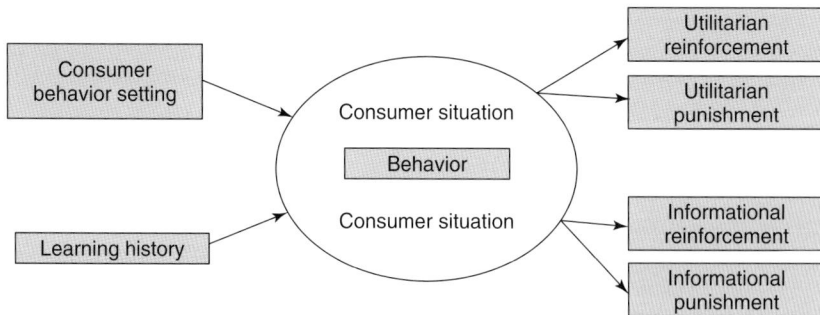

Figure 1 Summative behavioral perspective model.

those that are utilitarian in nature and those that are symbolic. Utilitarian reinforcement consists in the direct usable, economic, and technical benefits of owning and consuming a product or service, while informational reinforcement inheres in benefits of ownership and consumption, which are usually social in nature and consist in the prestige or status as well as the self-esteem generated by ownership and consumption. The driver of the cheapest car available is principally concerned with the utilitarian benefits that all cars provide: most obviously, door-to-door transportation. Informational reinforcement, on the other hand, is more likely to involve a lifestyle statement by which the consumer seeks to convey his or her social status or to bolster esteem and/or reported feelings of self-esteem. The driver of a Porsche not only clearly gets from A to B in it but also receives social esteem and status from others as well as personally conferred self-esteem. These constitute symbolic rewards of consumption. Most products have an element of both the instrumental and the symbolic. A mobile phone not only provides communications services when and where the consumer wants them; because it has interchangeable colored cases, it may also signal to that consumer's social group that he or she is "cool" (or, a year later, "not so cool").

Patterns of reinforcement, based on combining high and low levels of utilitarian reinforcement and high and low levels of informational reinforcement, suggest four operant classes of consumer behavior (Figure 2). The four broad classes of consumer behavior can be inferred as follows. (i) *Accomplishment* is consumer behavior reflecting social and economic achievement: acquisition and conspicuous consumption of status goods, displaying products and services that signal personal attainment. (ii) *Hedonism* includes such activities as the consumption of popular entertainment. (iii) *Accumulation* includes the consumer behaviors involved in certain kinds of saving, collecting, and installment buying. (iv) *Maintenance* consists of activities necessary for the consumer's physical survival and welfare (e.g., food) and the fulfillment of the minimal obligations entailed in membership of a social system (e.g., paying taxes). Both types of reinforcers figure to differing extents in each of the four classes. Adding in the scope of the current behavior setting leads to the eightfold way depicted in Figure 3, which shows the variety of contingency categories that exclusively constitute a functional analysis of consumer behavior. We take a closer look at the four broad operant classes of consumer behavior with the added complexity of consumer behavior-setting scope added in.

Accomplishment. In an open setting, this consists, in general, in the *purchase and consumption of status goods*: luxuries and radical innovations such as exotic vacations and iPhones. The items in question are possessed and used for the pleasure or ease of living they confer, the well-being they make possible for the individual; they thereby provide extensive hedonic rewards. As status symbols, their conspicuous consumption strengthens the behavior in question. They attest directly, and often publicly and unambiguously, to the consumer's attainments, especially economic. Goods in this category are usually highly differentiated – by novel function in the case of innovations, by branding in the case of luxuries. In a closed setting, accomplishment can be generally described as *fulfillment*, personal attainments gained through leisure, often with a strong element of recreation or excitement as well as achievement. It might, for instance, include both the completion of a

	High utilitarian reinforcement	Low utilitarian reinforcement
High informational reinforcement	Accomplishment	Accumulation
Low informational reinforcement	Hedonism	Maintenance

Figure 2 Operant classes of consumer behavior defined by pattern of reinforcement.

Behavior setting scope

Closed ◄──────────► Open

		CC2		CC1
Accomplishment	Fulfillment		Status consumption	
		CC4		CC3
Hedonism	Inescapable entertainment		Popular entertainment	
		CC6		CC5
Accumulation	Token-based consumption		Saving and collecting	
		CC8		CC7
Maintenance	Mandatory consumption		Routine purchasing	

Figure 3 BPM contingency matrix.

personal development seminar and gambling in a casino, both of which are maintained by high levels of utilitarian and informational consequence in fairly closed settings.

Hedonism. In an open setting, this consists of *popular entertainment*: viewing TV game shows, which provide near-constant utilitarian reward, or reading mass fiction, which contains a sensation on almost every page. iPods and, in their day, DVDs have made such reinforcement more immediate to the point of ubiquity. Mass culture presents frequent and predictable, relatively strong and continuous hedonic rewards, which are not contingent on long periods of concentrated effort. The arrangement of reinforcers is such that viewing, listening, or reading for even a short interval is likely to be rewarded. Informational feedback is more obvious on some occasions than others, as when game shows allow the audience to

pit their own performances against that of the competing participants, but it is not the main source of reward. Hedonism in closed settings often consists of inescapable entertainment and amelioration. The behaviors in question are potentially pleasurable but may become irksome because they are unavoidable. Consumption of these products and services may be passive rather than active. An example arises when long-haul airline passengers purchase meals and movies along with their travel. The meals are usually consumed, like the in-flight movies, which follow them, without alternative. The setting, which cannot be other than highly restrictive for safety reasons, is further closed by the pulling of blinds, the disappearance of cabin staff, the impossibility of moving around the plane, and the attention of fellow passengers to the movie. To try to read or engage in other activities may even invite censure.

Accumulation. In an open setting, accumulation is *saving and collecting*: purchases for which payments are made prior to consumption – installments for a holiday, which can only be taken once the full amount has been paid. Discretionary saving with the intention of making a large purchase once a certain amount has accumulated is also included as are promotional deals requiring the accumulation of coupons or other tokens before a product or service can be obtained. The immediate reward is informational, feedback on how much one has accumulated, how close one is to the ultimate reinforcer. Accumulation occurring in a closed setting may be described, in general terms, as *token-based buying* which also involves collecting – via schemes in which payment for one item provides tokens with which future rewards are obtained. The points earned by frequent flyers constitute informational reinforcers; some hotels offer gifts to frequent customers who accumulate points on each stay. The setting is relatively closed, because once one becomes a member of the scheme there is an incentive to remain in it.

Maintenance. In an open setting, maintenance is *routine purchasing and consumption* including buying goods necessary for survival as in the habitual purchasing of groceries at a supermarket. Comparatively, few such consumers are brand loyal in the sense of always choosing the identical brand in a long sequence of shopping trips. There is so much choice that the consumer enjoys considerable discretion among versions of the product. Maintenance in closed settings is *mandatory purchase and consumption* and includes consumer behaviors necessary to remain a citizen: the payment of taxes for public goods, payments into pension schemes, payments (as in the United Kingdom) of TV licenses.

RESEARCH

Early applications of the BPM were as an interpretive device; issues central to consumer research were examined not within the usual cognitive framework but from a behavioral perspective: the relationship between consumers' attitudes and behavior, the adoption

of innovations, spending, consuming and saving, "green" consumption, and the nature and influence of marketing management were interpreted within the new framework (Foxall, 2009). Most of this work was conducted within an ambience of testing out behavior analysis by comparing it with the conventional information processing accounts of consumer choice, a desire to promote a clash of competing explanations. Four strands of later research exemplify the empirical testing of the model: the prediction of consumers' emotional responses to retail and consumption environments, the application of matching and maximization techniques to consumer choice, the analysis of consumer demand (behavioral economics), and experimentation.

Emotional response. The first aim was to test the model as a whole, to understand whether (and if so how) the three structural variables of setting scope, utilitarian reinforcement, and informational reinforcement interacted. Eight empirical studies conducted in a variety of cultural settings employed a tripartite classification to emotion based on Mehrabian and Russell's theory of environmental psychology in which the central emotions are pleasure, arousal, and dominance. Measures of these emotions were hypothesized as predictable in consumer contexts defined by the BPM, so that utilitarian reinforcement was expected to generate pleasure, which implied satisfaction and utility; informational reinforcement to be associated with arousal, which reflects behavioral feedback; and the scope of the consumer behavior setting would correspond to dominance, i.e., being in control. The results of this work confirm the predictions (Foxall, 2005). The expectations of a larger pleasure score for higher utilitarian reinforcement; similarly, a larger arousal score was found for greater informational reinforcement; and a larger dominance score characterized a more open consumer behavior setting scope. The results indicate that by using the pleasure, arousal, and dominance measures as predicted verbal responses to the consumer situations defined by the BPM contingency matrix, it is possible to make useful predictions of consumer behavior.

Matching and maximization. *Matching* is the tendency of animals and humans to distribute their responses between two choices in proportion to the patterns of reward programmed to be contingent on each choice. The key dependent variable is not the single response that needed contextual explication in terms of a single contingent reinforcer: it was the relative frequency of responding, which he or she explained by reference to the relative rate of reinforcement obtained from the behavior. Animals with two opportunities to respond (pecking key A or key B), each of which delivers reinforcers (food pellets) on its own reinforcement schedule, allocate their responses on A and B in proportion to the rates of reward they obtain from A and B. This phenomenon has been replicated in numerous species including humans and has found applications in behavior modification and organizational behavior management, to name but two relevant fields. In particular, it provides a framework for the behavioral analysis of consumption. The phenomenon is particularly well researched in contexts that require an individual to allocate a limited period between two choices, each scheduled to produce reward at a different rate.

Most choices for human consumers require the allocation of a fixed income between alternative choices, each of which exacts a different monetary sacrifice. In this case, responses take the form of surrendering money in varying amounts, while the reward is the receipt of a fixed amount of the good in question. Price is the ratio of units of money that must be exchanged for units of the good. Both matching and maximizing theories make a similar prediction of behavior on such schedules: the individual will maximize by exclusively selecting the schedule that provides the higher return. Studies of animal choice confirm this prediction. The reason is that, given the parameters of matching in the context of consumer choice, where the schedules that govern performance are close analogs of the ratio schedules imposed in the operant laboratory, both maximization and matching theories predict a similar pattern of choice, one that eventuates in maximization and matching by virtue of the expectation that consumers will always select the cheapest alternative when selecting among brands. The expected behavior

pattern is, therefore, exclusive choice of the more favorable schedule. Although there is some evidence that this is generally the case, there are frequent exceptions in that consumers sometimes buy the most expensive option or, on the same shopping trip, purchase both cheaper and dearer versions of the same product, something that animal experiments, which demand discrete choices in each time frame, do not permit their subjects. In other words, the marketing system adds complications to the analysis that cannot be anticipated within the original context of the behavioral economics research program. Even behavioral economics research with human consumers in real-time situations of purchase and consumption (token economies and field experiments) have not been able to incorporate such influences on choice as a dynamic bilateral market system of competing producers who seek mutually satisfying exchanges with consumers whose high levels of discretionary income make their selection of suppliers not only routine but also relatively cost free. Behavioral economics experiments with human consumers have at best been able to incorporate only a portion of the full marketing mix influence on consumer choice. It has typically been possible to employ price as a marketing variable but not the full panoply of product differentiation, advertising and other promotional activities, and competing distribution strategies, which are the dominant features of the modern consumer-oriented economy. Moreover, because it is the marketing mix, rather than any of its elements acting in isolation from the rest, that influences consumer choice, such experiments have been unable to capture the effect of this multiplex stimulus on purchasing and consumption.

Our analyses found that brand competition was generally marked by ideal matching, while product choices, as demonstrated here by wine and cola purchases by some degree of under-, over-, or antimatching. Relative demand curves were generally downward sloping (Foxall *et al.*, 2007). Consumers maximized by purchasing the least expensive of the brands composing their considerations sets. Where there were exceptions from the predictions of matching and maximizing theories, they occurred for reasons peculiar to the marketing context: first, because the composition of consumers' consideration sets often meant that their selections were among premium priced, higher quality brands, or at least those more highly differentiated through promotional activity, rather than among all of the brands that made up the product category.

An interesting outcome of the application of matching theory to consumer choice is the finding that brands can be defined in terms of their substitutability, while product groupings and categories whose members are independent or complementary are indicated by under-, over-, or antimatching present further evidence on this. We benefit here from making a distinction between utilitarian and informational or symbolic reinforcement, which goes beyond the usual distinction between primary and secondary reinforcers. In the case of brands, it is inevitable that they will tend to be substitutes in so far as they are functionally similar (almost identical in terms of physical formulation), that is, in terms of utilitarian reinforcement, and complements in so far as they are differentiated by branding, that is, in terms of informational reinforcement or social symbolism. Branding is an attempt to reduce the perceived substitutability of brands by altering their value to the consumer on the basis of their social significance (e.g., increasing the status of their owners and users) or psychological significance (e.g., enhancing the self-esteem of those who own and use them).

The *pattern of reinforcement* (the pattern of low-to-high utilitarian reinforcement and low-to-high informational reinforcement produced by buying or using a product) is an analytical category that takes the place in interpretive behaviorism occupied by that of the schedule of reinforcement in the experimental analysis of behavior. Because patterns of reinforcement differ and because informational reinforcement increases the complementarity of brands within a product category, nonprice elements of the marketing mix come to the fore. The study of brand choice indicates that the multidisciplinarity of behavioral economics can usefully be extended by the inclusion of results and perspectives from marketing research. Behavioral economics is supported by the research in that its analyses and conclusions are shown to apply to human consumers in situations of free choice; behavioral economists should appreciate, however, the conclusions

of marketing researchers to the effect that most consumers are multibrand purchasers, and that marketing considerations other than price influence choice. Marketing researchers may need to take note of the import of price differentials in brand choice. The behavioral mechanism of choice that underlies the molar patterns of consumer choice depicted here appears to be momentary maximization of benefit, a result that is consistent with melioration or overall maximization. However, the lesson of the research is that brand choice is reinforced by two sources of reward, *utilitarian*, which derives from the functional benefits of the good, and *informational* or *symbolic*, which derives from the psychological and cultural meanings, which goods acquire through their participation in social interactions and, by derivation, through advertising and other means to branding. The recognition of both sources of reinforcement is the key requirement for both marketing researchers and behavioral economists.

Consumer demand analysis.   The point of the discussion of pattern of reinforcement and plasticity of demand is not to dismiss such stalwarts of economic analysis as elasticity of demand. Rather, having established the usefulness of the former types of interpretive construct to consumer behavior analysis, the aim should be to operationalize them and relate them to the standard constructs. This has been one of the tasks of work on consumer demand analysis within the BPM context. Much of the work on demand analysis has involved comparison of the buying patterns of consumers grouped by their predominant purchasing of brands having specific patterns of informational and utilitarian reinforcement.

Observed decreases in the quantity bought with increases in prices, indicated by negative elasticity coefficients, may be associated with different response patterns by different groups. The tendency to buy larger quantities when prices are lower may be related to one or more of the following three patterns: (i) buying larger quantities of a product when its price was below its usual, average, price rather than when its price was above its average price (i.e., intra-brand or absolute elasticity); (ii) buying larger quantities when buying brands belonging to cheaper, lower informational levels than when buying brands belonging to more expensive, higher informational levels (i.e., informational interbrand or relative elasticity); and (iii) buying larger quantities when buying brands belonging to cheaper, lower utilitarian levels than when buying brands belonging to more expensive, higher utilitarian levels (i.e., utilitarian inter-brand or relative elasticity). These phenomena have been investigated in two studies, employing different sets of consumer panel data, which have borne out these extensions to matching analysis in the context of consumer choice.

The possibility of combining matching and elasticity of demand analyses has led, most recently, to the testing of an equation that relates amount spent to quantity bought, util-itarian reinforcement obtained, informational reinforcement obtained, and price paid (which detects promotions). The results strongly support the view that economic demand is influ-enced not only by the amount purchased but by the variables posited by the BPM – utilitarian reinforcement, informational reinforcement, and aversive consequences – all of which can be shown to influence amount spent (Foxall *et al.*, 2007; special issue of JOBM, 2010).

Experimental analyses. Numerous studies in the experimental analysis of behavior are rele-vant to the development of consumer behavior analysis (see, inter alia, Foxall, 2002). However, several recent approaches to the experimental analysis of consumer behavior are of particular interest to the progress of the model and research program. The first is the use of simulated shopping malls to test predictions of matching theory in a consumer context. A series of exper-iments investigated the influence of various marketing elements (e.g., price and service level measured in terms of delay) on the spending behavior of buyers of consumer products. This work is significant not only for its contribu-tion to consumer behavior analysis but also for its insights into the nature of economic psychology, that is, the manner in which the all-too-often-separated disciplines of economics and psychology, and biobehavioral consumer research might be integrated. The integration is achieved in this case through foraging theory.

Although it is only one of a number of important outcomes of this kind of investigation, the finding that the price of a product may be viewed as a temporal factor by which foraging may be under-stood is valuable for further research that treats temporally extended consumption by humans in terms of foraging (see special issue of JoEP, 2003).

The constant need in experimental work that is designed to have some impact on the interpretation of complex behavior is to move gradually closer to empirical investigations of choice that permit field experimentation; in this way, the rigor of experimental manipulations and the links with the principles of behavior analysis can be retained while the focus of research more closely resembles the kinds of day-to-day behavior exhibited by consumers in natural settings. An interesting approach to this is found in experimental work on the influence of the base price of products on the amount of time prospective consumers spend on search. Observation of consumers during the prepur-chase phase of their purchase sequence not only permits in-store methodologies to be evaluated in the context of consumer behavior analysis but also yields the result that search behavior is more extensive for higher-priced items. In-store experimentation within the consumer behavior analysis framework has also been undertaken, as well as simulated store choices to test the effects of both utilitarian reinforcement and informa-tional reinforcement on consumer preference (JOBM, 2010).

DEVELOPMENT

The original aim of the research program – to ascertain the epistemological status of a radical behaviorist model of consumer choice – has been fulfilled. Not only is such a model feasible, it has provided unique interpretations of consumer behavior and permitted the prediction of such aspects of consumer choice as brand and product selection. In addition, it has explained such behaviors to the extent of identifying the contingencies that shape them: both utilitarian and informational reinforcement, and the scope of the consumer behavior setting. Wider aspects of the explanation of consumer behavior have not proved amenable to this kind of theorizing, however. Such features of behavior as its continuity and its relationship to the personal level of explanation including subjective experience require the use of intentional language and this implies a different mode of explanation from the extensional approach on which radical behaviorism is based (Foxall, 2004b). The use of the BPM as an interpretive device is also enhanced by the incorporation of intentionality. This does not mean that the original formulation of the model is superseded: it presents a means of predicting and potentially influencing consumer behavior that is not available from other sources. And it fulfills the expectations of a model of consumer choice that radical behaviorism itself would entertain. But the more general demands of consumer research as a social science can be implemented by the development of intentional and cognitive versions of the model (Foxall, 2007). The main point of these developments is to ascertain the nature of intentional and cognitive explanations of consumer choice respectively, a program that parallels the original aim with respect to behaviorist explanation. As a part of this quest, the application of the BPM to new areas such as intertemporal decision making, compulsion, impulsivity, and addiction, and the nature of the marketing firm continues apace.

ACKNOWLEDGMENT

The author is grateful to other key players in the research program who include Erik Arntzen, Asle Fagerstrom, Donald Hantula, Victoria James, Mike Nicholson, Jorge Oliveira-Castro, Sarah Xiao, Valdimar Sigurdsson, Teresa Schrezenmaier, and Mirella Yani-de-Soriano.

See also *choice models; consumer brand loyalty; demand elasticity; emotion; perception of brand equity*

Bibliography

Davison, M. and McCarthy, D. (1998) *The Matching Law: A Research Review*, Lawrence Erlbaum, Hillsdale.
Foxall, G.R. (2002) *Consumer Behavior Analysis: Critical Perspectives in Business and Management*, Routledge, London and New York.
Foxall, G.R. (2004a) *Consumer Psychology in Behavioral Perspective*, Beard Books, Frederick.
Foxall, G.R. (2004b) *Context and Cognition: The Interpretation of Complex Behavior*, Context Press, Reno.
Foxall, G.R. (2005) *Understanding Consumer Choice*, Palgrave Macmillan, New York.
Foxall, G.R. (2007) *Explaining Consumer Choice*, Palgrave Macmillan, New York.
Foxall, G.R. (2009) *Interpreting Consumer Choice: The Behavioral Perspective Model*, Routledge, New York.
Foxall, G.R., Oliveira-Castro, J.M., James, V.K., and Schrezenmaier, T.C. (2007) *The Behavioral Economics of Consumer Brand Choice*, Palgrave Macmillan, New York.
Herrnstein, R.J. (1997) *The Matching Law: Papers in Psychology and Economics*, Russell Sage Foundation, New York, Harvard University Press, Cambridge, MA.
Kagel, J.H., Battalio, R.C., and Green, L. (1994) *Economic Choice Theory: An Experimental Analysis of Animal Behavior*, Cambridge University Press, Cambridge.
Staddon, J.E.R. (ed.) (1980) *Limits to Action: The Allocation of Individual Behavior*, Academic Press, New York.
JOBM (2010) *Journal of Organizational Behavior Management*, **30** (2).
JoEP (2003) *Journal of Economic Psychology*, **23**, 5. Special issues of two journals contain accounts of recent theoretical and empirical advances.

consumer behavior and services marketing

Dawn Iacobucci

INTRODUCTION

Let us take a simple consumer behavior process and see how it is studied and modified by services marketing scholars. In particular, let us begin with the basic, vanilla-flavored consumption model, in which a consumer (i) identifies some desire, (ii) searches for means of satisfying that desire, (iii) makes a choice and a purchase, and (iv) afterward reflects upon that purchase. This article elaborates on the stages of this process with an eye toward identifying the special concerns of the services marketing researcher.

WHAT IS SERVICE MARKETING?

Presumably, the reader of this volume will walk away with a strong and clear understanding and appreciation of the explication of the consumption process. What is new to this article is the twist on services. Hence, a starting point is to clarify what is meant by services marketing. While the phrase *services marketing* is rather general, it tends to mean one of two things: a researcher is studying either customer service or some consumption phenomenon in a service industry.

The breadth of services marketing is part of what makes teaching services fun because the cases and applications run the gamut from customer service in, say, an automobile dealership, where the focus of the purchase is a good, or a call center, where the focus is often on service recovery, to fairly routine and familiar services such as hotels and restaurants, to the more sophisticated services such as in the health care or legal professions.

The range of applicability can be explained in part from the philosophy that just about every purchase contains some element of service. In the early days, services marketing scholars made a point of distinguishing services (e.g., dry cleaning) from goods (e.g., shampoo) to highlight the conceptual differences worthy of study. Contemporary thinking is that very few things exist that have not been processed in some manner (e.g., perhaps coal or wheat), and that the value-added processing is itself service. This argument of the pervasiveness of services seems to be getting more difficult to challenge as so much of the value-added element is information-based, both in B2C and B2B markets.

WHAT IS DIFFERENT ABOUT SERVICES?

There are several dimensions along which services have been distinguished from goods, or along which the service element of a purchase can be distinguished from whatever goods might be transacted in the purchase. The acronym "SHIP" is helpful to remember the primary dimensions: the "S" stands for "simultaneity of production and consumption," the "H" for "heterogeneity," the "I" for "intangibility," and the "P" for "perishability." Let us break these down, and then examine how each impacts the consumption process.

Simultaneity: Services are simultaneously produced and consumed. For example, a masseur creates an experience as the consumer experiences it. Massages are not stored in a spa, waiting to be pulled off a shelf when a customer buys one. The interaction between the service provider and the client is key to the service being customized and therefore optimally pleasing to the customer. The fact that services unfold in real time has several implications for the consumption process, as discussed below.

Heterogeneity: Services are also said to be heterogeneous. The idea is that one customer's experience is likely to differ from that of another. One person may rave about a masseuse, whereas another might find that provider's techniques too light or too deep, and he/she may not leave the spa as satisfied as the first customer. This type of difference is due to customer variability; on a large scale, we would call these segment preference differences. Other differences are attributable to the service providers having different styles and talents. Still other sources of variability are more temporary – a customer or service provider may be in a bad mood, and have an "off" day. As these examples illustrate, heterogeneity in customer experiences is largely attributable to the service encounter being an interpersonal interaction. Marketing managers responsible for services have a much greater challenge than those overseeing goods; people are harder to manage than machines. We will see shortly how marketers try to compensate in the consumption process.

Intangibility: Services are also said to be more intangible than goods. A 17-year-old girl who bought the book *Twilight* has a tangible proof of purchase. Another, who went to see the movie, has no visible evidence of the movie experience, except, perhaps, for swoony eyes. Many purchases are of course a mix of the tangible and intangible. Imagine an evening dining out – there exists both the tangible (food, restaurant appearance) and the intangible (attentiveness of the wait-staff, ambience). Most people's largest purchases – a house and a car – include the physical purchase of the dwelling or the vehicle, as well as less-tangible elements, such as financing, insurance, and maintenance. For those two purchases, the tangible might seem to dominate the intangible. For another large household purchase, a kid's education, the intangible seems to dominate the tangible. These examples notwithstanding, expensive purchases are not always those dominated by goods – divorces are services and they are also expensive. Health care is a service and it can be costly. We now discuss what marketers make of intangibility.

Perishability: The final piece of the SHIP acronym is perishability, and this aspect of services derives in part from the first, the simultaneity of production and consumption. The potential service provision during lull times cannot be realized during peak times; it has perished. For example, the airplane leaves the ground with some empty seats that can never be regained, or a tax consultant's hours during a slow month cannot be recaptured in early April. Now let us blend these service dimensions with the consumption process.

WHAT ARE THE IMPLICATIONS FOR THE CONSUMPTION PROCESS?

In this section, we take the properties of simultaneity, heterogeneity, intangibility, and perishability and consider their effects on the service encounter. Recall the basic consumer behavior process: needs identification, information search, choice and purchase, and postpurchase reflection. We will treat the process in temporal order.

Needs Identification. While some services require special skills (e.g., tax attorney, psychiatrist), there are many services that customers can provide for themselves, should they choose to do so (e.g., lawn-mowing, ride to the airport). When customers choose to outsource and buy a service, there must be a reason why paying another to execute the service is superior to doing it oneself. The trade-off is usually some combination of time, expertise, and convenience. For example, most of us could mow our lawns, if we wanted to: we would start up a mower, push the machine back and forth, and so on. However, most of us are busy enough that we would assess a trade-off of time and value, and conclude that

it is worth it to hire someone to take care of the landscaping.

Yet while it is true that we seem to be getting busier and busier, there is a seemingly counter trend, and that is the growth of self-services (Meuter *et al.*, 2005). Many grocery chains offer self-service checkouts. At the outset, checking oneself out might seem to take more time than letting someone else scan the items, but when the lines for the checkers are long, the same principle of time-famine motivates customers to do the work themselves – it is faster. There is no price discount (or premium) for self-checkout. There are also no superior skills required of the checker than the customer. Hence, the self-service checkout is altogether more convenient.

As the effects of information technology seem omnipresent, here too, smart software can begin to simulate the expertise that a regular customer lacks and who would have traditionally sought a professional. There are a variety of software packages that facilitate our lives: some prompt us to calculate proper taxes, others assist in writing wills, other software functions as a dietitian, and still other programs serve as tutors when learning foreign languages.

The challenge in the future will be to determine those purchases for which we will continue to buy a service provider's time and expertise, and those for which we will enjoy the consumption of the activity itself. Marketers for service providers will have the challenge of demonstrating even greater value in the time and money saved, and the additional expertise and value-added elements that the service provider may bring to the customer.

Information Search. For reasons that will become clear shortly, services marketers have always made much of the expectations that customers hold when they enter the service encounter. Marketers try to shape expectations through various communications, for example, advertising, public relations, and information posted online. Yet unlike shopping for a laptop or automobile, where we might seek comparisons among brands as conducted and reported by experts, a good part of services are experiential. That services are experiential is attributable in part to the intangibility quality, an essence that is difficult for an expert to convey.

The challenge to marketers is to take the intangibility, which is difficult to grasp by customers because it is abstract and ethereal, and make it more concrete. As a result, marketers are encouraged to use symbols in their advertising and logos to express their benefits more tangibly (e.g., "You're in 'good hands' with AllState"; "Like a 'good neighbor,' State Farm is there"). The abstraction also leads customers to believe that the purchase might be somewhat risky, as they do not know quite what to expect. Accordingly, some marketers have demonstrated success in showing customers videos that preview the service they are about to experience so as to help them understand more precisely what to expect (Bitner et al., 1997).

Customers who have experience with a particular service provider will naturally have information from which they derive expectations for future interactions. Lacking direct experience, customers are thought to rely on word-of-mouth from trusted sources, such as friends or coworkers. Indeed, services marketers have long posited the very likely greater importance of word-of-mouth for services than for the purchase of goods. As online social networks thrive, we can expect this form of tailored communication to only grow in strength. Marketers have not yet come upon the winning formula for monetizing a presence in such spaces, but with time, no doubt, will do so.

Another prepurchase phenomenon in services that receives much consideration is queuing, the one tool in a marketer's arsenal that approximates the inventorying of goods. While a movie theater might not be able to seat more than 200 patrons on a Friday night for an opening of some new, wildly anticipated movie, it can encourage moviegoers to attend at another showing, by making another time slot more desirable, such as by lowering prices. Restaurants similarly take reservations to try to manage fluctuating demand. Yield management is a near science at the airlines, though not without error, as overbooking experiences will attest. In fact, marketers look to levers such as price to increase or decrease demand, so as to more optimally match supply, in the provision of many kinds of services (Desiraju and Shugan, 1999).

Choice and Purchase. The purchase of a service is far more complicated than the purchase of most goods. The complications are first due to the heterogeneity, due to the fact that the service encounter is frequently an interaction between two people, the customer and service provider, both of whom can introduce noise or error into the system. There is not much that a marketer can do to control the behavior of a customer, but the behavior of the front-line employee serving that customer leads marketing to a nexus with human relations. To ensure smooth service encounters, marketers have emphasized the importance of supervisors and companies being selective in hiring service providers and in training them (Heskett, Sasser, and Schlesinger, 1997), empowering them (Schneider and Bowen, 1995), and keeping them motivated (Rust and Chung, 2006).

The complications of services marketing purchases are also due to the aspect of services being simultaneously produced and consumed. One implication of the fact that services unfold in real time is that the customer's evaluation of the service – the service experience, the front-line service provider, or the service firm brand – is comprised of many "moments of truth" (Carlzon, 1989). All these elements, whether large and central (e.g., a dental exam), or smaller and seemingly peripheral (e.g., the availability of parking near the dentist's office), factor into the customer's overall assessment of the service encounter. To manage the multitude of process issues, services marketers have encouraged the use of flow charts to explicate the consumer experience down to the last detail, as well as the behind-the-scenes operational elements which facilitate a smooth customer service flow (Lovelock and Wirtz, 2006; Fisk, Grove, and John, 2007; Bitner, Ostrom, and Morgan, 2008). Note too that the real-time process can be potentially advantageous – it can allow for the customization of the transaction for superior service, or for the recovery of impending service failure for at least minimally acceptable levels of service quality.

As brand building is all the rage, it is important to see the implications of the heterogeneity and simultaneity on this marketing effort. It is difficult to build a brand, much less an excellent brand, when it is difficult to assure the consistency of the quality of the purchase experience. In services marketing, one form of brand building is the distribution channel of the franchise system. In franchising, the attempt is to sell a service system that is as standardized, replicable, and as consistent as possible. Some succeed – those with a large portion of tangible character (e.g., some hotel or restaurant chains), or with heavy assistance of information technology (e.g., tax assistance offices). However, while brand building might be an admirable goal for such straightforward services, it would likely be more difficult to brand a professional service. In the professions, one touts the reputation, that is, the brand, and hopes that all the service providers deliver at the heights implied and expected. If the members of the profession have been hired selectively and well trained, perhaps the service can be seamless and of consistently high quality.

Postpurchase Reflection. Services marketing adheres rather uniformly to the model known variously as the *disconfirmation paradigm* of customer satisfaction or the *gap model* of service quality (Oliver, 2009; Zeithaml, Parasuraman, and Berry, 2009). In this model, a customer is thought to come to the service encounter with certain expectations, and judges the quality of the encounter against those expectations. If the customer's expectations are met, it is predicted that the customer is satisfied. If the experience is much better than the expectations, it is predicted that the customer is delighted. If the experience does not hold to the expectations, the customer is expected to be dissatisfied.

It is in this evaluative phase that we see why marketers pay attention to expectations. Some admonish to "manage expectations" (downward), so that the service provider can meet or exceed them. However, downward management is counter to the marketing impulse of bragging in advertising.

The comparative judgment model got attention very early as services marketers struggled with the implications of services being intangible, and therefore quality being difficult, or at least subjective to evaluate. Marketers overseeing goods of many kinds, from consumer packaged goods to electronics to durables, rode a wave in the 1980s of total quality management, which specified, among other things, accuracies in processes and outcomes. Manufacturers of corn flakes can say they want 10 ounces of flakes

per box, and if they set their machinery properly, that is what they will get. Marketers responsible for a high quality service encounter struggle with such standards. What should be measured and managed that serve as cues to good quality? In the late 1990s, many companies would brag, "We answer our customer service calls within three rings," which of course begs the question, "What is the quality of the customer service provided once the phone is picked up?" As a result, the evaluation of customer satisfaction or service quality remains largely subjective, perhaps as it should be, if we marketers truly believe customers should have the last word.

As the consumption process of the service encounter is extended over time, it is natural to take the evaluation and generalize it as well. Loyalty systems thrive in services, at least in those sectors where switching costs are not high. Whether it is a free coffee for every 10th purchase, upgrades for sufficient air miles, shorter queuing systems for preferred insurance packages, or discounts for the use of retail cards, services marketers have embraced loyalty programs. In turn, when the resulting information capture is used creatively, true customer relationship management can further enhance the customer's share of heart and wallet dedicated to the particular service provider.

Conclusion

Consumers are not thought of as behaving all that differently in a service encounter compared to how they behave when purchasing a good. However, the service encounter itself is a more complicated purchase. Accordingly, as the services marketing literature matured, the research and writings gave opportunity to reflect on new issues.

As stated at the outset, most purchases have some element of goods and some element of services transacted. The question is a matter of the proportions of each. As a result, the theories and research findings of the services marketing scholars are relevant and very broadly applicable.

Bibliography

Bitner, M.J., Ostrom, A.L., and Morgan, F.N. (2008) Service blueprinting: a practical technique for service innovation. *California Management Review*, **50** (3), 66–94.

Bitner, M.J., Faranda, W.T., Hubbert, A.R., and Zeithaml, V.A. (1997) Customer contributions and roles in service delivery. *International Journal of Service Industry Management*, 8 (3), 193–205.

Carlzon, J. (1989) *Moments of Truth*, Harper & Row, New York.

Desiraju, R. and Shugan, S.M. (1999) Strategic service pricing and yield management. *Journal of Marketing*, **63** (1), 44–56.

Fisk, R.P., Grove, S.J., and John, J. (2007) *Interactive Services Marketing*, Southwestern, Dallas, TX.

Heskett, J.L., Sasser, W.E. Jr., Schlesinger, and L.A. (1997) *The Service Profit Chain*, Free Press, New York.

Lovelock, C. and Wirtz, J. (2006) *Services Marketing*, 6th edn, Prentice-Hall, New York.

Meuter, M.L., Bitner, M.J., Ostrom, A.L., and Brown, S.W. (2005) Choosing among alternative delivery modes: an investigation of customer trial of self-service technologies. *Journal of Marketing*, **85**, 61–83.

Oliver, R.L. (2009) *Satisfaction: A Behavioral Perspective on the Consumer*, 2nd edn, McGraw-Hill, New York.

Rust, R.T. and Chung, T.S. (2006) Marketing models of service and relationships. *Marketing Science*, **25** (6), 560–580.

Schneider, B. and Bowen, D.E. (1995) *Winning the Service Game*, Harvard Business School, Boston, MA.

Zeithaml, V.A., Parasuraman, A., and Berry, L.L. (2009) *Delivering Quality Service*, Free Press, New York.

consumer brand loyalty

Richard L. Oliver

INTRODUCTION

This article describes the general field of consumer (customer) loyalty as it is currently conceptualized. Whereas the field has been approached from many perspectives, the most common appearing in the area of repeat purchasing, more psychologically based approaches are now coming into fruition.

Here, the underlying mechanisms of how consumers manifest, consciously or subconsciously, their loyalty mind-set are explored so that greater loyalty development and switching avoidance can be engendered. Readers interested in more detail and elaboration, including discussion of topics not covered here, should consult the author's original works (Oliver, 1997; Oliver, 2010) and an earlier conceptual article on loyalty determinants (Oliver, 1999).

CONSUMER BRAND LOYALTY

Oliver (1997, p. 392), had proposed the following definition as being consistent with conceptual and empirical evidence:

Customer loyalty is a deeply held commitment to rebuy or repatronize a preferred product or service consistently in the future, *despite* situational influences and marketing efforts having the potential to cause switching behavior (italics in original).

To put this consumer display of loyalty in perspective, an elaboration of the stages and their vulnerabilities, which will address the "despite" clause, brings what is known of loyalty to the recognition of a social extension, discussed later in this article.

Loyalty phases. The framework used here follows the cognition–affect–conation historical pattern of attitude engagement (Taylor, Hunter and Longfellow, 2006), but differs in the sense that consumers can become "loyal" or "locked" at each loyalty phase. Specifically, consumers are thought to first become loyal in a cognitive sense, then later in an affective sense, still later in a conative manner, and finally in a behavioral manner, described as *action inertia*.

Cognitive loyalty. In this first loyalty phase, the brand attribute information available to the consumer suggests that one brand is preferable to its alternatives. This stage is referred to as *cognitive* loyalty or loyalty based on brand belief only. Cognition can be based on prior or vicarious knowledge and recent experience-based information. Loyalty at this phase is directed toward the brand because of this "information" (attribute performance levels). This consumer state, however, is of a very shallow nature. If the transaction is routine, so that satisfaction (*see* CUSTOMER SATISFACTION) is not processed (e.g., trash pickup, utility provision), the reaches of loyalty are no deeper than mere performance, and "performance-only" models apply here. *If* satisfaction is processed, it becomes part of the consumer's experience and begins to take on affective overtones.

Affective loyalty.   At the second phase of loyalty development, the emergence of a liking or attitude toward the brand is required on the basis of cumulatively satisfying usage occasions. Commitment at this phase is referred to as *affective* loyalty (*see* EMOTION) and is encoded in the consumer's mind as cognition *and* affect. Whereas cognition is directly subject to counter-argumentation, affect is not as easily dislodged. Here, the brand loyalty exhibited is directed at the degree of affect for the brand. Like cognitive loyalty, however, this form of loyalty remains subject to switching as evidenced by the data showing that large percentages of brand defectors claim to have been previously satisfied with their brand, a phenomenon known as the *satisfaction trap* (Reichheld and Teal, 1996). Thus, it would be desirable if consumers were loyal at a deeper level of commitment.

Conative loyalty.   The next phase of loyalty development is the *conative* stage, as influenced by repeated episodes of positive affect toward the brand. *Conation*, by its definition, implies a brand-specific commitment to repurchase. Conative loyalty, then, is a loyalty state containing what at first appears to be the deeply held commitment to buy, noted in the loyalty definition. However, this commitment is to one's intention to rebuy (*see* CONSUMER INTENTIONS) the brand and is more akin to motivation. In effect, the consumer desires to repurchase, but like any "good intention," this desire may be an anticipated but unrealized action. At this point, commitment is an additional overlay to the prior cognitive and affective bases of loyalty.

Action loyalty.   The study of the mechanism by which intentions are converted to actions is referred to as *action control* (Kuhl and Beckmann, 1985). In the action control sequence, the motivated intention in the previous loyalty state is transformed into *readiness to act*. The action control paradigm proposes that this is accompanied by an additional *desire to overcome obstacles* that might prevent the action. Action is

seen as a necessary result of engaging both of these states. If this engagement is repeated, an "action inertia" develops, thereby facilitating repurchase.

Readers will note the correspondence between the two action control constructs, readiness to act and the overcoming of obstacles, to the loyalty definition presented earlier. Readiness to act is analogous to the "deeply held commitment to rebuy or repatronize a preferred product/service consistently in the future," while "overcoming obstacles" is analogous to rebuying "despite situational influences and marketing efforts having the potential to cause switching behavior." Thus, completing the earlier cognitive–affective–conative frameworks with a fourth, or action phase, brings the attitude-based loyalty model to the "behavior" of interest – the action state of inertial rebuying (*see* ATTITUDE–BEHAVIOR CONSISTENCY).

OBSTACLES TO LOYALTY: SWITCHING INCENTIVES

It may have occurred to the reader that true loyalty is, in some sense, fragile as long as alternatives are available. Competitors could (and do) take advantage of this position, engaging consumers via persuasive messages and incentives with the purpose of attempting to lure them away from their preferred offering. These verbal and physical enticements are the obstacles that brand or service loyalists must overcome. As may be evident at this point, the easiest form of loyalty to break down is the cognitive variety; the most difficult is the action state. Thus, the cognitive-to-action loyalty sequence brings the analysis closer to the emergence of "full" loyalty, but still may fail as each phase is subject to attack, as follows.

Cognitive loyalty.   In the case of cognitive loyalty, it has been noted that this level of loyalty is based on purely functional characteristics, primarily costs and benefits, and is thus subject to functional shortfalls. For example, in many areas, it has been shown that deteriorating performance, apart from dissatisfaction, is a strong enhancement to switch. Thus, cognitive loyalty is actually "phantom loyalty," as it is directed to benefits and costs and not to the brand. Costs (including prices), in particular, are a major component of brand switching at the cognitive level.

Before moving to affective loyalty, it is necessary to address the commonly observed breakdown in the satisfaction–loyalty link (i.e., the "trap"). Two situations are of note. The first is apparent disloyalty (switching) in the face of satisfaction and the second is apparent loyalty when encountering very low levels of satisfaction (dissatisfaction). The first is easily explained by cognitive loyalty that is overcome by attractive alternatives, as noted. The second is also easily explained by a phenomenon that has come to be known as *cognitive lock-in* (Büschken, 2004).

Lock-in can be achieved via many tactics. The most obvious is through a supply monopoly such as video game cartridges. At the interpersonal level, consumers have been known to become loyal to particular provider employees (e.g., salespeople). It is also known that normal consumer failings such as the sunk cost phenomenon and ordinary consumer learning are strong motivators to stay with an otherwise dissatisfying provider. Working in parallel with these influences is the notion of simple fear of the unknown. These are all reasons for firms to "ensnare" consumers so that they are held through "captive loyalty."

Affective loyalty.   Barring lock-in, affective loyalty can become susceptible to dissatisfaction with the cognitive elements of a purchase, thereby inducing attitudinal shifts. A concurrent effect of dissatisfaction is the increased attractiveness of alternatives, as noted. Thus, affective loyalty is first subject to the deterioration of its cognitive base, causing dissatisfaction, which has deleterious effects on the strength of one's attitude toward a brand, and hence, affective loyalty. It is also possible for competitive communications to use imagery and association to enhance the desirability of alternative brands while degrading that of the present brand.

Conative loyalty.   Although conative loyalty brings the consumer to a stronger level of loyalty commitment, it has its vulnerabilities nonetheless. Although a consumer at this phase can weather some small number of dissatisfactory episodes, the consumer's motivation to remain committed can be "worn down" by barrages of competitive messages, particularly if they enhance the perceived severity of experienced dissatisfaction, a phenomenon called *prejudice*.

This occurs, not only via marketing communications, but also through social pressure from one's environment. In fact, it has been shown that social norms vastly dominate satisfaction (dissatisfaction) in the prediction of switching intentions (Roos, 1999). Additionally, competitive product trial, via samples, coupons, or point-of-purchase promotions, may be particularly effective here as the consumer has only committed to the brand, but has not committed to avoiding trial of new offerings. Thus, the conatively loyal consumer has not developed the "resolve" to intentionally avoid consideration of competitive brands.

At this juncture and perhaps before action loyalty manifests itself, the firm has achieved *product superiority*. Here, the firm has engendered enhanced liking – even an established preference – for its brand because of quality (information) and continued ability to satisfy. Additionally, the consumer is committed to its repurchase in the future. But, the consumer has not reached the state of resistance, resilience, and the overcoming of obstacles and adversity necessary for lasting loyalty to emerge.

Action loyalty and the beginning of fortitude.   When reaching the action phase of brand attachment, however, the consumer has generated both the focused desire to rebuy a brand and only that brand, and has also acquired the skills necessary to overcome threats and obstacles to this quest. This consumer would be expected to routinely "tune out" competitive messages, to engage in effortful search for the favored brand, and to possibly even shun the trial of competitive brands. Marketers with action-loyal segments need not expend great sums on retention as, theoretically, their consumers would be governed by "inertial" repurchasing. Aside from deteriorating performance, a potential switching inducer at all stages, only insurmountable unavailability would cause this consumer to try another brand.

With the emergence of the action phase, it appears that the formula for loyalty has been largely crafted; later, this state will be referred to as *consumer fortitude*. It is intended that the action-loyal consumer has a deep commitment to repurchase, so much so that such behavior may be guiding itself in some habituated manner. But habituation is not the loyalty of interest. Rather, the quest is for a version of loyalty fitting the description of devotion "against all odds." When found, the state of consumer fortitude is achieved whereby the consumer fervently desires the consumable in a prohibitive, exclusive relationship. This should be a natural occurrence experienced by the consumer and not one created by the marketer.

It is to be borne in mind, however, that it is the province of competition to gain the consumer's attention so as to hear its communications. One major tactic by which this is accomplished, common in one or another way in all loyalty phases, is the creation of dissatisfaction with the current brand. In fact, the role of satisfaction in loyalty formation and defection can now be more fully specified. In the same way that satisfaction is a building block for loyalty, primarily at the affective loyalty stage, dissatisfaction is its Achilles tendon – for it is here that the competition can strike through the creation or facilitation of dissatisfaction at every stage.

Interpersonal loyalty: additional effects in services. Historically, discussion of loyalty effects has focused largely within the context of product marketing. With the possible exception of fan clubs, industries having a large service component were still thought to be governed by loyalty to the core deliverable. Thus, Starbucks' loyalty is to its product and business model and not to its baristas (service providers). With recognition of the strong interpersonal component of services, loyalty now takes on additional dimensions of a much more binding and even overriding nature. Little research had been available in this new area, save for a small number of sources. This oversight has reversed itself with a number of insights beyond that of the more generic topic of service delivery, primarily with regard to service contact personnel (e.g., Price and Arnould, 1999).

Loyalty programs. We now discuss the emergence of *loyalty programs* that have sprung up since the time of early grocery store promotions. The issue now is that of program-based repetitive purchasing and its link to the mind-set of "true loyalty." One question that must be answered, then, is that of the role of mechanical incentives or rewards in loyalty apart from habit formation, but including inertial states that tend to persist until their exuberance wears off. It is not clear that loyalty programs are quite so "malleable."

The evidence for the success of such programs can be assessed along the four stages of progression. Do purchasing rewards pass the test of cognitive through action sequencing with the attendant behavioral building blocks? The answer given here is "no." Can reward programs be made to provide sufficient structure so that the consumer can become loyal to something such as loyalty to the program and loyalty to the behavior of pursuing its rewards? Possibly "yes." The interesting aspect of this analysis is that insights may be gained into the pursuit of "true" consumer loyalty.

Cognition in loyalty programs. Most rewards programs are based on lock-in principles. Consumers are given participation points that accumulate over time. Programs that give immediate rewards without long-term implications (such as discounts) do little other than condition the consumer to expect future discounts. Moreover, the reward must have value in and of itself or must add value to the basic consumable. Carnival prizes, for example, are too fleeting a reward to the consumer to have lasting value. In contrast, higher order values (e.g., attainment) do have lasting value either in terms of self-esteem or social approval. Thus, card levels (silver, gold, platinum) or club achievement identification (million dollar, million mile) may work. Tangibles (upgrades, free flights) work for the moment and are good future "carrots." But few of these have lasting implications for the firm.

Loyalty to the prize simply does not engender loyalty to the firm. The firm becomes an instrument, an enabler. Sports is a good example of the many forms of "loyalty to," and an industry that is now in the early throes of programmatic "loyalty." What is the object of the loyalty target? Is it the sport itself, the statistics (including win/loss), team identity, local spirit, the crowd (fans), becoming one of the fans, the camaraderie, or the new incentives that teams are deploying, including preferred seating, among others. And one should not forget the entertainment venue of music, one of the most addictive pursuits due to its biological origin.

Now, if sports and music need some level of minimal incentives, tangible or not, what of truly mundane consumables such as air travel? And what of ordinary everyday purchasing where credit card programs hold sway? The essential value of a reward is similar to all valued consumables. As promotions, they should take on the characteristic of a desired, wanted, or needed item. But simple wanting satisfies only at the cognitive level. Loyalty "icons" must give pleasure in anticipation, in receipt, in use, in ownership, and in further desire. If rewards are viewed as a collection or accumulation, this in and of itself must be of value.

Affect in loyalty programs. This discussion would be incomplete if the next level of affective loyalty were omitted. Does a program enhance the liking one expresses toward the firm? This is where loyalty programs begin to falter. Unless the program rewards can transfer the pleasure of the reward to the pleasure of consuming the sponsor's deliverable, the program becomes available to any competitor. And what if the program becomes the product? When consumers begin buying Crackerjacks for the prizes and discard the product, the product becomes the prize, of little essential value. People begin taking flights for the next flight they will obtain or to complete the requirements for a free flight of even greater value or to stave off expiration.

The next two phases, conative and action loyalty, remain as goals, but are easily hidden or mimicked. In some sense then, the loyalty progression bifurcates at affective loyalty into a true psychological progression where the stages are in synchrony or into a false appearance of loyalty where consumers go through the motion of being committed and then repeat-purchase. At this point, without a psychological measurement metric, the mechanical and psychological loyalty patterns appear identical. From the firm's perspective, it won't be known which-is-which until true loyalty is allowed to emerge. This can

be observed with either of any of a variety of "acid tests" such as termination of the program, comparison to a control market without the program, or lack of defections to competitors with equal or better programs.

The data are universally discouraging with a small number of exceptions (e.g., Dowling and Uncles, 1997). What is clear is that programs increase purchasing in the classic carrot and stick fashion. What is not clear is whether revenues net of the additional costs are profitable and these data are not available except anecdotally. It is also clear that heavy current purchasers are most favorably affected and benefit at the costs of less frequent purchasers. Besides, strategically, programs are necessitated, and costs incurred, when faced with close competitors with programs.

CONSUMPTION COMMUNITIES

Three new perspectives on customer loyalty are proposed, stated as questions: (i) Can the consumer elect to be self-isolated from alternative consumable overtures so that competitive information is blocked or screened? (ii) Can the consumer be socially integrated in an exclusive environment that envelopes and directs the consumer's choices in a satisfying way? (iii) Can the consumer effect a self-identity that corresponds only to selected brand(s) *within* the environment? These issues speak to the "community" of loyalty (*see* BRAND COMMUNITY), singularly in the case of self-isolation, communally in the case of the environment, and both in the case of a preclusive lifestyle.

Dimensions of the framework. Picture a 2×2 table representing the dimensions on which these new issues are based. The vertical dimension reflects the degree of "individual fortitude," or the degree to which the consumer fights off competitive overtures based on his/her allegiance to the brand and not on marketer-generated "information." Despite an artificial break in this continuum into high (top row) and low (bottom row) categories, it is acknowledged that loyalty commitment develops with the advancement of stages in the four-phase model. At the lowest levels of fortitude, the consumer has only brand-related information. At the highest levels of fortitude, the consumer has developed the action inertia discussed previously, and has *also* developed a fierce defense against competitive encroachment that approaches "blind faith."

The horizontal dimension of the table would illustrate low and high phases of community and social support (McMillan, 1996). Here, the community provides the impetus to remain loyal either because it is enticing in a passive sense or because it proactively promotes loyalty. This dimension is crossed with that of individual fortitude so that the high-high cell contains the apex of loyalty and the low-low cell the weakest case of more vulnerable "loyalty," basic product superiority.

Product superiority, the weakest form of loyalty in this new framework, has already been discussed in cognitive, affective, conative, and action terms. This reflects the traditional view of loyalty as resulting from high quality and/or product superiority, both of which are believed to generate a strong sense of brand-directed preference. At some point in the cognitive–affective–conative–action chain, the consumer will cross the threshold from "low" consumer fortitude to "high," largely on the basis of the degree of immunization against competition that may have developed. The perspective taken here, however, provides further conceptual content in the high-fortitude (and low-social support) quadrant. In addition to the consumer's desire to rebuy on the basis of superiority, this framework suggests that he or she will also wish to rebuy based on determination or "determined self-isolation," that is, the consumer desires an exclusive relation with the brand and does not wish to be "courted" by other suitors.

The low-fortitude, high-social-support quadrant represents "village envelopment," in that it is analogous to the ever-popular concept of "it takes a village." Here, the consumer is sheltered from outside influences, nurtured in the use of selected and protected brands, and provided integrated and routinely updated consumption systems. The common computer platform and networking environment supported by most businesses is an example of this concept. The distinguishing feature here is that the consumer is a passive acceptor of the brand environment.

Lastly, the high-high quadrant, referred to as *immersed self-identity*, contains the combined influences of fortitude and social support. Here, the consumer has intentionally targeted (or has been targeted by) the social environment because it is consistent with and supports the self-concept. In effect, the consumer "immerses" his or her self-identity in the social system of which the brand is a part. This is a synergistic situation and is self-sustaining. The consumer fervently desires the product or service association, affiliates with the social setting knowing that it will be supportive of this association, and, at the limiting extreme is rewarded by the social system for his or her patronage. Religious institutions are good exemplars of this situation, although other secular social settings are equally illustrative such as fan clubs and alumni organizations.

It should be noted that the defining characteristics of these new perspectives are not directly under the control of management, but can be facilitated by it. They go beyond the cognitive–affective–conative–action sequence, because they transcend it. They tap into the socioemotional side of loyal consumption and closely access its "meaning," as discussed next.

Self-isolation as a sustainer of loyalty. Crossing the threshold from a belief in product superiority to brand-directed determinism and personal fortitude is a somewhat nebulous process. The transitioning mechanism is not well understood, even for areas of life where determinism is frequently observed (e.g., romance, religion, politics). One potential threshold transition phase is that of attachment. Attachment is something more than satisfaction as it requires states of satisfaction reinforcements over time until the "glue is set." This is an apt description since glue, being a chemical/mechanical adhesive, has resilience until the breaking strength is breached. Brand attachments, particularly those of "human brands," are not necessarily monogamous, can withstand bouts of dissatisfaction, and display commitment without being "ultimate." Still, this consumer may very likely be immune from competitive overtures, is unlikely to be swayed from determined repurchasing, may defend the brand fiercely, and would most probably promote the brand to others.

The social organization: the village.   In its pure form, the village is a social alliance whereby the primary motivation to become loyal on the part of each consumer is to be one with the group and the primary motivation of the group overseers is to please their constituency. In this situation, the consumer becomes a (willing) participant because of the attention provided by its members. In the limiting case, the product/service is not the "consumable." Rather, it is the camaraderie provided by the social organization. Good examples of this are the numerous varieties of clubs including internet communities of all types.

This concept goes by many names in its various literatures, but is perhaps best exemplified as the aforementioned *consumption community*, on the basis of the widely observed notion that individuals feel a sense of community when they share the same consumption behaviors. More to the point, when they espouse and own the same brand, these groupings are known as *brand communities* (Muniz and O'Guinn, 2001). Note that the previous "club" examples are somewhat weaker forms of the social collective envisioned here as they largely assume only that the mere knowledge of shared consumption is sufficient to generate a consumption community. Thus, it appears that the social dimension of the proposed framework, much like the fortitude dimension, is a continuum and some of the examples given "drift" to either the weaker or stronger side.

Individual and social integration: fully bonded loyalty.   The final, high-high quadrant in the table encompasses a blend of personal identity with the cultural milieu surrounding the consumable. This situation is distinguished from the previous example of the village because, in the present case, the cultural/social environment may assume a passive or stationary, although enticing, role. Here, the consumer is drawn to the consumable environment as opposed to the situation where the environment defines consumption for the consumer, although this does occur. The main distinguishing feature of this cell is that the consumer finds a "natural match" with both the consumable and its environment.

This is a particularly healthy situation for the firm as the product/service is inextricably embedded within some portion of the consumer's psyche as well as his/her lifestyle. The consumable is now part and parcel with one's self-identity and with his/her social identity, that is, the individual cannot conceive of him/herself as whole without it. At the extreme, the object is present intensionally and extensionally. Here, the consumer would say that the object is "part of me" and that it is an "extension of me." He or she lives it. Strong examples include sects with religious overtones and cults, although consumables in the more ordinary consumption domain are clearly candidates. Common examples include products, services, and even images supported by fans with various levels of group identification. Typically, the identity of the consumer is not known to the team, artist, and so on. The allure of the larger consumption icon is sufficient to "hold" the consumer to the loyalty state.

This concludes the discussion of loyalty influences beyond the cognitive-to-action framework. A consumer's willingness to rebuy or repatronize cannot reach ultimate extremes until she/he is willing to adore and commit unfailingly to a product/service. Beyond this, the necessary additional adhesion stems from the social bonding of a consumption community and the synergy between the two. In essence, the consumer wants to be loyal, the social organization wants him/her to be loyal and, as a result, the two may become symbiotic. The role of satisfaction in loyalty formation, which has not been discussed in this section, is addressed next.

What is the relation between satisfaction and loyalty?.   In Oliver (1999), a number of plausible relations were suggested linking satisfaction and loyalty. The appropriateness of these in light of the evidence offered is now discussed. The first, suggesting that satisfaction and loyalty are two manifestations of the same concept, is easily dismissed. From the many avenues of discourse presented and the definition of loyalty, it should be clear that the two concepts are distinctly separate. Satisfaction is a fairly temporal postusage state for one-time consumption or a repeatedly experienced state for ongoing consumption that reflects how the product or service fulfilled its purpose. Thus, satisfaction is *delivered* to the consumer. Loyalty, in contrast, is an *attained* state of enduring preference to the point of determined defense.

A second suggests that satisfaction is an essential ingredient for the emergence of loyalty, a third only that it is necessary, and another that there is an ambiguous overlap across the two. There is merit to these perspectives as no perspective discussed here entertains loyalty development without early or concurrent satisfying episodes. While it may be that satisfaction is not a core element of loyalty, particularly after loyalty has set, it is difficult to entertain loyalty development without satisfaction at some level, however small. The endurance of loyalty is another matter, however.

This brings this discussion to a dynamic perspective, which suggests that satisfaction becomes "transformed" into loyalty, after which they share virtually no common characteristics. This is truly an extreme position for it suggests that loyalty can never return to mere satisfaction. Indeed, some have suggested that there is a threshold at which loyalty can "revert" to *dissatisfaction* in the face of repeatedly unsatisfactory purchase episodes. Sometimes referred to as *catastrophe models*, discontinuous jumps are posited within an ordinarily continuous relationship, which is what many assume.

The reason for the ambivalence as to which conception is most accurate is that, even in the perspective taken here, there remain variants of loyalty. In addition to the cognitive-to-action sequence, it is suggested that there are now different degrees of loyalty depending on how many of the synergistic factors presented here are involved. Immersion-based loyalty is supported by the convergence of product, personal, and social forces and the consumer displaying this state has logical, personal, and communal loyalty sustainers. At the same time, competition is easily thwarted by these same forces. Removing any or one of these lowers the consumer's resistance to competitive persuasion. Loyalty supported only by the social environment permits the consumer to look beyond its borders. Loyalty supported only by fortitude is susceptible to "relapse" such as self-doubt, second thoughts,

competitive onslaught, and repetitively unpleasant dissatisfactory experiences. Furthermore, as discussed throughout this article, loyalty supported only by product information is subject to competitive counterinformation.

Thus, the dynamic model comes closest to the perspective taken here except that satisfaction does not transform into loyalty as much as it is a seed requiring nurturance. These are the analogies to personal determination and social support. Without these additional factors, satisfaction, much like the seed, stays dormant. The consumer remains satisfied, but does not progress beyond that state. Even a flash of sustenance – like the flash of delight – will not begin the transformation process. Once the seed sprouts, it will grow if the requisites are there. Only the mature version contains the strength of survival despite lapses in its base form, namely, dissatisfaction.

The translation of loyalty to profits.   The study of satisfaction as a precursor of loyalty, and exploration of the concept of loyalty itself, brings the discussion to what many considered to be the ultimate goal – profit. Until recently, insufficient data were available to establish the "much talked about" relationship between satisfied and loyal consumers and a firm's profits. While many working in the satisfaction field had assumed that the relationships between satisfaction and loyalty and between loyalty and profits are inherently intuitive and self-evident, others provide arguments to the contrary.

The reader may remember when stock market valuation models contained only financial and accounting data. They still do. It may seem strange indeed that the customer is not represented beyond mere sales (revenue) in these calculations. True, backward trends are analyzed and forecasts are made based on "hard" data. However, we now have equally hard data on customer satisfaction across industries and countries over time (Johnson *et al.*, 2001). Moreover, it is now recognized that the same customer satisfaction data statistically and significantly add to the explanation of changes (variation) in stock valuations (Morgan and Rego, 2006). Then what of loyalty?

Perhaps the greatest effect of loyalty on profit is the direct influence of a steady stream of future customers. In a manner similar to discounted cash flows, guaranteed future customers allow firms to budget offensive and defensive competitive efforts, to time tactical market moves, and to weather severe attacks by competitors until an appropriate strategy can be mapped. Moreover, since loyal customers, in the pristine case, require little, if any, marketing attention, efforts can be redirected toward product improvement and service enhancement. In the limiting condition, if a firm had an optimal number of perfectly loyal customers who, by definition, could not be swayed away, the firm's marketing costs would be zero. These findings no doubt will be buttressed by new work in the area as these conclusions are explored on a continuing basis.

Bibliography

Büschken, J. (2004) *Higher Profits Through Customer Lock-In: A Roadmap*, TEXERE (Thomson), Mason.

Dowling, G.R. and Uncles, M. (1997) Do customer loyalty programs really work? *Sloan Management Review*, **38**, 71–82.

Johnson, M.D., Gustafsson, A., Andreassen, T.W. *et al.* (2001) The evolution and future of national customer satisfaction index models. *Journal of Economic Psychology*, **22**, 217–245.

Kuhl, J. and Beckmann, J. (1985) *Action Control: From Cognition to Behavior*, Springer-Verlag, Berlin.

McMillan, D.W. (1996) Sense of community. *Journal of Community Psychology*, **24**, 315–325.

Morgan, N.A. and Rego, L.L. (2006) The value of different customer satisfaction and loyalty metrics in predicting business performance. *Marketing Science*, **25**, 426–439.

Muniz, A.M. Jr and O'Guinn, T.C. (2001) Brand community. *Journal of Consumer Research*, **27**, 412–432.

Oliver, R.L. (1997) *Satisfaction: A Behavioral Perspective on the Consumer*, Irwin/McGrawHill, New York, M.E. Sharpe, Armonk, NY.

Oliver, R.L. (1999) Whence consumer loyalty. *Journal of Marketing*, **63** (Special Issue), 33–44.

Oliver, R.L. (2010) *Satisfaction: A Behavioral Perspective on the Consumer*, 2nd edn., M.E. Sharpe, Armonk, NY.

Price, L.L. and Arnould, E.J. (1999) Commercial friendships: service provider-client relationships in context. *Journal of Marketing*, **63**, 38–56.

Reichheld, F.F. and Teal, T. (1996) *The Loyalty Effect: The Hidden Force Behind Growth, Profits, and Lasting Value*, Harvard Business School Press, Boston.

Roos, I. (1999) Switching processes in customer relationships. *Journal of Service Research*, **2**, 68–85.

Taylor, S.A., Hunter, G.L., and Longfellow, T.A. (2006) Testing an expanded attitude model of goal-directed behavior in a loyalty context. *Journal of Consumer Satisfaction, Dissatisfaction and Complaining Behavior*, **19**, 18–39.

consumer categorization

Barbara Loken

CATEGORIZATION CONSTRUCTS AND DEFINITIONS

A *consumer category* is "a set of products, services, brands, or other marketing entities, states, or events that appear to the consumer, related in some way" (Loken, Barsalou, and Joiner, 2008). The types of categories studied in marketing include *taxonomic* categories such as *product* categories (e.g., "snack foods") and *brand* categories (e.g., "Coach"). Consumers also have *goal-derived* categories, which focus on a desired outcome such as "ways to chat with my friends", and might include telephone, Facebook, and email as category members (Ratneshwar *et al.*, 2001).

Category members have *graded structure;* they vary probabilistically in how representative or *prototypical* they are of the category. For example, Coach handbags are more typical and a better example of the Coach brand category than Coach sunglasses. Prototypical category members tend to be better liked, have more ideal or favorable category features, and are encountered more frequently, than atypical members (Loken and Ward, 1990; Veryzer and Hutchinson 1998; Viswanathan and Childers, 1999).

CATEGORY STABILITY AND FLEXIBILITY

Research on consumer categories yields several conclusions (see Loken, Barsalou, and Joiner, 2008, for a review). First, categories are both *stable* and *flexible*. A consumer's concept of Crest as a prototypical toothpaste brand stays relatively stable over time, and consumers would generally agree that toothpaste (rather than "dental hygiene") is a *"basic level"* of categorization. Category membership and representation are also flexible, shifting with the context. For example, the prototypical beverages "at a football game" are different from those "at an opera intermission". Consumers' goals often motivate their categorizations (Ratneshwar *et al.*, 2001). The goal-relevant attribute of "sophistication" may drive category membership of beverages at the opera but not at football games. Category experts tend to show more category flexibility and greater use of subcategories than novices (Cowley and Mitchell, 2003), and consumers categorize differently depending on their cultural self-view as either Eastern or Western (Jain, Desai, and Mao, 2007).

Brand categories (e.g., Kashi products) are flexible in that atypical extensions (e.g., Kashi candy) "fit" the category better under some conditions than others. When consumers are in a good mood, or seeking variety or risk, they rate moderately atypical brand extensions as better category members. People accept more moderately atypical category members when a brand category is broad (e.g., Healthy Choice) than narrow (e.g., Campbell's). However, extremely atypical category extensions (e.g., Kashi electronics) are viewed as atypical regardless of the context. *Assimilation-contrast* processes also can explain flexibility of category members (cf. Schwarz and Bless, 2007).

CATEGORY INFERENCES

A second conclusion is that consumers use category information to make inferences about new category members. Consumers transfer beliefs and attitudes about a brand (e.g., the Coach brand is associated with "leather" and "designer status") to a new brand extension (e.g., a new Coach pink leather belt) when the brand extension is viewed as similar to, or a good fit for, the brand.

Third, consumers use information about new category members to make inferences and judgments about the overall category. A new BMW hybrid might increase consumers' beliefs that BMWs have "good gas mileage"

or decrease beliefs that BMWs have "excellent performance". Failed extensions in near product categories and successful extensions in far product categories affect brands, particularly when other information is inaccessible.

SUBCATEGORIZATIONS

Fourth, consumers use *subtypes* or subgroupings of categories to more finely differentiate a category. For example, Apple *subbrands* might include MP3 players (iPod), handheld computers (iPhone), laptop computers (iMac), and musical software (iTunes). Marketers use subbrands to call attention to unique or innovative features, and these subbrands sometimes develop into strong categories of their own. When a subbrand has multiple members (e.g., multiple electric cars in the vehicle category), consumers are more likely to position a new product within this subbrand (Lajos *et al.*, 2009).

Fifth, consumers enjoy products more and *satiate* less quickly when they categorize at a lower or *subordinate* level (Redden, 2008). For example, enjoyment of jelly beans continues longer when the candy is categorized specifically (e.g., orange, cherry) than generally (e.g., jelly bean). Subcategorizations focus people's attention on differences between category members. Having multiple subcategories (e.g., on a store shelf) signals variety, which can increase consumers' sense of self-determination and overall satisfaction (Mogilner, Rudnick, and Eyengar, 2008) but can also bias choices (Fox, Ratner, and Lieb, 2005).

ACKNOWLEDGMENT

Thanks to Joe Redden for comments and suggestions on an earlier draft.

Bibliography

Barsalou, L.W. (1985) Ideals, central tendency, and frequency of instantiation as determinants of graded structure in categories. *Journal of Experimental Psychology: Learning, Memory, and Cognition*, 11, 629–654.

Cowley, E. and Mitchell, A.A. (2003) The moderating effect of product knowledge on the learning and organization of product information. *Journal of Consumer Research*, 30, 443–454.

Fox, C.R., Ratner, R.K., and Lieb, D.S. (2005) How subjective grouping of options influences choice and allocation: diversification bias and the phenomenon of partition dependence. *Journal of Experimental Psychology: General*, **134** (4), 538–551.

Jain, S.P., Desai, K.K., and Mao, H. (2007) The influence of chronic and situational self-construal on categorization. *Journal of Consumer Research*, **34** (1), 66–76.

Lajos, J., Katona, Z., Chattopadhyay, A., and Sarvary, M. (2009) Category activation model: a spreading activation network model of subcategory positioning when categorization uncertainty is high. *Journal of Consumer Research*, **36** (1), 647–650.

Loken, B. (2006) Consumer psychology: categorization, inferences, affect, and persuasion. *Annual Review of Psychology*, **57**, 453–485.

Loken, B., Barsalou, L.W., and Joiner, C. (2008) Categorization theory and research in consumer psychology: category representation and category-based inference, in *Handbook of Consumer Psychology* (eds C.P. Haugtvedt, P.M. Herr, and F.R. Kardes), Psychology Press, New York.

Loken, B. and Ward, J. (1990) Alternative approaches to understanding the determinants of typicality. *Journal of Consumer Research*, **17**, 111–126.

Meyers-Levy, J. and Tybout, A. (1989) Schema congruity as a basis for product evaluation. *Journal of Consumer Research*, **16**, 39–54.

Mogilner, C., Rudnick, T., and Eyengar, S.S. (2008) The mere categorization effect: how the presence of categories increases choosers' perceptions of assortment variety and outcome satisfaction. *Journal of Consumer Research*, **35** (2), 202–215.

Ratneshwar, S., Barsalou, L.W., Pechmann, C., and Moore, M. (2001) Goal-derived categories: the role of personal and situational goals in category representations. *Journal of Consumer Psychology*, **10** (3), 147–158.

Redden, J.P. (2008) Reducing satiation: the role of categorization level. *Journal of Consumer Research*, **34** (5), 624–634.

Schwarz, N. and Bless, H. (2007) Mental construal processes: the inclusion/exclusion model, in *Assimilation and Contrast in Social Psychology* (eds D.A. Stapel and J. Suis), Psychology Press, Philadelphia, pp. 119–142.

Veryzer, R.W. and Hutchinson, J.W. (1998) The influence of unity and prototypicality on aesthetic responses to new product designs. *Journal of Consumer Research*, **24** (4), 374–393.

Viswanathan, M. and Childers, T.L. (1999) Understanding how product attributes influence product categorization: development and validation of fuzzy set-based measures of gradedness in product categories. *Journal of Marketing Research*, **36** (1), 75–94.

consumer creativity

James Burroughs

Creativity is widely defined as the production of outcomes that are both novel and effective for the given context or issue. Thus, novelty and functionality form the two core dimensions of creativity. The definition of *consumer creativity* follows from the more general definition as a "departure from conventional consumption practice in a novel and functional way" (Burroughs and Mick, 2004, 403). This form of creativity could include the consumer devising a new use for an existing product, altering the form of a product to improve its performance or appearance, or combining two or more products in a unique way.

TWO FORMS OF CREATIVE CONSUMPTION

Instances of individuals exhibiting creativity in consumer behavior are widespread, and generally fall into one of two categories: consumer problem solving and consumer self-expression. In the first instance, the impetus for the creativity is supplied by the environment. Some type of constraint (a lack of time, money, or product availability, being the three most common; Moreau and Dahl, 2005; Bagozzi and Warshaw, 1990) prompts the individual to design his or her own consumption solution. For example, a consumer may lack a necessary ingredient for a recipe and may be forced to improvise, or a consumer who is unable to afford expensive home furnishings may use creativity to take a more affordable product and augment it to look more expensive. Many new product ideas have their origins in consumer creativity (VonHippel, 1986) (*see* CONSUMER INNOVATIVENESS), and the potential for tapping consumers as a creative resource (customer cocreation) has attracted considerable attention in recent years.

A second type of consumer creativity is more expressive in nature, such as the alteration of a car or clothing to make a statement about one's individual identity or the culture in which they are a part. Though this creativity is always embedded in a social network, it is not prompted by the environment per se, but rather comes from within the individual (Holt, 1997; Kates, 2002). Creativity is essential to every person's sense of self-worth, including feelings of autonomy, competence, and relatedness (Deci and Ryan, 2000); in modern society, these needs are increasingly met through consumption behaviors. Because this form of consumer creativity is not evoked to solve an immediate problem, the second dimension is more aesthetic than functional in nature.

There can be considerable overlap between these two forms of consumer creativity and there is no reason that an act of creativity that is highly aesthetic cannot also come in response to a very practical consumption problem. Similarly, mundane problems can be solved in very elegant ways. For this reason, it has been suggested that researchers may want to adopt a three-dimensional view of consumer creativity (i.e., novelty, functionality, and aesthetics), at least in some instances.

ANTECEDENTS OF CREATIVE CONSUMPTION

In addition to trying to understand when and why consumers may engage consumption creatively, research has also tried to understand the factors responsible for producing more creative outcomes. In other words, why are some consumers more creative than others? While a full review of all the contributing factors to creativity is not possible in this article (see Burroughs, Moreau, and Mick, 2008), four are particularly noteworthy: analogical reasoning, intrinsic motivation, domain knowledge, and risk taking.

Generally, creativity is held to flow from a confluence of interacting factors rather than any single factor. However, one factor has captured more interest and intrigue from researchers than perhaps any other, and this is analogical reasoning. Almost by definition, creativity involves taking an idea from a disparate domain and recognizing its relevance to a completely different situation. Individuals who are able to think analogically or metaphorically (as opposed to literally), consistently come up with more creative responses to consumption issues (Burroughs and Mick, 2004; Dahl and Moreau, 2002). That said, we still have very limited understanding of this fascinating cognitive process and its role in creativity.

Two less-explored but important areas of consumer creativity are domain knowledge and risk taking. The role of domain knowledge for creativity is controversial. Some advocate that a knowledge foundation is necessary for new insights to occur (Weisberg, 1999) (see KNOWL-EDGE ACCESSIBILITY). However, others have found that too much knowledge leads to rigid thinking and is therefore detrimental to creativity. This has resulted in the inverted-U hypothesis, that creativity in an area is optimized by substantial but not overwhelming knowledge. Finally, creativity is an emergent and uncertain enterprise; thus individuals who are creative exhibit a high tolerance for ambiguity, as well as a proclivity for novelty seeking and risk taking (Sternberg and Lubart, 1996).

Another important factor is intrinsic motivation. Intrinsic motivation is sustained and intense interest in a consumption activity out of curiosity or enjoyment. Because people often engage in acts of consumption because they enjoy them (for example, a hobby), and because thinking creatively is mentally taxing, intrinsic interest is essential to the sustained effort needed to bring a potentially creative idea to fruition (Amabile, 1996).

PROCESS FACTORS IN CREATIVE CONSUMPTION

Finally, a nascent area of research is trying to understand the creative process, or how creative outcomes come about. Largely based on the cognitive tradition, creativity is widely believed to have four stages: exploration, fixation, incubation, and insight (Ward, Smith, and Finke, 1999). Exploration is a preparatory stage during which many combinations of ideas and possibilities are explored (mentally and sometimes physically). Fixation is when a consumer becomes entrenched in thinking about a consumption problem or issue in one way, which often leads to mental blocks and frustration. The consumer eventually becomes fatigued and desists, at which point the process enters the incubation period. Though the consumer is no longer actively thinking about the problem, the brain continues to unconsciously contemplate it. However, the linkages that were so tightly held are now relaxed allowing new and more distal mental linkages to form. The result can be an abrupt and wholly unanticipated new approach or solution, known as the *moment of insight* (Burroughs, Moreau, and Mick, 2008). As with many other areas of creative cognition, how the brain is able to accomplish this remarkable feat is still largely a mystery.

In sum, creativity is a useful, multifaceted, and underdeveloped issue in consumer behavior. There are many opportunities for research on this topic.

See also *creativity; consumer innovativeness; knowledge accessibility; lead users*

Bibliography

Amabile, T.M. (1996) *Creativity in Context*, Westview Press, New York.

Bagozzi, R.P. and Warshaw, P.R. (1990) Trying to consume. *Journal of Consumer Research*, **17**, 127–140.

Burroughs, J.E. and Mick, D.G. (2004) Exploring antecedents and consequences of consumer creativity in a problem-solving context. *Journal of Consumer Research*, **31** (3), 402–411.

Burroughs, J.E., Moreau, C.P., and Mick, D.G. (2008) Toward a psychology of consumer creativity, in *Handbook of Consumer Psychology* (eds C.P. Haugtvedt, P.M. Herr, and F.R. Kardes), Erlbaum, New York, pp. 1011–1038.

Dahl, D.W. and Moreau, P. (2002) The influence and value of analogical thinking during new product ideation. *Journal of Marketing Research*, **39**, 47–60.

Deci, E.L. and Ryan, R.M. (2000) The what and why of goal pursuits: human needs and the self-determination of human behavior. *Psychological Inquiry*, **11** (4), 227–268.

Holt, D.B. (1997) Poststructuralist lifestyle analysis: conceptualizing the social patterning of consumption in postmodernity. *Journal of Consumer Research*, **23**, 326–350.

Kates, S.M. (2002) The protean quality of subcultural consumption: an ethnographic account of gay consumers. *Journal of Consumer Research*, **29**, 383–399.

Moreau, C.P. and Dahl, D.W. (2005) Designing the solution: the impact of constraints on consumer creativity. *Journal of Consumer Research*, **32**, 13–22.

Sternberg, R.J. and Lubart, T.I. (1996) Investing in creativity. *American Psychologist*, **51** (7), 677–688.

Ward, T.B., Smith, S.M., and Finke, R.A. (1999) Creative cognition, in *Handbook of Creativity* (ed. R. Sternberg), Cambridge University Press, New York, pp. 189–212.

Weisberg, R.W. (1999) Creativity and knowledge: a challenge to theories, in *Handbook of Creativity* (ed. R.J. Sternberg), Cambridge University Press, New York, pp. 226–250.

VonHippel, E. (1986) Lead users: a source of novel product concepts. *Management Science*, **32**, 791–805.

consumer decision making

Haiyang Yang and Ziv Carmon

INTRODUCTION

The standard benchmark for models of consumer decision making against which all other models are typically compared is that of *homo economicus* (economic man). This elegant model suggests that consumers are rational actors who evaluate all relevant choice alternatives, assess the utility (value) that each can provide, and choose the one that they expect to provide the most utility. Different versions of this prescriptive model vary in their assumptions and in their descriptive fidelity (the extent to which they accurately describe how consumers actually think and behave), but on the whole, that view of consumer decision making is overly simple. For example, it assumes that consumers are sophisticated thinkers who process information effectively, efficiently, and without bias, and know their preferences.

Decades of descriptive research about consumer judgment and decision making shows that consumers systematically deviate from this model in important ways. Consumers' capacity to process information is limited, yet they commonly face a great deal of information and must therefore trade-off the accuracy of their decisions and the mental effort involved. Rather than choosing the optimal option (the one that they expect will maximize utility), many tend to select an option that is "good enough". Moreover, consumers often do *not* know their preferences. They construct rather than reveal their preferences when those are elicited, and these constructed preferences are sensitive to the decision context and the manner in which these preferences are elicited (Bettman, Luce, and Payne, 1998). In addition, consumers are influenced by meta-goals such as a desire to manage negative emotions like potential regret or conflict, or the extent to which their choice seems easy to justify. Complicating the picture further, rather than simply maximizing pleasure and minimizing pain, consumers sometimes pursue higher order goals such as bolstering their self-esteem, achieving a sense of mastery, or seeking deeper meaning.

In this chapter, we review some of the current knowledge on consumer decision making, highlighting a few ways in which consumers deviate from *homo economicus*. The review is *very* selective as we were restricted in how much we could write and cite, allowing us to cover and to acknowledge few of the papers that contributed to the body of knowledge that we describe. In the following sections we first discuss the impact of decision task and context on consumer preference, and then look at how the interplay of affect and cognition shapes consumer decision making. We also review factors influencing consumers' forecasts of future consumption experiences and discuss the relationship between utility maximization behavior and consumer well-being.

Decision Task and Context

Decisions are easy when consumers know what they want. Unfortunately that is frequently not the case; there are many instances in which consumers have but a sense of what they prefer, and must construct their preferences "on the fly" when a judgment or a choice is called for. Because consumers are affected by a variety of perceptual and judgmental biases, and since they are also often unable or unwilling to invest much time, effort, or attention in constructing their preferences, these preferences can be sensitive to how they were elicited. Examples of significant preference elicitation characteristics discussed below include choice set size, attribute quantity, option similarity and justifiability, presentation format, and response mode.

Choice set size and attribute quantity. Consumers who face a complex judgment or decision frequently use heuristics, decision strategies that simplify the task and are hoped to lead to a decision that is close to the best possible one (see Bettman, Luce, and Payne, 1998). Some heuristics avoid trading off attributes against one another. Such strategies are named *noncompensatory*, as an advantage in one attribute cannot compensate for a disadvantage in others. A lexicographic strategy is a notable example: consumers select the option with the highest value on the attribute that they consider most important, ignoring information about other attributes (in case of ties, they also consider the second most important attribute, etc.). Elimination by aspects is another noncompensatory strategy: consumers screen the choice options, and at each round of screening they select the most important attribute and eliminate options that do not exceed a minimum level on that attribute; this process continues until a single option remains. Compensatory strategies, on the other hand, do trade-off among attributes: a high value on one attribute can thus compensate for a low value on another. An example of a compensatory strategy is weighted adding: consumers evaluate each attribute of an option and compute a weighted total score for the option; after obtaining the scores for all the options in the set, consumers can then identify the option with the highest rating. Note that the examples we describe are "pure" strategies, whereas in reality, consumers may use a mixture of strategies or simplified variants of the strategies for a given decision.

Consumers tend to believe that to reach a good decision it is desirable to examine many alternatives, and seek as much information as they can reasonably find about these choice alternatives. However, information about many attributes or choice sets consisting of many options can make decisions too difficult. To illustrate, Iyengar and Lepper (2000) found that more consumers were drawn to a sampling booth of gourmet jams when it displayed 24 different types of jams, compared to when only 6 types were displayed. However, when only 6 jams were displayed more purchases were made – 10 times more than when 24 jams were displayed. These researchers also found that consumers were more satisfied with their choices when they chose from smaller sets of options. In conclusion, it appears that although people often want more options and more information, these are not necessarily beneficial.

Option similarity and justifiability. Consumer decisions are influenced by the extent to which choice options seem similar to one another. For instance, consider consumers choosing between two shirts: *A* that is comfortable to wear but not very stylish, and *B* that is stylish but not so comfortable. Adding to the choice set another shirt, *C*, that is slightly less comfortable and stylish than *A*, but more comfortable than *B*, can increase the attractiveness and relative choice share of shirt *A*. This phenomenon, known as the *asymmetric dominance effect* (attraction effect), violates the economic principle of regularity: adding an alternative to a choice set should not increase the choice share of any option in the original set (Huber, Payne, and Puto, 1982). This effect occurs because presence of the dominated option (shirt *C*) increases the appeal of the dominating option (shirt *A* in our example) as contrast between the former and the latter options helps the trade-off between the different dimensions (style and comfort) appear more favorable to the dominating option (shirt *A*) versus the alternative (shirt *B*).

Consumers are influenced by the extent to which they feel that they can easily justify their decisions, a notion named *reason-based choice*. This notion predicts a variety of interesting phenomena, such as a preference for so-called compromise options (Simonson, 1989). To illustrate, consider our shirt example; if we add to the original choice set of shirts *A* and *B* a shirt *D* that is more comfortable but less stylish than *A* and *B*, both the attractiveness and choice probability of shirt *A* are likely to increase. This is because consumers tend to find choosing an intermediate option (shirt *A*) easier to justify than extreme options (shirt *B* and *D*). This phenomenon is known as the *compromise effect* or *extremeness aversion*.

Presentation format. Consumer decision making is often influenced by how information is organized and presented, as consumers tend to focus on the information that is explicitly displayed and use it in the form that it

is displayed. For example, consumers can use price information better when product and price information is presented in a list sorted by unit price than when the same information is displayed in a traditional store setting, price tags on product shelves (Russo, 1977). That said, consumers do sometimes restructure information to make it more suitable for decision making when it seems too arduous to follow the given format.

Information can be displayed so as to establish different standards of comparison (referred to as *reference points*), which, in turn, influence consumer decision making. For example, if consumers are offered a full-featured product and asked to delete features that they do not want, they tend to choose significantly more features than if they are given a base model and asked to add the features they desire (Park, Jun, and MacInnis, 2000). This tendency has been attributed to two important notions in consumer decision making: reference dependence and loss aversion. According to reference dependence, consumers evaluate options by comparing them to reference points rather than evaluating them in absolute terms. In our example, the configuration that consumers first see serves as the reference point against which subsequent configurations are compared. The notion of loss aversion suggests that giving up an item, a feature, or a level of a feature, hurts more than acquiring the same thing feels good; in other words, losing something looms larger than gaining the same thing (Kahneman and Tversky, 1979). In our example, loss aversion drives consumers to add more features than they detract.

Loss aversion can also lead to a preference for the status quo. For instance, in countries where organ donation is the default decision (status quo) and people are given the option to opt out, consent rates tend to be very high, while in countries that generally seem comparable where the default decision is not to donate (an alternative status quo) and people can choose to opt in, consent rates are much lower (3–20 times lower according to Johnson and Goldstein, 2003).

Even arbitrary reference points can impact decision making. For example, Tversky and Kahneman (1974) used a roulette wheel to randomly generate a number, then asked participants in their experiment whether the number of African countries in the UN was higher or lower than that number, and then asked the participants to estimate the actual number of African UN member countries. Those who first saw a large (roulette derived) number estimated the number of African countries in the UN as significantly greater than those who saw a small (roulette derived) number.

More recent research showed that arbitrary anchors can also influence assessments of a sequence of items. The subsequent valuations tend to be "coherent" with respect to perceived differences among the products, "the entire pattern of valuations can easily create an illusion of order, as if it is being generated by stable underlying preferences" (Ariely, Loewenstein, and Prelec, 2003, p. 73). For example, the willingness to pay for a single bottle of wine was shown to be heavily influenced by an arbitrary number, but bids for multiple units of the same wine followed a reasonable logic: if willingness to pay for one bottle was $X, the willingness to pay for two bottles was a bit less than 200% of $X, for three bottles it was a bit less than 150% of the bid for two bottles, and so on. This phenomenon was named *coherent arbitrariness*, as the first bid is arbitrary but subsequent bids follow a coherent pattern.

Consumers' judgment of an option can also be shaped by whether the option is presented and evaluated separately or jointly with other options; if a choice option is rated favorably in singular evaluation, consumers may prefer the option less if the option is evaluated jointly with other options; conversely, if the option is not rated very positively in singular presentation and evaluation, its rating may improve in joint judgment (Hsee and Leclerc, 1998).

Meta-cognitive experiences related to presentation format can also influence choice. As an example, when choice information is presented in a fuzzy, difficult-to-read font, the resulting perceptual difficulty (of reading) can be attributed to the choice set. Consumers may infer that choosing between the options is difficult, and this can increase the likelihood of choosing to put off a decision (choice deferral) (Novemsky *et al.*, 2007).

Response mode.   Procedure invariance, another important principle in the classical economic decision-making paradigm, requires that equivalent preference elicitation procedures elicit the same preferences. A well-known violation of procedure invariance is the prominence effect (Tversky, Sattath, and Slovic, 1988): prominent (important) attributes are weighed more heavily when people choose among options than when they evaluate the same options in other ways, such as matching. Price matching, for example, asks for the price level at which the options will be equally attractive. To illustrate, when choosing between two programs to reduce traffic accident fatalities, one saving more lives but costing more than the other, people weigh saved lives (the more prominent attribute) more heavily than cost. They therefore tend to choose expensive programs saving more lives, reflecting high willingness to pay to save a life. But when asked a price matching question, such as at what price the program saving more lives is equivalent to the inexpensive program saving fewer lives (the price beyond which the less expensive program saving fewer lives is preferred), they indicate a price roughly proportional in cost per life saved, reflecting lower willingness to pay to save a life.

As another example, consumers' value assessment of the same item can vary greatly depending on how it is assessed. For instance, the highest sum consumers will pay to obtain an item is typically very different from the lowest sum for which they will part from the item. This is true even if potential differences between buyers and sellers (such as liquidity constraints and information asymmetries) are controlled for, and although both types of value assessments should reflect the value that the consumer associates with owning the item. This robust phenomenon (see Maddux et al., in press, for discussion on variation across cultures), named the *endowment effect* (Kahneman, Knetsch, and Thaler, 1990), is due to a combination of factors. One is loss aversion. Another is that buyers and sellers use different heuristics to assess value, each focusing on and thus assessing different aspects of the potential transaction. Buyers focus on the money they stand to forgo should the transaction take place, and thus consider such things as opportunity costs (e.g., other things they could purchase with the money). Sellers, on the other hand, focus on the item that they would forgo should the transaction take place (Carmon and Ariely, 2000).

As yet another example, hedonic dimensions are weighed less heavily in acquisition decisions (which of several options to obtain) than in forfeiture decisions (which of several options to forgo). To illustrate, consumers wishing to buy a chocolate bar and an equally priced notepad, but who can only afford one, are more likely to buy the chocolate when choosing which option to forgo (e.g., if they have both items in their shopping cart when they notice the budget constraint) than when choosing which to select (e.g., if they have neither item in the cart when they notice the budget constraint; Dhar and Wertenbroch, 2000).

AFFECT IN DECISION MAKING

Affect can have considerable impact on consumer decision making. Choices can be so affect-laden that trade-offs among them evoke strong unpleasant emotions. Some consumer decisions reflect reluctance to experience such emotions. For example, consumers sometimes choose to maintain a status quo so as to avoid the unsettling emotions involved with agonizing over which option they should choose instead (Luce, 1998).

Affective state.   Affect can significantly influence decision-making processes. Positive affect can sometimes lead to more efficient decision making, for example. Also, when in a positive mood, consumers can decide more quickly and search less for redundant information. When experiencing negative emotions, on the other hand, consumers may seek to make accurate choices to improve how they feel, and may thus engage in more systematic, effortful information processing (Isen, 2001).

How consumers feel as they decide can also color their evaluations. For example, when assessing an object, consumers partly infer their assessment from how the product experience "seems to feel." This is referred to as the "how-do-I-feel-about-it heuristic," or "affect-as-information" (Pham, 1998; Schwarz and Clore, 1988). Incidental emotions (having little to do with the evaluated product, such as gloominess on a cloudy day), can affect how consumers feel at that point in time and can

thus contaminate their product assessments, as consumers partly infer their evaluations from how they feel when they assess the product. Thus, positive incidental emotions can lead to more favorable assessments and the opposite is true of negative incidental emotions. Such effects of incidental emotions can be reduced if their true source is made salient. For example, negative effects of gloominess during a cloudy day on product assessment can be reduced if consumers are first explicitly asked what the weather is like then.

Anticipated regret.   Anticipated emotions can also influence consumer decision making. For example, when consumers try to predict how they would feel if they were to have made a poor decision, they are more likely to purchase a product that is currently on sale rather than wait for a better sale; they are also more likely to choose higher priced well-known brands (Simonson, 1992). Bar-Hillel and Neter 1996 describe another interesting example of the impact of anticipated affect: participants were first given a lottery ticket and then asked if they would exchange the ticket for another that had objectively better odds. Surprisingly, most participants did not want to trade due to the regret they expected to feel if their original ticket won. More generally, consumers' concerns about the regret that they might feel should their choice turn out badly drive them to seek "safe" choices (*see* EMOTION).

SELF-CONTROL

Consumers regularly face choice situations involving indulgent and utilitarian options. They often choose the short lived satisfaction that comes from indulging themselves at the expense of their longer term goals and interests, even when the negative consequences of their decisions are clear. Owing to the so-called "hot-cold empathy gap," consumers often fail to predict such transgressions when they are in a "cold state" – removed from the tempting situation, in physical distance, in time, or in their thoughts. Being in such a cold state, it is easy to mispredict one's ability to act virtuously in the face of temptation. Worse yet, lapses are often exacerbated by visceral states such as feeling significant deprivation, hunger, or lust

(Loewenstein, 1996). For example, consumers who shop for food while they are hungry, tend to buy more than they would otherwise purchase, or will want to consume.

Wertenbroch (1998) distinguishes between vice and virtue goods. Vices (such as rich chocolate cake, or cigarettes) are typically preferred to virtues (such as fresh broccoli, or fat free versions of fatty foods) when consumers focus on the immediate consequences of consumption. To solve their self-control problems, consumers sometimes proactively ration their decisions. For example, they sometimes ration purchase quantity, limiting their stock of vice goods and thus consumption opportunities. Consumers of vice goods seeking to regulate their behavior may thus agree to pay higher unit price (for instance, avoid buying cigarette cartons despite the expected savings). Interestingly, some consumers become so future-oriented that they find it difficult to indulge (Kivetz and Simonson, 2002); to cope with this difficulty, they sometimes precommit to indulge (for example, choose luxury items rather than cash of equal or greater value, as a reward from a loyalty program).

Consumer decision making is shaped by spontaneous affect as well as by cognitive processes. When consumers' cognitive resources are constrained, they are more likely to choose options with higher immediate affective rewards (e.g., chocolate cake); conversely, when processing resources are less constrained, consumers are more likely to choose options with more favorable cognitions (e.g., fruit salad; Shiv and Fedorikhin, 1999). If options are presented vividly (e.g., real chocolate cake and fruit salad are physically placed in front of the consumer), even consumers with sufficient cognitive resources to elaborate on their decisions are likely to be swayed by affective considerations and choose to indulge (*see* IMPULSIVE AND COMPULSIVE BUYING).

MISFORECASTING CONSUMPTION EXPERIENCES

Another reason consumers often fail to select those options that seem best for them is that they often mispredict their satisfaction with their choices. In this section, we discuss examples of prediction errors that can lead to suboptimal decisions.

Consumers' decisions often rely on intuitive predictions about future consumption experiences. Forecasts of how satisfied consumers will be with the consequences of their choices can unfortunately be quite poor. To illustrate this, Kahneman and Snell (1992) asked participants in an experiment to consume a serving of plain yogurt every day for eight days. The participants incorrectly predicted increasing dislike of yogurt, whereas most came to like it more (or dislike it less). Note that this experience of eating yogurt is quite familiar, suggesting that consumers may fair more poorly when it comes to experiences with which they are less familiar.

Another reason that consumers tend to mispredict which decisions will be most satisfying for them has to do with a distinction between how a consumption episode is experienced as it happens and how it is summarized and remembered in retrospect. When consumers retrospectively summarize a consumption episode, they tend to focus only on a few key characteristics, such as the rate at which the experience became more or less pleasant over time, the intensity of the most extreme sensation, and the sensation at the final moment of the experience (Ariely and Carmon, 2000). Summary evaluations tend to represent only few aspects of the actual experience, and can thus be poor representations of the actual episode. Nevertheless, they are the best predictor of future decisions.

Incorrect but self-fulfilling expectations. Consumers' assessment of consumption experiences are influenced by their expectations, as the latter serve as a standard against which the actual experience is compared. Some expectations are based on widely held but incorrect beliefs, such as the notion that lower prices reflect lower quality (in this example the reality is that the empirical correlation between price and quality is negligible). Interestingly, in some instances, expectations that are incorrect can nevertheless be self-fulfilling.

For example, consumers who paid a discounted price for an energy drink that was said to increase mental acuity, derived less benefit from consuming the product (they were able to solve fewer puzzles) versus those who purchased the same product at its regular price (Shiv, Carmon, and Ariely, 2005). Similarly, Lee, Frederick, and Ariely (2006) asked patrons of a pub to evaluate the "MIT Brew" which was made of regular beer to which a few drops of balsamic vinegar was added. When the ingredients were revealed before participants sampled the brew, few liked it. However, when participants received the information immediately after they had sampled the brew, they rated the beer highly and were more likely to choose the special brew over regular beer. In other words, only when they (incorrectly) expected the beer to taste badly did it in fact taste that way.

Impact bias. Impact bias occurs when consumers "overestimate the intensity and duration of their emotional reactions to future events" (Wilson and Gilbert, 2005, p. 131). Focalism, the tendency to fixate on certain attributes or events but ignore (or under weigh) others, is one of the causes of the impact bias. For example, Schkade and Kahneman (1998) found that although people's self-reported life satisfaction was similar whether they lived in the Midwest or in California, when asked to rate a similar person living at the other location, they thought Californians would be more satisfied than Midwesterners. This was explained by people's assessments focusing too heavily on the salient qualities of California (climate and cultural opportunities), and largely ignoring other important determinants of happiness. As another example, consumers tend to recall atypical instances (e.g., the worst experience at a restaurant) and may rely on those rare instances in forecasting how they will react to future consumption events.

A related cause of impact bias is a tendency to neglect or underweigh adaptation to changes in circumstances. In a provocative example, Brickman, Coates, and Janoff-Bulman (1978) describe data suggesting that lottery winners are no happier than the average person, and people who became paralyzed in an accident are no less happy than the average person, a year after the dramatic change to their lives. While this example is controversial and may well over-state people's ability to adapt, due to difficulties in measuring and comparing happiness across

people, the general point that, people tend to underestimate their ability to adapt, is widely accepted.

Projection bias. Consumer decisions are also influenced by a projection bias, the inability to sufficiently consider how their preferences may change when circumstances become different (Gilbert, Gill, and Wilson, 2002). For example, when in a "hot" state such as hunger or thirst, consumers tend to overweigh the impact of temporary visceral factors on projections of needs and wants (Loewenstein, 1996). For example, when sexually aroused, men are significantly more willing to engage in unsafe and morally questionable sexual behaviors than they would otherwise consider. (Ariely and Loewenstein, 2006).

IRONIC EFFECTS OF TRYING TO CHOOSE WELL

Consumers' attempt to choose the very best alternative has interesting consequences for their satisfaction. Studies by Wilson *et al.* (1993) suggest that careful consideration of choices can cause consumers to pay more attention to less important criteria, and therefore choose less satisfying options. Ironically, maximization (seeking the best option) can not only result in normatively better decision outcomes (e.g., better paying jobs) but also in more negative subjective evaluations of the outcomes (e.g., lower job satisfaction). The lower satisfaction of maximizers is said to be due to heavier reliance on criteria that seem objectively important rather than criteria that feel important to them, and greater fixation on unrealized options (Iyengar, Wells, and Schwartz, 2006). Furthermore, those who maximize tend to be more affected by upward social comparisons (naturally dissatisfying comparisons to others who are in a better position), and experience more depression and regret.

Sometimes consumers experience buyers' regret, unsettling displeasure with having made a choice. Ironically, this is common with choices over which consumers extensively elaborated (made an effort to determine the very best option). This happens because elaboration can induce feelings of attachment to the choice options, a sense of prefactual possession of those options. When consumers eventually choose, they effectively lose the prefactual ownership of nonchosen options, which evokes negative feelings associated with loss and increases the appeal of forgone options compared to their appeal before the choice was made (Carmon, Wertenbroch, and Zeelenberg, 2003).

Similarly, over time, satisfaction with the chosen outcome can decrease for those consumers who considered alternatives before they chose. Ironically, satisfaction with a randomly assigned option, as well as satisfaction of consumers who did not consider alternatives, tends to remain comparatively stable (Ritov, 2006). On a related note, when consumers make hyperopic choices (choices emphasizing long- rather than short-term benefits) of virtue over vice, they may experience increasing regret over time because time attenuates emotions of indulgence guilt, but accentuates wistful feelings of missing out on hedonic pleasures, leading to intensified regret (Kivetz and Keinan, 2006) (*see* CONSUMER WELL-BEING).

SUMMARY

Many thoughtful researchers still defend the view that consumer decisions should be considered rational. In contrast, there is a large and growing body of evidence suggesting that consumers are not the *homo economicus* that the classical economic paradigm portrays. Consumers are limited by finite mental capacity; in many situations they have only a sense of what they prefer and must therefore construct their preferences on the fly, and those preferences tend to be contingent on the characteristics of the decision task and context. Consumers' decisions are often swayed by the affect they experience and anticipate and by their predictions regarding future consumption experiences that are often inaccurate. Consumers' attempt to seek utility-maximizing outcomes, ironically, may harm rather than improve their well-being. Although these insights do not yet make up a coherent theory of consumer decision making, they do suggest that *Homo sapiens*' rationality is predictably fallible.

Consumers' decision biases and errors, such as those we review here, can lead to suboptimal decisions. That said, consumers' decisions are often "good enough." In part this is because the heuristics that consumers use are often reasonably effective, and partly since many decisions, including ones in which consumers invest much energy are largely inconsequential, either because the decision is between good alternatives or because the decision is of little real importance. However, in some situations errors can have serious consequences (such as failing to save enough for retirement). The notion of Libertarian Paternalism (Thaler and Sunstein, 2008) proposes that " ... knowledge of how people think be used to design choice environments that make it easier for people to choose what is best for themselves, their families and their society." For example, a simple change to employees' default decision so that they regularly contribute money to their retirement savings account unless they choose to opt out (instead of the default being not to save unless they choose to opt in) could greatly help combat failure to save enough for retirement. The paternalistic flavor is controversial, though its proponents point out that it does *not* affect the freedom to choose.

In conclusion, the debate over whether and to what extent consumer decisions can be considered rational has spurred a large body of research yielding many insights into how consumers decide. Beyond that, however, approaches such as that of Libertarian Paternalism, using research on customer decision making to help consumers, seem more productive. We hope that future research will not only work toward developing a complete theory of consumer decision making but also shed more light on how this knowledge can be used to help consumers become better decision makers.

Acknowledgment

We thank Jim Bettman and Itamar Simonson for helpful comments and suggestions.

Bibliography

Ariely, D. and Carmon, Z. (2000) Gestalt characteristics of experiences: the defining features of summarized events. *Journal of Behavioral Decision Making*, **13**, 191–201.

Ariely, D. and Loewenstein, G. (2006) The heat of the moment: the effect of sexual arousal on sexual decision making. *Journal of Behavioral Decision Making*, **19**, 87–98.

Ariely, D., Loewenstein, G., and Prelec, D. (2003) Coherent arbitrariness: stable demand curves without stable preferences. *Quarterly Journal of Economics*, **118**, 73–105.

Bar-Hillel, M. and Neter, E. (1996) Why are people reluctant to trade lottery tickets? *Journal of Personality and Social Psychology*, **70**, 17–27.

Bettman, J.R., Luce, M.F., and Payne, J.W. (1998) Constructive consumer choice processes. *Journal of Consumer Research*, **25**, 187–217.

Brickman, P., Coates, D., and Janoff-Bulman, R. (1978) Lottery winners and accident victims: is happiness relative? *Journal of Personality and Social Psychology*, **36**, 917–927.

Carmon, Z. and Ariely, D. (2000) Focusing on the forgone: why value can appear so different to buyers and sellers. *Journal of Consumer Research*, **27**, 360–370.

Carmon, Z., Wertenbroch, K., and Zeelenberg, M. (2003) Option attachment: when deliberating makes choosing feel like losing. *Journal of Consumer Research*, **30**, 15–29.

Dhar, R. and Wertenbroch, K. (2000) Consumer choice between hedonic and utilitarian goods. *Journal of Marketing Research*, **37**, 60–71.

Gilbert, D.T., Gill, M., and Wilson, T.D. (2002) The future is now: temporal correction in affective forecasting. *Organizational Behavior and Human Decision Processes*, **88**, 430–444.

Hsee, C.K. and Leclerc, F. (1998) Will products look more attractive when evaluated jointly or when evaluated separately? *Journal of Consumer Research*, **25**, 175–186.

Huber, J., Payne, J.W., and Puto, C.P. (1982) Adding asymmetrically dominated alternatives: violations of regularity and the similarity hypothesis. *Journal of Consumer Research*, **9**, 90–98.

Isen, A.M. (2001) An influence of positive affect on decision making in complex situations: theoretical issues with practical implications. *Journal of Consumer Psychology*, **11** (2), 75–85.

Iyengar, S.S. and Lepper, M.R. (2000) When choice is demotivating: can one desire too much of a good thing? *Journal of Personality and Social Psychology*, **79**, 995–1006.

Iyengar, S., Wells, R., and Schwartz, B. (2006) Doing better but feeling worse: looking for the "best" job undermines satisfaction. *Psychological Science*, **17**, 143–150.

Johnson, E.J. and Goldstein, D.G. (2003) Do defaults save lives? *Science*, **302**, 1338–1339.

Kahneman, D., Knetsch, J.L., and Thaler, R.H. (1990) Experimental tests of the endowment effect and the Coase Theorem. *Journal of Political Economy*, **98**, 1325–1348.

Kahneman, D. and Snell, J. (1992) Predicting a changing taste: do people know what they will like? *Journal of Behavioral Decision Making*, **5**, 187–200.

Kahneman, D. and Tversky, A. (1979) Prospect theory: an analysis of decisions under risk. *Econometrica*, **47**, 313–327.

Kivetz, R. and Keinan, A. (2006) Repenting hyperopia: an analysis of self-control regrets. *Journal of Consumer Research*, **33**, 273–282.

Kivetz, R. and Simonson, I. (2002) Self control for the righteous: toward a theory of precommitment to indulgence. *Journal of Consumer Research*, **29**, 199–217.

Lee, L., Frederick, S., and Ariely, D. (2006) Try it, you'll like it: the influence of expectation, consumption, and revelation on preferences for beer. *Psychological Science*, **17**, 1054–1058.

Loewenstein, G. (1996) Out of control: visceral influences on behavior. *Organizational Behavior and Human Decision Processes*, **65** (3), 272–292.

Luce, M.F. (1998) Choosing to avoid: coping with negatively emotion-laden consumer decisions. *Journal of Consumer Research*, **24**, 409–433.

Maddux, W.W., Yang, H., Falk, C. *et al.* (in press) For whom is parting with possessions more painful? Cultural differences in the endowment effect. *Psychological Science*.

Novemsky, N., Dhar, R., Schwarz, N., and Simonson, I. (2007) Preference fluency in choice. *Journal of Marketing Research*, **44**, 347–356.

Park, C.W., Jun, S.Y., and MacInnis, D.J. (2000) Choosing what I want versus eliminating what I don't want: the effects of additive versus subtractive product option framing on consumer decision making. *Journal of Marketing Research*, **37**, 187–202.

Pham, M.T. (1998) Representativeness, relevance, and the use of feelings in decision making. *Journal of Consumer Research*, **25**, 144–159.

Ritov, I. (2006) The effect of time on pleasure with chosen outcomes. *Journal of Behavioral Decision Making*, **19**, 177–190.

Russo, J.E. (1977) The value of unit price information. *Journal of Marketing Research*, **14**, 193–201.

Schkade, D. and Kahneman, D. (1998) Does living in California make people happy? A focusing illusion in judgments of life satisfaction. *Psychological Science*, **9**, 340–346.

Schwarz, N. and Clore, G.L. (1988) How do I feel about it? Informative functions of affective states, in *Affect, Cognition, and Social Behavior* (eds K.Fiedler and J. Forgas), Hogrefe International, Toronto, pp. 44–62.

Shiv, B., Carmon, Z., and Ariely, D. (2005) Placebo effects of marketing actions: consumers may get what they pay for. *Journal of Marketing Research*, **42**, 383–393.

Shiv, B. and Fedorikhin, A. (1999) Heart and mind in conflict: interplay of affect and cognition in consumer decision making. *Journal of Consumer Research*, **26**, 278–282.

Simonson, I. (1989) Choice based on reasons: the case of attraction and compromise effects. *Journal of Consumer Research*, **16**, 158–174.

Simonson, I. (1992) The influence of anticipating regret and responsibility on purchase decisions. *Journal of Consumer Research*, **19**, 105–118.

Thaler, R.H. and Sunstein, C.R. (2008) *Nudge: Improving Decisions about Health, Wealth, and Happiness*, Yale University Press, New Haven .

Tversky, A. and Kahneman, D. (1974) Judgment under uncertainty: heuristics and biases. *Science*, **185**, 1124–1130.

Tversky, A., Sattath, S., and Slovic, P. (1988) Contingent weighting in judgment and choice. *Psychological Review*, **95**, 371–384.

Wertenbroch, K. (1998) Consumption self-control by rationing purchase quantities of virtue and vice. *Marketing Science*, **17**, 317–337.

Wilson, T.D. and Gilbert, D.T. (2005) Affective forecasting: knowing what to want. *Current Directions in Psychological Science*, **14**, 131–134.

Wilson, T.D., Lisle, D.J., Schooler, J.W. *et al.* (1993) Introspecting about reasons can reduce post-choice satisfaction. *Personality and Social Psychology Bulletin*, **19**, 331–339.

consumer desire

Richard P. Bagozzi

As a scientific concept, desire is relatively new in consumer research. Two construals of desires have been proffered by consumer researchers. One is championed by Belk and colleagues (e.g., Belk, Ger, and Askegaard, 1997, 2003). These authors conceive of desires as "belief-based passions that involve longing, yearning, and fervently wishing for something" and can be expressed in metaphors for "hunger (or thirst), sexual lust, and addiction" (Belk, Ger, and Askegaard, 1997, p. 24). Belk, Ger, and Askegaard (2003) characterize desire as "a powerful emotion" (p. 343) observed in a state of tension between feelings of seduction and morality (p. 345) and distinguish it from wants and needs (p. 328). While derived from grounded

research with consumers, this conceptualization of desires seems overly narrow, limited too much to biological kinds of desire, and exclusionary of less intense forms of everyday desire functioning in consumer behavior.

A second conceptualization of desire, while overlapping with that formulated by Belk, Ger, and Askegaard (2003), comes from the subfields of philosophy known as the *philosophy of mind* and the *philosophy of action* (e.g., Bishop, 1989; Davis, 1997; Mele, 2003). Davis (1997) distinguishes between volitive and appetitive desires. A volitive desire is "synonymous with *want*, *wish*, and *would like*, and appears as a *transitive verb* in sentences like 'I desire to … ' and 'I desire … '" (Davis, 1997, p. 136, emphasis in original). For example, "John would like to apply to Harvard" and "Mary wants intellectual stimulation in a movie" are volitive desires. By contrast, an appetitive desire has "the near synonyms *appetite*, *hungering*, *craving*, *yearning*, *longing*, and *urge*, and appears as a *noun* in sentences like 'I have a desire to … ' and 'I have a desire for … ,' [moreover] objects of appetitive desire are *appealing*, things we *view with pleasure*" (Davis, 1997, p. 136, emphasis in original). For instance, "Silvia has a longing for her birthplace" and "Paul has a craving for sushi" are appetitive desires. Davis points out that volitive and appetitive desires are logically independent and can exist empirically in distinct ways:

> We often want to eat, for social or nutritional reasons, when we have no appetite and view the prospect of eating without pleasure. We desire to eat, but have no desire to. On the other hand we may have a ravenous appetite and find the prospect of eating terribly appealing and yet not want to eat because we are on a diet. (1997, p. 136)

Bagozzi (1992, pp. 183–194) proposed that desires are fundamental psychological events or states (distinct from cognitive, evaluative, and affective reasons for acting) that convert reasons for acting into intentions to act. Such desires have been termed *behavioral desires* or *action desires*. Mele (1995) calls such desires *extrinsic desires* (i.e., desiring to act as a means to an end). Desires also exist as intrinsic desires (i.e., desiring something for its own sake or as an end;

Mele, 1995). An important form of intrinsic desires is goal desires.

Desires perform three functions. First, they motivate our goal intentions and our behavioral or action intentions (*see* CONSUMER INTENTIONS). One way they do this is automatically and nonconsciously or nondeliberatively through what Damasio (1994, pp. 173–174) called the *somatic-marker hypothesis*. That is, prior to conscious processing of pros and cons characteristic of rational decision making, people experience pleasant or unpleasant feelings that highlight options and create either positive or negative biases, which favor or eliminate options from consideration. Such unconscious processes influence or bias a number of antecedents to decision making and indeed can form the basis for certain desires. It is likely that declarative knowledge processed rationally by consumers (with regard to facts, alternative goals and brands, consequences of consumption, and various expectations one has) is influenced by unconscious preference biases residing in the brain and arising from previous emotional experience associated with similar decision problems. Bechara *et al.* (1997) present research showing that such covert processes bias decision making prior to cognitive evaluation and reasoning and without awareness occurring on the part of decision makers. The authors suggested that the unconscious processes guide or shape behavior, before conscious processing commences, and function to produce better decisions, especially to the extent that learning accumulates as a consequence of previous rewards and punishments, which become stored as nondeclarative dispositional knowledge. It is possible that some desires, especially appetitive ones, develop in this way and become the basis for goal desires and even some behavioral desires.

Now consider a second function of desires. People are often aware of their desires, and desires seem to function consciously in many decision-making settings. This is especially true for volitive desires. It is common for a decision maker to have many reasons for action, some of which might even conflict or constitute reasons for not acting in the very same decision context. In such cases, desires serve to integrate or summarize a decision maker's overall felt urge to act as a function of multiple, mixed reasons

for action. Reasons for action are appraised, combined, and transformed into a motivation to act. Whether this happens as a deterministic resultant of competing forces in response to reasons for action, or follows learned rules of weighting and consolidation, remains to be studied. But in the face of multiple reasons for acting and not acting, in which some reasons are determinative whereas others are not, people subjectively experience and express their final felt urge to act.

A third function for desires is to induce an intention; a goal desire incites a goal intention, and a behavioral desire evokes an implementation intention. (*see* CONSUMER INTENTIONS). Desires harbor energy in an action-tendency or consummatory sense, but without precise direction and without a personal commitment to act. Intentions provide precise direction and personal commitment in this sense. These are the primary differences between desires and intentions. Yet another distinction is that intentions, but not desires, can entail a plan to act, though not all intentions necessarily contain or imply plans. Perugini and Bagozzi (2004) explored additional distinctions between desires and intentions.

Left unchecked, desires tend to influence intentions. This happens for goal intentions as well as for action or behavioral intentions (*see* CONSUMER INTENTIONS). An important issue for research is how desires are self-regulated (*see* Bagozzi, 2006 and SELF-REGULATION). As we becomes aware of our desires, we may reflect upon them and apply self-evaluative standards. In this regard we may ask ourselves (figuratively or literally) whether we are the sort of person who should have, and act, on these desires. The answer may encompass a decision to cancel, override, or postpone implementation of the desire through intention formation. The decision might be influenced by one's social, moral, or self-conscious emotions (e.g., pride, gratitude, guilt, shame, embarrassment, contempt, disgust, anger), by one's ethics, moral beliefs, or character, by one's personal or social identity, or by one's feelings of empathy, love, or affection for another person implicated by the desire one way or the other. In parallel way, a person might come to question why he/she has no desire for a goal or to act and then embrace such a desire as a function of determinants similar to those mentioned in the aforementioned sentence.

Bibliography

Bagozzi, R.P. (1992) The self-regulation of attitudes, intentions, and behavior. *Social Psychology Quarterly*, **55**, 178–204.

Bagozzi, R.P. (2006) Explaining consumer behavior and consumer action: from fragmentation to unity. *Seoul Journal of Business*, **12**, 111–143.

Bechara, A., Damasio, H., Tranel, D., and Damasio, A. (1997) Deciding advantageously before knowing the advantageous strategy. *Science*, **275**, 1293–1295.

Belk, R.W., Ger, G., and Askegaard, S. (1997) Consumer desire in three cultures: results from projective research, in *Advances in Consumer Research*, vol. **24** (eds M. Brucks and D.J. MacInnis) Association for Consumer Research, Provo, pp. 24–28.

Belk, R.W., Ger, G., and Askegaard, S. (2003) The fire of desire: a multisided inquiry into consumer passion. *Journal of Consumer Research*, **30**, 326–351.

Bishop, J. (1989) *Natural Agency: An Essay on the Causal Theory of Action*, Cambridge University Press, Cambridge.

Damasio, A.R. (1994) *Descartes' Error: Emotion, Reason, and the Human Brain*, Avon Books, New York.

Davis, W.A. (1997) A causal theory of intending, in *Philosophy of Action* (ed. A.R. Mele), Oxford University Press, Oxford, pp. 131–148.

Mele, A.R. (1995) Motivation: essentially motivation-constituting attitudes. *Philosophical Review*, **104**, 387–423.

Mele, A.R. (2003) *Motivation and Agency*, Oxford University Press, Oxford.

Perugini, M. and Bagozzi, R.P. (2004) The distinction between desires and intentions. *European Journal of Social Psychology*, **34**, 69–84.

consumer expertise

Eric M. Eisenstein

INTRODUCTION

Consumer learning has been a focus of research in models of consumer behavior since the early days of marketing as an academic discipline. Research on consumer knowledge and expertise is more recent (e.g., Alba and Hutchinson, 1987), but both streams of investigation share a heritage within cognitive psychology. However, within psychology, the topics of learning and expertise have had quite different research foci. Models of learning have been explored in tasks ranging from those performed by animals (e.g., pigeons and rats) to complex skills available only to humans (e.g., reading, driving, language acquisition). Many of the paradigms that have been used to investigate learning involve laboratory experiments in which subjects are "trained up" to be expert in some (usually fairly simple) task. Thus, in psychology, research into learning has largely focused on the earliest stages of learning – moving from zero or near-zero expertise to some greater level. Cognitive psychologists have traditionally viewed expertise as the end result of many years of learning and practice, and the paradigms used to identify expertise have tended toward observational studies in which learning has occurred naturally over many years rather than in the laboratory (Chi *et al.*, 1988; Shanteau, 1988a). In contrast to cognitive psychology, in consumer research neither expertise nor learning has received extensive attention, and the paradigms that have been used have not typically been the same as those used in cognitive psychology. Among other differences, in consumer research learning and expertise have generally been treated as closely related to each other.

What is expertise?   Historically, there has been little agreement on the definition of expertise, which has hampered research. The layman's conception of expertise generally suggests broad-based, superior problem solving skills. This conception was shared by early researchers, who conceived experts as general problem solvers, but this formulation was short-lived, because it was soon discovered that learning experiences are bound to a specific environment, and that the superior performance of experts is tied to a domain. Initially in the concrete domain of chess, and then in many other domains, it became apparent that expertise depends critically on detailed, domain-specific knowledge, and that transfer of expertise is remarkably more difficult than expected. Therefore, when we discuss expertise, researchers are in agreement that we are really discussing human performance in a specific environment. However, there is still considerable disagreement on the definition of expertise as a construct.

Shanteau's (1988a, 1988b) Theory of Expert Competence remains the most widely accepted definition of expertise, and it provides a road map for examining consumer expertise. For the moment, let us assume the existence of a group of experts, and defer the thorny question of how one would determine who is a bona fide expert. Given the existence of at least some experts, competence will be based on five factors: domain knowledge, psychological traits, cognitive skills, decision strategies, and task characteristics. From the point of view of marketing, these characteristics can be mapped onto typical situations faced by consumers to determine the likelihood of achieving expert level consumer performance.

Adequate *domain knowledge* is a prerequisite for expert performance. It is likely that familiarity (repeated experience with the product or category) is necessary to develop adequate domain knowledge. However, it is obvious that mere memorization of facts in laundry list fashion is insufficient to achieve expert decision making performance. This is because accuracy depends critically on the linkages between stored facts, and creating and learning the linkages among stored facts is a kind of metaknowledge that is not simply declarative. Alternatively such linkages could be thought of as a separate skill requiring enrichment of the mind's ability to identify similarities and patterns, and to use that similarity function to recruit decision-relevant facts from long-term memory.

Experts require specific *cognitive skills* in order to achieve high levels of performance. The exact composition of these cognitive skills depends on the specific task. For example, the task may require retrieving items from a large number of previously stored cases, the ability to perform well under pressure, or the ability to quickly recognize patterns, among other skills. Clearly, aspiring experts will have an advantage on tasks which load on these skills to the extent that their cognitive abilities match the task requirements. In addition to cognitive skills, expertise requires mastery of specific *decision strategies*, which help experts to overcome cognitive limitations. Within consumer research, considerable research effort has been devoted to the simplifying heuristics that consumers use to consider, eliminate, and choose among presented options, and how decision strategies vary with various task characteristics such as amount of information, number of attributes, number of options, and so on. Payne, Bettman and Johnson's (1993) adaptive decision maker is perhaps the classic example of this type of research (*see* CONSUMER DECISION MAKING). Research in this stream has generated robust findings that demonstrate that novice consumers frequently ignore large amounts of relevant information and are susceptible to various decision biases that arise as a result of heuristic processing. Payne *et al.*, and other researchers working within their effort-accuracy paradigm, explicitly exclude experts from consideration, and there has been little additional work done to determine what modifications to the basic theory would be necessary for expert consumers.

The role of *task characteristics* is often overlooked in the study of expertise, both in psychology and in marketing. Many have argued that characteristics of the task are critical in determining whether there will be any bona fide experts in the domain (i.e., people who are consistently superior). A common observation is that in some domains experts perform at very high levels, but in other domains, performance is not significantly different from novices. In general, task characteristics that predict good performance include repetitive tasks that are based on static, agreed-upon stimuli, with timely, veridical, feedback available, and a stationary underlying model, in which the unmodelable error in the environment is low. Task characteristics that suggest poor performance with little evidence of objective expertise include dynamic stimuli or stimuli with little agreement about which are important, nonstationary underlying processes, where feedback is either unavailable, nonveridical, delayed, or ambiguous.

Shanteau proposed that experts also possess certain *psychological traits*, such as "self-presentation – the creation and maintenance of a public image," (Shanteau, 1988b). This proposition is controversial, because there are charlatans and hucksters who are surprisingly adept at the art of self-presentation. However, surprisingly, such traits may be highly relevant when discussing consumer expertise. This is because most people have a friend or acquaintance who knows "everything" about cars, computers, stereos, food, stocks, or other common consumer goods, and one characteristic of such "consumer mavens" is that they are able to maintain (and perhaps develop) the self-presentation of expertise (*see* OPINION LEADERSHIP AND MARKET MAVENS). Consumer research has not extensively investigated the role of these consumer experts, except in thinking about them as early adopters in Bass and similar diffusion frameworks.

Applying this framework to consumer expertise, we should expect the development of expertise across a wide variety of consumer tasks. For example, many consumers buy "collectables." Some collectable purchases are priced using a typical retail take-it-or-leave-it formats. However, many collectables are sold at auction (e.g., on eBay) and others are sold at yard sales, flea markets, and other similar venues, which are not fixed price settings. Under such circumstances, we would expect that consumer expertise would develop, with some consumers able to accurately value objects within their domain of expertise. Similarly, experienced shoppers are likely to develop a reasonable sense of where to go for the cheapest product, if it is commonly purchased (though store choice is not usually determined by a single good). In other circumstances, it is unlikely that consumers will develop substantial expertise. For example, people infrequently negotiate over automobiles, little feedback is available to the consumer after the deal, and the relevant attributes change over time. Therefore, we would expect very little expertise to develop among ordinary consumers in this market.

In many domains in which expertise has been studied, expert participants are typically at the highest levels of learning or achievement within the field. By contrast, in consumer research, investigations of expertise have generally involved comparisons of more knowledgeable and less knowledgeable consumers without requiring that the more knowledgeable consumers be experts in the sense of representing the highest attainable levels of knowledge (e.g., grand masters in chess, professional judges of agricultural products, medical doctors, and meteorologists). This focus on "relative" rather than "absolute" expertise is natural because many (arguably most) important problems in consumer behavior involve the very earliest stages of learning from experience (e.g., the adoption of innovations, transitions from trial to repeat purchases, and differences between light and heavy users). Thus, the emphasis in this article is on the integration of learning and expertise on the effects of relative differences in consumer knowledge on questions of consumer behavior.

BENEFITS AND COSTS OF CONSUMER EXPERTISE

One reason that the definition of expertise remains open and controversial is that there are starkly conflicting research results associated with the study of experts across domains and research paradigms. Among decision scientists, the results of many carefully controlled studies of experts (as defined by credentials, schooling, years of experience, and peer consensus) paint a dismal picture of expertise, revealing a robust finding that experts are no better than novices in objective performance (see Meehl, 1954, for a seminal and comprehensive overview). These findings stand in sharp contrast to the findings of cognitive psychologists. In psychological research on experts, the robust finding is that experts dominate novices in almost every aspect of cognitive processing, such as measures of cognitive structure, memory or recall for facts, analytic processing, information use and selection, inference, problem solving strategy choice, effort and automaticity, ability to deal with complexity, and elaborative reasoning. Camerer and Johnson (1991) dubbed these contrasting results the "process-performance paradox" (i.e., experts dominate on tests of cognitive process, but fail to achieve better results). Before attempting to resolve this paradox, it will be useful to review the benefits and potential costs of expertise.

COGNITIVE STRUCTURE

Cognitive structure refers to the way in which factual knowledge is organized in memory. As product familiarity increases, especially from nonuser to user of a product, cognitive structure is acquired (*see* THE ROLE OF SCHEMAS IN CONSUMER BEHAVIOR RESEARCH). The most common forms of cognitive structures studied in consumer research are based on psychological research into naturally occurring categories, because product categories, consisting of brands, products, and attributes are generally learned from experience in the same way that naturally occurring taxonomic categories are learned. There are a number of widely accepted theories that are borrowed from cognitive psychology in such research. First, most product categories behave similarly to what Rosch and her colleagues (Rosch *et al.*, 1976) termed "basic level categories," meaning that objects (products) are named at this level and that people can identify objects as belonging to a basic level more quickly than those belonging to a nonbasic level. The essential characteristic of basic level categories is that, at the basic level, within-category similarity and between-category dissimilarity are maximized (e.g., the basic level category is "bird," not the subcategory "raptor" or "finch," and also not the supercategory "vertebrate" or "animal"); *see* CONSUMER CATEGORIZATION. It is easy to see how typical markets encourage classification structure at the basic level: insofar as product categories are defined as collections of substitutes that compete with each other to fulfill the same consumer needs, it is natural that such products will be quite similar to each other, and dissimilar to products that do not fulfill those needs. As expertise increases, knowledge about subordinate categories increases and information at this level is processed as efficiently as at the basic level (thus, ornithologists would be almost equally fast when classifying "raptor" or "finch"). There has been little research in marketing to determine the extent to which the most typical products within a category are also the best products, or how this perception varies with expertise. However, marketing researchers have reached conclusions similar to those of cognitive psychologists, in that expert consumers have substantially different and more elaborate cognitive structures than novices, as well as the attendant advantages in processing speed.

MEMORY

One common characteristic of experts in all domains is better memory for domain-relevant facts, which is at least partially because of experts' more elaborate, better-organized, and differentiated, cognitive structures. Classic studies of chess experts showed that grand masters could remember game configurations far better than novices, but only when shown board configurations that could be obtained in real games (Chase and Simon, 1973). Similar results have been obtained in a wide variety of fields, providing strong evidence for the superiority of experts over novices in recall. Although a very small amount of this research has been specifically called consumer research (or conducted by consumer researchers), most investigations have used consumer markets or activities to define the continuum of expertise. For example, there have been extensive studies on expert versus novice players of games (e.g., chess, bridge, and go), sports (e.g., baseball, basketball, football, figure skating, and field hockey), as well as studies of hobbyists who follow these sports (i.e., people who follow baseball or basketball carefully, especially statistics related to the game). In consumer research, researchers have demonstrated the superiority of expert recall for attributes, attribute values, and the relationships between them. Studies by researchers in cognate fields have replicated the memory superiority effect in business and academic contexts, such as computer programming, mathematical proofs, physics problems, and medical diagnosis. Memory superiority, almost by definition, leads to more completely and perfectly informed consumers, and ought to improve decision making.

In general, research demonstrates that expert consumers are better able to process new information about products, are therefore more resistant to the biasing effects of advertisements, and as a result, they make objectively better decisions (however, this is not universally true, see the section Negative Consequences of Expertise).

ELABORATIVE THINKING

In addition to better organization and memory for information acquired directly from product experiences, experts sometimes exhibit higher levels of reasoning and problem solving within their domains of expertise. The most frequent, important, and researched type of problem solving that occurs within the context of consumer expertise is the ability to infer the ultimate benefits and costs of a product based on its objective features and technical specifications, which leads to the concomitant ability to use these inferences to solve the problem of satisfying specific needs. For example, consumers are constantly faced with the task of evaluating products' attributes and determining the appropriate weights to apply to the attributes in order to maximize the consumption utility of a specific usage occasion. The research consensus is that experts are considerably more accurate than novices in making feature-to-benefit inferences, whether for themselves or when serving as an agent for another party. Expertise also reduces perceived complexity, increases the utility of the ultimate choice, and experts extract differentially more utility in complex situations than novices.

OTHER POSITIVE EFFECTS OF EXPERTISE

One surprising finding in the research on expertise is that, contrary to conventional beliefs, experts use approximately the same number of cues, or pieces of information, in their reasoning as novices. However, what information is used varies significantly between experts and novices. It appears that for many tasks, variable selection is more important than the weighting assigned to those variables. As a result, in many fields, especially consumer oriented decisions, experts perform better than novices in choosing what information to examine, where to invest time in searching for additional information, and in making an ultimate decision.

In addition to better choices of attributes or cues to examine, experts also use substantially different problem solving strategies than novices. Among other major differences, novices tend to reason backward from a goal, whereas experts tend to classify the problem as a certain type, and then proceed forward using tools that are appropriate for the identified problem-class. This effect is particularly evident in concrete domains such as solving math, physics, or computer programming problems, as well as in games such as chess, bridge, and go. However, these games probably represent a good analogy for many types of consumer decision making. As in games, many consumer decisions are made from a strongly constrained set of options, where specific rules reduce the combinatorial space to a far smaller number (e.g., cellular phones). Hence, we should expect that expert consumers are able to reason forward rather than backward, and that this change in reasoning strategy at least partially accounts for the robust finding that expert consumers are better able to choose products appropriate to the usage situation (see the section Elaborative Thinking).

Experts have overlearned many of the skills they use. This is a double-edged sword. On the one hand, overlearning leads to automaticity, reduced effort, reduced perception of complexity, and a general reduction in effort with little or no loss of accuracy. However, automatic processing has downsides, including attentional blindness to possible environmental changes (*see* HABIT IN CONSUMER BEHAVIOR elsewhere in this volume, and the section Negative Consequences of Expertise).

NEGATIVE CONSEQUENCES OF EXPERTISE

When humans believe that they have learned something, they become more confident in their answers (whether or not anything has in fact been learned in the sense of objective measures of accuracy). Unfortunately, it appears to be a nearly universal truth that the rate of increase in confidence outstrips the actual increase in accuracy (it may be noted that this does not prevent experts from being more accurate than novices, merely that there is an interaction such that they are frequently more overconfident). The correspondence between actual accuracy and confidence is called *calibration*, and most studies have found experts to be at least as poorly calibrated as novices (see Alba and Hutchinson, 2000, for a comprehensive review). This effect has been replicated in medicine, law, psychology, sports, and among undergraduates (who were assumed to have more expertise in their major than in other areas). The notable exceptions to this finding have been in examinations of professional meteorologists and world-class bridge players, leading some to speculate that large numbers of repetitions with immediate outcome feedback is necessary for calibration to be improved by experience. However, as a stylized fact, acquisition of expertise does little to reduce the overconfidence that plagues most human decision making. Given that consumer decision making environments rarely feature the type of task characteristics associated with meteorology or bridge (i.e., neither large numbers of repetitions nor immediate outcome feedback), it seems likely that consumer experts will exhibit overconfidence and lack of calibration, perhaps in greater amounts than novices.

Confidence and calibration are particularly important in the consumer domain, because confidence has been shown to be a strong predictor of consumer preferences and choice, and confident consumers are less susceptible to manipulation by advertising and other marketing techniques. The fact that confidence and learning become increasingly disassociated as expertise (and experience or familiarity) increases is therefore problematic. In particular, overconfidence among consumer experts is likely to slow the diffusion of new information into the marketplace to the extent that novice consumers rely on word of mouth and the opinions of expert consumers as a major source of prepurchase information (e.g., in high tech industries). Furthermore, the increased reach of individual experts' opinions that has resulted from Internet-based social networking is likely to make word of mouth more important in novices' decision making. Thus, social networking will likely exacerbate any negative effects associated with overconfidence.

Another possible negative consequence of expertise is that it may inhibit the spontaneous recognition of a change in the underlying environment under some circumstances (Wood and Lynch, 2002). For example, if an expert consumer has learned that attributes *a*, *b*, and *c*, are associated with some positive outcome, it may be more difficult for such an expert to detect the fact that *c* has become a negative, or merely less positive than it used to be. On the other hand, experts still appear to dominate novices in speed of learning, adapting to, and recognizing such changes if they are cued that a change may have occurred. Owing to the interaction,

any potential disutility of expertise depends on the relative levels of cued and uncued changes in the environment – a topic that is essentially unstudied.

EXPLAINING EXPERT PERFORMANCE

Given the slow computational speed of the human brain, it is reasonable to ask how experts are capable of bringing relevant information, inferential techniques, and other specialized skills to bear on problems as quickly as they are observed to do.

Computation rate versus knowledge base size. Experts are called upon to process complex decision inputs and to make accurate decisions quickly. There are two general ways to approach this problem: retrieval from memory and search. Retrieval from memory is a fast and relatively effortless process for humans: conditional on a match between the current situation and a past situation that has been stored in long term memory, retrieval is rapid and automatic. If it is discovered that there is no good match in memory, however, a slower "computational" or exhaustive search through the space of possible answers ensues to discover an appropriate course of action. Search is effortful and slower, but it is the foundation of general problem solving ability. There is an obvious trade off between knowledge and search. Building an extensive database of cases and committing them to memory is time intensive, though the costs can potentially be spread out; learning procedural knowledge is frequently easier, but the actual computation is more effortful. The retrieval-search continuum represents the difference between the *cost of learning*, which is borne in the past, and the *cost of thinking*, which is incurred at the time of decision (Shugan, 1980; Eisenstein, 2002).

A robust finding is that expert performance is largely based on retrieval, not search. Experts pattern match and recall from memory, whereas novices tend to think extemporaneously. Therefore, the cost of expertise is a high cost of learning, not a cost of thinking (indeed, automaticity may reduce the cost of thinking!). This finding provides the explanation for why expertise has been found to be domain-specific and difficult to transfer to even analogous problems:

the stored cases and exemplars in memory are strongly bound to a particular domain. Moreover, even for analogous problems, relevant examples must be recalled and matched, and the associative "recall key" is equally, or more strongly, bound to a domain. To provide an idea of the power of retrieval as compared to search (and therefore of experts' decision making vs novices'), we can examine the case of chess, which has been called the *drosophila* of expertise. In chess, humans can process approximately one node (essentially a potential move) per second. By contrast, computers can search nearly 200 million nodes per second. Yet, human experts compete on nearly equal terms with such computers, in spite of a hundred-million-fold difference in processing speed. In order to accomplish this feat, it has been estimated that human experts store 50 000 to 100 000 positions in memory, and simultaneously possess a highly developed sense about when each is applicable. Although the number of stored exemplars may differ by domain, it is quite likely that similar effects would be revealed in many other areas of human expertise, from appraising collectables or houses to estimating the price of cars. For consumer experts, it seems likely that similar "databases" of facts, usage occasions, outcomes, and so on, are stored by experts, whereas novice consumers must attempt to reason their way through at the time of decision. However, little research attention has been given to investigating this question.

Learning to be an expert. Expertise cannot occur without learning. As discussed previously, a large knowledge base that allows experts to draw on a larger store of memorized facts is one difference that explains a portion of expert-novice performance differences. The large knowledge base allows experts to employ a case-based judgment strategy. Case-based strategies rely on the impressive human ability to automatically and relatively effortlessly judge similarity between cases. Using such a strategy, an expert compares the attributes of the current case to those stored in long-term memory, and the expert then reports a judgment for the current case that matches the judgment made in the stored case (or a weighted average of prior responses). This strategy has been shown

to be common in fields such as law, medicine, automobile and other fault diagnostics, and chess. It is likely to be employed by experts in other domains as well (e.g., case studies are often used in MBA programs, and it is likely that business people use them as well). Case-based strategies are most useful and accurate in highly predictable environments because, in such environments, any individual case will be quite similar to the stored cases to which it is most similar. Using a case-based strategy, individual differences in the number of cases stored in long-term memory and in the veridicality of the similarity metric will underlie differences in observed expertise. The utility of a large set of stored cases begs the question of how novices accrete these cases in memory en route to becoming an expert. Cases can be observed and committed to memory either through deliberate instruction or from experience, and experiential learning may be intentional or incidental.

Instruction is one of the most common ways that people become expert in a domain. For example, someone can take a course on computer programming and master recursion, or a doctor can attend medical school and become better than a novice at diagnosis. Instruction tends to be the primary path to skilled performance in most scientific and technical fields, which makes sense because these are fields in which "practice makes perfect" and in which there is an established base of facts and relationships to be mastered. Experience is another route to skilled performance, though the literature suggests that it is a much less successful path than instruction (see Klayman, 1988 for a comprehensive review). When learning from experience, the norm is that people identify small numbers of cues and utilize simple rules for combining them. However, occasionally people do appear to learn complex rules from experience as they become expert. For example, it has been shown that there exist experts at predicting the outcome of horse races, and these experts used complex configural rules, learned from experience, that they could not articulate (and their expertise extended to making money at it).

Unfortunately for consumers, most consumer expertise is likely to be gained through experience. There are likely some exceptions where learning about a product category through a guide or magazine article is the norm. Learning from experience is more difficult than learning by instruction, and the likelihood of developing expertise from experience is greatest when the general conditions that have been identified for the development of expertise are satisfied. First, the outcome and the feedback relating to that outcome should be unambiguous. Second, the feedback about whether the prediction was correct should be immediate (delayed feedback is not particularly useful). Third, the number of experiences should be "large." For example, learning how to appraise used cars is a skill that is likely to be learned from experience. However, in order to learn to accurately price used cars, the would-be expert must observe hundreds or even thousands of used car auctions, each time comparing his predicted price to the actual selling price, updating and adding to his knowledge base. For consumers, these characteristics can be used to predict domains in which substantial expertise will develop, but these predictions are complicated by substantial heterogeneity in the availability and quality of feedback. Many consumer tasks provide ambiguous feedback, subject to a substantial delay between purchase and consumption (and therefore feedback), and a modest number of consumption opportunities. Other consumer decisions have the opposite characteristics. Moreover, for some types of feedback, such as the utility associated with using the product, it might be easy to obtain feedback that is well-suited to the development of expertise, but it might be difficult to pay appropriate attention to the feedback, as when consumption occurs in a distracting environment such as a party, or with children screaming. Because the focus of research in marketing has been almost exclusively on studying people, rather than decision environments, we know little about the quality of feedback that is encountered by consumers.

Regardless of the quality of feedback, extensive research in both psychology and in marketing has demonstrated that raw experience or degree of familiarity is a poor predictor of expert performance. Some of this effect is owing to a subtlety in the definition of "experience." Most people think of experience as the amount of time spent "doing" an activity. For example, if someone had shopped for tennis racquets over a 20-year period, they would say that they had 20 years of experience shopping for racquets. However, experience is necessary but not sufficient to lead to improved performance. The critical link between experience and expertise appears to be the intention to learn from the experience, and at a more granular level, the precise goal associated with learning (Eisenstein and Hutchinson, 2006). This linkage occurs because learning goals define what constitutes feedback (particularly important in real-world environments in which the feedback is ambiguous), and intentionality directs attention to feedback and to discrepancies between the intended and actual outcomes. In the expertise literature, experience gained with the explicit goal of identifying discrepancies between one's mental model and the true state of the world is called *practice*, and in contrast to mere experience, time spent practicing is highly correlated with objective performance. In situations in which practice is not the norm, learning may still occur incidentally or unintentionally. This type of learning can be extremely powerful, and may lead to accurate judgments in relatively simple, deterministic domains, but it is generally not adequate for the development of expertise in most environments. Moreover, one of the hallmarks of incidental learning is the inability of subjects to articulate their reasoning process, which limits its usefulness in many decision problems.

In the development of consumer expertise, there remains an open question as far as how often consumers practice their buying skills, as opposed to simply experiencing outcomes. Certain consumer skills may be subject to substantial deliberate practice, for example searching for the lowest price on the Internet. However, some consumer activities are almost never practiced (e.g., learning attribute-price relationships in a grocery store, in which we have found that people cannot recall prices 30 seconds after purchase, much less at the time of consumption). There may also be individual differences in the degree to which identical consumer experiences are viewed as opportunities for learning, practice, and skill development (e.g., when dining out, some people are careful to taste wine with the intention of learning an attribute–quality relationship, whereas others are content simply to experience the wine).

Incentives.   In laboratory studies of experts, feedback is frequently combined with an incentive to get the answer correct. In the real world, such incentives take the form of arbitrage opportunities, promotions, or other payoffs for getting the answer right. Neither the mere existence of feedback nor the addition of incentives is sufficient to guarantee the development of expertise, and in some cases, incentives reduce the rate of learning. In many consumer environments, the incentives are obvious (saved money, increased utility through superior match between product and usage). Most people, including most economists, assume that incentives will increase effort, motivation, and persistence. However, incentives are not universally helpful, and additional effort does not always result in improved performance or learning. The effects of incentives are complex and vary depending on characteristics of the task and the learning environment. In general, incentives improve performance in tasks where increased effort is likely to result in better performance, such as memory or recall tasks, clerical tasks, and motor tasks (the latter two because they are otherwise boring, and incentives help to maintain effort). Since incentives primarily affect motivation, incentives are unlikely to have an effect when intrinsic interest in the task is high. Perhaps surprisingly, incentives frequently degrade performance in tasks that require flexibility in thinking and in tasks for which it would be better to rely on automatic processes (e.g., "choking" in sports, test anxiety). Moreover, incentives have been shown to exacerbate large classes of documented cognitive biases (e.g., representativeness, accessibility) and perceptual illusions. However, research has demonstrated that additional motivation to perform well is helpful mainly in tasks where little cognitive effort is required. Additional research has shown, however, that if incentives are too "exacting," meaning that subjects are strongly penalized for errors, then incentives reduce performance and the rate of learning. Thus, as in the case of feedback, the specific characteristics of decision making tasks are critically important

in making predictions about the relationship between incentives and the development of expertise. Since incentives primarily affect motivation, one could hypothesize that incentives would be most important for the quotidian tasks consumers encounter. Perversely, however, these everyday tasks are likely to be the least important in people's lives, and also less likely to have significant incentives associated with them. Finally, in the development of consumer expertise, there are always the incentives of increased utility and decreased cost, but there has been little or no investigation of whether consumers perceive their decision milieu in these economic terms.

CONCLUSIONS AND FUTURE RESEARCH

At the outset, the question of whether there are bona fide experts was deferred, as was a satisfactory explanation for the process-performance paradox. Decision scientists have purportedly shown that experts are not superior to novices, and that experts are frequently bested in accuracy by "simple linear models." These facts are so entrenched in the decision science literature that some researchers have argued that "all anyone needs to know is which variables to look at, and then how to add" (Dawes and Corrigan, 1974).

In spite of the dismal view of experts painted by decision scientists, there are good reasons to believe that bona fide experts do exist, both in the consumer domain and in other fields that have been the frequent whipping boys of researchers (e.g., medicine). Although the evidence is mixed, taken as a whole it generally supports the superiority of experts over novices. This statement is not without caveats. The common conception of expertise is sociological – an expert is anyone agreed to be an expert. This definition is directly related to Shanteau's notion of self-presentation, and his argument that members of a field should determine who the experts are by acclamation. It may be argued that the *sine qua non* of expertise is objective accuracy. The risk with this definition is that it is tautological: experts are found only where there is demonstrable superiority in accuracy. Although this is literally true, an accuracy requirement is actually much more stringent, and more useful, because it rules out the possibility of expertise in the absence of well-defined outcomes, agreed upon by independent observers, and a gold-standard of "correctness." This requirement has the effect of eliminating the concept of expertise from many fields, because in many domains, such a standard does not exist, and it may not be possible to construct one. This is particularly true in fields for which conditions that are believed to encompass a "spectrum" of manifestations (depression, autism, Asperger's, schizophrenia), as well as for matters of taste (what does it mean for a wine or a meal to be "good"? or one operating system to be "easier to use" than another?). In both cases, what would serve as the standard of accuracy? Similarly, this definition would exclude (correctly, it may be argued) anyone from being an expert astrologer or alchemist.

In future research, the findings of lack of expert performance should be challenged. Although there have been many studies conducted by decision scientists, the vast majority have used a small set of experimental paradigms. The set of experimental paradigms should be expanded. Moreover, many (if not most) studies that have examined expert-novice differences have done so in extremely limited contexts. For example, an expert and a novice might be asked which of two options is a better match for a certain usage situation, or which of two diseases is the correct diagnosis. Such tasks minimize experts' advantages in cognitive structure, problem solving strategies, and memory because the researcher who selected the problem has already narrowed the decision space down to only a few options. By contrast, the reason that laypeople think of experts as general problem solvers is that real experts are frequently called upon to sift through an enormous number of possibilities in order to isolate the handful that are worthy of further investigation. To use a medical analogy, once the options have been narrowed down to only flu or pneumonia, almost anyone could be taught to diagnose which is more likely. However, real doctors are instead presented with a patient who has a wet cough, fever, and feels weak. The number of pathogens that produce such symptoms is probably in the hundreds. Most will resolve without incident, but bacterial pneumonia can kill within 24 hours. Decision scientists can claim that there is no advantage to

expertise, but given the symptoms above, one will seek out an experienced infectious disease doc – and when the cards are on the table, so will they.

Bibliography

Alba, J.W. and Hutchinson, J.W. (1987) Dimensions of consumer expertise. *Journal of Consumer Research*, **13** (4), 411–454.

Alba, J.W. and Hutchinson, J.W. (2000) Knowledge calibration: what consumers know and what they think they know. *Journal of Consumer Research*, **27** (2), 123–156.

Camerer, C.F. and Johnson, E.J. (1991) The process-performance paradox in expert judgment: how can experts know so much and predict so badly? in *Toward a General Theory of Expertise: Prospects and Limits*, (eds K.A. Ericsson and J. Smith), Cambridge University Press, New York.

Chase, W.G. and Simon, H.A. (1973) Perception in chess. *Cognitive Psychology*, **4** (1), 55–81.

Chi, M.T.H., Glaser, R. and Farr, M.J. (eds) (1988) *The Nature of Expertise*, Lawrence Erlbaum Associates, Hillsdale, NJ.

Dawes, R.M. and Corrigan, B. (1974) Linear models in decision making. *Psychological Bulletin*, **81** (2), 95–106.

Eisenstein, E.M. (2002) Action-based reasoning: the cost of learning and the benefit of thinking less. University of Pennsylvania Vol. Dissertation Abstracts International. Philadelphia: Dissertation Abstracts International.

Eisenstein, E.M. and Hutchinson, J.W. (2006) Action-based learning: goals and attention in the acquisition of market knowledge. *Journal of Marketing Research*, **43** (2), 244–258.

Klayman, J. (1988) On the how and why (not) of learning from outcomes, in *Human Judgment: The SJT View* (eds B. Brehmer and C.R.B. Joyce), Elsevier Science Publihers B.V, North Holland.

Meehl, P.E. (1954) *Clinical Versus Statistical Prediction; A Theoretical Analysis and A Review of the Evidence*, University of Minnesota Press, Minneapolis, MN.

Payne, J.W., Bettman, J.R. and Johnson, E.J. (1993) *The Adaptive Decision-maker*, Cambridge University Press, Cambridge.

Rosch, E.H., Mervis, C.B., Gray, W.D., Johnson, D.M. and Boyes-Braem, P. (1976) Basic objects in natural categories, *Cognitive Psychology*, **8**, 382–439.

Shanteau, J. (1988a) Psychological characteristics and strategies of expert decision makers. *Acta Psychologica*, **68**, 203–215.

Shanteau, J. (1988b) Psychological characteristics and strategies of expert decision makers. *Acta Psychologica*, **68** (1–3), 203–215.

Shugan, S.M. (1980) The cost of thinking. *Journal of Consumer Research (pre-1986)*, **7** (2), 99.

Wood, S.L. and Lynch, J.G. (2002) Prior knowledge and complacency in new product learning. *Journal of Consumer Research*, **29** (3), 416–426.

consumer information processing

Hélène Deval and Frank R. Kardes

Marketing researchers and marketing managers spend enormous resources on monitoring, predicting, understanding, and influencing the behavior of consumers. This requires investigating the effects of marketing communications at each stage of consumer information processing: attention, comprehension, evaluation, memory, and choice (Wyer, 2008). Consumers can use virtually any type of cue, attribute, or knowledge as information, and this information is processed sequentially to facilitate judgment and decision making.

ATTENTION

Consumers are limited information processors (Kardes *et al.*, 2011). They often lack the motivation, capacity, or opportunity to analyze the judgmental implications of all relevant pieces of information. It is therefore critically important to capture their attention and interest. Specific goals influence the amount of processing and lead consumers to focus selectively on certain products or services. A given product or service is valued more heavily when it is goal relevant (valuation effect) and consumers tend to ignore goal-irrelevant products (devaluation effect, Markman and Brendl, 2005). The devaluation effect is typically much larger than the valuation effect. For example, even money is devaluated when hunger, thirst, or some other need is highly salient, even if money could indirectly help satiate that need.

Regardless of their relevance to a specific goal, some stimuli are conspicuous and therefore capture attention automatically (Kardes, 1994). Specifically, salient and vivid stimuli are highly noticeable and difficult to ignore. The vividness of a stimulus depends on the properties of the stimulus itself. It is determined by concreteness, emotional interest, and psychological proximity, independent of the context or background (e.g., the color red is a vivid color). Salience is determined by a difference in the background – contextually novel, unexpected, complex, or moving stimuli stick out (e.g., a red package surrounded by gray packages on a shelf is salient but the same package becomes nonsalient if surrounded by other red packages). Not surprisingly, advertisers are well aware of the importance of capturing the attention of consumers and so constantly try to create novel and salient ads that capture consumers' attention and interest. For example, ads that have a surprise element, such as mystery ads that hide the identity of the product till the end of the ad, are attention drawing (Kardes *et al.*, 2011). For unfamiliar brands, mystery ads help build a strong category-brand association in memory because withholding the identity of a brand arouses curiosity. This strong category-brand association results in the activation of a brand whenever the product category is brought to mind. Similarly, ads that use multiple variations on a theme, and ads that use upward camera angles are contextually salient and capture interest. In the same way, unusual packages, such as cylinders for Pringle's potato chips, plastic eggs for L'eggs panty hose, and 15-packs for Strohs beer, are salient and attention drawing. Salience effects are reduced when involvement or motivation for accuracy is high (Kardes *et al.*, 2011).

COMPREHENSION

Comprehension is the ability to interpret and assign meaning to information by relating it to knowledge already stored in memory (Wyer, 2008). It involves the formation of inferences that enable consumers to grasp the meaning of a product claim without systematically considering and evaluating each possible meaning of each word presented in the message (Kardes *et al.*, 2008). For example, instrumental inferences (the statement "he pounded a nail into the wall" implies that a hammer was used) facilitate communication. Interpretive inferences usually involve very little effort, making it difficult for the consumer to discriminate between the information that was actually presented and interpretative inferences based on this information (Kardes, 1994).

Prior knowledge leads to selective processing of knowledge-consistent information. Take two people that have opposite opinions about computers – one is a PC user and the other is a Mac user. It is likely that the PC will perform better on some dimensions (e.g., it is cheaper) and the Mac will perform better on other dimensions (e.g., it is more reliable). Both computer users will use prior knowledge and will selectively process the information that supports their original opinion, and, consequently, the same message will be interpreted in different ways by different consumers.

Similarly, most consumers assume that price and quality are highly correlated, and this assumption leads consumers to focus on information that is consistent with this hypothesis (Kardes *et al.*, 2008; Posavac *et al.*, 2005). Consequently, recognition and recall performance is better for high-price/high-quality brands and low-price/low-quality brands than for brands that do not confirm the original hypothesis. This leads to overestimation of the strength of the relation between price and quality. This overestimation increases the willingness of consumers to spend. Overestimation is reduced only when selective processing is discouraged owing to low cognitive load, random information presentation, or a low need for cognitive closure. The need for cognitive closure refers to a preference for a definite answer to a judgmental problem, any answer rather than ambiguity, inconsistency, or confusion (Kruglanski and Webster, 1996). Selective processing, anchoring, priming, primacy, heuristic reasoning, and stereotyping effects decrease as the need for cognitive closure decreases.

When processing effort is low, consumers are more prone to the effect of misleading advertisements using claims that are literally true but figuratively false. The claim "Brand X may help whiten your teeth" is literally true: the product may or may not help whiten your teeth. Yet, because in everyday language *may*

is interpreted as *usually*, the claim is figuratively false. Likewise, consumers are prone to infer that the claim "Women who look younger use Oil of Olay" indicates that "Women who use Oil of Olay look younger" (Kardes, 1994). This is known as "confusion of the inverse," which occurs frequently in everyday reasoning.

Low processing effort also results in other types of biases, like the truth effect (Kardes, 1994). The perceived validity of a statement increases with mere repetition independently of its objective validity. Because consumers might be unwilling or unable to judge the validity of a statement directly, they use other cues such as familiarity to assess the validity of a product claim. If people feel that they have heard the claim before, they assume that the claim is probably true even if they cannot remember where they heard it in the first place. The truth effect leverages this relation between familiarity and perceived validity: repetition increases familiarity, and in turn, familiarity increases perceived validity. The truth effect has obvious implications with respect to the effects of repetitive advertising on the perceived validity of product claims. This effect is less pronounced when processing is high because consumers are more likely to recognize that the impression of familiarity is because of repetition.

EVALUATION

After a product has captured consumer attention and interest, and after the information about the product has been understood, consumers assign a value to it in order to determine how much a product is worth to them (*see* ATTITUDES; PERSUASION). Selective processing leads consumers to focus on positive aspects of positively evaluated products and negative aspects of negatively evaluated products (Kardes *et al.*, 2011). Returning to our example of the PC user and the Mac user, selective processing has implications for the evaluation of products. The Mac user evaluates Macintosh computers positively and PCs negatively. He will therefore focus on the positive aspects of a Mac. Conversely, he will focus on negative aspects of a PC.

Selective processing can also induce product attribute information distortion. In this case, the information that does not support an initial preference is not ignored but its value is simply discounted while the importance of information supporting the initial preference is enhanced. When more than one product is present and consumers are encouraged to identify the product that is the leader, one alternative becomes the focal alternative. When consumers begin to prefer tentatively one alternative over others, the attributes of the focal alternative are rated as more important or as more favorable, relative to attribute ratings assessed in a pretest or a control group. One piece of information that would otherwise be interpreted as neutral might be interpreted as supportive of the leader. Information distortion can amplify the pioneering brand advantage or increase preference for an inferior alternative when attribute information is presented in a manner that leads to an early preference advantage for that alternative.

Most of the biases described previously leverage the lack of involvement and/or motivation to carefully process information (see CONSUMER INVOLVEMENT). Fortunately, consumers do not always process information using heuristics and low effort. Important decisions are likely to be guided by judgments and evaluations formed on the basis of a systematic analysis. Dual process models, such as the elaboration likelihood model (ELM) or the heuristic systematic model, suggest that there are two qualitatively different routes to persuasion: a high involvement route in which consumers think a lot (i.e., the central route of the elaboration likelihood model and the systematic route of the heuristic/systematic model) and a low involvement route in which consumers think very little (i.e., the peripheral route of the elaboration likelihood model and the heuristic route of the heuristic/systematic model; Chaiken and Trope, 1999).

The ELM suggests that when involvement is high, and when the ability to think about an ad is high, consumers are likely to follow the central route to persuasion by focusing on information that is most central to or important for forming an accurate attitude. Consumers are less prone to process the information passively. Instead, consumers are likely to elaborate on a persuasive message by generating their own support arguments or counterarguments. Strong arguments and strong reasons for forming a particular attitude are particularly persuasive when consumers follow the central route to persuasion. Attitudinal judgments formed on the basis of highly compelling arguments are likely to be enduring, resistant to change, and more likely to influence behavior.

When involvement is low or when the ability to think about an ad is low because of distraction, a lack of relevant knowledge, time pressure, and so on, consumers are likely to follow the peripheral route to persuasion without evaluating the quality of the arguments supporting or refuting a given position. Following the peripheral route to persuasion by focusing on peripheral or superficial information makes it easy to form an opinion without much thought. Many different types of superficial cues may be used. Attractive, likable, and expert sources seem trustworthy, so if these sources say that an advertised brand is a good product, consumers often believe these sources rather than spending a lot of time thinking about the attributes and benefits of the product (see SOCIAL INFLUENCE). Furthermore, positive moods and feelings often transfer to the advertised brand when consumers follow the peripheral route to persuasion. Consumers tend to form weak attitudes that are not accessible from memory, not long lasting, not resistant to change, and that have a weak influence on other judgments and behavior.

The ELM indicates that facts and reason are important when consumers follow the central route to persuasion, but not when consumers follow the peripheral route to persuasion. The model also indicates that celebrities, authority figures, humor, and pleasant background music and scenery are important when consumers follow the peripheral route to persuasion, but not when consumers follow the central route to persuasion. Hence, consumers use different types of information depending on which route to persuasion they are following. Furthermore, the central route to persuasion leads consumers to form strong attitudes that are accessible from memory, persistent, resistant to change, and that have a strong influence on other judgments and behavior (Haugtvedt and Kasmer, 2008; see CONSUMER INTENTIONS).

MEMORY

Availability refers to information that is stored in memory, and accessibility refers to the "activation potential" of the available information (Wyer, 2008). Accessibility depends on the strength of the association between stored knowledge and situational cues, the recency with which information has been acquired or last activated, the frequency of prior activation, and the intensity with which information has been processed (see KNOWLEDGE ACCESSIBILITY). Rather than using all relevant information stored in memory, consumers frequently use the subset that has been activated or primed by stimulus cues. The priming paradigm consists of two phases: first, consumers are exposed to a stimulus that increases the accessibility of the primed construct; second, consumers perform a seemingly unrelated task and their judgments or behaviors are assessed. When the applicability of a priming stimulus relative to a target is high, the stimulus influences subsequent judgments and behaviors concerning the target.

A wide variety of marketing communications have been shown to serve as priming stimuli (e.g., ads, Internet messages, salesperson interactions, retail environments, consumer magazines), and these priming stimuli have been shown to influence a wide variety of judgments (e.g., expensiveness, evaluative, and likelihood judgments) and mind-sets (e.g., comparing brands in one product category can increase purchase intentions in a different product category). Consumers often overestimate the likelihood of occupations (e.g., doctors, lawyers), objects (e.g., luxury cars, swimming pools), and behaviors (e.g., having wine with dinner, incidence of crime) shown frequently on television. This is particularly the case for heavy viewers, despite the fact that most consumers do not believe that television reflects reality accurately. With respect to evaluation, priming can result in either assimilation (a shift in judgment of a target toward the priming stimulus) or contrast (a shift in judgment of a target away from the priming stimulus), depending on the degree of overlap between the priming stimulus and the target. Assimilation occurs when overlap is high, and contrast occurs when overlap is low.

There is usually a considerable gap between the point of time at which information about products or services is encountered and the point of time at which this information is used in order to make a purchase decision. That is why it is of crucial importance to understand the role of memory in decision making (see CONSUMER MEMORY PROCESSES). Memory enables past experiences and learning that occurred long ago to influence current behavior. Memory is often compared to a computer (Kardes et al., 2011). A computer has a hard drive that can store a large amount of inactive files. A computer also allows users to retrieve a file from the hard drive and make it active so that the file can be processed (e.g., edited or used). Similarly, people have a long-term memory system that stores a large amount of inactive data or knowledge. To use this knowledge, people must retrieve it from long-term memory and bring it in into short-term, active memory so that the information can be processed. The transfer from the short-term memory to the long-term memory happens through rehearsing the information. The entire thinking and reasoning occurs in short-term memory, and only a small amount of information can be held in short-term memory; consistent with Miller's magic number seven, consumers cannot hold more than seven brands in their short-term memory (Kardes et al., 2011). If this information is not used, it can be lost in as little as 18 seconds. By contrast, long-term memory appears to store an unlimited amount of information permanently.

Memory can have an impact on diverse dimensions of brand choice: the brands included in the consideration set, what information will be used to evaluate the considered brands, and how the information will be used. Three general types of brand choice can be distinguished (Lynch and Srull, 1982). First, stimulus-based choice involves the selection of one brand from a set of brands that are actually present at the time of choice. For example, consumers in a grocery store might occasionally consider the brands that are on the shelves directly in front of them, not considering any brand retrieved from memory. Purely memory-based choice involves electing a brand from a set of brands stored in memory. Good examples of this type of choice include picking a restaurant before one leaves home. In between these two alternatives, mixed brand choice involves both alternatives that are physically present and alternatives that are retrieved from memory. This type of choice happens when consumers compare products from different stores that carry different brands (Kardes, 1994).

The usual comparison of memory to a computer does not imply that memory is infallible. For example, forgetting occurs. Forgetting is not because of information loss or decay. Instead, forgetting occurs because we cannot find the information we are trying to find during memory search. In addition, information held in long-term memory can also be distorted or changed over time (Kardes et al., 2011).

Selective processing also influences how information is stored in memory. Advertising can change the manner in which products are experienced. Subjective product experiences are ambiguous and might be interpreted in multiple ways. When an ad states that a particular brand of soda tastes sweet and refreshing, consumers frequently test this hypothesis by searching for hypothesis-consistent information in their memory (i.e., confirmation that the soda is indeed sweet and refreshing), and this leads to premature confirmation of the advertisement claim. When the ad precedes the experience, it sets expectations that will guide the interpretation of the product experience. Learning from experience becomes difficult because prior beliefs and current experiences are perceived as more consistent than they actually are. Conversely, current belief might bias memory. For example, a consumer might be led to believe that product A is better than product B. But, if at a later time, the consumer is led to believe product B is better than product A, the consumer is likely to distort his memory and report that he thought that product B was superior all along. Selective search can occur for stimulus information or for information stored in memory, depending on the timing of the ad and the consumption experience.

Most retail settings offer only a limited set of brands, and the brands that are offered often determine which brands are included in consumers' consideration sets, or the group of brands that are considered for purchase by consumers. Consumers are more likely to focus on immediately available brands and neglect unmentioned brands in singular judgment task (Kardes et al., 2011).

The neglect of unmentioned brands increases as the number of brands presented increases because of part-list cuing-induced inhibition (Kardes et al., 2011). This type of inhibition is different from intentionally blocking or suppressing examples available from memory. It occurs when just some brands are presented and consumers are trying to recall as many brands as possible. The brands presented inhibit the recall of other brands. Similarly, advertising reduces the ability of consumers to recall attribute information pertaining to competing brands. Inhibition of nonfocal brands also occurs when focal brands are physically present (as in grocery stores) rather than mentioned only by name. When no brands are mentioned by name, consumers are forced to generate their own consideration sets via memory search, and this leads to a strong advantage to brands enjoying strong brand-category associations in memory. Consumers often demonstrate selective memory for previously chosen products.

CHOICE

All the previous stages of information processing (attention, comprehension, and memory) are important in order to make a purchase decision (i.e., a choice). Selective processing often leads consumers to focus on one brand. Leveraging the effect of part-list cuing, marketers often try to influence which brands and how many brands consumers will include in their consideration sets. Marketers also leverage other effects, such as the attraction effect and the compromise effect (Kardes et al., 2011; see CONSUMER DECISION MAKING).

The attraction effect is based on the principal that a given brand seems more attractive when it is compared to inferior brands and less attractive when compared to superior brands. Hence, marketers want consumers to compare their brands to inferior brands. This can be done in a selling situation or using comparative advertising and promotion where the target brand is shown to be superior to other brands on some dimension. Alternatively, the attraction effect can come into play when a firm has multiple brands in its product line. For example, when a company markets a relatively expensive product, it might appear as too expensive when presented with no point of comparison. As a result, few consumers might choose to purchase the product. If the company introduces a more expensive product that competes directly with the first product, the original product might appear as more reasonably priced and much more attractive. This gives the impression to consumers that they save money while the characteristics of the original product remain unchanged.

Another way to improve the evaluation of a target brand is to make this brand seem like an average, or a good compromise, relative to other brands in the consideration set. A compromise brand seems average on all important attributes or features; other brands often have some really good features and some really bad features, but a compromise brand does not seem to have any very bad features and is at least acceptable on all features. Hence, the compromise brand seems like a safe choice and the compromise effect, or the increased likelihood of buying a compromise brand, is particularly likely to occur when consumers are concerned about avoiding a bad decision. Brands that are intermediate or "average" in terms of price, quality, and number of features are frequently chosen from the consideration set, and they are chosen even more frequently when we have to justify our choice to others. Because it is often easier to justify the purchase of intermediate rather than extreme brands, such a choice might also reduce post-decision regret. Of course, almost every brand can appear to be a compromise brand depending on what brands serve as points of comparison. Advertising and promotion campaigns that encourage consumers to compare a seemingly average brand to more extreme brands increase the influence of the compromise effect.

Selective processing leads consumers to use a number heuristics to make choices (Kardes et al., 2011). An important aspect of making a purchase decision is based on the ability to predict the future performance of a product. Although the ability to make predictions is very important, research evidence suggests that people are not very good at making them. This is because people often unknowingly use heuristics

to generate predictions. Such heuristics include the representativeness heuristic, the availability heuristic, the simulation heuristic, and anchoring-and-adjustment heuristic.

People using the representativeness heuristic make predictions based on the perceived similarity between a specific target and a general category. Consumers can make mistakes when they focus on superficial similarities between an object and a category (e.g., focusing on irrelevant similarities like package color and graphics). People using the availability heuristic make predictions based on the ease with which instances are retrieved from memory. For example, if an event is highly memorable and easy to remember (a service failure), it might overpower the availability of other less memorable events (e.g., several flawless interactions with the same service provider). If it is easy to remember, it seems more likely to occur. This will affect the prediction of consumers if they have to interact again with the same service provider. People using the simulation heuristic make predictions based on the ease with which an event or a sequence of events can be imagined or visualized. Such a heuristic has important implications for health-care marketing. Consumers with high blood pressure often forget to take their medicine because the symptoms usually are not that bad and this makes it difficult to imagine that their condition is serious. People using the anchoring-and-adjustment heuristic make predictions based on a first impression or an initial judgment (or anchor) and then shift (or adjust, or fine-tune) this judgment upward or downward depending on the implications of the imagined possibilities. Unfortunately, we usually fail to adjust enough and the effect of the anchor can remain more impactful than it ought to be. As a consequence the final judgment is often close to the initial impression.

In addition to heuristic that influence predictions related to decision making, there are also heuristic strategies related specifically to consumer choice (Kardes et al., 2011). These heuristics include the lexicographic heuristic, the elimination-by-aspects heuristic, the additive-difference heuristic, the conjunctive and disjunctive heuristics, and the frequency of good and bad features heuristic.

Consumers using the lexicographic heuristic (or single-attribute heuristic) compare all brands on one attribute, and choosing the brand that performs the best on that single attribute, generally ignoring the other attributes. If there is a tie, consumers examine the next most important attribute to break the tie.

Another choice heuristic is the elimination-by-aspects heuristic. Consumers simply reject brands that do not have a key feature that they want. Next, consumers would focus on a different attribute and reject all brands that do not meet their requirements on this attribute, and so on. Consumers using the additive-difference heuristic compare two brands at a time (rather than all brands) on one attribute at a time and subtract the difference. Subtraction is performed on all relevant attributes and each attribute is weighted for importance – each difference is multiplied by the importance of the attribute. Each weighted score is then summed to arrive at an overall score for each brand.

Choice heuristics do not always involve making comparisons across brands. Sometimes we focus on one brand at a time and no comparisons are performed. Examining one brand at a time is easy, and if the first brand seems satisfactory you might buy it without examining any other brands. Consumers using the conjunctive heuristic set a minimum value for all relevant attributes and select the first brand that meets this value for all relevant attributes. Consumers using the disjunctive heuristic set an acceptable value, rather than a minimum value, for all relevant attributes and select the first brand that meets this value on one attribute, rather than all of the attributes. The frequency of good and bad features heuristic is a strategy in which consumers form a simple attitude toward each brand alternative by counting the number of good product features, counting the number of bad product features, and choosing the brand with the largest number of good product features.

CONCLUSION

Consumer judgment and decision making is influenced by a large and complex set of variables that capture the attention and interest of consumers; influence how consumers acquire, retain, and revise product knowledge; and influence how product knowledge is used to ultimately make judgments and decisions. Selective processing is likely to have an impact on every stage of consumer information processing (e.g., selective attention, selective encoding, selective retrieval). Dual process models emphasize that effortful information processing, which reduces selective processing, heuristic processing, and the biases resulting from selective or heuristic processing, depends on the motivation and ability to process information carefully. Consumer information processing has important implications for understanding how consumers make judgments and decisions, and how policymakers can help consumers make better judgments and decisions.

Bibliography

Chaiken, S. and Trope, Y. (eds) (1999) *Dual-Process Theories in Social Psychology*, Guilford, New York.

Haugtvedt, C.P., Herr P.M. and Kardes F.R. (eds) (2008) *Handbook of Consumer Psychology*, LEA/Psychology Press, New York.

Haugtvedt, C.P. and Kasmer, J.A. (2008) Attitude change and persuasion, in *Handbook of Consumer Psychology* (eds C.P. Haugtvedt, P.M. Herr and F.R. Kardes), LEA/Psychology Press, New York, pp. 419–459.

Kardes, F.R. (1994) Consumer judgment and decision processes, in *Handbook of Social Cognition*, Vol. 2 (eds R.S. Wyer and T.K. Srull), Lawrence Erlbaum Associates, Hillsdale, NJ, pp. 399–466.

Kardes, F.R., Cronley M.L. and Cline T.W. (2011) *Consumer Behavior*, South-Western College Publishing, Cincinnati.

Kardes, F.R., Herr P.M. and Nantel Jacques (eds) (2005) *Applying Social Cognition to Consumer-Focused Strategy*, Lawrence Erlbaum Associates, Mahwah.

Kardes, F.R., Posavac, S.S., Cronley, M.L. and Herr, P.M. (2008) Consumer inference, in *Handbook of Consumer Psychology* (eds C.P. Haugtvedt, P.M. Herr and F.R. Kardes), LEA/Psychology Press, New York, pp. 165–191.

Kruglanski, A.W. and Webster, D.M. (1996) Motivated closing of the mind: 'Seizing' and 'freezing'. *Psychological Review*, 103, 263–283.

Lynch, J.G. Jr., and Srull T.K. (1982) Memory and attentional factors in consumer choice: concepts and research methods. *Journal of Consumer Research*, 9, 18–37.

Markman, A.B. and Bendl, C.M. (2005) Goals, policies, preferences, and actions, in *Applying Social Cognition to Consumer-Focused Strategy* (eds F.R. Kardes, P.M. Herr and J. Nantel), Lawrence Erlbaum Associates, Mahwah, pp. 37–51.

Posavac, S.S., Fitzsimons, G.J., Kardes, F.R. and Sanbonmatsu, D.M. (2005) Implications of selective processing for marketing managers, in *Applying Social Cognition to Consumer-Focused Strategy* (eds F.R. Kardes, P.M. Herr and J. Nantel.), Lawrence Erlbaum Associates, Mahwah, pp. 37–51.

Wyer, R.S. (2008) The role of knowledge accessibility in cognition and behavior: implications for consumer information processing, in *Handbook of consumer psychology* (eds C. Haugtvedt, P.M. Herr and F.R. Kardes), Psychology Press, New York, pp. 31–76.

consumer innovativeness

Gerard J. Tellis and Eden Yin

Consumer innovativeness is a construct that deals with how receptive consumers are to new products. Knowledge of consumer innovativeness is crucial for a firm's success given that new products are essential for future growth and success, cost millions of dollars to develop, and their life cycles are becoming increasingly short.

Research on consumer innovativeness is extensive, and yet it has achieved little consensus in definition, measurement, and findings. Consumer innovativeness has been defined as a predisposition or propensity to buy or adopt new products (Midgley and Dowling, 1978; Hirschman, 1980; Steenkamp *et al.*, 1999; Tellis, Yin and Bell, 2009), a willingness to change (Hurt *et al.*, 1977; Im *et al.*, 2003), or a preference for new and different experiences (Hirschman, 1980; Raju, 1980; Venkatraman and Price, 1990).

The measurement of consumer innovativeness has varied greatly across studies partly because of the variation in its definition. The main scales developed to measure this construct are life innovativeness scales and adoptive innovativeness scale. An example of the former is the ability to introduce newness in one's life (Kirton, 1976). Examples of the latter are measuring innovativeness as a tendency to buy new products,

which include Raju's scale (1980), Goldsmith and Hofacker's scale (1991), and Baumgartner and Steenkamp's (1996) exploratory product acquisition scale. One problem of these scales is that they have a large number of multiple items that are not substantially different from each other. Thus, the discipline can benefit from a parsimonious measure of consumer innovativeness.

On the basis of a review of the literature, Tellis, Yin and Bell (2009) identify at least ten dimensions of consumer innovativeness: novelty seeking, risk taking, variety seeking, opinion leadership, stimulus variation, habituation, nostalgia, suspicion, effort, and frugality. The first five of these are positively valenced while the latter five are negatively valenced. In a test of these dimensions across 15 countries of the world, Tellis, Yin and Bell (2009) found that the positively valenced measures are prone to social desirability bias and yea saying, while the negatively valenced measures do not suffer from such a bias. Indeed, they found that three or four of the negatively valenced measures could provide a reasonably good estimate of consumer innovativeness across cultures and countries.

Another important measure used to capture consumer innovativeness is a concept called sales takeoff. *Sales takeoff* is the first dramatic increase in the sales of a new product in the early stage of its life cycle. Sales takeoff often marks the beginning of the growth stage of a product's life cycle and can signal its future evolution into a mass market product. Tellis, Stremersch and Yin (2003) and Chandrasekaran and Tellis (2008) use the time to takeoff as a measure for consumer innovativeness across countries. Their finding indicates that clear country clusters of consumer innovativeness emerge based on time to takeoff. For example, in Europe, Scandinavian countries are the most consumer innovative, followed by mid-European countries, and then Mediterranean countries.

Researchers have found some demographic correlates of consumer innovativeness are significant: age, income, education, gender, and mobility. For example, Steenkamp *et al.* (1999) found age to be significant and Steenkamp and Burgess (2002) found income and gender to be significant drivers of consumer innovativeness. In the largest cross-country study on consumer innovativeness, Tellis, Yin and Bell (2009) found age, education, gender, income, and mobility to be significant drivers of consumer innovativeness. Their study is based on data from 5569 consumers across 15 major nations and 9 languages.

Demographics aside, consumer innovativeness is category specific. In particular, women are more eager to buy new home appliances, cosmetics, and food and grocery products, while men are more eager to buy new automobiles and sporting goods. Younger consumers are more eager to buy automobiles than other age groups. Highly educated consumers are more eager to buy financial service (Tellis, Yin and Bell, 2009). Consumer innovativeness also varies across countries and categories. For example, Japanese are most prone to buy new electronics, Brazilians to buy cosmetics, and Swedes to buy food products (Chandrasekaran and Tellis, 2008; Tellis, Yin and Bell, 2009).

See also *choice models; consumer decision making*

Bibliography

Baumgartner, H. and Steenkamp, J.-B.E.M. (1996) Exploratory consumer buying behavior: conceptualization and measurement. *International Journal of Research in Marketing*, 13, 121–137.

Chandrasekaran, D. and Tellis, G.J. (2008) The global takeoff of new products: culture, wealth, or vanishing differences. *Marketing Science*, 27 (5), 844–860.

Goldsmith, R.E. and Hofacker, C.G. (1991) Measuring consumer innovativeness. *Journal of the Academy of Marketing Science*, 19 (3), 209–222.

Hirschman, E.C. (1980) Innovativeness, novelty seeking, and consumer creativity. *Journal of Consumer Research*, 7 (3), 283–295.

Hurt, H.T., Joseph, K. and Cook, C.D. (1977) Measuring consumer innovativeness. *Journal of the Academy of Marketing Science*, 19 (3), 209–221.

Im, S., Bayus, B.L. and Mason, C.H. (2003) An empirical study of innate consumer innovativeness, personal characteristics and new product adoption behavior. *Journal of the Academy of Marketing Science*, 31 (1), 61–73.

Kirton, M. (1976) Adaptors and innovators: a description and measure. *Journal of Applied Psychology*, 61 (5), 622–629.

Midgley, D.F. and Dowling, G.R. (1978) Innovativeness: the concept and its measurement. *Journal of Consumer Research*, 4, 229–242.

Raju, P.S. (1980) Optimum stimulation level: its relationship to personality, demographics, and exploratory behavior. *Journal of Consumer Research*, 7, 272–282.

Steenkamp, J.-B.E.M. and Burgess, S.M. (2002) Optimum stimulation level and exploratory consumer behavior in an emerging consumer market. *International Journal of Research in Marketing*, 19 (2), 131–150.

Steenkamp, J.-B.E.M., Hofstede, F. and Wedel, M. (1999) A cross-national investigation into the individual and national cultural antecedents of consumer innovativeness. *Journal of Marketing*, 63, 55–69.

Tellis, G., Stremersch, S. and Yin, E. (2003) The international takeoff of new products: the role of economics, culture and country innovativeness. *Marketing Science*, 22 (2), 188–208.

Tellis, G., Yin, E. and Bell, S. (2009) Global consumer innovativeness: cross-country differences and demographic commonalities. *Journal of International Marketing*, 17 (2), 1–22.

Venkatraman, M.P. and Price, L.L. (1990) Differentiating between cognitive and sensory innovativeness. *Journal of Business Research*, 20 (4), 293–315.

consumer intentions

Richard P. Bagozzi

An *intention* has been defined as a *person's commitment, plan, or decision to carry out an action or achieve a goal* (Eagly and Chaiken, 1993), and in fact has been used synonymously at times with choice, decision, and plan. All these usages more generally fall under the label *volition*. Psychologist Ajzen (1991, p. 181) conceives of intentions rather broadly as "indicators of how hard people are willing to try, of how much of an effort they are planning to exert." This definition seems too broad in that it encompasses (i) motivation, which is better construed as an antecedent of intention and (ii) planning, which constitutes a mental activity or process that often occurs after one forms an intention to pursue a goal or perform an action.

The need for a narrower definition of intention can be seen in Lewin's (1951, pp. 95–96) specification of the role of volition in action: "[A] complete intentional action is conceived as follows: Its first phase is a motivational process, whether a brief or a protected vigorous struggle of motives; the second phase is an [mental] act of choice, decision, or intention, terminating this struggle; the third phase is the consummatory intentional action itself." This clearly differentiates intention from motivation and action and situates it between these concepts: motivation→intention→action.

The most common type of intention is the personal or I-intention to pursue a goal or perform an action by oneself. Notice that one can have an intention to pursue a goal, accomplish an end, or produce an outcome ("I intend to lose body weight") or an intention to execute an act ("I intend to buy a new LED television"). Both goal intentions and action intentions can be expressed noncontingently, as phased above, or contingently (e.g., "I intend to buy a new LED television, as soon as the price drops below $3000").

Gollwitzer proposed an important kind of intention, which he termed, *implementation intentions* (e.g., Gollwitzer and Brandstätter, 1997). These involve planning when, where, and how to act. Typically, a gap in time, often significant, exists between intention formation and behavioral execution. Implementation intentions serve cognitively to provide mental representations of opportunities to act and volitionally "create strong mental links between intended situations and behavior" and "in the presence of the critical situation, the intended behavior will be elicited automatically" (Gollwitzer and Brandstätter, 1997, p. 196). Thus one's intention to buy milk at the end of the day, made in the morning before work begins, may be recalled by the sight of a favorite store that one passes while returning home from work and enacted straight away. Because intentions frequently form first and lead to planning, many researchers might prefer to term "implementation intentions," *planning*, to allow for separate mental states and processes in this regard.

Intentions might lead directly to action straight away or after a gap in time. But they also have been shown to differ in degree of well-formedness and to be moderated in

their effects by level of effort required in action execution and by correspondence or independence between goal commitment and planning. Further, various mediators may occur between intentions and behavior, such as the need to deal with temptations, impediments, weakness-of-will, and monitoring progress in goal pursuit. For a review of moderators and mediators of the intention-action linkage, *see* Bagozzi (2006a, p. 19ff).

A common role for intentions in so-called goal-directed action is to bridge desires and their downstream effects. The consumer core captures this role of intentions and can be expressed as follows: goal desire→goal intention→action desire→action intention→action (see Bagozzi, 2006b). An important way that self-regulation occurs is in the management of the desire-to-intention links sketched above (see Bagozzi, 2006a, 2006b). Here desires are modulated through the imposition of personal standards of conduct, ethics, or moral imperatives. (*see also* SELF-REGULATION; CONSUMER DESIRE).

Recently the meaning of intentions has been expanded to include shared or collective intentions (Bagozzi, 2000, 2005). Thus, for example, persons in an intimate relationship might speak of "our intention to see Tchaikovsky's Swan Lake"; a football player may mention "the team's plan to implement a new defensive scheme"; corporation spokespersons might announce "the firm's hostile intention to take over another firm"; and the President of a country might remark that "our people intend to eliminate poverty by 2020." These examples – referring, respectively, to a two-person dyad, a small group, an organization, and a collectivity – illustrate that people often use social notions of intentions in ordinary speech, whether referring to informal or formal groups.

There are two types of collective intentions. One is a personal intention to do something with a group of people or contribute to, or do one's part of a group activity (e.g., "I intend to prepare the holiday dinner with my sisters"). Notice that a person can have an intention to act as an actor, yet the action can be self-construed as an individual act performed alone (an I-intention to do an individual act by oneself) or as a member of a group (an I-intention to do one's part of a group act). The latter is one type of collective action.

A qualitatively different form of a collective intention is what might be called a *we-intention*. A we-intention is a collective intention rooted in a person's self-conception as a member of a particular group (e.g., an organization or institution) or social category (e.g., one's gender or one's ethnicity), and action is conceived as either the group acting or the person acting as an agent of, or with, the group. A we-intention can be expressed in two forms: a shared we-intention articulated in the form of "I intend that our group/we act" (e.g., "I intend that our family visit Sea World, San Diego, next vacation") or a communal we-intention explicated in the form, "We (i.e., "I and the group to which I belong") intend to act" (e.g., "We intend to sponsor an exchange student in our home next year"). Collective intentions open up new avenues for exploring consumer behavior and are grounded in plural subject theory (Bagozzi, 2000, 2005).

Traditionally, such psychological determinants of behavior as attitudes, motives, emotions, values, felt social pressure, self-efficacy, and perceived behavioral control have been conceived to work through intentions to influence behavior. More recently desires have been considered to be proximal causes of intentions, channeling the effects of multiple psychological determinants (see consumer desires in this volume).

Bibliography

Ajzen, I. (1991) The theory of planned behavior. *Organizational Behavior and Human Decision Processes*, **50**, 179–211.

Bagozzi, R.P. (2000) On the concept of intentional social action in consumer behavior. *Journal of Consumer Research*, **27**, 388–396.

Bagozzi, R.P. (2005) Socializing marketing. *Marketing: Journal of Research in Management*, **1**, 101–110.

Bagozzi, R.P. (2006a) Consumer action: automaticity, purposiveness, and self-regulation, in *Review of Marketing Research* (ed. N.K. Malhotra) Sharpe, Armonk, pp. 3–42.

Bagozzi, R.P. (2006b) Explaining consumer behavior and consumer action: from fragmentation to unity. *Seoul Journal of Business*, **12**, 111–143.

Eagly, A.H. and Chaiken, S. (1993) *The Psychology of Attitudes*, Harcourt Brace Jovanovich, Fort Worth.

Lewin, K. (1951) *Field theory in social science*, Harper and Row, New York.

Gollwitzer, P.M. and Brandstätter, V. (1997) Implementation intentions and effective goal pursuit. *Journal of Personality and Social Psychology*, **73**, 186–199.

consumer involvement

Judith Lynne Zaichkowsky

Involvement is a motivational variable in consumer behavior and can be defined as *A person's perceived relevance of the object based on inherent needs, values and interests* (Zaichkowsky, 1985, 1986). Involvement is used to describe the level of consumer interest, search, or complex decision making toward an object. The object of involvement may be a product, a service, a situation, or an advertisement. Low involvement implies inertia, and high involvement implies a great deal of activation and it is found to influence consumer decision making and interactive communications. A consumer's level of involvement can be used as a segmenting variable to further target the market by marketing managers.

The history of the term *involvement* in the marketing literature has two major roots: one in the advertising research literature (Krugman, 1965, 1967) and the other in the consumer behavior literature (Howard and Sheth, 1969). In applying learning theory to TV copy testing, Krugman 1965 found that when a series of ads were presented, those presented first and last were better remembered than those ads in the middle of the series. This finding showed the same primacy and recency effects found by Hovland 1957 in the learning of non-ego involving material. Krugman hypothesized what advertising and non-ego involving material had in common were low levels of involvement, and operationalized it as the number of "bridging experiences, connections or personal references" per minute that the viewer made between his own life and the advertisement. Therefore personal involvement impacted on response to advertising.

Consumer involvement in the marketing and consumer behavior literature grew out of the realization that a great deal of consumer behavior does not involve extensive search for information or a comprehensive evaluation of choice alternatives (Olshavsky and Granbois, 1979). The consumer makes dozens of mundane decisions and choices each day and it is inappropriate to assume consumers actively process and think about each decision (Kassarjian, 1978). In this domain, many studies looked at the act of purchase, in addition to the product category itself, and determined the situations of purchase were highly influential in determining the level of consumer decision making activity (Clarke and Belk, 1978).

Because involvement was discussed in terms of products, advertisements, and purchase situations, early quantitative studies used various manipulations or single item measures and outcomes to represent and capture the concept. In a response to the plethora of definitions and measures, Zaichkowsky (1985) proposed a single definition and semantic differential scale to be used across all domains to capture the abstract concept of involvement on one dimension. Laurent and Kapferer (1985), on the other hand, proposed a measurement of product involvement which captured five facets or dimensions of product involvement: personal interest, importance of negative consequences, subjective probability of mispurchase, pleasure value, and sign value. These two studies represented the beginning of a long debate on how best to measure involvement.

It was clear that involvement was not only cognitive, but could also be emotional in nature (Petty, Cacioppo, and Schumann, 1983). The original Zaichkowsky Personal Involvement Inventory (PII) was later reduced to 10 items (Zaichkowsky, 1994) which better represented a balance of cognitive and emotional involvement items. This revised PII fitted in well with the idea that there are four quadrants in consumer behavior research: low and high involvement on one axis, and emotional and cognitive involvement on the other (Vaughn, 1988).

In recent years, the research literature indicates the concept of consumer involvement is widely embraced across a multiple of disciplines from agriculture (e.g., Verbeke and Vackier,

2004) to information systems (e.g., Koufaris, 2002). The role of involvement in consumer behavior has been so well accepted that it is completely incorporated in the field and no textbook in consumer behavior seems complete without a discussion of the topic.

Bibliography

Clarke, K. and Belk, R. (1978) The effects of product involvement and task definition on anticipated consumer effort, in *Advances in Consumer Research*, vol. 5 (ed. H.K. Hunt), Association for Consumer Research, Ann Arbour, pp. 313–318.

Hovland, C.I. (1957) *The Order of Presentation in Persuasion*, Yale University Press, New Haven.

Howard, J.A. and Sheth, J.N. (1969) *The Theory of Buyer Behavior*, John Wiley & Sons, Inc., New York.

Kassarjian, H.H. (1978) Presidential address, in *Advances in Consumer Research*, vol. 5 (ed. H.K.Hunt), Association for Consumer Research, Ann Arbour, pp. 31–34.

Koufaris, M. (2002) Applying the technology acceptance model and flow theory to online consumer behavior. *Information Systems Research*, 13, 205–223.

Krugman, H.E. (1965) The impact of television advertising involvement. *Public Opinion Quarterly*, 29, 349–356.

Krugman, H.E. (1967) The measurement of advertising involvement. *Public Opinion Quarterly*, 30, 583–596.

Laurent, G. and Kapferer, J.N. (1985) Measuring consumer involvement profiles. *Journal of Marketing Research*, 22, 41–53.

Olshavsky, R. and Granbois, D.H. (1979) Consumer decision making-fact or fiction? *Journal of Consumer Research*, 6, 93–100.

Petty, R.E., Cacioppo, J.T., and Schumann, D. (1983) Central and peripheral routes to advertising effectiveness: the moderating role of involvement. *Journal of Consumer Research*, 10, 135–146.

Vaughn, R. (1988) How advertising works: a planning model revisited. *Journal of Advertising Research*, 26 (1), 57–66.

Verbeke, W. and Vackier, I. (2004) Profile and effects of consumer involvement in fresh meat. *Meat Science*, 67, 159–168.

Zaichkowsky, J.L. (1985) Measuring the involvement construct. *Journal of Consumer Research*, 12, 341–352.

Zaichkowsky, J.L. (1986) Conceptualizing involvement. *Journal of Advertising*, 15 (2), 4–14.

Zaichkowsky, J.L. (1994) The personal involvement inventory: reduction, revision, and application to advertising. *Journal of Advertising*, 23 (4), 59–70.

consumer materialism

Marsha L. Richins

Consumer materialism refers to the importance that a consumer places on the acquisition and possession of material objects. In the consumer-behavior literature, materialism is usually considered to be a personal value, meaning that it affects the priorities in people's lives and the choices they make. Materialists believe that acquisition of material goods is a desirable and effective way to achieve important life goals. Thus, a materialist is more likely than others to see acquisition as a way to attain happiness, develop relationships with others, achieve status and a sense of self worth, and reach other important life goals. Richins and Dawson (1992) identified three elements that constitute materialism: the belief that acquisition is necessary for happiness, the tendency to judge the success of one's self and others by their possessions, and the centrality of acquisition and possessions in one's life. Because materialism is a value orientation and not a behavior, it is independent of financial status and is readily observed in both developed and developing economies. Materialism is most commonly measured by the material values scale (Richins, 2004).

Materialism should not be confused with conspicuous consumption, which is the ownership and display of status objects to enhance one's relative standing and inspire envy. While some materialists engage in conspicuous consumption, it is possible to have materialistic values without engaging in this particular behavior, particularly if status is not an important life goal for a consumer.

Although the formulation of materialism described above is the dominant one in consumer behavior, there are some alternative conceptualizations that should be recognized. Kasser (2002), a psychologist, has equated materialism with the pursuit of wealth, attractiveness, and social recognition and has looked especially at the negative effects of these goal pursuits on well-being. Inglehart (2008), a political scientist, has conducted extensive cross-national research over several decades to investigate the relative emphasis members of a society place on *material values* (defined as the importance one places on

economic and physical security) and *postmaterial values* (the priority assigned to such things as free speech and a greater say in government decisions). A third approach (Belk, 1985) views materialism as a combination of the personality traits of envy, nongenerosity, and possessiveness.

Materialism has important implications for society as a driver of personal consumption, and thus of economic growth. It also has personal implications because of its negative association with well-being (Christopher, Saliba, and Deadmarsh, 2009), strength of personal relationships, and altruistic behavior. Because of materialism's importance, much has been written about its potential causes. Commonly, high materialism levels have been attributed to insufficiently bridled capitalism coupled with a consumer society that is endorsed and facilitated by marketing firms, assisted by mass media. A lack of spirituality is also often alluded to. The preponderance of writings on the causes of materialism is speculative in content, and in any event the construct itself and the systems in which it is embedded are too complex to assign a single causal variable. However, some empirical research has provided insight by examining potential influences on individuals' materialism levels, including media exposure (Shrum, Burroughs, and Rindfleisch, 2005), early family environment (Flouri, 2004), and peer influences (Roberts, Manolis, and Tanner, 2009). The developmental progression of materialistic tendencies in children has also been investigated (Chaplin and John, 2007).

Materialism is associated with many variables of interest to marketers, including a preference for status goods and unique products, the centrality of visual aesthetics when making a product choice, willingness to purchase counterfeit products, impulse buying, and other decision variables. It is also associated with a greater willingness to go into debt to purchase discretionary goods, lower levels of frugality, compulsive spending, and with perceived financial distress and conflict between spouses.

Bibliography

Belk, R.W. (1985) Materialism: trait aspects of living in the material world. *Journal of Consumer Research*, **12**, 265–280.

Chaplin, L.N. and John, D.R. (2007) Growing up in a material world: age differences in materialism in children and adolescents. *Journal of Consumer Research*, **34**, 480–493.

Christopher, A.N., Saliba, L., and Deadmarsh, E.J. (2009) Materialism and well-being: the mediating effect of locus of control. *Personality and Individual Differences*, **46**, 682–686.

Flouri, E. (2004) Exploring the relationship between mothers' and fathers' parenting practices and children's materialist values. *Journal of Economic Psychology*, **25**, 743–752.

Inglehart, R.F. (2008) Changing values among western publics from 1970 to 2006. *West European Politics*, **31**, 130–146.

Kasser, T. (2002) *The High Price of Materialism*, MIT Press, Cambridge.

Richins, M.L. (2004) The material values scale: a re-inquiry into its measurement properties and the development of a short form. *Journal of Consumer Research*, **31**, 209–219.

Richins, M.L. and Dawson, S. (1992) A consumer values orientation for materialism and its measurement: scale development and validation. *Journal of Consumer Research*, **19**, 303–316.

Roberts, J.A., Manolis, C., and Tanner, J.F. Jr. (2009) Interpersonal influence and adolescent materialism and compulsive buying. *Social Influence*, **3**, 114–131.

Shrum, L.J., Burroughs, J.E., and Rindfleisch, A. (2005) Television's cultivation of material values. *Journal of Consumer Research*, **32**, 473–479.

consumer memory processes

Kathryn R. Mercurio and Mark R. Forehand

Consumer memory involves the encoding, storage, and retrieval of information related to products and services. The strongest consumer brands are those that have high brand awareness, whereby consumers easily recognize the brand (aided awareness) and can also recall the brand in the absence of cues (unaided awareness). Following associative network models of memory (Anderson and Bower, 1973), consumer memory is generally described as a massive network of interconnected ideas and concepts. The probability that any particular piece of information will be retrieved is dependent on the strength of association between the information and other connected concepts that are activated in the environment. When numerous pieces of information are integrated into a given associative network, the probability of successful recall of any particular piece of information may drop. For example, memory performance often lessens in the presence of competing information from competitive advertising (Keller, 1991) or from contextual interference (Kumar and Krishnan, 2004).

Consumer memory performance is critically influenced by the depth with which new information is encoded and the context in which the encoding takes place. For example, brands that are encoded in conjunction with parent categories and are considered more prototypical members of a category are usually easier to recall than are less representative brands (Mao and Krishnan, 2006). Brand concept maps have shown that the core brand associations that define a brand's image are connected not only to brand but also to secondary associations outside the brand (John *et al.*, 2006). These secondary associations provide an initial indication of the concepts that are likely to trigger memories for the brand in the external environment. There are also a number of marketing-controlled factors at the time of encoding that influence memory performance including message source (Kirmani and Shiv, 1998), persuasion (Drolet and Aaker, 2002), order effects (Cunha, Janiszewski, and Laran, 2008), virtual product experience (Schlosser, 2006), sponsorship (Cornwell *et al.*, 2006), mode of encoding – visually, verbally, and so on (Vanhuele, Laurent, and Drèze, 2006), and repetition (Appleton-Knapp, Bjork, and Wickens, 2005).

The states a consumer is in during encoding and retrieval can also significantly influence the consumer's ability to retrieve learned information. Within an associative network, activated states can serve as central units or nodes in a semantic network and a reoccurrence of a state can, therefore, trigger improved recall of information associated with that state (Cowley, 2007). Two accepted models of state-based memory are state dependency and state congruency. State-dependent learning models suggest that memory performance improves when information learned under a particular activated state is retrieved while that state is again activated, regardless of whether the learned information is related to the state. In contrast, state congruent models propose that memory performance is driven by a match between an individual's state at retrieval and the a priori association of the learned content with the activated state (Fiedler, 2000). In advertising contexts that feature content ambiguously associated with a state, memory performance is only apparent when the same state is active at encoding and retrieval and the content is moderately related to the state (Mercurio and Forehand, 2009).

One way of improving memory performance in consumer contexts is to provide retrieval cues that activate critical information nodes that can in turn facilitate retrieval of closely associated information. Although these cues generally improve memory performance, they can also hinder long-term memory if the consumer becomes dependent on the cue for retrieval and does not reinforce the required retrieval pathways (Forehand and Keller, 1996).

Consumer memory is a dynamic and complex process and given the role of memory in almost all aspects of consumer behavior it is important to understand the marketing factors that facilitate or hinder memory performance. Memory performance depends on the ability to encode information into long-term memory, retain the information over time, and retrieve previously stored memory. As shown by the associative network model of memory, factors present at encoding and retrieval can influence the strength of association between brands and new information and thereby significantly influence subsequent recall and recognition of consumer information.

Bibliography

Anderson, J.R. and Bower, G.H. (1973) *Human Associative Memory*, Winston, Washington, DC.

Appleton-Knapp, S.L., Bjork, R.A., and Wickens, T.D. (2005) Examining the spacing effect in advertising: encoding variability, retrieval processes, and their interaction. *Journal of Consumer Research*, 32, 266–276.

Cornwell, B.T., Humphreys, M.S., Maguire, A.M. et al. (2006) Sponsorship-linked marketing: the role of articulation in memory. *Journal of Consumer Research*, 33, 312–321.

Cowley, E. (2007) How enjoyable was it? Remembering an affective reaction to a previous consumption experience. *Journal of Consumer Research*, 34, 495–505.

Cunha, M.V., Janiszewski, C., and Laran, J. (2008) Protection of prior learning in complex consumer learning environments. *Journal of Consumer Research*, 34, 850–864.

Drolet, A. and Aaker, J. (2002) Off-target? Changing cognitive-based attitudes. *Journal of Consumer Psychology*, 12, 59–68.

Fiedler, K. (2000) Towards and integrative account of affect and cognition phenomena using the BIAS computer algorithm, in *Feeling and Thinking: The Role of Affect in Social Cognition* (ed. J.P. Forgas), Cambridge University Press, New York.

Forehand, M.R. and Keller, K.L. (1996) Initial retrieval difficulty and subsequent recall in an advertising setting. *Journal of Consumer Psychology*, 5, 299–323.

John, D.R., Loken, B., Kim, K., and Monga, A.B. (2006) Brand concept maps: a methodology for identifying brand association networks. *Journal of Marketing*, 43, 549–563.

Keller, K.L. (1991) Memory and evaluation effects in competitive advertising environments. *Journal of Consumer Research*, 17, 463–476.

Kirmani, A. and Shiv, B. (1998) Effects of source congruity on brand attitudes and beliefs: the moderating role of issue relevant elaboration. *Journal of Consumer Psychology*, 7, 25–47.

Kumar, A. and Krishnan, S. (2004) Memory interference in advertising: a replication and extension. *Journal of Consumer Research*, 30, 602–611.

Mao, H. and Krishnan, H.S. (2006) Effects of prototype and exemplar fit on brand extension evaluations: a two-process contingency model. *Journal of Consumer Research*, 33, 41–49.

Mercurio, K.R. and Forehand, M.R. (2009) An interpretive frame model of state dependent learning: the moderating role of content–state association. *Journal of Consumer Research*, under review.

Schlosser, A.E. (2006) Learning through virtual product experience: the role of imagery on true and false memories. *Journal of Consumer Research*, 33, 377–383.

Vanhuele, M., Laurent, G., and Drèze, X. (2006) Consumers' immediate memory for prices. *Journal of Consumer Research*, 33, 163–172.

consumer neuroscience

Hilke Plassmann, Carolyn Yoon, Fred M.
Feinberg, and Baba Shiv

BACKGROUND

The past decade has seen tremendous progress in academic research at the nexus of neuroscience, psychology, business, and economics. Even five years prior to that, fewer than a half-dozen papers appeared with keywords "neuroscience" and "decision making." Presently, across these parent disciplines, the yearly count stands around 200, and is doubtless accelerating. The twin births of neuroeconomics and decision neuroscience has generated wide-ranging, ongoing debates on whether these hybrid fields benefit their parent disciplines and, within them, what forms these benefits might take (Shiv *et al.*, 2005). Their joint aim is to adapt tools and concepts from neuroscience – combined with theories, formal models, rich empirical data, and tested experimental designs from the decision sciences – to develop a neuropsychologically sound theory of how humans make decisions, one that can be applied to both the natural and social sciences.

A group of consumer psychologists is now dedicated to investigating consumer research questions with methodological and conceptual approaches from neuroscience. This emergent field, consumer neuroscience, is described in detail in this article. A primary, and critical, distinction is between "consumer neuro-science," which refers to academic research at the intersection of neuroscience, psychology and marketing, and "neuromarketing," which refers to practitioner and popular interest in neuro-physiological tools – such as eye tracking, skin conductance, electroencephalography (EEG), and functional magnetic resonance imaging (fMRI) – to conduct company-specific market research. This article briefly details recent methods in neuroscience used by consumer researchers, presents basic ideas in consumer neuroscience as demonstrated by a variety of preliminary findings, and concludes with an outlook for the future of consumer neuroscience research.

METHODOLOGICAL APPROACHES IN NEUROSCIENCE

Many distinct methods are used in neuroscience to study neural processes underlying human behavior. Because each method has its own strengths and weaknesses, robust research findings typically arise from studies using several different techniques to shed light on the same question. A core defining precept is that neurophysiological methods measure responses of either the central or the peripheral nervous system. Most research in the nascent field of consumer neuroscience has availed of methods capturing changes, or manipulating activity, in the central nervous system, specifically, in the brain. However, physiological measures are hardly new to consumer research; even 30 years ago, researchers had measured skin conductance and eye movements to understand motivation and involvement in consumer behavior. Many peripheral physiological reactions can be readily measured, and used to make inferences about both neural functioning and correlated behavior. For example, pupil dilation is correlated with mental effort; blood pressure, skin conductance, and heart rate are correlated with anxiety, sexual arousal, mental concentration, and other motivational states; and emotional states can be reliably measured by coding facial expressions and recording movements of facial muscles.

Recent technological advances in measuring and manipulating brain activity allow us to observe in real time the neural processes under-lying consumer decision making via functional brain imaging techniques. Most brain imaging research involves within-subjects comparisons of people performing different tasks; an "exper-imental" task (A) and a "control" task (B). The difference between changes in brain activity measured during A and B indicates parts of the brain that are differentially activated by A (this is often referred to as the "subtraction approach"). One of the oldest imaging methods, EEG, measures electrical activity on the brain's surface using electrodes attached to the skull. EEG records timing of activity very precisely (resolution about 1 ms), but spatial resolution is poor, so that localizations when recording brain activity in subcortical areas that are small (e.g., the amygdala) can be problematic.

Positron emission topography (PET) is a newer technique that records positron emissions after a weakly radioactive blood injection. It does not measure brain activity directly, but rather metabolic changes linked to differentials in brain activity. PET offers better spatial resolution than EEG, but poorer temporal resolution and, because of rapid radioactive decay, it is limited to shorter tasks. However, PET usually requires averaging over fewer trials than fMRI, the method most widely used in consumer neuroscience. fMRI measures local changes in the ratio of oxygenated to deoxygenated hemoglobin. This ratio tracks neural activity because the brain effectively "overshoots" in providing oxygenated blood to active parts of the brain. Oxygenated blood has different magnetic properties than deoxygenated blood, giving rise to the signal picked up by fMRI (the so-called blood-oxygen-dependent-level, or BOLD, signal). Unfortunately, the signal-to-noise ratio of fMRI is, to date, fairly poor, so drawing tight inferences requires repeated sampling and many trials.

Yet another approach is single neuron recording, which tracks smaller scale neural activity (by contrast, fMRI measures activity of circuits consisting of thousands of neurons). In single neuron recordings, tiny electrodes are inserted into the brain, each measuring the firing of one specific neuron. Since these electrodes can damage neurons, the method is restricted to animal and special human populations, for therapeutic reasons (e.g., epileptic patients undergoing neurosurgery). Owing to its experimental use on animals, single neuron measurement has so far shed far more light on basic emotional and motivational processes than on higher-level ones, such as cognitive control. Regardless, the great body of extant research in neurobiology based on animal work (e.g., in rats and nonhuman primates) can directly inform theorizing in consumer neuroscience. Owing to functional and structural similarities in human and animal brains, the "animal model" has proved highly useful in the past, the main difference being a cortex enfolding the mammalian brain responsible for higher cognitive functions. Thus, owing to partial functional overlaps in subcortical areas, studying lower level processes, such as

motivational signals during simple decision making, is also informative for understanding human decision making. An advantage of animal work is the ability to perform manipulations (e.g., stimulation) to make causal inferences, and also to allow single neuron recordings as direct measures of neuronal activity, which are not possible with fMRI or PET.

The oldest neuroscientific approach applied to understand human decision making, and among the cornerstones in decision neuroscience, is studying patient populations with brain lesions. Localized brain damage, often produced by accidents and strokes, and patients who underwent radical neurosurgical procedures, are an especially rich source of insights. If patients with known damage to area X perform a particular task more poorly than "normal" patients, this suggests that area X may be vital in performing that task. "Virtual lesions" can also be created by transcranial magnetic stimulation (TMS), which creates temporary local disruption to brain regions using magnetic field stimulations.

CONCEPTS AND PRELIMINARY FINDINGS

Consumer neuroscience evolved alongside wide-ranging developments in behavioral decision-making research and cognitive neuroscience, with the common goal to better understand various elements of consumers' evaluation and purchase decision processes (for a recent review, see Kenning and Plassmann, 2008). In consumer behavior research, neuroscience has received considerable attention for at least two reasons. First, neuroscience can be viewed as a new *methodological tool*, a "finer scalpel" to dissect decision-making processes without asking consumers directly for their thoughts, evaluations, or strategies. Second, neuroscience can be viewed as a source of *theory generation*, supplementing traditional ones from psychology and economics proper. Most of the remainder of this article is devoted to discussing these two perspectives.

Neuroscience as methodological tool. Methodological approaches in consumer research have tended to make heavy use of qualitative methods and survey measures to assess how experimental manipulations influence consumers' attitudes and behavior. This has served the field well, having led to a rich body of empirical data and cohesive theoretical foundations. When relying on stimulus-organism-response models from psychology, consumer researchers must, however, take certain "black-box" conceptualizations of brain processes on faith. This raises several caveats that neuroscience might help to address.

First, neuroscience measurements, though they may be intrinsically noisy, have a strong advantage over surveys and self-reports in regard to potential biases. Since neuroscientific methods measure brain activity and its correlates directly – rather than relying on what subjects tell us what they think of how they are thinking it – they may offer more reliable indices of certain variables important to consumer researchers. Consider research on emotions and their role in consumer decision making. Emotions play an important role in consumer research, but are notorious for being difficult to induce via clever experimental manipulation, owing to their partially unconscious nature and great response heterogeneity across subjects. Neuroscientific research suggests that we cleave the concept of emotion into two parts, emotional states that can be measured through physiological changes (such as autonomic and endocrine responses), and feelings, the subjective and largely ineffable experience of emotions (Bechara and Damasio, 2005). The emotional states themselves depend on basic (implicit) brain mechanisms, which are rarely available for conscious cognitive introspection. A similar division could well be made for motivational processes. Another general area where neuroscience may offer substantial measurement benefits concerns when consumers undertake rapid information processing (e.g., viewing a visually dense TV ad) or enacting speedy habitual choices (e.g., selecting which sort of eggs or milk to buy at the supermarket). For example, prior research that used steady state, visually evoked potentials (similar to EEG) to understand memory systems underlying ad recall found that changes in brain activity in certain frontal brain regions, while viewing TV ads, predict long-term memory for those ads. Habitual choices were investigated by Milosavljevic et al. (2009), whose subjects engaged in a fast perceptual choice task between very familiar food items, during which eye

positions were acquired with the help of an eye tracker. They found that subjects were able to make value-based choices (i.e., consistent with subjects' preferences) within "a blink of an eye" (as fast as 400 ms).

Second, some preliminary consumer research uses brain imaging to *validate marketing scales*. A guiding principle is that brain imaging is too costly a tool to squander on large-scale surveys, but could be used to ask the "right" questions to get at the underlying (neuro)psychological phenomena. For example, a recent study by Dietvorst et al. (2009) used fMRI to investigate neural activity in brain regions associated with "theory-of-mind" abilities (i.e., MPFC, temporo-parietal junction, temporal pole) in salespeople, combining it with surveys and other traditional methodologies to develop a new scale for assessing salespeople's interpersonal mentalizing skills.

Third, fortifying existing models of consumer decision-making with neuroscientific data may help them make *better predictions* about consumer behavior. An early effort in this direction is by Knutson et al. (2007), who combined neural and attitudinal measures to predict consumers' purchases. The authors decomposed the purchasing process into three steps – (i) viewing a product, (ii) viewing product and price information, (iii) pressing buttons to indicate whether one wishes to buy the product at the end of the experiment – and investigated neural correlates of the preference formation stages (i, ii) and the price processing stage (ii). They found that product preference correlated positively with activity changes in, amongst other areas, the nucleus accumbens (NAcc), a region thought to be involved in reward prediction mechanisms, and that net value (WTP-price) correlated positively with activity changes in the medial prefrontal cortex (MPFC), anterior cingulate cortex (ACC), and frontopolar cortex. During the choice stage (iii), purchasing correlated negatively with activation in the bilateral insula, a region known to be involved in risk and pain processing, and positively with activity changes in the ventromedial prefrontal cortex (VMPFC), a region shown to encode preference signals at the time of choice. When distinguishing purchased-item trials from non-purchased-item trials, the authors found significant differences in NAcc activation during preference formation, and both MPFC and insula deactivation during price processing, in line with their *a priori* hypotheses. They then estimated brain activity in these three regions of interests and entered them as covariates in a logistic regression, along with self-report measures of preference and net value, to predict subsequent purchasing decisions. Results indicated that the full model (i.e., including the neural measures) was a significantly better predictor than one including only self-report measures.

This idea has been further developed by recent work combining behavioral decision-making research with machine-learning algorithms used in computational neuroscience. Computational neuroscience attempts to understand mental processing so as to allow a computer to mimic the way the brain functions during these processes. It has been used extensively to model simple learning algorithms in humans, among other areas. A recent first attempt to follow this path in consumer neuroscience (Tusche and Haynes, 2009) investigated how implicit brain processes could predict hypothetical purchasing decisions using multivariate decoding. They found that activity changes in the insula and the MPFC – specifically, while one group of subjects was exposed to various cars and asked how much they liked each (referred to by the authors as a condition where attention was shifted to cars, but not to purchasing) and while another group of subjects was asked to respond to a fixation cross that sometimes was displayed on a car background (referred to as condition with neither attention to cars nor to purchasing) – predicted at the end of the experiment whether or not subjects wished to purchase the cars in question.

A similar approach using eye-tracking data as physiological measures, coupled with models from computational neuroscience of vision, has started to be applied in advertising research; extensions relying on additional neurophysiological measures and more detailed computational models have recently been suggested by Milosavljevic and colleagues (e.g., Milosavljevic *et al.*, 2009). Indeed, studies of which brain areas (and/or other physiological measures, such as eye movements) are involved

during certain tasks could well be enhanced by the use of machine-learning algorithms for predictive analysis.

Fourth, consumer researchers have begun to apply neuroscientific methods to test the abilities of *competing behavioral theories* to explain various phenomena. Although this has been the most common application of neuroscientific methods in consumer research to date, space limitations allow for only a few selected studies to be discussed. An early example is Yoon *et al.* (2006), who used fMRI to test whether semantic judgments about products and persons are processed similarly, finding that, contrary to several extant theories in marketing, they tend not to be. Specifically, when judgments of persons activated the MPFC, a region that in prior studies had been implicated in person processing, judgments of brands differentially activated the left inferior frontal cortex, an area known to be associated with object processing. Plassmann *et al.* (2008) used fMRI to study whether information that creates expectations about how good a product should taste (e.g., its price or brand) does so via postconsumption rationalizing or via changes in actual taste perceptions. The authors found the latter – that changing the prices of otherwise identical wines affected brain regions involved in interpreting taste pleasantness while the wines were being sampled. Hedgcock and Rao (2009) used fMRI to investigate different theories of how consumers make trade-offs between goods or services that differ on the utilities for single attribute, but whose overall utilities are similar, that is, are judged as equally good or bad across multiple dimensions. Prior research had confirmed that "asymmetric dominance" can lead to consistent violations of the regularity axiom: that introducing an alternative that is normatively irrelevant (because it is dominated by the existing alternatives) to the choice set can *increase* the choice probability of a nearby, dominating option. The authors found that activity patterns differed across conditions (e.g., higher in the dorsolateral part of the prefrontal cortex and the ACC vs higher in the amygdala, MPFC, and parietal lobule), supporting the existence of trade-off aversion.

Weber *et al.* (2009) investigated whether increased happiness, as opposed to alternative explanations consistent with rational choice theory, can explain why consumers judge the value of money on the basis of actual amount of currency (nominal value) and not on the bundle of goods it can buy (real value), the so-called "money illusion." The authors found that brain areas thought to be involved in the anticipation and experience of reward, namely the ventral medial portions of the prefrontal cortex (PFC), showed higher activity changes when subjects displayed the money illusion. These findings were interpreted to suggest that the money illusion is based on changes in reward- or happiness-related neural activity, and thus cannot be fully accounted for by standard "homo economicus" theories of rational choice.

Two other recent papers investigated the neural basis of the "endowment effect": why we value goods we own more than (identical or equivalent) goods we do not. Vast theorizing has attended the endowment effect, ranging from a higher attraction to goods in one's possession (possibly owing to familiarity, or overestimating positive and underestimating negative features) to an aversion of losing what one tangibly possesses. Knutson *et al.* (2008) compared situations where subjects sold various products, bought different products, and made purchasing decisions for yet other products, all while their brains were scanned using fMRI. They found that, in both the selling and buying conditions, product preferences correlated with activity changes in the striatum (more precisely, the NAcc), a region known to be involved in reward prediction. The authors found no difference in NAcc activity in the selling versus buying conditions during what they refer to as the "product preference formation stage" (i.e., the point when subjects were exposed to items and prices), evidence against the theory that owned goods are more attractive or "sticky." In addition, the authors did not find activation in the insula (a region known to be involved in pain and risk processing, and so related to loss aversion) to correlate with product preference in selling versus buying trials. However, in "sell" trials specifically, individual differences in insula activity for preferred products *did* predict the extent to which subjects' indifference points for selling differed from the mean indifference point of buying (referred to by the authors as "endowment effect estimates"). The authors

offer this as evidence of some role for insula activity, and thus for loss aversion as antecedent to the endowment effect. The second paper, De Martino *et al.* (2009), used fMRI to investigate the neural basis of within-subjects differences in WTA (willingness-to-accept)–WTP (willingness-to-pay) for lottery tickets, when subjects either owned (i.e., acted as seller) or did not own (i.e., acted as buyer of) the ticket. On a behavioral level, they found a systematic increase in the minimum selling prices, as compared to maximum buying prices, for a ticket with the same expected value. On a neural level, they found that the magnitude of WTP (in the buying condition) was encoded in the medial OFC (orbitofrontal cortex), and the magnitude of WTA (in the selling condition) in the lateral OFC. As the medial OFC has been found to encode increases and decreases in WTP during purchasing decisions across several fMRI studies (Plassmann *et al.*, 2007), and the lateral OFC was found to be responsive to the price (and thus the net value) of a good and to the anticipation of monetary losses, the authors suggest this finding as in line with the theory that, in the selling condition, transactions were perceived as potential losses. Interestingly, Knutson *et al.* (2008) found a partly overlapping area to be involved in the value comparison portion of the preference formation stage (i.e., only that time interval when subjects are exposed to the buying/selling price, a moment when subjects potentially started to think of their WTP/WTA in monetary units, rather than overall product preference, and compare it to the price, thus computing utility of the offer, i.e., whether or not it is a "good deal"). They found that the subjects showed increased activity changes in the VMPFC (among other areas) when they perceived the offer to be a good deal. However, it seems that the lateral part of the PFC did not react in the same way as in the study by De Martino *et al.* (2009), which could be owing to the fact De Martino *et al.* looked at neural correlates of within-subjects endowment effects, whereas Knutson *et al.* studied between-subject effects.

Of special note is that De Martino *et al.* (2009) also computed the difference between a "context-free" subjective value measure and a (either buying or selling) "context–biased" one, and found the bilateral ventral striatum to correlate with increasing deviations from the unbiased value in the selling condition and decreasing deviations in the buying condition. The authors interpret this finding as evidence for the fact that the ventral striatum tracks the magnitude to which the subject's stated price deviated from the subject's true, unbiased value of the ticket in the selling and buying condition (i.e., reference dependent values) similar to a reward prediction error signal. Taken together, the findings of these two studies suggest that the endowment effect is related to negative emotional signals in the brain before and during the actual experience of endowment effects, supporting the loss aversion hypothesis consistent with prospect theory.

Neuroscience in Consumer Behavior Theory Generation. Consumer researchers have now begun to base hypotheses directly on *theories from neuroscience*. A recent example is Wadhwa *et al.* (2008), who investigated the impact of food sampling on subsequent consumer behavior, and compared two *a priori* hypotheses: the first – concordant with marketing practitioners, health experts, and much folk wisdom – that sampling a food will lead to lower subsequent consumption, and a second, rival hypothesis based on physiological theories of "reverse-alliesthesia," that as drive states affect the incentive value of relevant rewarding stimuli, a consumption cue high in incentive value (such as sampling a food) can strengthen drive states like hunger and, thereby, lead to an increase in the urge to engage in reward-seeking behaviors (such as eating more, or increasing other consumption-related behaviors). A series of behavioral experiments support predictions arising from the notion of reverse-alliesthesia – sampling a food or beverage items high in incentive value can in fact make individuals more likely to engage in reward-seeking behaviors, independently from specific reward type. Specifically, sampling a drink high in incentive value (e.g., Hawaiian Punch) not only leads to increased consumption of other drinks (e.g., Pepsi), but also to consumers giving higher desirability ratings for hedonic food, hedonic nonfood, and on-sale items, compared with those who had not sampled the high-incentive drink. Subsequent studies by the same authors investigate how motivational behavior impacts goal striving. In particular, they argue that if experiencing a hedonic cue enhances subsequent reward-seeking behaviors, then the induced motivational drive is also likely to enhance pursuit of a subsequent goal (defined as a representation of an internal state associated with a desirable outcome). For example, experiencing a hedonic cue (e.g., being exposed to romantic pictures) is likely to make one persist longer on a subsequently adopted intellectual goal of solving anagrams. Thus, unlike much of the extant research that has focused on how factors related to the goal state (e.g., desirability) can influence its pursuit, the focus here is on how factors *unrelated* to the goal state (e.g., incidental brief experiences with hedonic cues) can enhance subsequent goal pursuit. The authors' hypotheses are based on neuroscientific evidence (in rats and humans) of how the dopamine system works, that is, any hedonic cue that leads to enhanced dopamine activity could also motivate behaviors aimed in pursuit of a subsequently adopted goal associated with a desirable outcome.

Can cognitive neuroscience benefit from consumer research? Having detailed why consumer researchers are increasingly interested in joining forces with neuroscientists, let us briefly suggest how they might repay the debt, that is, "what's in it for neuroscientists?" In neuroscience, a number of developments led to a "cognitive revolution" that set the stage for the field of *cognitive* neuroscience, specifically. One major concern in early neuroscientific work was that it was largely descriptive in nature, and led to multiple isolated theories resistant to integration into a general, normative theory. An important advance came via the introduction of signal detection theory, a first attempt to relate neuronal activity directly to behavior in the field of vision science. We believe it is possible that sophisticated *formal models* from decision science and economics might help cognitive neuroscience establish a body of normative theory regarding how different types of decisions are enacted in the brain. A similar approach is currently used in so-called "model-based fMRI" studies, which investigate neural correlates of decision–making variables by integrating models from economics and behavioral decision to aid in statistical data modeling.

Several pioneering neuroscientific studies on emotion and decision making were conducted using lesion patients, discovering impairments during simple economic decision-making tasks for patients with lesions specifically in the ventromedial portion of the PFC (for a review, see Bechara *et al.*, 2000). This represented something of a milestone for interdisciplinary work at the intersection of neuroscience, psychology and behavioral decision science, and stimulated a great deal of subsequent research. An opportunity for neuroscientists in this area is the possibility to combine the *wealth of empirical data* and *formal experimental design methods* from decades of work in behavioral decision science and studies on lesion patients. Although tasks have to be adapted to the specific requirements of patient work, experimental and empirical findings about observed behavior can be readily transferred to patient studies. This potential of behavioral decision research for neuroscience becomes slightly more complicated for brain imaging studies using fMRI, owing to the requirement for repeated measures. Nevertheless, behavioral protocols and empirical knowledge from behavioral decision science have greatly benefited the study of neural correlates of decision making. A prime example is a study of Plassmann *et al.* (2007) that used a design from behavioral economics, the Becker-de-Groot-Marchack auction, to sample trial-by-trial incentive compatible and nonhypothetical psychometric measures (here, economic preferences in the form of WTP bids) to correlate in real-time with repeated neurometric measures (here, changes in BOLD-signal). The authors found that activity in the medial orbitofrontal cortex and dorsolateral prefrontal cortex correlate with the magnitude of the subjects' WTP.

SUMMARY AND FUTURE DIRECTIONS

In this article we introduced the genesis, core concepts, and preliminary empirical findings of the nascent field of consumer neuroscience. The future of the field, and its eventual reception,

will depend on the insights and benefits it can generate in concert with its parent disciplines. We believe it will be crucial that researchers within the field of consumer neuroscience adopt a multimethod approach, including not only different neuroscientific tools but also traditional behavioral (laboratory) and field experiments, to transcend the limitations of mere correlational results subject to inverse inference and causation. Ideally, consumer neuroscience research will be able to link hypotheses about specific brain mechanisms (location, activation, direction, connectivity) to both unobservable intermediate variables (utilities, beliefs, goals, etc.) and observable behavior (such as choices), using a variety of different methodological approaches from neuroscience, statistical modeling, and social science proper.

Two emergent trends deserve special mention. First, computational, model-based consumer neuroscience studies will become increasingly crucial, as statistical approaches themselves become ever more sophisticated, from mapping functional connectivity to the use of multivariate statistics to decoding algorithms from computational neuroscience for predictive analysis. Second, a recent development of clear relevance to consumer neuroscience is the study of individual differences based on genetic information (often referred to as "imaging genetics"). Imaging genetics is the study of how genetic differences lead to individual differences in the morphology and functions of the brain, and thereby differences in behavior. The rapid proliferation of inexpensive, personalized genetic information should make such studies increasingly accessible and informative for consumer researchers.

The old saw goes that prediction is difficult, especially about the future. And so it is with consumer neuroscience, whose large time, financial, and learning-curve costs may appear to place it beyond the current reach of many consumer behavior researchers. We anticipate that the inevitable waning of these barriers over the coming decade will produce a flowering of interest in understanding the neural bases and correlates of consumer behavior, and encourage our fellow researchers to wade enthusiastically into this exciting, growing area of inquiry.

122   consumer well-being

See also *consumer decision making;consumer information processing;implicit consumer cognition*

Bibliography

Bechara, A. and Damasio, A.R. (2005) The somatic marker hypothesis: a neural theory of economic decision making. *Games and Economic Behavior*, **52**, 336–372.

Bechara, A., Tranel, D. and Damasio, H. (2000) Characterization of the decision-making deficit of patients with ventromedial prefrontal cortex lesions. *Brain*, **123** (11), 2189–2202.

De Martino, B., Kumaran, D., Holt, B., and Dolan, R.J. (2009) The neurobiology of reference-dependent value computation. *Journal of Neuroscience*, **29**, 3833–3842.

Dietvorst, R.C., Verbeke, W.J.M.I., Bagozzi, R.P. *et al.* (2009) A Sales Force– Specific Theory-of-Mind scale: tests of its validity by classical methods and functional magnetic resonance imaging. *Journal of Marketing Research*, **46** (5), 653–668.

Hedgcock, W. and Rao, A.R. (2009) Trade-off aversion as an explanation for the attraction effect: a functional magnetic resonance imaging study. *Journal of Marketing Research*, **46**, 1–13.

Kenning, P.H. and Plassmann, H. (2008) How neuroscience can inform consumer research. *IEEE Transactions on Neural Systems and Rehabilitation Engineering*, **16**, 532–538.

Knutson, B., Rick, S., Wimmer, G.E. *et al.* (2007) Neural predictors of purchases. *Neuron*, **53**, 147–156.

Knutson, B., Wimmer, G.E., Rick, S. *et al.* (2008) Neural antecedents of the endowment effect. *Neuron*, **58**, 814–822.

Milosavljevic, M., Huth, A., Rangel, A. and Koch, C. (2009) Ultra-rapid Consumer Choices. California Institute of Technology working paper.

Plassmann, H., O'Doherty, J. and Rangel, A. (2007) Orbitofrontal cortex encodes willingness to pay in everyday economic transactions. *Journal of Neuroscience*, **27**, 9984–9988.

Plassmann, H., O'Doherty, J., Shiv, B. and Rangel, A. (2008) Marketing actions can modulate neural representations of experienced pleasantness. *Proceedings of the National Academy of Sciences of the United States of America*, **105**, 1050–1054.

Shiv, B., Bechara, A., Levin, I. *et al.* (2005) Decision neuroscience. *Marketing Letters*, **16** (3–4), 375–386.

Tusche, A. and Haynes, J.D. (2009) Brain signals reveal implicit consumer choices. Neuroimage, Special Issue Proceedings of the Organization for Human Brain Mapping Conference.

Wadhwa, M., Shiv, B. and Nowlis, S.M. (2008) A bite to whet the reward appetite: the influence of sampling on reward-seeking behaviors. *Journal of Marketing Research*, **45**, 403–413.

Weber, B., Rangel, A., Wibral, M. and Falk, A. (2009) The medial prefrontal cortex exhibits money illusion. *Proceedings of the National Academy of Sciences of the United States of America*, **106**, 5025–5028.

Yoon, C., Gutchess, A.H., Feinberg, F. and Polk, T.A. (2006) A functional magnetic resonance imaging study of neural dissociations between brand and person judgments. *Journal of Consumer Research*, **33**, 31–40.

consumer well-being

Aaron Ahuvia, Crystal Scott, and Elif Izberk Bilgin

Early measures of consumer well-being (CWB) equated it with a person's quantity of consumption, such that the level of well-being in a society can be summarized by its gross domestic product (GDP) per capita. In the 1960s, this reliance on GDP came under criticism by the social indicators movement, which argued for a more holistic view of human well-being beyond GDP, by including factors such as health, education, and crime rates in measures of social progress (*see* SOCIETY, CULTURE, AND GLOBAL CONSUMER CULTURE). This focus on diversifying *objective* indicators of well-being beyond GDP was further augmented in the 1970s by large-scale survey research on *subjective* indicators of well-being (SWB), such as happiness and life satisfaction. Our knowledge of subjectively experienced aspects of CWB increased dramatically in the 1990s as the rapidly growing research in positive psychology and behavioral economics brought attention to subjective well-being in all domains of life.

Income is a good proxy of a person's overall consumption level, and hence a commonly used indicator of CWB. Income, and hence consumption, is strongly linked to objective measures of well-being such as health, longevity, and education. But the link between income and subjective indicators of well-being such as happiness is much weaker and more complex (Ahuvia, 2008a, 2008b). At very low income levels where basic human needs are not met, increases in income produce lasting improvements in happiness. And at all income levels, increases in income produce *short term* increases in happiness. However, at even moderate income levels where basic needs have been met, the relationship between income and *long term sustained* happiness is extremely weak. In general, studies show that differences in income explain between 2 and 5% of individual differences in SWB, thus leaving upward of 95% of the difference between individuals in SWB to be explained by other factors such as genetics, social relationships, and the way people think about the events in their lives.

Why does increased consumption among the nonpoor fail to produce much lasting happiness? Is the problem that consumption just does not work, or is it that most people are not consuming in the right way? Spending money has been shown to produce the most lasting happiness when the money is spent on (i) charitable donations (Dunn, Aknin, and Norton, 2008), (ii) things which help foster social relationships (Lyubomirsky, 2007), and (iii) experiences as opposed to physical objects (Van Boven and Gilovich, 2003), so long as the experience was purchased with the primary goal of acquiring a life experience. Apparently, watching television is not such an experience, as it is negatively associated with CWB (Frey, Benesch, and Stutzer, 2007). Finally, there is also evidence that a good way to turn money into happiness is not to spend it at all, as savings is a good psychic investment (Headey, Muffels, and Wooden, 2008).

CWB is not only influenced by how much people spend and how they spend it, but also by their general attitudes about consumption. Higher levels of materialism are associated with lower levels of SWB (Ahuvia and Wong, 2002). Furthermore, though close social relationships are strongly linked to SWB, just thinking about money puts people in a frame of mind in which they are less inclined to reach out to others or offer others their help (Vohs, Mead, and Goode, 2006).

Marketing, and in particular advertising, has inspired controversy around its relationship to CWB (Klein, 2002; Schor and Holt, 2000). Advocates for marketing stress its role in researching consumer needs and aligning production to meet those needs (*see* MARKETING'S CORPORATE RESPONSIBILITY and STAGES OF MARKET DEVELOPMENT). These advocates also emphasize the role of marketing in generating sales, and from them profits, employment, and the other benefits of a healthy economy. Finally, they argue that advertising increases CWB by providing consumers with needed information, and by enhancing the value consumers receive from products by investing the products with symbolic meanings (e.g., coolness, masculinity, etc.) which consumers find desirable. Critics of marketing, on the other hand, argue that marketing decreases CWB by increasing materialism, creating consumer desires in order to fill them, shifting consumers' priorities away from more rewarding nonconsumer activities, promoting racial and gender stereotypes, and promoting unrealistic norms for physical attractiveness or professional success which lead to disappointment and reduced SWB.

Bibliography

Ahuvia, A.C. (2008a) Wealth, consumption and happiness, in *The Cambridge Handbook of Psychology and Economic Behaviour* (ed. A. Lewis), Cambridge University Press, pp. 199–226.

Ahuvia, A.C. (2008b) If money doesn't make us happy, why do we act as if it does? *Journal of Economic Psychology*, **29** (4), 491–507.

Ahuvia, A.C. and Wong, N. (2002) Personality and values based materialism: their relationship and origins. *Journal of Consumer Psychology*, **12** (4), 389–402.

Dunn, E.W., Aknin, L.B., and Norton, M.I. (2008) Spending money on others promotes happiness. *Science*, **319** (5870), 1687–1688.

Frey, B.S., Benesch, C., and Stutzer, A. (2007) Does watching TV make us happy? *Journal of Economic Psychology*, **28** (3), 283–313.

Headey, B., Muffels, R., and Wooden, M. (2008) Money does not buy happiness: or does it? A reassessment based on the combined effects of wealth, income and consumption. *Social Indicators Research*, **87** (1), 65–82.

Klein, N. (2002) *No Logo*, Picador, New York.

Lyubomirsky, S. (2007) *The How of Happiness: A Scientific Approach to Getting the Life You Want*, Penguin, New York.

Schor, J.B. and Holt, D.B. (2000) *The Consumer Society Reader*, The New Press, New York.

Van Boven, L. and Gilovich, T. (2003) To do or to have? That is the question. *Journal of Personality and Social Psychology*, **85** (6), 1193–1202.

Vohs, K.D., Mead, N.L., and Goode, M.R. (2006) The psychological consequences of money. *Science*, **314** (5802), 1154–1156.

consumers' need for uniqueness

Ayalla A. Ruvio

Consumers often use possessions to differentiate themselves from other consumers. This tendency of using possessions to project a unique identity has been conceptualized as consumers' need for uniqueness (CNFU). The theoretical basis of CNFU is rooted in the more general theory of the need for uniqueness (NFU), which focuses on people's perceptions of and reactions to their similarity to others (Snyder and Fromkin, 1980). NFU theory postulates that individuals continuously evaluate their degree of similarity or dissimilarity to others and act on such evaluations. Individuals will normally attempt to maintain moderate uniqueness from others and will actively avoid being too similar or too different from others. High levels of similarity or dissimilarity will result in unpleasant feelings, reducing the individuals' self-esteem (Fromkin, 1972), and will trigger emotional and behavioral reactions. However, the magnitude of such reactions will vary across individuals and situations and will be determined by the individuals' level of NFU. The stronger it is, the greater the individuals' sensitivity to similarity and the more different from others they will want to be (Fromkin, 1972). However, the desire for uniqueness does not ignore social norms and is constrained by the need for social assimilation and approval (Snyder and Fromkin, 1980).

Building on the notion that possessions are an extension of one's POSSESSIONS AND SELF, CNFU reflects the individual's propensity for acquiring, using, and disposing of possessions in order to construct and maintain a unique self and social image (Tian, Bearden and Hunter, 2001). Tian, Bearden and Hunter (2001) conceptualized CNFU as a behavioral construct with three facets. Creative choice counterconformity captures the individual's tendency to use socially acceptable products and brands in order to create a distinct personal image (Snyder and Fromkin, 1980). Unpopular choice counterconformity postulates that individuals who seek to differentiate themselves from others may do so by using products that are not entirely within group norms, and will risk social disapproval (Tian, Bearden and Hunter 2001). Finally, avoidance of similarity reflects the individual's intentional avoidance of popular and commonly used products and brands. Such individuals lose interest in, avoid purchasing, or discontinue using those brands when they become commonplace (Tian, Bearden and Hunter, 2001). Tian and her colleagues (2001) developed a 31-item scale to measure the enduring trait of CNFU. A shorter 12-item version was later validated by Ruvio, Shoham and Makovec-Brencic (2008) in different cultural settings.

Empirical studies established that individuals will tend to display their uniqueness more in identity-relevant domains and in situations that pose a threat to their sense of distinctiveness (Berger and Heath, 2007). CNFU was also found to be related to a variety of consumption behaviors such as shopping innovativeness (*see* CONSUMER INNOVATIVENESS), opinion leadership and market mavenism, optimum stimulation level, status consumption, individualism, choice of shopping venues, preferences for unique exterior product design, and preferences for scarce and customized products (e.g. Clark and Goldsmith, 2005; Ruvio, Shoham and Makovec-Brencic, 2008; Tian, Bearden and Hunter, 2001).

Bibliography

Berger, J. and Heath, C. (2007) Where consumers diverge from others: identity-signaling and product domains. *Journal of Consumer Research*, **34**, 121–134.

Clark, R.A. and Goldsmith, R.E. (2005) Market Mavens: psychological influences. *Psychology and Marketing*, **22** (4), 289–312.

Fromkin, H.L. (1972) Feelings of interpersonal undistinctiveness: an unpleasant affective state. *Journal of Experimental Research in Personality*, **6** (2–3), 178–182.

Ruvio, A., Shoham, A. and Makovec-Brencic, M. (2008) Consumers' need for uniqueness: short-form scale development and cross-cultural validation. *International Marketing Review*, **25** (1), 33–53.

Snyder, C.R. and Fromkin, H.L. (1980) *Uniqueness: The Human Pursuit of Difference*, Plenum, New York.

Tian, K.T., Bearden, W.O. and Hunter, G.L. (2001) Consumers' need for uniqueness: scale development and validation. *Journal of Consumer Research*, **28** (3), 50–66.

cross-cultural psychology of consumer behavior

Minkyung Koo and Sharon Shavitt

INTRODUCTION

As new global markets emerge, and existing markets become increasingly segmented along ethnic or subcultural lines, the need to market effectively to consumers who have different cultural values has never been more important. Thus, it is no surprise that in the last several years, culture has rapidly emerged as a central focus of research in consumer behavior. This development followed on the heels of extensive social psychological research on culture, which provided a strong theoretical foundation for the consumer-behavior studies that followed.

What is culture?   Culture consists of shared knowledge that provides the standards for perceiving, believing, evaluating, feeling, comm-unicating, and acting among those who share a language, a historical period, and a geographic location. As a psychological construct, culture can be studied in multiple ways – across nations, across ethnic groups within nations, across individuals within nations (focusing on cultural orientation), and across situations through the priming of cultural values. The dimensions of individualism versus collectivism, independence versus interdependence, and analysis versus holism have in recent years received significant research attention. This attention has resulted in a great number of studies revealing both antecedents and consequences of the cultural differences between East Asian and North American cultures. As discussed subsequently, regardless of how culture is studied, cultural distinctions have important implications for advertising content, persuasiveness of appeals, consumer motivation, and consumer judgment processes.

Article scope and overview   This article reviews major cultural constructs and theoretical implications of cultural differences in consumer information processing, judgments, and choices. Our review is necessarily selective, focusing on findings specific to the consumer domain rather than providing a general review of cultural differences (for an excellent general review, see Wyer, Chiu, and Hong, 2009). It should also be noted that because of space limitations, this article does not cover some major topics in cross-cultural consumer behaviors such as self-regulation and risk-taking, as well as methodological issues such as response styles and biases (Shavitt, Lee, and Torelli, 2009; Shavitt, Torelli, and Wong, 2009).

In this article, the cultural constructs of individualism/collectivism and the independent/interdependent self-construals associated with them are given special attention because extensive research has demonstrated the implications of these distinctions for processes and outcomes relevant to consumer behavior. The most recent refinements to these constructs are briefly reviewed in an attempt to identify additional cultural variables likely to enhance the understanding of cross-cultural consumer behavior. We also review cultural differences in thinking styles as a major emerging cultural distinction and focus on their implications for consumer-behavior research. Finally, we close with a review of cross-cultural differences in advertising content and the persuasiveness of appeals.

KEY CONSTRUCTS AND DIMENSIONS OF CULTURE

Individualism versus collectivism.   The constructs of *individualism* and *collectivism* represent the most broadly used dimensions of cultural variability for cross-cultural comparison. In individualistic cultures, people value independence from others and subordinate the goals of their in-groups to their own personal goals. In collectivistic cultures, in contrast, individuals value interdependent relationships to others and subordinate their personal goals to those of their in-groups (Hofstede, 1980; Triandis, 1995). The key distinction involves the extent to which one defines the self in relation to others. In individualistic cultural contexts, people tend to have an independent self-construal whereby the self is defined as autonomous and unique. In collectivistic cultural contexts, by contrast, people tend to have an interdependent self-construal whereby the self is seen as inextricably and fundamentally embedded within a larger social network of roles and relationships (Markus and Kitayama, 1991).

National cultures that celebrate the values of independence, such as the United States, Canada, Germany, and Denmark, are typically categorized as individualistic societies in which an independent self-construal is common. In contrast, cultures that nurture the values of fulfilling one's obligations over one's own personal wishes, including most East Asian and Latin American countries, are categorized as collectivistic societies in which an interdependent self-construal is common (Hofstede, 1980; Triandis, 1995).

A large body of research in psychology has demonstrated the many implications of individualism/collectivism and independent/interdependent self-construals for social perception and social behavior (Markus and Kitayama, 1991; Triandis, 1995). These findings indicate consistently that individualists and people with an independent self-construal are oriented toward products and experiences that promote achievement and autonomy, offer personal benefits, and enable expression of one's distinctive qualities. On the other hand, collectivists and people with an interdependent self-construal are oriented toward products and experiences that allow one to avoid negative outcomes, maintain harmony and strong social connections with others, and dutifully fulfill social roles.

Although a given self-construal can be more chronically accessible in a particular culture, cultures generally provide sufficient experiences with independent and interdependent views of the self to allow either type of self-construal to be primed (Oyserman, Coon, and Kemmelmeier, 2002; Oyserman and Lee, 2007). Numerous studies have established that these activated self-views impact judgments in ways that parallel cross-national differences (Shavitt, Lee, and Torelli, 2009), for instance, by activating distinct self goals (Lalwani and Shavitt, 2009). People in general, and especially bicultural people, can readily switch back and forth between independent and interdependent cultural frames in response to their contexts. For instance, Lau-Gesk (2003) found that independent (interdependent) self-construals were temporarily activated when bicultural consumers were exposed to individually focused (interpersonally focused) appeals.

In sum, the distinctions between individualistic and collectivistic societies, and independent and interdependent self-construals, are crucial to the understanding of cross-cultural differences in consumer behavior. The studies to be reviewed here offer extensive evidence that these cultural classifications have fundamental implications for consumption-related outcomes.

Refined individualism versus collectivism. The conceptualizations of individualism and collectivism, and independence/interdependence, have historically been broad and multidimensional, summarizing a host of differences in focus of attention, self-definitions, motivations, emotional connections to in-groups, as well as belief systems and behavioral patterns (Hofstede, 1980; Oyserman, Coon, and Kemmelmeier, 2002). In addition, recent studies have proposed useful refinements to these broader cultural categories (Shavitt, Lee, and Torelli, 2009). These studies suggest that the nature and meaning of individualism and collectivism varies across gender and ethnic lines, as well as across family groupings and institutions. Although the breadth of the individualism-collectivism constructs lends integrative strengths, research indicates that further refinements of these categories can enhance the prediction of consumer behavior.

The horizontal/vertical distinction. Within the individualism-collectivism framework, Triandis *et al.* (Triandis, 1995; Triandis and Gelfand, 1998) have recently introduced a further distinction between societies that are *horizontal* (valuing equality) and those that are *vertical* (emphasizing hierarchy), and a scale to measure these orientations at the individual level. The horizontal/vertical distinction emerges from the observation that American or British individualism differs from, say, Norwegian or Danish individualism in much the same way that Japanese or Korean collectivism differs from the collectivism of the Israeli kibbutz. Specifically, in vertical individualist (VI) societies (e.g., United States and Great Britain), people strive to become distinguished and acquire status via competition (Shavitt, Torelli and Wong, 2009); whereas in horizontal individualist (HI) cultural contexts (e.g., Sweden and Norway), people value uniqueness but are not especially interested in becoming distinguished and achieving high status (Nelson and Shavitt, 2002). In contrast, in vertical collectivistic (VC) societies (e.g., Korea and Japan), people emphasize the subordination of their goals to those of their in-groups, submit to the will of authority, and support competitions between their in-groups and out-groups. Finally, in horizontal collectivist (HC) cultural contexts (e.g., exemplified historically by the Israeli Kibbutz), people see themselves as similar to others, and emphasize shared goals and sociability, but instead of submitting to authority, their view of power focuses on benevolence and helping others (Shavitt, Lee, and Torelli, 2009).

However, the modal comparisons in consumer research are between the United States (VI) and any of a number of Pacific Rim countries (VC). This means that much of what is known about consumer behavior in individualistic and collectivistic societies reflects vertical forms of these syndromes and may not generalize, for example, comparisons between Sweden (HI) and Israel (HC) or other sets of horizontal cultures. As an example, conformity in product choice, as examined by Kim and Markus (1999), may be a tendency specific to VC cultures, in which deference to authority and to in-group wishes is stressed. Much lower levels of conformity may be observed in HC cultures, which emphasize sociability but not deference (Triandis and Gelfand, 1998). Thus, differences in consumers' conformity between Korea (VC) and the United States (VI) may not characterize broad individualism-collectivism differences, because levels of product conformity in

HC contexts might not exceed those in HI contexts.

Indeed, several recent studies of this horizontal/vertical cultural distinction have provided evidence for its value as a predictor of new consumer psychology phenomena and as a basis for refining the understanding of known phenomena (Shavitt *et al.*, 2006). For instance, Lalwani, Shavitt, and Johnson (2006) showed that differences in the self-presentational responses observed for individualists and collectivists are mediated at the individual level by the horizontal but not the vertical versions of these cultural orientations. This suggests that culturally linked self-presentational efforts reflect distinct goals of being seen as self-reliant and capable (valued in HI contexts) versus sociable and benevolent (valued in HC contexts).

Further evidence for the value of the horizontal-vertical distinction comes from a study of country-of-origin effects. Gürhan-Canli and Maheswaran (2000) demonstrated that the tendency to favor products from one's own country over foreign products emerged more strongly in Japan (a VC culture) than in the United States (a VI culture). Mediation analyses using individual consumers' self-rated cultural values further indicated that only the vertical aspect of individualism and collectivism accounted for the country-of-origin effects in Japan. In other words, the collectivistic tendency to favor one's own country's products appeared to be driven by cultural values that stress hierarchy, competition, and deference to in-group wishes, not by values that stress interdependence more generally.

In line with this, as noted earlier, research suggests that mental representations of power in terms of status and competition versus benevolence differ reliably between vertical and horizontal cultural backgrounds and orientations. These differences impact consumer information processing and the interpretation of power-related stimuli (Shavitt, Lee, and Torelli, 2009). Finally, content analyses of magazine advertisements in several countries suggested that status-oriented themes of hierarchy, luxury, prestige, and distinction were generally more prevalent in societies presumed to have vertical cultural profiles (e.g., Korea, Russia) than a horizontal cultural profile (Denmark) (Shavitt et al., 2006).

Culture and thinking styles.   East Asian and North American cultural differences have been well documented in social psychological research, especially in terms of the differences in individualistic-collectivistic values and independent-interdependent self-systems (Markus and Kitayama, 1991). Many of these cross-cultural studies of consumer behavior have provided evidence that advertising (such as magazine ads, Internet advertising, and TV commercials) from Western cultures is in general more individualistic and less collectivistic than advertising from Asian cultures (Morling and Lamoreaux, 2008), and that consumers from Western cultures are more likely to be persuaded by individualistic ads and those from East Asian cultures are more likely to be persuaded by collectivistic ads (Han and Shavitt, 1994). However, relatively little research has been done on cross-cultural differences in consumers' thinking orientations. The following section provides a general review of cultural differences in thinking styles in addition to the findings of relevant studies of consumer behavior and advertising effects.

Analytic versus holistic thinking.   Broadly speaking, Westerners tend to adopt an analytic thinking style that emphasizes the independence of individual objects, whereas East Asians tend to adopt a holistic view emphasizing that the world is composed of interrelated elements (Nisbett et al., 2001). The analytic style of Westerners and the holistic style of East Asians have been demonstrated in various cognitive domains such as attention, causal reasoning, perception of change, tolerance of contradiction, and categorization.

The analytic style of attention is field independent (mainly oriented toward an object itself), whereas holistic attention is field dependent (focused on the relationship between objects and/or the field in which they are embedded) (Nisbett et al., 2001). This difference in the orientation of attention is also seen in the way East Asians and Westerners perceive and explain social events. East Asians tend to assume that each element in the world is somehow intertwined, and thus an event or object can be understood only in the context of the whole set of relevant factors. By contrast, Westerners tend to explain a certain event in terms of direct causal links, thereby considering fewer reasons than East Asians, who tend to consider a broader set of reasons, regardless of their relevance to the event (Choi et al., 2003).

Furthermore, in explaining causality of a social event, analytic thinkers tend to focus on the internal dispositions of an actor, whereas holistic thinkers tend to consider a broader set of reasons (including both dispositional and contextual information) and are therefore less likely to attribute an outcome to an actor's internal characteristics (Nisbett et al., 2001). This has implications for brand judgments, as well. Monga and John (2007) found that negative publicity influences analytic (vs. holistic) thinkers more heavily, and thus changes their beliefs about a brand to a greater degree because analytic thinkers are less likely to consider contextual information, and thus are more likely to attribute negative product information to the brand.

From the analytic perspective, objects exist independently, and thus the essence of the objects is stable over time. This assumption promotes a linear perception of change in which no drastic deviation is expected in the pattern of stability or change of a phenomenon (Nisbett, 2003). By contrast, the holistic view of the world assumes that objects are interrelated, and therefore it is less likely that a phenomenon will remain stable over time. This perspective results in a cyclic perception in which people tend to predict fluctuating trends for an event. For example, in predicting future stock-market trends and making investment decisions, Canadians are more likely to make judgments based on recent trends than are Chinese people; thus, when compared to the Chinese, Canadians are more willing to buy stocks when they are in an increasing trend and less willing to buy when stock prices are decreasing (Ji, Zhang, and Guo, 2008).

The cyclic perception of change and expectation of instability prevalent among East Asians renders a Yin-Yang belief that a characteristic of an object can potentially transform into its opposite. Consequently, East Asians tend to hold a dialectical perception in which apparently opposing concepts can simultaneously be true and can peacefully coexist (Nisbett *et al.*, 2001). When confronted with opposing propositions, East Asians tend to resolve contradictions by choosing a middle ground, whereas Westerners to rely on formal logic in resolving contradictions by choosing one of the opposing propositions. For example, US consumers tend to resolve incongruities with an attenuation strategy in which one piece of information is favored over another inconsistent piece of information. In contrast, Hong Kong Chinese consumers tend to follow an additive strategy in which both pieces of information are combined to influence judgments (Aaker and Sengupta, 2000).

East Asians and Westerners also perceive conflicting emotions in different ways. For example, Bagozzi, Wong, and Yi (1999) showed that Chinese tend to hold a dialectical perception that pleasant and unpleasant emotions can be experienced at the same time. Thus, their frequency judgment for pleasant emotions is positively correlated with their frequency judgment for unpleasant emotions. By contrast, this study found that for Americans the perceived frequency of pleasant emotions is inversely correlated with the perceived frequency of unpleasant emotions. Schimmack, Oishi, and Diener (2002) analyzed 38 nationalities and demonstrated that this cultural difference results from dialectical thinking, not from a difference in individualistic-collectivistic values. Moreover, Williams and Aaker (2002) demonstrated that opposing emotions (e.g., both happiness and sadness) in persuasion appeals elicit more positive attitudes among Asian Americans than among European Americans.

Westerners pay more attention to individual objects and attribute causality to them, whereas East Asians focus more on the field. Westerners are more accustomed to formulating rules that govern internal properties of objects and tend to categorize things by applying those rules. In contrast, East Asians organize objects on the basis of their relationship to other objects or to the field (Nisbett, 2003), and therefore they tend to categorize objects according to their overall similarities. Thus, when presented with pictures of a panda, a monkey, and a banana, East Asians tend to categorize the monkey and banana together based on the relationship between the two, whereas Westerners tend to categorize the

panda and monkey into one group based on the traits that characterize them (Ji, Zhang, and Nisbett, 2004).

Cultural differences in the way people categorize objects (rule/trait-based vs. similarity/relationship-based) also appear in the way they organize and store brand information. For example, Ng and Houston (2006) showed that Americans are less likely to retrieve brand exemplars (i.e., specific products or subcategories) than brand beliefs (i.e., general descriptive or evaluative thoughts), whereas the reverse was the case for Singaporeans. These results emerged from an analytic tendency to focus on "global beliefs" abstracted from prior product experiences and a holistic tendency to focus on contextual and incidental details about the product. Similarly, Monga and John (2008) found that, compared to Americans, Indians tend to perceive a higher degree of fit between a parent brand (e.g., Kodak) and its brand extension (e.g., Kodak filing cabinet, Kodak greeting cards), and to evaluate the brand extension more positively. This result reflects Indians' holistic tendency to base their judgments more heavily on the relationships between brand extensions and parent brands than do their American counterparts.

A variety of methods and techniques have been developed to measure cultural differences in thinking styles (Choi, Koo, and Choi, 2007; Ji, Zhang, and Nisbett, 2004; Monga and John, 2007), including responses to cognitive tasks, scenarios and questions, physiological measures, a scale, and analyses of various cultural products. Furthermore, priming an independent versus interdependent view of self has also been found to promote analytic and holistic modes of thinking, respectively. For example, people primed with an independent self-view were more likely to focus on a focal object and thus were better at finding an embedded figure by separating the figure from its background than were those primed with an interdependent self-view (see Oyserman and Lee, 2007, for a review).

Additional dimensions. Numerous other cultural distinctions deserve further attention in consumer research. A focus upon these relatively under-researched constructs as antecedents may allow for broadening the range of cultural differences beyond those currently investigated. For instance, Schwartz's (1992) circumplex structure of values, which is highly robust cross-nationally, parallels the HI, VI, HC, VC typology and offers a particularly detailed and comprehensive basis for classification. In his large-scale studies of work values, Hofstede (1980) derived three other dimensions of cultural variation in addition to individualism: *power distance* (acceptance of power inequality in organizations, a construct conceptually relevant to the vertical/horizontal distinction), *uncertainty avoidance* (the degree of tolerance for ambiguity or uncertainty about the future), and *masculinity/femininity* (preference for achievement and assertiveness versus modesty and nurturing relationships). Indeed, individualism was the second dimension identified by Hofstede (1980), whereas power distance emerged as the first dimension. A few marketing-oriented studies have employed Hofstede's nation-level classifications (Shavitt, Lee, and Torelli, 2009), but more potential remains for identifying consequences for consumer judgments and behaviors. For instance, uncertainty avoidance has been conceptualized as a syndrome related to anxiety, rule orientation, need for security, and deference to experts (Hofstede, 1980). As such, one might speculate that the level of uncertainty avoidance in a culture will predict the tendency for advertisements to use fear appeals or appeals to safety and security, and the tendency for advertisements to employ expert spokespersons. Differences along this cultural dimension may also predict patterns in the diffusion of product innovations, particularly innovations whose purchase entails a degree of risk.

CULTURE AND PERSUASIVE APPEALS

Most research on cultural influences on judgment and persuasion has examined the implications of individualism/collectivism or independent/interdependent self-construals. In general, the findings suggest that the prevalence or the persuasiveness of a given type of appeal matches the cultural value orientation of the society (Shavitt, Lee, and Torelli, 2009). For instance, appeals to individuality, personal benefits, and achievement are usually more prevalent and persuasive in individualistic compared to collectivistic cultures, whereas appeals to group benefits, harmony, and conformity are usually more prevalent and persuasive in collectivistic compared to individualistic cultures. Such evidence for "cultural matching" in the nature of appeals has been followed by studies examining the distinct psychological processes driving persuasion across cultures. These studies suggest that culture can affect how people process and interpret product-related information. It can determine the type of information that is weighed more heavily for making judgments (e.g., product attributes vs other consumers' opinions). However, brand and product characteristics can constrain the role of cultural variables in information processing and persuasion, with some brands and products serving as stronger carriers of cultural values (Shavitt, Torelli and Wong, 2009).

Cultural differences in the content of message appeals. Cross-cultural content analyses of advertisements can yield valuable evidence about distinctions in cultural values. For instance, American advertisers and consumer researchers often assume that consumer learning about the brand precedes other marketing effects, such as liking and buying the brand. Thus, advertisements that attempt to teach the consumer about the brand are typical in the United States, although other types of advertisements are also used.

In contrast, as Miracle (1987) suggested, the typical goal of advertisements in Japan appears very different. There, advertisements tend to focus on "making friends" with the audience and showing that the company understands their feelings. The assumption is that consumers will buy once they feel familiar with and have a sense of trust in the company. Because Japan, Korea, and other Pacific Rim countries are collectivist cultures that tend toward implicit and indirect communication practices (Triandis, 1995), Miracle suggested that the mood and tone of commercials in these countries will be particularly important in establishing good feelings about the advertiser. Several studies have supported these notions, showing that advertisements in Japan and Korea, compared to those in the United States, rely more on symbolism, mood, and aesthetics and less on direct approaches such as brand comparisons (Shavitt, Lee, and Torelli, 2009). The ads may be equally informative about the brand across cultures. It is the type of appeal that will vary.

For instance, a content analysis of magazine advertisements revealed that in Korea, compared to the United States, advertisements are more focused on family well-being, interdependence, group goals, and harmony, whereas they are less focused on self-improvement, ambition, personal goals, independence, and individuality (Han and Shavitt, 1994). However, as one might expect, the nature of the advertised product moderated these effects. Cultural differences emerged strongly only for products that tend to be purchased and used along with other persons (e.g., groceries, cars). Products that do not tend to be shared (e.g., health and beauty aids, clothing) are promoted more in terms of personal, individualistic benefits in both countries.

Paralleling the overall cross-national differences, a content analysis by Kim and Markus (1999) indicated that Korean advertisements, compared to US advertisements, were characterized by more conformity themes (e.g., respect for collective values and beliefs) and fewer uniqueness themes (e.g., rebelling against collective values and beliefs). Website content in Eastern and Western countries also appears to differ in the emphasis on individual versus collective activities (Shavitt, Lee, and Torelli, 2009).

Finally, it is important to note that, in countries experiencing rapid economic growth, advertising content does not necessarily reflect existing cultural values, instead promoting new, aspirational values such as individuality and modernity. For instance, in China, in recent years, westernized ad appeals are increasingly common. Appeals to youth/modernity, individuality/independence, and technology are especially salient in Chinese advertisements that target the younger generation (Zhang and Shavitt, 2003). Similarly, during a period of rapid transition in South Korea's economy (1968–1998), content analysis of advertisements revealed substantial shifts toward individualistic, modernity-oriented appeals (Han and Shavitt, 2005).

Cultural differences in judgment and persuasion. Research suggests that the persuasiveness of appeals may mirror the cultural differences in their prevalence. An experiment by Han and Shavitt (1994) showed that appeals to individualistic values (e.g., "Solo cleans with a softness that you will love") were more persuasive in the United States and appeals to collectivistic values (e.g., "Solo cleans with a softness that your family will love") were more persuasive in Korea. Again, however, this effect was much more evident for products that are shared (laundry detergent, clothes iron) than for those that are not (chewing gum, running shoes).

Zhang and Gelb (1996) found a similar pattern in the persuasiveness of individualistic versus collectivistic appeals in an experiment conducted in the United States and China. Moreover, this effect appeared to be moderated by whether the advertised product is socially visible (camera) versus privately used (toothbrush). Finally, Wang and Mowen (1997) showed in a US sample that individual differences in separateness/connectedness self-schema (i.e., the degree to which one views the self as independent of or interconnected with important others) predicts attitudes toward individualistic versus collectivistic ad appeals for a credit card. Thus, cultural orientation and national culture have implications for the effectiveness of appeals. However, such cultural differences would only be anticipated for those products or uses that are relevant to both personal and group goals.

Cultural differences in persuasion are also revealed in the diagnosticity of certain types of information. For instance, Aaker and Maheswaran (1997) showed that consensus information regarding other consumers' opinions is not treated as a heuristic cue by Hong Kong Chinese (as it is in the United States) but is instead perceived and processed as diagnostic information. Thus, collectivists resolve incongruity in favor of consensus information, not brand attributes. This would be expected in a culture that stresses conformity and responsiveness to others' views. On the other hand, cues whose (low) diagnosticity is not expected to vary cross-culturally (e.g., number of attributes presented) elicit similar heuristic processing in the United States and Hong Kong.

Finally, because cognitive associations with power vary with horizontal and vertical cultural orientations and with ethnicity, as noted earlier, Torelli *et al.*, found differences in the interpretive processes and mindsets triggered when power is salient. Specifically, people whose cultural orientation predisposes a status-oriented view of power activate cognitive processes that facilitate defending their power, such as reasserting control by confirming prior stereotypes about a brand. In contrast, people whose cultural orientation predisposes a benevolence-oriented view of power activate cognitive processes that facilitate helping others, such as by forming accurate, careful impressions of brands (Shavitt, Torelli and Wong, 2009).

Conclusions

As marketing efforts are increasingly globalized, understanding cross-cultural consumer behavior has become a key focus of consumer research. In recent years, research in consumer behavior has addressed a broadening set of cross-cultural issues and dimensions. Research has provided an enhanced understanding of the relations between culture and self-construal, motivation, thinking style, and consumer persuasion. Research has also begun to address the psychological mechanisms underlying cross-cultural differences in consumer judgments, and the products and contexts for which these differences are most likely to be observed. Understanding cultural differences has become crucial for effective marketing and advertising. In future research, it will be important to further distinguish cultural similarities and differences in consumer judgments, identify within-culture or subgroup differences that parallel between-culture differences, and explore their rich implications in consumer behavior.

Acknowledgments

Preparation of this article was supported by Grant #1R01HD053636-01A1from the National Institutes of Health, Grant #0648539 from the National Science Foundation, and Grant #63842 from the Robert Wood Johnson Foundation to Sharon Shavitt.

Bibliography

Aaker, J.L. and Maheswaran, D. (1997) The effect of cultural orientation on persuasion. *Journal of Consumer Research*, 24 (3), 315–328.

Aaker, J.L. and Sengupta, J. (2000) Addivity versus attenuation: the role of culture in the resolution of information incongruity. *Journal of Consumer Psychology*, 9 (2), 67–82.

Bagozzi, R.P., Wong, N., and Yi, Y. (1999) The role of culture and gender in the relationship between positive and negative affect. *Cognition and Emotion*, 13 (6), 641–672.

Choi, I., Dalal, R., Kim-Prieto, C., and Park, H. (2003) Culture and judgement of causal relevance. *Journal of Personality and Social Psychology*, 84 (1), 46–59.

Choi, I., Koo, M., and Choi, J. (2007) Measuring the analytic vs. the holistic thinking style. *Personality and Social Psychology Bulletin*, 33 (5), 691–705.

Gürhan-Canli, Z. and Maheswaran, D. (2000) Cultural variations in country of origin effects. *Journal of Marketing Research*, 37 (3), 309–317.

Han, S.-P. and Shavitt, S. (1994) Persuasion and culture: advertising appeals in individualistic and collectivistic societies. *Journal of Experimental Social Psychology*, 30 (4), 326.

Han, S. and Shavitt, S. (2005) Westernization of cultural values in Korean advertising: a longitudinal content analysis of magazine ads from 1968-1998, in *Advances in consumer research*, Vol. 32 (eds G. Menon and A.R. Rao), Association for Consumer Research, Provo, UT, pp. 249–250.

Hofstede, G.H. (1980) *Culture's Consequences: International Differences in Work-Related Values*, Sage, Newbury, Park.

Ji, L.J., Zhang, Z., and Guo, T. (2008) To buy or to sell: cultural differences in stock market decisions based on stock price trends. *Journal of Behavioral Decision Making*, 21 (4), 399–413.

Ji, L.J., Zhang, Z., and Nisbett, R.E. (2004) Is it Culture, or is it language? Examination of language effects in cross-cultural research on categorization. *Journal of Personality and Social Psychology*, 87 (1), 57–65.

Kim, H.S. and Markus, H.R. (1999) Deviance or uniqueness, harmony or conformity? A cultural analysis. *Journal of Personality and Social Psychology*, 77 (4), 785–800.

Lalwani, A.K. and Shavitt, S. (2009) The "me" I claim to be: cultural self-construal elicits self-presentational goal pursuit. *Journal of Personality and Social Psychology*, 97 (1), 88–102.

Lalwani, A., Shavitt, S., and Johnson, T.P. (2006) What is the relation between cultural orientation and socially desirable responding? *Journal of Personality and Social Psychology*, 90 (1), 165–178.

Lau-Gesk, L.G. (2003) Activating culture through persuasion appeals: an examination of the bicultural consumer. *Journal of Consumer Psychology*, **13** (3), 301–315.

Markus, H.R. and Kitayama, S. (1991) Culture and the self: implications for cognition, emotion, and motivation. *Psychological Review*, **98** (2), 224–253.

Miracle, G.E. (1987) Feel-Do-Learn: an alternative sequence underlying Japanese consumer response to television commercials, in *Proceedings of the L.A. Conference of the American Academy of Advertising* (ed. F.G. Feasley), The University of South Carolina, Columbia.

Monga, A.B. and John, D.R. (2007) Cultural differences in brand extension evaluation: the influence of analytic versus holistic thinking. *Journal of Consumer Research*, **33** (4), 529–536.

Monga, A.B. and John, D.R. (2008) When does negative brand publicity hurt? The moderating influence of analytic versus holistic thinking. *Journal of Consumer Psychology*, **18** (4), 320–332.

Morling, B. and Lamoreaux, M. (2008) Measuring culture outside the head: a meta-analysis of cultural products. *Personality and Social Psychology Review*, **12** (3), 199–221.

Nelson, M.R. and Shavitt, S. (2002) Horizontal and vertical individualism and achievement values: a multi-method examination of Denmark and the U.S. *Journal of Cross-Cultural Psychology*, **33** (5), 439–458.

Ng, S. and Houston, M.J. (2006) Exemplars or beliefs? The impact of self-view on the nature and relative influence of brand associations. *Journal of Consumer Research*, **32** (4), 519–529.

Nisbett, R.E. (2003) *The Geography of Thought: How Asians and Westerners think Differently..., and Why*, Free Press, New York.

Nisbett, R.E., Peng, K., Choi, I., and Norenzayan, A. (2001) Culture and systems of thought: holistic versus analytic cognition. *Psychological Review*, **108** (2), 291–310.

Oyserman, D., Coon, H.M., and Kemmelmeier, M. (2002) Rethinking individualism and collectivism: evaluation of theoretical assumptions and meta-analyses. *Psychological Bulletin*, **128** (1), 3–72.

Oyserman, D. and Lee, S.W.-S. (2007) Priming 'culture': culture as situated cognition, in *Handbook of Cultural Psychology* (eds S. Kitayama and D. Cohen), Guilford Press, New York, pp. 255–282.

Schwartz, S.H. (1992) Universals in the content and structure of values: theoretical advances and empirical tests in 20 countries, in *Advances in experimental social psychology*, Vol. 25 (ed. M.P. Zanna), Academic Press, San Diego, pp. 1–65.

Shavitt, S., Lalwani, A.K., Zhang, J., and Torelli, C.J. (2006) The horizontal/vertical distinction in cross-cultural consumer research. *Journal of Consumer Psychology*, **16** (4), 325–356.

Shavitt, S., Lee, A., and Torelli, C. (2009) New directions in cross-cultural consumer psychology, in *The Social Psychology of Consumer Behavior, a volume in the series, Frontiers of Social Psychology* (eds M. Wänke, A.W. Kruglanski, and J.P. Forgas) Series Editors, Psychology Press, New York, pp. 227–250.

Shavitt, S., Torelli, C., and Wong, J. (2009), Identity-based motivation in a consumer context. *Journal of Consumer Psychology*, **19** (3), pp. 261–266.

Schimmack, U., Oishi, S., and Diener, E. (2002) Cultural influences on the relation between pleasant emotions and unpleasant emotions: Asian dialectic philosophies or individualism-collectivism? *Cognition and Emotion*, **16** (6), 705–719.

Triandis, H.C. (1995) *Individualism and collectivism*, Westview Press, Boulder.

Triandis, H.C. and Gelfand, M.J. (1998) Converging measurement of horizontal and vertical individualism and collectivism. *Journal of Personality and Social Psychology*, **74** (1), 118–128.

Wang, C.L. and Mowen, J.C. (1997) The separateness-connectedness self-schema: scale development and application to message construction. *Psychology and Marketing*, **14** (2), 185–207.

Williams, P. and Aaker, J. (2002) Can mixed emotions peacefully co-exist? *Journal of Consumer Research*, **28** (4), 636–649.

Wyer, R.S., Chiu, C.-Y., and Hong, Y.-Y. (eds) (2009). *Understanding Culture: Theory, Research and Application*, Psychology Press, New York.

Zhang, Y. and Gelb, B.D. (1996) Matching advertising appeals to culture: the influence of products' use conditions. *Journal of Advertising*, **25** (3), 29–46.

Zhang, J. and Shavitt, S. (2003) Cultural values in advertisements to the Chinese X-generation: promoting modernity and individualism. *Journal of Advertising*, **32** (1), 23–33.

customer satisfaction

Richard L. Oliver

INTRODUCTION

This article describes the general field of consumer (customer) satisfaction behavior as it is currently conceptualized. Though the field has been researched from many perspectives, the most common appearing in the areas of satisfaction attribute (feature) *surveys* and customer satisfaction *strategy* (*see* CUSTOMER SATISFACTION/DISSATISFACTION), more psychologically based approaches are now practiced.

Here, the underlying mechanisms of how consumers construct, consciously or subconsciously, their satisfaction conclusions are explored so that greater satisfaction fostering and dissatisfaction avoidance can be ensured. Readers interested in greater detail and elaboration, including discussion of topics not covered here, should consult the author's original work (Oliver, 2010) and an earlier short treatise on satisfaction research (Oliver, 2006).

CUSTOMER SATISFACTION DEFINED

Recent interpretations in the consumer domain now couch satisfaction as a fulfillment response. Fulfillment implies that a consumption goal is known, as in basic motives of hunger, thirst, and safety. However, observers of human behavior understand that these and other goals can be and frequently are modified and updated in various ways. Thus, consumer researchers have moved away from the traditional meaning of satisfaction and now pursue this concept as the consumer experiences and describes it.

In Oliver (2010, p. 8), the following definition has been proposed as being consistent with the conceptual and empirical evidence:

> Satisfaction is the consumer's fulfillment response. It is a judgment that a product or service feature, or the product or service itself, provided (or is providing) a pleasurable level of consumption-related fulfillment, including levels of under- or over-fulfillment.

Here, pleasurable implies that fulfillment gives pleasure or reduces pain. Thus, individuals can be satisfied so as to return to normalcy, as in the removal of an aversive state. Moreover, fulfillment is not necessarily limited to the case of met needs. Overfulfillment can be satisfying if it provides additional unexpected pleasure; and underfulfillment can be satisfying if it gives greater pleasure than one anticipates in a given situation. Note that if the word "displeasure" is substituted for pleasure in the satisfaction definition, dissatisfaction results. Thus, the displeasure of underfulfillment

typically is dissatisfying and overfulfillment may be dissatisfying if it is unpleasant – "too much of a good thing."

A SATISFACTION MODEL USEFUL FOR CURRENT THINKING

At this point, it would be helpful to envision the framework upon which this discussion is based. If one can construct the antecedents of the satisfaction response, that is, how a consumer mentally constructs satisfaction, many conceptual nuances will be revealed. Perhaps the most useful model of this process is the expectancy disconfirmation framework that proceeds as follows. The model assumes that consumers have prior expectations of the product or service performance.

Expectations, whether measured before or after consumption (predicted or recalled retrospective expectations), and performance are compared to form an "objective" (or gap) disconfirmation level; objective disconfirmation provides the basis for a subjective interpretation of this expectation-performance difference, and subjective disconfirmation is one direct cause of satisfaction. Additionally, there may exist a direct effect of performance on satisfaction not channeled through disconfirmation. This represents the "expectancy disconfirmation with performance model."

The performance of features (attributes). In a familiar research scenario, consumers are asked to retrospectively rate the product or service on the degree to which each feature was delivered. Concurrently, the consumer may be asked to rate the product on an overall basis or on satisfaction. Despite the ubiquity of this method, problems are inherent in its implementation. One is that the list of features cannot be exhaustive for all consumers. A second problem arises from the disparate goals (needs) of consumers. Another problem is that of the relevance of features at different stages of decision-making.

Satisfaction drivers versus choice criteria. In pursuing the reasons behind the consumer's satisfaction response, it should be borne in mind that the researcher's goal is to determine the correct feature list of *satisfaction drivers*, as opposed to product or service *choice criteria*. A common mistake is that of assuming the features consumers use in selecting a product from a list of alternatives are identical to the set of features that play into satisfaction and dissatisfaction judgments.

Thus, for this reason, customer satisfaction researchers (*see* CUSTOMER-SATISFACTION RESEARCH) are advised to determine satisfiers and dissatisfiers independently of choice determinants. Additionally, this also illustrates why a satisfaction measure is preferred to one of, say, attitude (*see* ATTITUDES) or quality, if consumer satisfaction is the goal of the firm. Both attitude and quality judgments are used in choice and thus may give a distorted picture of the features most strongly related to satisfaction.

Expectations and their role in satisfaction.   Generally, an expectation is an anticipation of future consequences based on prior experience and other many and varied sources of information. Expectations can also be described as a *comparative referent* for performance. The reason is that performance alone is an unreferenced concept. Meaning is attached only when performance can be compared to some standard. In fact, any number of referents can be used in later satisfaction assessments, but they become channeled into expectations when the product or service is purchased. The concept of needs, discussed previously, is one of the many referents available to consumers. These same consumers, however, will pursue only those products that they *expect* to fulfill their needs.

Frequently, consumers express different variations of what they would prefer a product to deliver. At one level, they may have an ideal perception of a product offering, something they wish they could receive in a perfect world. Others, or the same consumers at a different time, expect only what they believe the firm's product can or will deliver. Researchers have referred to these two different perceptions as *ideal* and *predicted* expectations or, alternatively, as *should* and *will* or *desired* and *likely* outcomes.

A number of research investigations have established that consumers do indeed recognize and use multiple levels of expectations or standards. Among the most common of these are studies investigating the influence of normative (should) and predicted (will) expectations, or

alternatively, ideal and expected referents. The results of all studies tend to be similar. When the ideal or should level of expectations was the referent, satisfaction was lower than when actual expected or predicted expectations were used. Moreover, these studies generally conclude that consumers do entertain multiple standards and that inclusion of more than just the predicted level may improve a model's ability to understand satisfaction.

Disconfirmation and its role in satisfaction.   When consumers compare performance to their expectations, the response of *disconfirmation*, more specifically, disconfirmation of preperformance standards, results. Because the early work in consumer satisfaction was conducted with predictive expectations as a standard, the phrase "disconfirmation of expectations" or "expectancy disconfirmation" has come to apply to this concept. Many standards consumers bring to the consumption experience can be disconfirmed, so an alternative phrase to describe the discrepancy from a standard could be simply "disconfirmation."

However, because the phrase "disconfirmation" without a valence qualifier is ambiguous as to direction, the phrase "negative disconfirmation" is commonly used to refer to the negative discrepancy that occurs when performance is below standard, and "positive disconfirmation" is used to refer to the positive discrepancy that occurs when performance is above standard. When performance is equal to standards or expectations, a simple confirmation of expectation exists.

Disconfirmation is "generic" with numerous applications. For example, the entire consumption experience can be judged on the degree to which it was better or worse than was expected, as can individual attributes. Other possibilities include dimensions (attribute groups) of performance and the benefits (good aspects) reaped from consumption as separate from the problems (bad aspects) encountered.

Objective (calculated) versus subjective disconfirmation.   Early attempts to measure disconfirmation used a discrepancy or "gap" approach. That is, separate survey sections were used to capture, first attribute expectations and, later attribute performance perceptions. Then the performance scores were subtracted from their respective expectation scores and these "gaps" were added. The logic is direct. When attribute performance was higher than its respective expectation, the gap is positive and is considered favorable. Similarly, when expectations were higher, the gap was negative and unfavorable. Satisfaction should increase as the positivity of the gap score increased and it should decrease (contributing to dissatisfaction) with the negativity of the gap score.

Is there evidence for the superiority of subjective disconfirmation (better/worse than) over calculated disconfirmation in the prediction of satisfaction? Yes. A number of studies have examined both the calculated and single-score varieties of disconfirmation, most using rating scale scores. The results of all studies were similar with the majority of the evidence suggesting that the subjective version of disconfirmation correlates more highly with satisfaction scales than do the discrepancy scores. Moreover, when analyzed in an ordering of cause and effect, the following configuration of concepts, as shown in Equation (1), is consistently found to best fit the data:

$$\text{calculated disconfirmation}$$
$$\Longrightarrow \text{subjective disconfirmation}$$
$$\Longrightarrow \text{satisfaction} \qquad (1)$$

This sequence of events forms the basis for the expectancy disconfirmation model of consumer satisfaction discussed here. As shown, this sequence portrays a calculated expectation–performance discrepancy (if performed) as input to the consumer's subjective interpretation of this difference. The subjective interpretation then becomes the most immediate antecedent of satisfaction. If no "objective" score is available, then a subjective judgment is "sensed." Expectations and performance are implicitly incorporated in the disconfirmation judgment in this sequence.

Operation of disconfirmation in the satisfaction model.   Reviews of studies measuring disconfirmation in various forms are now available to suggest that it is a powerful predictor

of satisfaction, even when combined with expectation and performance in the manner discussed (Yi, 1990; Szymanski and Henard, 2001; Oliver, 2010). In fact, disconfirmation typically dominates expectation and frequently dominates performance in terms of the strength of effect. There are times, however, when both performance and disconfirmation are input to the same regression that the disconfirmation effect is obscured (becomes nonsignificant). The reason is multicolinearity as disconfirmation is a performance-based concept and both the performance and disconfirmation variables may be highly correlated. When this happens, two regressions must be run separately – the first containing performance and the second containing disconfirmation in its stead.

SHORT-TERM CONSEQUENCES OF SATISFACTION

Intention to repurchase.   One of the most common results of satisfaction/dissatisfaction is a stated intention (*see* CONSUMER INTENTIONS) to repurchase (or not) in the future. Sometimes, this is posed in surveys in a hypothetical sense as in "if you were in the market for a (generic product), how likely would you buy a (specific brand)?" These scales are ubiquitous in the literature; in particular, it is unusual not to see them being used because the researcher rarely can observe repetitive behavior in a cross-sectional one-shot survey. In commercial research, however, intention scales may not be needed because actual repeat behavior is more easily obtained.

Still another version of intention is the degree to which the consumer splits purchasing between alternatives. Similar to multibrand loyalty, consumers may intend to repatronize one of a set of acceptable alternatives, such as in restaurant dining. In this case, an intention to repatronize a particular establishment is more akin to a probability across choices as opposed to a probability within a choice. It is known, however, that stated intentions without behavioral validation are very unreliable. Consumers frequently overstate their intentions due to a positivity bias in consumer responding. In lieu of other measures of satisfaction validation, however, intention data may be among the best measurement modalities one can achieve.

Complaining/praising.   Perhaps the most neglected, infrequently found satisfaction-related concepts in satisfaction surveys are complaining and its polar opposite, praising. This is surprising as the complaining literature is vast and, in fact, was the first of the satisfaction concepts to be extensively studied. Complaining is important because, unlike dissatisfaction, complaining is a behavior. While dissatisfaction and complaining are related, they have been found to be imperfectly correlated. Not all dissatisfied consumers complain so that those who do are very disaffected. Nor are all "complainers" dissatisfied as they may be simply motivated to provide feedback to a firm so that it may improve a current marketplace offering.

In the same vein, the extent of complimenting or praising – the related bipolar concept of complaining – may also be of value to the firm. Praising is not as frequent as complaining, but it does occur. One might view it in the context of an extreme expression of satisfaction, having information value to the firm beyond high performance and satisfaction ratings. This could be particularly important in the service industry where many and varied service providers are involved.

Word of mouth and recommendations.   Word of mouth (WOM) is the third post-satisfaction concept discussed here. The nature of recommendations is very closely intertwined with WOM. While WOM can consist of praising or damning (to other consumers as opposed to the firm or its representatives), recommendations are targeted communications to potential purchasers. Note that "recommendations" is a general term and can be either positive (to buy) or negative (not to buy).

OTHER SATISFACTION-RELATED COMPARATIVE REFERENTS

The following are briefly mentioned here because they appear prominently in overall perspectives on the satisfaction response (Oliver, 2010).

Quality.   The quality literature (*see* QUALITY FUNCTION DEPLOYMENT (QFD)) predates the satisfaction concept and, in some sense, promoted the emergence of focused attention on satisfaction. In effect, it is a comparison of performance to standards of excellence or perfection as in the four criteria of diamond evaluation (cut, clarity, color, karat weight). The number of citations to this concept is legend, and justice would not be served if any were listed as prototypical.

Equity/inequity.   Equity, a comparison of performance to fairness standards, is similarly well-vested. Only a small number of satisfaction studies are available that tackle the core concept (e.g., Oliver and Swan, 1989). Most address unfair pricing (Campbell, 1999), or subdimensions, such as interactional fairness (Blodgett, Hill, and Tax, 1997).

Regret.   Regret is of recent vintage, at least in consumer behavior, and is a comparison of performance to "what might have been." Relying heavily on the concept of forgone alternatives, a complete summary can be found in Zeelenberg and Pieters (2007).

Value.   This article ends with the concept of value which has taken two forms in the consumer literature. The most common is that of performance compared to sacrifice in acquisition, in effect, a benefit versus cost perspective (Zeithaml, 1988). The second is that of performance against goal attainment, or the second derivative of performance – its intended consequences (Woodruff and Gardial, 1996). The latter is later subdivided into usage consequences and/or mere possession effects.

There is much more to the study and meaning of satisfaction and more is yet to come, as further discovery on this vast concept continues.

Bibliography

Blodgett, J.G., Hill, D.J., and Tax, S.S. (1997) The effects of distributive, procedural, and interactional justice on postcomplaint behavior. *Journal of Retailing*, **73**, 185–210.
Campbell, M.C. (1999) Perceptions of price unfairness: antecedents and consequences. *Journal of Marketing Research*, **36**, 187–199.

138 customer satisfaction

Oliver, R.L. (2006) Customer satisfaction research, in *The Handbook of Marketing Research: Uses, Misuses, and Future Advances* (eds R. Grover and M. Vriens), Sage, Thousand Oaks, pp. 569–587.

Oliver, R.L. (2010) *Satisfaction: A Behavioral Perspective on the Consumer*, 2nd edn, M.E. Sharpe, Armonk, NY.

Oliver, R.L. and Swan, J.E. (1989) Consumer perceptions of interpersonal equity and satisfaction in transactions: a field survey approach. *Journal of Marketing*, **53**, 21–35.

Szymanski, D.M. and Henard, D.H. (2001) Customer satisfaction: a meta-analysis of the empirical evidence. *Journal of the Academy of Marketing Science*, **29**, 16–35.

Woodruff, R.B. and Gardial, S.F. (1996) *Know Your Customer: New Approaches to Understanding Customer Value and Satisfaction*, Blackwell Publishers, Cambridge.

Yi, Y. (1990) A critical review of consumer satisfaction, in *Review of Marketing 1990*, (ed. V.A. Zeithaml.), American Marketing Association, Chicago, pp. 68–123.

Zeelenberg, M. and Pieters, R. (2007) A theory of regret regulation 1.0. *Journal of Consumer Psychology*, **17** (1), 3–18.

Zeithaml, V.A. (1988) Consumer perceptions of price, quality, and value: a means-end model and synthesis of evidence. *Journal of Marketing*, **52**, 2–22.

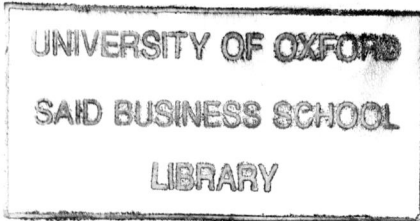

E

emotion

Julie A. Ruth

OVERVIEW AND DEFINITION OF EMOTIONS IN CONSUMER BEHAVIOR

Emotions are psychological states of readiness that encompass thoughts, subjective feelings, physiological changes, expressive behaviors, and action tendencies (Bagozzi, Gopinath, and Nyer, 1999). The specific character of the subjective feeling – for example, love, pride, excitement, anxiety, fear, guilt, or anger – is associated with systematic patterns of appraisals the consumer makes about the event in the light of implications for well-being. In addition to appraisals, emotions have a felt, experiential component that is accompanied by physiological processes such as heightened arousal. Emotions are often communicated physically through gestures or facial expressions, allowing emotions to spread to others, and may result in the consumer taking specific actions to adapt to the situation at hand.

Consistent with approaches in psychology, consumer research distinguishes between emotions and related constructs such as affect and mood. Emotions typically have a target, such as the consumer being exposed to a TV ad that elicits guilt or a consumer experiencing anger in light of a provider's inept service delivery. In contrast, affect is conceptualized as a feeling state that is largely undifferentiated beyond its positive or negative valence, or as an umbrella term that encompasses a set of more specific feeling phenomena such as emotions, moods, and/or attitudes. Moods are conceptualized as lower in intensity than emotions and are less differentiated due to their lack of a specific target and lack of correspondence with specific appraisals and action tendencies (Bagozzi, Gopinath, and Nyer, 1999; Cohen, Pham, and Andrade, 2008).

Emotions can be experienced in anticipation of, during, or after consumption episodes such as fear in response to an ad identifying risks to family safety, delight and regret upon making a good or poor decision respectively, or anger when receiving poor or prejudiced customer service. Consumers can also experience a mix of emotions such as fear, joy, regret, and excitement in conjunction with skydiving or viewing horror movies. Using frameworks of emotion developed in psychology as a foundation, Richins (1997) developed a set of descriptors reflecting the emotions consumers may experience when anticipating, acquiring, or possessing and using products. The Consumption Emotion Set (CES) includes multiple scale items associated with 16 emotions: anger, discontent, worry, sadness, fear, shame, envy, loneliness, romantic love, love, peacefulness, contentment, optimism, joy, excitement, and surprise. Richins also shows that consumers associate different emotions with different types of possessions. For example, sentimental objects such as heirlooms and mementos are associated with love, and recreational products such as stereo equipment are associated with positive emotions including excitement. In contrast, vehicles are associated with a combination of positive and negative emotions such as joy, pride, anger, excitement, worry, and guilt.

The next section describes the ways in which appraisals, coping, and goal striving are related to consumers' experience of emotions.

CONSUMERS' EXPERIENCE OF EMOTIONS

Appraisals. Emotions typically arise in conjunction with appraisals consumers make in situations of personal significance. Appraisals are evaluative judgments and interpretations of the meaning and importance of elements of the situation at hand. Appraisals may be conscious or may occur automatically upon perception. Johnson and Stewart (2005) synthesize appraisal theories drawn from psychology and suggest that six appraisals differentiate and inform the experience of discrete consumer emotions: (i) direction of goal congruence (i.e., positive or negative); (ii) agency, or the extent to which the locus of responsibility and control resides with the consumer, some other entity, or beyond anyone's responsibility and control; (iii) certainty; and (iv) normative or moral compatibility. In addition, appraisals of (v) goal importance and (vi) degree of goal congruence are linked to the intensity of emotional experience.

Different emotions are characterized by systematic patterns of appraisals. For example, as shown in research on gift exchange, gift recipients experience love in pleasant, goal-congruent gift-exchange situations in which certainty and other-agency are relatively high and self-agency is low. In contrast, recipients experience anger in unpleasant, goal-incongruent exchange circumstances in which certainty and other-agency are high and self-agency is low. It is also important to note that, although there is evidence that appraisals can be causal in their influence on emotions, other mechanisms can elicit emotions. For example, noncognitive methods such as bodily feedback or unconscious priming have also been shown to elicit specific emotions.

Coping. Emotion regulation is aimed at coping with the implications of a given situation for the consumer and his or her goals and well-being (*see* MOTIVATION AND GOALS; CONSUMER WELL-BEING). Coping is the means by which an individual identifies and assesses the adaptive potential and significance of various actions. Of critical importance is the assessment the consumer makes in light of the actual situation compared to the desired one. Two appraisals are particularly important at this stage of emotion formation: goal relevance and goal congruence, or the extent to which the consumer perceives a personal stake in the situation at hand and the

degree to which the event facilitates or inhibits this stake.

A prominent view suggests that two broad categories of coping strategies are available. Problem-focused coping aims at maintaining the original goal and taking action to attain the goal or maintain its achievement. Emotion-focused coping, on the other hand, involves an attempt to reframe the situation by shifting appraisal(s) and/or revising the goal. Such revisions in appraisal or goals shift the emotional reaction in light of the situation. For example, the angry consumer who lodges a complaint in order to resolve a negative situation may be activating problem-focused coping. In contrast, a consumer may be able to shift emotions from anger to disappointment through use of an emotion-focused coping strategy if he/she reframes the situation by strengthening beliefs that the service provider was not in control of a negative outcome.

Recent research shows that consumers frequently rely on both emotion-focused and problem-focused coping strategies and may do so even within the same consumption episode. Further, some coping strategies may satisfy both emotion- and problem-focused coping goals. Duhachek (2005) reviews the psychological literature on coping and provides evidence for three broad categories of coping strategies used by consumers: (i) cognitive or behavioral (e.g., engaging in rational thinking about the situation, trying to make the best of the situation through positive thinking, or taking action to resolve the situation); (ii) expressive support seeking (e.g., engaging in emotional venting to others, seeking instrumental assistance from others, or seeking emotional support from others); and (iii) avoidance coping (e.g., avoiding the situation or denying it). Duhachek also shows that coping strategies are dependent on the specific emotion the consumer experiences and the consumer's beliefs about coping efficacy. For example, high self-efficacy consumers show a tendency to enact expressive support-seeking coping strategies when experiencing fear in contrast to active coping strategies when experiencing anger.

Goal striving and action tendencies. Closely related to coping is action tendency, which is a readiness to engage in or disengage from interaction with an object to bring the situation in line with goals. Anticipated emotions serve a role in goal striving through prompting intentions, plans, and decisions of how to allocate resources in order to move toward goal attainment (*see* MOTIVATION AND GOALS; CONSUMER INTENTIONS). Specific emotions also provide consumers with valuable feedback about their progress toward goal attainment. Happiness, for example, is perceived by consumers as a signal that a goal has been achieved, whereas sadness is a signal that goal achievement has not been attained.

Much as emotions arise in response to patterns of appraisals, there is evidence that patterns of action readiness also correspond with distinct emotions. Although positive (negative) consumption emotions may stimulate positive (negative) behavioral intentions, their shared valence is not the only factor that shapes behaviors. The nature of the consumer's goals also shapes action tendencies. Pride, for example, is associated with goal attainment, but it can occur in the light of achieving either promotion or prevention self-regulatory goals. Research shows that consumers who experience pride in conjunction with prevention goals (e.g., striving to avoid paying extra money for a purchase) are less likely to repurchase than those with promotion goals (e.g., striving to obtain a discount as means to gain money), whereas there are no differences in repurchase behavior among consumers who experience low levels of pride in conjunction with either prevention or promotion goals.

THE ROLE OF EMOTION IN FOUR DOMAINS OF CONSUMER ACTIVITY

Emotions play important roles in many domains of consumer activity. Four key domains are consumer response to advertising, consumer decision making, purchase and service situations, and possession and usage.

Emotions and advertising persuasion. The majority of research on the role of emotion in advertising has focused on two aspects of persuasion: (i) the nature and effects of emotions evoked in response to ads; and (ii) how consumers process and evaluate ads that appeal on the basis of emotion (*see* ADVERTISING MESSAGE APPEALS; PERSUASION; ATTITUDES; ADVERTISING EFFECTIVENESS).

Ad-evoked feelings have been shown to systematically shape attitudes the consumer develops and holds toward the ad and brand. For example, Edell and Burke (1987) present a scale measuring emotional responses toward ads and find three factors underlying these responses: upbeat feelings such as delight, happiness, and pride; negative feelings such as anger and irritation; and warm feelings such as hope and having been moved by the ad. These positive and negative emotional responses to ads can co-occur and, along with cognitive responses, influence the formation of attitudes toward the ad and indirectly influence brand attitudes. Emotional responses to ads have been found to be more important determinants of attitude toward the ad than thoughts under low involvement conditions, whereas both cognitive and emotional responses are important under high involvement conditions.

Turning to consumer response to emotional appeals, these ads affect persuasion through eliciting a sufficiently high level of emotion that attracts attention and prompts consumer processing of the message, which in turn contributes to behavioral intentions. For example, research has shown that negative emotional appeals can prompt positive outcomes, as when a negative emotional ad highlights the needs of abused children. These types of prosocial appeals elicit consumer feelings of sadness, anger, fear, and empathy. Stronger felt negative emotions tend to prompt greater feelings of empathy, which in turn facilitate intentions to help.

An inverted U-shaped pattern of effects of emotional appeals on persuasion is sometimes observed. In such instances, attitudes toward the ad and brand are relatively favorable under moderate levels of the elicited emotion and less favorable under either low or high levels of emotional response. For example, research shows that fear appeals that elicit low levels of the emotion are low in persuasion because they prompt insufficient elaboration of the threat or harm referred to in the ad. Likewise, appeals that elicit high levels of fear are also low in persuasion because they prompt an overly high level elaboration of the threat or harm that interferes with processing the recommendations for action to alleviate the fear. In contrast, appeals calibrated to elicit a moderate level of the emotion appear to strike an effective persuasive balance because the consumer is able to both elaborate on the threat and process the recommended action. Interventions that enhance the likelihood of elaboration, such as self-referencing, can increase persuasiveness of low-fear appeals, and elaboration-reducing interventions can likewise increase the persuasiveness of high-fear appeals (Keller and Block, 1995). Some research has also observed a similar pattern for appeals intended to elicit positive emotions, such as humorous appeals. Low levels of humor can be weak in attracting consumer attention, and very high levels of humor can distract the consumer from processing the marketing message. Moderate levels of positive emotion elicited through humor appears to strike an effective balance in attracting attention and prompting processing while leading to positive attitude formation.

Appraisal-related dimensions of emotional ads also influence persuasion. Whether an ad refers to high or low consumer agency, for example, shapes male consumers' attitudes toward the ad. Males form less favorable attitudes toward ads depicting a low self-agency emotion, such as peacefulness or tenderness, when viewing with another male. This result is attributed to the incongruence between the low-agency emotion and male stereotypes, which are made salient by the viewing circumstances. In contrast, ad attitudes are more favorable when males are exposed to either a low-self agency ad with a female viewing partner or when exposed under any viewing condition to an ad depicting a stereotype-congruent, high-agency emotion such as excitement or joy. Females do not display differential responses to high-versus low-agency emotional ads.

Members of different cultural groups may also process and evaluate emotion-based ads in systematically different ways. Consumers from collectivist cultures rather than individualistic ones have more favorable attitudes toward ego-focused (e.g., pride, happiness) versus other-focused (e.g., empathy, peacefulness) emotional appeals and brands. Consumers' motivation to process explains this somewhat counterintuitive pattern of results. That is, ads that are incongruent with cultural values are relatively novel and thus attention getting, which yields greater liking; ads that are easier to process because the appeals are consistent with cultural values are less novel and hence less attractive.

Some ads contain a mix of positive and negative emotional appeals, such as those combining happiness and sadness. Williams and Aaker (2002) find evidence that mixed appeals yield less favorable attitudes among consumers with a lower propensity to accept duality compared to those with a higher propensity, such as Anglo–Americans and Asian–Americans, respectively. Liking and recall of emotional ads tends to be higher among older compared to younger consumers. Further, ads focusing on avoiding negative emotions are liked and recalled more by older consumers and also younger consumers who hold a limited compared to longer time horizon.

Emotions and decision making.   Emotions have been found to exert a variety of influences in consumer decision making through the signals they provide with respect to the consumer's movement toward goals and managing the situation at hand (*see* CONSUMER DECISION MAKING). Whereas considerable research examines ambient affect as a context effect (see Cohen, Pham, and Andrade, 2008), other research investigates a more central role of emotions in decision-making processes. According to an "affect-as-information" model, consumers may evaluate products by holding a target representation in mind and asking, "How do I feel about it?" From this theoretical perspective, consumers' emotions are considered to be valid sources of information.

When holding the target experience in mind, such as a consumer considering, "Should I go shopping this afternoon?", a target that elicits positive feelings leads to more favorable evaluations than a target that elicits negative emotions. The extent to which consumers rely on such feelings in decision making depends on (i) the heuristic value of feelings, (ii) their representativeness, and (iii) their perceived relevance (Pham, 1998). Specifically, feelings are more likely to be used when feelings have value as a type of heuristic, such as situations where few other sources of information are available or when feelings can be used to simplify the decision process. For example, the consumer may elect to eliminate from a choice set all alternatives that are not associated with positive feelings. Whether consumers rely on such feelings also depends on the extent to which feelings are believed to be representative of the target. Consumers are less likely to rely on them if they believe the feelings have not been elicited by the target itself, as when happiness is associated with the weather rather than the target consumption experience. Finally, consumers tend to rely on feelings when they are regarded as more relevant to the target, such as situations where consumers have experiential motives compared to instrumental ones. Consumers who tend to process in a sensory or visual manner also display a tendency to act in accordance with the affect-as-information framework.

While research has largely observed a carry-over effect of emotional valence on judgment and choice, more recent studies argue that specific emotions give rise to specific cognitive and motivational processes that are systematically related to patterns of effects of emotions on decision making. Specifically, consumer emotions of the same valence, such as anger and sadness, can have different effects on judgment and choice because key appraisals and core experiential themes associated with them differ. Likewise, emotions of different valences may even have similar effects on judgments if they share other key appraisals and core themes.

Still, many choice decisions are in and of themselves difficult for consumers and elicit negative emotions. In their model of choice trade-off difficulty, Luce, Bettman, and Payne (2001) suggest that consumers appraise choice situations in light of goals and emotional content. They show that negative task-related emotions arising in situations involving difficult emotional trade-offs lead to various forms of coping that are either directed toward the problem or the emotion. If processing resources are limited, emotional reactions that are evoked spontaneously by an alternative in the choice set tend to have a greater impact on decision making and choice than cognitive reactions. In these constrained processing conditions, consumers tend to choose alternatives that are superior on an emotion-related rather than a cognitive dimension.

In contrast to trade-off difficulty, in other instances consumers may doubt whether what they yearn for is possible and thus find that their feelings of hope are threatened (de Mello, MacInnis, and Stewart, 2007). Consumers experience hope as a positive-valenced emotion that is elicited in situations that are uncertain but hold the possibility of achieving a goal-congruent outcome. If consumers lose confidence in a hoped-for outcome, they tend to engage in motivated reasoning when processing information about a product touted to enable goal achievement. That is, they tend to produce more self-serving product judgments, seek out product-supportive information sources, make biased assessments of information credibility, exhibit weaker distinctions between high- and low-credibility product information, and place less weight on negative information.

Kidwell, Hardesty, and Childers (2008) recently developed the Consumer Emotional Intelligence Scale (CEIS) to measure individual differences in consumers' ability to skillfully use emotion-based information in information processing and decision making (see CONSUMER INFORMATION PROCESSING; CONSUMER DECISION MAKING; EMOTIONAL INTELLIGENCE). The scale consists of items measuring four underlying dimensions of consumer emotional intelligence: *perceiving* emotions accurately; *facilitating*, or the ability to access and use emotions in mental processes; *understanding* emotions and their meaning; and *managing* emotions in the process of achieving desired outcomes. Consumers with higher compared to lower levels of emotional ability and confidence in this ability tend to make higher compared to lower quality choices.

Emotions arising in purchase and service settings.
Psychological aspects of emotions in purchase and service settings. Emotions that arise in product purchase or service delivery shape the consumer's assessments of satisfaction, complaint behavior, and word-of-mouth communications (see CONSUMER BEHAVIOR AND SERVICES MARKETING; CUSTOMER SATISFACTION). Research has largely found that the experience of positive emotions

increases satisfaction while the experience of negative emotions decreases satisfaction, over and above the influence of expectations, product performance, and disconfirmation processes. Products that meet or exceed consumers' hedonic wants and fulfill promotion goals also tend to increase delight, which in turn contributes toward more favorable word-of-mouth and repurchase intentions.

Negative emotions arising from purchase have been the subject of numerous studies. Regret, for example, is experienced when the consumer makes the judgment that a foregone alternative performs better than the chosen alternative (Tsiros and Mittal, 2000). Consumer regret and satisfaction have been shown to have different antecedents, moderators, and consequences. Regret tends to be experienced when the consumer recognizes a better but forgone option and engages in counterfactual thinking in conjunction with a chosen outcome that is negative and irreversible. Whereas regret and satisfaction both directly influence repurchase intentions, the influence of regret on complaint intentions is mediated by satisfaction. Although research has generally found that consumers experience more regret when deciding to make a change from the status quo compared to maintaining it, feelings of regret can be mitigated if the consumer reflects and concludes that the decision was appropriate under the circumstances.

There is evidence of systematic relations between appraisals, emotions, and the coping strategies that consumers employ in negative purchase situations. Yi and Baumgartner (2004) find that two dimensions explain the appraisal, emotion, and coping patterns of consumers experiencing anger, disappointment, regret, or worry in purchase: (i) the extent to which the consumer believes the problem can or cannot be managed; and (ii) the extent to which the consumer can manage or not manage the emotion itself. In anger experiences, where responsibility and control are attributed to another party and the situation is deemed changeable, a high problem-focus/low emotion-focus coping strategy of confrontation is likely to be used. In disappointing purchase situations associated with unmet expectations and a situation that is beyond the control of the consumer or other party, low problem-focus/low emotion-focus coping strategies such as disengagement are likely to be enacted. When consumers blame themselves and experience regret in purchase, they tend to engage in acceptance and positive reinterpretation coping strategies, which are low in problem-focus and high in emotion-focus. Worry, on the other hand, arises in consumption situations where the future is uncertain, and so a variety of coping strategies are enacted, depending on perceptions of control over the situation.

Numerous studies have also examined negative emotion experienced in service failures (see CONSUMER BEHAVIOR AND SERVICES MARKETING). Consumers make assessments about the characteristics of the failure, which are in turn associated with different emotions such as anger or regret. When consumers appraise a goal-incongruent situation as having been caused by the service provider, consistent with its characteristic appraisal and action tendency patterns, the consumer is more likely to experience anger than regret and exhibit more retaliatory behaviors. Whereas marketers' recovery efforts that are designed to reduce consumer anger are associated with a reduction in consumers' retaliatory behavior, recovery efforts that aim to shift blame from the service provider to the consumer typically result in increased consumer anger and retaliatory behavior. Moreover, consumers' negative emotions such as anger or exasperation are highly predictive of their negative word-of-mouth behavior. Consumers' positive emotions, in contrast, are not related to their negative word-of-mouth behavior in these situations.

Social aspects of emotions in purchase and service settings. Many purchase and service contexts involve the presence of other people. How does that social situation affect consumer emotions? How is the consumer affected by another person and that individual's emotional state? Some research argues that emotional contagion occurs when one person "catches" the emotion being experienced and expressed by another person, so that the emotion of the receiver converges with that of the sender. Recent findings suggest that the role played by an emotion sender – a fellow consumer versus an employee – and the authenticity of the sender's emotional display influence how the emotional message is received by consumers. For example, Howard and Gengler (2001) find that emotional contagion occurs when happiness transfers from senders to receiving consumers who have positive relational bonds with senders. The facial expression of senders must be visible in order for receiving consumers to mimic the smiling and experience the happy emotion, which in turn has a positive impact on receivers' attitudes toward products that are present in the situation. Research on employee–customer interactions shows that employees' emotional displays can also trigger changes in customers' emotions but that, in addition to the bond established between employees and customers, the correspondence in employee/customer emotions may depend on the authenticity of employees' emotional display rather than the mere act of smiling itself.

Consumer emotions are also affected by brief interactions with unacquainted others or even a noninteractive "mere" presence of others in a shopping environment. Dahl, Honea, and Manchanda (2005) show that consumers who interact briefly with a salesperson compared to those who do not are more likely to experience guilt if they do not ultimately make a product purchase. Consumers are also more likely to experience embarrassment in purchasing an embarrassing product in the presence of another. Several other factors affect the degree to which consumers experience embarrassment in purchasing embarrassing products: the frequency of the potentially embarrassing situation's occurrence, the severity of the social threat, and the consumer's public self-consciousness. Likewise, the presence or absence of others can affect the experience of anger in service failure situations. Consistent with research on the salience of felt ethnicity in numerical minority social conditions, Baker, Meyer, and Johnson (2008) find that service failures elicit higher levels of anger among black consumers when no other black customers are present compared to situations where several other black consumers are present, or compared to white consumers in either condition.

Emotions arising in possession and usage. Studies examining various aspects of possession and usage have found emotions to be central to these experiences in two noteworthy ways. First, mixed emotions are common because consumption experiences almost always involve multiple and sometimes conflicting attributes and goals. Second, possession and usage contexts are often social in nature, and so interpersonal and social factors may be more salient in the experience and effects of emotions in these types of consumption settings.

The recent work on indulgent consumption acknowledges the importance of positive and negative emotions, showing that their effects are dependent on the specific combination of mixed emotions that consumers experience. With indulgent consumption, both prudent and impulsive consumers experience a mix of positive and negative emotions such as excitement and frustration. Yet prudent, but not impulsive, consumers also tend to experience negative self-conscious emotions such as guilt and shame. As time elapses after indulging, impulsive consumers are more likely to feel residual effects of their positive emotions as their negative feelings dissipate, whereas negative emotions including self-conscious feelings tend to persist for prudent consumers while their positive emotions dissipate. As a result, prudent compared to impulsive consumers are less likely to indulge when given a subsequent opportunity to do so (*see* IMPULSIVE AND COMPULSIVE BUYING).

The nature of emotions experienced in consumption also affects memory, where mixed consumption experiences involving both positive and negative emotions are more difficult to recall accurately than unipolar ones. In addition, over time consumers remember mixed emotion experiences as less mixed, a finding that highlights a type of memory decay that does not occur with unipolar emotion experiences. The felt conflict of mixed emotions appears to explain this decay. The memory bias is also more evident among Anglo-American compared to Asian-American consumers, consistent with other research regarding cultural differences regarding acceptance of duality.

At first glance, consumers' pursuit of consumption experiences laden with negative emotions, such as horror movies, would seem to be counterintuitive. Research shows that viewing horror movies elicits both negative and positive emotions in consumers predisposed to viewing horror movies. In contrast, only negative emotions are activated among consumers who typically avoid these types of consumption activities. Although similarly high levels of negative emotions are felt by both types of individuals, consumers with a protective orientation that provides psychological distance or detachment are able to experience positive emotions as well (see Cohen, Pham, and Andrade, 2008).

Turning to social aspects of consumption, some research has examined the correspondence between the emotions consumers experience and the relationships they hold with others including family, friends, and acquaintances. For example, gift exchange oftentimes elicits a mix of emotions, such as joy and love in being acknowledged as a gift recipient but also the anxiety a recipient may experience in being the center of attention and obligated to conform to dramatic scripts associated with rituals like baby showers or holiday observances. As a result, valence alone does not explain the relationship impact of gift exchange. For example, research shows that gift recipients who perceive that the relationship with the giver is strengthened typically feel a mix of positive and negative emotions such as joy in the relationship heading in a desired direction but fear of the unknown that lies ahead in the relationship. Recipients who believe already-strong relationships are affirmed typically experience positive emotions in gift-exchange processes (Ruth, Otnes, and Brunel, 1999).

With a focus on participation in rituals, Otnes, Lowrey, and Shrum (1997) explore the nature of consumer ambivalence, defined as the simultaneous or sequential experience of multiple emotional states that are shaped by the consumer's interaction with social or cultural phenomena in market-oriented contexts and that influence prepurchase, purchase, or postpurchase attitudes and behavior. Four antecedents of consumer ambivalence emerge in their study of consumer participation in wedding planning: a gap between expectations and actual experience, overload in decision-making processes, role conflict with

others, and conflicts among customs and/or values. These antecedents are associated with specific coping strategies that consumers use to manage their ambivalent feelings such as striving to assertively resolve gaps between expectations and reality regarding products or retailer services, or compromising to deal with role conflicts.

LOOKING FORWARD

Much of the extant research in our field has adopted a psychological perspective, concerned with the individual consumer's experience of emotion and its effect on other individual-level phenomena such as the consumer's attitudes, choices, assessments of satisfaction, and goals (*see* ATTITUDES; CONSUMER DECISION MAKING; CUSTOMER SATISFACTION; MOTIVATION AND GOALS). Yet, it is important to note that consumer behavior frequently occurs within interactions with service providers, friends, family, and even strangers in servicescapes and shopping environments. Building on extant research with a psychological foundation, recent studies of the social aspects (*see* SOCIAL INFLUENCE) of emotional experience and expression provide a strong platform for expanding research on how consumer emotions are elicited and shared between and among consumers and marketing agents such as service providers and sales personnel. Such initiatives could address how such emotions affect interpersonal phenomena, for instance, assessments of interpersonal relationship quality, trust, and commitment.

Such initiatives could also contribute to our understanding of how consumer emotions contribute to and shape the meanings and emotional attachments consumers have with brands and BRAND COMMUNITY, the ways in which consumers experience and express nostalgia, and other emotion-based aspects of possession and usage. In addition, recent conceptualizations emphasizing the perspective that emotions are informative and help consumers to function and adapt to changing situations provide promising directions for new knowledge insights on emotions in consumer behavior.

Bibliography

Bagozzi, R.P., Gopinath, M. and Nyer, P.U. (1999) The role of emotions in marketing. *Journal of the Academy of Marketing Science*, **27** (2), 184–206.

Baker, T.L., Meyer, T. and Johnson, J.D. (2008) Individual differences in perceptions of service failure and recovery: the role of race and discriminatory bias. *Journal of the Academy of Marketing Science*, **36** (4), 552–564.

Cohen, J.B., Pham, M.T. and Andrade, E.B. (2008) The nature and role of affect in consumer behavior, in *Handbook of Consumer Psychology* (eds C.P. Haugtvedt, P.M. Herr and F.R. Kardes), Lawrence Erlbaum, New York, pp. 297–348.

Dahl, D.W., Honea, H. and Manchanda, R.V. (2005) Three Rs of interpersonal consumer guilt: relationship, reciprocity, reparation. *Journal of Consumer Psychology*, **15** (4), 307–315.

de Mello, G.E., MacInnis, D.J. and Stewart, D.W. (2007) Threats to hope: effects on reasoning about product information. *Journal of Consumer Research*, **34** (2), 153–161.

Duhachek, A. (2005) Coping: a multidimensional, hierarchical framework of responses to stressful consumption episodes. *Journal of Consumer Research*, **32** (1), 41–53.

Edell, J.A. and Burke, M.C. (1987) The power of feelings in understanding advertising effects. *Journal of Consumer Research*, **14** (3), 421–433.

Howard, D.J. and Gengler, C. (2001) Emotional contagion effects on product attitudes. *Journal of Consumer Research*, **28** (2), 189–201.

Johnson, A.R. and Stewart, D.W. (2005) A reappraisal of the role of emotion in consumer behavior: traditional and contemporary approaches, in *Review of Marketing Research* (ed. N.K. Malhotra), M. E. Sharpe, Armonk, NY, pp. 1–33.

Keller, P.A. and Block, L.G. (1995) Increasing the persuasiveness of fear appeals: the effect of arousal and elaboration. *Journal of Consumer Research*, **22** (4), 448–459.

Kidwell, B., Hardesty, D.M. and Childers, T.L. (2008) Consumer emotional intelligence: conceptualization, measurement, and prediction of consumer decision making. *Journal of Consumer Research*, **35** (1), 154–166.

Luce, M.F., Bettman, J.R. and Payne, J.W. (2001) *Emotional Decisions: Tradeoff Difficulty and Coping in Consumer Choice*, University of Chicago Press, Chicago.

Otnes, C.C., Lowrey, T.M. and Shrum, L.J. (1997) Toward an understanding of consumer ambivalence. *Journal of Consumer Research*, **24** (1), 80–93.

Pham, M.T. (1998) Representativeness, relevance, and the use of feelings in decision making. *Journal of Consumer Research*, **25** (2), 144–159.

Richins, M.L. (1997) Measuring emotions in the consumption experience. *Journal of Consumer Research*, **24** (2), 127–146.

Ruth, J.A., Otnes, C.C. and Brunel, F.F. (1999) Gift receipt and the reformulation of interpersonal relationships. *Journal of Consumer Research*, **25** (4), 385–402.

Tsiros, M. and Mittal, V. (2000) Regret: a model of its antecedents and consequences in consumer decision making. *Journal of Consumer Research*, **26** (4), 401–417.

Williams, P. and Aaker, J.L. (2002) Can mixed emotions peacefully coexist? *Journal of Consumer Research*, **28** (4), 636–649.

Yi, S. and Baumgartner, H. (2004) Coping with negative emotions in purchase-related situations. *Journal of Consumer Psychology*, **14** (3), 303–317.

environmental consumer behavior

John A. McCarty, L. J. Shrum, and Tina M. Lowrey

Environmental consumer behavior, or more commonly, "green" consumer behavior, refers to a general class of behaviors (and their underlying processes) involved in purchasing, using, and disposing of products and services with the intention of improving the environment. A variety of activities can be considered under this umbrella. Probably the two most prominent ones are the extent to which consumers buy products that are environmentally friendly and the extent to which they dispose of product waste in an environmentally responsible manner. From a perspective of environmental activities, these two are related in that the disposal of waste (e.g., recycling of paper) provides some of the materials for the production of environmentally friendly products. Thus, in the materials life cycle (*see* FAMILY LIFE CYCLE) (Shrum, Lowrey, and McCarty, 1996), from the manufacturing of products and their packaging through consumer use to the disposal or recycling of the products and/or packaging, these two consumer actions (green buying and recycling) are the behaviors by which consumers can have the greatest potential impact on the environment.

Although a variety of polls over the last couple of decades show that consumers desire to become more "green" and are concerned about the environment, such findings are not always consistent with what consumers do (*see* ATTI-TUDE–BEHAVIOR CONSISTENCY), particularly in the area of buying green. For example, a 2007 global survey by McKinsey & Company (Bonini and Oppenheim, 2008) showed that 87% of the respondents indicated that they were concerned about the environment; however, only 33% reported that they bought or would buy green products. Thus, engaging in environmentally responsible behaviors, like other behaviors, is only partially determined by individuals' values, ATTITUDES, and intentions. There are a number of other factors that may facilitate or impede green behavior. In particular, polls typically show that consumers' reluctance to buy green relates to several key impediments: eco-friendly products are perceived as more expensive than other product offerings; eco-friendly products are perceived as less effective than other alternatives; and consumers are often skeptical of the claims made by environmentally friendly brands.

Besides buying green products, the other major way that consumers can act on their concern for the environment is to recycle the waste from the products they purchase. Like buying green, however, concern for the environment is but one of the factors that relate to the extent to which consumers will recycle materials such as paper, glass, and plastic. In terms of facilitating or inhibiting factors, the perceived convenience of recycling appears to facilitate the extent to which consumers recycle (McCarty and Shrum, 2001). Municipalities and organizations have caught on to this, and over the years there have been increased efforts to ease the burden on consumers to recycle. From the times when consumers had to take recyclables to special locations or bring recyclables to recycling drives at specific times, most cities now provide containers for recycling materials that are picked up at regular intervals.

Although making recycling more convenient increases recycling rates, it is still critical for consumers to believe that it is important. In fact, research has shown that consumers who feel that recycling is important tend to perceive it as less inconvenient, compared with those who do not feel it is important (McCarty and Shrum, 2001). The belief that recycling is important is driven, to some degree, by a variety of social and personality variables, such as values and attitudes; thus, these individual difference variables are critical to the success of consumer recycling.

Researchers have searched for antecedents of consumers' beliefs about the importance of recycling and pro-environmental behavior more generally. It appears that psychographic and personality variables show a stronger relationship with recycling attitudes than do demographic variables such as age and income (Straughan and Roberts, 1999). In particular, variables that are related to recycling include materialism (the extent to which one attaches importance to possessions), collectivism (the extent to which one believes in the importance of the group over the individual), and locus of control (the extent to which people believe that they control their lives rather than that they are controlled by external forces). Those who are more materialistic tend to have more negative attitudes toward the environment than do those who are less materialistic (Kilbourne and Pickett, 2006). Those who are more collectivistic tend to believe that recycling is more important than do those who are less collectivistic (McCarty and Shrum, 2001). People with an internal locus of control tend to believe that recycling is more important than do those who have an external locus of control (McCarty and Shrum, 2001). Presumably, those with an internal locus believe that their environmental efforts will have an impact and thus believe that such activities can be important.

Bibliography

Bonini, S. and Oppenheim, J. (2008) Cultivating the green consumer. *Stanford Social Innovation Review*, 6, 56–61.

Kilbourne, W. and Pickett, G. (2006) How materialism affects environmental beliefs, concern, and environmentally responsible behavior. *Journal of Business Research*, **61**, 885–893.

McCarty, J.A. and Shrum, L.J. (2001) The influence of individualism, collectivism, and locus of control on environmental beliefs and behavior. *Journal of Public Policy and Marketing*, **20**, 93–104.

Shrum, L.J., Lowrey, T.M., and McCarty, J.A. (1996) Using marketing and advertising principles to encourage pro-environmental behaviors, in *Marketing and Consumer Research in the Public Interest* (ed. R.P. Hill), Sage Publications, Thousand Oaks, pp. 197–216.

Straughan, R. and Roberts, J. (1999) Environmental segmentation alternatives: a look at green consumer behavior in the new millennium. *The Journal of Consumer Marketing*, **16**, 558–575.

F

family buying

James W. Gentry

Both "family" and "buying" are complex terms. For example, the question of how to define family has gained increasing relevance in postmodernity. "Family" may entail an intact nuclear family, three or four generations under one roof, a gay/lesbian couple, a single parent with children, a step-family, a single person with a network of exceptionally close ties, or even other household types. Most legal definitions are similar in substance to that of the US Census Bureau: "a family is a group of two people or more (one of whom is the householder) related by birth, marriage, or adoptions and residing together." We prefer the broader definition provided by Galvin, Bylund, and Brommel (2004, p. 6): "networks of people who share their lives over long periods of time bound by ties of marriage, blood, or commitment, legal or otherwise, who consider themselves as family and who share a significant history and anticipated future of functioning in a family relationship."

"Buying" too has complex meanings, as it involves much more than just the act of purchase. Also embedded in the term are issues of perceived need/desire for the product/service/experience; information search about the stimulus, including where to find it; transportation to the store or event, or the ordering of the item by mail, phone, or Internet; the payment for the item; its use and maintenance after purchase; its disposal (especially intergenerationally, see CHILDHOOD SOCIALIZATION AND INTERGENERATIONAL INFLUENCES); and the satisfaction with the memories created.

While Alderson (1957) noted that the family should be the unit of analysis in consumer research, the vast majority of family research in marketing has focused on the individual or, more precisely, on "family" decision making as the linear combination of individual preferences. Much emphasis in consumer family research has been paid to relative influence, in an effort to identify the individual most likely to make the particular decision. Measurement of "relative influence" has usually taken on an either/or perspective, using a competitive framework rather than a cooperative one more likely in the family context, and precluding investigation into constructs such as "shared influence." Thus, family consumer research has focused on individual members (Commuri and Gentry, 2000), usually the mother, rather than on interactions within the family. More recent work, however, has relied less on pencil and paper instruments and more on qualitative data that provide deeper insight into processes. An exemplar of such research was Epp (2008), who interviewed the family as a whole, as individual members, in dyads, and in triads in the context of vacation planning.

Family consumer research is an extremely dynamic phenomenon. Family gender norms are changing rapidly owing to societal changes (see MARKETING AND FEMINISM) such as the increasing number of households in which the wife makes a higher salary than her husband (over one-third now). Globalization is making the world smaller, and marketers are increasingly dealing with family decision making throughout the world. The most common format in the United States is the nuclear family, whereas family in the developing world is far more extended. At the same time, technology changes are having profound effects on roles within the family; for instance, consider the relative computer knowledge levels, which are generating more influence for teenagers in terms of many search processes. Family buying is a complex topic which will continue to challenge consumer researchers far into the future.

Bibliography

Alderson, W. (1957) Marketing Behavior and Executive Action, Irwin.

Commuri, S. and Gentry, J.W. (2000) Opportunities for family research in marketing. *Academy of Marketing Science Review*, **4** (5), 1–26. http://www.amsreview.org/articles/commuri08-2000.pdf

Epp, A.M. (2008) Yours, Mine, and Ours: How Families Manage Collective, Relational, and Individual Identity Goals in Consumption, (January 1, 2008), http://digitalcommons.unl.edu/dissertations/AAI3297655

Galvin, K.M., Bylund, C.L. and Brommel, B.J. (2004) *Family Communication: Cohesion and Change*, 6th edn, Allyn & Bacon, New York.

family life cycle

Catherine A. Cole, Dhananjay Nayakankuppam, and Jayati Sinha

The family life cycle (FLC) emerged as a fundamental marketing concept in the 1950s. Subsequent research on the concept addressed two questions: (i) how many different stages are there in the FLC? (Wells and Gubar, 1966; Murphy and Staples, 1979; Gilly and Enis, 1982; Du and Kamakura, 2006, 2008) and (ii) how do stages in the FLC affect household expenditure, savings, and the mix of products consumed? (see Redondo-Bellon, Royo-Vella, and Aldas-Manzano, 2001 for a review).

For managers, the FLC concept has obvious practical appeal. Stages of the FLC often replace the chronological age of the head of the household as a useful segmenting variable because households within the same FLC stage spend money in similar ways, while households in different FLC stages spend money in different ways. Furthermore, because the proportion of households at different FLC changes across time in predictable ways, the FLC stage can be used as an independent variable in models forecasting primary demand for certain products such as day care or food consumption at home.

However, we suggest that there is a need to better understand the theoretical underpinnings of the FLC model. If the concept is merely an agglomeration of a set of correlated demographic variables, it has little theoretical appeal – its value mainly lies in collapsing a large number of variables into a smaller set, thereby making it more practical and useful. Thus, differences in consumption across different categories formed through the agglomeration of these demographic variables might reflect cohort effects, or shifts in consumption patterns as a function of changing circumstances (for e.g., childcare consumption, and perhaps minivan purchases, are obviously precipitated by the birth of a child). A more interesting question might be to examine shifts in consumer processes as a function of the life cycle. This is an important issue because it is not just circumstances that change and dictate consumption – there are also real social changes brought about in consumer decision processes and these could dictate consumption in much more subtle and powerful ways. More importantly, these changes are not obvious and could thus result in counterintuitive effects. For example, could the preferences of children influence the preferences of parents, and vice versa?

We start by providing a review of the extant literature on the consumption life cycle. We then review criticisms of this concept. We also propose a framework that might be useful in examining how life cycle might influence consumer processes. Finally, we report briefly on one study from our labs in which we studied how children might influence parent preferences and how household environmental variables (such as parenting style) may account for heterogeneity in preferences among households at the same stage of the FLC.

THE CURRENT HOUSEHOLD/FAMILY LIFE-CYCLE MODEL

The assumption underlying the current FLC model is that family changes (marriage, birth of children, breakup of marriage, etc.) impact both the income and the expenditures of households. On the basis of variables such as age and labor activity of the household head, marital status, and age of youngest child, we can classify families into different stages. The stages of the FLC remain at heart a multidimensional variable resulting from combining other unidimensional ones.

Stages of the FLC. Conceptually, the FLC has evolved over time, primarily through increases in the number of stages and through increases in the flexibility of households in moving between stages. The early years established the conceptual bases of the FLC, utilizing family composition as the organizing theme. Starting in the 1940s and 1950s, the FLC models incorporated new variables as further stages were added to the model. In the more recent literature, FLC models have evolved away from the notion that households pass through an orderly progression of stages (Wells and Gubar, 1966) to the notion that households pass back and forth between stages in a more disorderly pattern (Gilly and Enis, 1982).

Table 1 summarizes the life stages of four prominent models. Wells and Gubar's (1966) model utilizes the criteria of marital status, age of head of household (HH), age of youngest child, the presence of dependent children, and whether the HH is part of the labor force. The model identifies nine consecutive stages through which an individual passes: bachelor, newly married couple, full nest I–II–III, empty nest I–II, solitary survivor in labor force, and solitary survivor retired.

Murphy and Staples (1979) propose 14 stages linked by multiple paths based on marital status and presence of children. Murphy and Staples (1979) sought to incorporate nontraditional families in response to the evolving family unit. The model considered new classification variables, such as adding the category divorced in marital status and parsing some of the other variables in a more fine-grained manner (e.g., HH age was divided into three bands as opposed to the two in the Wells and Gubar model). This model allowed the age of the children to be classified as (younger than 4, from 4 to 12, and between 13 and 18) to allows substages. The modifications reduced the number of nonclassifiable households to less than 20% in the United States and less than 30% in the United Kingdom.

The Gilly and Enis (1982) model, which includes 13 stages, incorporates nontraditional unmarried cohabiting-couple households and remarriages. Like the Murphy and Staples (1979) model, the Gilly and Enis model is not a single sequence model. Instead, households can move in both directions along various routes. This model represents most HHs since it excludes only 2.8% on the same data of the US Bureau of Census. Wilkes (1995) proposed a 15-stage hybrid of the Wells and Gubar and the Gilly and Ennis typologies.

Du and Kamakura (2006) empirically developed a 13-stage model, which is summarized in Table 1. Instead of a priori defining stages, they empirically identify life stages using a hidden Markov model on household data that include characteristics such as marital status, age, and employment, and information about household size including the number of other adults and the presence of children at different ages. One interesting variable that emerges in their life-stage characterization is whether the household has children in college. Intuitively, this variable should influence household consumption because tuition often represents a major household expenditure. The data, supporting the life-stage model, were collected from a panel of approximately 8000 households in the United States that were tracked annually from 1968 through the present.

Ability of the FLC to predict consumption. Evidence is accumulating that household/FLC stage affects both the size of the consumption budget and household spending priorities for a broad variety of categories including home ownership, entertainment, energy, and other expenditures (Lansing and Morgan, 1955; Wells and Gubar, 1966; Fritzsche, 1981; Schaninger and Danko, 1993; Wilkes, 1995; Redondo-Bellon, Royo-Vella, and Aldas-Manzano, 2001; Du and Kamakura, 2008). While the reports are too numerous to review extensively, we summarize a few findings. Lansing and Morgan (1955) as well as Wells and Gubar (1966) report that income, expenditures on durable goods, assets, debts, and subjective feelings about financial position differ at different life-cycle stages. Fritzsche (1981) reports that after controlling for income and the number of people in the household, young

Table 1 Comparison of the stages of four family life–cycle models.

Wells and Gubar (1966)	Murphy and Staples (1979)	Gilly and Enis (1982)	Du and Kamakura (2006, 2008)
Bachelor stage; young, single, not living at home	Young (below 35) single	Bachelor I: under 35 years of age	Co/So: young single/married couple, no child, HH age 22–30
	Young (below 35) divorced, no children	—	S1: single/divorced, no child, HH age 26–42
Young, married, no children	Young (below 35) married without children	Young couple under 35 years of age	—
Full nest I, youngest child under 6	Young (below 35) married with children	Full nest I: couple, child under 6, HH under 35	C1: couple, children less than age 7, HH age 25–35
	Young (below 35) divorced with children	Single parent I: child under 6, HH under 35	S2: Divorced/single, children under age 18, HH age 27–41
Full nest II: youngest child 6+	Married, children, HH age 35–64	Full nest II: couple, children 6+, HH under 35	C2: Family (5+), children under age 15, HH age 33–41
		Single parent II: children 6+, HH under 35	C4: Family (3–4), children age 7+, HH age 33–44
	Middle aged (35 to 64) divorced with children	Single parent III: HH 35–64	S3: Divorced/widow (2–3), children age 14+, college kids, HH age 44–62
	Middle aged (35 to 64) married without children	Childless couple: age 35–64	—
	Middle aged (35 to 64) divorced without children	Bachelor II: age 35–64 years	—
Full nest III: older married couples with dependent children	—	Delayed full nest: couple HH age 35–64, child under 6	C3: family (5+), children age 7+, college kids, HH age 40–50
		Full nest 3 HH age 35–64, children 6+	C5: family (3–4), children age 14+, college kids, HH age 45–57

Table 1 (*Continued*).

Wells and Gubar (1966)	Murphy and Staples (1979)	Gilly and Enis (1982)	Du and Kamakura (2006, 2008)
Empty nest I: older married couples, no children living with them, head in labor force	Middle aged (35–64) married without dependent children	—	C6: Couple with no dependent children (age 51–73)
Empty nest II: older couple, no children at home, retired	Older (above 64) married	Older couple: 65+	C7: Family (2–3), no children under 18 or in college, HH age 63–77, retired.
Solitary survivor, working	Older (above 64) unmarried	Bachelor III: 65+	S4: Divorced/single, empty nest, HH age 49–71, working/ retired
Solitary survivor, retired	—	—	S5: (Widowed) empty nest, HH age 66–84, retired

singles in the Wells and Gubar (1966) FLC classification consume less energy than households at any other stage of the FLC (except for gasoline). Du and Kamakura (2006) analyze discretionary spending across a wide range of expenditure categories. They find that the lowest levels of expenditures are observed for older households with single, divorced, or widowed heads, while the highest are observed for large households with children. They also find allocation differences across households. For example, the top tax- and rent-paying FLC stages are households (single/divorced or young couples) with no children. In summary, there are budget and budget allocation differences across the FLC.

Criticisms of the FLC concept.   While much research has verified that FLC is a discriminating variable of consumption and expenditure in a wide range of products and services, there are a number of shortcomings. There is considerable uncertainty about the generalizability of these models. They require frequent updating in the face of social trends that change the dynamics that presumably underlie the different stages. Further, these models have been developed primarily within the US context and are difficult to apply in other countries with different

social contexts. For example, Redondo-Bellon, Royo-Vella, and Aldas-Manzano (2001) present plausible reasons for modifying the model for the Spanish environment and develop a model with 11 stages. Wells and Gubar (1966) note that these models may not generalize across social classes because, as sociologists have noted, there may be differences in consumption goals. Finally, stages of FLC may not affect consumption of all products and services.

Other problems with the concept include the observation that no two investigators have yet agreed on the numbers and types of stages. This makes comparing the results from one study with those from another difficult. Additionally, within a single study, the researcher often has difficulty defining categories. If they are defined too narrowly, they will include a very small portion of the respondents, but if they are too broad, they will squeeze everyone into a few categories. Most models do not cover all possible types of families, nor are the identified types of families always mutually exclusive. For example, the Wells and Gubar (1966) model does not include household with children older than 17, single people older than 44, or widows with children living at home. Similarly, the Murphy and Staples (1979) model excludes families with children aged above 18, single parent households with a nondivorced parent, and those over 64 living with their children. The Gilly and Enis (1982) model treats cohabiting and married couples as the same, although their consumption patterns may differ.

Additionally, in all the models, older adults are typically lumped together in one or two stages depending on marital status. However, this categorization may mask substantial differences in the older population (those still working, living independently vs those supported by assisted living) that may account for differences in expenditures. Also, these models often do not incorporate the labor force participation of both partners.

Additionally, Commuri and Gentry (2000) raise the point that the most interesting changes in consumer behavior may be observed as households move between stages, not once they reach equilibrium in a stage. Finally, because most research on the FLC uses cross-sectional rather than longitudinal research, cohort effects may explain the observed pattern of results.

An overall problem is the focus on outcome (decisions) rather than processes (decision making). On the one hand, researchers frequently check whether the FLC model does better in predicting outcomes than socioeconomic variables such as size of the household, and characteristics of the main wage earner such as education level, job status, age, and income (Redondo-Bellon, Royo-Vella, and Aldas-Manzano, 2001). However, the models have neither identified underlying mechanisms,

which explain how families make decisions, nor have they identified how these mechanisms might change across the FLC to explain different outcomes. In other words, there is little evidence suggesting that the FLC stage determines consumption.

PROPOSED NEW MODEL

Figure 1 contrasts the current and a proposed new FLC model. We propose a new model based on the following linkages: changed circumstances → life-cycle stage → (information processing, memory, attitudes) → behavior → consumption.

Because most people grow up in a family and continue as adults to live in social units, we believe that families have a pervasive influence on consumer behavior. We think that research in this area should shift from identifying characteristics of different life-cycle stages and consumption outcomes to analyzing how life-cycle stage affects the decision process.

Our proposed model suggests questions regarding a variety of interesting factors: how does life-cycle stage affect information processing, memory, attitudes, and behavior? For example, one difference that might emerge between different household types is the time pressure felt. It would be reasonable to predict that increases in the time pressure felt would reduce the amount of information processing for major household purchases. These changes in the time pressure felt might affect memory, attitudes, behavior, and consumption outcomes.

Current family life cycle model		
Changed circumstances in terms of partner status presence/age of children age of head of household	→	Life cycle stage → Consumption

Proposed new model			
Changed circumstances →	→	Life cycle stage	→ Information processing → Memory → Attitudes → Behavior → Consumption

Figure 1 The current and proposed new household/family life cycle model.

Thus, in this example, the underlying variable of interest is not so much the stage of the FLC, but the time pressure felt by members of the household.

In the next section, we narrow down on a specific topic: the influence of college children on parents. Typical models of the FLC minimize this flow because the adult children are no longer living at home.

EXAMPLE RESEARCH: COLLEGE STUDENTS' INFLUENCE ON THEIR PARENTS' CONSUMPTION BEHAVIOR

The study we describe represents part of a larger effort to investigate how adult children "socialize" their parents, which represents a twist on traditional socialization theory, because we are not studying how adults influence their children's brand choices but how children shape the choices of the adults. Specifically, we study the amount of attitudinal convergence between adult children and their parents for different brands in different product categories. We expect that attitudinal convergence will vary across different types of product categories and across different types of families.

Product category. In our research, we invest-igated four different types of products: high-technology products, joint family use products, products used for individual purposes, and fast-moving consumer goods. We expect a family's opinions about brands in the high-technology products and in the joint family use categories to converge the most, but for different reasons. If a product is consumed by a family, then the family will confer about the brand and consumption is likely to be correlated – so there will likely be a convergence of attitudes. If a product is a high-technology product, then we expect the college-age student to influence the older parent – the college-age child is likely to be perceived as having expertise in the category and his/her preferences and recommendations would thus be more influential. However, for products consumed for individual purposes and for fast-moving consumer goods, it is likely that members of the household are less likely to discuss the brand choice and preferences

with each other and there will thus be a divergence in family opinions. This leads to H1: attitudinal convergence will be higher for high technology products and for products that are consumed jointly and lower for frequently purchased consumer goods and items consumed for personal use. However, more important for the point we are making (namely, that these effects on attitudes are mediated through social processes), we suggest that this influence of college-age students on parents will surface only in certain kinds of households.

Family environment variables as moderators. Households within the same stage of the FLC may differ on constructs that capture family dynamics, such as nurturance, communication style, and parenting style.

Nurturance. We assessed parental warmth or nurturance using an 18-item scale with five-point Likert-type items measuring the degree to which a parent describes his/her interaction with his/her children as being warm, affectionate, and encouraging. Thus, nurturance is likely to create an atmosphere where children are more comfortable about expressing their preferences, which could thus influence parents. Thus, while we expect greater attitudinal convergence within families for technology products and joint-consumption products, we expect this to be particularly the case in families high on nurturance (H2).

Communication style. Prior research sugg-ests that communication within the family affects children's influence. We use a communication encouragement scale, which is composed of four five-point Likert-type statements measuring the degree to which a parent believes that children should be free to candidly express their own views and disagree with their parents when they feel like it. Prior research reports that parents scoring high on the communication encouragement scale are more likely to talk to their children about consumer issues. Parents are likely to be exposed to the opinions and attitudes of their children, leading to the greater possibility of influence, depending on the extent to which children are free to express their opin-ions. Thus, while we expect greater attitudinal convergence within families for technology products and joint-consumption products, we expect this to be particularly the case in families high on communication style (H3).

Parental style. Parenting style refers to a group of attitudes toward the child that influence the emotional climate in which the child is raised. Prior research reports that parental style affects both children's choice of influence strategy and their degree of influence indirectly through children's perceptions of parental power. The scale can be viewed as being made up of three subscales: demandingness, emotional responsiveness, and psychological autonomy granting. The demandingness dimension reflects the extent to which parents direct their children's development through maturity, and expectations, close supervision, discipline, and confrontation when a child disobeys. The responsiveness dimension is the extent to which parents encourage their children's individuality by staying attuned to and supporting their children's needs. The autonomy-granting subscale reflects the parental attitude toward the child having an independent point of view. Thus, while we expect greater attitudinal convergence within families for technology products and joint-consumption products, we expect this to be particularly the case in families high on parenting style, especially on the responsiveness and autonomy-grating dimensions (H4).

Method.   A total of 115 student participants took part in the study for partial course credit. They proceeded to fill out a questionnaire designed to assess their attitudes toward a variety of targets as well as containing scales designed to assess family environment – parenting-style scale. Each student addressed a questionnaire to one parent. This questionnaire assessed the parent's attitudes toward the same targets as well as their assessments of the family environment – scales to measure nurturance and communication style.

Analytic approach.   Since the data have a nested design (with attitudes of parents and children toward various brands nested within families), with brands at the lower level (level 1) and family characteristics at the higher level (level 2), we adopted a hierarchical modeling technique. This technique is, in essence, a mixed model incorporating fixed as well as random effects, to incorporate heterogeneity. Thus, attitudes toward any stimuli are presumed to be the result of not only characteristics at level 1 (product category) but could also result from the fact that the attitudes come from a certain social unit with interdependencies. This approach allows us to explicitly test for the hypothesized cross-level interaction, where family characteristics (at level 2) impact attitudes of both constituents (at level 1).

For the purposes of the analysis, a deviance score was calculated for each target of judgment by squaring the difference between the parent and child's attitudes. This represents the degree of convergence in family opinion – that is, the higher the deviance score, the greater the divergence in opinion (or the lower the convergence in attitudes). Thus, the deviance scores for a number of targets are nested within families that vary on the family environment variables. One can then estimate whether there is significant heterogeneity (i.e., do families differ significantly in their deviance scores across targets?). This separates the variance components across the two levels of analysis. One can then examine whether the deviance is impacted by product category, by family environment variables, and, importantly, by the cross-category interaction that has been hypothesized.

Results.
Brand attitudes.   A null model yielded significant heterogeneity across families (estimate $= 5.85$, $z = 5.59$, $p < 0.0001$) and an intraclass correlation of 0.153, revealing that about 15% of the variance was at level 2 (at the level of the families). Adding the product-type variable yielded a significant main effect, F $(3, 342) = 12.64$, $p < 0.0001$. As predicted in H1, the deviance scores for technology $(M = 1.7)$ and joint decisions $(M = 1.8)$ were smaller than those for fast-moving consumer goods $(M = 3.7)$ and personal items $(M = 2.4)$. The next models added the perceptions of influence. Both parent's $(F (1, 1723) = 98.85$, $p < 0.0001)$ and children's $(F (1, 1724) = 78.91$, $p < 0.0001)$ perceptions of influence yielded main effects. We next proceeded to add the family environment variables.

Nurturance.   Consistent with H2, analyses yielded a significant cross-level nurturance X product-type interaction, F (3, 1719) = 3.29, $p < 0.02$. This interaction is graphed in Figure 2, and shows that, consistent with the hypothesis, high-nurturance families have more convergent brand attitudes on the target categories than low-nurturance families. Families low in nurturance show little convergence across all categories, while families high on nurturance show a significant convergence in the target categories.

Communication encouragement style. Consistent with H3, a main effect for communication style, F (1, 113) = 8.11, $p < 0.01$,

was qualified by a significant cross-level product-type X-communication-style interaction, F (3, 1719) = 7.71, $p < 0.0001$. The interaction is graphed in Figure 3 and shows that families that scored high on communication encouragement scale had higher convergence of attitudes toward brands than families that scored low on this scale in the target categories.

Parenting style.   The main effects emerged for responsiveness, ($b = -0.85$), F (1, 113) = 3.26, $p < 0.07$, autonomy granting, ($b = -1.3$) F (1, 113) = 10.98, $p < 0.0001$, and demandingness, ($b = -0.75$), F (1, 113) = 4.89, $p < 0.03$. As predicted in H4, these main effects

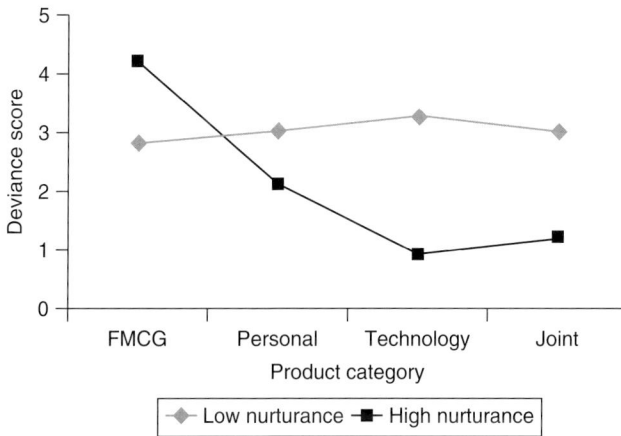

Figure 2 Nurturance × product-type interaction.

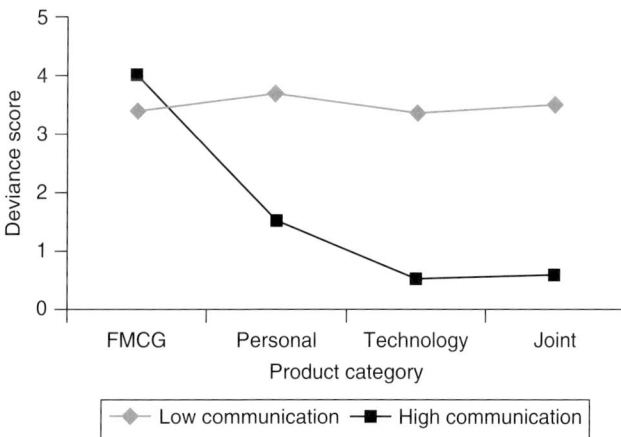

Figure 3 Communication style × product-type interaction.

were all moderated by significant cross-level interactions with product type (all interactions significant at least at $p < 0.01$ level). These interactions are graphed in Figures 4–6.

Discussion. Analyses suggest that there is considerable convergence in attitudes within families. This suggests that there are, indeed, theoretically meaningful differences in the social processes that accompany FLC stages. DINKs (double income–no kids) households, for instance, cannot be subject to the kinds of influence we have just outlined. This suggests that it might be worthwhile trying to explicate the social changes that accompany FLC stages and the impact these have on various consumer processes (information processing, memory, attitudes, etc.).

While it is difficult to parse out the direction of influence (is the convergence due to parents influencing children or children influencing parents) with the correlational data reported here, there appear to be the following reasons to think that children do influence parents' attitudes, at least to some extent. First, the pattern of influence across the product types is more suggestive of children influencing parents. For example, the technology items were chosen as those that children would be more likely to have experience in (e.g., MP3 players, computers, etc.). Second, we asked participants for the extent of influence they thought they

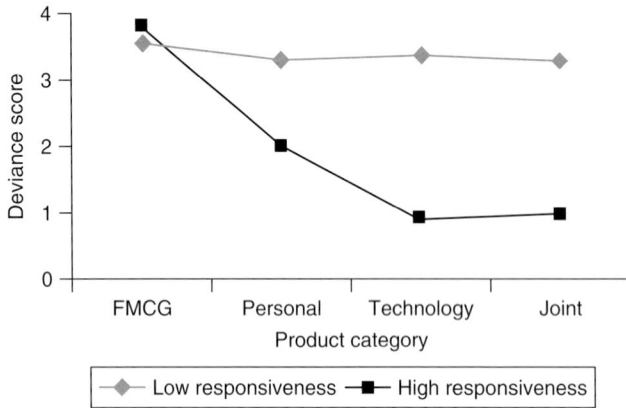

Figure 4 Parent's responsiveness × product-type interaction.

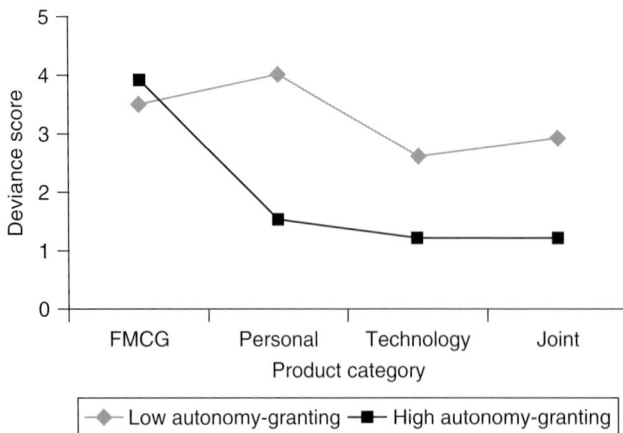

Figure 5 Parent's autonomy-granting × product-type interaction.

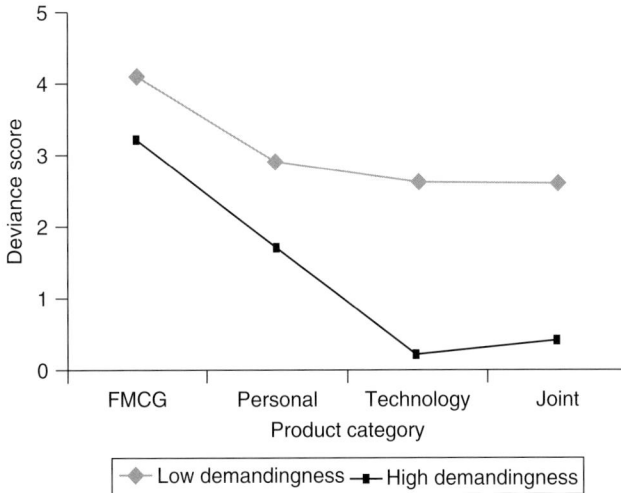

Figure 6 Parent's demandingness × product-type interaction.

had on their parents for each of the targets of judgments. Children actually had fairly accurate perceptions of when they had an influence on their parent's attitudes – that is, their impression was that they were more likely to have influenced their parents' attitudes on the technology and joint-consumption items than the other categories. Third, the pattern of moderation by the family environment variables lends further credence to this idea – the family environment variables were chosen as theoretical constructs that would suggest a greater propensity for children to express their opinions about products – this further supports the notion that children were likely to have influenced their parent's attitudes.

CONCLUSION

We conclude by observing that there are several important directions for future research. First, prior research has identified meaningful parameters to use to classify households into life stages. These variables include demographics such as marital status, age of the HH, employment status of the HH, and age of children (if any). Future researchers should use available sophisticated methodologies such as the hidden Markov models used by Du and Kamakura (2006) to empirically identify the most common

types of households in a market and to estimate the probabilities that a household will follow an expected life path. Such an analysis could, for example, help school districts better predict enrollment trends at local elementary schools. Second, research needs to continue to identify how these emerging FLC stages influence consumption outcomes. However, such work would be enhanced if it were based on theoretically derived hypotheses about why consumption priorities shift across the FLC. Third, more research needs to be directed toward households in transition from one stage to the next stage. Households in transition may share characteristics such as a high degree of uncertainty about consumption priorities. Finally, and perhaps most importantly, more research on group consumer decision making would shed light on the processes that underlie consumption decisions made at each stage of the FLC. It is likely that such research will uncover considerable heterogeneity among families at the same life-cycle stage. Our lab study, for example, suggests that variables related to family dynamics, such as parenting style, may explain some of the heterogeneity. We believe there are many exciting unanswered questions about how family decision making changes across the FLC.

Bibliography

Commuri, S. and Gentry, J. (2000). Opportunities for family research in marketing. *Academy of Marketing Science Review*, 8. Available at: http://www.amsreview.org/articles/commuri08-2000.pdf.

Du, R.Y. and Kamakura, W.A. (2006) Household life cycles and lifestyles in the United States. *Journal of Marketing Research*, 93, 121–132.

Du, R.Y. and Kamakura, W. (2008) Where did all that money go? Understanding how consumers allocate their consumption budget. *Journal of Marketing*, 72, 109–131.

Fritzsche, D. (1981) An analysis of energy consumption patterns by stage of family life cycle. *Journal of Marketing Research*, 18, 227–232.

Gilly, M.C. and Enis, B.M. (1982) Recycling the family life cycle: a proposal for re-definition, in *Advances in Consumer Research*, vol. 9 (ed. A. Mitchell), Association for Consumer Research, Ann Arbor, MI, pp. 271–276.

Lansing, J.B. and Morgan, J.N. (1955) Consumer finances over the life cycle, in *Consumer Behavior*, vol. 2 (ed. L.H. Clark), New York University Press, New York, pp. 36–51.

Murphy, P. and Staples, W. (1979) A modernized family life cycle. *Journal of Consumer Research*, 6, 612–638.

Redondo-Bellon, I., Royo-Vella, M. and Aldas-Manzano, J. (2001) A family life cycle model adapted to the Spanish environment. *European Journal of Marketing*, 35, 612–638.

Schaninger, C.M. and Danko, W.D. (1993) A conceptual and empirical comparison of alternative household lifecycle models. *Journal of Consumer Research*, 19, 580–594.

Wells, W. and Gubar, G. (1966) Life cycle concept in marketing research. *Journal of Marketing Research*, 3, 355–363.

Wilkes, R.E. (1995) Household lifecycle stages, transitions and product expenditures. *Journal of Consumer Research*, 22, 27–42.

H

habit in consumer behavior

Leona Tam

A habit is a behavioral disposition in which past responses are triggered directly by associated context cues. Consumer habits can be triggered by a wide array of cues in purchase and consumption contexts, including physical settings, presence of others, mood, time of day, and actions that immediately precede a habitual response. Thus, the theater environment may trigger popcorn consumption, or a visit from family around dinnertime might trigger a trip to Olive Garden.

How is habit formed? Consumer habits are formed when purchases and consumptions are repeated under similar circumstances. Such repetitions strengthen the cognitive associations between consumer responses and purchase and consumption contexts. When habits have formed, perception of the familiar cues activates a representation of the practiced, habitual response in memory. Given this reliance on cues, consumer habits are maintained when cues in the purchase and consumption contexts remain stable. Habits change when the cues are altered or when consumers are motivated and able to inhibit their automatic responses to the cues.

Even when consumers intend to try new brands and thereby change their established brand habits, they may continue to repeat past purchase and consumption activities when those responses are cued automatically by stable features of the environment. Because habits are automatically brought to mind in the appropriate circumstances, they tend to be repeated unless consumers are willing and able to exert effortful control to inhibit the activated response and

to select a new one, or when the circumstances triggering habitual responses are changed.

Owing to the automaticity in consumer habits, consumers' habits do not necessarily change through altering behavioral intentions. How can consumers change their habits? One possibility is to take advantage of the *habit discontinuity effect*, or the disruption in habits that naturally occurs when people change life contexts. Change in performance contexts can shift consumer habits out of an automatic mode so that purchase and consumption become more deliberate and guided by consumer intentions. With changes in performance contexts, the habitual behavior may no longer be automatically brought to mind, and people may be released to act in ways consistent with their intentions and preferences. Marketers could target interventions to change consumers' habits to use competing brands for times at which consumers undergo naturally occurring changes in habit contexts, for example, when consumers relocate and may not have access to old retail outlets and associated brands. Retailers like Home Depot and Bed Bath & Beyond offer discounts as incentives to encourage patronage of consumers who have recently relocated. This strategy should effectively attract habitual consumers of competitor's brands whose habits are disrupted because of relocation.

Habitual consumers can also undertake to change their response to context cues, but not without sufficient regulatory strength to inhibit habits. In the implication of the willpower required for habit inhibition, marketers may wish to set up promotions and other sales events so that consumers repeatedly purchase and use their brand in ways that foster habit formation. Once formed, habits persist because they require willpower effort to inhibit. Illustrating such a promotion, a consumer recently received in the mail six $10 coupons for a new grocery store. Each coupon was valid for one week, and the coupon promotion was held over a period of six consecutive weeks. In order to use the coupons, she went to that grocery store every week, despite that there was another store she preferred. After six weeks, when all the coupons were used, she found herself going automatically to the new grocery store for the next shopping trip. She had formed a habit to frequent the new store, and, especially after a depleting day at work, it was easier to follow that habit than to inhibit it and choose another store.

Consumer habits are sometimes referred to as low involvement decision making, given the lack of effortful processing in consumer habit performance. However, consumers often repeat important purchases and consumptions and thus form habits. Health conscious consumers purposefully go to a salad bar for lunch on weekdays and are very likely going to form a strong habit to do so after a few weeks of repetitions. Therefore, consumer habits are not limited to products of low involvement to consumers. The critical distinction between habits and brand loyalty for marketers lies in whether repeated purchase and consumption reflect the repetition of a particular response (habits) or whether they reflect an evaluative disposition that can guide repetition of a variety of brand responses (loyalty). Thus, for marketers, managing habitual customers requires different programs than those that are typically used to manage loyalty. Managing habits involves changing or maintaining the cue or the response to a cue, while managing loyalty involves improving or changing consumers' brand evaluation or favorability.

See also *consumer behavior analysis; consumer brand loyalty; implicit consumer cognition; self-regulation*

Bibliography

Beatty, S.E. and Kahle, L.R. (1988) Alternative hierarchies of the attitude-behavior relationship: the impact of brand commitment and habit. *Journal of the Academy of Marketing Science*, **16** (2), 1–10.

Ji, M.F. and Wood, W. (2007) Purchase and consumption habits: not necessarily what you intend. *Journal of Consumer Psychology*, **17** (4), 261–276.

Johnson, E.J., Bellman, S. and Lohse, G.L. (2003) Cognitive lock-in and the power law of practice. *Journal of Marketing*, **67** (2), 62–75.

Kaas, K.P. (1982) Consumer habit forming, information acquisition, and buying behavior. *Journal of Business Research*, **10** (1), 3–15.

Khare, A. and Inman, J.J. (2006) Habitual behavior in American eating patterns: the role of meal occasions-link. *Journal of Consumer Research*, **32** (4), 567–575.

Murray, K.B. and Häubl, G. (2007) Explaining cognitive lock-in: the role of skill-based habits of use in consumer choice. *Journal of Consumer Research*, **34**, 77–88.

Tam, L., Bagozzi, R.P. and Spanjol, J. When planning is not enough: the self-regulatory effect of implementation intentions on changing snacking habits. *Health Psychology*. (in press)

Tam, L., Wood, W. and Ji, M.F. (2009) Brand loyalty is not habitual, in *Handbook of Brand Relationships* (eds J. Priester, D. MacInnis and C.W. Park), ME Sharpe.

Verplanken, B., Walker, I., Davis, A. and Jurasek, M. (2008) Context change and travel mode choice: combining the habit discontinuity and self-activation hypotheses. *Journal of Environmental Psychology*, **28** (2), 121–127.

Wirtz, J., Mattila, A.S. and Lwin, M.O. (2007) How effective are loyalty reward programs in driving share of wallet? *Journal of Service Research*, **9** (4), 327–334.

Wood, W. and Neal, D.T. (2007) A new look at habits and the habit-goal interface. *Psychological Review*, **114** (4), 843–863.

Wood, W., Quinn, J. and Kashy, D. (2002) Habits in everyday life: thought, emotion, and action. *Journal of Personality and Social Psychology*, **83**, 1281–1129.

Wood, W., Tam, L. and Guerrero Witt, M. (2005) Changing circumstances, disrupting habit. *Journal of Personality and Social Psychology*, **88** (6), 918–933.

hedonism: gratification is value

Barry J. Babin and Mitch Griffin

Mill's *Utilitarianism* impresses upon us the fact that gratification is tied to consequences. In other words, one finds value in activities because those activities may bring future contentment. Does anyone really want a root canal? Consumers seek this service because the end result will be greater contentment because of a lack of pain. While this notion is the received view of most consumer behavior – consumers are solving problems through their activities – the fact is that this utilitarian value in no way precludes the more nascent idea that value is also realized from the immediate gratification of these activities in and of themselves (Babin, Darden, and Griffin, 1994). An automobile is purchased because the consumer is able to address the task of transporting oneself, the family, and effects from one place to another. This utilitarian gratification will be realized in the future. However, the actual act of purchasing an automobile can also be directly gratifying. This is particularly true for the car enthusiast, but even a novice will likely feel some excitement taking a new (preferably expensive) car out for a test spin. This immediate happiness produces gratification, which is hedonic value.

The contrast between consumer activities characterized by hedonism, or experiencing things for the value of the experience itself, with activities performed because they are means to future ends, or workings of utilitarian value, provides a great deal of insight into consumers' behavior. For instance, consider the interplay between time and consumption. Although a topic that is not particularly well studied, most marketing management practice addressing time issues is directed toward reducing the time that it takes for a consumer to receive a service or accomplish a task. This is the utilitarian view. Hedonic value, in contrast, releases the consumer from the bounds of time in the sense that hedonism has no time cost. This does not mean that time does not pass, but the time invested now yields value because of the immediate gratification provided, rather than lacking or even diminishing consumer value.

One might ask, which of the two is greater, hedonism or utilitarianism? This is an empirical question (Babin and Attaway, 2000), but it also is a question that misleads to the extent that it casts these as opposing values. Marketers must provide experiences that provide high value and examples can be found where the provision is accomplished through predominantly utilitarianism (i.e., Wal-Mart) or hedonism (i.e., Disney). But perhaps the best route to truly great marketing is the provision of high utilitarian *and* high hedonic value. Consider how the modern day spa provides services a consumer might have previously received by visiting a hair salon, a nail salon, a massage therapist, a dermatologist, and so forth to receive the same amount of utilitarian value. But, these spas also provide an instantaneously gratifying experience. The consumer can experience hedonism. Fortunately for marketers, this added value is also associated with added payments by the consumer. When the two become inseparable, the experience of the extrinsic value provided by products and services provides intrinsic value in itself, the value experience is maximized.

Eventually, Mill (1861) argues that value is captured in contentment or happiness. Happiness eventually wins out as a greater and more interesting value being ephemeral yet powerful. People will sacrifice current contentment for greater happiness. Interestingly, marketing practice and theory devotes a great deal of attention toward satisfaction and less toward hedonism. Contentment is not nearly as motivating. The state of contentment itself is indicative of homeostasis and thus lacks motive power. However, hedonism leads to attachment and the desire to reexperience the gratification. Thus, perhaps consumer researchers would be well served to consider the relative power of value, particularly hedonic value, over satisfaction.

See also *brand value; consumer desire; customer lifetime value (CLV); customer solutions; emotion; international retailing; luxury brands versus other brand categories; variety-seeking*

Bibliography

Babin, B.J. and Attaway, J.P. (2000) Atmospheric affect as a tool for creating value and gaining share of customer. *Journal of Business Research*, **49**, 91–99.

Babin, B.J., Darden, W.R. and Griffin, M. (1994) Work and/or fun? Measuring hedonic and utilitarian shopping value. *Journal of Consumer Research*, **19**, 644–656.

Mill, J.S. (1861) in *Utilitarianism*, (ed. R. Crisp (1998)), Oxford University Press, Oxford.

how consumers respond to price information

Kent B. Monroe

PROCESSING OF PRICES AS NUMERICAL INFORMATION

We use numbers virtually every day in our lives, for example, as a form of identification of ourselves, to make telephone calls, or to pay a bill. However, the apparent ease with which we use numbers hides the fact that very complex cognitive processes are required to recognize numerical stimuli, or to make numerical comparisons or calculations. In this section, we review research results that help us understand the complexity of processing price information.

Complexity of numerical cognition processes. Number processing involves the ability to mentally manipulate sequences of words or symbols according to fixed rules. This process is of interest when a consumer is calculating or estimating the numerical difference between two prices, or adding the surcharge of shipping and handling to determine the total cost of the purchase. To compare prices, or judge the differences in prices requires that we access and manipulate a mental model of quantities similar to a mental number line. Approximation is the process by which Arabic or verbal numerals are first converted into an internal magnitude representation in our minds. This encoding is automatic, fast, and independent of which number is encoded.

When numbers are used to denote amounts, such as prices, the magnitude of the number becomes meaningful. When a price is encoded as a magnitude, either the exact value or an approximation of the exact value of the price is encoded and represented in memory. Given this encoding, we are interested in learning how people process price information when making price comparisons, when discriminating between two prices, whether the oddness of a price influences processing, and how a series of numbers that comprise a price may be remembered.

Comparing and discriminating numbers. The *distance effect* indicates that it takes longer to decide that 8 is larger than 6 than to decide that

8 is larger than 2. Moreover, the *magnitude effect* indicates that, for equal numerical distance, it is easier to discriminate small numbers (e.g., 1 vs 2) than larger numbers (e.g., 8 vs 9). The digit 5 has a special status in our numbering system. The digits 2, 3, and 4 are initially encoded as small, while the digits 6, 7, and 8 are encoded as large. That is, the mental representation of numbers below 10 is divided into numbers above and below 5. Thus, in a price comparison, task people first automatically encode the two prices independently and then classify the prices as "small" or "large" (Monroe and Lee, 1999).

When judging which number in a pair is *larger*, people find the task easier when both numbers are large than when both are small. The opposite is true when people have to decide which item is smaller. It has been shown that when people are trying to determine which of the two numerals is larger, it is an easier task if the larger of the compared numerals is displayed in larger font size. Similar results occur when people are trying to determine the smaller of compared numerals and the smaller numeral is displayed in smaller font size (Coulter and Coulter, 2005).

As suggested above, some processing of price information may be more automatic than others. Also, price comparisons in the lower price range (i.e., smaller numbers involving fewer digits), which are more typical for most supermarket purchases, may be more likely to be processed automatically. Moreover, identifying whether a specific price is higher than another price will be processed faster when that price is indeed higher than the comparison or reference price.

The left digit and price endings effects. Research has demonstrated that under a variety of different tasks and judgments, even digits are processed faster and/or more accurately than odd digits. Possible reasons for this odd price effect on consumer behavior can be divided into effects of *price perception* (how people encode price information into their minds) and effects of *price cognition* (how people process and interpret the price information).

Consumers have a tendency to underestimate 99¢-ending prices. Given that consumers seem to have more difficulty recalling odd-ending prices than round prices (e.g., $300) could imply that odd-ending prices are not encoded completely or that $300.00 is easier to encode as a magnitude than $299.99. One reason is prices ending in 99¢ are more difficult to process and as a result people may encode an approximation of the price rather than the precise price. Also, people tend to misperceive the difference between two prices when the left-most digits differ, odd price endings are used, and computations are necessary to determine the magnitude of difference (Manning and Sprott, 2009; Thomas and Morwitz, 2009). Knowing that perceived price has *meaning* that differs from its objective meaning in terms of perceived monetary sacrifice suggests that using inappropriate price endings could have unwanted implications for sellers.

Thus far, we have considered only a single price for a product or service, what are called *unidimensional prices*. However, offers often are provided with multiple price attributes. For example, an automobile may be advertised with a price for the vehicle, along with a combination of monthly payments, amount of down payment, and effective interest rate. Catalog and Internet offers typically quote selling prices and shipping and handling charges. When there are multidimensional prices, additional computations are required to evaluate the offer, some of which can be difficult. Also, some retail price promotions provide multiple discounts, for example, 40% off all merchandise with an extra 15% off if purchased at a certain time. When odd price endings are used, or when an item has a complicated price, for example, $23 977, these types of offers affect consumers' abilities to evaluate prices and to know exactly what they are paying for the item. The computational difficulty associated with multidimensional pricing is influenced by the price ending used, the perceived numerical distance between comparative prices, as well as the calculations necessary to determine the price to be paid.

Remembering prices.   Previous research has attempted to determine the extent that consumers do remember prices they have paid assuming that consumers are *consciously* involved in their purchasing behaviors and that product evaluations and choice decisions are a function of what information is accessible in memory. What is accessible in memory often is measured by

what consumers *can consciously remember*. The notion is that consumers frequently make judgments that a particular item is "too expensive" or "a real bargain" based on some prices that they recall from past shopping experiences, and these recalled prices form a basis on which the consumers' reference price is formed.

However, research measuring consumers' ability to remember prices of recently purchased items report that a relatively low proportion of consumers can accurately recall prices of recently purchased products (Monroe and Lee, 1999). Such research evidence could lead to the conclusion that consumers do not consciously attend to price information when either considering or actually making purchase decisions. Nevertheless, a shopper who does not recall the price of, say, the box of snack bars she just put into her cart may tell the interviewer that it is expensive. Thus, consumers may encode price information into memory in different representational forms.

Consumers may process and retrieve price information either consciously or nonconsciously. When price information is processed consciously, consumers pay attention to the price, make judgments regarding the value of the product using information that is either present in the external environment or retrieved from memory, and finally make a purchase decision. When consumers consciously process the actual price information, a magnitude representation of the price and their evaluative judgment may be transferred from working memory into long-term memory (Vanhuele, Laurent, and Dreze, 2006).

Alternatively, it is possible that only their comparative or evaluative judgments, and not the actual price information, are transferred into long-term memory. In this case, the consumers would not be able to recall the actual price when asked to do so at a later point in time. This scenario is consistent with the idea that an evaluation of a product may be more easily remembered than the price when the evaluation is formed at the time of exposure (Adaval and Monroe, 2002). When price information is processed nonconsciously, the consumer does not pay particular attention to the prices. Nonetheless, a judgment regarding the value of the product and a purchase decision may have been made. When nonconscious processing of price information occurs, the consumer may not be able to recall the price of the product at a later time, but she may still be able to indicate that the product is "too expensive," "a bargain," or "reasonably priced," indicating that the price information has been processed and evaluated. Thus, consumers' price comparisons and evaluations are affected by price information to which they have been previously exposed, even though they may not consciously remember the actual prices relevant to their judgments.

REFERENCE PRICES

Price judgments are comparative in nature. That is, for consumers to determine that a price is acceptable, too high, or low, that price must be compared to another price, whether that other price is in memory or available nearby. The other price serves as a comparison standard or reference price. Researchers have proposed and provided evidence for the existence of reference prices (Mazumdar, Raj, and Singh, 2005). These propositions have been based on adaptation-level theory and assimilation-contrast theory (social judgment theory).

Adaptation-level theory.   Adaptation-level theory assumes that stimuli are judged with respect to internal norms (*adaptation levels*) representing the combined effects of present and past experiences. For any consumer, the adaptation-level price for a specific product category is a function of the frequency distribution of prices for that category, the relative magnitude of the prices, the range of prices, and the dispersion of prices from the average price. It is influenced by past experience and by the sequence that the consumer observes the prices for the category. The concept of adaptation level or reference price supports the important point that *consumers judge or evaluate prices comparatively*; that is, the acceptability of a price is judged by comparison to another price.

When considering how consumers perceive prices, it has to be borne in mind that perception is relative. In other words, a specific price is compared to another price, or a reference price. When sellers advertise both the offered price and a (higher) comparative regular price, they

are suggesting a reference price for consumers' comparisons. To convince consumers to use the higher price as a reference price, sellers may include such words as "formerly", "regularly," and "usually," to describe the higher price. The judgment of acceptability depends not only on consumers' price expectations but also on information provided in promotions or advertisements.

Assimilation-contrast theory.   Similarly, the basic tenet of assimilation-contrast theory is that new stimuli encountered by an individual are compared against a background of experience with the stimuli category. This experience forms an individual's reference scale that serves as a basis for the individual to compare and evaluate other stimuli *perceived as related to* the reference stimuli.

If a new price is encountered for evaluation, it may also serve as an anchor in that it may result in a changing of the reference scale. Both adaptation-level theory and assimilation-contrast theory suggest that the reference price range should move in the direction of this new price. If the new price is relatively high, the reference price range moves toward the new price and the previously lower prices become further away from the reference price scale. If judgments of these previously perceived low prices in the category do not change when the new price is encountered, an *assimilation effect* is said to occur. The assimilation effect occurs because the new price is perceived as similar to the reference prices. However, if the new price moves the reference price range sufficiently higher, the original low prices will be perceived as lower than previously, and a *contrast effect* is said to occur.

The prevailing range of prices for a product category affects the consumer's reference price for that category. Since the width of the price range is affected by the lowest and highest price (end prices) in the range, these two end prices also affect price judgments. Thus, there are three different price cues affecting price judgments: the reference price, the lowest price, and the highest price in the range of prices available for judgment. Prices used by consumers to judge other prices (reference price, end prices) are called *anchoring stimuli*. By *price judgment* we mean a consumer's assessment of whether a price is too low, just right (acceptable), or too high.

In summary, a reference price is any price in relation to which other prices are perceived. These two theories clearly suggest that a reference "price" is actually an internally held judgment scale concerning prices for a product-price category.

PRICE THRESHOLDS

Absolute price thresholds. An important concept introduced in our discussion of reference price was the *acceptable price range*. This concept implies that a consumer has a lower price threshold and that there are prices greater than $0, which are unacceptable because they are considered to be too low, perhaps because consumers are suspicious of the product's quality. Also, it is recognized that at specific points in time there is a maximum price that consumers are willing to pay for a product or service (upper price threshold). The important point is that there is not just one acceptable price for a product or service; instead, there is some range of acceptable prices.

Variations in the level and width of consumers' acceptable price ranges are influenced by a number of factors. For a specific product category, the upper acceptable price threshold is lower if consumers perceive that there are similar alternative offerings available. However, if customer satisfaction increases or consumers become more loyal, then the upper threshold tends to be higher. Conversely, if customer satisfaction declines leading to lower consumer loyalty, consumers' upper price threshold would become lower. If consumers are not knowledgeable about prices for a product category, their acceptable price ranges tend to be relatively narrow and their lower and upper acceptable price limits tend to be lower than more knowledgeable consumers. Consumers who infer quality on the basis of price tend to have higher acceptable price levels, higher upper acceptable price limits, and wider acceptable price ranges. Finally, consumers who are consciously concerned about prices tend to have lower acceptable price levels, lower upper acceptable price limits, and narrower acceptable price ranges (Monroe, 2003).

Differential price thresholds. Usually a consumer has alternative choices available for a purchase and selects from among these choices. The prices of these alternative choices may provide cues that facilitate the decision process. However, even if the numerical prices are different, it cannot be assumed that the prices are *perceived* to be different. Hence, the problem becomes one of determining the effect of *perceived price differences* on consumer choice.

The perception of a price change or difference depends on the magnitude of the change or difference. Also, people are more sensitive to perceived price increases than to decreases. The immediate implication is that consumers will be more sensitive to price changes for some products, that is, have lower differential price thresholds. But, for other products, a similar price change may not be perceived. The differential price issue is how the price of one product is perceived to differ from the price of another offering that consumers believe is an alternative choice to consider. These alternative products could be sold by different sellers competitively or they could be alternative models of the product sold by a single seller.

PRICE AND CONSUMERS' PERCEPTIONS OF VALUE

Behavioral research has provided explanations of how people form value judgments and make decisions when they do not have perfect information about alternatives. These findings further our understanding of why consumers may be more sensitive to price increases than to price decreases, and how they respond to comparative price advertisements (e.g., regular price $65, sale price $49), coupons, rebates, and other price promotions.

In this section, we return to the idea that people seldom are good information processors and that they often take shortcuts (decision heuristics). These shortcuts may lead to errors in judgment and choice, but they may also facilitate the choice process. Several of these decision heuristics can help us understand how price influences perceptions of value and eventual product choice. First, the *context* of the purchase decision, including the way the offer is presented, *frames* the consumer's evaluation and choice. For example, the way a sale is advertised will influence consumers' judgments about the value of the offer. The context of the place of purchase affects a consumer's internal reference price or expectations about prices in that place.

Another important point is the *anchoring* effect mentioned earlier. As we observed earlier, the order of price presentation anchors consumers' judgments as do the low or high prices in a product line. Also, people tend to adapt to prices that are presented as the original prices. For example, antique dealers often over-price their items, anticipating that consumers will want to negotiate over the price. The initial high price serves as an anchor, and generally the negotiated price is higher than it would have been without this initial high anchor price. Prices that are irrelevant to the considered purchase can anchor judgments about what is acceptable to pay for an item (Nunes and Boatwright, 2004).

Perceived value represents a trade-off between consumers' perceptions of quality and sacri-fice. The degree that consumers believe there is a price–quality relationship influences their value perceptions and willingness to buy. When comparing prices, consumers' judgments are influenced by the relative or perceived differ-ences between the actual or offer price and the reference price. Using these points about price perception, we now show how perceived price influences consumers' judgments of value.

The price–perceived quality relationship. Con-sumers do not use price solely as a measure of cost (sacrifice). They also use price as an indicator of product quality (Rao and Monroe, 1989). Consumers are assumed to assess product or service quality by the use of cues. Prod-ucts, services, or stores can be conceptualized as consisting of an array of cues that may serve as indicators of quality. Consumers may use these cues if the cues help them predict the quality of the product or service and when they have confidence that they can use and judge the cues accurately. *Extrinsic cues* are product-related attributes – price, brand name, packaging, but they are not part of the product. *Intrinsic cues* are also product-related attributes, but they cannot be changed without altering the physical proper-ties of the product. Consumers rely on extrinsic cues and intrinsic cues when evaluating quality.

When consumers become familiar with a product they are more likely to use intrinsic cues rather than price or other external cues as indica-tors of product quality. However, highly familiar consumers (experts) use either price or intrinsic cues as indicators of quality, depending on whether their knowledge includes information about the reliability of price as a quality indicator. That is, if consumers know that there is a posi-tive price–quality relationship in the market, they will probably use price as a quality indicator. It has been argued further that if consumers know that there is a weak price–quality relationship in the product market, they will be more likely to use intrinsic product cues to assess product quality. Thus, the strength of the use of price or other external cues, such as brand or store name, as indicators of product quality, depends on the relative perceived differences between different cues and the degree that consumers know about the product and actual price–quality relationships.

The price–perceived monetary sacrifice relation-ship. A consumer's perceptions of the sacri-fice, "give up," or loss incurred by paying the monetary price for a product may vary according to a variety of situations and conditions. For example, does a consumer perceive paying $90 for a dental cleaning to be an equivalent sacri-fice as paying $90 for a ticket to a concert or sporting event? Indeed consumers may perceive equivalent monetary prices as representing very different sacrifices.

For some products or services, consumers would prefer not to make the expenditure. Thus the perceived sacrifice of paying a specific price for some products is psychologically more "painful" than others, even though the mone-tary outlay may be equivalent. Thus, the more the consumers are reluctant or hesitant to spend money on certain products, the more likely are they to search for bargains or lower prices, and they will be more sensitive to price changes and to price differentials between alternative choices.

If consumers believe that sellers have incre-ased prices to take advantage of an increase in demand, or a scarcity of supply, without a corresponding increase in costs, then such price increases would be perceived to be unfair (Bolton, Warlop, and Alba, 2003; Xia, Monroe, and Cox, 2004). In situations where one category of consumers receive the benefit of a lower price for an equivalent product or service but another category of consumers do not, the price-disadvantaged consumers may perceive that the price they pay is unfair (Haws and Bearden, 2006). Such situations typically occur when sellers provide discounts for consumers with certain characteristics, for example, age or preference status. Further, if there is no perceived discrepancy between the effort that these favored consumers make to qualify for the lower price relative to the disadvantaged consumers, then they will be receiving the same benefits as the disadvantaged consumers but incurring a smaller monetary sacrifice. Similarly, if consumers perceive that the prices they pay are higher than their comparable reference group, then such prices are likely to be perceived to be unfair.

Thus, a price judged as unfair can lead to lower perceptions of value and a reduction in willingness to pay; that is, a perceived disadvantaged price inequity, or a loss, increases consumers' perceptions of sacrifice, thereby decreasing their perceptions of value and willingness to buy.

INTEGRATING PRICE, QUALITY, AND SACRIFICE INFORMATION

When consumers use price as an indicator of cost or sacrifice, increasing price has the effect of reducing perceived value for the product or service. On the other hand, if consumers use price as an indicator of quality or benefits, increasing price has the effect of increasing perceived value. We know that consumers generally are not able to assess perfectly product or service quality (the ability of the product to provide satisfaction). We also know that perceptions of monetary sacrifice for the same specific price may vary according to whether the price is perceived to be fair, the context in which the price is presented, the consumers' acceptable price range, and the extent that consumers are concerned about price. We also understand that perceived value represents a mental trade-off between consumers' perceptions of quality and sacrifice and is positive when perceptions of quality are greater than their perceptions of sacrifice.

A very important issue is how consumers are able to integrate these different bits of information to determine their overall perceptions of value. In other words, information about the product or service attributes and benefits represents positive information (i.e., what the consumer gains from acquiring the product or service). Considering price as an indicator of cost represents negative information (i.e., what the consumer gives up when acquiring the product or service). Attempting to integrate positive and negative information simultaneously to determine an overall value judgment is a difficult mental task.

Although we have not been able to clarify the exact nature of this trade-off between perceived quality and sacrifice, there are some important implications given what we do know. The weight consumers attach to quality and sacrifice depends on the relative magnitude of the product's price. Generally, both quality and sacrifice are perceived to be low when price is perceived to be relatively low, and to be high when price is perceived to be relatively high. However, when evaluating a low-priced product, consumers appear to weigh quality more heavily than sacrifice, thus judging the product as low in value. Yet, when judging a high-priced product, consumers tend to weigh sacrifice more heavily than quality, again judging the product as low in value. These generalizations assume that consumers have sufficient motivation and cognitive resources to process the price and other attribute information to determine product value (Suri and Monroe, 2003). However, these assumptions about motivation and available cognitive resources are not always correct.

DECOMPOSING PERCEIVED PRODUCT VALUE

The overall perceived value of a product being evaluated is its (i) *acquisition value* (the expected benefit to be gained from acquiring the product less the net displeasure of paying for it) and (ii) *transaction value* (the perceived merits or fairness of the offer or deal) (Grewal, Monroe, and Krishnan, 1998).

Acquisition value. Consumers' perceptions of acquisition value represent a cognitive trade-off between the benefits they perceive in the product and the sacrifice they perceive to be required to acquire the product or service by paying the monetary price of the product. In part, the perceived benefits of a product are related to the consumers' judgments about the product's quality. Lacking perfect information about the inherent quality of the product, many consumers tend to believe that there is a positive relationship between a product's price and its quality ("You get what you pay for"). Thus, other things remaining the same, a higher priced product would be perceived to provide more benefits because of its higher perceived quality. However, at the same time, a higher price increases consumers' perceptions of their sacrifice. Thus, within some range of prices, the perceived benefits in the product will be larger than the perceived sacrifice, and consumers will perceive that there is positive acquisition value in the product. Generally, the greater the perceived acquisition value, the greater is the likelihood that consumers would be willing to purchase the product. However, besides evaluating the product's value, consumers also evaluate the offer itself.

Transaction value.　*Transaction value* is defined as the consumers' perceived merits of the offer or deal. Of concern here is how consumers evaluate a purchase situation in which the consumer gains a product but gives up the money paid for the product. Consumers first *judge* the value of the offer and then *decide* whether to make a purchase. To explain the role of price in this process, three price concepts are used. The *perceived benefit* of the product is equivalent to the utility inherent in the *maximum acceptable price* the consumer would be willing to pay. The *acquisition value* of the product is the perceived benefits of the product at this maximum price compared to the actual selling price, that is, $p_{max} - p_{actual}$. The *transaction value*, or the perceived merit of paying the actual price, is determined by comparing the consumer's reference price to the actual price, that is, $p_{ref} - p_{actual}$. Transaction value is positive if the actual price is less than the consumer's reference price, zero if they are equal, and negative otherwise.

Researchers have discovered that when transaction value is present it enhances acquisition value, but does not directly influence consumer

behavior (Grewal, Monroe, and Krishnan, 1998). Thus, acquisition value is determined by the consumers' perceptions of quality or benefits to be received plus perceived transaction value, which represents the comparison of the selling price to the consumers' reference price. One important implication of the finding that perceived transaction value enhances consumers' perceived acquisition value is consumers need to feel confident that they either can determine quality prior to purchase, or they can infer quality because the various signals of quality used by the sellers are appropriate indicators of quality.

SUMMARY

Throughout this article, we have developed a behavioral explanation of how consumers perceive price and how these perceptions influence their perceptions of value. Adaptation-level theory indicates not only that there is a reference price but also that it changes. Reference price is affected by contextual effects such as frequency of previous price changes, consumers' expectations about future prices, the order that price information is presented to consumers, the advertisement of prices, and the intensity of price promotion.

Assimilation-contrast theory indicates that there is a range of acceptable prices. This theory also suggests that the acceptable price range may be affected by the amount of price variation for a product category as perceived by consumers. Another implication derived from assimilation-contrast theory is that there is likely to be a range of prices around the reference price within which little change in demand is likely in response to a price change, that is, the price resulting from the price change may not be perceived as very different.

Finally, the psychological argument recognizes that people respond differently to perceived gains and perceived losses and suggests that consumers are more sensitive to price increases (perceived loss) than to price decreases (perceived gain). However, once the price difference (i.e., $p_{ref} - p$) is perceived to be important by the consumer, there is likely to be a more noticeable change in demand. These price differences can occur because of either a price increase or decrease, or because of comparative price advertising in which the seller provides an external reference price for comparison.

See also *brand value; consumer memory processes; customer analysis; demand elasticity; pricing strategy*

Bibliography

Adaval, R. and Monroe, K.B. (2002) Automatic construction and use of contextual information for product and price evaluations. *Journal of Consumer Research*, 28, 572–587.

Bolton, L.E., Warlop, L., and Alba, J.W. (2003) Consumer perceptions of price (un)fairness. *Journal of Consumer Research*, 29, 474–491.

Coulter, K.S. and Coulter, R.A. (2005) Size does matter: the effects of magnitude representation congruency on price perceptions and purchase likelihood. *Journal of Consumer Psychology*, 15, 64–76.

Grewal, D., Monroe, K.B., and Krishnan, R. (1998) The effects of price-comparison advertising on consumers' perceptions of acquisition value, transaction value, and behavioral intentions. *Journal of Marketing*, 62, 46–59.

Haws, K.L. and Bearden, W.O. (2006) Dynamic pricing and consumer fairness perceptions. *Journal of Consumer Research*, 33, 304–311.

Manning, K.G. and Sprott, D.E. (2009) Price endings, left-digit effects, and choice. *Journal of Consumer Research*, 36, 328–335.

Mazumdar, T., Raj, S.P., and Singh, I. (2005) Reference price research: review and propositions. *Journal of Marketing*, 69, 84–102.

Monroe, K.B. (2003) *Pricing: Making Profitable Decisions*, McGraw-Hill/Irwin, Burr Ridge.

Monroe, K.B. and Lee, A.Y. (1999) Remembering versus knowing: issues in consumers' processing of price information. *Journal of the Academy of Marketing Science*, 27, 207–225.

Nunes, J.C. and Boatwright, P. (2004) Incidental prices and their effect on willingness to pay. *Journal of Marketing Research*, 41, 457–466.

Rao, A.R. and Monroe, K.B. (1989) The effect of price, brand name and store name on consumers' perceptions of product quality: an integrative review. *Journal of Marketing Research*, 26, 351–357.

Suri, R. and Monroe, K.B. (2003) The effects of time constraints on consumers' judgments of prices and products. *Journal of Consumer Research*, 30, 92–104.

Thomas, M. and Morwitz, V.G. (2009) Heuristics in numerical cognition: implications for pricing, in *Handbook of Pricing Research in Marketing* (ed. V. Rao), Edward Elgar Publishing, pp. 132–149.

Vanhuele, M., Laurent, G., and Dreze, X. (2006) Consumers' immediate memory for prices. *Journal of Consumer Research*, 33, 163–172.

Xia, L., Monroe, K.B., and Cox, J.L. (2004) The price is unfair! A conceptual framework of price fairness perceptions. *Journal of Marketing*, 68, 1–15.

implicit consumer cognition

Patrick T. Vargas and Sangdo Oh

Advertisers worry about clutter; they worry about getting their message noticed amid all the other messages aimed at consumers. Some estimates suggest that the average American is exposed to over 3000 advertisements each day. It would be impossible for even the most motivated and patient consumer to wade through all of that information attentively. Fortunately for advertisers, focused attention may not be absolutely necessary. Consumers may be affected by information outside of their conscious awareness. There is a large and growing body of psychological and consumer research demonstrating that people need not intentionally process information to be affected by it. In this article, we offer a brief review of research on implicit consumer cognition.

Implicit cognition (*see* KNOWLEDGE ACCESSIBILITY), more generally, refers to the influence of past experience without conscious recollection or awareness of the influencing experience. For example, consider a classic study of memory (Warrington and Weiskrantz, 1970). Amnesiacs have difficulty with short-term memory. When shown a list of words for study and later asked to recall words from the list, amnesiacs perform substantially worse than non-amnesiacs. However, on certain types of tests, amnesiacs show roughly the same evidence of prior exposure to the studied words as non-amnesiacs. These are implicit tests, in which the memory "test" is presented as a simple task to be completed rather than an explicit demand for conscious recollection, for example, word stem completion: deter_ _ _ _ could be either detergent or deterrent. Amnesiacs and non-amnesiacs

that had recently studied a list of words including the word detergent are more likely to use detergent to complete the stem. Thus, amnesiacs show evidence of prior exposure to the words, at almost exactly the same rate as non-amnesiacs, but only on implicit measures of memory.

Implicit consumer cognition may be defined as the unacknowledged or misidentified influence of prior experience on consumer-related judgment and behavior. In this article, we review research on implicit consumer cognition. We begin with an overview of implicit measures, with a focus on how they may be applied to marketing and consumer behavior; and then we address implicit processes and effects, including topics such as subliminal persuasion and priming.

IMPLICIT MEASURES OF ATTITUDES

ATTITUDES are central to the study of marketing and consumer behavior. Consumers rarely choose products or patronize services that they dislike, so it is important for marketers to engender positive attitudes. Advertising agency Saatchi & Saatchi conceptualizes brand strength in terms of "lovemarks," employing ideas like love, respect, inspiration, sensuality, and intimacy. Very often consumers report definitive attitudes toward brands, sometimes positive and sometimes negative. Traditionally, attitudes are measured using explicit, self-report measures, in which respondents indicate on, say 10-point scales, how much they like or dislike an object (semantic differential scales). Other explicit attitude measures present respondents with a series of valenced statements about an object, and respondents are asked to indicate their level of agreement with the statements (Likert-type scales), or select a few statements that most closely match their own feelings (Thurstone scales). However, sometimes research participants may be unwilling to express their true feelings, or, in some cases, they may not know how they really feel about some object. In these cases, researchers have turned to implicit measures of attitudes.

Like implicit measures of memory (described briefly, above), implicit measures of attitudes are presented to research respondents simply as tasks to be completed. Respondents' performance on the task can then be used to infer their attitudes. In one early consumer study involving an implicit measure, respondents were simply given a seven-item grocery shopping list and asked to make some judgments about the woman who made the list (Haire, 1950). There were actually two versions of the list: one version contained Maxwell House drip coffee, and the other version contained Nescafe instant coffee. The lists were identical in all other respects. Half of the research participants received the Maxwell House version of the list and the other half received the Nescafe version of the list. Those who received the Nescafe version were more likely to describe the woman who wrote the list as "lazy," "a poor planner," and a "bad wife." These characteristics strongly suggest that consumers had negative attitudes toward Nescafe instant coffee. Implicit measures of attitudes have come a long way since 1950.

Two of the most popular contemporary measures are computer-based and rely on millisecond differences in response times. The Implicit Association Test (IAT, see Greenwald et al., 2009) is presented to respondents as a series of classification tasks. Four categories of stimuli are presented sequentially on a computer screen, and respondents must categorize the stimuli as quickly as possible by pressing one of two keys associated with the different categories. Initial trials of a typical IAT involve two categories, for example, good and bad, or fruit and cigarettes. Respondents must press one key if the stimulus is a good word or picture, and another key if the stimulus is a bad word or picture. Some subsequent trials involve all four categories, forcing respondents to pair categories on the keys. For example, one block of trials may require respondents to press

one key if the stimulus is either fruit-related or good, and another key if the stimulus is either cigarette-related or bad. A later block of trials will reverse the pairings, requiring respondents to press one key if the stimulus is either cigarette-related or good, and another key if the stimulus is either fruit-related or bad. In this example, we refer to these blocks of trials as consistent (fruit/good and cigarettes/bad) and inconsistent (cigarettes/good and fruit/bad). For most Americans, categorizing the consistent trials would be easier, and faster, than categorizing the inconsistent trials. Average response times for each block of trials can be calculated, and the difference between these times is known as the *IAT effect*. It is really a measure of the strength of an individual's associations between the concepts used in the task. If someone finds it easier to associate fruit/good and cigarettes/bad than cigarettes/good and fruit/bad, we can infer that they have relatively favorable attitudes toward fruit, and relatively negative attitudes toward cigarettes.

The IAT has generated an enormous amount of research. A recent review of the research considered 184 distinct studies involving a total of 14,900 respondents (Greenwald et al., 2009). A meta-analysis of these studies revealed that the IAT was moderately correlated with a wide variety of different behaviors, judgments, and physiological measures ($r = 0.274$). In the domain of consumer preferences (40 studies involving 3257 respondents), the IAT showed a slightly higher correlation with relevant outcomes ($r = 0.323$). Studies of political preference (11 studies, 2903 respondents) obtained average IAT-criterion correlations of 0.483; studies of alcohol and drug use (16 studies, 1718 respondents) obtained average IAT-criterion correlations of 0.221.

A second popular, computer-mediated implicit measure of attitudes relies on priming (see Wittenbrink, 2007). Measuring attitudes with priming also involves the sequential presentation of stimuli on the screen, and requires respondents to categorize the stimuli as quickly and accurately as possible. Again, respondents categorize the stimuli using two keys, each assigned to one of the two categories – usually one key for "good" and one key for "bad." The judgment task is influenced by the brief presentation of an attitude object immediately prior to the task, a prime. Reusing the example from above, a prime (picture of a cigarette or picture of a piece of fruit) would appear very briefly on the screen, and disappear, replaced with a good or bad word. The respondent's task is to categorize that target word. In general, people are faster to categorize the target words when they have been preceded by an evaluatively consistent prime. So, for example, people would be faster to categorize a good word when it is preceded by an image of grapes, than to categorize a bad word when preceded by an image of grapes. Likewise, they would be faster to categorize a bad word when a picture of a cigarette precedes it, than to categorize a good word when a picture of a cigarette precedes it. However, someone who loves cigarettes and hates fruit would likely be faster to categorize cigarette → good and grapes → bad, compared to grapes → good and cigarette → bad. This priming measure has also been used in a wide variety of studies, and reliably predicted relevant behaviors and judgments. This measure has been shown to work when the primes are presented subliminally – so the procedure can be administered to respondents who are completely unaware of the attitude objects under consideration.

There are dozens of implicit measures in use now, each with different characteristics. Many of these implicit measures do not require millisecond-resolution for response times, and may therefore be easier to use in the absence of dedicated computer software. One such measure is the Affect Misattribution Procedure (AMP; Payne et al., 2005). This measure is procedurally similar to the priming measure, but does not require respondents to categorize target stimuli. In the AMP, respondents are presented with a prime, that is, some attitude object (e.g., grapes or cigarettes), which then disappears from the screen and is replaced by some neutral, abstract stimulus (e.g., a Chinese ideograph). Respondents then have to indicate how much they like the ideograph. Their responses are influenced by the primes. Ideographs that are preceded by pleasant primes are rated as more favorable than those that are preceded by unpleasant primes.

This effect occurs even when respondents are explicitly warned that the primes could influence their judgments, and instructed to try to prevent that from happening.

Other implicit measures are even easier to implement, requiring only willing respondents, a pencil, and some paper (see Vargas, Sekaquaptewa, and von Hippel, 2007). These measures come in many different forms, and have been used to predict judgments and behaviors, as well. One such measure involves presenting respondents with sentence beginnings, and simply asking respondents to complete the sentence in any way that is grammatically correct. Some of the sentence beginnings are constructed so that they violate or confirm commonly held beliefs, like the belief that Toyota automobiles are very reliable: "Paul's Toyota broke down ..." or "The odometer on Paul's Toyota was approaching 150 000 miles ..." Because people have a natural tendency to explain unexpected events, their completed sentences often imply favorable or unfavorable attitudes toward the targets. Thus, someone who had favorable attitudes toward Toyota might be inclined to try to explain the Toyota's breakdown ("... because Paul drove like a madman."), but not the Toyota's resiliency ("... and he expected it to last for another 150 000 miles."). Someone with negative attitudes toward Toyota might be expected to show the opposite pattern – explaining sentence beginnings featuring good things about Toyota ("... because Paul was the luckiest guy on the planet."), and simply continuing sentence beginnings featuring bad things about Toyota ("... and Paul knew he wouldn't get to the job interview in time.").

As noted above, implicit measures have typically been reserved for use when explicit attitude measures are not expected to perform well, such as when social desirability concerns would influence respondents to report so-called politically correct attitudes, rather than their true feelings. At least one type of paper-and-pencil implicit measure has also been shown to predict unique variance in behavior, beyond what can be predicted by traditional explicit measures – even when the attitude object under consideration is not a socially sensitive topic. Attitudes are complex constructs, with many different facets, each of which may play some unique role in driving behavior. Implicit measures most likely tap different components of attitudes than explicit measures (Gawronski and Bodenhausen, 2006). Traditional, explicit measures are believed to assess propositional components of attitudes – essentially, these are evaluative statements about some object that are stored in memory, such as, "I believe that Apple is a good brand." Response-time-based implicit measures are believed to assess stored evaluations that are automatically activated by the presence of some attitude object. A crude example of an automatically activated concept can be seen in the facility with which "butter" comes to mind when someone says "bread and…" Bread and butter have been paired together so often that invoking bread automatically activates the concept of butter. In the same way that bread and butter are linked, many attitude objects are linked to evaluations (e.g., puppies + good). These evaluations may not be consciously endorsed, but they are automatically activated in the presence of the attitude object, and this activation is reflected in the speed with which someone might categorize rainbows as good following a cuddly puppy prime in a priming implicit measure.

Research on implicit attitude measures is exceptionally fast-moving. In 1995, there were fewer than 10 published articles on implicit attitudes, but just a decade later there were nearly 100 articles published on the topic. It is an exciting area that continues to develop, and is likely to have an increasingly profound impact on consumer research.

IMPLICIT PROCESSES

As noted above, people cannot possibly consciously process all the advertising and marketing-related stimuli they encounter, much less than all the other stimuli they are faced with. A great deal of cognition goes on outside of our conscious awareness. When it comes to consumer cognition, we can lack conscious awareness of (i) environmental stimuli that may influence our behavior; (ii) automatic cognitive processes that are driving our behavior; and (iii) outcomes, including preferences, judgments, behaviors, emotions, and so forth (Chartrand,

2005). In this section, we review additional work on implicit consumer cognition, beginning with the influence of environmental stimuli that are outside of conscious awareness.

Lacking awareness of stimuli. "I saw a subliminal advertising executive, but only for a second," (attributed to Steven Wright, comedian). One of the greatest obstacles to successfully marketing goods and services is the consumer's resistance to new information and persuasion (*see* CHOICE MODELS) attempts. When consumers are aware of persuasive intent, they are much more likely to try to counterargue, disengage, or otherwise refuse to go along with the would-be persuader. From a marketer's perspective, it would be great to be able to bypass consumers' resistance to persuasion, and just plant ideas to like and buy specific brands directly in the consumers' minds. From a consumer perspective, the prospect of marketers bypassing our ability to resist is terrifying – it would be just a short step from mind control.

For these reasons, marketers and consumers, alike, seem to share a fascination with the idea of bypassing the conscious mind, persuading without allowing any opportunity to resist. This idea ostensibly came to fruition in September 1957, when James Vicary announced that he had used subliminal persuasion to increase popcorn and soda sales. Vicary claimed to have subliminally presented messages ("Eat popcorn" and "Drink Coca-Cola") during a movie. The messages, presented at 1/3000th of a second, were well below the threshold for conscious perception – moviegoers would not have even realized that they had been commanded to eat and drink. And Vicary claimed that this technique increased sales of popcorn and soda in the theater by 18.1 and 57.5%, respectively. The implications of this "experiment" were profoundly troubling. It would be a few years before *The Manchurian Candidate* was popularized (the book was published in 1959; the film debuted in 1962), but by using Vicary's technique one could imagine nudging an unsuspecting public to do any number of things – work harder for less pay, vote for a crooked politician, discriminate or even wage war against some unfortunate group.

The public was nervous. Letters and editorials appeared in the news, Congress and the Federal Communications Commission discussed the ethical implications of subliminal persuasion, and the National Association of Broadcasters banned SUBLIMINAL ADVERTISING. The public disquiet turned out to be unfounded. Attempts to duplicate Vicary's claims were unsuccessful, and in a 1962 interview in *Advertising Age* Vicary admitted that his claim was bogus. He had made the claim in an effort to promote a company in which he was a partner, the Subliminal Projection Company. Despite no solid evidence in support of subliminal persuasion, the concept remained firmly embedded in the public mind.

Several best-selling books promoted the idea of subliminal persuasion, including Vance Packard's (1957) *The Hidden Persuaders*, and Wilson Brian Key's luridly titled, *Subliminal Seduction: Are You Being Sexually Aroused by this Picture?* (1973) and *The Clam-Plate Orgy: And Other Subliminals the Media Use to Manipulate Your Behavior* (1980). Surveys reveal that roughly three-fourths of Americans are aware of subliminal advertising, and of those who are aware nearly all believe it is actually used, and close to half believe that they may be susceptible to subliminal advertising.

The truth about subliminal persuasion is a little more down-to-earth. For one thing, the term *subliminal* is very often misused in the general media. Steven Wright's clever line about a subliminal advertising executive exemplifies this misuse. The term subliminal evokes the limen, which is the threshold, or point, at which a stimulus evokes a sensation. A subliminally presented stimulus is one that evokes no sensation in the respondent; that is, the respondent has no conscious sense of having seen (or heard, smelled, tasted, touched) the stimulus. Mr. Wright would not have perceived a truly subliminal advertising executive. As well, the limen varies among people, such that one person's subliminal stimulus may be another's supraliminal (consciously perceived) stimulus; the limen also varies within individuals, so that stimuli presented at the same level of intensity may evoke a response at some times, but no response at other times. Objectively operationalizing a subliminal stimulus is therefore

quite difficult. Most researchers have opted for a more subjective approach, in which a stimulus is considered subliminal if the respondent cannot notice its presentation (even when they are highly motivated to do so, such as when they are offered cash incentives for correctly identifying the presence of a stimulus).

Subliminal stimuli should be differentiated from transformed stimuli, or unattended stimuli. The former are distorted, blurred, or otherwise degraded so as to be less recognizable; the latter may be clearly recognizable, but are not intended to serve as focal points for attention. An auditory example of transformed stimuli might be music in which different lyrics are audible when played in reverse. An auditory example of unattended stimuli is when different messages are played in left and right headphone channels, while the respondent is instructed to attend to just one channel. Many of the examples used in books by Key and Vicary are transformed, or unattended, rather than strictly subliminal; so most of the claims by Key and Vicary are misinformed, at best, and downright misleading, at worst.

Good, solid evidence for subliminal persuasion is scarce, but it does exist. A review of over 150 mass media articles and over 200 academic papers obtained no solid support for subliminal persuasion (Pratkanis and Aronson, 1992). The articles were seriously flawed in a variety of different ways, making it difficult to infer valid and reliable effects of subliminal stimuli. However, several recent academic articles have offered some evidence that subliminally presented stimuli can have an impact on consumer behavior.

In one study, participants watched an episode of *The Simpsons*. Half of the participants were presented with subliminal primes pertaining to thirst, and the other half were not. Participants who were exposed to the thirst primes later rated themselves as being thirstier than those who were not exposed to the thirst primes (Cooper and Cooper, 2002). In another study, the researchers experimentally manipulated thirst by having all of the participants eat cookies and having half of the participants then drink a glass of water. Next, participants were subliminally exposed to thirst-related words, or words unrelated to thirst. In this study, there was no effect of the thirst prime on participants' self-reported thirst; however, in a fake taste test, participants who were both thirsty and primed with thirst-related words drank the most Kool-Aid (Strahan, Spencer, and Zanna, 2002). In yet another study, researchers experimentally manipulated participants' thirst, and then subliminally exposed participants to a particular brand of beverage or neutral words. Participants who were thirsty and exposed to neutral words expressed no preference for one beverage over another, but those who were thirsty and exposed to the branded beverage showed a marked preference for the brand of beverage that had been subliminally primed (Karremans, Stroebe, and Claus, 2006).

Work on subliminal persuasion continues, but the evidence to date suggests that subliminally presented stimuli most definitely cannot induce moviegoers to get up during a film, go to the concessions stand, and buy a tub of popcorn and a Coca-Cola. Subliminal stimuli seem to be most influential when people are already motivated to engage in some behavior – the subliminal stimuli tend to nudge people further in the direction in which they are already leaning.

Lacking awareness of cognitive processes. Supraliminal stimuli can also influence consumer judgment, emotion, and behavior. A popular classroom demonstration of this effect begins with a list of words that students are instructed to memorize: ocean, waves, gravity, beach, and moon. In order to prevent students from rehearsing the words (the most common strategy for memorizing a handful of items), the instructor asks students a series of questions and instructs them to answer each question aloud. "Name a brand of automobile." In a crowded classroom, the response is an indistinguishable rumble of different brands. "Name a brand of shoes." Again, the response is an indistinguishable rumble. After a few more questions the instructor says, "Name a brand of laundry detergent." The class responds, almost unanimously, "Tide."

When asked about the surprising unanimity of the Tide response students often volunteer that Tide is a brand leader, or that their family uses Tide, or that it just came to mind. Usually, at least one student will also make the connection between the list of words and the conceptually

related brand name. The word list serves as a prime, increasing accessibility of the concept of tides. When an opportunity to use the accessible concept arises, many students will do so. In theory, the laundry detergent brand "Cheer" could be elicited by using the words stadium, fan, mascot, game, and team. Priming is an example of a case where people are aware of some stimulus, but generally unaware of the cognitive processes mediating their behavior, or that the prime has had an influence on their behavior (for a thorough review of accessibility effects, see Wyer, 2008).

Priming a familiar brand increases the likelihood that the brand enters the consumers' consideration set and is selected as a final choice (Coates, Butler, and Berry, 2006). A single exposure to a previously unfamiliar brand name is sufficient to induce a reliable increase in the selection rate of the primed brand over already familiar brand names. A similar effect has been demonstrated with auditory stimuli. Hearing a brand name once may be enough to increase a brand's familiarity. Increased feelings of familiarity may provoke consumers to misattribute their familiarity of the brand to an assumption that the brand is popular and well known. If the exposure context is unable to be retrieved, the brand name tends to be considered an existing established brand (Holden and Vanhule, 1999). Even asking consumers about their general purchase intentions (e.g., how likely are you to buy a new automobile?) can increase the likelihood that they make a purchase (Morwitz and Fitzsimons, 2004). This "mere-measurement" effect seems to operate, like more traditional priming effects, by increasing the accessibility of relevant attitudes and beliefs about the object in question.

Priming has been shown to directly influence consumer behavior, as well. Participants primed with prestige goals were more likely to choose relatively expensive and prestigious socks with the Nike brand; participants primed with thrift goals were more likely to choose relatively inexpensive and less prestigious socks with the Hanes brand (Chartrand *et al.*, 2008). Primes do not have to be presented supraliminally in order to have an effect on behavior: participants subliminally primed with the Apple computer logos showed higher creativity scores than those exposed to IBM logos, and participants primed with the Disney channel reported more honest responses to social undesirable questions than did those primed with E! (Entertainment network; Fitzsimons, Chartrand, and Fitzsimons, 2008).

Implicit memory. Marketers have primarily focused their attention on retrieval, or explicit memory (Shapiro and Krishnan, 2001). Explicit memory is assessed via respondents' conscious recollection of a prior exposure to some stimulus, and an intentional attempt to access the information acquired previously. A great deal of consumer behavior is driven by explicit memory (e.g., "Remember to buy eggs and milk," and "I liked the pie at that restaurant."), but implicit memory also has an important role in consumer behavior. *Implicit memory* may be defined as the unintentional, unconscious retrieval of previously acquired information. It is frequently observed by increased performance on indirect tasks that do not demand conscious recollection of past experience. An example of an implicit memory test comparing amnesiac and non-amnesiac respondents was provided at the beginning of this article.

In assessing ADVERTISING EFFECTIVENESS, Lee (2002) argued that there are two distinct types of implicit memory, perceptual and conceptual, and that these distinct types of implicit memory can be tapped by different measures. She created conceptual primes by having respondents read brand names in sentences (i.e., in a context where conceptual features are salient), and perceptual primes by having respondents read brand names in isolation (i.e., perceptual features of the brand name are salient). Further, consumer behavior was differentially impacted by conceptual and perceptual primes; the former increased the likelihood that consumers would select a primed brand from memory, whereas the latter increased the likelihood that consumers would select a primed brand from a physical layout of different brands. This result has important practical implications for advertisers: when customers are expected to retrieve different product alternatives from memory, persuasive messages should provide relevant contexts to motivate elaborative processing of the brand

or product. Otherwise, displaying a prominent product image (perceptual cues) might be a better strategy.

Researchers have supported implicit memory measures as alternatives to explicit recall tasks by showing dissociations between explicit and implicit measures. When participants were asked to do dual tasks (i.e., listen to a short story audio program while advertisements were displayed on slides), their inability to keep their attention focused on the advertisements at the moment of exposure caused different memory performance later in the explicit recall tasks. The number of correct recognitions among participants who were asked immediately after the exposure was quite high (significantly greater than chance levels); however, those who received the recognition task after a week failed at explicit memory retrieval. On the contrary, indirect memory measures were unaffected by either the week delay or attentive states. Overall, implicit tasks revealed an increased likelihood of choosing the advertised brands in all conditions (Shapiro and Krishnan, 2001).

Advertising and product placement seem to have independent and distinct effects on implicit and explicit memory. It is not yet clear whether information that is consciously accessible (explicit memory), and consciously inaccessible (implicit memory) can have additive, or interactive, effects on consumer behavior, but future research should illuminate further effects of implicit memory.

Lacking awareness of behavior. Perhaps one has found oneself unpacking groceries at home, feeling surprised at finding an item come out of his/her grocery bag that he/she does not remember selecting from the shelf: a jar of peanut butter or some Ziploc baggies. Certainly most people have, at one time or another, found themselves parking their own car in their own driveway without any conscious recollection of driving the last few miles home. We have an astounding ability to conduct routine behaviors on autopilot. Riding a bicycle is a remarkably complex task involving the coordinated tasks of steering, balancing, pedaling, breathing, and so on – and it is a task that most people can do without even thinking about it. These are examples of behavior without awareness.

People may be unaware of different aspects of their behavior. Often we are unaware of basic physiological processes, such as breathing. At other times, we are unaware of simple nervous habits, such as repetitive foot tapping. We may also be unaware that a behavior is contingent upon some previous event, such as the effect of a prime. Studying behavior that is outside of awareness is difficult because there are so many ways in which behavior may be outside of awareness – there is no generally agreed upon conceptualization of what, exactly, behavior without awareness actually means.

Still, it is interesting to consider how, and the extent to which, consumer behavior operates outside of conscious awareness. This is an undeveloped area that is wide open for future researchers. As a whole, implicit consumer cognition is a relatively new area of research, so there are numerous gaps where researchers may add substantial contributions. It is an exciting and quickly developing area, with new findings appearing in academic journals monthly.

Bibliography

Chartrand, T. L. (2005) The role of conscious awareness in consumer behavior. *Journal of Consumer Psychology*, **15**, 203–210.

Chartrand, T.L., Huber, J., Shiv, B., and Tanner, R.J. (2008) Nonconscious goals and consumer choice. *Journal of Consumer Research*, **35**, 189–201.

Coates, S., Butler, L., and Berry, D. (2006) Implicit memory and consumer choice: the mediating role of brand familiarity. *Applied Cognitive Psychology*, **20**, 1101–1116.

Cooper, J. and Cooper, G. (2002) Subliminal motivation: a story revisited. *Journal of Applied Social Psychology*, **32**, 2213–2227.

Fitzsimons, G., Chartrand, T., and Fitzsimons, G. (2008) Automatic effects of brand exposure on motivated behavior: how apple makes you "think different". *Journal of Consumer Research*, **35**, 21–35.

Gawronski, B. and Bodenhausen, G.V. (2006) Associative and propositional processes in evaluation: an integrative review of implicit and explicit attitude change. *Psychological Bulletin*, **132**, 692–731.

Greenwald, A.G., Poehlman, T.A., Uhlmann, E.L., and Banaji, M.R. (2009) Understanding and using the implicit association test: III. Meta-analysis of predictive validity. *Journal of Personality and Social Psychology*, **97**, 17–41.

Haire, M. (1950) Projective techniques in marketing research. *Journal of Marketing*, **14**, 649–656.

Holden, S.J.S. and Vanhuele, M. (1999) Know the name, forget the exposure: brand familiarity versus memory of exposure context. *Psychology and Marketing*, **16**, 479–496.

Karremans, J.C., Stroebe, W., and Claus, J. (2006) Beyond vicary's fantasies: the impact of subliminal priming and brand choice. *Journal of Experimental Social Psychology*, **42**, 792–798.

Lee, A. (2002) Effects of implicit memory on memory-based versus stimulus-based brand choice. *Journal of Marketing Research*, **39**, 440–454.

Morwitz, V.G. and Fitzsimons, G.J. (2004) The mere-measurement effect: why does measuring intentions change actual behavior? *Journal of Consumer Psychology*, **14**, 64–74.

Payne, B.K., Cheng, C.M., Govorun, O., and Stewart, B.D. (2005) An inkblot for attitudes: affect misattribution as implicit measurement. *Journal of Personality and Social Psychology*, **89**, 277–293.

Pratkanis, A.R. and Aronson, E. (1992) *Age of Propaganda: The Everyday Use and Abuse of Persuasion*, W. H. Freeman/Times Books/Henry Holt & Co., New York.

Schacter, D., Chiu, C.-Y., and Ochsner, K. (1993) Implicit memory: a selective review. *Annual Reviews in Neuroscience*, **16**, 159–182.

Shapiro, S. and Krishnan, S. (2001) Memory-based measures for assessing advertising effects: a comparison of explicit and implicit memory effects. *Journal of Advertising*, **30**, 1–13.

Strahan, E.J., Spencer, S.J., and Zanna, M.P. (2002) Subliminal priming and persuasion: striking while the iron is hot. *Journal of Experimental Social Psychology*, **38**, 556–568.

Vargas, P.T., Sekaquaptewa, D., and von Hippel, W. (2007) Armed only with paper and pencil: "Low-Tech" measures of implicit attitudes, in *Implicit Measures of Attitudes* (eds B. Wittenbrink and N. Schwarz), Guilford Press, New York, pp. 103–124.

Warrington, E.K. and Weiskrantz, L. (1970) Amnesia: consolidation or retrieval? *Nature*, **228**, 628–630.

Wittenbrink, B. (2007) Measuring attitudes through priming, in *Implicit Measures of Attitudes* (eds B. Wittenbrink and N. Schwarz), Guilford Press, New York, pp. 17–58.

Wyer, R.S. (2008) The role of knowledge accessibility in cognition and behavior: implications for consumer information processing, in *Handbook of Consumer Psychology* (eds C. Haugtvedt, F. Kardes, and P. Herr), Erlbaum, Mahwah, pp. 31–76.

impulsive and compulsive buying

Ronald J. Faber

Impulsive and compulsive buying are terms that are frequently confused for each other, but represent behaviors that differ greatly in regard to their frequency, cause, outcome, and severity. Impulsive buying is a more common and ordinary behavior. Virtually everyone makes a purchase on impulse (without much deliberation) from time to time. Some do this more frequently than others. Nonetheless, almost everyone finds that sometimes they are able to resist the desire to buy on impulse and at other times they give in to this impulse. It has been suggested that impulse buying occurs when desire for a product or brand outweighs one's willpower to resist (Hoch and Loewenstein, 1991).

On the other hand, compulsive buying is a psychological disorder where one experiences an urge to buy that cannot be controlled. Failing to act on this urge creates increasing tension for the individual which only dissipates with buying. Frequently, this urge is triggered by negative events or feelings. Ultimately, this behavior leads to extreme negative consequences (financial and/or personal) for the individual (Faber and Christenson, 1996; O'Guinn and Faber, 1989). Many compulsive buyers never use the items they purchase.

IMPULSE BUYING

Historical development of impulse buying. Early research on impulse buying in the 1950s and 1960s viewed it as occurring anytime a consumer made any unplanned purchase. As a result, research sought to classify certain types of products as impulse items and looked at what store characteristics encouraged impulse buying. This approach changed in the 1970s as researchers began to realize that all products could be purchased impulsively. As a result, research on impulse buying began to focus on characteristic of individuals, rather than of products or stores, and to define the term as a sudden and powerful urge in the consumer to buy immediately (Rook and Hoch, 1985; Rook, 1987).

Correlates and causes of impulse buying. Factors that influence both the desire for a product and willpower to resist this desire are related to situations when impulse buying occurs (Hoch and Loewenstein, 1991). Proximity to a purchase can increase wanting for an item. Thus one technique to reduce impulse buying is to walk away from an item and only buy it if you still want it as much several minutes later. Another factor that correlates with impulse buying is mood state. People indicate they are much more likely to buy on impulse when in a positive mood (Rook and Gardner, 1993).

Willpower has also been shown to effect impulse buying. Vohs and Faber (2007) showed that people were more likely to buy on impulse when their self-regulatory resources (willpower) were diminished. Engaging in self-regulation in some other domain increases the likelihood people will buy on impulse. Thus, not shopping after a long, difficult day and keeping shopping trips short can help people to cut down on impulse buying.

COMPULSIVE BUYING

Historical development of compulsive buying. Compulsive buying was initially discussed in the psychiatric literature under the term *onomania* almost 100 years ago (Kraeplin, 1915). However, there was little discussion of it from the mid-1920s until the late 1980s when researchers in the United States, Canada, and Germany all began to report on this problem (d'Astous, Maltais, and Roberge, 1990; O'Guinn and Faber, 1989; Scherhorn, Reisch, and Raab,1990). The Compulsive Buying Scale (Faber and O'Guinn, 1992) was developed to distinguish compulsive buyers from other consumers. Using this measure with a national probability sample, Koran *et al.* (2006) estimated that 5.8% of the US population may be compulsive buyers.

Correlates and causes of compulsive buying. Many compulsive buyers have personal or family histories of other problem behaviors such as alcoholism and drug abuse, eating disorders, and impulse control disorders. The most commonly reported correlates of compulsive buying are psychological ones. Numerous studies have found that compulsive buyers are perfectionists, and have low self-esteem and high levels of depression and anxiety. Compulsive buying seems to provide temporary relief from these negative feelings, but ultimately makes compulsive buyers feel even worse about themselves. Thus, compulsive buying appears to be more about obtaining short-term relief from negative feelings than about a desire for specific goods. Several studies have found that compulsive buying is unrelated to income.

See also *consumer desire; consumer materialism; consumer well-being; emotion; possessions and self; self-regulation*

Bibliography

d'Astous, A., Maltais, J. and Roberge, C. (1990) Compulsive buying tendencies of adolescent consumers, in *Advances in Consumer Research*, vol. 17 (eds M.E. Goldberg, G. Gorn and R.W. Pollay), Association for Consumer Research, Provo, pp. 306–312.

Faber, R.J. and Christenson, G.A. (1996) In the mood to buy: differences in the mood states experienced by compulsive buyers and other consumers. *Psychology and Marketing*, 13, 803–820.

Faber, R.J. and O'Guinn, T.C. (1992) A clinical screener for compulsive buying. *Journal of Consumer Research*, 19, 459–469.

Hoch, S.J. and Loewenstein, G.F. (1991) Time inconsistent preferences and consumer self-control. *Journal of Consumer Research*, 18, 492–507.

Koran, L., Faber, R.J., Aboujaoude, E. *et al.* (2006) Estimated prevalence of compulsive buying in the United States. *American Journal of Psychiatry*, 163 (10), 1806–1812.

Kraeplin, E. (1915) *Psychiatrie*, 8th edn, Verlag Von Johann Ambrosius Barth, Leipzig.

O'Guinn, T.C. and Faber, R.J. (1989) Compulsive buying: a phenomenological exploration. *Journal of Consumer Research*, 16, 147–157.

Rook, D.W. (1987) The buying impulse. *Journal of Consumer Research*, 14, 189–199.

Rook, D.W. and Gardner, M.P. (1993) In the mood: impulse buying's affective antecedents. *Research in Consumer Behavior*, 6, 1–28.

Rook, D.W. and Hoch, S.J. (1985) Consuming impulses. *Advances in Consumer Research*, 12, 23–27.

Scherhorn, G., Reisch, L.A. and Raab, G. (1990) Addictive buying in West Germany: an empirical study. *Journal of Consumer Policy*, 13, 355–387.

Vohs, K. and Faber, R.J. (2007) Impulse buying: a result of self-regulatory resource depletion. *Journal of Consumer Research*, 33 (4), 537–548.

K

knowledge accessibility

Robert S. Wyer, Jr.

GENERAL CONSIDERATIONS

Definition. Knowledge is accessible in memory if it comes to mind quickly and easily in the course of pursuing a goal to which it is relevant. As such, it is distinguished from *availability*, which refers to the existence of knowledge in memory. The distinction is important in light of the fact that people are normally neither motivated nor able to bring all of the knowledge they have accumulated that is relevant to a judgment or decision they make. Rather, they retrieve and use only a subset of this knowledge that comes easily to mind, ignoring other knowledge that is equally applicable but less easily accessible.

Theoretical formulations of the determinants and consequences of knowledge accessibility depend on the type of knowledge in question. *Declarative* knowledge includes single concepts that are used to interpret individual pieces of information, configurations of attributes that are used in combination as a basis for identifying a stimulus as a member of a more general category, beliefs, and attitudes. It can also include sequences of temporally and thematically related events. Some sequences characterize specific experiences one has had and constitute stories that are retrieved and communicated to others. Other, more general (prototypic) sequences can be used to infer the cause of a new event or to predict its likely consequences. These latter sequences can constitute *implicit theories* about the social or physical world. Other sequences may specify the steps required to attain a particular objective.

In addition, *procedural* knowledge concerns the sequences of cognitive or motor behavior that have been acquired through learning and are performed automatically when the configuration of stimuli with which they are associated are experienced. These procedures can include those that operate on declarative knowledge in the course of attaining a particular objective.

Determinants of accessibility. The accessibility of knowledge in memory typically increases with both the recency and the frequency with which it has been activated and used in the past. Individuals who search memory for knowledge that is relevant to a goal they are pursuing presumably compile a set of features that specifies the type of knowledge required, and these features cue the retrieval of previously acquired units of knowledge that have the features in common.

If concepts and knowledge have been used recently, they typically come to mind more quickly and easily than other, equally relevant concepts and knowledge. Therefore, they are more likely to be used in attaining a goal to which they are relevant. For example, a person may evaluate a luxury car more favorably if (s)he has recently been asked to judge the aesthetic appeal of a series of paintings (thereby increasing the accessibility of aesthetics-related criteria) than if (s)he has recently been asked assess the speed and memory capacity of a computer (thus activating concepts associated with functional utility).

However, the likelihood of knowledge coming to mind in the course of goal-directed activity is also a function of the *frequency* with which it has been used in the past. Thus, concepts and knowledge that have been used very frequently over a period of time become *chronically* accessible in memory and, in the absence of other considerations, may be applied rather than other, potentially applicable but less accessible cognition.

Underlying processes.   The situational and individual difference factors that determine the accessibility and use of knowledge are well documented. However, ambiguities continue to surround the cognitive processes that underlie their effects. These processes depend on both the type of knowledge in question and the theory of memory one assumes.

The processes that underlie the accessibility of declarative knowledge are most commonly conceptualized with reference to a spreading activation model of associative memory (Collins and Loftus, 1975; but see Wyer and Srull, 1989, for an alternative). According to this model, concepts and units of knowledge are represented in memory by nodes and the associations between them by pathways that connect them. When a unit of knowledge is activated (that is, thought about), excitation spreads from the node at which it is located to other nodes along the pathways connecting them. When the excitation that has accumulated at one of these nodes exceeds a certain threshold value, the knowledge at this node is activated (comes to mind). When this knowledge is no longer thought about, the excitation that exists at the node dissipates. However, it takes time to dissipate entirely. Therefore, if a relatively short period of time has elapsed, residual activation may still exist at the node. Consequently, the knowledge is more likely to be reactivated by excitation that is transmitted to it from other sources (e.g., new stimulus information, or a directed search of memory for goal-relevant knowledge).

These processes govern the conscious use of declarative knowledge in the course of goal-directed activity. They also capture the conscious identification and use of a goal-directed procedure under conditions in which more than one strategy is potentially applicable. However, cognitive and motor procedures are often applied automatically, with little, if any, deliberation. These procedures, which constitute procedural knowledge, can be conceptualized as a set of *productions*, or learned "if [X], then [Y]" rules, where [X] is a configuration of externally or internally generated stimulus features and [Y] is a sequence of cognitive or motor acts that are elicited automatically when the preconditions specified in [X] are met (Anderson, 1983).

Productions can guide the cognitive and motor activity in a large number of situations, ranging from the generation of speech to driving a car or using a word processor. However, the activation of a production depends on the particular set of concepts and declarative knowledge that is accessible in memory at the time and, perhaps fortuitously, happens to be included among the features that compose a production's precondition [X]. Thus, to borrow an example from Bargh, Chen, and Burrows (1996), experimental participants who fortuitously have the concept "slow," accessible in memory as a result of thinking about the elderly, are likely to walk more slowly to the elevator upon leaving the experiment.

METHODOLOGICAL CONSIDERATIONS

The effect of knowledge accessibility on judgments and behavior has generally been investigated using *priming* techniques, that is, participants are typically asked to perform a task or engage in activity that requires the use of a particular concept, thus increasing its accessibility in memory. The effects of this activity on judgments and behavior in an unrelated situation are then observed. Furthermore, concepts and knowledge can often be activated subliminally in the course of performing an unrelated task.

However, concepts and knowledge can also become chronically accessible in memory as a result of their frequent application over an extended period of time. Thus, for example, cultural differences in the interpretation of information and the construal of its implications can be a reflection of differences in the chronic accessibility of concepts and knowledge that result from frequent exposure to them in the course of growing up. Although the effects of priming concepts and knowledge on their accessibility in memory can temporarily override the effects of their chronic accessibility, the latter effects are likely to predominate after a period of time has elapsed.

The role of awareness.   Individuals are not always conscious of why a piece of knowledge comes to mind, and are likely to attribute it to the type of object they are judging or the decision they are called upon to make. Consequently, when two or more units of knowledge are equally useful in attaining a particular objective, objectively irrelevant factors that influence their relative accessibility in memory can determine which is applied, and this can occur without awareness that the influence has occurred.

In fact, when individuals *are* aware that concepts and knowledge come to mind for reasons that have nothing to do with the stimuli being judged, they may intentionally avoid using them. As a result, the cognitions are less likely to be applied than they might otherwise be. On the other hand, conscious attempts to suppress a concept or unit of knowledge require thinking about the knowledge to be suppressed. Thus, ironically, knowledge may become more accessible in memory as a result of the attempts to suppress it, and, consequently, it may be *more* likely to be used once active attempts to suppress it no longer exist. Thus, for example, individuals who actively avoid using a person's ethnicity or social status as a basis for judgment in order to comply with sanctions imposed in one situation are more likely to use the stereotype in responding to a different person once the sanctions are lifted (Bodenhausen and Macrae, 1998).

Individuals are normally aware that they are applying certain criteria in arriving at a judgment or decision, but are nonetheless unaware of why they applied these particular criteria rather than others that are equally applicable. However, behavior of the sort that is governed by productions can be activated and applied without awareness of the behavior itself. Thus, as in the earlier example, activating concepts associated with the elderly may stimulate people to walk slowly without awareness of their walking speed. Similarly, if a driver who is on the way to the store happens to think about a meeting she has the next day, these thoughts may activate a product that leads her to wind up in front of her office rather than at her intended destination.

APPLICATIONS

The effects of stimulus information on behavior and decisions can be localized at several stages of processing, including the attention to information, its comprehension, inference, and evaluation, and the generation of an overt response or behavioral decision. The following review of representative research on the effects of knowledge accessibility at each stage of processing provides an indication of the range of phenomena in which knowledge accessibility plays a role. (For a more detailed discussion of this research, see Förster and Liberman, 2007; Wyer, 2008.)

Attention and search processes.   Effects of declarative knowledge accessibility. When individuals receive specific items of information about an object for the purpose of making a judgment, they may first interpret information in terms of more general concepts that the information exemplifies. However, information that can be interpreted in terms of concepts that are accessible in memory are likely to be more quickly identified and encoded in terms of them than is information that is less easily interpreted. This selective encoding can influence the judgments that are ultimately made.

The concepts that are accessible in memory are likely to be influenced by the goal that individuals are pursuing at the time. The selective attention to information that exemplifies these concepts can influence judgments of the object to which the information refers. For example, individuals who receive information about a person's behavior for the purpose of deciding whether the person is an extrovert may activate attributes of an extrovert and identify information that exemplifies these attributes, ignoring information that describes attributes of an introvert. Consequently, they are likely to judge the person as more extroverted than might otherwise be the case. Similarly, consumers who are asked to decide which of several products they like most may focus their attention on favorable attributes, whereas those who are asked to decide which they dislike most are more likely to focus on unfavorable attributes. Thus, the first group of subjects is likely to judge the products as a whole more favorably than the second group.

Attributes that happen to be accessible in memory for goal–irrelevant reasons can have similar effects. For example, exposing individuals to news stories that concern either domestic or foreign affairs can affect the criteria that individuals used to assess the performance of the United States President. Similarly, priming concepts associated with either taste or health can influence the criteria that consumers use to evaluate a product they encounter in an ostensibly unrelated situation.

Effects of activating procedural knowledge. Other studies show that the procedures that individuals use to search for information can be influenced by the procedures they have employed in the course of performing other, unrelated activities. For example, individuals who have previously rank ordered stimuli from high to low along a dimension, which requires a consideration of stimuli with high values before stimuli with low values, use a similar strategy when scanning an array of information they encounter later (i.e., the prices of hotels in a given city, or individual consumers' ratings of a product's quality). Consequently, they make higher estimates of the implications of the information than do individuals who have previously ranked stimuli from low to high (Shen and Wyer, 2008). (This, of course, occurs only when individuals do not have the time or motivation to consider all of the information available.)

Comprehension processes.   Effects of declarative knowledge accessibility. When people receive information that can be interpreted in different ways, the interpretation they give to it is likely to be determined by the applicable concepts that are most accessible in memory at the time. Thus, for example, exposing individuals to the words such as "adventurous" or "reckless" in the course of performing an ostensibly unrelated color–naming task can influence the concept they use to interpret information that a person wants to cross the Atlantic in a sailboat and, therefore, can influence the evaluation of this person. Similar effects can occur when the concepts used to interpret the behavioral information are primed subliminally.

Accessible concepts and knowledge can have more general effects. For example, statements

that appear anomalous when encountered out of context (e.g., "The haystack was important because the cloth would rip") are given meaning, and consequently are better remembered, by preceding them with a single word (e.g., "parachute"). The word apparently activates a complex body of knowledge that permits recipients to construct a mental picture of the situation in which the statement makes sense.

A consideration of the impact of knowledge accessibility on the interpretation of information increases in importance by virtue of the fact that once this interpretation is made, it is used as a basis for later judgments of the information's referent independently of the information itself. Moreover, this tendency increases over time. For example, priming a concept of hostility may lead a target person to be judged as hostile on the basis of behavior that exemplifies this concept. However, this effect is greater a day after the original information is presented than it is immediately afterwards. Similarly, once a person has been judged as honest on the basis of information that he told his girlfriend that her hairstyle was ugly, the person is judged as more kind than he would be if this initial judgment had not been made, and this tendency also increases over time (Carlston, 1980).

People's reliance on their interpretation of information rather than the information itself can produce distortions of memory. Research on eyewitness testimony (Loftus, 1975) indicates that individuals who have been shown a picture of an automobile accident make higher estimates of the car's speed if the question they are asked refers to the car "smashing into the tree" than if it refers to "hitting the tree." Furthermore, they are more likely to mistakenly remember that there was broken glass in the picture in the first case. Participants apparently reconstruct a mental image of the accident that is consistent with implications of the verbal description they are given and later use this reconstruction as a basis for their recall rather than the original picture they saw.

The chronic accessibility of concepts and knowledge can also affect the interpretation of information. The accessibility of these concepts can arise in part from the frequency of using them in the course of daily life. Thus, for example, music majors are more likely than physical education majors to interpret an ambiguous passage as pertaining to the rehearsal of a string ensemble rather than a game of cards. However, the physical education majors are relatively more likely to interpret a passage as being about a wrestling match rather than a jail break (Anderson *et al.*, 1977).

Assimilation and contrast effects. Primed concepts are more likely to be used as a basis for interpreting information only when the information is sufficiently ambiguous that the concept can plausibly be applied to it. If the possible meanings the information can have do not fall within the range to which the concept is applicable, the concept may be used as a standard of comparison, leading it to have a contrast effect. Thus, for example, exposing participants to the names of moderately hostile individuals may lead a target's ambiguous behavior to be interpreted as more hostile than it would otherwise be, but exposing them to extreme exemplars of hostility (e.g., Adolf Hitler) may lead the behavior to be interpreted as *less* hostile than it would otherwise be. Correspondingly, consumers typically judge the price of a product, which is unambiguous, to be less expensive if they have previously been exposed to high prices than if they have been exposed to low prices. Furthermore, this is true even when the primed values are conveyed subliminally (Adaval and Monroe, 2002).

Effects of procedural knowledge accessibility. People may employ different strategies in comprehending information. Some individuals, for example, may have a disposition to interpret information in terms of semantic concepts regardless of the modality in which the information is conveyed. Others, however, may be disposed to construct visual images on the basis of the information even when the information is conveyed verbally. These dispositions, which can be either chronic or situationally primed, can influence the impact of the information. For example, individuals with a disposition to form visual images from verbal information may find it difficult to construct an image of an unfamiliar product and to organize descriptions of its attributes into this image. Thus, they may evaluate the product less favorably persons who process the information semantically.

Furthermore, individuals with a disposition to form visual images may have difficulty processing ad information about an object (e.g., a hotel resort) if it is described from different perspectives (e.g., that of someone inside vs outside the hotel) and may evaluate the object less favorably than those who interpret the individual items in terms of semantic concepts without forming visual images.

A second processing style with implications for consumer judgment and decisions concerns the disposition to comprehend information items individually or in relation to one another or the context in which they are found. This disposition, like the disposition to process information verbally or visually, can be either chronic or situationally induced. For example, stimulating people to think of themselves as individuals or in relation to others can be induced by asking them to use either "I" or "we" repeatedly in a sentence construction task. Once activated, these self-referent processing styles can influence the processing of information in quite unrelated domains. For example, inducing individuals to think of themselves in relation to others increases their memory for the positions of physical objects in a stimulus array independently of memory for the items themselves. It also increases their memory for contextual features of a stimulus array as well as the focal object.

The effects of priming independent versus relational thinking are paralleled by the effects of chronic differences in the accessibility of these thinking styles. North Americans typically think of themselves as independent of others, whereas Asians tend to think of themselves in relation to others. These chronic differences in self-construal, like situationally induced differences, are manifested in more general differences in thinking style (Nisbett, 2003). Thus, when asked to group stimuli (e.g., a man, a woman, and a child), Westerners are likely to group them on the basis of category membership (putting the man and woman together, as both are adults) whereas Asians are more likely to group them on the basis of their relation to one another (e.g., to group the woman with the child because the woman takes care of the child). Furthermore, although Asians and Westerners are equally able to identify and remember differences in the central features of a picture, Asians are more likely to remember peripheral, contextual features of the stimuli as well.

Inference and evaluation.   Beliefs. When individuals are asked to report their belief that a statement is true, they are likely to search memory for previously acquired knowledge that has implications for its validity. However, they normally retrieve and use only a small subset of their knowledge that comes to mind quickly and easily. This knowledge may often include a semantically equivalent statement they have encountered at an earlier point in time. However, although individuals often remember having encountered such a statement before, they are less likely to remember where or when they did so. In such instances, they may base their judgment on the statement's familiarity. This, in turn, may depend on the ease with which the statement comes to mind.

Thus, if knowledge bearing on a statement's validity has been encountered recently and, therefore, is easily accessible in memory, individuals may often infer that the statement is true without considering the source of this information. For example, people are likely to judge a proposition to be true if they encountered it in a questionnaire they had completed a few days before. Similarly, they are likely to judge a fictitious person to be well known if his/her name was encountered in a different context 24 hours earlier. Perhaps more interesting is evidence that when consumers have been repeatedly exposed to an advertising claim along with an assertion that the claim is false, they later report this as more likely to be true than they would if they had never been exposed to it at all.

When a previously acquired representation of the statement to be judged does not come quickly to mind, individuals are likely to search for other relevant knowledge that bears on its validity. In doing so, they may retrieve and use only a subset of this knowledge that is most accessible in memory, assuming that it is representative of the larger subset that they have acquired and not considering other information that may be applicable. Thus, to give a simple example, they may report a stronger belief that drinking coffee is desirable if they are asked in the morning (when the knowledge that it wakes you up is easily accessible) than if they are asked late at night (when the fact that it gives you insomnia is more accessible).

Individuals' estimates of the likelihood of an event can often be based on their perception of the frequency of its occurrence and this perception, in turn, may depend on the ease with which exemplars of the event come to mind. Shrum, Wyer, and O'Guinn (1998) provide evidence of this in research on the effects of watching television on perceptions of social reality, that is, individuals typically overestimate the incidence of objects and events in the real world when the events occur frequently on television. Furthermore, this tendency increases with the amount of television they watch. Thus, for example, heavy television viewers are more likely than light viewers to overestimate the incidence of violent crime, the number of lawyers and doctors, and the number of individuals who have swimming pools in their backyard.

The assumption that these effects are mediated by the ease with which instances come to mind is strengthened by evidence that when instances are difficult to generate, they can have a negative effect on judgments that is independent of the number that are actually identified (Schwarz, 2004). Thus, for example, individuals report less favorable evaluations of a product after generating many favorable attributes of it (which is difficult to do) than after generating only a few such attributes (which is easy).

Attitudes. Attitudes toward an object, event, or state of affairs are often inferred from estimates of its desirability. Like beliefs, they can sometimes be based on the subset of knowledge that comes to mind most quickly. Although this knowledge can often include a previously formed evaluation of the stimulus in question, other judgment-relevant knowledge can be retrieved and used as well. To this extent, the stability of an attitude depends on whether the same or a different subset of previously acquired knowledge happens to come to mind each time the attitude is reported. In some cases, a recent behavior that has implications for one's attitude may be retrieved and used independently of other criteria. Thus, individuals who have recently volunteered to advocate a position on an issue may later recall this behavior and infer that they favor the position without considering other attitude-relevant knowledge they have acquired (Bem, 1972).

A major source of information about one's attitude toward a stimulus can be one's affective reactions to it. That is, an individual can have positive or negative reactions to a stimulus as a result of encounters with it in the past, and thinking about the stimulus can reelicit these feelings. These feelings can then be used as a basis for evaluating it. However, individuals are often unable to distinguish clearly between the affect that is actually elicited by an object they are judging and the feelings they are experiencing for other, perhaps irrelevant reasons. Consequently, extraneous affect that is elicited by thinking about an unrelated past experience, or by objectively irrelevant features of the situation in which an object is judged (e.g., the weather, or music that happens to be playing) can influence judgments of the object (Schwarz and Clore, 1996). In the product domain, the affect that is elicited by a picture of a product can influence consumers' evaluations of the product independently of more specific attribute information that they encounter later (Yeung and Wyer, 2004).

Decision processes.   The implications of the effects of knowledge accessibility for consumer behavior are particularly evident at the decision stage of processing. Research on these effects has concerned both the criteria that individuals bring to bear on their decisions and the procedures they employ when making these decisions.

Effects of declarative knowledge. When the products that consumers consider purchasing have both desirable and undesirable attributes, their choices can depend on which type of attribute they weight more heavily. Suppose one product has a very favorable attribute but also a very unfavorable one. However, a second has a moderately favorable attribute and a moderately unfavorable one. In this case, consumers who focus on favorable attributes are likely to choose the first product, whereas consumers who are concerned with negative attributes are likely to choose the second.

These dispositions may be either chronic or induced by situational factors that are quite irrelevant to the decision to be made. For example,

calling individuals' attention to a discrepancy between their actual self concept and their ideal self appears to stimulate a *promotion* focus, that is, a tendency to think about positive consequences of their behavior. In contrast, calling individuals' attention to a discrepancy between their actual self and standards established by others stimulates them to think about avoiding negative consequences. The latter, *prevention* focus can also be induced by increasing individuals' awareness of their membership in a group, thus activating thoughts about social responsibility and decreasing the willingness to take risks. Once activated, these dispositions influence choice behavior in situations that are unrelated to the situations that gave rise to them.

Cultural differences in the tendency to focus on positive or negative decision consequences have also been identified, that is, North Americans are disposed to focus on the positive features of choice alternatives, whereas Asians are more concerned about the avoidance of negative features. However, these cultural differences may only be apparent if situational factors (e.g., the language in which individuals are communicating, or the need to give a reason for their choices) increase the accessibility of culture-related norms and values (Briley, Morris, and Simonson, 2000, 2005).

Effects of procedural knowledge. Making a purchase decision can involve three steps: deciding whether to make a purchase, deciding which of several alternatives to buy, and deciding how to implement the purchase (e.g., to pay by cash or credit card). Although these steps often occur in sequence, increasing the accessibility of later steps in the sequence can sometimes lead consumers to apply these steps without performing the earlier ones. For example, consumers may think about how to pay for a product without thinking about whether they actually want to purchase it. Similarly, they may consider which product to choose without thinking about whether they want to buy anything at all. To this extent, activating concepts associated with later stages in the decision process may lead consumers to apply these concepts without performing earlier steps, and this can affect their likelihood of making a purchase.

Thus, for example, consumers who are induced to make a small purchase early in an experimental session are more inclined to make a second purchase later in the session than they otherwise would be. Furthermore, inducing consumers to state a preference for one of two choice alternatives can induce a "which to choose" mind-set that increases their likelihood of making a purchase without considering the option of buying nothing at all. Moreover, this is true even if the preferences they report initially pertain to products that are quite different from the ones considered in their later purchase decision and, in fact, do not have to concern products at all (that is, reporting preferences for wild animals, like reporting preferences for products, can increase the likelihood of purchasing snacks that are on sale after the experiment; see Xu and Wyer, 2008).

Overt behavior. The subset of knowledge that is accessible in memory can influence overt behavior as well as judgments and decisions. Moreover, this influence can occur without awareness. A number of studies by Bargh (1997) and his colleagues provide evidence. For example, individuals who have been primed with concepts associated with rudeness in a sentence construction task are more likely to interrupt an experimenter's conversation with a graduate student in order to return a questionnaire. Similarly, individuals who have been primed with concepts associated with the elderly walk more slowly to the elevator after leaving the experiment. Subliminally exposing Caucasian students to faces of African Americans (who are stereotypically associated with aggressiveness) increases their nonverbal manifestations of irritation when they were asked to repeat a boring task. These and other studies suggest that priming semantic concepts activate a production that elicits overt behavior without awareness.

Bibliography

Anderson, J.R. (1983) *The Architecture of Cognition*, Harvard University Press, Cambridge.

Anderson, R.C., Reynolds, R.E., Schallert, D.L., and Goetz, E.T. (1977) Frameworks for comprehending discourse. *American Educational Research Journal*, **14**, 367–381.

Adaval, R. and Monroe, K.B. (2002) Automatic construction and use of contextual information for product and price evaluations. *Journal of Consumer Research*, **28**, 572–588.

Bargh, J.A. (1997) The automaticity of everyday life, in *Advances in Social Cognition*, Vol. 10 (ed. R.S. Wyer), Erlbaum, Mahwah, pp. 1–62.

Bargh, J.A., Chen, M., and Burrows, L. (1996) Automaticity of social behavior: direct effects of trait construct and stereotype activation on action. *Journal of Personality and Social Psychology*, **71**, 230–244.

Bem, D.J. (1972) Self-perception theory, in *Advances in Experimental Social Psychology*, Vol. 6 (ed. L. Berkowitz), Academic Press, New York, pp. 1–62.

Bodenhausen, G.V. and Macrae, C.N. (1998) Stereotype activation and inhibition, in *Advances in Social Cognition*, Vol. 11 (ed. R.S. Wyer), Erlbaum, Mahwah, pp. 1–52.

Briley, D.A., Morris, M., and Simonson, I. (2000) Reasons as carriers of culture: dynamic versus dispositional models of cultural influence on decision making. *Journal of Consumer Research*, **27**, 157–178.

Briley, D.A., Morris, M.W., and Simonson, I. (2005) Cultural chameleons: biculturals, conformity motives and decision making. *Journal of Consumer Psychology*, **15**, 351–362.

Carlston, D.E. (1980) Events, inferences and impression formation, in *Person Memory: The Cognitive Basis of Social Perception* (eds R. Hastie, T. Ostrom, E. Ebbesen *et al.*), Erlbaum, Hillsdale, NJ, pp. 89–119.

Collins, A.M. and Loftus, E.F. (1975) A spreading-activation theory of semantic processing. *Psychological Review*, **82**, 407–428.

Dijksterhuis, A. and Bargh, J.A. (2001) The perception-behavior expressway: automatic effects of social perception on social behavior, in *Advances in Experimental Social Psychology*, Vol. 33 (ed. M.P. Zanna), Academic Press, San Diego, pp. 1–40.

Förster, J. and Liberman, N. (2007) Knowledge activation, in *Social Psychology: Handbook of Basic Principles*, 2nd edn (eds A.W. Kruglanski and E.T. Higgins), Guilford, New York, pp. 201–231.

Higgins, E.T. (1996) Knowledge activation: accessibility, applicability, and salience, in *Social Psychology: Handbook of Basic Principles* (eds E.T. Higgins and A. Kruglanski), Guilford, New York, pp. 133–168.

Loftus, E.F. (1975) Leading questions and the eyewitness report. *Cognitive Psychology*, **7**, 560–572.

Nisbett, R.E. (2003) *The Geography of Thought: How Asians and Westerners Think Differently*, Free Press, New York.

Schwarz, N. (2004). Metacognitive experiences in consumer judgment and decision making. *Journal of Consumer Psychology*, **14**, 332–348.

Schwarz, N. and Clore, G.L. (1996) Feelings and phenomenal experiences, in *Social Psychology: A Handbook of Basic Principles* (eds E.T. Higgins and A. Kruglanski), Guilford, New York, pp. 433–465.

Shen, H. and Wyer, R.S. (2008) Procedural priming and consumer judgments: Effects on the impact of positively and negatively valenced information. *Journal of Consumer Research*, **34**, 727–737.

Shrum, L.J., Wyer, R.S., and O'Guinn, T. (1998) The effects of watching television on perceptions of social reality. *Journal of Consumer Research*, **24**, 447–458.

Taylor, S.E. and Fiske, S.T. (1978) Salience, attention and attribution: top of the head phenomena, in *Advances in Experimental Social Psychology*, Vol. 11 (ed. L. Berkowitz), Academic Press, New York, pp. 249–288.

Wyer, R.S. (2008) The role of knowledge accessibility in cognition and behavior: implications for consumer information processing, in *Handbook of Consumer Psychology* (eds C. Haugtvedt, P. Herr, and F. Kardes), Erlbaum, Mahwah, pp. 31–76.

Wyer, R.S. and Srull, T.K. (1989) *Memory and Cognition in its Social Context*, Erlbaum, Hillsdale, NJ.

Xu, A.J. and Wyer, R.S. (2008) The comparative mindset: from animal comparisons to increased purchase intentions. *Psychological Science*, **19**, 859–864.

Yeung, C.W.M. and Wyer, R.S. (2004) Affect, appraisal and consumer judgment. *Journal of Consumer Research*, **31**, 412–424.

M

marketing and feminism

Elizabeth C. Hirschman

The development of feminist theory in marketing has an uneven history. During the 1990s researchers published some key papers and articles which helped gain a foothold for feminist thought (see e.g., Bristor and Fischer, 1993; Hirschman, 1993; Stern, 1993).

This effort was expanded by a growing set of feminist researchers during the 1990s to incorporate ecofeminism (Dobscha and Ozanne, 2001), gender roles (Penalosa, 1994), gay and lesbian studies (Penalosa, 1996) and critiques of marketing ideology as essentially masculine (Penalosa, 1994). These diverse lines of research were consolidated in an edited volume (Catterall, Maclaran, and Stevens, 2000) which effectively summarized the state of theorization and application of feminism in marketing over the prior decade.

During the past decade, that is, 2001–2010, feminism has been expanded further into marketing areas such as environmentalism (Dobscha and Ozanne, 2001; Scott and Penalosa, 2006), queer studies (Scott and Penalosa, 2006), and critical theory (Maclaran *et al.*, 2008). However, feminist research has not made the advances one would have expected, given its early theoretical potency and intrinsic applicability to a wide set of marketing phenomena. In particular, little attention has been directed toward the economic progress of women in marketing careers or, indeed, within the academy, itself (for an exception, see Penalosa, 2000). For example, women have served as editors of the *Journal of Consumer Research*. However, they have not acted in a similar capacity in *the Journal of Marketing, Journal of Marketing Research*, or *Journal of Public Policy and Marketing*.

A portion of this slowdown is likely attributable to the redirecting of research attention toward critical theory, generally, and even more recently toward transformative research agendas on the part of feminist marketing scholars (see e.g., Catterall, Maclaran, and Stevens (2005, 2006)). However, the larger part may be due to a "feminist generational gap."

The majority of productive feminist scholars in marketing matured as researchers during the early 1990s, a time period during which feminism played a more active role in academic discourse and public awareness. Over the past decade, while the ranks of women scholars in marketing have doubled, there has been little interest among these newcomers to apply feminist thought in their research agendas. Indeed, many may see little or no need for feminism on either a personal or academic level. Sadly, this viewpoint on their part is mistaken, as there are still ongoing gender discrepancies in salary, promotion, and the larger academic reward structure, as for example, journal editorships.

Further, as Scott (2009); Dolan and Scott (2009) has argued, there are many pressing issues for women in developing countries which tend to be given little attention by feminist researchers in Western Europe and North America. Among these are legal restrictions on women's rights to own property and work outside the home, very insufficient access to health care and education, and restrictions on travel. Recent initiatives to provide basic health care and employment opportunities have the potential to remake the lives of hundreds of millions of women around the world (Scott, 2009). Thus, there remains much important work to be done and a reawakening of interest in the relationship between feminism and marketing would be of great value to the field – and the lives of women – in many ways.

See also *sex in advertising; subcultures*

Bibliography

Bristor, J.M. and Fischer, E. (1993) Feminist thought: implications for consumer research. *Journal of Consumer Research*, **19**, 518–527.

Catterall, M., Maclaran, P. and Stevens, L.L. (1997) Marketing and feminism: a bibliography and suggestions for further research. *Marketing Intelligence and Planning*, **15** (7), 67–80.

Catterall, M., Maclaran, P. and Stevens, L.L. (eds) (2000) *Marketing and Feminism: Current Issues and Research*, Routledge Interpretive Marketing Research series, Routledge, London.

Catterall, M., Maclaran, P. and Stevens, L.L. (2005) Postmodern paralysis: the critical impasse on feminist perspectives on consumers. *Journal of Marketing Management*, **21** (5-6), 489–504.

Catterall, M., Maclaran, P. and Stevens, L.L. (2006) The transformative potential of feminist critique in consumer research. *Advances in Consumer Research, Association for Consumer Research*, **33**, 222–226.

Dobscha, S. and Ozanne, J.L. (2001) An ecofeminist analysis of environmentally sensitive women. *Journal of Public Policy and Marketing*, **20** (2), 201–214.

Dolan, C. and Scott, L.M. (2009) Lipstick evangelism: avon trading circles and gender empowerment in South Africa. *Gender and Development*, **6**, 203–218.

Hirschman, E. (1993) Ideology in consumer research, 1980 and 1990: a marxist and feminist critique. *Journal of Consumer Research*, **19** (4), 537–555.

Maclaran, P., Catterall, M., Stevens, L. and Hamilton, K. (2008) *Reinstating Wider Social Critique in Research on Gender and Consumer Behavior*, Association for Consumer Research conference on Gender Marketing and Consumer Behavior, Boston.

Penalosa, L. (1994) "Crossing boundaries, drawing lines": a look at gender trouble in marketing research. *International Journal of Research in Marketing*, **11**, 359–379.

Penalosa, L. (1996) We're here, we're queer and we're going shopping. *Journal of Homosexuality*, **31** (1/2), 9–41.

Penalosa, L. (2000) You've come a long way baby? Negotiating Feminism in the Marketing Academy in the US, in *Marketing and Feminism*, (eds M. Catterall, P. Maclaran and L. Stevens), Routledge, London, 39–50.

Scott, L.M. (2009) The double X economy. *Business at Oxford*, **10**, 13–17.

Scott, L.M. and Penalosa, L. (2006) Matriarchal marketing: a manifesto. *Journal of Strategic Marketing*, **15**, 309–323.

Stern, B.B. (1993) Feminist literary criticism and the deconstruction of ads. *Journal of Consumer Research*, **19** (4), 556–566.

motivation and goals

Hans Baumgartner and Rik Pieters

Motivation deals with the question of why consumers do the things they do. It is frequently contrasted with cognition and affect. While cognition refers to the thinking aspect of functioning, and affect to the feeling aspect, motivation deals with the wanting or striving aspect. Two issues are involved: what people want (the direction of motivation) and how much they want something (the force of motivation). Psychological constructs such as needs, motives, desires, wishes, values, drives, and goals all fall within the purview of motivation. It is frequently difficult to distinguish between these constructs precisely, but in general needs and motives are higher level reasons for engaging in a behavior, usually thought to be limited in number so that classifications of human needs and motives can be developed. Desires and wishes tend to refer to lower level wants, often ones whose feasibility may be questionable, with desires being stronger than wishes. Values are high-level ideals that are considered socially desirable by some segments of society, and they may be used as criteria for evaluating objects, events, and behaviors. Drives are hypothetical internal states (often arising from a discrepancy between a desired and actual state and considered to be aversive) that impel people to action and energize behavior. Finally, goals are internal representations of desirable states that people try to attain (approach goals) and undesirable states that they try to avoid (avoidance goals).

In this article, we focus on goals as the central construct of motivation and use the notion of goal in a general sense ranging from relatively concrete aims that provide specific direction for behavior to more abstract purposes (including motives, needs, and values) that imbue subordinate goals with affect. We emphasize the directional aspect of motivation, since involvement (which captures the intensity aspect) is covered in a separate chapter. We start the presentation with a discussion of goal structure and then move to the dynamics of goal pursuit, including both conscious and nonconscious goal setting and goal striving.

THE STRUCTURE OF GOALS

Structural approaches to the study of motivation are well established (see Austin and Vancouver, 1996; Carver and Scheier, 1998; Heckhausen, 1991). These frameworks describe different levels of motivations that people are assumed to have, either in general or in a specific situation, ranging from concrete to abstract motivations, and the linkages between motivations at the same or different levels in the hierarchy in terms of their associative, temporal, conditional, or causal relationships. We begin our discussion with two approaches that are well known but usually not mentioned under the rubric of goals (Maslow's hierarchy of needs and Schwartz's classification of values), although they are closely related since needs and values can be conceived as high-level goals. We then describe means-end chain analysis and its extension to modeling consumer goal structures. We end with a brief discussion of purchase motives.

Needs and values.   In general, needs and values are abstract motivational constructs that are linked to the more concrete goals that consumers have in specific life-domains and situations.

Maslow's hierarchy of needs.   Maslow (1943) proposed a famous theory of motivation that posits five basic human needs: physiological needs (hunger, thirst, sex), safety needs, love needs (belonging, affection), esteem needs (including both self-esteem based on achievement or independence and esteem from others based on prestige or appreciation), and need for self-actualization. The five needs are hypothesized to be organized into a "hierarchy of relative prepotency" such that lower order needs have to be satisfied before higher order

needs can emerge. Applied to marketing, and as described in consumer behavior textbooks, the theory suggests that products are differentially relevant to the five needs (e.g., insurance presumably satisfies the need for safety) and that when appealing to consumers' needs, account has to be taken of where in the need hierarchy a target segment is situated. Among the criticisms of the theory are that the posited hierarchy of prepotency may not be valid and that the theory may not be cross-culturally applicable. Importantly, interest in the basic needs proposed by Maslow has been growing in recent years, with specific theories and measures being developed for each of them, such as the need to belong (Baumeister and Leary, 1995). In the domain of consumer behavior, Belk, Ger, and Askegaard (2003) provide a rich framework of needs and wants and their connections to consumer passions.

The structure of values.   Particularly for purposes of market segmentation, research on values has a long tradition in marketing. Market segmentation aims to identify groups of consumers with similar within-group and different between-group "preferences." Values are considered such abstract "preferences" that give direction to consumer behavior in a wide range of situations. The most sophisticated framework is Schwartz's (1992) work on universals in the content and structure of values. Extending Rokeach's (1973) structural theory of instrumental (lower level) and terminal (higher level) values, Schwartz distinguishes 10 different value types, corresponding to basic human motivations. The value types can be arranged in a circular order to reflect their compatibilities and conflicts. Furthermore, the 10 value types can be grouped into four higher order value domains (roughly four quadrants of a circle): self-enhancement (achievement, power) versus self-transcendence (universalism, benevolence), and conservation (tradition, conformity, and security) versus openness to change (self-direction, stimulation), with hedonism falling between the openness to change and self-enhancement values. Schwartz also constructed an instrument in which participants rate over 50 individual values based on importance, and research using this instrument, involving cultures from around the globe, suggests that the hypothesized structure of values may be universal.

Hierarchical conceptualizations of goals.
Means-end chain analysis. A hierarchical approach to goals, which was developed in marketing and builds on some of the earlier work on values, is means-end chain theory (Reynolds and Olson, 2001; see also Huffman, Ratneshwar, and Mick, 2000). According to means-end chain theory, consumers purchase products because these products (via their need–satisfying attributes) help them attain certain values. Specifically, product attributes (both concrete attributes such as a car's horsepower and more abstract attributes such as its sportiness) have certain functional (e.g., being able to drive fast) and psycho-social (e.g., being admired by others) consequences of product use, which ultimately relate to important instrumental (e.g., being independent, imaginative) and terminal (e.g., pleasure, sense of accomplishment) values. The task of marketers is to uncover the salient means-end connections for a product category of interest (via data collection techniques such as laddering), and the resulting hierarchical value map (HVM) can then be used to segment the market and develop positioning strategies that will appeal to the chosen target segments, by emphasizing self-relevant attributes, consequences, and values and the linkages between them.

Goal structures as means-end chains.
Pieters, Baumgartner and Allen (1995) extended the means-end chain approach to the modeling of consumer goal structures (see also Bagozzi and Dholakia, 1999; Baumgartner and Pieters, 2008). The notion that goal-directed behavior is structured hierarchically is a common assumption in research on goals (Austin and Vancouver, 1996). Pieters and his coauthors specifically assume that behavior is usually controlled by a basic-level goal (e.g., losing weight, purchasing a new car) at an intermediate level in the goal hierarchy (which identifies *what* the consumer is trying to do), but that in order to understand behavior more completely, one also needs to know *how* the consumer is trying to attain this goal (the subordinate goal or operation level) and

why he or she is trying to attain this goal (the superordinate goal or motivation level). Interestingly, the goal hierarchy is closely related to two important goal features, namely, their desirability and importance on the one hand and their feasibility on the other hand. Superordinate goals are relevant for understanding why goals are desirable and important to people, whereas subordinate goals are critical for evaluating the feasibility of goal pursuit. Importantly, the three levels in the goal hierarchy are not fixed but flexible, depending on person and task characteristics. Different consumers in different circumstances may be guided by goals at different levels in the hierarchy (ranging from wanting to avoid sugary snacks at a rather concrete level to wanting to have a more attractive body or better self-esteem at a very abstract level), and this determines which goals are subordinate and superordinate relative to the basic-level goal.

Consumers' decision making goals and purchase motives. Consumer behavior researchers have considered goals that guide decision making and the processing of other marketing stimuli (e.g., ads). For example, Bettman, Luce, and Payne (1998) proposed four goals (maximizing decision accuracy, minimizing decision effort, minimizing negative emotions during decision making, and maximizing the ease of justification of a decision) that are relevant to decision making. However, surprisingly little research has investigated the motives that underlie consumers' buying behavior (i.e., why consumers make certain buying decisions, not how they make them). Recently, Baumgartner (2010) conducted a comprehensive review of prior classifications of purchase behavior and proposed a new, empirically based typology derived from consumers' categorization of 44 purchase motives. The full typology consists of eight different purchase behaviors corresponding to the eight cells of a $2 \times 2 \times 2$ cross-classification of three orthogonal dimensions: functional versus psycho-social purchases; low versus high purchase involvement; and spontaneous versus deliberate purchases.

As might be expected, purchases that are made spontaneously and entail little effort and care (this includes casual purchases at the functional end and impulsive purchases at the psycho-social end of the continuum) are not well-defined in terms of purchase motives (i.e., buying things more or less mindlessly or based on convenience vs making unplanned or impulsive purchases). Spontaneous purchases that are higher in purchase involvement include promotional purchases (based on functional motives of getting a good deal) and exploratory purchases (based on psycho-social motives of variety, change, and curiosity).

Deliberate purchases made with little involvement comprise repetitive purchases (characterized by functional motives of loyalty, habit, routine, and familiarity) and hedonic purchases (characterized by psycho-social motives of sensory gratification and simple liking/wanting). Deliberate purchases higher in purchase involvement include extended purchase decision making (based on utilitarian motives such as logical problem solving and a concern with performance, quality, and value) and symbolic purchase behavior (involving psychological motives of wanting to express one's personality and feeling good about oneself and social motives of projecting a certain image, attaining status, and being socially accepted).

Conscious Goal Pursuit

Although they are often intertwined in practice, we distinguish two separate stages of goal pursuit: goal setting and goal striving (Bagozzi and Dholakia, 1999; Baumgartner and Pieters, 2008; Heckhausen, 1991). The discussion of goal setting will focus on the decision to pursue the basic-level goal, where the consumer commits to pursuing a goal. But, of course, goals also have to be set during goal striving at lower levels of the hierarchy, consistent with our earlier discussion about flexibility in means-end chains of goals. Once a consumer has formed an intention to pursue a particular goal (avoiding sugary snacks before dinner or eating less during the week), steps are taken to strive toward the chosen goal. According to Heckhausen (1991), goal setting is a motivational process of deciding whether or not to pursue a given goal, or choosing between conflicting goals, whereas goal striving is a volitional process focused on reaching the desired goal. We emphasize goals that are pursued

deliberately in this section, but we touch upon subconscious goal pursuit too.

Goal setting. Sometimes consumers do not set goals themselves but pursue goals that are "assigned" to them (e.g., buying a wedding present using a gift registry, using someone else's shopping list to buy groceries). But often consumers set their own goals, although rarely in a social vacuum. Usually, the goal-setting process is conceptualized as some variant of subjective-expected utility or expectancy-value theory. The notion is that consumers consider the consequences of pursuing a goal, taking into account both the desirability of the outcomes emanating from goal achievement ("part utilities" or "evaluations") and the feasibility of reaching the goal and/or the outcomes associated with the goal ("expectations" or "beliefs"). In addition, other influences are sometimes considered as well. A well-known framework, which was originally developed for explaining and predicting volitional behaviors (e.g., buying a soft drink, going out for dinner, voting for a certain candidate) but which has often been applied to goals (e.g., losing weight, donating blood), is the theory of reasoned action or TRA (Fishbein and Ajzen, 1975). According to this theory, behavior is a function of a person's intention to engage in the behavior, which in turn depends on the person's attitude toward the act and the subjective norms governing the behavior (i.e., the expectations of relevant others and the person's motivation to comply with these expectations). Attitudes toward the behavior are determined based on a person's evaluation of the consequences of engaging in the behavior weighted by the likelihood that the behavior in question will lead to these consequences. Applied to goals, the theory suggests that consumers will form a goal intention (which implies a commitment to reach the goal) if the goal is evaluated favorably by the decision maker (i.e., the outcomes associated with goal achievement are valued highly and it is deemed likely that reaching the goal will lead to these outcomes) and if relevant others are in favor of the decision maker's goal pursuit.

Bagozzi and Warshaw (1990) reformulated TRA to make it more relevant for explaining goal pursuit. This so-called theory of trying assumes that in the context of goal-directed behavior the relevant dependent variable is consumers' attempts to reach the goal in question (i.e., trying), that trying is preceded by a conscious decision to try (intention to try), and that intention to try is a function of attitude toward trying, social norms toward trying, and the frequency of past trying. Attitude toward trying depends on considerations of desirability and feasibility involving success and failure at attaining the goal as well as attitudes toward the process of goal pursuit.

Expectancy-values models have typically been applied to single behaviors and goals, but they can be extended to the choice between behaviors and goals by assuming that the behavior or goal with the highest subjective utility and/or the highest behavioral/goal intention is selected. When choosing between multiple goals, conflicts may arise. There are at least three types of conflict: approach–approach conflict (several goals are desirable, such as taking a vacation or having a baby), avoidance–avoidance conflict (one goal has to be adopted, but all choices have undesirable features, such as cleaning up the garage or painting the house) and approach–avoidance conflict (a goal has both desirable and undesirable features, such as spending one's savings when taking a vacation). Goal conflicts are omnipresent in everyday consumer behavior, but surprisingly little is known about how consumers cope with such conflicts.

Goal striving.
Goal striving with single goals.   Once a consumer has formed a goal intention, which implies a commitment to attain the goal, a course of action aimed at reaching the goal has to be planned, the plan has to be implemented, progress toward goal achievement has to be monitored, and if difficulties are encountered, decisions have to be made about whether goal pursuit should be continued, reconsidered, suspended, or abandoned (see Baumgartner and Pieters, 2008).

With simple behaviors and goals, such as those usually studied with TRA, goal striving is not an issue, particularly if the necessary behaviors have been enacted frequently in the past. However, when goal achievement requires a sequence of more complex behaviors, the consumer has to develop a plan for goal pursuit. One tool for planning is mental simulation. Two types of mental simulations have been distinguished in the literature. Outcome simulation involves imagining the consequences of reaching the goal, and particularly anticipated emotional reactions to goal success and goal failure can serve a useful motivational function for energizing goal pursuit. More relevant for planning purposes are process simulations, in which the consumer imagines the steps necessary to reach the desired end. Prior research shows that engaging in process simulations is more beneficial for goal attainment than engaging in outcome simulations (see Baumgartner and Pieters, 2008).

In a tradition strongly rooted in German psychology (Heckhausen, 1991), Gollwitzer and his associates (e.g., Gollwitzer, 1996) have argued that implementation intentions and an implemental mind-set are useful tools for enacting goal-directed behaviors. Implementation intentions are self-instructions to execute certain behaviors when a particular situation is encountered (i.e., I will do x when situation y arises). They are effective because relevant behaviors are linked to critical situations so that encountering the critical situation automatically triggers the relevant behavior or activates relevant plans in working-memory, which also increases the likelihood of enacting the intention. In a similar way, an implemental mindset has been found to facilitate the enactment of goal-relevant behaviors because instead of deliberating the pros and cons of potential courses of action (which is characteristic of a deliberative mindset), the consumer focuses single-mindedly on the execution of behaviors necessary for goal achievement, and doubts about feasibility and desirability are put aside.

Consumers need to self-regulate during goal pursuit (i.e., they have to stay focused on striving toward the goal and not be distracted by momentary temptations, and they have to be able to resume goal pursuit after an interruption). Following Baumeister (see Baumeister *et al.*, 2008, for a recent review), self-regulation involves monitoring goal progress with regard to standards and it requires self-regulatory strength. Since people's capacity for self-regulation is limited, engaging in self-regulation is ego-depleting. Various tasks have been shown to result in ego depletion, including making choices between consumer products and trading off quality and price. Furthermore, ego depletion has been demonstrated to make it more difficult for consumers to control their eating and spending, among other things, and it may lead to the use of simplistic decision strategies such as choosing options based on the attraction effect.

The final step of goal striving is the evaluation of goal achievement. If the goal is an outcome goal ("buying a Porsche sports car"), goal pursuit is terminated when the goal has been reached (i.e., the consumer has purchased the car). However, when the goal is a process goal ("learning to drive a Porsche like the pros"), goal pursuit consists of a continuous process of goal monitoring and involves attempts to either ensure goal progress or maintain adherence to appropriate standards.

If the consumer encounters difficulties during goal striving, several coping strategies are available. These include putting additional effort into goal striving, revising the initial plan, suspending the goal, or abandoning the goal. Research has shown that emotions play an important role in alerting people to those aspects of goal pursuit that require attention, and emotions are also an important consequence of goal success and goal failure (see Baumgartner and Pieters, 2008, for details).

Goal striving with multiple goals. In practice, consumers usually do not pursue single goals, but have to juggle multiple goals. One question is how they accomplish this multiple-goal pursuit over time. Will they first pursue one goal, and then move on to the next, in an orderly sequence? An integrative model of the dynamics of multiple-goal pursuit was recently proposed by Louro, Pieters, and Zeelenberg (2007). These authors argue that, when several goals compete for resources (i.e., the goals do not conflict intrinsically, but compete for the same resource pool), effort allocation to the focal goal is a joint function of the valence of goal-relevant emotions and people's proximity to the goal. When goal progress is slower (faster) than expected and people therefore experience negative (positive) emotions, less (more) effort will be allocated to the focal goal when goal

attainment is distant, whereas more (less) effort will be allocated to the focal goal when goal attainment is near. Furthermore, the proposed effects are mediated by people's expectancies of success, such that either positive emotions (when the goal is distant) or negative emotions (when the goal is close) lead to moderate expectancies of success, which maximize effort allocation relative to situations of low or high expectancies of success. In other words, positive emotions have a facilitating effect on goal pursuit when people are far away from the goal ("It is still a long way, but I'm doing well"), whereas negative emotions encourage goal pursuit when people get close to the focal goal ("It's so close, but I'm doing badly"). The reason is that these are the situations in which goal attainment is uncertain but plausible and allocation of effort promises to further goal progress. In three studies involving goals that compete for consumers' attentional and time resources, such as dieting and studying, Louro, Pieters, and Zeelenberg (2007) found support for these predictions.

Regulatory focus theory in goal pursuit. A motivational theory that has had a substantial impact on consumer research is regulatory focus theory (e.g., Pham and Higgins, 2005). The theory distinguishes two types of regulatory orientations. When people are in a promotion focus, they are concerned with accomplishments, the relevant self-guide is the ideal self (one's hopes and aspirations), and behavior is sensitive to the presence and absence of positive outcomes. In contrast, when people are in a prevention focus, they are concerned with safety, the relevant self-guide is the ought-self (one's duties and obligations), and behavior is sensitive to the presence and absence of negative outcomes. Research has shown that, consistent with these different outcome foci, promotion-oriented consumers have a preference for products signaling luxury and technical innovation, whereas prevention-oriented consumers assign greater value to safety and reliability. In addition, consumers prefer decisions for which there is a match between their regulatory orientation and the means of goal pursuit (value from fit). This occurs when a goal is pursued in an eager fashion (taking chances and avoiding missed opportunities) under a promotion orientation or in a vigilant fashion (being careful and avoiding mistakes) under a prevention orientation. Because of the dual emphasis of the theory on outcome value and value from fit, the theory is relevant for both goal setting and goal striving and has proven useful in areas as diverse as message framing and persuasion, emotional reactions to past and future decision outcomes, and cultural differences in conceptions of the self (independent vs. interdependent self-views).

NONCONSCIOUS GOAL PURSUIT

Thus far we have emphasized consumers' conscious pursuit of goals when a goal is set deliberately and consumers are fully aware of their attempts to strive toward the goal. Many important consumer behaviors are consistent with this process, such as when somebody decides to buy a new car or books a flight to spend the holidays with family. However, it is possible for goals to be activated outside of consumers' awareness, and even the process of goal striving may occur subconsciously. The idea of subconscious goal pursuit is an old one and in the 1950s and 1960s the term *motivation research* actually referred to the study of the hidden motives underlying purchase and consumption. Motivation research fell into disrepute and except for occasional forays into subliminal persuasion (following the journalistic report of James Vicary about the effectiveness of subliminally flashing "eat popcorn" on a movie screen), researchers showed little interest in nonconscious influences on consumer behavior. However, recently there has been a new surge of interest in automatic influences on human behavior in general and consumer behavior in particular (see Bargh, 2002; Chartrand *et al.*, 2008).

According to this perspective, processes that are functionally similar to goal setting and goal striving can occur without conscious awareness. First, cues in the environment, which have become strongly associated with certain goals through past exposure, can activate goals automatically. In laboratory studies, nonconscious activation is usually achieved through subliminal priming, in which participants are exposed to goal concepts so

briefly that they are not consciously aware of the priming stimuli, or supraliminal priming, in which participants are exposed to goal concepts in the context of an ostensibly unrelated study. The real-world analog of such manipulations would be situations in which the consumer happens to get exposed to symbols that are associated with certain goals (e.g., prestige and status when seeing a store sign for Nordstrom). Prior research shows that the nonconscious activation of a goal can indeed affect consumer choices (e.g., priming prestige vs thrift increases the choice of a higher priced product).

Second, not only can goals become activated nonconsciously, but the entire process of goal pursuit can occur outside conscious awareness. The reason is that the steps necessary to reach the goal (the means of goal achievement) have been automatized and once the goal is activated, the associated action plan is enacted as well. Furthermore, this nonconscious goal pursuit exhibits many of the features characteristics of conscious goal striving. When a goal is unfulfilled, motivational strength increases over time, whereas when a goal has been achieved, motivational strength decreases. In addition, similar to conscious goals, nonconscious goals increase people's persistence when there are obstacles to goal achievement, and they encourage resumption of goal-directed behavior after interruption. For example, in the study in which either a prestige or thrift goal was primed, choice of the higher priced product as a function of the prestige prime increased when the time interval between the goal priming and the choice task was longer. Overall, there is now convincing evidence that at least relatively simple goals can be activated automatically and that the ensuing goal pursuit can also occur without consumers' conscious awareness.

CONCLUSION

Despite the importance of motivation and goals for understanding consumer behavior, the wanting or striving aspect of psychological functioning was not at the forefront of research for many years. However, motivation has experienced a renaissance recently, and goal concepts, both conscious and nonconscious, are now employed quite frequently in published research. We hope that this renewed emphasis will motivate additional research to deepen our understanding of consumer behavior, and that the current essay contributes to this goal.

See also *consumer desire; consumer intentions; consumer involvement; optimum stimulation level; self-regulation*

Bibliography

Austin, J.T. and Vancouver, J.B. (1996) Goal constructs in psychology: structure, process, and content. *Psychological Bulletin*, **120**, 338–375.

Bagozzi, R.P. and Dholakia, U. (1999) Goal setting and goal striving in consumer behavior. *Journal of Marketing*, **63** (Special issue), 19–32.

Bagozzi, R.P. and Warshaw, P.R. (1990) Trying to consume. *Journal of Consumer Research*, **17**, 127–140.

Bargh, J.A. (2002) Losing consciousness: automatic influences on consumer judgment, behavior, and motivation. *Journal of Consumer Research*, **29**, 280–285.

Baumeister, R.F. and Leary, M.R. (1995) The need to belong: desire for interpersonal attachments as a fundamental human motivation. *Psychological Bulletin*, **117**, 497–529.

Baumeister, R.F., Sparks, E.A., Stillman, T.F. and Vohs, K.D. (2008) Free will in consumer behavior: self-control, ego depletion, and choice. *Journal of Consumer Psychology*, **18**, 4–13.

Baumgartner, H. (2010) A review of prior classifications of purchase behavior and a proposal for a new typology, in *Review of Marketing Research*, vol. 6 (ed. N.K. Malhotra), M.E. Sharpe, Armonk, NY, 3–36.

Baumgartner, H. and Pieters, R. (2008) Goal-directed consumer behavior: motivation, volition and affect, in *Handbook of Consumer Psychology* (eds C.P. Haugtvedt, P.M. Herr and F.R. Kardes), Lawrence Erlbaum, New York, pp. 367–392.

Belk, R.W., Ger, G. and Askegaard, S. (2003) The fire of desire: a multisited inquiry into consumer passion. *Journal of Consumer Research*, **30**, 326–351.

Bettman, J.R., Luce, M.F. and Payne, J.W. (1998) Constructive consumer choice processes. *Journal of Consumer Research*, **25**, 187–217.

Carver, C.S. and Scheier, M.F. (1998) *On the Self-regulation of Behavior*, Cambridge University Press, New York.

Chartrand, T.L., Huber, J., Shiv, B. and Tanner, R.J. (2008) Nonconscious goals and consumer choice. *Journal of Consumer Research*, **35**, 189–201.

Fishbein, M. and Ajzen, I. (1975) *Belief, Attitude, Intention, and Behavior: An Introduction to Theory and Research*, Addison-Wesley, Reading, MA.

Gollwitzer, P.M. (1996) The volitional benefits of planning, in *The Psychology of Action* (eds P.M. Gollwitzer and J.A. Bargh), Guilford, New York, pp. 287–312.

Heckhausen, H. (1991) *Motivation and Action*, 2nd edn, Springer, Berlin.

Huffman, C., Ratneshwar, S. and Mick, D.G. (2000) Consumer goal structures and goal-determination processes, in *The Why of Consumption: Perspectives on Consumer Motives, Goals, and Desires* (eds C. Huffman, R. Ratneshwar and D. Mick), Routledge, London, pp. 9–35.

Louro, M.J., Pieters, R. and Zeelenberg, M. (2007) Dynamics of multiple-goal pursuit. *Journal of Personality and Social Psychology*, **93**, 174–193.

Maslow, A.H. (1943) A theory of human motivation. *Psychological Review*, **50**, 370–396.

Pham, M. and Higgins, E.T. (2005) Promotion and prevention in consumer decision-making: State of the art and theoretical propositions, in *Inside Consumption: Frontiers of Research on Consumer Motives, Goals, and Desires*, (eds S. Ratneshwar and D.G. Mick), Routledge, New York, pp. 8–43.

Pieters, R.G.M., Baumgartner, H. and Allen, D. (1995) A means-end chain approach to consumer goal structures. *International Journal of Research in Marketing*, **12**, 227–244.

Reynolds, T.J. and Olson, J.C. (eds) (2001) *Understanding Consumer Decision Making: The Means-end Approach to Marketing and Advertising Strategy*, Lawrence Erlbaum, Mahwah, NJ.

Rokeach, M. (1973) *The Nature of Human Values*, The Free Press, New York.

Schwartz, S.H. (1992) Universals in the content and structure of values: theoretical and empirical tests in 20 countries, in *Advances in Experimental Social Psychology*, Vol. 25 (ed M. Zanna), Academic Press, New York, pp. 1–65.

O

online consumption

David Mazursky and Gideon Vinitzky

In view of its fast growth, little doubt remains about the central role that online consumption plays in practically every aspect of our marketing world. Much of the research interest in recent years has focused on whether the key consumer decision-making rules that we acquired over decades of research can be easily applied in the online consumption context, or alternatively, whether it involves unique characteristics which challenge our accumulated knowledge and predictions about how consumers behave. The emerging literature indicates that the on-line shopping process possesses several unique characteristics that distinguish it from other forms of transactions.

The study of on-line shopping focuses mainly on the effects of technological aspects of the Internet on consumers' experience, motivation to engage in the process, the unique process dynamics, and postconsumption behavior. The literature developed so far mentions two technological features of the Internet as affecting the way people make their purchases and the outcome of consumption: interactivity and vividness (Steuer, 1992). Although the literature offers different definitions of the interactivity concept (Rafaeli, 1990; Steuer, 1992) and different dimensions based on various theoretical frameworks, it is agreed that most web sites offer dimensions that enable consumers to hold instant-response dialogues with the electronic interface and salesperson, simulating a regular conversation between human beings. The second characteristic of the technological environment is vividness, defined as the clarity of information received by consumers in the virtual world (Steuer, 1992).

Researchers suggest that interactivity and vividness promote the experience of telepresence, defined as consumers' feeling when located within the Internet environment (Steuer, 1992). Telepresence enables consumers to enjoy the actual process of navigating the site and is characterized by intrinsic motivation. Hoffman and Novak (1996) suggest that the interaction between the consumer and the purchase interface has an effect beyond that of the information in the shop, thus promoting the experience of flow, that is, the complete engagement with and immersion in an activity (Hoffman and Novak, 2009). The research states that the flow experience is more a characteristic of consumers in purchase tasks than of computer users on surfing tasks who have no purchase intentions and that the flow experience promotes exploratory, curiosity, and discovery behavior (control and perceived behavioral control, and learning).

What motivates consumers to engage in on-line shopping? From the financial aspect, buying on-line enables consumers to visit a large number of shops, increases the choice range of various products, increases competitiveness and gains from reduced prices (Bakos, 1997; Lynch and Ariely, 2000). From the cognitive aspect, consumers expect to benefit from the reduced cost of cognitive search (Lurie, 2004; Häubl and Trifts, 2000; Alba *et al.*, 1997), affecting also their sensitivity to price and quality (Lynch and Ariely, 2000). From the hedonic perspective, researchers suggest that on-line transactions provide consumers with types of pleasure that are similar to traditional transactions (Menon and Kahn, 2002) as well as other sources of enjoyment, for example, convenience and entertainment, that are uniquely associated with on-line purchasing (Childers *et al.*, 2001).

One of the most significant barriers to consumer entry when purchasing on-line is the concern of trust. Trust is a psychological state expressing reliance on another person or organization to do that what is required. Researchers state that trust is a multidimensional psychological concept that includes cognition, affect, and behavior (Johnson and Grayson, 2005). More concretely, factors affecting trust include site features (Shankar and Sultan, 2002), familiarity with the company and its reputation (Yoon, 2002), information security features (Belanger, Hiller, and Smith, 2002), ease of use, and expertise (Fogg *et al.*, 2001). At the same time, trust-motivating factors are distinctively affected by various product categories and interpersonal differences (Bart *et al.*, 2005).

Research on the dynamics of the on-line shopping process suggests that consumers demonstrate various search patterns stemming from the features of the interface (Mazursky and Vinitzky, 2005). Three-dimensional purchase interfaces were found to promote a structured search process, which is more continuous and more compatible with physical shopping, while two-dimensional purchase interfaces were found to promote less structured search, which is quicker yet different from the search pattern characteristic of buying in a traditional shop.

On the basis of the preference construction approach (Bettman, Luce, and Payne, 1998), researchers suggest that consumer preferences change during the purchase process in line with various aspects of the purchase environment. Häubl and Trifts (2000) propose that the default values that appear in search agents affect the features examined in the purchase process. Mandel and Johnson (2002) found that the background color of a web site can serve as priming the criteria involved in product selection and that it affects the weight given to these criteria in the process of product choice.

The postconsumption factors consist of satisfaction, loyalty, and word-of-mouth communication. Studies offer various models for examining consumer satisfaction upon purchasing on-line. Szymanski and Hise (2000) suggest that the surfer's convenience, the products offered, site design, and financial safety issues, have an effect on satisfaction. Cheung and Lee (2005) focused on the quality of the various components containing the information displayed in the shop and how the system functions. Turban *et al.* (2008) expanded this model and added the component of quality of service provided on site. Surfer satisfaction, in turn, was found to impinge on a variety of shopping related aspects, including word-of-mouth (Parish, Holloway, and Wang, 2005; Chevalier and Mayzlin, 2006), trust (Bart *et al.*, 2005), and loyalty (Bolton, Kannan, and Bramlett, 2000; Floh and Treiblmaier, 2006).

The ease of access to a variety of alternative shops offering the same services (Lynch and Ariely, 2000) contributes positively to consumer loyalty. Keaveney and Parthasarathy (2001) suggest that previous consumer behavior patterns on the site (e.g., use of services), attitudes, involvement, and demographic variables, distinguish between consumers' loyalty status. Other factors found to promote loyalty are the quality of services on the site (Chen and Hitt, 2002), consumer commitment (Pavlou and Gefen, 2004), and trust (Park and Kim, 2006).

However, experiences in on-line shopping may not always be positive. Presumably because of the relative ease to express negative feedback (in comparison with other forms of transaction), such activity is highly prevalent and has intrigued researchers' interest. The nonpositive pattern of postshopping behavior may involve revenge, negative rumor, and negative word of mouth. For example, writing negative on-line reviews may even lead to harming of sales (e.g., Chevalier and Mayzlin, 2006)

Finally, despite the noticeable progress in the study of on-line shopping behavior, its unique infrastructure represents an important research area both for studying on-line shopping, as well as for serving as a proxy for learning the way consumers form decisions in shopping behavior, in general. This infrastructure involves presenting information, prompting a decision, and echoing postconsumption reactions, all in vivo, and in a relatively condensed time framework, enabling tracking and analyzing the process. This is quite a unique setting compared with other forms of transactions such as in physical stores, where tracking this process generally involves tools that are largely artificial and inaccurate. In addition, the growing direct linking possibilities from the shopping activity to other network systems such as social networks, available in on-line shopping formats, further increase their research potential. The outlook is indeed promising, although possible barriers such as intercultural and language issues need to be carefully considered in planning future research.

See also *customer satisfaction; e-commerce and Internet marketing; marketing functions on the Internet; social networks*

Bibliography

Alba, J.W., Lynch, J., Weitz, B. *et al.* (1997) Interactive home shopping: consumer, retailer, and manufacturer incentives to participate in electronic marketplaces. *Journal of Marketing*, **61**, 38–53.

Bakos, J.Y. (1997) Reducing buyer search cost: implication for electronic marketplaces. *Management Science*, **43** (12), 1676–1693.

Bart, Y., Shankar, V., Sultan, F. and Urban, G.L. (2005) Are the drivers and role of online trust the same for all web sites and consumers? A large-scale exploratory empirical study. *Journal of Marketing Research*, **69** (4), 133–152.

Belanger, F., Hiller, J.S. and Smith, W.J. (2002) Trustworthiness in electronic commerce: the role of privacy, security, and site attributes. *Journal of Strategic Information Systems*, **11** (3,4), 245–270.

Bettman, J.R., Luce, M.F. and Payne, J.W. (1998) Constructive consumer choice processes. *Journal of Consumer Research*, **25** (3), 187–217.

Bolton, R.N., Kannan, P. and Bramlett, M.D. (2000) Implications of loyalty program membership and service experiences for customer retention and value. *Journal of the Academy of Marketing Science*, **28** (1), 95–108.

Chen, P. and Hitt, L. (2002) Measuring switching costs and the determinants of customer retention in Internet-enabled businesses: a study of the online brokerage industry. *Information Systems Research*, **13** (3), 255–274.

Cheung, C.M.K. and Lee, M.K.O. (2005) The Asymmetric Impact of Website Attribute Performance on User Satisfaction: An Empirical Study. Paper presented at the Hawaii International Conference on System Sciences, Big Island, Hawaii.

Chevalier, J.A. and Mayzlin, D. (2006) The effect of word of mouth on sales: online book reviews. *Journal of Marketing Research*, **43** (3), 9.

Childers, T.L., Carr, C.L., Peck, J. and Carson, S. (2001) Hedonic and utilitarian motivations for online retail shopping behavior. *Journal of Retailing*, **77** (4), 511.

Johnson, D. and Grayson, K. (2005) Cognitive and affective trust in service. Relationships. *Journal of Business Research*, **58** (4), 500–507.

Floh, A. and Treiblmaier, H. (2006) What keeps the e-banking customer loyal? A multigroup analysis of the moderating role of consumer characteristics e-loyalty in the financial service industry. *Journal of Electronic Commerce Research*, **7** (2), 97–110.

Fogg, B.J., Marshall, J., Laraki, O. *et al.* (2001) What makes web sites credible? A report on a large quantitative study. *ACM SIGCHI*, **3** (1), 61–67.

Häubl, G. and Trifts, V. (2000) Consumer decision making in online shopping environments: the effects of interactive decision aids. *Marketing Science*, **19** (1), 4–21.

Hoffman, D.L. and Novak, T.P. (1996) Marketing in hypermedia computer- mediated environment: conceptual foundation. *Journal of Marketing*, **60**, 50–68.

Hoffman, D.L. and Novak, T.P. (2009) Flow online: lessons learned and future prospects. *Journal of Interactive Marketing*, **23** (1), 23–34.

Keaveney, S. and Parthasarathy, M. (2001) Customer switching behavior in online services: an exploratory study of the role of selected attitudinal, behavioral, and demographic factors. *Journal of the Academy of Marketing Science*, **29** (4), 374–390.

Lurie, N.H. (2004) Decision making in information-rich environments: the role of information structure. *Journal of Consumer Research*, **30** (4), 473–486.

Lynch, J. and Ariely, D. (2000) Wine online: search costs affect competition on price, quality and distribution. *Marketing Science*, **19**, 83–103.

Mandel, N. and Johnson, E.J. (2002). When web pages influence choice: effects of visual primes on experts and novices. *Journal of Consumer Research*, **29** (2), 235–245.

Mazursky, D. and Vinitzky, G. (2005) Modifying consumer search processes in enhanced on-line interfaces. *Journal of Business Research*, **58** (10), 1299.

Menon, S. and Kahn, B. (2002) Cross-category effects of induced arousal and pleasure on the Internet Shopping Experience. *Journal of Retailing*, **78** (1), 31–40.

Parish, J.T., Holloway, B.B. and Wang, S. (2005) The role of cumulative online purchasing experience in service recovery management. *Journal of Interactive Marketing*, **19** (3), 54–66.

Park, C. and Kim, Y. (2006) The effect of information satisfaction and relational benefit on consumers' online shopping site commitments. *Journal of Electronic Commerce in Organizations*, **4** (1), 70–90.

Pavlou, P. and Gefen, D. (2004) Building effective online marketplaces with institution-based trust. *Information Systems Research*, **15** (1), 37–59.

Rafaeli, S. (1990). Interacting with media: para-social interaction and real interaction, in *Mediation, Information and Communication: Information and Behavior* (ed. B.D. Ruben and L.A. Lievrouw), pp. 125–181, Vol. 3.

Shankar, G.L.U. and Sultan, F. (2002) Online trust: a stakeholder perspective, concepts, implications and future directions. *Journal of Strategic Information Systems*, **11** (3-4), 325–344.

Steuer, J. (1992) Defining virtual reality dimensions determining telepresence. *Journal of Communication*, **42** (4), 73–93.

Szymanski, D.M. and Hise, R. (2000) E-satisfaction: an initial examination. *Journal of Retailing*, **76** (3), 309–322.

Turban, E., Lee, J.K., KIng, D. *et al.* (2008) *Electronic Commerce*, 1st edn, Prentice Hall, New Jersey.

Yoon, S.-J. (2002) The antecedents and consequences of trust in online purchase decisions. *Journal of Interactive Marketing*, **16** (2), 47–63.

opinion leadership and market mavens

Ronald Earl Goldsmith

SOCIAL COMMUNICATION AND CONSUMER BEHAVIOR

Consumers use information to make shopping and buying decisions. They get some of this information from marketer-dominated sources such as advertisements, salespersons, brochures, packages, web pages, and promotions. Another and perhaps more important source of information comes in the form of social communication (*see* SOCIAL INFLUENCE). This is the influence consumers have on other consumers. Also termed *non-marketer-dominated* sources, the influence of other consumers can be passive, where consumers simply observe others and imitate them, or active, where consumers talk to each other, seeking or offering advice and information as part of everyday life (Weimann, 1994).

This final form of social communication is often termed *word of mouth*. Word of mouth can be incidental, where topics covering products, advertisements, stores, brands, and buying can be part of ordinary conversations. Consumers can also actively seek advice and information from other consumers or they can actively give information. The former describes opinion seeking and the latter opinion leadership. Opinion leaders are consumers who actively transmit information to other consumers either on their own initiative or after information seekers solicit them. Some consumers called *market mavens* are especially involved in the marketplace (*see* CONSUMER INVOLVEMENT). They are knowledgeable and actively influence other consumers. Because opinion leaders and market mavens exert such a powerful influence on sales, marketers are keen to identify them and to persuade them to promote their brands.

OPINION LEADERSHIP

Most opinion leadership takes the form of product category or domain-specific opinion leadership where consumers spread word of mouth about specific types of products, such as clothing, movies, cars, food, and so on (Flynn, Goldsmith, and Eastman, 1996). The chief antecedent or motivator for opinion leadership is likely involvement, or the interest, enthusiasm, and excitement consumers feel for their favorite categories. Opinion leaders are not only involved in their favorite domains, they are knowledgeable about them, widely exposed to marketer-dominated sources of information, eager to buy new products in the domain (*see* CONSUMER INNOVATIVENESS), and motivated to influence others. Opinion leadership occurs both off-line in the physical world as well as online in cyberspace, especially in SOCIAL NETWORKS where a small number of enthusiastic consumers dominate the flow of information across the network (Iyengar, Van den Bulte, and Valente, 2008).

In addition, some consumers act as general opinion leaders where their influence cuts across several domains (Keller and Berry, 2003). This general type of opinion leadership suggests that some consumers are especially important in the spread of information through social connections. The most thorough examination of this general marketplace behavior occurs in the research stream devoted to market mavenism.

MARKET MAVENS

Market mavens were first described by Feick and Price (1987, p. 85) as: "individuals who have information about many kinds of products, places to shop, and other facets of markets, and initiate discussion with consumers and respond to request from consumers from market information." Since then, researchers have extended the understanding of this phenomenon. Market mavens cannot be especially defined by their demographics, but do thrive in different countries around the world (Chelminski and Coulter, 2007). These consumers pay close attention to ads and brands, they like to shop, they think about shopping and buying, they like to talk to others about ads, stores, products, shopping, and consuming in general. They clip and trade coupons. They know the best places to buy and actively recommend them to their friends. They are aware of and eager to buy new products. They act as general opinion leaders but differ from them through their greater engagement in the marketplace and variety of market-related behaviors.

Bibliography

Chelminski, P. and Coulter, R.A. (2007) On market mavens and consumer self-confidence: a cross-cultural study. *Psychology and Marketing*, **24** (1), 69–91.

Feick, L.F. and Price, L.L. (1987) The market maven: a diffuser of marketplace information. *Journal of Marketing*, **51**, 83–97.

Flynn, L.R., Goldsmith, R.E., and Eastman, J.K. (1996) Opinion leaders and opinion seekers: two new measurement scales. *Journal of the Academy of Marketing Science*, **24** (2), 137–147.

Goldsmith, R.E., Flynn, L.R., and Goldsmith, E.B. (2003) Innovative consumers and market mavens. *Journal of Marketing Theory and Practice*, **11** (4), 54–65.

Iyengar, R., Van den Bulte, C., and Valente, T.W. (2008) Opinion Leadership and Social Contagion in New Product Diffusion. Report No: 08-120, Marketing Science Institute, Cambridge.

Keller, E.B. and Berry, J.L. (2003) *The Influentials: One American in Ten Tells the Other Nine How to Vote, Where to Eat, and What to Buy*, Free Press, New York.

Weimann, G. (1994) *The Influentials*, State University of New York Press, Albany.

opportunities and challenges in social marketing

Alan R. Andreasen

BRIEF HISTORY

Social marketing has two points of origin, one in the practical world and one in academia. The first instance of application of marketing concepts and tools in a social context is found in family planning programs in India in the late 1960s. Despite significant inputs of international aid, families in underdeveloped and developing countries were becoming worse off because family size growth was outpacing economic growth. At the time, public health programs were minimally effective in part because of their poor reputations and frequent inaccessibility.

A visiting professor at the Indian Institute of Management at Calcutta (IIMC), Peter King, along with businessmen, IIMC professors, and the Ford Foundation brought out the document "Proposals for Family Planning Promotion: A Marketing Plan" in 1964. The concept was to package and advertise branded, donated products and have them distributed by six cooperating international marketers including Hindustan Lever, Lipton, and Union Carbide. The Nirodh program became the world's largest social marketing effort and remained so until the mid-1990s.

In the same period as the Nirodh start-up, the marketing faculty at Northwestern University fomented a sea change in the academic view of marketing by proposing that it be broadened beyond its commercial confines, arguing that "every organization performs marketing-like activities whether or not they are recognized as such … marketing is a pervasive activity that goes considerably beyond the selling of toothpaste, soap and steel." Two key members of the Northwestern faculty, Philip Kotler and Gerald Zaltman, focused on a particular set of applications which they called for the first time *social marketing* (Kotler and Zaltman, 1971).

Initial academic opposition to the broadening concept (marketing implies "markets") quickly retreated and a number of academics in the United States, many of whom were influenced by the social unrest provoked by the Vietnam war, began to investigate and write about social marketing applications. At the same time, select advertising and public relations organizations such as Porter Novelli began to take on clients with social challenges and existing consulting organizations such as The Futures Group, Population Services International, and the Academy for Educational Development also secured social marketing contracts from government agencies such as USAID (United States Agency for International Development), CDC (Centers for Disease Control and Prevention), and the World Bank.

The growth of interest in social marketing on the scholarly and practical sides approximated a typical diffusion process which is still in the growth phase. Research and applications grew relatively slowly at first because, on the academic side, articles of top journal quality were slow in appearing and, on the practical side, because clients were often unfamiliar with or confused about the concept. Both impediments have largely been overcome.

There are now at least eight textbooks and various specialized volumes. The field has its own journal, the *Social Marketing Quarterly*, and social marketing articles routinely appear in the *Journal of Consumer Research*, *Journal of Public Policy and Marketing*, and other major journals around the world. There are reading books on social marketing ethics, annual conferences, and special sessions within other mainstream conferences that are now devoted to social marketing. Chapters on social marketing appear in books in nonmarketing disciplines such as health promotion and health communication. Social marketing as a strategic platform has been introduced into US agencies like the Centers for Disease Control and Prevention and into a range of UK programs of the National Health Service.

DEFINITIONAL CHALLENGES

One of the early – and in one respect continuing – problems for social marketing was confusion about what the term meant and how it differed from nonprofit marketing, socially responsible marketing, social advertising and, most recently, social network marketing. In the earliest period, social marketing was seen as product marketing (as in the family planning work and later in many child survival medical interventions). However, the field slowly evolved to encompass service applications (mammography screening and drug counseling campaigns) and eventually "pure behaviors" (recycling and walking more). Along the way, given the dominance of health applications, it faced challenges to differentiate itself from health education or health communication. A further of source of confusion was scholars and promoters who claimed that it encompassed the marketing of *ideas*, which led critics to argue that it was just a fancy version of advocacy or propaganda. Many asked: "Isn't this what the Advertising Council has been doing since World War II?"

By the mid-1990s, a consensus emerged around the fundamental notion that the objective was to influence *behavior* and not just attitudes or knowledge. It was argued that the commercial marketers whose concepts and tools social marketers apply do not settle for program impacts solely on knowledge and attitudes. If marketing efforts do not result in sales, marketing managers or advertising agencies are not rewarded and campaigns – even products and brands – are scrapped. This author's own definition is that social marketing is the application of commercial marketing concepts and tools to influence the voluntary behavior of target audiences to improve their lives or the society of which they are a part. It is made clear that the goal is to influence *problem* behaviors; not simply behaviors like voting, charitable giving, or attending the arts. The latter fall into the realm of nonprofit marketing more broadly construed.

The focus on behavioral outcomes also distinguishes it from social advertising which has communication goals which may be needed to provoke or assist a behavioral outcome. It is also distinguishable from social network marketing which also can be a tool of social marketing but is not equivalent to it.

Two more definitional challenges revolve around social marketing strategy rather than tactics. The first is whether social marketing can be used to promote racial discrimination or Aryan superiority. The author's own view is that social marketers are behavior influence specialists – as are marketers in the private sector. The choice of objectives and overall goals of some strategy is not their province – although they may provide advice on feasibility. Social marketers need to make ethical choices about the strategies to which they lend their talents – as do commercial marketers asked to promote cigarette brands.

The second strategic issue is whether social marketing should focus solely on individuals or groups exhibiting – or likely to exhibit – problem behaviors, what is often referred to as *downstream* targets. Michael Rothschild (1999) proposed that social marketing scholars and researchers pay more attention to the distinction made by MacInnis, Moorman, and Jaworski (1991) that behaviors – both commercial and social – require three preconditions – the *motivation* to act, the *opportunity* to act, and the *ability* to act (often denoted by the acronym MOA). The obesity crisis has provided a particularly compelling example of the need to focus strategically not just on overweight kids and their families but also on what social marketers call *upstream* targets – school administrators who can change cafeteria menus, banish soft drink machines, and add physical education classes, or city council members who can provide playgrounds or increase police protection in areas where obese kids might play.

In his most recent book Andreasen, (2007), the author has made the case that social marketing has a proper role to play in influencing upstream targets as well as those who exhibit – or might exhibit – problem behaviors. This point deserves expansion here.

"CONSUMER" BEHAVIOR

First, a conceptually important distinction in social marketing is that its definition focuses on "target audiences" and not "consumers." The distinction was made early on, in part, to make the application of marketing concepts and tools more palatable to those in the social sector who considered marketing as somehow evil. However, it also reflects the fact that the objective of many social marketing campaigns is not "consumption." The focus is behavior. In the private sector, the behavior in question is acquisition and consumption of specific goods or services by *consumers*. In social campaigns, such as those directed at exercise or recycling, it is

confusing – even off-putting – to imply that the goal is to influence some sort of "consumption." As a consequence, this author has advocated the more general – and more encompassing – term of *target audience behavior*, a term that subsumes both commercial and social objectives.

This is not merely a semantic challenge. It may be argued that marketing is all about influencing behavior. Creating intellectual silos, wherein social marketing is seen as somehow different and a special (and minor) area of application of marketing concepts and tools, is a taxonomic construct that inhibits the opportunity to create a more generic view of the field. That is, we should ourselves, as behavior influence researchers, seek commonalities across behavioral contexts. For example, rather than dividing the field into purchasing and social behaviors, would we not advance the field further if we ask more generic questions about behavioral influence? For example, how does achieving the goal of *starting* a behavior differ from *continuing* a behavior or *switching* a behavior? What do we know about stopping a behavior? Is preventing someone from engaging in a behavior (stealing videos, using drugs, engaging in risky sex) different from getting them to start a behavior? Are there general principles that apply across sectors in starting or switching behaviors?

Further, if influencing behavior is our strength, then can we consider efforts to influence upstream individuals a legitimate subject of interest? Is getting a city council member to vote "yes" to fund a school playground in a poor neighborhood an example of influencing target audience behavior? What of cafeteria managers, editorial directors at TV stations, or the person who decides what information goes on menu boards at a Burger King? The author's argument is that the answer is yes and, further, many of these situations would present opportunities to study *stopping* behavior in more depth.

There are already a number of commonalities in the way that marketing managers in both sectors approach their behavioral challenges. The commercial concept of value creation, for example, is equally relevant in both sectors. A social marketer seeks to offer target audiences compelling value propositions comprising attractive benefits and minimal costs so as to provoke a desired behavioral outcome in which benefits are exchanged for costs (Bagozzi, 1978; Bagozzi and Warshaw, 1990). Thus, the truth® campaign of the American Legacy Foundation has the goal of inducing teenagers not to take up smoking (a behavioral outcome). The campaign offers the target audience *benefits* such as a sense of pride in not being manipulated by the tobacco industry and a feeling of comradeship in being part of an "anti-tobacco movement of teens." These benefits have been found to more than compensate for the costs of not having specific (smoker) friends or enduring the taunts of teen smokers who implicitly argue that smoking is "cool."

The future of "consumer behavior" research should include special issues of major journals and conference sessions on switching, stopping, and starting behaviors along with those on brand preference, cognitive processing, and customer satisfaction. Further, one would hope that scholars interested in the latter topics would, from time to time, ask whether and how their theories and findings would apply in different realms, not just in the commercial marketplace.

TARGET AUDIENCE BEHAVIORAL RESEARCH

Social marketing comprises an area of application of marketing concepts and tools similar to B2B marketing and services marketing. Textbooks and strategic plans therefore insist on thorough target audience research in planning interventions, pretesting of such interventions, and regularly tracking progress.[1] Social marketing applications also urge sophisticated segmentation approaches and close attention to positioning and branding possibilities.

The research in the area of social marketing divides into three broad categories. First, there are macrolevel evaluation studies that seek to ascertain whether a particular intervention yielded desired effects and, where possible, which elements of the specific campaign seemed to have been most impactful. Second, there are midlevel studies of particular tactics, typically variations on communication approaches. Third, there are microlevel studies that seek to discover mental processing pathways between inputs and desired effects.

Typical of macrolevel research is an evaluation of 54 social marketing programs carried out

in 2006 by Stead *et al.* (2007). The authors' conclusions are characteristic:

> A majority of the interventions, which sought to prevent youth smoking, alcohol use and illicit drug, use reported significant positive effects in the short term. Effects tended to dissipate in the medium and longer term, although several of the tobacco and alcohol interventions still displayed some positive effects two years after the intervention. These results are broadly comparable with systematic reviews of other types of substance use prevention interventions ... . The evidence is more mixed for adult smoking cessation, although small numbers of programmes were nonetheless effective in this area. There is modest evidence of impact on levels of physical activity and psychosocial outcomes, with an apparently weaker effect on physical activity related physiological outcomes.

Two well-funded campaigns in the United States that represent social marketing success stories are the VERB campaign of the Centers for Disease Control and Prevention and the truth® campaign of the American Legacy Foundation. The VERB campaign used sophisticated branding and media approaches focused on children 9–13 years as well as upstream influencers. It used "commercial marketing methods to advertise being physically active as cool, fun, and a chance to have a good time with friends." Baseline and 1-year follow up surveys of 3120 parent–child dyads were conducted in 2002 and 2003. Huhman *et al.* (2005) concluded that "The VERB campaign achieved high levels of awareness in 1 year." They also noted particularly marked effects on the behavior of younger children, girls, children whose parents had less than a high school education, children from urban areas that were densely populated, and children who were "low active at baseline." (Ironically, after spending $339 million over 5 years, funding for this successful campaign was withdrawn in 2006).

The truth® campaign has a much longer history. It began under the Florida State Government with funding from one of four early settlements of state suits against the tobacco industry and migrated to the American Legacy Foundation which was created with funding from the subsequent master settlement negotiated with 48 states and the District of Columbia.

The campaign achieved dramatic effects on smoking initiation in Florida, results that are paralleled in research on the national campaign (Farrelly *et al.* 2002).

Midlevel and microlevel social marketing research studies both exhibit a key difficulty in modeling and understanding social marketing effects at the micro and campaign level. Despite an earlier argument that marketing is all about behavior, whatever the sector, it is the case that behaviors to be influenced in the social sector often have one of three characteristics:

1. There is no observable behavior that one can measure that would mark behavioral outcomes – for example, not smoking and not using drugs.
2. The objective is to instill a future pattern of repeated behaviors – for example, exercising regularly, advancing girls' education and employment in developing countries, regularly taking one's medicine, and recycling.
3. The major benefit constitutes an expectation (promise?) of something that takes place many years in the future – for example, a longer life – or that comprises a "nonoutcome" such as a stroke or breast cancer both of which may be perceived as probabilities of such outcomes.

As a consequence, considerable focus in social marketing research has been on measuring and tracking *intentions* to behave. Fortunately, these intentions have been a key measure in commercial consumer behavior research especially in microlevel consumer behavior experiments. It has also been a particular focus in the area of health marketing where perhaps 80–85% of social marketing applications have been initiated. The latter has the important advantage for those eager to conduct target audience research in social marketing that there exists a significant body of theory and research, much of it seeking to explain or predict socially important behavior from measures of intentions.

A useful summary of much of this work is provided in the comprehensive 2006 meta-analysis by Webb and Sheeran (2006) of 47 experimental studies of the linkage between intentions and behavior change.[2] The models

that undergirded many of these studies will be familiar to traditional marketing scholars. Eighty-one percent were grounded in one of four models. The most common (29%) was Fishbein and Ajzen's Theory of Reasoned Action (TRA) or the modification in Ajzen's Theory of Planned Behavior (TPB). This was followed by Bandura's social-cognitive theory (21%), Ronald Rogers' Protection Motivation Theory (18%), and Hochbaum and Rosenstock's Health Belief Model (13%). As most consumer behavior researchers know, the TRA/TPB models specify that intentions and ultimately behaviors are driven by three factors: (i) beliefs about outcomes and the evaluation of those outcomes; (ii) normative beliefs about the wishes of significant others and the motivation to comply with those wishes; and (iii) self-efficacy – "control beliefs and perceived power." Other factors that can influence these three central components as well as factors that potentially impact the link between intentions and behavior are summarized by Fishbein and Cappella (2006). The potential modifiers between intentions and behavior are environmental factors and skills and abilities. Six sets of background factors can influence behavioral, normative, and control beliefs. These are

- past behavior;
- demographics and culture;
- attitudes toward targets (stereotypes and stigma);
- personality, moods, and emotions;
- other individual difference variables (perceived risk);
- intervention exposure and media exposure.

Bandura's model focuses primarily on self-efficacy beliefs – one's ability to act and to secure a specific outcome. Roger's Protection Motivation Model emphasizes individual perceptions of vulnerability to health threats and appraisals of their coping skills – the perception of the efficacy and costs of recommended responses, The Health Belief Model is similar in that it assesses individual's perceptions of health threats and their ability to favorably respond to them. These models are often used by social marketing researchers as in Pechmann *et al.*'s use of the protection motivation model to assess the effectiveness of antismoking advertisements on adolescents (Pechmann *et al.*, 2003).

All of these models focus on factors influencing intentions. Webb and Sheeran (2006) particularly focused on the extent to which intentions actually led to behavior. Three sets of factors were considered: the theoretical base and the methods and perceived sources of the intervention. Of potential future research interest was the finding that intentions were less predictive of behavior under two conditions – prior habit formation and social reactions to the particular health behavior.

Social reactions have been of particular interest to Robert Cialdini and colleagues. Cialdini found that perceived social norms have a strong effect on actual behaviors. Ironically, he also found that subjects in their studies perceived norms to be much less influential than they actually were (Kallgren, Reno, and Cialdini, 2000; Nolan *et al.*, 2008).

Many approaches to socially important behaviors have considered intentions as a variable represented as probabilities of action. To augment this approach, Prochaska and DiClemente introduced what they called the *Transtheoretical Model of Behavior*. The focus of this approach is that, for the high involvement kinds of behaviors that are the focus of much social marketing research, it is more reasonable to think of target individuals proceeding not in a single step from considering a behavior to acting on it (or not). Rather, these researchers proposed that target audiences proceed through six "stages of change." These are as follows:

- Precontemplation – where the target audiences are either unaware of the need for the behavior or consider it not of relevance for them.
- Contemplation – where they are actively considering the action – a stage that can take considerable time and which has been thought of as "early" and "late" contemplation.
- Preparation – where the individuals have decided to go forward and are, perhaps, assembling the necessary skills, social support, and the like to accomplish the behavior.

- Action – where the individuals are undertaking their initial attempts at behavior change (which may be all that is needed, for example, securing an important inoculation).
- Maintenance – where the individuals take up a new pattern of behavior and, preferably, make it a habit.
- Termination – either abandoning or completing a course of action.

Their model has been applied with considerable success to such behaviors as smoking, drinking, condom use, responsible eating, and exercise (Prochaska, DiClemente, and Norcross, 1992; Prochaska and Velicer, 1997).

RECENT DEVELOPMENTS

The twenty-first century has seen a number of significant developments that raise important opportunities for research. First, as noted earlier, social marketers have begun to pay more attention to environmental factors that often provide significant social influence. Social norms (already cited) are one set of factors. Social norms, of course, are themselves not fixed. They both evolve over time and are themselves potentially capable of being influenced. In this regard, the author has suggested elsewhere that social marketers investigate the formation and influence of social agendas. Important precursors of social influence may be the relative importance of the behavior on the general public agenda. Such agendas ebb and flow in particular stages and are very often influenced by media agendas.

A second recent focus that reflects attention to upstream factors is the attention to behavioral economics. This line of thinking stems from conservative thinkers who are reluctant to promote strong campaigns to change behaviors but, instead, argue for changes in environmental conditions that can "nudge" people toward doing the right thing (Thaler and Sunstein, 2008). Wansink's series of studies on such influences on overeating suggest possible courses of research along these lines (Wansink, 2004).

A third development has been an expansion of the areas of interest beyond health care. As environmental issues rise on political or public agendas, more social marketers are exploring intervention alternatives. McKenzie-Mohr and

Smith (1999) have emphasized that such issues call for much more attention to community involvement in solutions. In a different realm, Lusardi, Keller, and Keller (2009) have used social marketing concepts to study financial decision making.

A fourth important development is the merging of social marketing interests with those of social entrepreneurs including corporations. In recent years, private sector businesses have increasingly become interested in bringing about social change (Hess, Rogovsky, and Dunfee, 2002). They do so, not because they are generous and big – hearted – although they may be – but because they envision potential strategic payoffs to their own bottom lines. For example, Hindustan Lever has found that it could create a longer lasting, smaller bar of Lifebouy soap, thereby combating sanitation challenges and expanding the total market. Coca Cola found that it needed to bring its marketing and promotional skills to bear on the HIV/AIDS crisis in Africa where it found many of its workers afflicted with the disease.

FUTURE RESEARCH NEEDS

As several leading scholars with interests in social marketing have said, the potential for innovative research in noncommercial settings is significant. Part of this is due to several characteristics of the behaviors that social marketers are attempting to influence. Among these are behaviors where

1. there are no concrete products or services involved – for example, exercise;
2. they are really *non* behaviors – for example, not smoking, not engaging in violence against spouses or children, and not using drugs;
3. they promise unobservable benefits (without instrumentation) – for example, lowered blood pressure;
4. they promise benefits long in the future – for example, longer life from exercise or better diets and a happier retirement from today's savings;
5. they often require significant trials before success is achieved – for example, stopping smoking or losing weight;

6. the behaviors are heavily influenced by significant others – for example, health practices of young African women under the watchful eyes of their mothers-in-law;
7. the benefits of the behavior accrue to others while the costs are personal – for example, recycling;
8. interventions are constrained by public scrutiny or by social norms – for example, HIV/AIDS campaigns in many countries and family planning initiatives by the US government (especially under conservative administrations).

There is also an intriguing challenge that, to the author's knowledge, has not been addressed in consumer behavior studies in commercial settings. This is the fact that, in social marketing campaigns, there are often multiple *types* of target audiences that will be affected by a particular campaign or tactic but may not respond in the same way. Resources for social marketing campaigns come from five principal sources: revenues from clients (e.g., Goodwill clothing sales), funding by foundations, government contracts, individual donations, volunteer commitments, and various forms of involvement by corporations. Typical consumer behavior research assesses responses – or likely responses – for a single type of target – consumers. In nonprofit contexts, it may be that volunteers or donors will respond differently (and perhaps negatively) to tactics that are positively effective with donors or foundations. What if alternative AIDS campaign messages yield different responses from at-risk populations, volunteers, and corporate partners? How does one choose among them?

Branding is potentially highly valuable for social marketing programs. It has been used to brand specific products (e.g., Nirodh condoms) or services (Family of the Future health clinics). However, there are two problems for campaigns that do not involve products or services. What, for example, should branding's role be in tackling the obesity problem? Is there "customer value" to be derived from branding an intervention to get someone eating better or exercising more? Will there be more frequent or more lasting outcomes if a target audience member follows the recommended behaviors of a branded social marketing campaign? Are slogans – *Don't Mess with Texas* or *Click It or Ticket* – equivalent of brands?

Another challenge alluded to above is the fact that many desirable social outcomes require that the target audience adopt a different behavioral pattern – often over a lifetime – whether it is a better diet, regular exercise, condom use, recycling, and so on. Experience shows that lifestyle changes often suffer setbacks and reversals. Sometimes, it is because the behavior seems difficult (regular exercise) or because outcomes are not obvious on a daily basis (lowered blood pressure). How does one study cognitive processes yielding not just a one-time behavior but a pattern of future behaviors? Useful beginnings are found in Bagozzi and Warshaw's, 1990 "theory of trying." More recent research by Kahn and Luce (2003) may add to this by looking at the role of feedback on continued behavior, in their case, the impact of "false positives" from mammographies on repeated test-taking.

Another research need is to pay more attention to intervention strategies other than communications and message alternatives. It is understandable that those describing and investigating social marketing interventions would focus on communications. Clever and unconventional advertising approaches are seductive as a means of describing and bragging about campaign performance. (Indeed, the author's colleagues have observed that his own writings often exhibit this tendency.) There are three fundamental problems with this distorted emphasis.

First, it offers ammunition to those who argue that we bring nothing to problematic areas that are already dominated by communications specialist. Second, it sorely underutilizes marketing's robust armamentarium – for example, other elements of the "4Ps." In the early family planning programs, a critical contributor to success was the establishment of far flung and *reliable* distribution networks for family planning products. This was essential to a poor mother seeking to limit her family size because she could rely on the availability of a new cycle of oral pills when she had enough money to buy another round. Equally important was the pricing of family planning products. Research has shown that free products

are perceived as of lower quality and reliability than products (and services) that cost something, but how much? Rules of thumb were used initially but this is one of those realms where careful target audience research by marketing scholars could not only help organizations make tactical decisions about pricing but also broaden our understanding and interpretation of pricing signals by the poor and not-so-poor. Such research would also have the virtue of fueling arguments against social critics who rail against social marketing approaches that charge anything to the poor as immoral.

Third, it reinforces the myopic view that all that is needed for the desired behavioral influence that the target audience be sufficiently motivated. However, as Rothschild and others keep emphasizing and the cognitive models of Fishbein and others make clear, social behaviors also require that target audiences have the ability and opportunity to act and keep acting. This requires social marketing scholars to pay greater attention to influencing the behaviors of upstream target audiences, not typically considered to be "consumers" in the way the term is construed in traditional texts. That is, for a society to have major impact on childhood obesity, school administrators have to provide better lunches and breakfasts and safer school playgrounds. Similarly, McDonald's marketers need to bring marketing skills to the problem and legislators (sometimes) have to pass laws requiring better food labeling, bans on transfats and/or funding for new parks and bike paths.

If consumer behavior research is about influencing behaviors to increase desirable organizational outcomes (more profits, more donations, or more grants) and if we extend our consideration to the task of improving individual and societal welfare, then can we not consider a school administrator an important target audience whose behavior is needed to yield better social outcomes? If so – as I believe it is – then this opens up a dramatic new array of opportunities to study a whole new class of targets and potentially advance our understanding of how marketing's 4Ps can influence target audiences to protect the poor from poverty and disease, improve the world's physical environments, and improve the health and financial well-being of all.

ENDNOTES

[1] This contrasts with historical social science approaches to project research that emphasized benchmarking and project-end evaluations.

[2] The 47 studies were selected out of a broader universe of 221 studies in that both intentions and behavior were measured and that the latter measures were separated in time. That is, intentions were measured and behavior was tracked at some later point.

Bibliography

Andreasen, A.R. (2007) *Social Marketing in the 21st Century*, Sage, Thousand Oaks.

Bagozzi, R.P. (1978) Marketing as exchange: a theory of transactions in the marketplace. *American Behavioral Scientist*, **21**, 535–556.

Bagozzi, R.P. and Warshaw, P.R. (1990) Trying to consume. *Journal of Consumer Research*, **17**, 127–140.

Farrelly, M.C., Healton, C., Davis, K.C. *et al.* (2002) Getting to the truth: evaluating national tobacco countermarketing campaigns. *American Journal of Public Health*, **92**, 901–907.

Fishbein, M. and Cappella, J.N. (2006) The role of theory in developing effective health communications. *Journal of Communications*, **56**, S1–S17.

Hess, D., Rogovsky, N., and Dunfee, T.W. (2002) The next wave of corporate community involvement. *California Management Review*, **44** (2), 110–125.

Huhman, M., Potter, L.D., Wong, F.L. *et al.* (2005) Effects of a mass media campaign to increase physical activity among children: year-1 results of the VERB campaign. *Pediatrics*, **116**, 277–284.

Kahn, B.E. and Luce, M.F. (2003) Understanding high-stakes consumer decisions: mammography adherence following false alarm test results. *Marketing Science*, **22** (3), 393–410.

Kallgren, C.A., Reno, R.R., and Cialdini, R.B. (2000) A focus theory of normative conduct: when norms do and do not affect behavior. *Personality and Social Psychology Bulletin*, **26**, 1002–1012.

Kotler, P. and Zaltman, G. (1971) Social marketing: an approach to planned social change. *Journal of Marketing*, **35**, 3–12.

Lusardi, A., Keller, P.A., and Keller, A. (2009) New ways to make people save: a social marketing approach, in *Overcoming the Saving Slump: How to Increase the Effectiveness of Financial Education and Saving Programs* (ed. A. Lusardi), University of Chicago Press, Chicago.

MacInnis, D.J., Moorman, C., and Jaworski, B.J. (1991) Enhancing and measuring consumers' motivation, opportunity and ability to process brand information from ads. *Journal of Marketing*, **55**, 32–53.

McKenzie-Mohr, D. and Smith, W. (1999) *Fostering Sustainable Behavior: An Introduction to Community-Based Social Marketing*, New Society Publications, New York.

Michie, S., Johnson, M., Francis, J. *et al.* (2008) From theory to intervention: mapping theoretically derived behavioural determinants to behavior change techniques. *Applied Psychology: An International Review*, **57** (4), 660–680.

Nolan, J.M., Schultz, P.W., Cialdini, R.B. *et al.* (2008) Normative social influence is underdetected. *Personality and Social Psychology Bulletin*, **34**, 913–923.

Pechmann, C., Zhao, G., Goldberg, M.E., and Reibling, E.T. (2003) What to convey in antismoking advertisements for adolescents: the use of protection motivation theory to identify effective message themes. *Journal of Marketing*, **67**, 1–18.

Prahalad, C.K. (2004) *The Fortune at the Bottom of the Pyramid: Eradicating Poverty Through Profits*, Wharton School Publishers, Philadelphia.

Prochaska, J.O., DiClemente, C.C., and Norcross, J.C. (1992) In search of how people change: applications to addictive behaviors. *American Psychologist*, **47** (9), 1102–1114.

Prochaska, J.O. and Velicer, W.F. (1997) The transtheoretical model of health behavior change. *American Journal of Health Promotion*, **12**, 38–48.

Rothschild, M.L. (1999) Carrot sticks, and promises: a conceptual framework for the management of public health and social issues behavior. *Journal of Marketing*, **63**, 24–37.

Sly, D.F., Hopkins, R.S., Trapido, Ed., and Ray, S. (2001) Influence of a counteradvertising media campaign on initiation of smoking: the Florida "truth" campaign. *American Journal of Public Health*, **91** (2), 233–238.

Thaler, R.H. and Sunstein, C.R. (2008) *Nudge: Improving Decisions about Health, Wealth, and Happiness*, Yale University Press, New Haven.

Stead, M., Gordon, R., Angus, K., and McDermott, L. (2007) A systematic review of social marketing effectiveness. *Health Education*, **107** (2), 126–191.

Webb, T.L. and Sheeran, P. (2006) Does changing behavioral intentions engender behavior change? A meta-analysis of the experimental evidence. *Psychological Bulletin*, **132** (2), 249–268.

Wansink, B. (2004) Environmental factors that increase the food intake and consumption volume of unknowing consumers. *Annual Review of Nutrition*, **24**, 454–479.

optimum stimulation level

Jan-Benedict E. M. Steenkamp

The Construct of Optimum Stimulation Level

The notion that human behavior is sometimes instigated by the mere desire to attain a satisfactory level of stimulation has figured prominently among psychological theories investigating motivational tendencies as causes of people's actions (Berlyne, 1963; Zuckerman, 1994). People tend to prefer intermediate levels of stimulation, referred to as the *optimal stimulation level* (*OSL*) in the literature. There are reliable individual differences in the amount of stimulation considered optimal by a given person, which appear to be affected by social learning factors as well as biochemical substances (Zuckerman, 1994).

To attain a satisfactory level of stimulation, a person may engage in exploration of the environment. As stated by Berlyne (1963, p. 288), exploratory behavior is "an end in itself" "with" the sole function of changing the stimulus field." Psychologists have studied exploratory tendencies extensively, and the general finding has been that people with higher OSLs engage in exploratory behaviors to a greater extent than people with lower OSLs (see Zuckerman (1979, 1994) for reviews).

Measurement. Several self-report measures have been developed to assess OSL, among them the 40-item Arousal Seeking Tendency (AST) scale, and its revised version, the 32-item AST-II scale, the 95-item Change Seeker Index (CSI), the 40-item Sensation Seeking Scale, version V (SSS-V), and the 80-item Novelty Experiencing Scale (NES). Despite the different labels, all scales load on the underlying construct of OSL (Steenkamp and Baumgartner, 1992). AST-I/II, SSS-V, and NES scales specify subfactors, but research has indicated that their factorial structure is generally unstable. Consumer researchers have, therefore, almost invariably used summated scores on the total scale. The reliability of the summated scores on each scale is high.

Steenkamp and Baumgartner (1992) concluded that CSI is the preferred instrument,

based on extensive psychometric and nomological tests. However, with 95 items, CSI is much too long to be of practical use in most research applications. To address this issue, Steenkamp and Baumgartner (1995) developed a 7-item short-form version of the CSI scale. The 7-item scale has better psychometric properties and nomological validity than the original, 95-item scale. These items are listed in Table 1.

Relevance of Optimum Stimulation Level to Understanding Consumer Behavior

The consumer behavior literature has been dominated by the information processing paradigm, in which it is assumed that the consumer purposefully solves problems in order to achieve goals. However, since the seminal article by Holbrook and Hirschman (1982), researchers have increasingly recognized that many consumer behaviors are not (solely) purposeful in this sense, but also contain a strong exploratory component. For example, a consumer may not only buy a new product because she/he believes that the product is of better quality (information processing perspective) but also because she/he likes the excitement of trying out something new (exploratory perspective). As such, the exploratory perspective adds to our understanding of consumer behavior.

The fact that psychological research has uncovered that exploratory tendencies are related to a person's characteristic need for stimulation suggests that OSL may be a major determinant of consumer behaviors with strong exploratory elements. Indeed, a growing body of research has shown that OSL is an important factor in explaining a wide variety of consumer behaviors with an exploratory component. Consumers seeking thrills, adventure, disinhibition, new experiences, fantasies, cognitive or sensory stimulation, escape from boredom, and alternation among familiar things have been identified as engaging in exploratory consumer behaviors in order to raise their level of stimulation in life (Baumgartner and Steenkamp, 1996; Celsi, Rose, and Leigh, 1993; Holbrook and Hirschman, 1982; Raju, 1980; Steenkamp and Baumgartner, 1992; Steenkamp

Table 1 Items of CSI short-form scale.

1. I like to continue doing the same old things rather than trying new and different things.[a]
2. I like to experience novelty and change in my daily routine.
3. I like a job that offers change, variety, and travel, even if it involves some danger.
4. I am continually seeking new ideas and experiences.
5. I like continually changing activities.
6. When things get boring, I like to find some new and unfamiliar experience.
7. I prefer a routine way of life to an unpredictable one full of change.[a]

[a]This indicates reverse-coded item. Items are rated on a 5-point scale, ranging from -2 (completely false) to $+2$ (completely true) or from 1(completely disagree) to 5 (completely agree).

and Burgess, 2002; Steenkamp, ter Hofstede, and Wedel, 1999).

High OSLs have a greater preference for emotionally charged stimuli such as fear-arousing ads (Steenkamp, Baumgartner, and Van der Wulp, 1996) and have a greater interest in pursuing fantasies and fun (Holbrook and Hirschman, 1982). They engage more often in information search out of curiosity, generate more curiosity-based thoughts when exposed to ambiguous ads, and experience greater tedium during repeated exposure to the same ad (Baumgartner and Steenkamp, 1996; Steenkamp and Baumgartner, 1992). High OSLs exhibit more variety seeking and have a greater interest in knowing about novel or complex products and brands out of curiosity (Raju, 1980). OSL is related positively to a person's tendency to try out new retail outlets (Mittelstaedt et al., 1976) and to his/her willingness to purchase new products and brands (Baumgartner and Steenkamp, 1996; Gielens and Steenkamp, 2007; Steenkamp and Gielens, 2003). Steenkamp and Burgess (2002) provide evidence that OSL does not only have relevance for understanding behavior of Western consumers but also holds great promise for understanding the behavior of consumers in emerging markets.

CONCLUSION

OSL is firmly grounded in psychological theory and can be measured reliably with self-report measures. OSL is of great relevance for understanding consumer behavior, both in high-income countries and in emerging markets. While it is generally believed that general personality traits have little explanatory value for consumer behavior, OSL is clearly an exception. Since many consumer behaviors have an exploratory component, the theoretical potential of OSL is substantial. Therefore, consumer researchers are encouraged to include OSL more often in their research design.

Bibliography

Baumgartner, H. and Steenkamp, J.-B.E.M. (1996) Exploratory consumer behavior: conceptualization and measurement. *International Journal of Research in Marketing*, **13** (2), 121–137.

Berlyne, D.E. (1960) *Conflict, Arousal, and Curiosity*, McGraw-Hill, New York.

Berlyne, D.E. (1963) Motivational problems raised by exploratory and epistemic behavior, in *Psychology: A Study of Science*, vol. 5 (ed K. Sigmund), McGraw-Hill, New York, pp. 284–364.

Celsi, R.L., Rose, R.L., and Leigh, T.W. (1993) An exploration of high-risk leisure consumption through skydiving. *Journal of Consumer Research*, **20**, 1–23.

Gielens, K. and Steenkamp, J.-B.E.M. (2007) Drivers of consumer acceptance of new packaged goods: an investigation across products and countries. *International Journal of Research in Marketing*, **24**, 97–111.

Holbrook, M.B. and Hirschman, E.C. (1982) The experiential aspects of consumption: consumer fantasies, feelings, and fun. *Journal of Consumer Research*, **9**, 132–140.

Mittelstaedt, R.A., Grossbart, S.L., Curtis, W.W., and Devere, S.P. (1976) Optimum stimulation level and the adoption decision process. *Journal of Consumer Research*, **3**, 84–94.

Raju, P.S. (1980) Optimum stimulation level: its relationship to personality, demographics, and exploratory behavior. *Journal of Consumer Research*, **7**, 272–282.

Steenkamp, J.-B.E.M. and Baumgartner, H. (1992) The role of optimum stimulation level in exploratory consumer behavior. *Journal of Consumer Research*, **19**, 434–448.

Steenkamp, J.-B.E.M. and Baumgartner, H. (1995) Development and cross-cultural validation of a short form csi as a measure of optimum stimulation level. *International Journal of Research in Marketing*, **12**, 97–104.

Steenkamp, J.-B.E.M., Baumgartner, H., and Wulp, E.V. (1996) Arousal potential, arousal, stimulus attractiveness, and the moderating role of need for stimulation. *International Journal of Research in Marketing*, **13**, 319–329.

Steenkamp, J.-B.E.M. and Burgess, S.M. (2002) Optimum stimulation level and exploratory consumer behavior in an emerging consumer market. *International Journal of Research in Marketing*, **19**, 131–150.

Steenkamp, J.-B.E.M. and Gielens, K. (2003) Consumer and market drivers of the trial rate of new consumer products. *Journal of Consumer Research*, **30**, 368–384.

Steenkamp, J.-B.E.M., ter Hofstede, F., and Wedel, M. (1999) A cross-national investigation into the individual and national cultural antecedents of consumer innovativeness. *Journal of Marketing*, **63**, 55–69.

Zuckerman, M. (1979) *Sensation Seeking: Beyond the Optimal Level of Arousal*, Lawrence Erlbaum, Hillsdale.

Zuckerman, M. (1994) *Behavioral Expressions and Biosocial Bases of Sensation Seeking*, Cambridge University Press, New York.

P

persuasion

Michal Herzenstein

Persuasion is an active attempt to change beliefs, attitudes, preferences, or behaviors. The extent of persuasion is measured by changes to the above (measured before and after the persuasion attempt). This article focuses on various approaches to persuasion.

COGNITIVE APPROACHES

Persuasion will take place if cognitive processing, conscious or unconscious, has occurred. An example for conscious cognitive approaches is comparative judgment theory, which suggests that nothing is judged in isolation and everything can be seen as good or bad depending on what it is compared with (framing and prospect theory, Tversky, and Kahneman, 1979; contrast and assimilation effects, Hovland, Harvey, and Sherif, 1957). Examples for unconscious cognitive processes are implicit memory (Schacter, 1987) and mere exposure theories (Zajonc, 1968) that show that even under conditions of limited processing resources, exposure can influence judgment (albeit without awareness).

AFFECTIVE APPROACHES

People are persuaded because the communication evokes certain affects. Both positive affects (such as humor, love, or pride) and negative affects (such as fear, disturbance, or unpleasantness) are commonly induced. Persuasion occurs because people try to maintain their positive moods or avoid negative moods. One important theory that explains how to use emotions in persuasion is classical conditioning.

On the basis of Pavlov's experiments with dogs, this theory suggests that pairing brands with positive unconditioned stimuli (familiar stimuli that automatically produce affective responses) will elicit the desired affective response toward the brand itself (rather than the stimuli). For example, a brand is paired with a familiar and loved tune in a commercial (Gorn, 1982). The tune elicits positive emotions that are paired with the brand. Afterwards, when the brand is encountered without the tune (i.e., in the store) it elicits the same emotions.

MOTIVATIONAL APPROACHES

Persuasion happens when people wish to be persuaded. Subtle motivational techniques are preferred over obvious persuasion attempts (Kardes, 2001). The most relevant principle is consistency – people like consistency and dislike inconsistency. They dislike it so much that they are willing to change beliefs, attitudes, and behaviors in order to eliminate the inconsistency. A famous example of this principle is cognitive dissonance (Festinger, 1957), which suggests that people strive for attitude–behavior consistency. When attitudes are inconsistent with past behaviors (dissonance), an unpleasant tension is produced, which motivates people to reduce that dissonance. The result is a shift in attitudes that increases attitude–behavior consistency.

SELF-PERSUASION

Persuasion that results from elaboration on the true merit of the brand leads to strong accessible attitudes, and therefore is preferred over persuasion that results from peripheral cues such as music or humor. Self-persuasion approaches try to understand how persuasive communications induce people to think more extensively about the brand or advocated position. One of the most useful models is the elaboration likelihood model of persuasion (ELM) (Petty and Cacioppo, 1981). ELM proposes two routes to persuasion: the central route – requires effortful processing of the message; and the peripheral route – requires minimal thinking. The central route leads to strong accessible attitudes, but it will be taken only when the recipient is both motivated and able to elaborate on the message.

SOCIAL INFLUENCE

Communicators who wish to move people in their direction should appeal to a limited set of deeply rooted human drives and needs. According to Cialdini (2001) there are six principles that lead to persuasion. (i) Liking – sellers should like their customers. People like people who like them, and they are more likely to say yes to them because they feel they are in good hands. (ii) Reciprocity – people want to give back to those who have given to them. Companies who give their clients something meaningful, tailored, and unexpected are often repaid. (iii) Social proof – people like to follow the crowd. Use the many to persuade the few. (iv) Consistency – when people make a public commitment, they almost always back those words with actions. (v) Authority – people like to follow the lead of legitimate experts. (vi) Scarcity – people are afraid to miss out or lose by not choosing something scarce.

In conclusion, persuasion can be attained in various ways, and choosing the proper appeal is crucial. Any communicator who wishes to move people in his or her direction should exercise some "detective work" and seek out the right time, and the right place, to put the right approach to use with his/her target audience (Cialdini, 2001).

See also *attitudes; emotion; implicit consumer cognition; social influence*

Bibliography

Cialdini, R.B. (2001) Harnessing the science of persuasion. *Harvard Business Review*, **79** (9), 72–79.

Festinger, L. (1957) *A Theory of Cognitive Dissonance*, Row and Peterson, Evanston.

Gorn, G.J. (1982) The effect of music in advertising on choice behavior: a classical conditioning approach. *Journal of Marketing*, **46**, 94–101.

Hovland, C.I., Harvey, O.J., and Sherif, M. (1957) Assimilation and contrast effects in reactions to communication and attitude change. *The Journal of Abnormal and Social Psychology*, **55** (2), 244–252.

Kardes, F.R. (2001) *Consumer Behavior and Managerial Decision Making*, Pearson Education, Inc., Upper Saddle River.

Petty, R.E. and Cacioppo, J.T. (1981) *Attitudes and Persuasion: Classic and Contemporary Approaches*, William C. Brown, Dubuque.

Schacter, D.L. (1987) Implicit memory: history and current status. *Journal of Experimental Psychology: Learning, Memory, and Cognition*, **13**, 501–518.

Tversky, A. and Kahneman, D. (1979) Prospect theory: an analysis of decision under risk. *Econometrica*, **47** (2), 263–291.

Zajonc, R.B. (1968) Attitudinal effects of mere exposure. *Journal of Personality and Social Psychology*, **9** (2), 1–27.

possessions and self

Russell Belk

The concept of extended self (Belk, 1988) posits that there is first an atomized individual self that radiates out into the world by means of both tangible possessions and other people to whom one feels connected. This notion can be traced to William James (1890) who observed that

> A man's Self is the sum total of all that he CAN call his, not only his body and psychic powers, but his clothes and his house, his wife and his children, his ancestors and friends, his reputation and works, his lands, and yacht, and bank account. All these things give him the same emotions. If they wax and prosper, he feels triumphant; if they whither and die away, he feels cast down, – not necessarily in the same degree for each thing, but in much the same way for all (291–292).

Belk (1987, 1988) presents various primary and secondary evidence demonstrating that we regard our possessions as constitutive parts of our selves and that both things and people are commonly perceived as varying in their centrality as components of our self conception. When our key definitional objects are people, we construe the self in a more aggregate way. Thus, our children's accomplishments or setbacks are felt as our own and our parents' behaviors can be a source of pride or shame for us as children. Aggregate extended self provides one mechanism to explain why we are more willing to share with those whom we regard as a part of us ("sharing in") than with others ("sharing out") (Belk, 2010). At a more extended aggregate level it helps to understand why our sports team's, university's, or nation's achievements or failures can bring us pleasure or pain.

A related concept is that of attachment to possessions (Belk, 1992; Kleine and Baker, 2004). Because certain possessions are seen as more central to our sense of self, they are protected more, shared less, cared for better, and mourned more when they are lost or damaged. Even internal bodily organs are less likely to be donated when they are seen as more central to our identity (Belk, 1987). An additional individual characteristic that is related to unwillingness to share possessions is materialism (Belk, 1985; CONSUMER MATERIALISM). *Materialism* is the belief that having or not having desired possessions is a primary source of happiness or unhappiness in life. Theorized subcomponents of materialism include nongenerosity and possessiveness, both of which help explain why more materialistic people may be less generous in sharing their possessions with others. Ironically, despite materialists' beliefs that possessions contribute to feelings of well-being, those who are more materialistic tend to be less happy and report lower feelings of well-being than those who are less materialistic. Although it might seem that those who eschew acquiring or upgrading possessions in favor of experiences might be less attached to possessions, experiences too can be regarded possessively and as self-extending. This is the case, for instance, when we claim bragging rights to places we have visited and things we have done. And even those who practice voluntary simplicity may be attached to those things they own, perhaps even more than those who have more things, but regard them more superficially. In

this sense, a wasteful society of abundance may cause a problem in which we are insufficiently materialistic rather than overly so.

POSSESSIONS AND IDENTITY

It should not be assumed however that possessions reflect on us only in terms of their quantity or monetary worth. Rather, the choice of particular possessions and groups of possessions help to define our lifestyles, group affiliations, and perceived personalities. Because the meanings of possessions are defined socially as well as by marketing in an age of branded and increasingly global commodities, the role of particular possessions in identity and impression formation is a changing one. Fashions, novelty, affordability, and the adoption patterns of others all influence these image-related aspects of possessions. Moreover, it is seldom a single good that provides a recognizable identity, but instead a particular ensemble or constellation of goods allows recognition of coherent patterns that can be interpreted as conveying consumption meanings. It takes a coherent and recognizable set of possessions to make an intelligible statement about our identity. In addition, it is not only ownership of certain things or affiliations with certain people that conveys meanings. If the consumer does not have the requisite knowledge or skill to deploy these goods or interact with these people effectively, their possession or affiliation will fail to allow us to bask in their glory. For example, knowing the right wines to order or having the right acquaintances may not be enough to convey sophistication if the consumer is unable to master a meaningful conversation about viniculture or topics of interest to the people who might otherwise enhance our image by virtue of our association with them.

One important study of favorite self-expressive possessions was a three-generation study carried out in Chicago by Csikszentmihalyi and Rochberg-Halton (1981). The youngest, largely teenaged, generation treasured things that helped them perform (e.g., musical instruments, sports equipment). Their 40- to 50-year-old parents favored things that showed their status or power (e.g., automobiles, gadgets). And their grandparents cited objects that showed their connections to friends and family members (e.g., photographs, gifts from others). While this was a cross-sectional study, other studies have found similar life-cycle differences in the meanings of things as well as the degree of materialism exhibited by different generations (*see* FAMILY LIFE CYCLE). Earlier in the life cycle, possessions may help the infant to define a separate identity from his or her mother and subsequently possessions may act as transitional objects like a security blanket to ease the separation from mother and home. Later in the life cycle, as we prepare for death, there is often an attempt among the middle class of the world to leave a legacy for children via heirlooms and other mementos that hopefully leave a trace of our life behind for subsequent generations (e.g., Price, Arnould, and Curasi 2000).

Because of their functions in potentially creating meaningful identities and links to other people over the life cycle, possessions in a society without fixed and inherited roles also help us to envision and enact different selves. Some of these different selves are situational, as when we don different shoes, clothes, and cosmetics to go to work, go to a play, or go running. But there are other self transformations and possession-related rites of passage that ease us through transitions related to aging, educational and career milestones, marriage, divorce, parenthood, sickness, mourning, and other changes in status, health, appearance, employment, and social connections. In cultures that value independence and self-determination, our desire for expressing uniqueness may be stronger than our desire for expressing affiliation. But normally, both of these forces shape our behavior and both are manifest in the products, brands, and experiences that we acquire as consumers. In efforts to defy aging or try on new personas we may change wardrobes, visit beauty spas, acquire cosmetic surgery, accumulate travel experiences, or simply change brands.

Because possessions are often central to our identity, the involuntary loss of possessions to theft or disaster is often traumatic. Wicklund and Gollwitzer (1992) theorize that at such times as well as when we otherwise feel a lessened sense of self, we attempt to shore up or reconstitute our identity through acquiring new possessions as an act of symbolic self completion. They found, for example, that MBA students who were less

secure about their job prospects were more likely to attempt to compensate by acquiring stereotypical business artifacts like new shoes and suits, expensive pens, and attaché cases. This can be seen as a case of trying to improve the image conveyed by the extended self and what we have rather than by what we do or the person we are in some deeper sense.

One approach to understanding the role of possessions in identity is to ask people to describe themselves. Although there are cultural differences in the responses people give to this question, in the West it might be common to list our name, age, sex, occupation, religion, and hometown first. But after that we might begin to list our consumption interests (e.g., musical tastes, sports allegiances, recreational preferences) and the family and friends with whom we identify (Belk, 1987). Maffesoli (1996) has suggested that the contemporary equivalents of tribal affiliations are the "brand tribes" with which we identify (*see* BRAND COMMUNITY). Thus, we might identify ourselves as being a member of the "cult" of Macintosh, a "Red Devil" supporter of Manchester United Football Club, a Phish Phan, or a Harley Davidson motorcycle rider. We may also display these allegiances through decals, signature clothing, and tattoos so that our affiliations are evident even in contexts where the focus of our loyalty is absent.

More subtly, we often express our moods, lifestyles, religions, personalities, political orientations, and much more by our choices of foods, clothing, homes, automobiles, and other visible consumption choices. There is a behavioral advantage in such attempts at nonverbal communication via consumption choices. Although it would be considered gauche, ostentatious, or crude to introduce yourself to other people by saying such things as "I am rich," "I am adventurous," "I've been to Bali," or "I am looking for love," such messages may be presented in more socially acceptable ways via our visible consumption choices. Nonverbal consumption choices are largely visual, but can also be olfactory, as with perfumes, incense, and cigarettes. Such material expressions of self are enacted largely through our possessions, but they can also involve such patronage choices in areas such as travel (e.g., first class, tour groups), clubs, restaurants, and retailers. And as we invest more of ourselves in digital representations and social networking sites (*see* SOCIAL NETWORKS), identity creation and expression can also include our photographs, web links, taste statements, virtual friendships, and other creative activities made visible to those who visit our Facebook page, website, or blog, as well as to those who receive our e-mails and text messages. With such means at our disposal, the lines of what is socially acceptable have been extended and more and more of our consumption and consumption-related aspirations have potentially become visible to others. Likewise, our network of other people who comprise a part of our extended self has also potentially become more readily apparent.

THE NATURE OF THE SELF

One take on the contemporary self is that we are not only adapting a more malleable extended self that is increasingly external to our physical self and personal traits, but is also more postmodern, fragmented, decentered, and uncertain. Rather than a singular coherent core self that is consistent throughout our lives, in this view, we have multiple selves that we can put on and take off just as we change our wardrobe and clothing. Although the original conception of the extended self envisioned a central core self with various aggregate levels that are more or less central to our identity as well as various possessions that are also regarded as more proximate or distal to our sense of self, there are other possibilities.

One alternative conception of self that is consistent with the postmodern idea of fragmented selves is that we have a flexible cast of selves that we can call up depending on the situation and the others to whom we are presenting our selves. Thus we behave, dress, eat, and talk differently in a job interview, with our parents, with our children, with our significant other, and with our friends. In a study (Tian and Belk, 2005) of the office place possessions of employees at a high-tech firm in the United States, it was found that their offices, cubicles, and desks were a battleground where conflicting loyalties to the firm and their families were played out. Family members sought to keep themselves foremost in the employee's thoughts through photographs, mementos, children's artworks, telephone calls, e-mails, and other reminders

and links. Meanwhile, the corporate culture of the firm made demands for offices uncluttered by such personal items and for some display of the corporate colors, especially when clients came to visit. In addition, the corporation's hold on employees was extended through expectations of employees putting in overtime hours as well as links to them outside of the office via telephone, e-mail, the Internet, pagers, and corporate events like picnics. Thus, rather than forming differing concentric levels of self, the familial and corporate selves engaged one another as adversaries competing for the employee/family member's time and devotion.

Another alternative to conceptualization of self that is more premodern than postmodern is when the nature of the self is more collective and inclusive rather than individual and exclusionary. For example, among the Iñupiaq of Alaska, it is believed that humans and whales share a kindred spirit (Bodenhorn, 2005). The whale gives itself to the people in order to sustain them, but its spirit does not die. Rather it returns again and again to feed the people when they are hungry. As Bodenhorn (2005) explains:

> What we are talking about here is neither the bounded individual nor performative fragmentary individuals who sound so postmodern. Instead we are talking about being part of a whole that is neither indistinguishable nor separate from it. The cosmology of the whale/human relationship is profoundly unifying (p. 91).

As Belk (1988) recognized, the concept of extended self is both Western and male. To the Iñupiaq sense, self is not an individualistic one radiating outward to incorporate more things and people in the environment. Rather, both the people and the environment are part of an integrated whole. The concept of individual ownership and possession is less relevant in this context and the alternative formulation of a giving holistic environment emphasizes the inseparability and interpenetration of people, animals, and the natural world.

THE NATURE OF POSSESSIONS

The nature of possessions seems much more fixed than the existential question of who we are. Yet, notions of property, ownership, and the more general issue of our relationship with the world around us are all less stable and immutable than might initially appear to be the case. For example, just as the concept of self can be more shared and mutual rather than individual, so can the concept of ownership. Communal owner- ship is a case in point here. What European settlers in North and South America derisively called *Indian giving* was merely a case of Native Americans viewing the land and its resources as jointly owned, or more properly as unowned and unownable by anyone (e.g., Parry, 1986). Similar differences in notions of property and systems of property rights imposed by colonialists have eventually led to conflicts on every continent. Although planned communal societies based on common ownership have often failed and been dismissed as utopian, the vision of communities based on shared ownership has lasted thou- sands of years. On a smaller scale, the sharing that takes place within families has likely lasted hundreds of thousands of years (Belk, 2010). Infants depend upon parental sharing for their survival. Children typically do not need permis- sion to eat from the family's food pantry, enter the family's home, or use most of the resources that the family owns. Nor, in using these pooled resources, do they incur a debt that must be specifically repaid. The family in its pooling and allocation of resources comes close to fulfilling Louis Blanc's prescription: from each according to his or her abilities and to each according to his or her needs.

This is not to say that the possessions of families are all held in common. What may have once been the family's joint participation in musical performance through singing, playing musical instruments, and dancing, has subse- quently been commodified through subsequent iterations as written music, phonograph record- ings, tape recordings, compact discs, music videos, and digital files. In the process, the former family possessions of radios, record players, VCR, and hi-fi systems have become privatized as his/her/their transistor radios, boom boxes, Walkman devices, iPods, and personal computer files. The same is true of many other former family-shared possessions and rituals including rooms, meals, televisions, and cars.

What is true in the family is true in society as well. On one hand, the rise of the Internet and the ability to give and receive digital files while losing nothing and expending little more than electricity has led to an economy in which the majority of music and films are now exchanged either freely or outside of authorized channels in the form of so-called pirated or counterfeit copies. This is truly an economy of sharing rather than proprietary ownership. The same is true of many other things that we regu- larly give away and consume thanks to the Internet: e-mails, instant messages, websites, bulletin boards, chat rooms, and blogs full of free advice, reviews, recipes, directions, maps, and so on. On the other hand, this free sharing of information has led to a rapid and expansive rise of intellectual property rights legislation designed to preserve the profits and proprietary ownership of music, films, genetic codes, soft- ware, and brand property, even (and especially) when it exists in the form of digital information (e.g., see Benkler, 2006). Mark Getty, chairman of Getty Images, has referred to intellectual property as the oil of the twenty-first century. No doubt there will be many more battles in the post-Napster post-Pirate Bay world of file-sharing and fair-use skirmishes, but mean- while entities like Google, Wikipedia, Linux, Flickr, Facebook, and others show how a nonpro- prietary sharing-based orientation toward infor- mation can still be an enormously successful business model. In an age of finite and dwindling resources, global warming, and vast inequalities between rich and poor, an economy of sharing looms as a highly enticing alternative to individ- ualistic property and ownership.

Perhaps the world of academic journal publishing offers a model of how sharing, at least in the case of ideas and information, can be a win–win situation. The open model of science that has prevailed since the scientific revolution is based on the premise that science will advance much faster and all will benefit if we publish and share our ideas openly rather than seeking to profit from them. So we submit accounts of our research to journals for which we and others volunteer our reviewing expertise without compensation. We sign over the copyright of our work to the journals that agree to publish it. And we are happy when someone references our work and builds on our ideas. None of this needs be done out of a spirit of altruism and generosity, for when our work is published and cited, when we are listed as a member of an editorial review board or an editor, and when we send hard or digital copies of our work to anyone who seeks them, we are publicizing ourselves and building our academic reputations. But we have found a way to do this by giving away our ideas and services with the facilitating help of publishers, journals, and web sites who stand to earn a profit in the process. However, even here we can see the beginning of a more proprietary attitude toward the ownership of such ideas. Especially in the sciences such as genetic research, and in certain applied fields like electrical engineering, universities, laboratories, and corporations all seek to protect their inventions through patents, copyrights, and other forms of intellectual property. Scientists are reluctant to publish their work until they are certain they will obtain the patent rights to their discoveries. Thus, even within the hallowed halls of academia, the battle for property rights is increasingly in evidence.

CREATING AND PROTECTING AN INTANGIBLE POSSESSION: THE BRAND

Consumers are not the only ones concerned with creating self meanings through objects in the marketplace. Marketers are critically interested in investing meanings in their intangible brands. The two processes – marketers instilling meanings in their brands and consumers using these brands to create and maintain their self meanings – are interdependent. Moreover, since marketers can only do so much in their attempts to create brand meanings, the completion of this process ultimately depends to varying degrees on consumers to cocreate meanings for the brands they acquire in the marketplace. For example, the image of a model of Nike basketball shoe or Apple iPod depends partly on who the various people are who are first to adopt these objects, their characteristics such as the coolness that others ascribe to them, and what they have to say about their new acquisitions. Therefore, when a marketer attempts to measure the personality or image of a brand, they are partly measuring the image of the consumers who use the brand. And consumers for their part depend on the meanings that marketers have been able to impart to their brands via design,

advertising, merchandizing, packaging, pricing, distribution, and other marketing activities. Celebrity endorsers often help in this process as well, as with the successes of Nike and Michael Jordan. It is easy to see this as a case of contagious magic in which the characteristics of the endorser transfer to the brand and from there hopefully to the purchaser of the goods being endorsed.

One category of goods where brand and user image is all-important is luxury goods. In fashions, accessories, handbags, luggage, fragrances, jewelry, and watches, luxury brands can sell for premium prices that can be as much as 10 times more expensive than average brands in these categories, or even more. Exclusivity, quality, and hip and elegant design are a part of the appeal of such goods, as is their exorbitant price and their sometimes limited availability. But their appeal also benefits from the image imparted through the use of celebrities and models promoting the brands, including Tiger Woods, George Clooney, Chris Jorgensen, Uma Thurman, Kate Moss, Naomi Campbell, and Scarlett Johansson. Contagious magic is no less implicated in luxury goods than it is for more moderately priced offerings. In the case of Louis Vuitton, celebrities are also sought in the art world for design collaborations (e.g., Takeshi Murakami, Stephen Sprouse) and the company also sponsors art exhibitions featuring the work of these and other artists. Such cobranding seeks to draw on the high cultural capital of associating with the world of fine art; something that would be lost for example in sponsoring NASCAR race cars. Luxury goods companies like Tag Heuer that do seek sports celebrity endorsements confine themselves to higher status sports like golf and tennis rather than boxing, for example. Thus just as consumers can enhance their self image by surrounding themselves with popular goods and people, so can luxury brands enhance their images through associating themselves with high-status people, events, and settings.

Given the coproduction of brand meanings by consumers and marketers of luxury goods, one problematic occurrence is counterfeiting. In this case, the much lower prices of counterfeit goods make them available to more people and less-affluent people than comprise the target market of the authentic brands. This creates a dilemma. On one hand, such counterfeit brand proliferation threatens to dilute the brand and reduce its exclusivity. But, on the other hand, to have a luxury brand that is not the object of counterfeiting would suggest that the brand is not sufficiently desirable to warrant imitation. France, the home of many luxury brands including those of Louis Vuitton Moët Hennessy, has enacted legislation that makes it a crime to be in possession of a counterfeit good, with penalties of up to 3000 Euros per item, plus jail time.

On the other hand, brands like Nike, Stussy, Hilfiger, Polo, and DKNY all tolerated, if not encouraged, counterfeit copies of their brands among members of hip-hop culture in New York City. Their reason is simple. Rather than selling an exclusive luxury image, they are selling cool. By associating their brands with rap music and cool kids, they are trying to endow the goods with coolness. Product placements with popular cool kids in schools are another way that such brands sometimes try to achieve cool status. And another tactic is to use cool celebrities. For example, in a 2006 ad in *Transworld Skateboarding*, Vans promotes a skateboarding shoe called the *Hosoi SK8-HI*. The only copy reads "Very Limited Edition, Available April 1." The ad shows an action shot of skateboarding star Christian Hosoi, for whom the shoe is named. In the same way that Nike was able to exploit Michael Jordan's coolness with the Air Jordan, Vans hopes that Hosoi's cool image will transfer to the shoe. His cool image derives not only from his prominent role in early California skateboard culture, but also from his drug-dealing past. He was imprisoned for three years and was released shortly before the ad ran. He also appeared in the Vans-financed film, *Dogtown and Z-Boys*, about the origins of skateboarding in southern California. Vans has successfully used their early popularity in skateboarding subculture in order to borrow the cool renegade image of skateboarders. They have parlayed this image with products centered on music and cool sports including surfing, snowboarding, BMX wakeboarding, motocross, and supercross. Other shoes have tried to create a cool image by showing ads with cool cars and their owners (e.g., K-Swiss, 310), adult film stars (e.g., Pony), or simply cool-looking people with tattoos and a look of cool indifference (e.g., GBX).

So it can be seen in these examples that the implications of possessions for self image can be commercial as well as personal. By focusing on extended self, celebrity endorsement, cool people, cool settings, and contagious magic, it is sometimes possible to build a brand into an aspirational prop for self image. If William Shakespeare and Erving Goffman are correct, all the world is a stage, and we increasingly rely on ensembles of branded consumer goods in order to try on the various roles that we imagine ourselves playing.

Conclusion

It is easy to condemn our reliance on possessions to enlarge our sense of self as being a shallow substitute for the alternative character-based sense of self that presumably hides behind our façade of consumer goods. Materialism, waste, excessive consumption, and the vicious cycle of striving to have the latest gadgets ultimately prove unfulfilling. And there is much to be said for striving for a simpler material lifestyle and reducing our ecological footprint, especially among those of us who have much more than we need in order to live comfortably. But despite these easy criticisms, possessions also play some very positive roles in our lives. By accumulating certain possessions, we are accumulating visual mnemonic cues to our pasts and potential cues to the meaning of our lives. These material cues often take the form of photographs, gifts, souvenirs, awards, and heirlooms, but they can as easily be a fragment of a song, the whiff or a perfume, or the taste of a particular food like Proust's lime-blossom tea and petite madeleines. At more aggregate levels of self, we also have national monuments, national buildings, flags, and other icons to remind us of our country's past.

Besides looking backward and reminding ourselves of who we are, possessions that we aspire to own can also provide goals that drive us forward in education, career, personal relationships, travel, and other spheres of life. Aesthetic objects can be a source of contemplation, relaxation, and reflection about who we are and what is important in life. We have come to rely on material goods in our rituals of birth, death, marriage, childbirth, and other rites of passage that help us get through life and feel that we are honoring life's sacred moments. Even in our so-called disposable age of ephemeral possessions, it is likely that some of our individual and collective possessions will outlive us. They are sometimes our link to immortality and parts of the trace that we leave behind that will help others remember us when we are gone. For academics, artists, writers, playwrights, poets, filmmakers, craftspeople, builders, cabinetmakers, and others who create, it is their creations that they hope will fulfill this function. For others, it may be any of the many goods that have become embedded in their lives and identities. But regardless of how humble or magnificent the object, the power of possessions lies not only in their role in our present lives, but potentially in the past and future as well.

Bibliography

Belk, R. (1985) Materialism: trait aspects of living in the material world. *Journal of Consumer Research*, **12** (3), 265–280.

Belk, R.W. (1987) Identity and the relevance of market, personal, and community objects, in *Marketing and Semiotics: New Directions in the Study of Signs for Sale* (ed J. Umiker-Sebeok), Mouton de Gruyter, Berlin, pp. 151–164.

Belk, R.W. (1988) Possessions and the extended self. *Journal of Consumer Research*, **15** (2), 139–168.

Belk, R.W. (1992) Attachment to possessions, in *Human Behavior and Environment: Advances in Theory and Research, Vol. 12, Place Attachment* (eds I. Altman and S., Low), Plenum Press, New York, pp. 37–62.

Belk, R.W. (2010) Sharing. *Journal of Consumer Research*. **34** (1), 1–20.

Benkler, Y. (2006) *The Wealth of Networks: How Social Production Transforms Markets and Freedom*, Yale University Press, New Haven, CT.

Bodenhorn, B. (2005) Sharing costs: an exploration of personal and individual property, equalities and differentiation, in *Property and Equality, Vol. 1: Ritualisation, Sharing, Egalitarianism* (eds T. Widlock and W.G. Tadesse.), Berghahn Books, New York, pp. 77–104.

Csikszentmihalyi, M. and Rochberg-Halton, E. (1981) *The Meaning of Things: Domestic Symbols and the Self*, University of Chicago Press, Chicago.

James, W. (1890) *The Principles of Psychology, Vol. 1*, Henry Holt, New York.

Kleine, S.S. and Baker, S.M. (2004) An integrative review of material possession attachment. *Academy of Marketing Science Review*, **1**, 1–39.

Maffesoli, M. (1996) *The Time of the Tribes: The Decline of Individualism in Mass Society*, D. Smith, trans., Sage, Thousand Oaks, CA.

Parry, J. (1986) The Gift, the indian gift and the 'Indian Gift'. *Man*, **21**, 466–471.

Price, L.L., Arnould, E.J., and Curasi, C.F. (2000) Older consumers' disposition of special possessions. *Journal of Consumer Research*, **27**, 179–201.

Tian, K. and Belk, R.W. (2005) Extended self and possessions in the workplace. *Journal of Consumer Research*, **32**, 297–310.

Wicklund, R. and Gollwitzer, P. (1992) *Symbolic Self-Completion*, Lawrence Erlbaum, Hillsdale, NJ.

S

self-regulation

Kathleen D. Vohs and Ayelet Fishbach

People are not passive, listless automatons waiting for stimuli to demand a response. They plan, organize, prioritize, and modify their behavior. They set goals. Broadly, these behaviors are called *self-regulation*. Self-regulation is a vital process of the self. The self-regulation process not only sets goals but also monitors progress, shifts to new goals as necessary, and manages a hierarchically structured system of multiple goals.

The consumption setting is an ideal context in which to situate self-regulation theory and research. After humans evolved to form groups that led to the formation of culture, the development of trade and the emergence of humans as *homo economicus* brought about advances in reproduction and survival, not to mention quality of life (*see* CONSUMER WELL-BEING).

The role of consumption is still crucial today but not in the same way. The press to study self-regulation in contemporary settings comes in large part from the abundance of temptations and urges. "Having it now" interferes with long-term goal strivings, many of which are centered around consumption. Financial goals influence spending and health goals influence food intake (Herman and Polivy, 1975). It is difficult to understate the importance of self-regulation in humans ancestral history and now.

DEFINITIONS

Terms: Cognitive scientists use the construct of basic level to describe the default category used to define objects. In the current case, the basic level constructs are self-regulation and self-control. Many scholars use these terms interchangeably to mean modulation of an incipient response. Often the definition tacitly includes a secondary component that a more suitable response will be substituted for the undesirable response. Modulations of responses can involve suppression (the most common) or amplification. It can even mean creating a response out of nothing (e.g., faking a smile when opening a disappointing gift). When scholars use the terms differently, they often take self-control to be the conscious form of response modification, whereas self-regulation can be nonconscious as well. At a broader level, some scholars have discussed self-management, which involves moving current goals up and down the priority list, the importance or salience of the goals often being determined situationally.

Scope: There are five general classes of responses that can be regulated. One can fixate one's attention (e.g., when driving in a Minnesota snowstorm), down- or up-regulate emotions (e.g., stifling a laugh), overcome an impulse (e.g., to eat the whole bag of cookies), suppress intrusive thoughts (e.g., do not think about an ex-lover), or guide behavior (e.g., throwing a dart to hit the bull's-eye). Eating, drinking, spending, sexuality, drug taking, avoiding exercise, and risky driving involve many or all of these foundational spheres of self-regulation and are but a few of the manifestations of self-regulation in a consumer culture.

Types: The current article cleaves the literature on self-regulation into two pieces: motivational versus social-cognitive inputs to self-regulation. It is no coincidence that one major distinction between types of self-regulation, namely controlled versus automatic processes, roughly corresponds to the degree to which they are energy-taxing (i.e., subject to motivation) and conscious. The automatic system guides behavior via well-learned (through practice or habit) or functional (i.e., evolutionary-based) action patterns. Owing to their ingrained nature, these responses are not said to take up energy or to be under conscious control. In contrast, consciously controlled processes cost energy to enact and involve a high degree of self-awareness. Hence, essential distinctions about broad types of self-regulation processes rest on the notion of motivation and cognition.

Process versus outcome: We emphasize the fact that self-regulation is a process, not an outcome. Too often, scholars conflate the process of attempting to reach a goal with the normative nature of the goal itself. Mostly people set goals that align with normative prescriptions for behavior, such as having positive relationships with others, adopting healthy behaviors, and being morally good, but not always. People can engage in self-regulation in order to get themselves to overeat, binge drink, or engage in risky sex acts. More novel, insightful, and predictive research will come from separating the process of self-regulation from the outcomes that the actors intend to achieve.

OVERVIEW

As mentioned, the article reviews research on self-regulation as falling into one of two camps: energy or motivational versus social-cognitive. Whether a theory focuses on self-regulation from a motivational or cognitive perspective suggests that different inputs, processes, and outcomes are considered relevant in each approach. Admittedly, though, the dividing line between these two camps is artificial, if readers think that one theory or another could be in a different camp they may be right. We do not intend to draw exact dividing lines. Rather, parsing the research into motivational versus cognitive emphases is meant to be a loose classification system in order to highlight theories that share features.

MOTIVATIONAL INPUTS TO
SELF-REGULATION

Motivation can loosely be defined as effort or energy that one puts toward a goal (*see* MOTIVATION AND GOALS). Freud's psycho-dynamic model has been the energy model with the greatest impact on the psychology of self-change. As the reader is probably noting already, that model has long since dominated scientific studies. Baumeister, a social psychologist who studies self-regulation, once quipped that, "energy models are so out of fashion that we [i.e., social scientists] aren't even against them anymore" (personal communication, March 16, 2004). Today's motivation research, while certainly not Freudian in nature, embraces energy as a central component that reorients behavior away from entrained routes and toward desired ends.

Cybernetic models.   Cybernetic models describe the process of self-regulation as discrepancy-closing. When a person identifies a desired end state, the motivational system calculates the size of the discrepancy between the present state and the desired state and guides action toward closing the gap. The acronym "TOTE", which stands for Test, Operate, Test, Exit, is often used to denote this process. According to this notion, once the person identifies a desired end state, the required effort to reach this state is assessed (Test), which leads people to put effort into achieving it (Operate), which requires another assessment of the distance (Test), which cycles around recursively until the process ends because the end state is achieved (Exit). For example, a woman may perceive she needs to go on a diet. She calculates how much weight to lose, trims calories and exercises, and steps on the scale from time to time. She stops dieting when the gap is closed either because she reached her goal (success) or altered it (likely due to repeated failed attempts).

Research by Carver and Scheier (1990) developed this feedback model into a comprehensive model of feedback loops. Their model highlights emotions as feedback for self-regulation. Positive emotions signal that the rate of closing the gap to goal attainment is faster than expected. In this case, people reduce their effort or "coast."

Negative emotions, conversely, signal that the rate of closing the gap is slower than intended. In this case, people increase their effort investment. An interesting implication of this model is that people will work harder toward a goal when they feel bad about it than when they feel good about it.

Limited-resource model of self-regulation. A recent model depicts self-regulation as being a function of a limited stock of energy. This energy is said to be involved in every act of self-regulation, which implies that it is easily taxed. When people are low in self-regulatory resources, they are said to be in a state of depletion (or ego depletion), which portends poor self-regulation subsequently. At last count, over 120 published experiments have shown the pattern that was predicted by the limited-resource model: after a person engages in self-regulation, ensuing attempts at self-regulation are less successful than if the person had not earlier engaged in self-regulation. The resource is renewable but unfortunately it does not seem to replenish itself with as much ease as it gets depleted.

The first papers on the limited-resource model established basic self-regulation findings (Baumeister *et al.*, 1998). In this work, participants would engage in one form of self-regulation (or not, for the neutral conditions) and then all participants would be tested in a different domain of self-regulation. Papers subsequent to those focused on boundary conditions of the model or mechanisms. Particularly germane to the current volume is work on breaking one's diet and impulsive spending as a function of self-regulatory resource depletion and decision making impacting self-regulation (*see* IMPULSIVE AND COMPULSIVE BUYING).

Controlling caloric intake is a perennial self-regulation problem and one that is especially interesting given that people cannot completely exit the eating cycle. That is, when studying other overconsumption problems, such as drug or nicotine addiction, one solution is to simply not consume the substance. This does not work with food intake. Hence, how people grapple with regulating eating is of special interest because people must indeed constantly regulate.

The limited-resource model was used to show that dieters, but not non-dieters, eat more when they have been taxed of their self-regulatory resources (Vohs and Heatherton, 2000). In a representative experiment, for instance, dieters and non-dieters were brought to the laboratory individually and were first asked to watch a boring movie about bighorn sheep. There were also snacks in the room that were either nearby the participant's chair or far away, and those snacks were either labeled as "off-limits" or "for the taking." Being bored made it likely, we thought, that participants would want to eat the snacks, but we knew from prior research that dieters may well be tempted but would not eat the snacks because they were fattening (chocolate candies, cookies, etc). In fact, we hypothesized that the greatest temptation would be for the participants for whom the snacks were nearby and allowed to be eaten. In this condition, not eating the goodies would require the most self-regulation. For dieters, we surmised that if they were reduced in the amount of self-regulatory resources they had, then later if we surprised them with another context in which they had to taste food (a taste-and-rate ice cream task), they would not be able to exert enough resources to curb their desire to indulge. We observed the expected pattern. As predicted, dieters who sat next to candies and were allowed to eat them – but held back because of their personal dieting goal – later ate the most ice cream during a ratings task. Non-dieters are not regulating in the domain of food intake, so their eating – in the initial phase and the ice cream eating test phase – is merely a function of internal cues and not because of depletion. This article raises a broad point about the limited-resource model of self-regulation and motivation: when people become depleted, they will not behave impulsively at random. What will come unglued is that which they are regulating the most: for dieters, this means that they should eat more when depleted, which are the findings of Vohs and Heatherton (2000). For consumers trying to curb their spending, this would mean purchasing. Vohs and Faber (2007) found exactly this pattern.

The studies testing impulsive spending as a result of self-regulatory resource depletion (*see* IMPULSIVE AND COMPULSIVE BUYING) are similar to the aforementioned studies on eating among dieters with one key difference. We argued in this article (Vohs and Faber, 2007) that everyone has an outside goal of reigning in spending (*see* CONSUMER MATERIALISM). In almost all situations, some self-control in buying is necessary in order to achieve other goals. People who think they have unlimited funds, such as celebrities, may soon discover that their funds have run dry (e.g., Mike Tyson's bankruptcy, Michael Jackson's debts). Hence, we claimed that most people have at least an implicit goal not to spend impulsively. This generalization meant that we expected to see unplanned spending (as a form of lax self-regulation) as a consequence of self-regulatory resource depletion as a main effect. Above and beyond this main effect, we also predicted that the buying behavior of people who are regulating in the domain of spending would be especially affected by resource depletion. As predicted, our experiments revealed that depletion condition and interaction of depletion condition with trait impulsive buying tendencies are major causes of impromptu spending. One representative experiment had participants in the ego depletion condition list out their thoughts for several minutes, with the exception that they were not allowed to think thoughts of a white bear. Other participants were allowed to think anything they wanted for the thought listing task, including a white bear. Hence, the former group has a thought suppression goal, whereas the latter does not. After the thought listing task, participants were shown 22 products that were said to be under consideration for inclusion in the university bookstore. We gave them $10 to spend in the mock bookstore or take home. The dependent measure was ad hoc spending in this spontaneous purchasing situation. As expected, participants who had been in the thought suppression condition spent more money and bought more items than participants in the no suppression condition. Moreover, participants who had chronic problems with overspending spent more than other participants when they had been depleted of their self-regulation resources. In short, controlling one's spending uses self-regulation, and when self-regulatory resources run low, unplanned and unnecessary spending is likely to occur.

The third domain that is especially relevant to the notion of consumer self-regulation is how choice influences self-regulation. The executive function of the self houses both self-regulation and decision making. As a consequence, making choices and controlling the self are likely to be interrelated (*see* CONSUMER DECISION MAKING). We posited that making choices would tax the self-regulation system in a manner similar to when people engage in self-regulation. That is, we predicted that self-regulatory abilities would be compromised after making choices. Eight studies supported this hypothesis (Vohs *et al.*, 2008).

In one study, participants in the choice condition (comprised primarily of first-year college students) were asked to select courses that they would take for their remaining years in college, whereas those in the no-choice condition simply reviewed the course catalog. Next, all participants were given time to study for an upcoming test purportedly to measure participants' intelligence. Participants in the choice condition practiced less (that is, procrastinated more) than those in the no-choice condition. In another experiment, participants in the choice condition were asked to make a series of binary choices between consumer products, such as a yellow candle versus white candle. Participants in the no-choice condition rated the same products on how often they had used such products but did not make choices. Then all participants were asked to keep their forearms in painfully cold water for as long as possible. As predicted, high choice participants were less able to endure the pain of cold water than no-choice participants. In a study that took place at a shopping mall, shoppers reported the extent they had made decisions during the day, including how many decisions, how much they deliberated and how personally responsible they felt for the decisions, which formed a latent variable that we called investment in choices. Later, shoppers were asked to complete arithmetic problems. The more choices shoppers reported having made, the fewer math problems they attempted, the less time they spent on them, and the more problems they got wrong.

Follow-up studies found that when people are depleted of their self-regulatory resources, they are more likely to buy hedonic products more than utilitarian products. These studies also confirmed the linkages between self-regulation and choice in a non-North American context (Western Europe), which is important because one would want to know that these effects occur outside of the United States and its plethora of choices. In sum, these studies suggest that the processes involved in decision making rest on the same mechanism that is used for self-regulation, which unfortunately exact significant intrapsychic costs.

OTHER MOTIVATIONAL INPUTS

Motivation has much to do with whether the actor thinks that he or she is capable of reaching the goal. One consumer model of goal attainment (Bagozzi and Dholakia, 1999) focuses on self-efficacy, which is the belief that a person can achieve what he or she wants to achieve. Self-efficacy is a construct somewhere between self-esteem (one's appraisal of oneself in terms of goodness or badness) and self-regulation (goal attainment) in that it involves self-perceptions of ability. Having the sense that one can meet valued goals is crucial to self-regulation success because it amps up the motivation to do so.

A small but growing literature on lay beliefs about the structure of self-regulation also points to the role of motivation. At a broad level, personal theories of self-regulation as a flexible, dynamic system has been found to benefit self-regulation.

Social Cognitive Inputs to Self-Regulation

Social cognitive models vary by whether they address the regulation of a single versus multiple goals. In addition, models that address regulation of multiple goals vary by whether they address goals that are of equal status (e.g., goals related to career and family) versus goals that pose a self-control dilemma (e.g., eating healthy and tasty). We offer a brief overview of some of the more prominent models in this domain.

Regulatory focus theory. Other research distinguishes between the different types of goals that individuals pursue and how they may evoke different processes of self-regulation. The most basic distinction exists between the goal to obtain pleasure versus avoid pain. For example, every

organism strives to get food as well as avoid danger (and stay alive). On the basis of this distinction, regulatory focus theory distinguishes self-regulation with a promotion focus, on the presence and absence of positive outcomes or gains, and self-regulation with a prevention focus, on the presence or absence of negative outcomes or losses. Individuals strive toward positive outcomes when pursuing advancement needs and aspirations (e.g., planning a vacation). They further strive to avoid negative outcomes when pursuing security needs and responsibilities (e.g., getting a fire alarm). Interestingly for many goals (e.g., personal hygiene), both frames are possible and individual differences as well as situational factors will determine which focus a person adopts.

According to regulatory focus theory, different processes characterize the different foci and they have different psychological consequences. In particular, the pursuit of promotion goals is oriented toward receiving gains, whereas the pursuit of prevention goals is oriented toward non-losses. The emotional consequences of pursuing promotion goals further differ from those of prevention goals. For promotion goals, successful pursuit results in happiness and failure results in sadness, because these emotions characterize the presence versus absence of gains. In contrast, for prevention goals, successful pursuit results in calmness and failure results in anxiety, because these emotions characterize the absence versus presence of losses. In addition, research finds that people enjoy pursuing a goal in a manner that sustains their regulatory focus, a phenomenon titled "regulatory fit" (Higgins, 2000). In particular, people prefer to use eager strategies toward promotion goals and vigilant strategies toward prevention goals.

Goal systems theory. Whereas the basic unit of research on self-regulation involves the pursuit of a single goal, people rarely hold only one goal at a time. Rather, they often need to juggle between several goals that compete with each other for resources (e.g., buying a house versus increase contribution to retirement) or that directly undermine each other (e.g., eating healthy and fatty food). Research on goal systems theory addresses the cognitive operations that govern the regulation of multiple goals. According to this research, goals are organized in associative networks, connecting higher order goals with lower level means of attainment. Each goal is associatively linked to several attainment means. Similarly, each means is connected to several goals that it can potentially serve. For example, the goal of having a good figure may be connected with the means of eating healthy food and exercising, and the means of exercising may be connected with goals of having a good figure and leading a healthy lifestyle. In addition, there are inhibitory links between unrelated goals or between unrelated means that potentially compete for resources.

There are several predictions that follow from this theory. For example, it assumes that the presence of potential means to a goal activates the corresponding goal, such that individuals will adhere to the goal upon encountering a means (or an opportunity) for goal pursuit. For example, the mindless impact of an advertisement on consumer choice may reflect such goal activation upon encountering cues for means of attainment. In addition, because competing goals inhibit each other, a focal goal can often lead to the inhibition of another alternative goal. In this way, the focal goal "*shields*" itself from alternative ones by directly reducing their accessibility (Shah, Friedman, and Kruglanski, 2002). Empirically, this inhibition is often reflected in the slowing down of lexical decision times to concepts that represent alternative goals. For example, activation of academic goals slowed down the lexical decision time to concepts related to alternative goals (e.g., exercising).

Other research on goal systems documents a desire for multiple goal attainment. Given the presence of several salient goals and limited motivational resources, individuals search for attainment means that are linked to the attainment of several goals simultaneously. For example, a person may prefer to dine out (vs. dine in) in order to satisfy both hunger and various social motives (to see and be seen, etc.), or commuters may choose to commute by bike (vs. car) in order to save money and keep in shape. Interestingly, however, as the number of goals attached to a given means increases, each association becomes weaker. The result is a dilution of the means–goal association, which may reduce the perceived effectiveness of the means with respect to the goal. That is, although individuals often seek means that are linked to multiple goals, they also find them less effective than those which serve fewer goals. In a demonstration of this *dilution effect*, Zhang, Fishbach, and Kruglanski (2007) found that when participants considered the different goals (e.g., building muscles and losing weight) that a single means (e.g., working out) could satisfy, an increase in the number of goals resulted in a reduction in the perception of the instrumentality of the means with respect to each goal. As a result, individuals sometimes choose means that are connected with fewer goals, because they believe these means are more effective. For example, participants in a study were less likely to use the writing function of a pen that had also been used as a laser pointer (vs. was not used as a laser pointer) when they only needed to write. It appears that the general preference for means that serve several goals diminishes and even reverses when a person focuses upon pursuit of a single goal.

DYNAMICS OF SELF-REGULATION

When individuals wish to successfully pursue several goals, they often take into account a sequence of actions that unfold over time. Then, completed actions in the past or upcoming actions in the future can both influence which goal an individual attends to in the present. In addition, missing actions in the past or the absence of plans to pursue a goal in the future will influence the decision to pursue a goal in the present.

Research on the dynamics of self-regulation (Fishbach and Dhar, 2005) attests that self-regulation follows a sequence of actions that either balances between several goals or highlights the pursuit of one, focal goal. According to this research, whether people balance or highlight depends on whether they represent actions that pursue a goal as an expression of their commitment to this goal or as a signal that progress was made. When actions express commitment, each action increases goal commitment and goal adherence, and hence people highlight the goal. However, when actions signals progress on a goal, each action decreases the perceived need for taking more actions, and hence people balance between their goal pursuits.

One factor that determines whether people represent goal actions as an expression of their commitment or as making progress is their degree of commitment certainty. When individuals are not sure whether the goal is valuable for them, they highlight by adhering more to a goal if they have done so before. But when individuals are already sure that the goal is valuable, they wish to monitor their level of progress and they adhere to a goal more if they have not done so since they perceive greater need to make progress. For example, shoppers who were buying luxuries, expressed greater interest to use a frequent buyer card that had a visual emphasis on completed purchases (using stamps) than on missing purchases (using punches), because completed purchases signaled that buying luxuries is valuable and promoted highlighting of the purchase behavior. In contrast, shoppers who were buying necessities were more likely to use a frequent buyer card if it emphasized missing (vs. completed) purchases, because missing purchases signal need for progress and promote balancing for the absence of purchases.

These findings have implications for pursuing group goals, when individuals join force with other group members, for example, when contributing to a charity. Research finds that first time donors are more likely to contribute if they receive information on accumulated contributions to date (vs. missing contributions to go), whereas returning donors are more likely to contribute if they receive information on missing contributions to go (vs. accumulated to date). The reason is that first time donors wish to evaluate whether the charity goal is valuable and their behaviors follows, or "highlights" others' contributions. Returning donors wish to evaluate the rate of progress on the charity goal and their behavior compensates or "balances" for others' contributions.

The arrangement of action alternatives also influences the dynamic of self-regulation individuals follow. Individuals often make selections from sets that include items that serve multiple goals. For example, they browse a television guide that includes educational shows and light sitcoms, or they go through highbrow news magazines and lowbrow fashion magazines on a newsstand. The arrangements of the alternatives influences people's perceptions of them as competing against versus complementing each other, which in turn influences the dynamics of self-regulation they would follow. In particular, separating items into two sets (e.g., two bowls), versus presenting them together in one set (e.g., one bowl), determines whether individuals perceive the items as conflicting versus complementary. When the items are presented apart, they seem conflicting and promote a highlighting dynamic of choice; when the items are together, they seem complementary and promote a balancing dynamic of choice.

These dynamics have unique consequences for situations in which the items on a set pose a self-control conflict. When goal and temptation alternatives (e.g., healthy and unhealthy foods) are presented apart from each other, they seem to compete against each other. As a result, people are more likely to resolve the conflict in favor of the goal alternatives in a dynamic of highlighting: they assign a greater value to goal alternatives (e.g., educational shows, news magazines) than to tempting alternatives and consistently choose goal alternatives for both immediate and future consumption. In contrast, when choice alternatives appear together and seem to complement each other, thus promoting balancing, people tend to resolve the self-control conflict in favor of the immediately gratifying temptation option. As a result, they value the tempting alternatives (e.g., watching sitcoms, reading lowbrow fashion magazines) more than the goal alternatives and prefer these tempting alternatives for immediate consumption, thereby postponing the consumption of goal alternatives to a future occasion. The reason tempting alternatives are selected first in this presentation format is that their value is immediate, whereas the value of the goal alternatives, although larger, is delayed. Thus, in a self-control conflict, a balancing dynamic would most often take the form of "first temptation then goal" rather than "first goal then temptation."

Counteractive control theory. Other cognitive models address the exercise of self-control and overcoming temptations. In particular, counteractive control theory (Fishbach and Trope,

2007) examines the processes of resolving goal conflict between an important long-term goal and a momentary temptation (e.g., saving and spending, eating healthy and enjoying fatty food, study and leisure). According to this theory, the process of counteracting temptations involves asymmetric shifts in motivational strength, namely an increase in the motivation to pursue a goal and a reduction in the motivation to pursue temptations. Such asymmetric shifts are often of conscious, deliberative nature, but they may involve nonconscious, implicit strategies that promote individuals' long-term interest without requiring conscious awareness. In addition, some strategies are behavioral and they act on the choice opportunities themselves (e.g., increasing the availability of goal items) while other strategies are more cognitive by nature, and they act on the representation of the choice opportunities (e.g., increasing the value of goal items).

Individuals employ behavioral counteractive strategies when they choose, for example, to make rewards contingent on undergoing uncomfortable (but helpful) medical tests and make penalties contingent on failing to do so. Using this strategy, they counteract the temptation to avoid the test. Another behavioral strategy involves precommitment to pursue goals and avoid temptations. For example, while grocery shopping, a consumer might suspect that having tempting sweets available in the kitchen will pose a problem and decide to purchase fruits instead. People further avoid temptations by maintaining physical distance from tempting objects, while ensuring proximity to objects associated with goals. For example, they will push away the liquor glass and pull toward them a glass of water, in order to stop drinking.

Other cognitive strategies alter the representation of goals and temptations. Thus, individuals often counteractively bolster their evaluations of goals and dampen their evaluations of temptation. For example, health-conscious individuals who were facing a choice between health bars and unhealthy chocolates evaluated the chocolates as less appealing than the health bars before choosing between the two, in order to secure making the "right choice." Individuals further promote goal pursuit by adopting a concrete representation of goals but an abstract representation of temptations, because the more concrete representation facilitates action. For example, in a study on the regulation of academic goals, students formed concrete behavioral plans to facilitate pursuit of their academic goals (Gollwitzer and Brandstätter, 1997). In another study on delay of gratification, children resisted the temptation to eat a marshmallow by thinking about it as an abstract cloud, thus cooling its appetitive influence (Mischel, Shoda, and Rodriguez, 1989).

Finally, similar patterns of asymmetric shifts exist for individuals' nonconscious self-control operations. For example, they nonconsciously boost the value of the goal while dampening the value of the temptation. In addition, implicit counteractive control entails changes in the accessibility of goals and temptations. Individuals shore up their goals by activating goal-related constructs in response to interfering temptations and by inhibiting temptation-related constructs in response to goal-related cues. For example, a study on college students demonstrated that subliminally presenting the word "television" reduced the time students took to subsequently recognize the goal-related word "study" (goal-related), and similarly presenting the word "study" increased the time students took to subsequently recognize the word "television" (Fishbach, Friedman, and Kruglanski, 2003).

Conclusions

The research reviewed in this article is aimed at offering two broad perspectives on self-regulation. One is motivational, the other cognitive. For the former, energy models are increasingly popular. Future work could, however, expand on the link between emotion and motivation as these two often interact in novel ways (e.g., urges and impulses as emotions; *see* CONSUMER DESIRE).

We encourage researchers to remember that self-regulation is a process, not an outcome. While it is true that most self-regulation acts are aimed at securing goals that will lead to normatively better, longer, and morally right lives, some do not. An emphasis on the process rather than the outcome will open new vantage points.

Problems because of failures of self-regulation seem to be taking over the Western (and, increasingly, Eastern) world. Drug and alcohol abuse, overeating, sexual improprieties, underachievement, insufficient exercise, Internet and video game addictions, violence, and crime are all linked through problems with self-regulation. Indeed, it is difficult to think of many behavioral problems that do not have a regulatory component. Against this backdrop, it is somewhat consoling that along with problems of self-regulation comes an increasing emphasis on the importance of research in this area.

Bibliography

Bagozzi, R.P. and Dholakia, U. (1999) Goal-setting and goal-striving in consumer behavior. *Journal of Marketing*, **63**, 19–32.

Baumeister, R.F., Bratslavsky, E., Muraven, M., and Tice, D.M. (1998) Ego depletion: is the active self a limited resource?. *Journal of Personality and Social Psychology*, **74**, 1252–1265.

Carver, C.S. and Scheier, M.F. (1990) Origins and functions of positive and negative affect. *A Control-process View. Psychological Review*, **97**, 19–35.

Fishbach, A. and Dhar, R. (2005) Goals as excuses or guides: the liberating effect of perceived goal progress on choice. *Journal of Consumer Research*, **32**, 370–377.

Fishbach, A., Friedman, R.S., and Kruglanski, A.W. (2003) Leading us not unto temptation: momentary allurements elicit overriding goal activation. *Journal of Personality and Social Psychology*, **84**, 296–309.

Fishbach, A. and Trope, Y. (2007) Implicit and explicit mechanisms of counteractive self-control, in *Handbook of Motivation Science* (eds J. Shah and W. Gardner), Guilford, New York, pp. 281–294.

Gollwitzer, P.M. and Brandstätter, V. (1997) Implementation intentions and effective goal pursuit. *Journal of Personality and Social Psychology*, **73**, 186–199.

Herman, C.P. and Polivy, J. (1975) Anxiety, restraint and eating behavior. *Journal of Abnormal Psychology*, **84**, 666–672.

Higgins, E.T. (2000) Making a good decision: value from fit. *American Psychologist*, **55**, 1217–1230.

Mischel, W., Shoda, Y., and Rodriguez, M.L. (1989) Delay of gratification in children. *Science*, **244**, 933–938.

Shah, J.Y., Friedman, R., and Kruglanski, A.W. (2002) Forgetting all else: on the antecedents and consequences of goal shielding. *Journal of Personality and Social Psychology*, **83**, 1261–1280.

Vohs, K.D., Baumeister, R.F., Schmeichel, B.J. et al. (2008) Making choices impairs subsequent self-control: a limited resource account of decision making, self-regulation, and active initiative. *Journal of Personality and Social Psychology*, **94**, 883–898.

Vohs, K.D. and Faber, R.J. (2007) Spent resources: self-regulatory resource availability affects impulse buying. *Journal of Consumer Research*, **33**, 537–547.

Vohs, K.D. and Heatherton, T.F. (2000) Self-regulatory failure: a resource-depletion approach. *Psychological Science*, **11**, 249–254.

Zhang, Y., Fishbach, A., and Kruglanski, A.W. (2007) The dilution model: how additional goals undermine the perceived instrumentality of a shared path. *Journal of Personality and Social Psychology*, **92**, 389–401.

social class

David K. Crockett

WHAT IS SOCIAL CLASS?

Although no single precise definition exists, most scholars acknowledge that social class is composed of a variety of factors such as wealth (especially inherited wealth), income, occupational status, educational attainment, and residence. Arnould, Price, and Zinkhan (2002, p. 181) provide a useful working definition: *social classes are groupings across society, broadly recognized by members of that society, involving inequalities, or certainly, differences in such areas as power, authority, wealth, income, prestige, working conditions, lifestyles, and culture.* Social class is by nature hierarchical, that is, groups and individuals receive unequal amounts of power, prestige, and esteem (i.e., status). Social class is pervasive, if often invisible. The mere mention of it may invite feelings of superiority among members of the elite, or feelings of uneasiness among those at the bottom of the status hierarchy.

One important component of social class is income. In fact many people think income is synonymous with class. However, even though income largely determines lifestyle at any given point in time it is a poor indicator of social class. In much of the developing world, accurate income data is difficult to obtain, and in developed nations income can fluctuate wildly over the life course (Leonhardt, 2005). Hence, instead of income many organizations and institutions use *purchasing power parities* to make cross-national comparisons where costs of living and currency values can be quite different.[1]

HOW DOES SOCIAL CLASS IMPACT CONSUMER BEHAVIOR?

Scholars have historically sought one-to-one relationships between income (usually indexed with education and occupation) and consumption, where high status consumers purchase brand X while lower status consumers purchase comparably more brand Y. In contemporary consumer culture however, the lowest and highest status consumers often choose the same products (Schor, 1998). Consequently, the old economic approaches are giving way to cultural approaches that generate insights about social class and consumption by focusing on *how* people consume rather than *what* they consume (Holt, 1998). People consume their way up the social class hierarchy by utilizing three types of status-generating resources: economic capital, social capital, and cultural capital (Bourdieu, 1984). Cultural approaches emphasize social and cultural capital (while economic approaches emphasize only economic capital). Social capital refers to membership in formal and informal reference groups. Cultural capital refers to skills, knowledge, tastes, and preferences derived indirectly from family background, class heritage, and common experience. Higher status comes from consuming in ways that signal a person's store of social and cultural capital relative to others.

WHAT ARE THE SOCIAL CLASS SEGMENTS?

The particular distribution of individuals into social class groupings varies widely from country to country. Most countries feature at least three segments (upper, middle, and working class), with the most fully formed class structures in the developed world. The upper class can include upper-upper and lower-upper subsegments. The former is usually characterized by inherited wealth, while the latter is often characterized by "nouveau riches" (or new money). Many, if not most consumption trends are

indexed to the tastes of these two subsegments (Schor, 1998). The upper middle class, despite lower stores of economic capital than the upper class, is typically more similar to the upper classes than to other members of the middle class in aspirational lifestyles, culture, and values. The remainder of the middle class is the primary target of most marketing efforts aimed directly at consumers. The majority of the world's people, however, belong to the working class or the chronically poor. Working-class consumers are difficult to characterize globally, other than by their very limited economic resources. In developed nations, they are thought to basically enjoy the core features of their current lifestyles and have little incentive to fundamentally alter them (other than to have more resources). Finally, the chronically poor or underclass largely lack access to most basic consumer choices. World Bank researchers estimate that one-quarter of the developing world fits in this group, living on less than $1.25 per day in 2005 prices (Chen and Ravaillion, 2008).

ENDNOTES

[1] The World Bank estimates purchasing power parities between countries (where data is available) and publishes the data at its website: http://web.worldbank.org/WBSITE/EXTERNAL/DATASTATISTICS/ICPEXT/0,,pagePK:62002243~theSitePK:270065,00.html

See also *consumer acculturation; consumer behavior across literacy and resource barriers; consumer materialism; consumer well-being; global consumerism and consumption; social class; social influence; social networks; society, culture, and global consumer culture; subcultures*

Bibliography

Arnould, E.J., Price, L.L. and Zinkhan, G. (2002) *Consumers*, McGraw Hill, New York.

Bourdieu, P. (1984) *Distinction: A Social Critique of the Judgment of Taste*, Harvard University Press, Cambridge, MA.

Chen, S. and Ravaillion, M. (2008) The Developing World Is Poorer Than We Thought, But No Less Successful in the Fight against Poverty, *Policy Research Paper #4703*, World Bank Development

Research Group, http: //econ. worldbank. org/ external/default/main?pagePK=64165259&theSite PK=469372&piPK=64165421&menuPK=64166093 &entityID=000158349_20080826113239] (accessed 31 May 2009).

Holt, D.B. (1998) Does cultural capital structure american consumption? *Journal of Consumer Research*, 25 (1), 1–25.

Leonhardt, D. (2005) A closer look at income immobility. (May 14) *New York Times* (online), http://www. nytimes.com/2005/05/14/national/class/15MOBI LITY-WEB.html?_r=1] (accessed 31 May 2009).

Schor, J.B. (1998) *The Overspent American: Upscaling, Downshifting, and the New Consumer*, Basic Books, New York.

social influence

Vladas Griskevicius and Robert B. Cialdini

Social influence involves the changing of a person's attitude or behavior through the doings of another person. Here we focus on the realm of consumer behavior and on the factors that cause one individual to comply with another's request. The starting point in ascertaining what are the most successful influence strategies was an investigation of the techniques that are most successful in professions dependent on their ability to induce compliance (e.g., salespeople, fund-raisers, advertisers, political lobbyists, cult recruiters, negotiators, and con artists). What emerged from this period of systematic observation was a list of six principles on which compliance professionals appeared to base most of their influence attempts: (i) *reciprocity* – repaying a gift, favor, or service; (ii) *consistency* – acting consistently with prior commitments; (iii) *social validation* – following the lead of similar others; (iv) *liking* – accommodating the requests of those we know and like; (v) *authority* – conforming to the directives of legitimate authorities; and (vi) *scarcity* – seizing opportunities that are scarce or dwindling in availability. A full account of the origins, workings, prevalence, and scientific evidence of these six principles is available elsewhere (Cialdini, 2009; Cialdini and Goldstein, 2004; see also Goldstein, Martin, and Cialdini, 2008). Here we provide a summary of the principles and the scientific evidence regarding how each principle functions to influence consumer behavior.

RECIPROCITY

Pay every debt as if God wrote the bill.
(Ralph Waldo Emerson)

One of the most powerful norms in all human cultures is that for reciprocity, which obligates individuals to return the form of behavior that they have received from another. For instance, we report liking those who report liking us; we cooperate with cooperators and compete against competitors; we self-disclose to those who have self-disclosed to us; we yield to the persuasive appeals of those who have previously yielded to one of our persuasive appeals; we try to harm those who have tried to harm us; and in negotiations, we make concessions to those who have offered concessions to us.

A *reciprocation rule* for compliance can be worded as follows: *One should be more willing to comply with a request from someone who has previously provided a favor or concession.* Under this general rule, people will feel obligated to provide gifts, favors, services, and aid to those who have given them such things first, sometimes even returning larger favors than those they have received. For example, restaurant servers who give two candies to guests along with the check increase their tips by 14.1%. A number of sales and fund-raising tactics also use this factor to advantage: the compliance professional initially gives something to the target person (e.g., a free sample), thereby causing the target to be more likely to give something in return. Often, this "something in return" is the target person's compliance with a substantial request.

The unsolicited gift, accompanied by a request for a donation, is a commonly used technique that employs the norm for reciprocity. One example is organizations sending free gifts through the mail. Including an unsolicited gift such as an individualized address labels can nearly double response rates. People often feel obligated to reciprocate even the smallest of gifts. For example, one study showed that people were more than twice as likely to fill out a lengthy survey when the request asking to complete the survey was accompanied by a handwritten Post-It note. Although such a note does not constitute a sizable gift, participants in the study recognized the extra effort and personal touch that this gesture required, and they felt obligated to reciprocate by agreeing to the request. Indeed, those who filled out the survey when it came with a handwritten sticky note returned it more promptly and gave more detailed answers.

A crucial aspect of successful reciprocity-based influence techniques involves activating the sense of obligation. The creation of obligation necessitates that the individual who desires to influence another needs to be the first to provide a gift or favor. It is noteworthy that this important aspect of reciprocity-based influence techniques is often misemployed. For example, numerous commercial organizations offer donations to charity in return for the purchase of products or services – a general strategy falling under the rubric of "cause-related marketing." Yet such tit-for-tat appeals often fail to engage reciprocity properly because influence agents do not provide benefits first and then allow recipients to return the favor. The suboptimal nature of such messages can be clearly seen in the results of an experiment in hotels, in which messages that urged guests to reuse their towels were varied systematically. Messages that promised a donation to an environmental cause if guests first reused their towels were no more effective than standard pro-environmental messages. Consistent with the obligating force of reciprocity, however, a message informing guests that the hotel had already donated increased towel reuse by 26%.

Reciprocal concessions. A variation of the norm for reciprocation of favors is that for reciprocation of concessions (also called the *door-in-the-face technique*). A requester uses this procedure by beginning with an extreme request that is nearly always rejected and then retreating to a more moderate favor – the one the requester had in mind from the outset. In doing so, the requester hopes that the retreat from extreme to moderate request will spur the target person to make a reciprocal concession by moving from initial rejection of the larger favor to acceptance of the smaller one. This reciprocal concessions strategy has been successfully used in fund-raising contexts where, after refusing a larger request for donations, people become substantially more likely than before to give the average contribution. This technique has also been used effectively to solicit blood donors, whereby potential donors were first asked about participating in long-term donor program. When that request was refused, the solicitor made a smaller request for a one-time donation. This pattern of a large request (that is refused) followed by a smaller request significantly increased compliance with the smaller request, as compared to a control condition of people who were asked only to perform the smaller one-time favor (50 vs 32% compliance rate).

Related to the door-in-the-face technique is the *that's-not-all technique*, which is frequently used by sales operators. An important procedural difference between the two techniques is that, in the that's-not-all tactic, the target person does not turn down the first offer before a better second offer is provided. After making the first offer but before the target can respond, the requester betters the deal with an additional item or a price reduction. This approach has been found to be useful in selling more goods during a bake sale. One reason that this technique works appears to be the target person's desire to reciprocate for the better deal.

SOCIAL VALIDATION

If you can keep your head when people all around you are losing theirs, you probably haven't grasped the situation
(Jean Kerr)

People frequently decide on appropriate behaviors for themselves in a given situation by searching for information as to how similar others have behaved or are behaving. This simple principle of behavior accounts for an amazingly varied army of human responses. For instance, research has shown that New Yorkers use it in deciding whether to return a lost wallet, hotel guests use it when deciding whether to reuse their towels, children with a fear of dogs use it in deciding whether to risk approaching a dog, amusement park visitors use it to decide whether to litter in a public place, audience members use it in deciding whether a joke is funny, National Park visitors use it when deciding whether to commit theft, pedestrians use it in deciding whether to stop and stare at an empty spot in the sky, and, on the alarming side, troubled individuals use it in deciding whether to commit suicide.

The *social validation rule* for compliance can be stated as follows: *One should be more willing to comply with a request for behavior if it is consistent with what similar others are thinking or doing.* Our tendency to assume that an action is more correct if others are doing it is exploited in a variety of settings. Bartenders often "salt" their tip jars with a few dollar bills at the beginning of the evening to simulate tips left by prior customers and, thereby, to give the impression that tipping with folded money is proper barroom behavior. Church ushers sometimes prime collection baskets for the same reason and with the same positive effect on proceeds. Advertisers love to inform us when a product is the "fastest growing" or "largest selling" because they do not have to convince us directly that the product is good; they need only say that many others think so, which seems proof enough. The producers of charity telethons devote inordinate amounts of time to the incessant listing of viewers who have already pledged contributions. The message being communicated to the holdouts is clear: "Look at all the people who have decided to give; it *must* be the correct thing to do."

Social validation techniques are most likely to be effective in situations that are objectively unclear, and when there are indications of multiple similar others engaging in the particular behavior. For example, research shows that people are strongly influenced by the behavior of others when deciding whether to conserve energy in their homes. However, the influence of others' conservation behaviors increased as those others become more similar to the actual home resident: whereas other citizens of the state have an effect on conservation, behavior was more strongly influenced by the residents of the same city, and even more strongly influenced by the residents of their own neighborhood. Thus, when people are unsure, they are most likely to look to and accept the beliefs and behaviors of

similar others as valid indicators of what they should believe and do themselves.

One tactic that compliance professionals use to engage the principle of social validation is called the *list technique*. This technique involves asking for a request only after the target person has been shown a list of similar others who have already complied. Studies show that when people are asked to donate money to charitable cause, those individuals who were initially shown a list of similar others who had already complied were significantly more likely to comply themselves. What's more, the longer the list, the greater was the effect.

CONSISTENCY

It is easier to resist at the beginning than at the end
(Leonardo Da Vinci)

Psychologists have long understood the strength of the consistency principle to direct human action. If we grant that the power of consistency is formidable in directing human action, an important practical question immediately arises: How is that force engaged? Psychologists think they know the answer – commitment. If a person can get you to make a commitment (that is, to take a stand, to go on record), that person will have set the stage for your consistency with that earlier commitment. Once a stand is taken, there is a natural tendency to behave in ways that are stubbornly consistent with the stand.

A *consistency rule* for compliance can be worded as follows: *after committing oneself to a position, one should be more willing to comply with requests for behaviors that are consistent with that position.* Any of a variety of strategies may be used to generate the crucial instigating commitment. One such strategy is the *foot-in-the-door technique*. A solicitor using this procedure will first ask for a small favor that is virtually certain to be granted. The initial compliance is then followed by a request for a larger, *related* favor. It has been found repeatedly that people who have agreed to the initial small favor are more willing to do the larger one, seemingly to be consistent with the implication of the initial action. For instance, home owners who had agreed to accept and wear a small lapel pin promoting a local charity were, as a consequence, more likely to contribute money to that charity when canvassed during a subsequent donation drive.

The foot-in-the-door technique is successful because performance of the initially requested action causes individuals to see themselves as possessing certain traits. For example, after taking and wearing the charity pin, subjects begin to see themselves as favorable toward charitable causes. Later, when asked to perform the larger, related favor of contributing to that charity, subjects would be more willing to do so to be consistent with the "charitable" trait they had assigned to themselves.

Other, more unsavory techniques induce a commitment to an item and then remove the inducements that generated the commitment. Remarkably, the commitment frequently remains. For example, the *bait and switch procedure* is used by some retailers who may advertise certain merchandise (e.g., a room of furniture) at a special low price. When the customer arrives to take advantage of the special, he or she finds the merchandise to be of low quality or sold out. However, because customers have by now made an active commitment to getting new furniture at that particular store, they are more willing to agree to examine and, consequently, to buy alternative merchandise there.

A similar strategy is often employed by car dealers in the *low-ball technique*, which proceeds by obtaining a commitment to an action and *then* increasing the costs of performing the action. The automobile salesperson who "throws the low ball" induces the customer to decide to buy a particular model car by offering a low price on the car or an inflated one on the customer's trade-in. After the decision has been made (and, at times, after the commitment is enhanced by allowing the customer to arrange financing, take the car home overnight, etc.), something happens to remove the reason the customer decided to buy. Perhaps a price calculation error is found, or the used car assessor disallows the inflated trade-in figure. By this time, though, many customers have experienced an internal commitment to

that specific automobile and proceed with the purchase.

Another approach to employing the consistency principle also has gained popularity among commercial compliance professionals. Rather than inducing a new commitment to their product or service, many practitioners point out existing commitments within potential customers that are consistent with the product or service being offered – a tactic called the *labeling technique*. In this way, desirable existing commitments are made more visible to the customer, and the strain for consistency is allowed to direct behavior accordingly. For example, insurance agents are frequently taught to stress to new home owners that the purchase of an expensive house reflects an enormous personal commitment to one's home and the well-being of one's family. Consequently, they argue it would only be consistent with such a commitment to home and family to purchase home and life insurance in amounts that befit the size of this commitment. Research of various kinds indicates that this sort of sensitization to commitments and to consequent inconsistencies can be effective in producing belief, attitude, and behavior change.

A more manipulative tactic than merely focusing people on their existing values is to put them in a situation where to refuse a specific request would be inconsistent with a value that people wish to be known as possessing. One such tactic is the *legitimization-of-paltry favors* (or even-a-penny-would-help) *technique*. Most people prefer to behave in ways that are consistent with a view of themselves as helpful, charitable individuals. Consequently, a fund-raiser who makes a request that legitimizes a paltry amount of aid ("could you give a contribution, even a penny would help") makes it difficult for a target to refuse to give at all; by doing so he/she risks appearing to be a very unhelpful person. Notice that this procedure does not specifically request a trivial sum; that would probably lead to a profusion of pennies and a small total take. Instead, the request simply makes a minuscule form of aid acceptable, thereby reducing the target's ability to give nothing and still remain consistent with the desirable image of a helpful individual. After all, how could a person remain committed to a helpful image after refusing to contribute when "even a penny would help"?

LIKING

The main work of a trial attorney is to make the jury like his client
   (Clarence Darrow)

A fact of social interaction that each of us can attest to is that people are more favorably inclined toward the needs of those they know and like. Consequently, a *liking rule* for compliance can be worded as follows: *One should be more willing to comply with the requests of liked individuals.* Could there be any doubt that this is the case after examining the remarkable success of the Tupperware Corporation and their "home party" demonstration concept? The demonstration party for Tupperware products is hosted by an individual, usually a woman, who invites to her home an array of friends, neighbors, and relatives, all of whom know that their hostess receives a percentage of the profits from every piece sold by the Tupperware representative, who is also there. In this way, the Tupperware Corporation arranges for its customers to buy from and *for* a friend rather than from an unknown salesperson. So favorable has been the effect on proceeds ($3 million in sales per day) that the Tupperware Corporation has wholly abandoned its early retail outlets, and a Tupperware party begins somewhere every 2.7 seconds. Indeed, the success of this strategy has inspired many companies to use parties to sell their products, including cosmetics, arts-and-crafts, and even video games. Most influence agents, however, attempt to engage the liking principle in a different way: before asking a request, they get their targets to like *them*. But how do they do it? It turns out that the tactics that practitioners use to generate liking cluster around certain factors that have been shown by controlled research to increase liking.

Physical Attractiveness. Although it is generally acknowledged that good-looking people have an advantage in social interaction, research findings indicate that we may have sorely underestimated the size and reach of that advantage. There appears to be a positive reaction to good

physical appearance that generalizes to such favorable trait perceptions as a talent, kindness, honesty, and intelligence. As a consequence, attractive individuals are more persuasive in terms of both changing attitudes and getting what they request. For instance, a study of Canadian Federal elections found that attractive candidates received more than two-and-a-half times the votes of unattractive ones. Equally impressive results seem to pertain to the judicial system. In a Pennsylvania study, for example, researchers rated the physical attractiveness of 74 separate male defendants at the start of their criminal trials. When, much later, the researchers checked the results of these cases via court records, they found that the better-looking men received significantly lighter sentences. In fact, the attractive defendants were twice as likely to avoid incarceration as the unattractive defendants. When viewed in the light of such powerful effects, it is not surprising that extremely attractive models are employed to promote products and services, that sales trainers frequently include appearance and grooming tips in their lessons, or that, commonly, con men are handsome and con women pretty.

Similarity. We like people who are similar to us. This fact seems to hold true whether the similarity occurs in the area of opinions, personality traits, background, or lifestyle. Not only has research demonstrated that even trivial similarities can increase liking and have profound effects on important decisions such as careers and marriage partners but also perceived attitude similarity between oneself and a stranger can automatically activate thoughts of kinship, inducing a person to behave prosocially toward that similar other. Consequently, those who wish to be liked in order to increase our compliance can accomplish that purpose by appearing similar to us in any of a wide variety of ways. For that reason, it would be wise to be careful around salespeople who just *seem* to be just like us. Many sales training programs urge trainees to "mirror and match" the customer's body posture, mood, and verbal style, as similarities along each of these dimensions have been shown to lead to positive results. Similarity in dress provides still another example. Several studies have demonstrated that we are more likely to help those who dress like us. In one study, done in the early 1970s when young people tended to dress either in "hippie" or "straight" fashion, experimenters donned hippie or straight attire and asked college students on campus for a dime to make a phone call. When the experimenter was dressed in the same way as the student, the request was granted in over two-thirds of the instances; but when the student and requester were dissimilarly dressed, a dime was provided less than half of the time. Another experiment shows how automatic our positive response to similar others can be. Marchers in a political demonstration were found not only to be more likely to sign the petition of a similarly dressed requester but also to do so without bothering to read it first.

Compliments. Praise and other forms of positive estimation also stimulate liking. Actor Maclain Stevenson once described how his wife tricked him into marriage: "She said she liked me." Although designed for a laugh, the remark is as much instructive as it is humorous. The simple information that someone fancies us can be a bewitchingly effective device for producing return liking and willing compliance. Although there are limits to our gullibility – especially when we can be sure that the flatterer's intent is manipulative – as a rule we tend to believe praise and to like those who provide it. Evidence for the power of praise on liking comes from a study in which men received personal comments from someone who needed a favor from them. Some of the men got only positive comments, some only negative comments, and some got a mixture of good and bad. There were three interesting findings. First, the evaluator who offered only praise was liked the best. Second, this was so even though the men fully realized that the flatterer stood to gain from their liking of him. Finally, unlike the other types of comments, pure praise did not have to be accurate to work. Compliments produced just as much liking for the flatterer when they were untrue as when they were true. It is for such reasons that salespeople are educated in the art of praise. A potential customer's home, clothes, car, taste, and so on, are all frequent targets for compliments.

Cooperation. Cooperation is another factor that has been shown to enhance positive feelings and behavior. Those who cooperate toward the achievement of a common goal are more favorable and helpful to each other as a consequence. That is why compliance professionals often strive to be perceived as cooperating partners of a target person. Automobile sales managers frequently set themselves as "villains" so that the salesperson can "do battle" on the customer's behalf. The cooperative, pulling together kind of relationship that is consequently produced between the salesperson and customer, naturally leads to a desirable form of liking that promotes sales.

SCARCITY

The way to love anything is to realize that it might be lost
(Gilbert Keith Chesterton)

Opportunities seem more valuable to us when they are less available. Interestingly, this is often true even when the opportunity holds little attraction for us on its own merits. Take, as evidence, the experience of Florida State University students who, like most undergraduates, rated themselves dissatisfied with the quality of their cafeteria's food. Nine days later, they had changed their minds, rating that food as significantly better than they had before. It is instructive that no actual improvement in food service had occurred between the two ratings. Instead, earlier on the day of the second rating students had learned that, because of a fire, they could not eat at the cafeteria for two weeks.

A *scarcity rule* for compliance can be worded as follows: *One should try to secure those opportunities that are scarce or dwindling.* With scarcity operating powerfully on the worth assigned to things, it should not be surprising that compliance professionals have a variety of techniques designed to convert this power to compliance. Probably the most frequently used such technique is the "limited number" tactic in which the customer is informed that membership opportunities, products, or services exist in a limited supply that cannot be guaranteed to last for long.

Related to the limited number tactic is the "deadline" technique in which an official time limit is placed on the customer's opportunity to get what is being offered. Newspaper ads abound with admonitions to the customer regarding the folly of delay: "Last three days." "Limited time offer." "One week only sale." The purest form of a decision deadline – right now – occurs in a variant of the deadline technique in which customers are told that, unless they make an immediate purchase decision, they will have to buy the item at a higher price, or they will not be able to purchase it at all. This tactic is used in numerous compliance settings. For example, a large child photography company urges parents to buy as many poses and copies as they can afford because "stocking limitations force us to burn the unsold pictures of your children within 24 hours." A prospective health club member or automobile buyer might learn that the deal offered by the salesperson is good for that one time; should the customer leave the premises, the deal is off. One home vacuum cleaner sales company instructs its trainees to claim to prospects that "I have so many other people to see that I have the time to visit a family only once. It's company policy that even if you decide later that you want this machine, I can't come back and sell it to you." For anyone who thinks about it carefully, this is nonsense: The company and its representatives are in the business of making sales, and any customer who called for another visit would be accommodated gladly. The real purpose of the can't-come-back-again claim is to evoke the possibility of loss that is inherent in the scarcity rule for compliance.

The idea of potential loss plays a large role in human decision making. In fact, people are generally more motivated by the thought of losing something than by the thought of gaining something of equal value. For instance, home owners told about how much money they could lose from inadequate insulation are more likely to insulate their homes than those told about how much money they could save. Similar results have been obtained on college campuses where students experienced much stronger emotions when asked to imagine losses rather than gains in their romantic relationships or grade point averages.

One naturally occurring example of the consequences of increased scarcity can be seen in the outcome of a decision by county officials in Miami to ban the use and possession of phosphate detergents. Spurred by the tendency to want what they could no longer have, the majority of Miami consumers came to see phosphate cleaners as better products than before. Compared to Tampa residents, who were not affected by the Miami ordinance, the citizens of Miami rated phosphate detergents as gentler, more effective in cold water, better whiteners and fresheners, and more powerful on stains. After passage of the law, they had even come to believe that phosphate detergents poured easier than did the Tampa consumers.

Other research has suggested that in addition to commodities, limited access to information makes the information more desirable and more influential. For example, wholesale beef buyers who were told of an impending imported beef shortage purchased significantly more beef when they were informed that the shortage information came from certain "exclusive" contacts that the importer had. Apparently, the fact that the scarcity news was itself scarce made it more valued and persuasive.

AUTHORITY

Follow an expert
  (Virgil)

Legitimately constituted authorities are extremely influential persons. Whether they have acquired their positions through knowledge, talent, or fortune, their positions bespeak of superior information and power. For most people, conforming to the dictates of authority figures produces genuine practical advantages. Consequently, it makes great sense to comply with the wishes of properly constituted authorities. It makes so much sense, in fact, that people often do so when it makes no sense at all.

Take, for example, the strange case of the "rectal earache" reported by two professors of pharmacy. A physician ordered eardrops to be administered to the right ear of a patient suffering pain and infection there. But instead of writing out the location "right ear" on the prescription completely, the doctor abbreviated it so that the instructions read "place in R ear." Upon receiving the prescription, the duty nurse promptly put the required number of eardrops into the patient's anus. Obviously, rectal treatment of an earache made no sense. Yet, neither the patient nor the nurse questioned it.

An *authority rule* for compliance can be worded as follows: *One should be more willing to follow the suggestions of someone who is a legitimate authority*. Authorities may be seen as falling into two categories: authorities with regard to the specific situation and more general authorities. Compliance practitioners employ techniques that seek to benefit from the power invested in authority figures of both types. In the case of authority relevant to a specific situation, we can note how often advertisers inform their audiences of the level of expertise of product manufacturers (e.g., "Fashionable men's clothiers since 1841"; "Babies are our business, our only business"). At times, the expertise associated with a product has been more symbolic than substantive, for instance, when actors in television commercials wear physicians' white coats to recommend a product. In one famous coffee commercial, the actor involved, Robert Young, did not need a white coat, as his prior identity as TV doctor Marcus Welby, MD, provided the medical connection. It is instructive that the mere symbols of a physician's expertise and authority are enough to trip the mechanism that governs authority influence. One of the most prominent of these symbols, the bare title "Dr.," has been shown to be devastatingly effective as a compliance device among trained hospital personnel. In what may be the most frightening study we know, a group of physicians and nurses conducted an experiment that documented the dangerous degree of blind obedience that hospital nurses accorded to an individual whom they had never met, but who claimed in a phone call to be a doctor. Ninety-five percent of those nurses were willing to administer an unsafe level of a drug merely because that caller requested it.

In the case of influence that generalizes outside of relevant expertise, the impact of authority (real and symbolic) appears equally impressive.

For instance, researchers have found that, when wearing a security guard's uniform, a requester could produce more compliance with requests (e.g., to pick up a paper bag in the street, to stand on the other side of a Bus Stop sign) that were irrelevant to a security guard's domain of authority. Less blatant in its connotation than a uniform, but nonetheless effective, is another kind of attire that has traditionally bespoken of authority status in our culture – the well-tailored business suit. One study found that three-and-a-half times as many people were willing to follow a jaywalker into traffic when he wore a suit and tie versus a work shirt and trousers.

SUMMARY

An important question for anyone interested in understanding resisting or harnessing the process of influence is, "which are the most powerful principles that motivate us to comply with another's request?" We suggested that one way to assess such power would be to examine the practices of commercial compliance professionals for their pervasiveness. In other words, if compliance practitioners made widespread use of certain principles, this would be evidence for the natural power of these principles to affect everyday compliance in the realm of consumer behavior. Six principles emerged as the most popular in the repertoires of the most effective compliance pros: reciprocity, social validation, consistency, liking, scarcity, and authority. Close examination of the principles revealed broad professional usage that could be validated and explained by scientific research, indicating that these six principles engage central features of the human condition in the process of motivating compliance.

Bibliography

Cialdini, R.B. (2009) *Influence: Science and Practice*, 5th edn, Allyn & Bacon, Boston.
Cialdini, R.B. and Goldstein, N.J. (2004) Social influence: compliance and conformity. *Annual Review of Psychology*, 55, 591–621.
Goldstein, N.J., Martin, S., and Cialdini, R.B. (2008) *Yes! 50 Scientifically Proven Ways to be Persuasive*, Free Press.

social networks

Jacob Goldenberg

A *social network* is usually defined as a graph of nodes, or actors, (e.g., in a marketing context, actors are individual consumers, families, or business entities) that are linked to each other in a meaningful way (e.g., through information exchange or friendship, in the case of individuals, or through trade or collaboration in the case of business entities). These networks are often complex, and social networks can be extremely large in marketing.

It is beyond the scope of this article to note all the works in this field. Several key terms are defined in the box.

In the last two decades, our understanding of social network properties has advanced significantly, and networks have become one of the most attractive fields of research for scholars of almost all social science disciplines, including computer sciences (computer-based networks), biology (e.g., networks of genes), physics, and chemistry. One of the most interesting features of network research is that researchers from diverse fields typically work on similar problems, use similar definitions, and they obtain consistent results concerning networks dynamics (as a result, a typical network paper includes references from multiple fields). Some examples of well-known network properties found to be common to many networks (briefly defined in the box) include a *high clustering coefficient* (Watts, 1999), *short distances or paths* (see Newman, 2001; Watts and Strogatz, 1998), a *scale-free degree distribution* (Albert and Barabasi, 2002; Amaral *et al.*, 2000; Barabási and Albert, 1999; Jeong *et al.*, 2000), and a common *betweenness centrality distribution* (Chen *et al.*, 2007; Kitsak *et al.*, 2007).

Social network literature can be classified into two research themes: (i) network formation (see among many others: Albert and Barabasi, 2002; Barabási and Albert, 1999; Davidsen, Ebel, and Bornholdt, 2002; Deroian, 2006; Kryssanov *et al.*, 2008; Kryssanov *et al.*, 2006; Watts, 1999; Zhang and Liu, 2006; Zhou and Mondragon, 2004) and (ii) information dissemination over networks and network connectivity (see among others: Brown, 1981; Goldenberg, Libai, and Muller, 2001; Goldenberg *et al.*, 2005; Kocsis and Kun, 2008; Rogers, Ascroft, and Rolling, 1970; Valente, 1995; Young, 2006).

In the first research stream, recent efforts have been applied to understand how network structures and properties emerge, and to identify the local rules of behavior that generate the formation of these structures. One topic of study in this stream is scale-free emergence. Barabási and Albert 1999 mapped the topology of a portion of the Web, and reported two findings: some nodes (termed *hubs*) had an exceptionally greater number of links than other nodes, and the number of links connecting to a single node followed a power-law distribution. After discovering that several other networks, including social and biological networks, typically had heavy-tailed degree distributions, they called this structure a *scale-free network*. Amaral *et al.* demonstrated that most real-world networks can be classified into two broad categories according to the slope of the distribution (usually plotted on a log–log scale). Barabási and Albert proposed the *preferential attachment* mechanism to explain the appearance of this power-law distribution. This mechanism (with many variations) essentially assumes that any new node joining the network has a higher probability to link to a node with a higher degree. Alternative mechanisms, such as transitivity (in which a friend of my friend is likely to become my friend), have also been since suggested.

Marketing literature is more strongly oriented to the second research stream (for a recommended review, see Van den Bulte and Wuyts, 2007), with a recent focus on information dissemination, accepted as the core process driving innovation adoption (see Godes *et al.*, 2005; Goldenberg *et al.*, 2005; Hogan, Lemon, and Libai, 2005; Rogers, 2003; Trusov, Bodapati, and Bucklin, 2008; Valente, 1995; Van den Bulte and Joshi, 2007; Van den Bulte and Wuyts, 2007; Watts and Dodds, 2007). For example, a special session on networks was held at a recent Marketing Science conference, to discuss networks and related issues such as network population sampling (Ebbes *et al.*, 2008), the role of spatial proximity in diffusion (Barrot *et al.*, 2008), the economic value of social interactions (Stephen and Toubia, 2010), and a study of pharmaceutical social networks (Iyengar, Valente, and van Den Bulte, 2008). Research has also empirically established the intuitive understanding that innovations propagate through peer recommendations and word of mouth, which are strongly dependent on the structure of the social network. Several additional interesting issues are presented briefly below.

THE STRENGTH OF WEAK TIES

Granovetter (1973) found that weak ties are sometimes more important than strong ties in information seeking and innovation dissemination. Strongly tied individuals form cliques that have a tendency to conformity. Owing to their fundamental similarity, any single clique member also knows more or less what the other members know. Therefore, to discover new information or gain new insights, clique members must look beyond the clique to other, more distant friends, and acquaintances. This weak-ties strength was found to have significant implications for consumer behavior issues.

SMALL WORLDS AND DEGREES OF SEPARATION

The scale-free structure is one explanation for evidence on the nature of the dissemination process and the role of high connectivity in this process: The hubs receive information first and spread it through the network. Another explanation is the small world structure and the high clustering coefficient (Watts and Strogatz, 1998).

The small world theory is based on the premise that any arbitrary pair of nodes in the network is linked by a genuinely short chain of individuals (nodes). The 1967 small world experiment by Milgram, 1967 gave rise to the famous phrase "six degrees of separation." In this experiment, a sample of individuals was asked to reach a specific target person by passing a message along a chain of acquaintances (all pairs were in the United States). Successful chains (which reached their destination) turned out to be approximately six steps long, which is remarkably short. Note, however, that this finding may be biased by the fact that the majority of chains in that study actually failed to complete. Despite claims of the experiment's

questionable methodology, it is widely accepted that a social network requires a small number of steps to connect all its members. A recent electronic small world experiment found that approximately five to seven degrees of separation are sufficient for connecting any two people through e-mail (Watts, 1999), although the majority of chains in this experiment were also not completed.

According to the small world model, most nodes are not neighbors of one another, but can be reached from any other node using only a small number of jumps. A small world network, where nodes represent people and edges (or links) that connect acquaintances, captures the phenomenon of strangers who become linked through a mutual acquaintance. Watts and Strogatz (1998) noted that networks can be classified according to two independent structural features: the clustering coefficient and shortest path (distance). Random networks, for example, exhibit a small shortest pathlength and a small clustering coefficient. Indeed, many real-world networks not only have a small average shortest pathlength but also a clustering coefficient significantly higher than expected by random chance. This alone explains the rapid dissemination of information that occurs over a network.

THE ROLE OF KEY INDIVIDUALS

Research suggesting that a relatively small number of people have substantial influence on the opinions and decisions of the majority can be traced back at least 50 years to the seminal work by Katz and Lazarsfeld (1955). Broadly speaking, influential people are thought to have three important traits: (i) they are persuasive (perhaps even charismatic); (ii) they know a lot (i.e., are experts); and (iii) they have large number of social ties, i.e., they know a lot of people.

Hyper-influential individuals (also known as *opinion leaders*, *mavens*, or *hubs*) are one class of consumers that has always attracted the attention of researchers and practitioners. Extensive studies of the behavior of agents in social systems have been conducted at the social and psychological level (Reingen and Kernan, 1986). While different terms for these agents are typically used interchangeably, the constructs are not identical. Opinion leaders and mavens (Coulter, Larence, and Price, 2002; Feick and Price, 1987) are thought to have expertise in their area of influence, while hubs are individuals whose distinctive feature is their large number of social ties.

The literature on opinion leaders is relatively broad and opinion leaders have been studied in a variety of areas including marketing, public opinion, health care, communication, education, agriculture, and epidemiology. Until recently, researchers have broadly concurred that opinion leaders can have a major impact on opinion formation and change, and that a small group of influential opinion leaders may accelerate or block the adoption of a product in an entire market. Since 2008, this point has triggered heated debate. Some argue that influentials (or more precisely, individuals who represent nodes with an exceptionally large degree) have only a marginal influence on adoption speed (e.g., Watts and Dodds, 2007), yet according to counterarguments, influentials adopt sooner than other people. This occurs not because they are innovative but rather because influentials are exposed earlier to an innovation due to their numerous social links (e.g., Goldenberg *et al.*, 2009). As a result, highly connected individuals have a significant impact on the overall adoption speed of an innovation and in some cases even on the ultimate market size.

Social network metrics

Betweenness: Betweenness reflects the extent to which a node connects other pairs of nodes in the network (through the shortest path).

Centrality: Centrality reflects the social "power" of a node, based on how well it connects the network. The more common centrality measures are *degree*, *betweenness*, and *closeness*.

Closeness: Closeness reflects the proximity of all other individuals in a network (directly or indirectly) to the node. Closeness is the inverse of the sum of the shortest distances between each node and every other node in the network.

Clustering coefficient: The clustering coefficient measures the likelihood that two acquaintances of a node are acquaintances themselves: if A knows both B and C, a high coefficient in this network implies that the probability that B knows C is high.

Degree: The degree is the number of ties connected to each node.

Density: Network density is the proportion of ties in a network relative to the total number of possible ties.

Pathlength: Pathlength is the distance between pairs of nodes in the network.

Scale-free network: Scale-free networks have a degree distribution that is easy to view as a power law: $n(\text{degree} = x) = -ax^y$.

Structural cohesion: Structural cohesion is measured by the minimum number of nodes required to dismantle a group of nodes.

Structural equivalence: Structural equivalence is the extent to which nodes share a common set of ties.

Bibliography

Albert, R. and Barabasi, A.L. (2002) Statistical mechanics of complex networks, *Reviews of Modern Physics*, **74** (1), 47–97.

Amaral, L.A.N., Scala, A., Barthélémy, M., and Stanley, H.E. (2000) Classes of small-world networks, *Proceedings of the National Academy of Sciences of the United States of America*, **97** (21), 11149–11152.

Barabási, A.L. and Albert, R. (1999) Emergence of scaling in random networks,. *Science*, **286** (5439), 509–512.

Barrot, C., Rangaswamy, A., Albers, S., and Shaikh, N.I. (2008) The Role of Spatial Proximity in the Adoption of a Digital Product, Working Paper.

Brown, L.A. (1981) *Innovation Diffusion: A New Perspective*, Methuen, London and New York.

Chen, Y.P., Paul, G., Cohen, R. *et al.* (2007) Percolation theory applied to measures of fragmentation in social networks. *Physical Review E*, **75** (4), 1–7.

Coulter, R.A., Larence, F.F., and Price, L.L. (2002) Changing faces: cosmetics opinion leadership among women in the new Hungary. *European Journal of Marketing*, **36** (11), 1287–1308.

Davidsen, J., Ebel, H., and Bornholdt, S. (2002) Emergence of a small world from local interactions: modeling acquaintance networks. *Physical Review Letters*, **88** (12), 1–4.

Deroïan, F. (2006) Formation of a communication network under perfect foresight. *Theory and Decision*, **61** (3), 191–204.

Ebbes, P., Zan, H., Rangaswamy, A., and Thadakamall, H.P. (2008) Sampling Large-Scale Social Networks: The Good, the Bad, and the Ugly, Working Paper.

Feick, L.F. and Price, L.L. (1987) The market maven: a diffuser of marketplace information. *Journal of Marketing*, **51** (1), 83–97.

Godes, D., Mayzlin, D., Chen, Y. *et al.* (2005) The firm's management of social interactions. *Marketing Letters*, **16** (3), 415–428.

Goldenberg, J., Libai, B., and Muller, E. (2001) Talk of the network: a complex systems look at the underlying process of word-of-mouth. *Marketing Letters*, **12** (3), 211–223.

Goldenberg, J., Shavitt, Y., Shir, E., and Solomon, S. (2005) Distributive immunization of networks against viruses using the 'Honey Pots' architecture. *Nature Physics*, **1**, 184–188.

Goldenberg, J., Sangman, H., Lehmann, D.R., and Weon-Hong, J.W. (2009) *The Role of Hubs in the Adoption Processes*, Hebrew university of Jerusalem, Jerusalem, Israel. working paper.

Granovetter, M.S. (1973) The strength of weak ties. *American Journal of Sociology*, **78** (6), 1360–1380.

Hogan, J.E., Lemon, K.N., and Libai, B. (2005) Quantifying the ripple: word-of-mouth and advertising effectiveness. *Journal of Advertising Research*, **44** (03), 271–280.

Iyengar, R., Valente, T., and van Den Bulte, C. (2008) *Opinion Leadership and Social Contagion in New Product Diffusion*, University of Pennsylvania. working paper

Jeong, H., Tombor, B., Albert, R., Oltvai, Z.N., and Barabasi, A.L. (2000) The large-scale organization of metabolic networks. *Nature*, **407** (6804), 651.

Katz, E. and Lazarsfeld, P.F. (1955) *Personal Influence; The Part Played by People in the Flow of Mass Communications. Glencoe, Ill*, Columbia University. Bureau of Applied Social, Research, Free Press.

Kitsak, M., Havlin, S., Paul, G. *et al.* (2007) Betweenness centrality of fractal and nonfractal scale-free model networks and tests on real networks. *Physical Review E*, **75** (5), 1–8.

Kocsis, G. and Kun, F. (2008) The effect of network topologies on the spreading of technological developments. *Journal of Statistical Mechanics-Theory and Experiment*, **P10014**, 1–13.

Kryssanov, V.V., Rinaldo, F.J., Kuleshov, E.L., and Ogawa, H. (2006) Modeling the Dynamics of Social Networks. *ICE-B*, 242–249.

Kryssanov, V.V., Rinaldo, F.J., Kuleshov, E.L., and Ogawa, H. (2008) A Hidden Variable Approach to Analyze "Hidden" Dynamics of Social Networks, in Why Context Matters.

Milgram, S. (1967) The small world problem. *Psychology today*, **2** (1), 60–67.

Newman, M.E.J. (2001) The structure and function of complex networks. *Structure*, **45** (2), 167–256.

Reingen, P.H. and Kernan, J.B. (1986) Analysis of referral networks in marketing: methods and illustration. *Journal of Marketing Research*, **23** (4), 370–378.

Rogers, E.M. (2003) *Attributes of Innovations and their Rate of Adoption and Innovativeness and Adopter Categories. Diffusion of Innovations*, Free Press, New York.

Rogers, E.M., Ascroft, J., and Rolling, N.G. (1970) *As Reported in Valente, Network Models of the Diffusion of Innovations*, Hampton Press, Cresskill.

Stephen, A.T. and Toubia, O. (2010) Deriving value from social commerce networks. *Journal of Marketing Research*, **47** (2), 215–228.

Trusov, M., Bodapati, A.V., and Bucklin, R.E. (2008) Determining Influential Users in Internet Social Networks, working paper.

Valente, T.W. (1995) *Network Models of the Diffusion of Innovations*, Hampton Press, Cresskill.

Van den Bulte, C. and Joshi, Y.V. (2007) New product diffusion with influentials and imitators. *Marketing Science*, **26** (3), 400–421.

Van den Bulte, C. and Wuyts, S. (2007) *Social Networks and Marketing*, Marketing Science Institute.

Watts, D.J. (1999) *Small Worlds: the Dynamics of Networks Between Order and Randomness*, Princeton University Press, Princeton.

Watts, D.J. and Dodds, P.S. (2007) Influentials, networks, and public opinion formation. *Journal of Consumer Research*, **34** (4), 441.

Watts, D.J. and Strogatz, S.H. (1998) Collective dynamics of 'small-world' networks. *Nature*, **393** (6684), 440–442.

Young, H.P. (2006) The Diffusion of Innovations in Social Networks, Economy as an Evolving Complex System, III, pp. 267–281

Zhang, S. and Liu, J. (2006) *From Local Behaviors to the Dynamics in an Agent Network*, Proceedings of the 2006 IEEE/WIC/ACM International Conference on Web Intelligence: IEEE Computer Society, Hong Kong, China, 572–580.

Zhou, S. and Mondragon, R.J. (2004) The rich-club phenomenon in the Internet topology. *IEEE Communications Letters*, **8** (3), 180–182.

subcultures

Robert V. Kozinets

Contemporary consumer culture is filled with a rich gallery of subcultural archetypes, including rappers, gangstas, punks, surfers, jocks, fanboys, goth girls, metalheads, Trekkers, and hackers. These subcultures provide meanings and practices that significantly structure consumers' identities, relationships, and behaviors in many ways. They offer up rich, meaningful, group identities that differentiate from, oppose, or even seek to subvert normal mainstream ways of speaking, thinking, and behaving. With their resistant, activist, symbolic characteristics, subcultures are closely related to counter-cultures and often serve as the source of countercultural images and identities. These images and identities are often absorbed by the advertising, entertainment, and marketing industries, and eventually become popularized and commonplace mainstream activities. Subcultures thus fuel the never-ending engine of differentiation that underlies contemporary consumer culture (Heath and Potter, 2004).

In consumer research or consumer cultural studies, subcultures have been related to sports and avocations, fantasy and escape, mass media fans, brand consumption, as well as gender and class (Belk and Costa, 1998; Celsi, Rose, and Leigh, 1993; Kozinets, 2001; Schouten and McAlexander, 1995). Different aspects of consumption-related subcultures have been emphasized by consumer researchers, including their mode of acculturation (Celsi, Rose, and Leigh, 1993), their self-selection and hierarchical, ethos-driven structure (Schouten and McAlexander, 1995), as well as their relationship to mass-mediated meanings and images, resistance, and activism, and online communities (Kozinets, 2001, 2002; Kozinets and Handelman, 2004).

John Schouten and Jim McAlexander (1995, p. 43) coined the useful term *subculture of consumption* to refer to and underscore the importance of these consumption-oriented groupings, defining the term as "a distinctive subgroup of society that self-selects on the basis of a shared commitment to a particular product class, brand, or consumption activity." They also summarized and suggested some key characteristics of these groups: their shared ethos, mythos, values, and beliefs; their social structure based on hierarchies of commitment and authenticity; their shared language and rituals; and the religious and transformational

aspects of the subcultures. However, linking consumer culture to the subcultures litera-ture (e.g., Hebdige, 1979) has drawn some criticism. Some argue that "the social groups investigated in the name of 'subcultures' are subordinate, subaltern or subterranean" or are "deviant," "debased," illegitimate or of lower socioeconomic status" (Thornton, 1997, p. 4) or that the term is ambiguous and negatively charged (Hannerz, 1992). A further critique holds that the term has been overextended to refer to a variety of different leisure activities and hobbies, rather than to actual ways of life or social forms. In response to these and related critiques in sociology and anthropology, a number of other conceptions, including "cultures of consumption" (Kozinets, 2001), "microcultures" (Hannerz, 1992), "brand communities" (Muniz and O'Guinn, 2001, *see* BRAND COMMUNITY), and "consumer tribes" (Cova, Kozinets, and Shankar, 2007) have been proposed and used.

Yet despite the ever-present ambiguities of the term, the concept of subcultures is still very useful to consumer researchers and others who are interested in understanding consumer behavior in its actual, lived sense. The term deals with an ambiguous, dynamic, and counter-cultural phenomenon with a long history, strong momentum, and deep ties to consumer culture. The underground connotations of the term *subculture*, its established links to foundational cultural studies literature, and its inherent flex-ibility will continue to inspire new generations of researchers for many years to come. As long as lifestyle, differentiation, self-transformation, and small group identities continue to play an important part of consumers' lives in contem-porary consumer culture, the concept of subcul-tures will help us to better understand the complex social world around us.

Bibliography

Belk, R.W. and Costa, J.A. (1998) The mountain man myth: a contemporary consuming fantasy. *Journal of Consumer Research*, **25**, 218–240.

Celsi, R.L., Rose, R.L., and Leigh, T.W. (1993) An explo-ration of high-risk consumption through skydiving. *Journal of Consumer Research*, **20**, 1–23.

Cova, B., Kozinets, R.V., and Shankar, A. (eds) (2007) *Consumer Tribes*. Butterworth-Heinemann, Oxford and Burlington.

Hannerz, U. (1992) *Cultural Complexity*, Columbia University, New York.

Heath, J. and Potter, A. (2004) *Nation of Rebels: Why Counterculture became Consumer Culture*, Harper Business, New York.

Hebdige, D. (1979) *Subculture*, Methuen, New York.

Kozinets, R.V. (2001) Utopian enterprise: articulating the meanings of Star Trek's culture of consumption. *Journal of Consumer Research*, **28**, 67–88.

Kozinets, R.V. (2002) The field behind the screen: using netnography for marketing research in online communities. *Journal of Marketing Research*, **39**, 61–72.

Kozinets, R.V. and Handelman, J.M. (2004) Adversaries of consumption: consumer movements, activism, and ideology. *Journal of Consumer Research*, **31**, 691–704.

Muñiz, A.M. Jr. and O'Guinn. T.C. (2001) Brand community. *Journal of Consumer Research*, **27**, 412–432.

Schouten, J.W. and McAlexander, J.H. (1995) Subcultures of consumption: an ethnography of the new bikers. *Journal of Consumer Research*, **22**, 43–61.

Thornton, S. (1997) General introduction, in *The Subcultures Reader* (eds K.Gelder and S., Thornton), Routledge, New York, pp. 1–7.

the role of schemas in consumer behavior research

Karen E. Flaherty and John C. Mowen

INTRODUCTION

Social and cognitive psychology researchers assume that because our information processing capabilities are limited, we develop abstract knowledge structures. One form of knowledge structure that has been extensively studied in both the psychological and consumer behavior literatures is the schema. A schema is defined as a *" ... cognitive structure that represents knowledge about a concept or type of stimulus, including its attributes and the relations among those attributes"* (Fiske and Taylor, 1991, p. 98). Schemas are an individual's preconceived notions or ideas about the world that are stored in memory.

The schema concept stems from a combination of Heider's (1958) balance theory and Asch's (1946) person perception research, wherein people are believed to form general holistic perceptions from discrete social encounters (Fiske and Taylor, 1991). The basic premise of schema–driven research is that in order to simplify reality, we develop categories (*see* CONSUMER CATEGORIZATION) in which to store information at a broader level rather than attempting to incorporate specific experiences and new information in a piecemeal fashion. In essence, schemas serve to ease our information management processes and social experiences. Categories are formed to help us discriminate among individuals, interpret information, and evaluate others. When evoked, schemata are believed to influence social perceptions and evaluations as well as behavior. While schema research focuses largely on understanding and

describing the result of the evoked schema on such outcomes, categorization research focuses on how instances are classified and categories (or schemas) are formed. In this article, we limit our discussion to schema research.

TYPES OF SCHEMAS

Various types of schemas have been studied across a number of disciplines, including social psychology, consumer behavior, marketing, and organizational behavior. For instance, categories and schemas have been proposed to capture individual's perceptions of themselves, other people, roles and occupations, and the situations they face. A person (or other) schema represents preconceptions of a variety of personality traits, social goals, and so on. For example, an individual may have a preconceived idea of what it means to be outgoing or competitive (e.g., Cantor and Mischel, 1979). A self-schema represents perceptions of the self, or the core of the self-concept (Markus and Wurf, 1987). Self-schemas tend to be more complicated than other schemas, and as a result people remember better self-relevant information (Kihlstrom *et al.*, 1988). Role schemas capture our understanding of the characteristics and behaviors that we expect of people in certain roles and positions, including both achieved (e.g., professor, graduate student, janitor) and ascribed (e.g., race, age, gender). Event schemas represent our expectations regarding how events ought to be sequenced – much like scripts (e.g., what should happen when you go to a wedding, a funeral, or a dinner party). These types of schemas and others that have been proposed in the literature all serve to guide our information processing and social encounters with greater efficiency and ease.

THE EFFECTS OF SCHEMAS

In general, people balance a schema stored in memory against actual evidence received in the environment. Thus, external information is weighed against internal preconceived notions. In addition, schemas affect how individuals encode, remember, and evaluate information that is encountered after an initial schema is evoked. When a new piece of information or a new encounter takes place, it evokes an existing schema. In turn, the schema impacts the person's attention to the information, how the person interprets the information, and the basic judgments that are formed from the information.

Attention.   Schemas affect what people notice. When an individual has a strong preconceived notion of a given subject or object (i.e., the schema is well developed), then the person is likely to pay close attention to schema-consistent information and to ignore schema-inconsistent information (Fiske and Neuberg, 1990). Schemas also minimize perceptions of differences across those within the schema (e.g., all scientists are alike) and increase perceptions of differences between schemas (e.g., scientists and janitors are very different).

Memory.   Schemas also affect what people remember (*see* CONSUMER MEMORY PROCESSES). In addition to its effects on attention, research suggests that when an individual has a well-developed schema, he or she is also more likely to remember schema-consistent information (Fiske and Neuberg, 1990). However, if an individual does not have a well-developed schema, then both consistent and inconsistent information will be processed and remembered. The individual is still attempting to form a solid perception of the category and as a result will attempt to integrate the new information.

Evaluations.   Immediate evaluative responses are a result of the affect triggered by categorization to a specific schema (Anderson and Cole, 1990). When actual data or evidence is encountered, an existing schema is evoked. When the evidence is consistent with the activated schema and the schema is positive, then a positive evaluation is triggered. Hence, there is a schema congruity effect (Mandler, 1982).

In effect, our evaluations are driven by the degree of schema (in)congruity that we perceive when encountering a new piece of evidence. The new evidence received in conjunction with the existing schema forms the evaluation. It should be added, however, that an increasing body of literature indicates that a moderate level of incongruity between a product and a more general product category can stimulate information processing. In turn, this can lead to more favorable evaluations in relationship to products that are congruent or extremely incongruent with the schema (Meyers-Levy and Tybout, 1989).

The next section of the article briefly reviews four key theoretical areas in schema research. We then identify several areas for future research.

FOUR KEY THEORETICAL AREAS

Researchers have employed schema theory as the foundation for investigating a variety of applied areas of consumer behavior, including advertising, personal selling, public policy, branding, and product management. Rather than reviewing research in these applied areas, however, we have chosen to investigate contributions of consumer and psychological researchers to four key theoretical areas: (i) the effects of the level of schema congruity, (ii) the relationship of semantic memory networks to schema, (iii) the effects of moderating variables, and (iv) the impact of self-schemas on consumers.

The effects of level of schema congruity.   A substantial number of studies have investigated the effects on information processing and evaluative judgments of the level of congruity between the schemas for a consumer product and its associated product category. In this case, congruity or incongruity may be defined as the extent to which the holistic configuration of attributes associated with an object and the configuration of the existing schema for the product category correspond (Mandler, 1982). In general, this research follows the logic developed by Fiske and colleagues (e.g., Fiske and Neuberg, 1990) in the social psychology literature, the work of Sujan (1985) in the consumer behavior literature, or Mandler's (1982) schema congruity hypothesis. This research suggests that when the product (or other object) matches the evoked schema, then affect transfer from the evoked category to the object occurs. In contrast, when a mismatch is perceived, more elaborate processing will be triggered. In other words, in the case of congruence (or a match), holistic processing based on the schema will take place; however, when incongruent (or a mismatch), judgments will be derived in a piecemeal fashion.

As a general statement, the literature suggests that people react positively when objects conform to expectations, and as a result are congruent with existing schema (e.g., Fiske, 1982). Mandler (1982) added to the literature, however, by proposing that objects that match the existing schema are unlikely to elicit deep cognitive processing. Therefore, the positive response generated by congruence will be weak. Conversely, when the object is incongruent with the existing schema, deeper cognitive processing is likely to be triggered. In some instances these incongruities can be easily resolved through a process in which the individual recognizes that the object is just another example of the category. Thus, the object is recognized as a special case of an existing category (i.e., subtyping). Alternatively, the object may be recognized as residing in another category (i.e., alternative classification). Mandler (1982), and later Meyers-Levy and Tybout (1989) in the consumer behavior literature, suggest that the process of rectifying perceptions of incongruity between the object and the evoked schema will influence evaluative responses, and the process of successfully resolving the inconsistency can lead to greater positive affect. In contrast, however, extreme incongruities that cannot be easily rectified are likely to result in a negative affect. Meyers-Levy and Tybout (1989) argue that the positive effect of moderate incongruity is lacking in studies taking the Fiske (1982) approach because the effect of the process or responding to incongruity is subtle and likely to be overwhelmed when general affect toward the product or existing schema is very strong.

Again, many consumer studies take this approach. For example, Braun-LaTour, Puccinelli and Mast (2007) apply Mandler's hypothesis to investigate the effects of mood and information overload on consumer processing of ads.

Their results indicate that reaction times are faster when categorizing congruent information than when categorizing incongruent information. Also, consumers in a positive mood were found to categorize faster.

The role of memory and semantic networks in schema research. Another approach adopted in the study of schemas involves the study of memory (*see* CONSUMER MEMORY PROCESSES) and semantic networks. For example, the spreading-activation theory or semantic processing proposed by Collins and Loftus (1975) is employed in social psychology and some consumer behavior research to better understand the role of memory in schemas. The spreading-activation model links concepts (or nodes) via a network. When one concept is activated, it spreads to other related concepts. Concept nodes are linked together and usually flow in both directions. Further, the links between the concept nodes will vary in "criteriality" or strength. Thus, it might be highly criterial that one concept is linked to another concept in memory (e.g., an apple node is linked to a fruit node so that an apple is recognized as a piece of fruit), but less criterial for it to be linked to another (e.g., the apple node is linked to a yellow color node). The theory suggests that when a concept node is activated, activation spreads to other nodes via the connected paths of the network. The level of activation decreases as it spreads further across the network. Thus, concepts further removed from the initial concept node that was activated will be weakly triggered while those closer are more strongly triggered. Furthermore, activation can only start at one node at a time, and activation goes away gradually or decreases over time.

Braun-LaTour and LaTour (2004) apply concepts from spreading-activation theory in an advertising study. They argue that when a consumer is exposed to an advertisement, brand-related concepts are activated. Concepts related to the spokesperson and/or the message may also be activated. Associations between the links become more automatic and stronger with repetition. Thus, a continuous ad campaign will result in better recall and recognition among consumers than a new campaign. Although not surprising, the results are consistent with schema congruity theory.

Moderation effects.   Consumer researchers have identified a number of variables that moderate consumers' schema processing strategies. For example, Yoon (1997) finds that older adults exhibit greater use of schema-based processing strategies than younger adults. However, this effect is found only during nonoptimal times of the day, which for older adults is during the evening hours. In contrast, younger adults engage in detailed processing strategies regardless of the time of day.

An important finding in the schema literature is the "moderate incongruity effect" in which people prefer an option that is moderately inconsistent with a product category schema to one that is congruent with the product category schema. In two studies, the effect is found to be moderated by other variables. First, Peracchio and Tybout (1996) find that the effect occurs to a greater extent when consumers have little prior knowledge of the product category. Thus, when consumers are knowledgeable of a product category, the "moderate incongruity effect" disappears. Campbell and Goodstein (2001) extend the research by investigating the role of perceived risk on the "moderate incongruity effect." Consistent with previous research, the authors find that moderate incongruity results in more detailed processing and evaluations that are more positive than in congruity conditions. However, perceived risk is found to moderate the effect. That is, the moderate incongruity effect is found only in low-risk product selection conditions. If perceived risk is high, then congruity (rather than moderate incongruity) leads to a more favorable evaluation.

The "moderate incongruity effect" is also investigated from the perspective of the elaboration-likelihood paradigm. In a study of ad-brand incongruency, Dahlén *et al.* (2005) find that when an ad is incongruent with a brand schema two things occur. First, the attitude toward the ad decreases. Second, brand attitude evaluations increase along with the amount of brand-related information processing. These effects are moderated, however, by the respondents' need for cognition, such that the increased brand attitude and information

processing occur only among the high need for cognition respondents. Consistent with these findings is research by Lee and Thorson (2008), who find that a moderate incongruence between celebrity and product schemas increases the persuasiveness of an endorsement, but the effect is most pronounced among participants with higher levels of product involvement. Both of these studies can be interpreted from within the elaboration-likelihood theory paradigm. That is, those higher in the need for cognition and those with higher levels of product involvement engage in greater levels of information processing, which allows the respondents to cognitively handle the information in the moderate incongruency conditions.

In an interesting study, Aggarwal and McGill (2007) investigate the role of schemas in evaluating anthropomorphized products. The results of their first two studies reveal that the greater the extent that a product matches the schema for what a human looks like, the more positive the evaluation of the product when the text of the ad anthropomorphizes the product. For example, in one of the experiments an automobile is depicted as talking to the consumer when the ad begins "Hi, I am a Lexus." A third study, however, shows that the findings depend upon whether the affective tag associated with the human schema is positive. Thus, if the human schema that is activated is negative, the evaluation of the brand becomes more negative. In the study, beverage bottles are shown in pairs. In the copy of the ad, the bottles are described as either good twins, who will make their parents proud, or as evil twins who will conquer your city. The results reveal that the affective tag of "good twins" versus "evil twins" moderates the results. Thus, the evaluation of the brand is enhanced in the "good twin" condition in comparison to the "evil twin" condition. This study is important because it shows that schema congruity can increase or decrease evaluations depending upon the affective tag associated with the schema that is evoked.

The role of self-schemas in consumer behavior.
Aaker's (1999) research on the effect of self-schemas on consumer attitudes toward a brand provides the foundation for additional work on self-schemas in a branding context. Aaker

proposes that the self (*see* POSSESSIONS AND SELF) is malleable and that one's self-schema is influenced by personality and situational factors. Various self-conceptions (i.e., self-schema) may be activated or deactivated depending on how salient they are, which can be influenced by the existing social situation or by the traits that are evoked by a particular experience or memory. In her research she focuses on those traits that are deemed to be schematic because they are at that moment descriptive or important to the individual. Consistent with social psychology research, Aaker argues that people maintain a self-schema because they desire consistency and positivity. When presented with information that is inconsistent with the self-schema, then individuals are less likely to accurately recall the information. Further, negative affect is more likely to result if self-relevant information is inconsistent with the self-schema.

Aaker (1999) proposes that a brand (and the set of personality traits that the brand embodies) often serves a "self-expressive" purpose for consumers. As consumers, we select and utilize brands that allow us to make a certain impression or that best represent us at a given point in time. As a result, consumers who are schematic on a particular personality trait should demonstrate a preference for brands that are also highly descriptive on that trait. Aaker refers to this as "self-congruity." While consumers' schematic traits typically guide their behavior, she also acknowledges that sometimes consumers' behaviors express who they wish to be (desired self) or strive to be (ideal self) rather than the actual self. Thus, each individual holds a variety of self-conceptions. She also suggests that depending on the current social situation, certain situational cues can become salient and influence the conceptualization of the self so that one trait self-schema is more acceptable than others. On the basis of these situational cues, people will tailor their behavior to match the trait that is primed by the situation (i.e., "situation congruity" takes place).

Batra and Homer (2004) adopt Aaker's schematicity framework in their research on brand image beliefs. They find that personality associations of celebrity endorsers serve to reinforce consumer beliefs about the brand. That is, if the spokesperson is perceived to be

fun or sophisticated, then the brand is likely to be perceived to be more fun or more sophisticated. For brand image beliefs to be evoked, the brand's schema needs to fit the consumer's schema. Consistent with these findings, Worth, Smith and Mackie (1992) find that brands are evaluated more favorably if the description of the brand matches the consumer's self-schema. More specifically, these authors found that the gender schematicity of the respondents is assessed in terms of its degree of masculinity versus femininity. Respondents prefer products whose description matches their self-perceived schema for masculinity or femininity. Similar findings are found for self-schema based upon the separateness–connectedness of the subjects (Wang and Mowen, 1997). Thus, respondents who rate themselves as more connected to others preferred products described in terms of their ability to bring people together. In contrast, respondents who rate themselves as more separated prefer products described in terms of their ability to help maintain the person's individuality.

DIRECTIONS FOR FUTURE RESEARCH

One direction for future research involves the investigation of the nature of self-schemas. In the development of the 3M Model of Motivation and Personality, Mowen (2000) and his colleagues (e.g., Mowen and Sujan, 2005) propose a control theory model in which a system of personality traits provides a schema for interpreting stimuli and outcomes as well as for influencing attitudes and behavior. Thus, traits do not operate in isolation of each other. Rather, in conjunction with situational forces, multiple traits combine to form a schema that influences attitudes and behaviors. Importantly, past research has tended to investigate how single personality traits (e.g., need for cognition or extroversion) influence evaluations if they are congruent or incongruent with the description of a product. For example, as noted earlier, masculinity–femininity and separateness–connectedness can be conceptualized as traits and have been shown to positively impact brand evaluations if appropriately matched to a product's description. To the present authors' knowledge, however, researchers have not investigated multiple traits acting together in experimental studies.

How can an advertisement, brand, or endorser simultaneously activate a schema associated with multiple traits? Consider the development of a television advertisement. These ads will have multiple elements, including a message, music, a situational context, and perhaps an endorser. Each ad component can be used to activate a different personality trait. For example, the message could be composed of high-quality arguments, which would appeal to an individual high in the need for cognition. Similarly, the music could be based upon a song that emphasizes togetherness (e.g., "Love Will Keep Us Together"), which would activate a connectedness trait. The situation could be composed of a party atmosphere in which an endorser who is shown to be highly gregarious, which would activate an extroversion trait. These ideas suggest that a critical aspect of developing TV ads is the art of combining music, copy, situation, and endorser so as to effectively activate schema that are maximally congruent the product's schema as well as the self-schema of the target audience. These ideas also illustrate the crudeness of present schema research, which looks at only one trait at a time.

The idea that multiple traits act to form a self-schema suggests the possibility of bringing science into the art of creating advertisements. We believe that the complex interaction among a multitrait person schema, a product schema, and a situational context is why the development of advertisements can be described as an art. One possibility for incorporating a greater level of science into the art, however, is by identifying the trait antecedents of the specific behavior that ad developers hope to influence. In the hierarchical structured 3M Model, these highly specific behavioral dispositions are called *surface traits*, which emerge in part from combination of deeper level traits, including situational, compound, and elemental traits.

Here is an example. Suppose that the advertiser is marketing a product that is positioned as the leader in its field. The goal is to attach a leadership schema to the product. This schema would be based upon traits that are associated with individuals having a strong leadership propensity. The goal would be to create an advertisement that portrays a product schema that is congruent with a leadership self-schema. Research by Flaherty *et al.* (2009) identifies the system of traits of individuals with high levels of leadership propensity. This self-schema includes the deeper level traits of competitiveness, self-efficacy, and the need for material resources. With this information it would be straightforward to create an advertisement that employs an endorser who is self-confident (i.e., indicating self-efficacy), that takes place in a luxurious setting (suggesting materialism), and that includes music suggesting competition (e.g., the song "Eye of the Tiger"). Schema theory suggests that such a high level of congruity between the product's schema and self-schema of the target market should enhance the effectiveness of the advertisement. Future research, however, is required to test these ideas.

A second arena for future research involves integrating the research on schema congruity with the literature on fit and the match-up hypothesis. For example, Till and Busler (2000) propose that a match-up occurs when there is a fit between the characteristics of the product spokesperson and the product that is endorsed. That is, when fit, match-up, or similarity occurs between two entities, there is a greater likelihood of the transfer of knowledge and affect from one stimulus to another. This idea is consistent with both spreading-activation theory and balance theory, which places the literature squarely within the domain of schema congruity.

The concepts of fit and match-up have been applied to numerous cases in which congruence is sought in the characteristics between two entities. Across the studies, however, the authors are inconsistent in whether they cite the literature on schema congruity. The following are examples of the topics of studies investigating stimulus congruity from the perspective of fit and/or match-up.

- Fit of endorser with product
- Fit of country-of-origin with product
- Fit of style of music with brand image of retail store
- Fit of music with advertising message
- Fit of product extension with brand

- Fit of brand image with social cause in cause-related marketing
- Fit of advertisement with TV program
- Fit of product with TV program
- Fit of product with an ambient scent/smell
- Fit of attractiveness of service provider with nature of the service.

Each of the pairs of entities can be investigated from the perspective of schema theory. As such, the two literatures should be integrated. Interestingly, while the authors of the studies focusing on match-up/fit will sometimes cite schema theory, the authors investigating phenomena from a schema congruity perspective far less frequently cite the literature on match-up/fit.

The present authors believe that a key goal for future research is the development of a general model that could be possibly called the "schema congruency theory." The model will require the development of an enhanced version of schema theory that is able to explain the effects of moderating variables as well as handle the multifaceted nature of schema. The new theory of schema congruence would then be able to explain and predict consumer reactions to the level of congruency, which includes issues of match-up/fit among stimuli, whether product-based, self-based, other person-based, and/or situation-based.

Bibliography

Aaker, J.L. (1999) The malleable self: the role of self-expression in persuasion. *Journal of Marketing Research*, **36**, 45–57.

Aggarwal, P. and McGill, A.L. (2007) Is that care smiling at me? Schema congruity as a basis for evaluating anthropomorphized products. *Journal of Consumer Research*, **34**, 468–479.

Anderson, S.M. and Cole, S.W. (1990) Do I know you? The role of significant others in general social perception. *Journal of Personality and Social Psychology*, **59**, 384–399.

Asch, S.E. (1946) Forming impressions of personality. *Journal of Abnormal and Social Psychology*, **4**, 1230–1240.

Batra, R. and Homer, P.M. (2004) The situational impact of brand image beliefs. *Journal of Consumer Psychology*, **14**, 318–330.

Braun, K.A. (1999) Post-experience effects on consumer memory. *Journal of Consumer Research*, **25**, 319–334.

Braun-LaTour, K.A. and LaTour, M.S. (2004) Assessing the long-term impact of a consistent advertising campaign on consumer memory. *Journal of Advertising*, **33**, 49–61.

Braun-LaTour, K.A., Puccinelli, N.M. and Mast, F.W. (2007) Mood, information congruency, and overload. *Journal of Business Research*, **60**, 1109–1116.

Cacioppo, J.T., Petty, R.E. and Sidera, J.A. (1982) The effects of a salient self-schema on the evaluation of proattitudinal editorials: Top-down versus bottom-up message processing. *Journal of Experimental Social Psychology*, **18**, 324–338.

Campbell, M.C. and Goodstein, R.C. (2001) The moderating effect of perceived risk on consumers' evaluations of product incongruity: preference for the norm. *Journal of Consumer Research*, **28**, 439–449.

Cantor, N. and Mischel, W. (1979) Prototypes in person perception, in *Advances in Experimental Social Psychology*, vol. 12 (ed. L. Berkowitz.), Academic Press, New York, pp. 3–52.

Collins, A.M. and Loftus, E.F. (1975) A spreading-activation theory of semantic processing. *Psychological Review*, **82**, 407–428.

Dahlén, M., Lange, F., Sjödin, H. and Törn, F. (2005) Effects of ad-brand incongruency. *Journal of Current Issues*, **27**, 1–12.

Fiske, S.T. (1982) Schema-triggered affect: applications to social perception, in *Affect and Cognition: The Seventeenth Annual Carnegie Symposium on Cognition* (eds M.S. Clark and S.T. Fiske), Lawrence Erlbaum, Hillsdale, NJ, pp. 55–78.

Fiske, S.T. and Neuberg, S.L. (1990) A continuum of impression formation, from category-based to individuating processes: influences of information and motivation on attention and interpretation, in *Advances in Experimental Social Psychology*, vol. 2 (ed. M.P. Zanna), Academic Press, New York, pp. 1–74.

Fiske, S.T. and Taylor, S.E. (1991) *Social Cognition*, 2nd edn, McGraw-Hill, New York.

Flaherty, E.T., Mowen, J.C., Brown, T.J. and Marshall, G.W. (2009) Leadership propensity and sales performance among sales personnel and managers in a specialty retail store setting. *Journal of Personal Selling & Sales Management*, **39**, 39–55.

Hastie, R. (1980) Memory for behavioral information that confirms or contradicts a personality impression, in *Person Memory: The Cognitive Basis of Social Perception* (ed. R. Hastie *et al.*), Erlbaum, Hillsdale, NJ, 155–177.

Heider, F. (1958) *The Psychology of Interpersonal Relations*, Wiley, New York.

Kahneman, D. (1973) *Attention and Effort*, Prentice-Hall, Englewood Cliffs, NJ.

Kanungo, R.N. and Pang, S. (1973) Effects of human models on perceived product quality. *Journal of Applied Psychology*, **57**, 172–178.

Kihlstrom, J.F., Cantor, N., Albright, J.S. *et al.* (1988) Information processing and the study of the self, in *Advances in Experimental Social Psychology*, (ed. L. Berkowitz), vol. 21, Academic Press, New York, pp. 145–180.

Lee, J.G. and Thorson, E. (2008) The impact of celebrity-product incongruence on the effectiveness of product endorsement. *Journal of Advertising Research*, **48**, 433–449.

Lynch, J. and Schuler, D. (1994) The matchup effect of spokesperson and product congruency: a schema theory interpretation. *Psychology & Marketing*, **11**, 417–445.

Macrae, C.N. and Bodenhausen, G.V. (2000) Social cognition: thinking categorically about others. *Annual Review of Psychology*, **51**, 93–120.

Mandler, G. (1982) The structure of value: accounting for taste, in *Affect and Cognition: The Seventeenth Annual Carnegie Symposium on Cognition* (eds M.S. Clark and S.T. Fiske), Erlbaum, Hillsdale, NJ, pp. 3–36.

Markus, H. (1977) Self-schema and processing information about the self. *Journal of Personality and Social Psychology*, **35**, 63–78.

Markus, H. and Wurf, E. (1987) The dynamic self-concept: a social psychological perspective, in *Annual Review of Psychology*, vol. 38 (ed. M.R. Rosenzweig and W. Porter), Annual Reviews Inc., Palo Alto, CA, pp. 299–337.

Meyers-Levy, J. and Tybout, A.M. (1989) Schema congruity as a basis for product evaluation. *Journal of Consumer Research*, **16**, 39–54.

Mowen, J.C. (2000) *The 3M Model of Motivation and Personality: Theory and Empirical Applications to Consumer Behavior*, Kluwer Academic Press, Boston, MA.

Mowen, J.C. and Sujan, H. (2005) Volunteer behavior: a hierarchical model approach for investigating its trait and functional motive antecedents. *Journal of Consumer Psychology*, **15**, 170–182.

Peracchio, L.A. and Tybout, A.M. (1996) The moderating role of prior knowledge in schema-based product evaluation. *Journal of Consumer Research*, **23**, 177–192.

Sujan, M. (1985) Consumer knowledge: effects on evaluation strategies mediating consumer judgments. *Journal of Consumer Research*, **12**, 31–45.

Sujan, M. and Bettman, J.R. (1989) The effects of brand positioning strategies on consumers' brand and category perceptions: Some insights from schema research. *Journal of Consumer Research*, **26**, 454–467.

Sujan, M., Bettman, J.R. and Sujan, H. (1986) Effects of consumer expectations on information processing in selling encounters. *Journal of Marketing Research*, **23**, 346–353.

Taylor, S.E. and Fiske, S.T. (1978) Salience, attention and attribution: top of the head phenomenon, in *Advances in Experimental Social Psychology*, vol. 11 (ed. L. Berkowitz's), Academic Press, New York, pp. 249–288.

Till, B.D. and Busler, M. (2000) The match-up hypothesis: physical attractiveness, expertise, and the role of fit on brand attitude, purchase intent, and brand beliefs. *Journal of Advertising*, **29**, 1–13.

Unnava, H.R. and Burnkrant, R.E. (1991) An imagery-processing view of the role of pictures in print advertisements. *Journal of Marketing Research*, **28**, 226–231.

Wang, C.L. and Mowen, J.C. (1997) The separateness-connectedness self-schema: scale development and application to message construction. *Psychology & Marketing*, **14**, 185–207.

Wheeler, S.C., Petty, R.E. and Biser, G.Y. (2005) Self-schema matching and attitude change: situational and dispositional determinants of message elaboration. *Journal of Consumer Research*, **31**, 787–797.

Worth, L.T., Smith, J. and Mackie, D.M. (1992) Gender schematicity and preference for gender-types products. *Psychology & Marketing*, **9**, 17–30.

Yoon, C. (1997) Age differences in consumers' processing strategies: an investigation of moderating influences. *Journal of Consumer Research*, **24**, 329–342.

V

variety-seeking

Aimee Drolet and Daniel He

Most of the choices consumers face are choices they face regularly and can be viewed fundamentally as being either consistent or inconsistent with their usual habits. On most of these occasions, consumers strive for consistency in their choices. Inconsistency can signal fickleness and fussiness or, even worse, moral and mental weakness. In contrast, consumers who display consistency in their choices are viewed positively, believed to possess personal strength and intellectual competency. Furthermore, consistency makes the task of choosing easier, as it takes less effort to make a choice that has been made before than to reconsider and choose differently. These are some of the benefits of behavioral consistency.

At the same time, the costs of inconsistency appear equally clear. Making the same choice repeatedly means experiencing the same result repeatedly. In one word, consistency is boring. Inconsistency in the form of choosing a variety of options can be stimulating and forestall satiation. It can also be perceived as creative and interesting by others. In short, sometimes inconsistency can be good, and consumers often embrace inconsistency by seeking to vary their behavior. Variety-seeking is a common consumer choice strategy.

The tendency to *variety-seek*, defined here as switching away from a choice made on a previous occasion, has been found in both interpersonal and intrapersonal consumer choice contexts. In interpersonal contexts, such as a group at a restaurant or bar, consumers will choose an option not chosen by other consumers in the group. They will order a different dish or drink even if their variety-seeking behavior will make them unhappier with their order (Ariely and Levav, 2000). And, in intrapersonal contexts, consumers will switch from choosing more-preferred options to less-preferred options despite lowered satisfaction (Simonson, 1990). Indeed, the tendency among consumers to seek variety in intrapersonal consumer contexts is pervasive enough that it extends beyond the choice of product options to the choice of product choice rules themselves (Drolet, 2002).

Why are consumers so motivated to seek variety in their choice making? Further, what factors moderate the tendency to seek variety? Specifically, what are the situational and person-specific factors that influence the degree to which consumers will endeavor to be consistent versus inconsistent in their choice behavior? This article addresses these questions.

REASONS CONSUMERS SEEK VARIETY

Researchers have offered several reasons why consumers are motivated to seek variety. Consumers seek variety for biological, utilitarian, and psychosocial reasons.

Biological reasons. At the most basic level, the tendency to variety-seek may be "hard-wired." Animal studies suggest that the desire to vary behavior is innate. Even after there is no new information to acquire through behavioral diversification, animals change their behavior, seemingly just for the fun of it. Likewise, people change their behavior because they can get bored with the repeating same experience over and over.

Smart producers of products respond to consumers' eventual boredom. For example, classical music, with its frequent repetitions and long movements, can sound tedious even to its own enthusiasts. The composer Joseph Haydn anticipated his own eighteenth century audience's boredom. He interspersed the gentle, melodic parts of the second movement in his Symphony No. 94 with sudden, thunderous bursts of music. Haydn later nicknamed the symphony the "Surprise Symphony" because the piercing notes he added grab listeners' attention with something different. They also wake up sleeping listeners.

Stimulation.   Whether the products are songs (Ratner, Kahn, and Kahneman, 1999) or snacks (Simonson, 1990), consumers crave something different and choose options that allow them to experience something different. Change is inherently stimulating, and the inherent need for stimulation can be met by changing behavior. By choosing options that have not been chosen before or recently, consumers can increase their level of stimulation. Accordingly, by satisfying their need for stimulation by variety-seeking in one product category, consumers' tendency to seek variety in another category is less (Menon and Kahn, 1995). Likewise, the need for stimulation can be met by having consumers make choices in complex environments (Menon and Kahn, 2002). In these environments, consumers are less likely to variety-seek.

Satiation.   Besides boredom, satiation is another negative psychological consequence of repeated choice. Consumers become satiated with products, and variety-seeking among products is a way to stave off satiation (McAlister and Pessemier, 1982). Consumers also become satiated with product attributes. For example, in an experiment by Mitchell, Kahn, and Knasko (1995), consumers choosing among chocolate candies chose more variety in the presence of a stimuli-congruent scent (chocolate) versus a stimuli-incongruent scent (flowers).

Utilitarian reasons.
Uncertainty reduction.   By choosing a mix of products with a mix of features, consumers can meet a mix of needs. Some needs may be known at the time of choice. However, some are not. Variety-seeking is a choice strategy that shields consumers from several sources of uncertainty. The future value of products and product features is one source of uncertainty consumers confront. For example, a consumer might not be able to predict the usefulness of a newly purchased product (e.g., GPS) or the usefulness of one of its features (e.g., voice activation). Another source of uncertainty is future preferences (Simonson, 1990). As consumers, we often do not know what our tastes will be in a year or even tomorrow. So, we cover our bets by choosing variety. We cast a wide net and widen our selection. By doing so, we are better able to cope with this source of uncertainty. Put differently, a strategy of variety-seeking has normative value if one assumes that, due to uncertainty about products and preferences, consumers are testing their utilities for choice options (McAlister and Pessemier, 1982) and choice rules over time (Drolet, 2002).

Simplify choice.   Variety-seeking is one way that consumers cope with tough choices. Variety-seeking makes good sense for both cognitive and emotional reasons. In complex environments, for example, where there are large numbers of product options each described along large numbers of product features, consumers may not have the sufficient cognitive wherewithal to solve choice problems (Mitchell, Kahn, and Knasko, 1995). Variety-seeking is a choice heuristic that frees up cognitive resources. For example, consumers can focus on the relative value of attributes, an easier task than calculating attribute value trade-offs.

Choice problems can be emotionally difficult as well. Choosing one option means forgoing others. Consumers anticipate regret and seek to reduce it. Anticipated regret also drives consumers' unwillingness to make attribute value trade-offs that are emotionally threatening. To consumers, the idea of trading off attributes relevant to their self goals (e.g., personal safety and financial well-being) is an inherently aversive one. For consumers, variety-seeking is one way to avoid having to do so.

Maximize global utility.   Variety-seeking makes normative sense if consumers are attempting to maximize global utility as opposed to local utilities (Kahn, Ratner, and Kahneman, 1997). When making a series of choices over time, consumers can choose to maximize the utilities associated with each choice made in the series (i.e., local utilities). Or, consumers can choose to maximize the utility associated with the entire series of choices (i.e., global utility). Maximizing local utilities presupposes that earlier choices have no effect on the satisfaction consumers experience from later choices. This may not always be the case, for example, because of satiation. However, maximizing global utility, that is the utility associated with the entire series of choices, may cause consumers to experience less overall satisfaction (Simonson, 1990).

Maximize retrospective utility. Variety-seeking also makes sense if consumers are attempting to maximize retrospective utility. Ratner, Kahn, and Kahneman (1999) provided evidence that this is sometimes the case. In their research, participants rated their memory for how much they enjoyed sequences of music that were more versus less varied. Participants' retrospective reports of their enjoyment were higher for the more-varied (vs less-varied) sequence, even though their online reports of their enjoyment were lower for the more-varied (vs less-varied) sequence.

Psychosocial reasons.
Norm conformity. Some variation in choice behavior is viewed more favorably by others compared to no variation in choice behavior. A moderate amount of variation suggests positive values, such as discerning taste, and adaptive personality traits, such as flexibility. In contrast, the complete absence of variation suggests negative values, such as indiscriminant judgment, and maladaptive personality traits such as rigidity. When in the presence of others, consumers who follow a norm of variety-seeking are viewed more positively by others compared to those consumers who do not (Ratner and Kahn, 2002).

Need to appear unique. Another psychosocial reason that consumers seek to vary their choice behavior stems from the desire to be unique. In interpersonal contexts, a consumer will make different choices over others because these choices advance the goal of portraying oneself as unique. The consumer who makes the same choices as others runs the risk of appearing to imitate them. A study by Ariely

and Levav (2000) supports this view. In their study, microbrewery patrons were offered the choice of one of the four free beer samples. In a "collective" condition, patrons ordered their samples one by one aloud to the waiter. Thus, each person in the group knew what each of the others ordered. In an "independent" condition, patrons wrote down their choice on individual menus. Thus, other persons in the group did not know what each person had ordered. Consistent with the view that consumers seek variety in order to portray themselves as unique, in both their own eyes and the eyes of others, patrons in the collective condition showed greater variety in their beer choices, suggesting they desired to be unique. They also expressed greater regret when asked if they wished they had made a different choice, suggesting that they had sacrificed their initial choice so as to be unique.

The variety-seeking in this study involved a sequence of individual choices. An implication of its results is that a consumer who is the first in a group to order can satisfy his or her own particular taste without having to worry about being perceived as unique since no one else in the group has chosen before him or her. Indeed, in follow-up tests, Ariely and Levav (2000) confirmed that consumers in the collective condition who were the first to order were just as satisfied as the consumers in the independent condition. Equal satisfaction implies that these consumers ordered the drink they most preferred and at the same time were able to appear unique. Consumers in the collective condition who were not the first to order may have appeared unique but were less satisfied with their drink order because their choice was contingent on the choices of others.

The desire to appear unique also plays a role in intrapersonal choice contexts. Behavioral change in oneself is associated with perceptions of oneself as unique. People who prize uniqueness separate themselves from others by maintaining a sense of "specialness." People can demonstrate specialness by choosing not to conform to standards of behavior set by others and also to standards of behavior they themselves set. Not conforming to one's own standards reveals a person to be unique as it represents a display of situational abnormality, one aimed at avoiding excessive similarity.

MODERATORS OF VARIETY-SEEKING BEHAVIOR

There are several situational and person-specific factors that moderate the tendency to seek variety and that determine the conditions under which this tendency is more versus less pronounced.

Situational factors.

Mood effects.   Past research has shown that positive mood increases variety-seeking. For example, Kahn and Isen (1993) manipulated participants' mood to be positive by giving them a bag of candy. These participants chose more variety compared to participants in a control condition.

There have been multiple explanations offered for the increasing effect of positive mood on the tendency to variety-seek. One explanation is that positive mood is associated with sensation-seeking and novelty-seeking, and variety-seeking is one way in which people can achieve these ends (Menon and Kahn, 1995). Another explanation is that positive mood increases heuristic processing, and variety-seeking is a choice heuristic that simplifies choice-making (Mitchell, Kahn, and Knasko, 1995). Negative mood is associated with systematic thinking and also monotonous behavior.

Relatedly, heuristic processing is associated with broadened thinking, whereas negative mood is associated with narrowed thinking. Kahn and Isen (1993) suggested that positive mood caused participants in their study to have a more optimistic view of consumption. Besides, positive mood's increasing effect on broadened thinking may lead participants to have a more flexible view as to what products fit in a category, thereby increasing the size of their consideration sets (i.e., the number of product options they would consider choosing).

Presence of others.   The presence of a group forces individuals to deal with different goals, goals that can be achieved solely by the individual and goals that are accomplished by both the individual and the group (see SOCIAL INFLUENCE). Because these two goals often oppose one another, it may not be possible to meet both if each requires the choice of a different option. For example, when we are at a restaurant with friends, we must choose between these goals: we can either satisfy our own taste by ordering a meal without considering what our friends have ordered or we can portray ourselves as unique by ordering a meal contingent on the orders of others. If uniqueness is the goal, the recommended strategy would be to order an option that our friends do not. If uniqueness is not the goal, the recommended strategy would be to order an option that our friends order.

Ratner and Kahn (2002) demonstrated that the presence of others influences which kind of strategy consumers tend to pursue. Specifically, they found that consumers were more likely to variety-seek when their consumption was public versus private. Their finding implies that variety-seeking is a salient social norm and that compliance with this norm increases social evaluations. When their behavior is being observed, consumers will choose more variety than they would otherwise. By choosing a variety of products, consumers can appear more interesting, for example, a trait that is socially valued.

Physical confinement.   Recent research by Levav and Zhu (forthcoming) found that a physically restrictive space causes consumers to seek more variety. A physically restrictive space arouses feelings of confinement and threatens personal freedom. As a result, consumers develop psychological reactance and try to reclaim their personal freedom by seeking variety. In their view, variety-seeking is a manifestation of the freedom to choose.

In one of their studies, participants were instructed to choose three out of ten candy bars from a bowl placed on top of a table. To get to the bowl, participants had to walk down either a wide aisle or a narrow aisle. They found that participants in the narrow aisle condition chose a greater variety of candy bars compared to participants in the wide aisle condition. In another experiment, participants were confined to either a narrow aisle room or a wide aisle room. They were asked to take a seat at the end of the room. Participants then learned about six charitable organizations – three more well-known and three less well-known – who were seeking donations. Participants were asked about their likelihood of donating to each. Participants in the narrow (vs. wide) aisle room were more likely to donate to the lesser-known charities. Some participants were also given the opportunity to make actual donations to the charities. Among those participants, the actual donation amount was higher in the narrow (vs wide) aisle condition. Levav and Rhu suggest that increased variety-seeking for the less well-known and more unique brands is the result of feelings of confinement and subsequent reactance to these feelings. Consistent with this suggestion, Levav and Rhu found that simply varying perceptions of confinement instead of actual physical confinement induces reactance and increases variety-seeking behavior.

Choice set size. An increase in the number of choice options can not only decrease a consumer's willingness to buy any option but can also lower the satisfaction with choices made from a larger set of choices. When the size of the choice set increases, it is increasingly difficult for consumers to make a choice among items. One low-effort way for consumers to resolve difficult choice problems is to choose a mix of items. As mentioned, by choosing a mix of items, consumers can raise the odds of choosing a most preferred item and an item that can meet unknown future consumer needs.

Decision timing. The timing of decisions is an important situational determinant of the tendency to variety-seek. Consumers tend to seek more variety when making multiple product purchases simultaneously versus sequentially. An experiment by Simonson (1990) illustrates the effect of decision timing on variety-seeking behavior. Student participants were asked to choose from a set of snacks at the beginning of a class meeting. There were three conditions. In a sequential choice condition, participants made one choice each week for three weeks. In a simultaneous choice for sequential consumption condition, participants made all three choices at one time but received only one item each week. In a third condition, known as the simultaneous choices for immediate consumption condition, participants made three choices simultaneously and received all three snacks at the end of class that same day. Those in the simultaneous choices for sequential consumption condition were significantly more likely to choose a variety

of snacks compared to those in the sequential consumption condition. Moreover, participants in the third condition who were given all three snacks the same day were even more likely to choose variety than participants in the other two conditions.

According to Simonson (1990), having to make multiple product purchases simultaneously versus sequentially forces the consumer to confront multiple sources of uncertainty, including the uncertainty due to the inability to predict future preferences accurately since preferences change over time as well as the uncertainty due to the inability to know which among a set of options is the most-preferred. With respect to the latter source of uncertainty, sequential choice making provides the consumer with the opportunity to update their preferences as each choice occasion passes.

Person-specific drivers.
Personality traits. Past research indicates that there are several personality traits associated with the tendency to seek variety versus avoid it. For example, the dispositional drive for stimulation predicts variety-seeking behavior. As mentioned above, a basic human need is the need for stimulation, and this need can be satisfied through varied behavior or the experience of novel stimuli. The extent to which stimulation is needed varies across individuals (*see* OPTIMUM STIMULATION LEVEL). Some people have a higher need for stimulation than others and are more likely to seek out new things. They do so by seeking variety.

Another personality trait that promotes the tendency of consumers to seek variety is the dispositional need for uniqueness. Consumers use rules to solve choice problems. Which rule consumers select from their repertoire of rules depends on various characteristics of choice problems. Past research has demonstrated that the rule consumers select is also independent of choice problem characteristics (Drolet, 2002). In particular, consumers who score high on the need for uniqueness scale tend to vary their selection of choice rules more than consumers who score low on the scale. Consumers who desire to see themselves as different from others can do so by avoiding repeated use of the same choice rule.

People vary in the dispositional tendency to be indecisive and this tendency is associated with increased variety-seeking behavior (Jeong, H.G., and Drolet, A. (2009) The indecisive consumer: delaying decision-making by seeking variety, unpublished research). Highly dispositionally indecisive individuals tend to view the prospect of choice as aversive. Choice-making for them is an experience filled with anxiety, worry, disappointment, and regret. Accordingly, they are reluctant to make choices and avoid doing so. As a result, choice is an activity that often ends in impasse and is deferred until later. In the meantime, the search for new alternatives and new information about alternatives can continue. Variety-seeking appears to be a strategy consumers use to delay a final choice and, as such, is a disproportionately attractive strategy for highly dispositionally indecisive consumers.

Given that chronic indecisiveness is associated with negative emotion, these results appear at odds with research that has found an increasing effect of positive mood on variety-seeking behavior (e.g., Kahn and Isen, 1993). A study by Jeong, H.G., and Drolet, A. (2009) (The indecisive consumer: delaying decision-making by seeking variety, unpublished research.) reveals that negative mood increases variety-seeking among consumers who are high in dispositional indecisiveness but not among consumers who are low in dispositional indecisiveness. Chronically indecisive consumers report feeling better after choosing a variety of products.

Culture. In individualist cultures such as Western cultures, uniqueness has a positive meaning. In contrast, in collectivist cultures such as East Asian cultures, uniqueness has a negative meaning. Not following group norms of behavior undermines the cohesiveness of a group (see CROSS-CULTURAL PSYCHOLOGY OF CONSUMER BEHAVIOR). When maintaining the strength of a social group is important, and it is especially so for members of collectivist cultures, people must sometimes suppress their personal preferences in the interest of group harmony. In individualist cultures, where personal preferences often take precedence over social preferences, the act of choice

is viewed as an act of self-expression. In collectivist cultures, the act of choice is not always associated with the self. These attitudes toward uniqueness and choice have important implications on the extent to which consumers seek variety. The tendency to variety-seek depends on consumers' cultural backgrounds.

Research by Kim and Drolet (2003) shows that consumers from individualist cultures tend to seek more variety compared to consumers from collectivist cultures. Specifically, in one study, US-born participants were more likely than Korean-born participants to vary the choice rules they used. Rule change behavior was not as apparent among Korean-born participants. Kim and Drolet hypothesized that this pattern of results is due to cultural differences in the value of uniqueness and the meaning of choice. In a different study, they used advertisements to prime uniqueness (or not) in both US-born and Korean-born participants. Consistent with their hypothesis, individuals exposed to advertisements with a uniqueness theme sought to vary their choice rule use more, regardless of cultural background. These findings raise the question of just how "hard-wired" the variety-seeking tendency is given that people's tendency to seek variety depends on cultural assumptions of choice and uniqueness.

Aging. There is some evidence that aging influences the tendency to seek variety depending on decision timing. In the research by Novak and Mather (2007), older adults chose more variety when making choices for immediate consumption than when making choices for future consumption. The amount of variety chosen by young adults did not differ when making choices for immediate versus future consumption.

Novak and Mather (2007) attribute this pattern of findings to older adults' increased emotion regulation abilities. As we age, we tend to focus more on positive information and less on negative information, and this change in focus influences choice. As a result, older adults tend to experience more positive mood. As discussed earlier, positive mood has been linked to increased variety-seeking behavior. If an initial experience is positive, and we would expect it to be more so for older adults who are better at focusing on positive aspects of experiences, an individual should be more willing to try out new things.

One reason older adults experience more positive mood is that they avoid potentially negative experiences. When not making choices in real time and there is no information as to whether the initial experience will be positive or not, older adults choose less variety. Again, there is uncertainty surrounding future preferences and this uncertainty is experienced as a negative one (Simonson, 1990). In the presence of this uncertainty, older adults might be more risk averse, seeking to avoid negative outcomes. They will gravitate toward the familiar. Consequently, they will seek less variety when making choices for future consumption.

CONCLUSION

Variety-seeking is a common consumer choice strategy. This article reviewed several reasons why consumers view variety-seeking as a useful choice strategy. In addition, this article reviewed several moderators of the tendency to choose a variety of options. Both situational and person-specific factors influence the amount of variety consumers will choose.

In predicting the amount of variety consumers will choose, it is important to consider the interaction among such factors. For example, a person-specific driver like the personality trait need for uniqueness predisposes consumers to seek variety. However, this relationship depends on another person-specific variable, culture, which influences the degree to which a person values uniqueness. In summary, in order to predict the amount of variety consumers will choose, it is important to understand why some consumers are attracted to variety-seeking as a choice strategy whereas others are not. To do so, one must take into account the conditions under which some consumers

are more or less likely to variety-seek than others.

Bibliography

Ariely, D. and Levav, J. (2000) Sequential choice in group settings: taking the road less traveled and less enjoyed. *Journal of Consumer Research*, **27**, 279–290.

Drolet, A. (2002) Inherent rule variability in consumer choice: changing rules for change's sake. *Journal of Consumer Research*, **29**, 293–305.

Kahn, B.E. and Isen, A.M. (1993) The influence of positive affect on variety seeking among safe, enjoyable products. *Journal of Consumer Research*, **20**, 257–270.

Kahn, B.E., Ratner, R.K. and Kahneman, D. (1997) Patterns of hedonic consumption over time. *Marketing Letters*, **8**, 85–96.

Kim, H.S. and Drolet, A. (2003) Choice and self-expression: a cultural analysis of variety-seeking. *Journal of Personality and Social Psychology*, **85**, 373–382.

Levav, J. and Zhu, R.J. (forthcoming) Seeking freedom through variety. *Journal of Consumer Research*.

McAlister, L. and Pessemier, E. (1982) Variety-seeking behavior: an interdisciplinary review. *Journal of Consumer Research*, **9**, 311–322.

Menon, S. and Kahn, B.E. (1995) The impact of context on variety-seeking in product choices. *Journal of Consumer Research*, **22**, 285–295.

Menon, S. and Kahn, B.E. (2002) Cross-category effects of induced arousal and pleasure on the internet shopping experience. *Journal of Retailing*, **78**, 31–40.

Mitchell, D.J., Kahn, B.E. and Knasko, S.C. (1995) There's something in the air: effects of congruent or incongruent ambient odor on consumer decision making. *Journal of Consumer Research*, **22**, 229–238.

Novak, D. and Mather, M. (2007) Aging and variety seeking. *Psychology and Aging*, **22**, 728–737.

Ratner, R.K. and Kahn, B.E. (2002) The impact of private vs. public consumption on variety seeking behavior. *Journal of Consumer Research*, **29**, 246–258.

Ratner, R.K., Kahn, B.E. and Kahneman, D. (1999) Choosing less-preferred experiences for the sake of variety. *Journal of Consumer Research*, **26**, 1–15.

Simonson, I. (1990) The effect of purchase quantity and timing on variety-seeking behavior. *Journal of Marketing Research*, **27**, 150–162.

Subject Index

Note: Headings in **bold** denote article titles.